HISTORY OF THE OLD CHERAWS

CONTAINING

AN ACCOUNT OF
THE ABORIGINES OF THE PEDEE

THE FIRST WHITE SETTLEMENTS
THEIR SUBSEQUENT PROGRESS, CIVIL CHANGES,
THE STRUGGLE OF THE REVOLUTION, AND
GROWTH OF THE COUNTRY
AFTERWARD

EXTENDING FROM ABOUT
A. D. 1730 TO 1810

WITH

NOTICES OF FAMILIES AND
SKETCHES OF INDIVIDUALS

BY THE

Right Rev. Alexander Gregg, D.D.
Bishop of the P. E. Church in Texas
Formerly Rector of St. David's Church, Cheraw, South Carolina

HERITAGE BOOKS
2012

HERITAGE BOOKS
AN IMPRINT OF HERITAGE BOOKS, INC.

Books, CDs, and more—Worldwide

For our listing of thousands of titles see our website
at
www.HeritageBooks.com

A Facsimile Reprint
Published 2012 by
HERITAGE BOOKS, INC.
Publishing Division
100 Railroad Ave. #104
Westminster, Maryland 21157

Originally published
Columbia, S.C.
The State Company
1925

— Publisher's Notice —
In reprints such as this, it is often not possible to remove blemishes from the original. We feel the contents of this book warrant its reissue despite these blemishes and hope you will agree and read it with pleasure.

International Standard Book Numbers
Paperbound: 978-0-7884-2705-3
Clothbound: 978-0-7884-9300-3

TO

THE DESCENDANTS OF THE FIRST SETTLERS ON THE UPPER PEDEE,

OF

THE WHIGS OF THE OLD CHERAW DISTRICT AND LIBERTY PRECINCT,

WHEREVER THEY ARE TO BE FOUND:

THIS TRIBUTE TO THE MEMORY OF THEIR FATHERS,

Is Respectfully Dedicated

BY

THE AUTHOR.

REFERENCES TO BISHOP GREGG'S "OLD CHERAWS."

"This work affords a noble illustration of what antiquarian research can accomplish in working up the local traditions in our extended country. It is a mine of historic information, into which few shafts have yet been sunk."—Dr. B. M. Palmer, in his "Life and Letters" of Dr. Thornwell, page 8, note.

McCrady, in his "South Carolina Under the Proprietary Government, 1670-1719," says:

"In 1867 the 'History of the Old Cheraws,' by the Rt. Rev. Alexander Gregg, D. D., was published. This work contains an account of the aborigines of the Pedee, the first white settlements, their subsequent progress, civil changes, the struggle of the Revolution, and growth of the country afterwards, from 1730 to 1810, with notices of families and sketches of individuals. It offers the most complete history of a given section of the State to be found."

INTRODUCTION.

THE Author was induced some years since, at the instance of the "Cheraw Lyceum," to investigate the history of the Indian tribes formerly inhabiting the valley of the Pedee.
In the course of his researches, some very interesting documentary matter connected with the first white settlers of this region was unexpectedly discovered, which led to renewed effort in that direction, and resulted in the collection from various sources of an amount of matter far beyond anything which the most sanguine hopes in the outset could have anticipated. This was the more gratifying, inasmuch as in the histories of the State and the published memoirs of some of the distinguished leaders of the Revolution, the region of the Upper Pedee, embraced within the limits of the Old Cheraw District, had literally found no place. It was far removed from Charles-town, as well as from the main routes of emigration, travel, and the Indian trade, all which tended to the west and north-westward, where the Cherokees held sway. None of the important battles of the Revolution were fought in this portion of Carolina, though it contributed largely to the number of those who took an active part in the strife. The operations of Marion were confined chiefly to the parts lower down on the river. Even Judge James, who served in early life under that distinguished partizan leader, remarks, in his "Life of Marion":—"As to the Old Cheraw District, where a

sanguinary warfare was waged between the Whigs and Tories under General Thomas, their leader, nothing is known, and it will, perhaps, remain ever unrecorded."

It may, therefore, be readily imagined with what delight the materials of this *unwritten* history were recovered, how the desire was naturally excited to give it publicity, and the pride justly felt by one in the region of his nativity, to rescue the noble deeds of those who had long since passed away, from oblivion.

After gathering materials for his narrative from every accessible source, and carefully collating them, the Author was called, in the providence of God, to make a permanent removal from the State of his birth and the scenes of his former labors. He has since found time to bring the work to completion, esteeming it a tribute of affection due to those ties and associations, ever so dear to man, which he has left behind him.

Though in the main a *local* history, and for that reason chiefly interesting to those who by nativity or descent are more immediately connected with this portion of Carolina, there is yet of necessity a close and continuous connexion throughout with the history of the State at large—*a history* which, except by the aid of such detailed accounts of particular localities, can never be fully written. Much, therefore, of general interest will be found in the following pages, more especially in the period which immediately preceded the Revolution, and during the progress of that eventful conflict. To the Whigs of the Old Cheraws, though with very few exceptions hitherto unknown to fame, must a conspicuous place be assigned, for the part they took in preparing the way for that early struggle for independence, and in its prosecution afterwards.

If omissions appear in the account of families which came at an early period to the Pedee, and are known to have taken an active and influential part in its subsequent history, it is to be attributed to the fact, which none can regret more than the Author, that after diligent and unremitting effort, information was either not to be obtained, or failed, after repeated application, to be procured from their descendants. It is a melancholy fact, indeed, as has been painfully experienced here in not a few instances, how little is known by their posterity of the third and fourth generations, of ancestors who are worthy of being held in honored remembrance. In this connexion facts could be given which would scarcely be credited. Too little attention has been generally paid to the preservation of such ancestral accounts, and of documentary matter, invaluable in connexion with the history of communities and public events of importance. To a few such collections which happily escaped the ravages of time, the Author has been largely indebted in filling up some of the links of his narrative. He is under weighty obligations to those who kindly furnished information and materials within their reach; also to others who gave him access to public libraries and the archives of the State, and desires in this lasting form to give expression to his acknowledgements.

In a local history like the following, much of minute detail as to persons and places is to be expected, constituting, as it does, one of the chief attractions of such a narrative. Where printed or documentary matter of permanent interest and value could be given in full as recorded, the object has been to present it literally in its original form, rather than in the language of the Author. In this way only can the materials necessary for general use in the future be preserved, and the labor of those to come in more important paths of historical inquiry be lightened. The hope is therefore cherished that the intrinsic value of the matter collected, not the style of its narration, may interest the reader. And if a work, begun and prosecuted under the constant pressure of other pursuits and labors, shall serve to make those for whom he has chiefly written, better acquainted with the history of their fathers, and do justice, though at so late a period, to the memory of the noble men who have gone before, the Author will feel that his effort is abundantly rewarded.

SAN ANTONIO, TEXAS,
April, 1867.

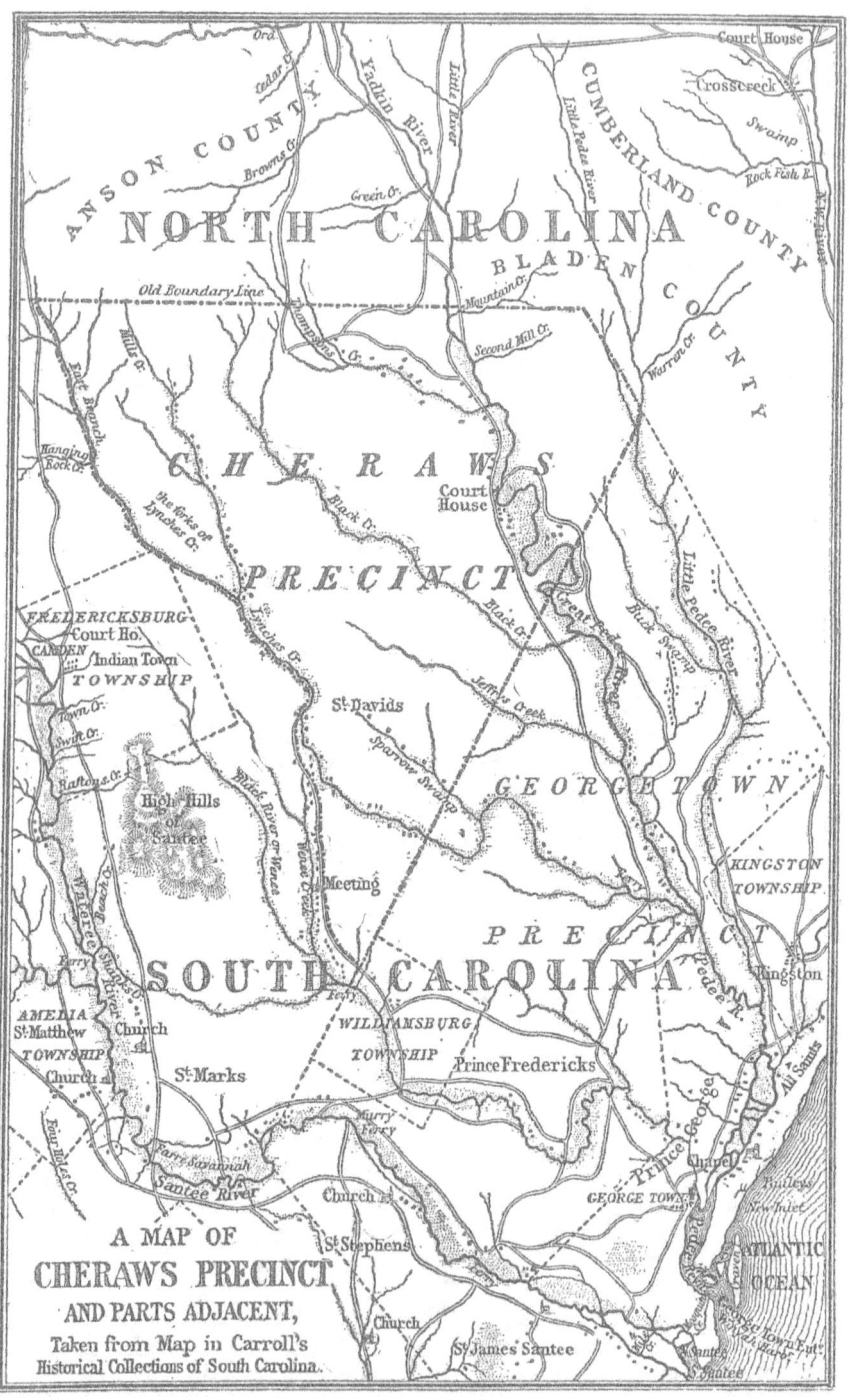

HISTORY

OF

THE OLD CHERAWS.

CHAPTER I.

Indian tribes in Carolina—Extent of their territory—Other tribes—Pedees—Kadapaws—Localities of each—Their origin—Advent of the Catawbas—Their tradition—Subsequent relation to tribes on the Pedee—Lederer's narrative—Localities identified—Sara, where—First mention in public records of tribes on the Pedee—Visit of the Cheraws to Charlestown—Governor's visit to the Congerees—Interview with Pedees—Governor Glenn writes to Governor Clinton—Evans's Journal—Cheraws visit Charlestown—Smallpox prevails—Removal of Cheraws and union with Catawbas—Catawba History—Languages of tribes on the Pedee—Meaning of "Cheraw"—"Pedee"—Indian remains on the Pedee—Indian habits and customs—Lawson's narrative—Last of Cheraws and Catawbas.

THERE is a sad chapter in the history of the New World: it is that relating to the Aborigines of America—a people, as all accounts agree, distinguished for many noble traits, but invariably degenerating in character and habit as they have come in contact with the "pale-faces," and taken up their mournful line of march towards the setting sun.

When first known to the colonists, South Carolina is said to have contained not less than twenty-eight tribes of Indians, with settlements extending from the ocean to the mountains. Of these tribes but a few names survive to mark the localities they once inhabited; and these, with such scattered remains as the waste of time and the levelling work of the white man have spared, are the only memorials left to tell of their early occupancy of the soil. Of the tribes which dwelt upon the Pedee and its tributaries, the Saras, or Saraws, as they were first called—afterwards Charrows, Charraws, and Cheraws—occupied the region still identified by the name: their territory extending thence to the coast, and along the coast from the Cape Fear to the Pedee. This extensive region has been assigned to the Cheraws by one of the most eminent ethnologists of America, as among the sites of the Indian tribes when first known to the Europeans, about the year 1600, along the coast of the Atlantic.*

If such was the extent of their territory at that early period, it would indicate a population which must have been greatly diminished, when, upon the approach of the Catawbas, a half century later, the supremacy of the Cheraws over the smaller tribes around them, and even over their own distinct nationality, would seem to have been lost, or at least unacknowledged. Within these early territorial limits of the Cheraws, and along the middle and lower parts of the valley of the river, must be assigned the Pedees; and about the mouth of the river, the Winyaws. The Kadapaws were found on Lynche's Creek, after the name of which tribe that stream was called in the Indian tongue. Of these, the Cheraws—however they may have been diminished in number by disease and war, or perchance by some dismemberment of their nation, and the removal of many, of which no record or tradition remains—continued to be the dominant race on the Pedee; the others having ever been reckoned among the smaller and inferior tribes. Of their origin nothing is known beyond the conjectures of ethnologists. They have been assigned, but upon what grounds does not appear, to the extensive family of Algonkins. These occupied that portion of North America on the east extending from 35° to 60° N. latitude, and reaching along the northern line of extension almost to the Pacific on the west. Beyond this, as the track of aboriginal descent and migration begins to be traced back, even conjecture is lost in a sea of uncertainty.

The tribes on the Pedee continued in their feeble and disconnected state (the Cheraws maintaining the supremacy) until the arrival of the Catawbas from the north, with the

---

*See map annexed, by the late Albert Gallatin, vol. i. of "Transactions of American Ethnological Society."

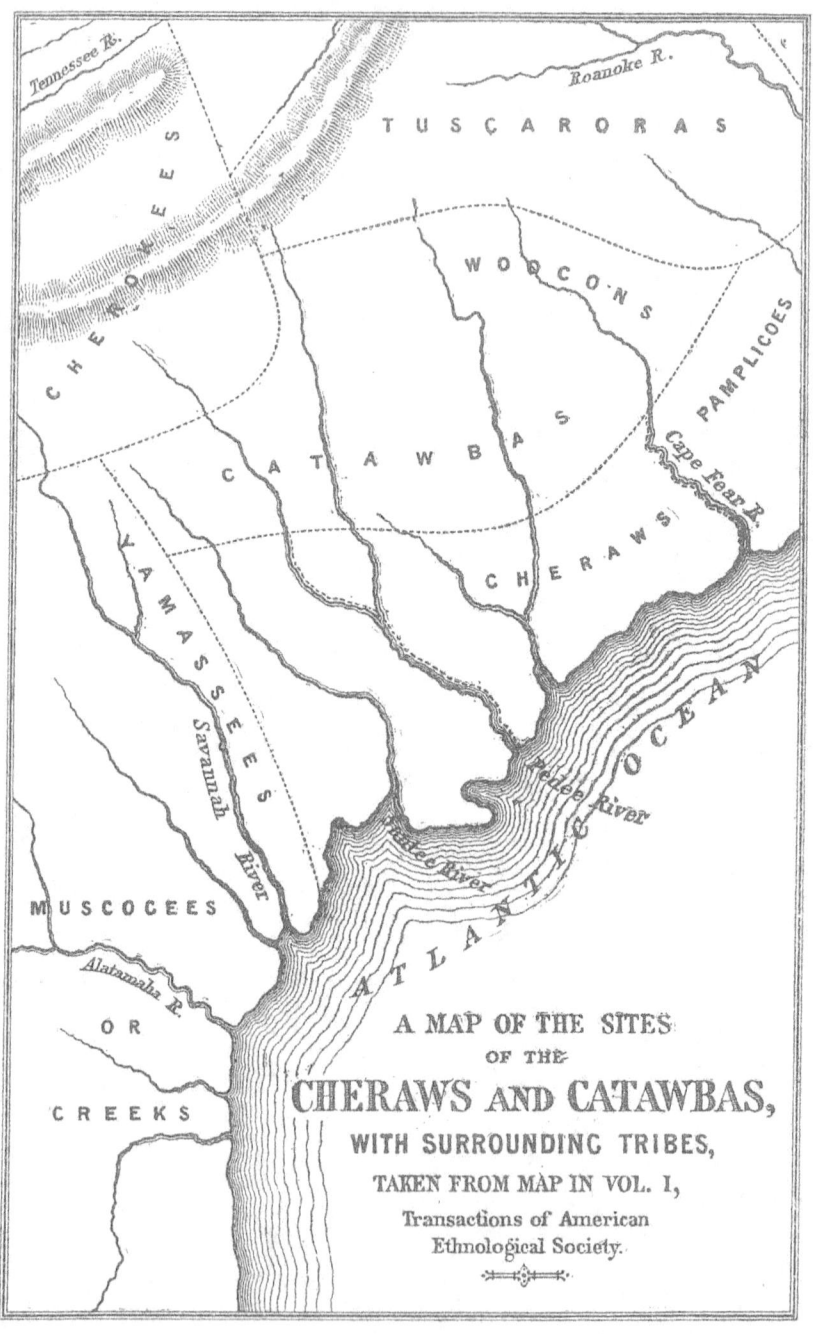

history of whom their own was ever after to be inseparably blended.

According to their tradition,* as it has been handed down to very recent times, the Catawbas, at a period prior or not long subsequent to the discovery and settlement of North America by the whites, occupied a region far to the northward, from whence, in course of time, they removed to the south. Being a numerous and warlike race, they vanquished the tribes with whom they came successively in conflict on the way, until they met the Cherokees on the banks of the river, afterwards called by their own name, Catawba.

Here, as the tradition relates, a sanguinary battle ensued between them, which lasted from morning until night, darkness alone serving to put an end to the conflict. The loss on both sides was heavy, though neither party gained the victory. They slept on the field of blood among their dead and wounded. With the approach of morning, propositions of peace were made by the Catawbas, and accepted by the Cherokees. According to the terms of the agreement, the former were to occupy the country east of the river, and the latter the territory on the west. Here they solemnly agreed to live together as brothers; and, after burying their dead, and erecting piles of stones as monuments alike of their common loss, and of the peace and friendship established between them, returned to their encampments, ever afterwards sacredly observing the terms of the compact. This tradition of the Catawbas is confirmed throughout by the fuller details which ethnological research has added to their history. They appear to have been a Canadian tribe, and to have left their ancient home about the year 1650, pursued by the Connewangas, a superior and more warlike tribe, with whom they had come in conflict. Forced thus to remove, they turned their faces to the southward, and fought their way, when necessary to do so, until they approached the head waters of the Kentucky River.

---

*For this interesting traditional account, as given by the Catawbas, the author is indebted to W. H. Thomas, Esq., of Qualla Town, No. Ca., who has been intimately connected with them, as their head man, or chief, since their removal to the western part of that State.

Here a separation took place, the larger number becoming absorbed in the great families of the Chickasaws and Choctaws.

The remainder of the tribe stopped in what was afterwards known as Bottetourt County, Virginia, but without making any permanent settlement.

They removed thence in the year 1660, continuing their journey to the south, and, as Adair wrote, "settled on the east side of a broad, purling river, that heads in the great blue ridge of mountains, and empties itself into Santee River, in Amelia township, then running eastward of Charlestown, disgorges itself into the Atlantic."

On the banks of this river, the Eswa Tavora (as it was called in the Indian tongue), they met the Cherokees, whose extensive territory ran thence to the westward, and there followed the sanguinary conflict, of which some account has been given.

In this battle 1000 of the bravest warriors were lost on each side, greatly reducing the force of the Catawbas, and doubtless making a permanent impression on their spirit as a warlike race, for which they had been so celebrated in the earlier periods of their history.

How the approach of the Catawbas was regarded by the Cheraws, and whether any conflict ensued between them, tradition does not inform us. The approach of a strong and formidable tribe was generally regarded by the Indians as a hostile demonstration and claim to dominion. Already, doubtless, the decline of the Cheraws had commenced and made such progress as to unfit them for contesting the claim to supremacy. It was to be the story of a continuous decline, and of a race scattered or absorbed into another superior to themselves, the beginning of the last and most mournful chapter in their history. A portion of the Cheraws, however, must have remained distinct and independent for more than a century later, as will be found in tracing their subsequent course. They were henceforth to be wanderers, the remains of their once extensive dominion, with those of the smaller tribes around them, having passed away to the Catawbas. The territory of the latter was placed at 34° north latitude, being bounded on the north and north-east by North Carolina; on the east and south by South Carolina; and about west and south-west by the Cherokee nation.*

The smaller tribes on the waters of the Pedee, appear after this period to have had but a nominal existence. They had doubtless degenerated through the operation of those wasting and destructive agencies at work in the history of the aboriginal races; and, in addition, had undergone the process, common among the Indians, of becoming absorbed in their conquerors or in the larger tribes around them.

In this instance they were merged chiefly in the Catawbas. About the year 1743, the language of the Catawbas is said to have consisted of twenty different dialects, of which the "Katahba" was the standard, or court dialect, the "Cherah" being another. Scarcely anything beyond a bare allusion to them by name is found relating to the tribes on the Pedee in the earliest accounts of the Indians of Carolina. With the exception of the Cheraws, they were reckoned among the smaller and inferior tribes, most of whom had then greatly degenerated and were rapidly approaching extinction. Brief allusions are found at an early period to the several tribes in the Acts of the Assembly, passed for the regulation and support of the Indian trade. The larger tribes on the northern and western boundaries of the Province engaged the attention of the Government almost exclusively. The Catawbas formed a sort of barrier against their incursions, and of them there is frequent mention.

Of the Cheraws the first distinct relation in any contemporaneous record, is found in the explorations of John Lederer, "in three several marches from Virginia to the west of Carolina and other parts of the Continent; begun in March, 1669, and ended in September, 1670."†

Such at least is the case, if we are to understand by "Sara," as he writes it, the locality of the "Saraws," as they were sometimes called, or Cheraw Indians. Thus, in

---
*Adair, p. 224.
†For a full account of this early American traveller, the reader is referred to Dr. Hawks' "History of No. Ca.," vol.ii. pp. 43—63, with maps annexed.

one of his journeys, Lederer says, "I departed from Watery the one-and-twentieth of June, and keeping a west course for near thirty miles, I came to Sara. Here I found the ways more level and easy. I did likewise, to my no small admiration, find hard cakes of white salt among them; but whether they were made of sea-water or taken out of salt-pits I know not, but am apt to believe the latter, because the sea is so remote from them. From Sara I kept a south-west course until the five-and-twentieth of June, and then I reached Wisacky. This three days' march was more troublesome to me than all my travels besides, for the direct way which I took from Sara to Wisacky is over a continued marsh overgrown with weeds, from whose roots spring knotty stumps, as hard and sharp as flint.

"I was forced to lead my horse most part of the way, and wonder that he was not either plunged in the bogs or lamed by those rugged knots. This nation is subject to a neighbor king residing upon the bank of a great lake called Ushery, environed of all sides with mountains and Wisacky marsh."*

There is great difficulty throughout Lederer's narrative, as Dr. Hawks more than once remarks, in determining the routes by which he passed and the localities described. If by "Watery," the Wateree of the present day is to be understood, he could not by going west thirty miles to "Wisacky," and thence three days' march by a south-west course to "Ushery," have reached the Santee; for by "Ushery" the Santee was meant, if the authority quoted by Dr. Hawks is correct: Col. Byrd, he adds, says that the Indians living on the Santee River were called "Usheries." If, on the other hand, amid the confusion of names which could not have been very well defined at that early period, we may understand by "Watery" the Pedee of the present day, a journey of thirty miles to the west would have brought Lederer to Lynche's Creek, the "Wisacky," and three days' march from thence south-westwardly along the swamp of Wateree, would have enabled him to reach the Santee, environed by the "High Hills" which have since become so famous, called by this early explorer, "Moun-

---

*Hawks' "History of N. C.," vol. ii. p. 49.

tains," and with an almost impenetrable swamp of vast extent, to which his description of a "marsh overgrown with reeds," would very well answer.

In support of this view, we find in Oldmixon's "History of Carolina," published in 1708, reason for supposing that the Pedee was then called by that name (Watery). Describing the six counties into which Carolina, North and South, was then divided, he begins with Albemarle, on the borders of Virginia. Then follows an account of Clarendon County, in which, he says, "is the famous promontory, called also Cape Fear, at the mouth of Clarendon River, called also Cape Fear River. The next river is named Waterey River, or Winyan, about twenty-five leagues distant from Ashley River; it is capable of receiving large ships, but inferior to Port Royal, nor is yet inhabited. There is another small river called Wingon River, and a little settlement honoured with the name of Charles-town, but so thinly inhabited that 'tis not worth taking notice of. We come now to South Carolina, which is parted from North by Zantee River. The adjacent county is called Craven County."*

It is evident that the "Waterey" here spoken of, was the Waccamaw, or the lower Pedee, and not the Wateree of the present day.

The Pedee being a much longer stream than the Waccamaw, it is not impossible that though the latter was known by the name of Waterey, or Winyan near its mouth, the former being supposed to form its extension higher up, was also in like manner designated. Dr. Hawks remarks, "Watery, Sara, Wisacky, and Ushery, would all appear to have been in South Carolina, the last directly west of Charles-town. If he made his journey then, entering the State somewhere in Robeson County, he must have crossed in a south-western line, and passing through Robeson County into South Carolina, must have traversed that State also in its entire width. The time occupied would not have been sufficient for it. Lederer's Itinerary presents difficulties which we confess we cannot satisfactorily solve."†

---

*Oldmixon's "History," in Carroll's Collections, vol. ii. p. 446.
†Hawks' "History of N. C.," vol. ii. p. 52.

If, as is here conjectured, Lederer passed through Robeson County into South Carolina, the supposition we have made will appear the more probable. And it brings to light the fact never before suggested or imagined, perhaps, that the Pedee, in the earlier days of aboriginal history, was known as "Sara." If it was so, the time and reason of the change to Pedee can be left to conjecture only.

It might have taken place after the advent of the Catawbas, and been brought about by them in order that such a standing memorial of the "Sara" dominion might be for ever obliterated; or, what is yet more probable, the "Sara" territory, once embracing the region higher up, but afterwards confined to the coast, the Pedees, if succeeding to it, would naturally have called the river after their own name.

The earliest mention in the provincial records of any of the tribes inhabiting the Valley of the Pedee, is found in the proceedings of the Council or Upper House of Assembly, December 15th, 1732.* It is in these words:—"Mr. Sanders and Mr. Waties came from the Lower House with the following message. We herewith send your Excellency a letter of great moment to this Government, relating to the murder of a Pedee Indian by one Kemp. We desire your Excellency to take the proper measures to prevent the ill consequences of it, by causing the offender to be apprehended and brought to justice, or otherwise as your Excellency shall see fit."

Upon reading the message from the Lower House of Assembly, and likewise the letter therein mentioned, complaining that one Kemp, or Camp, an overseer at Black River, or Georgetown, has barbarously murdered one of the Pedee Indians,

"Ordered,—That James Neale, Esq., Provost Marshal, do immediately attach the said Kemp, or Camp, and bring him before his Excellency, the Governor, in Charlestown, to be dealt with according to law, and that all Constables and other officers and subjects of his Majesty be aiding and

---

*"Council Journal," No. 5, p. 258, Secretary of State's Office, Columbia.

assisting to the said Provost Marshal in the execution of this order."

This proceeding of the House was based upon the following facts:—"Appeared before this Board, Thomas Burton and Wm. Kemp, and upon the affidavit of Thomas Burton, and the information of Wm. Kemp concerning the fact of an Indian fellow being killed, name Corn-White Johnny, his Excellency issued the following order. On the 17th January, 1733, in Council, upon hearing this day the information of William Kemp, relating to the death of Corn-White Johnny, and the affidavit of Thomas Burton, it is ordered that King Harry, Captain Billy, George and Dancing Johnny, and some of the relations of the deceased, be and appear before me, the second Wednesday in February next ensuing, to give an account of what they know of the death of the said Indian, and that Wm. Kemp do attend at the same time; likewise that Mr. John Thompson, jun., is desired to acquaint the said Indians of this order." This record is of interest now as evincing the jealous care exercised by the Provincial Government for the protection of those scattered and defenceless remnants of the Indian tribes whose domain was fast passing away from them, and who continued faithful to the whites to the close of their history.

Of the result of the proceedings referred to no further account appears.

We have next a brief, but interesting notice* of a visit made to Charles-town by a few of the leading men of the Cheraws and Catawbas in July, 1739:—"On Saturday last," said the *Gazette* of that day, "arrived in this town eleven of the chief men among the Catawbas and Cheraw Indians, who came to pay a visit to his Honour, the Lieutenant-Governor, and inform him that some time since a party of their people went out to war, and not meeting with their enemies, had cut off a white family on the

---

**South Carolina Gazette*, June 30—July 7th, 1739. For access to this invaluable historical collection—a complete file of the old *Gazettes*, commencing about 1730—the author is indebted to the courtesy of A. H. Mazyck, Esq., of the Charleston Library. Only a few of the earlier numbers of the *Gazette* are missing. At a later period a small portion was burned.

borders of Virginia; that upon complaint made to them of the said barbarous murder, they examined into the facts, and had put five of the ringleaders to death; and that they were determined to prosecute in the same rigorous manner any of their people who for the future should be found guilty of the like cruel practices. They met with a kind reception from his Honour the Lieutenant-Governor, and having received the usual presents from the country, they set out this day on their return home, well pleased and content."

The signal punishment visited by these tribes upon the murderers of the whites, indicated their fidelity to the Provincial Government, which continued to be as true as it was lasting.

Of the Pedees mention is made a few years later. "In Council, March 2nd, 1743, his Excellency, the Governor, signed the following order to Mr. Commissary Dart, viz., to provide for the Pedee Indians now in town, the following particulars, viz. :—

"*Presents.*—To the three head men, each of them, a gun and knife; to the others, each of them, a knife. For the three women, each of them, a looking-glass, twenty bullets, half a pound of vermillion to be divided among them.

"Also, an order on Col. Brewton, for ten pounds of gunpowder for use of said Indians."* The Pedees are mentioned again, with the Catawbas, in the following year. "In Council, 25th July, 1744, the Governor admitted four Pedee Indians to an interview in the Council Chamber, who informed his Excellency that seven Catawbas had been barbarously murdered by the Notchee Indians, who live among them, which horrible deed having been confirmed by Mr. Matthew Beard, who lives at Goose Creek, who had certain intelligence of the same, saying, that the said Catawbas being drunk near Fuller Cowpen, near the four holes, seven of them, while asleep, were murderd by the Notchees; which affair being taken into consideration, his Excellency, by the advice of his Majesty's Council, ordered the following letter to be despatched away, relating to that subject:—

---

*"Council Journal," No. 11, p. 133.

HISTORY OF THE OLD CHERAWS. 11

"So. Ca., July 28, 1744.

"Sir,—I have received information of an unlucky accident which happened about a week ago, at or near the store belonging to the late Major Fuller, somewhere about the Four Holes, where some Notchee Indians have fallen upon and killed five or six of the Catawbas, being instigated thereto by a person who keeps that store. The Catawbas, as I understand, have already set out to take their revenge, which has obliged the Notchees and Pedees to come further down among the settlements for shelter. I must therefore desire the favor of you to interpose in this matter, and to prevent, as far as you are able, any bloodshed, till this matter is fully enquired into. Then the guilty may be punished, and if you find it necessary, to interpose with the Militia in your parts to keep the peace. This I write at the desire of his Majesty's Council. I hear they are at Mr. Beard's Plantation, in the neighbourhood.

"I am, with truth, yours,
"JAMES GLEN.*

"To Hon. Wm. Middleton, Esq."

About two years after this, the Governor, as was usual when any difficulty occurred with the Indians, or to preserve their friendship and maintain a due influence over them, made a visit into the interior, at a certain place on the Congarees, appointed by him for an interview with the Catawbas, of which the following account was preserved.† "The Governor arrived at Congarees 27 April, 140 miles distance hence, where, on the bank of the Santee, the king and a few of the head men met him. Yenabe Yalangway, the King—the old leader, Captain Taylor, Nafkebee, and some others awaited on his Excellency. The next day the Governor addressed them. A place being erected for the Governor to sit under, and the Union Flag hoisted, our men were drawn out in two lines, through which the Indians marched, when they were received with drums beating and colours flying, and saluted with some small pieces of cannon: after they had all taken the Governor by the hand, and the King with some of his head-men, had placed himself near

*"Council Journal," No. 11, pp. 413, 414.
†*Gazette*, June 2, 1746.

his Excellency, a person was sworn truly to interpret all that should pass betwixt the Governor and the Indians; and then his Excellency addressed them in words, the purport of which was to dissuade them from agreeing to a proposition which had been made to them by some of the other Indian Nations to join in a French war against the people of Carolina. After which, presents were distributed, consisting chiefly of powder, guns, pistols, paint, &c. The Governor had that morning received an express from Mr. Brown (who trades amongst the Catawbas) acquainting him that some of the Pedees and Cheraws (two small tribes who have long been incorporated with the Catawbas), intended to leave them, which might prove of dangerous consequences at a time when they were so closely attacked by their enemies, the Northern Indians. Mr. Brown therefore entreated that, if possible, such a separation might be prevented.

The Governor ordered the rammers of all the pistols which he had delivered to the Indians to be laid upon the table, desiring that such as were Pedees and Charraws might advance, and they, being in a body near him, he spoke to them in these words:—"It gives me great concern, my friends, to hear that you entertain the least thought of leaving the Catawbas, with whom you have been so long and so closely united. This union makes you strong, and enables you to defend yourselves and annoy your enemies; but should you ever separate, you would thereby weaken yourselves, and be exposed to every danger. Consider that if you were single and divided, you may be broke as easily as I break this stick" (at the same time breaking one of the rammers); "but if you continue united together, and stand by one another, it will be as impossible to hurt or break you, as it is impossible for me to break these," (his Excellency then taking up a handful of rammers).

After this, they all promised to continue together in their camp. The Governor then directed himself to the King of the Catawbas, telling him that he would expect his answer. To which the King replied at some length, assuring the Governor of their continued friendship and fidelity.

The pledge of fidelity renewed on this occasion was

HISTORY OF THE OLD CHERAWS.

faithfully observed by these Indians throughout all their subsequent history. Though often tempted by artful representations and large promises to take up arms against the people of Carolina, they could never be persuaded to do so. Throughout the Indian wars, and the contest with the mother country, they continued steadfast in their devotion to their early friends and allies, well meriting the aid and protection extended to them by the State in the latter stages of their decline and weakness.

That the Pedees owned slaves, will appear from the following notice, published in the Gazette of the day, August 30—September 6, 1748:—

"Taken up by Michael Welch, overseer to the Subscriber, on an Island called Uchee Island, a Negro Fellow, who gives the following account of himself, viz., that he belonged formerly to Mr. Fuller, and was by him sold to Billy, King of the Pedee Indians; that the Catawba Indians took him from King Billy, and carried him to their nation; and that in endeavouring to make his escape from the Catawbas, he was lost in the woods, and had been so a considerable time before he was taken. He is a middle-sized Fellow, and a little pot-bellied; says his name is Fortune, but is suspected to have another name which he does not care to own. Any person having any right or property in the said Fellow, may apply to the Subscriber, now in Charlestown.

"ISAAC MARKSDALE."

The Pedees and other smaller tribes, who now led a wandering life, were in constant danger of being enticed off by the more powerful and hostile nations of Indians, to join them in their predatory excursions.

The following letters indicate the anxiety felt on the subject by the Catawbas, as well as by the Provincial Government at this period. The first* was addressed by the King of the Catawbas to his Excellency, James Glen, Esq.:—

"There are a great many Pedee Indians living in the settlements that we want to come and settle amongst us. We desire for you to send for them, and advise them to

---
*"Indian Book," vol. iii. pp. 163, 164, in Secretary of State's Office, Columbia, S. C.

this, and give them this string of wampum in token that we want them to settle here, and will always live like brothers with them. The Northern Indians want them all to settle with us; for, as they are now at peace, they may be hunting in the woods or straggling about, killed by some of them, except they join us, and make but one nation, which will be a great addition of strength to us.

"Catawbas, 21st November, 1752."

"The $\overset{\text{his}}{\times}$ King.
mark.

During the previous year—viz., May 24, 1751—Governor Glen had written to Governor Clinton, of New York, respecting the Congress of Indians to be holden at Albany, for the purpose of uniting the different friendly tribes, and preserving their friendship as a bulwark against the more hostile. Of that letter, the following extract will suffice:—

"Our first care," said Governor Glen, "ought to be to make all Indians that are friends with the English friends also among themselves; and for that reason I hope you and the other Governors and Commissioners will heartily join your interest in removing all the obstacles to a peace, in reconciling all the differences, and cementing together in a closer union the northern and southern Indians, under the name of Norw$^{\text{d.}}$ Indians. I include not only the six nations, the Delewares, and Susquehanna Indians, but all the different tribes who may be in friendship with them, particularly those on the Ohio River; as under the name of Southward Indians, I comprehend the Cherokees, the Catawbas, the Creeks (called sometimes Muscogee), the Chickesaws, and such part of the Chactaws as are in our interest, and all the tribes in friendship with these nations, or that live amongst our settlements, such as Charraws, Uchees, Pedees, Notches, Cape Fears, or other Indians; and I hope that all prisoners on each side will be mutually delivered back."*

On the 14th of October, 1755, John Evans made a visit to the Catawbas, by order of his Excellency, Governor Glen. From his journal the following extracts are taken,

*"Indian Book," vol. ii. p. 96.

and will be found chiefly interesting here, as containing some information respecting the Pedees:—

"October 17th.—Met a Catawba man and woman, and informed by them, that in the summer, the Cherrackees and Notchees had killed some Pedees and Waccamaws in the white people's settlements.

"18th.—I got into the Catawbas. King Hazler was gone a hunting the day before; the next morning they sent for him, and he came in that night.

"Before he got into the nation, I made it my care to inquire of the Pedees if they could not tell what people killed the Pedees at Goose Creek, where the boys were that was taken prisoners: answered, 'They could not tell who they were, but understood it was the Notchees and Cherokees that did the mischief.'

"21st.—The king and head men met, and desired to know what I was come for. I told them that there was two Pedee women killed and scalped, and two boys carried away from out of the settlements, and that it was done by some of their nation; and one Notchee, which was called the Notchee Doctor, and his Excellency, the Governor, had sent me to demand the boys; and I then and there demanded these boys. I further acquainted them that his Excellency, the Governor, desired that they would not come into the settlements without they were sent for. The white people might mistake them, and do them a mischief, believing them to be enemy Indians. I further said, that it was his Excellency, the Governor's pleasure, that the Catawba people should not attempt to carry away any of the Indians that are now living in the settlements up to their nation on any pretence whatever without his permission first. Their answer was, that old men should always speak truth; and that most of them were grey-headed; and they, for their parts, did not hurt the Pedees, and did not know or believe the mischief was done by any belonging to that nation; and further said, that when the Northward Indians were in their nation, they bound the same three women and two men; and the Catawbas released the three women, but the Northern Indians carried the men away.

"22nd.—I set out from the Catawba nation homeward,

and at night came to a camp of Pedees. I acquainted them with my errand to the Nation, and desired them to let me know, if they could, who it was that killed and scalped the Pedee women, and carried the boys away. Lewis Jones, their chief, answered, that soon after the Pedees were killed, he went down from the nation to the settlements to inquire what harm was done by Goose Creek. He met a Pedee Indian, named Prince, who lived in the settlements; and Prince told him, that a day or two before the mischief was done, there was five Cherokees and one Notchee seen to go by Monck's Corner, and Lewis John said, he did believe they scalped the women, and carried the boys away."*

The Cheraws, following the example of the Catawbas, were true to the English, as they continued to be to the colonists throughout the Revolution and afterwards.

They cheerfully endured the hardships of distant journeys when called upon for aid. In the *South Carolina Gazette* of June 2, 1759, this account was given:—"On Tuesday last, 45 Charraws, part of a Nation of Indians incorporated with the Catawbas, arrived in Town, headed by King Johnny, who brought to the Governor the scalp of a French Indian, which he had taken near Loyal-Henning. He and several others that are with him here, were with Gen. Forbes during the whole expedition against Fort Du Quesne. Their chief business seems to be, to see his Excellency and receive presents."

In the latter part of this year the great scourge of the red man appeared amongst them, and carried off many Indians in this part of the Province. In the *Gazette* of December 8th-15th, 1759, was this sad account of its ravages:—"It is pretty certain that the small-pox has lately raged with great violence among the Catawba Indians, and that it has carried off near one half of that Nation, by throwing themselves into the river as soon as they found themselves ill. This distemper has since appeared among the inhabitants at the Charraws and Waterees, where many families are down, so that unless especial care is taken, it must soon

---

*"Indian Book," vol. v. pp. 94, 95.

spread through the whole country, the consequences of which are much to be dreaded. The smallpox went almost through the Province in the year 1738, when it made prodigious havoc, and has ever since been kept out of it by the salutary laws enacted for that purpose." So destructive and rapidly exterminative had been this disease among the Indians from its first introduction, that its appearance brought on a spirit of phrenzy and desperation. Ignorant and grossly superstitious, they regarded it as a visible embodiment of the Spirit of evil—the sentence of wrath from heaven let loose upon them, from which there was no escape. In this state of mind the disease found abundant food for keeping itself alive and completing the work of destruction. The white families at the "Charraws" and "Waterees," who appear to have suffered severely at this period, were doubtless unprepared for such a visitant, and having not the means of prevention or cure at command, yielded for a time, like their savage neighbours, to the fell destroyer. At a later period, about the time of the Revolution, some of the Catawba warriors having visited Charlestown, there contracted the disease again, and returning, communicated it to their Nation, which, according to contemporaneous accounts, came well nigh being exterminated. It was after this, having been sorely thinned by disease, that they were advised by their friends to invite the Cheraws to move up and unite with them as one tribe. The Cheraws here spoken of by the writers of the day, must have been a part of the tribe which had maintained its independence probably in the region lower down the Pedee or on the coast, where they led a proud but feeble existence. That some of them should have refused to submit to what must have seemed to be the yoke of a foreign invader, is not surprising. But their doom was sealed. No longer able to maintain their isolated sway, or to resist the destructive agencies at work among them, a weak and declining remnant, like the Catawbas themselves, they gladly accepted the invitation to unite their future with that of their brethren who had gone before them.

And now was seen their last journey as the representatives of a nation of ancient renown.

Mournful as it was short, the march was soon ended; and henceforth these broken fragments were to constitute but one nation, under the name of Catawbas. For a while, as at the first, the Cheraws retained their own language, though ordinarily using the Catawba.

They lived in harmony together, their early feuds forgotten, and the jealousies of other days obliterated by those common wants and saddened recollections which were henceforth to mark their declining history. Within the memory of persons now living, a few of the Cheraws have visited the upper Pedee, to take a last look at the localities which their own traditions had identified as the homes of their fathers. About the year 1700, the Catawbas numbered 1500 warriors. Only a half century later this proud band had dwindled away to 400. Their principal settlement about this latter period was on the Wateree, where their country was described as being "an old waste field, seven miles in extent, with several others of smaller dimensions; which shows," it was added, "that they were formerly a numerous people, to cultivate so much land, with their dull stone axes, before they had an opportunity of trading with the English, or allowed others to incorporate with them."*

In 1787 they were the only organized tribe, under a distinct name of its own, in South Carolina.

Their town, "Catawba," contained then about 450 inhabitants, of which not more than 150 were fighting men. In 1798 they are said to have been in the habit of holding an anniversary meeting of a sadly interesting character. It was intended to commemorate their former greatness, by recounting the numbers and deeds of their ancestors, of which tradition had kept them informed.† Well might the Catawbas have been proud of that history. And well may South Carolina cherish the memory of a people who maintained their friendship and their active devotion inviolate throughout the long and trying period of conflicts waged successively with savage foes, and those of the same language and blood who came to reduce their American brethren to a state of worse than colonial vassalage!

*"Adair."
†"Barton's New View," p. 51.

Of the liberal provision made for the Catawbas in later times by the Legislature of South Carolina, it is unnecessary to speak.

A portion of them had removed at an earlier period to Buncome county, North Carolina, west of the Blue Ridge, and thither the miserable remnant, with few exceptions, followed a few years since. Reduced in numbers by disease and intermarriage, by the contracted territory to which they had been confined while yet unfitted by the slow process, through which the Indian must always pass, for agricultural pursuits; and withal, by those habits of idleness and dissipation which the custom of leasing their lands to the whites, and the consequent want of employment had subjected them; drunken and wandering from place to place, their condition became as abject as it had once been elevated among the red men of Carolina! "In this rapidly declining tribe," says an eminent authority of recent times, "we behold the remnant of the defeated, long-lost, and celebrated tribe of the Eries." It is hoped that their history, in the materials of which the public records of the State abound, will one day, as it deserves, be fully written.

Of the languages of the Indian tribes once inhabiting the valley of the Pedee, scarce a vestige is left, except the names of the rivers and a few localities. The same remark may be made of all the tribes which were found at the first approaches of the white man on the coast of Carolina, from Cape Hatteras to the Savannah.*

Of the meaning of "Cheraw," reasoning from the affinities of the Indian tongues, a probable conjecture may be hazarded. In Cherah, or Chera, as it seems at certain periods of Indian history to have been called, is found a close affinity with Chera-kee. In the language of the Chera-kees, Cherah, or Chera, means fire. If, then, as seems highly probable, Cherah is identical with Serah, or Saraw, or Sara—as Lederer called it—now Cheraw, it may be conjectured to have meant the fire town. The site of the present town of Cheraw, which has retained the name, with slight changes, from an early period, may have been the

---

*"Transactions of American Ethnological Society," vol. ii. p. 115.

scene of an extensive conflagration when occupied by the Indians; or, being situated on a high bluff, and visible as a point of observation and alarm for miles across, it may have been a signal station, as such prominent localities often were, to gain the knowledge of an enemy's approach, or other danger, and hence may have been called Cherah; in Cherokee, the fire-town: or, as may seem yet more probable, in another view; if, about the period of their first distinct existence as a tribe, being possible an offshoot from the Cherakees, at the era of some internal struggle and partial dismemberment of that once powerful and widely extended nation, the Cherahs, or Cheraws, were noted as fire-eaters, as some of the Indian tribes have been, the original of the name may be found in this circumstance—Cheraw meaning fire-eaters. After all, however, it is one of those points, the original of language in the aboriginal races, which, without the light of contemporaneous history, must ever remain involved in more or less of darkness and uncertainty.

Of the meaning of "Pedee," nothing is known. It has even been made a question whether the name is of Indian origin; and the opinion has been advanced that it is not, on the ground that it appears to have been unknown prior to the English colonial settlements. Hence it is conjectured that it was of subsequent origin, having had its beginning, perhaps, in the initials of a white man's name, as of Patrick Daly, for example—P. D.—first carved upon a tree, then Indianized, and so changed into Pedee, as we now have it. This theory, however, is wholly untenable.

That the name is not mentioned by the earliest writers, is readily accounted for by the fact that the Pedees, if ever a people of any note, had then become an insignificant tribe; whereas only the more powerful nations of Indians engaged attention at first, or were so much as known by name. The earliest mention of Pedee is found in the account of the Eleven Townships, one of which was to be laid out on that river. This was about the year 1731-32.* But then it was spoken of as having already been in familiar use. It was spelt, too, not as if it had come from two capital letters, the initials of a proper name.

*Carroll's "Historical Collections," vol. ii. p. 124.

Both the analogy and euphony of the Indian tongue indicate, beyond all doubt, that Pedee had the same original as Santee, Congaree, Wateree, Uchee, and Sewee, all of unquestionable Indian birth, and the names of neighbouring and cognate tribes. That the name Pedee does not appear in the earliest published accounts of Carolina may be attributed to the fact that for a considerable time after the first settlement of the Province, scarcely anything was known of that part of the State, because out of the line of the main route of travel, far in the interior, and at a later period only coming into notice.

Of the Indian remains on the Pedee which are still to be seen, though but little trace is left, there is nothing distinguishable from those in other parts of the State, of which full accounts have been given. In some instances these remains are so numerous as to indicate the existence of once populous settlements. These settlements, as usually the case with the aborigines, were made upon the banks of rivers and other large streams, on account of the fertility of the soil, for fishing purposes, and other facilities thereby afforded.

In most instances on the Pedee where these remains are yet to be seen, are found large collections of fragments of pot-ware of varied shapes, sizes, and devices. It is difficult even to conjecture why such quantities of these were deposited at points not far removed from each other. They could scarcely have been the result of large accumulations in those places where the pot-ware was made, for they are generally found to be well-finished specimens of their kind, and evidently parts of vessels which were once in use. Nor does it appear to be a well-founded opinion, sometimes advanced, that upon the sudden breaking up of the Indian settlements, for whatever cause, these vessels of ornament or use were heaped together in one confused mass, and with such other chattels as could not be removed, abandoned for ever. Their appearance indicates that they were broken by violence; and what is more remarkable, of all the specimens taken up at random in any single locality, scarcely any two are found to be exactly alike in outward device and finish.

The ornamental lines and figures on the exterior are in many cases well executed, and for the untutored savage, exhibit a high degree of art. The questions, how they were broken, why collected in such strangely-mingled masses, and why other remains, as the pipe, the arrow-head, the stone axe, &c., are not generally found among them, will remain unanswered; and like so much else we would fain know respecting these early occupants of the soil, continue perhaps among the secret things of their history.

A large vase or jar,* of three gallons' capacity, was washed up a few years since by the waters of a freshet on the east bank of the Pedee, in Marlborough district, near Spark's Ferry. It is in a state of almost entire preservation, but not so highly finished as are many of the broken specimens which have been recovered. Like those to which Lawson alludes, in his account of the Congerees, this jar has a hole in the bottom, not smoothly cut, but roughly and irregularly made, as if punched through by some blunt instrument after the vessel was finished. Lawson supposes that they were sometimes used for burial purposes, and that the holes were made in the bottom to let off the morbid juices of the body going to decay. Some of the specimens of pot-ware found are highly finished; and, upon the whole, appear to warrant the conclusion arrived at by the first and most thoughtful travellers among our Indian tribes, and since clearly demonstrated by the results of later explorations, that those whom the Europeans found, on their first discovery and settlement of the country, were not the ancient dwellers in this part of the new world.

"The earthen pots," says Lawson, "are often found under ground, and at the foot of the banks, where the water has washed them away. They are for the most part broken in pieces; but we find them of a different sort, in comparison of those the Indians use at this day, who have had no others ever since the English discovered America. The bowels of the earth cannot have altered them, since they are thicker, of another shape and composition, and

---

*This vessel was presented to the Cheraw Lyceum, by Col. J. D. Wilson, of Darlington.

nearly approach to the urns of the ancient Romans."* We are told that they made earthen pots of very different sizes, so as to contain from two to ten gallons; large pitchers to carry water, bowls, dishes, platters, basons, and a prodigious number of other vessels of such antiquated forms, that it would be almost impossible to describe them.

Some of the specimens, in a fragmentary form, and others in a state of preservation, which were found on the Pedee, are of different shapes, and curiously finished. Of these one is very small, not holding more than a gill, and seems to have been used for paint, or some other valuable liquid.

Another,† of which the lower portion only is left, has the exact shape, the outward finish, and as much the appearance of a pineapple as if it had been carefully fashioned after that as a model. The process of glazing was simple, and consisted in placing the vessels over a large fire of smoky pitch pine, which made them smooth and shining. "Their lands abounded in proper clay for that use, and even with porcelain, as has been proved by experiment." When first discovered on the coast, the Indians were found to cultivate a variety of grains and vegetables. The process of clearing their lands has been minutely described. Their stone axes, of which specimens have been found on the Pedee, resembled a wedge or smith's chisel, and weighed from one to two or three pounds. They twisted two or three tough hickory slips about two feet long round the notched head of the axe, and by means of this simple contrivance deadened the trees by cutting through the bark, after which they fell by decay, or having become thoroughly dry, were easily burned.

With these trees they kept up their annual holy fire. In the first clearing of their plantations they only barked the larger timber, cut down the saplings and underwood, and burned them in heaps. As the suckers put up, they chopped them off close by the stump, and so made fires to deaden the roots, till in time they also decayed. The burning of the grass and underwood in the forests is said to have been an ancient custom of the Indians. This may account for

*Lawson, pp. 169, 170.
†This was also presented to the Cheraw Lyceum by Col. Wilson.

the fact which has been mentioned in connexion with the first settlements by the whites in the interior, that in many places the woods were found open to such an extent that even small objects could be seen to a great distance. These burnings were practiced by the Indians, as we are told, "in order to allure the deer upon the new grass, as also to discover the impressions of their enemies' tracks in the new burnt ground, distinguishable to their women and children, in case the raven should be sick or out of the way (thus they call the look-out, whose business it is to recognise the avenues of their towns), who, as well as any other Indian (as they all apply themselves to hunting) are by practice so keen and precise, that they can distinguish and follow a track, be it of a white man, negro, Indian, or be it of a bear, deer or wolf, horse or cow, even on hard bottom, not admitting of impression so as on soft ground, although covered all over with leaves, so that the ground itself is not visible, and even bare of any grass or bushes, which by their irregular bend may indicate a creature—human or animal—having trod upon or brushed by it."* Having cleared their lands in the primitive manner before described, the Indians used, in planting and tilling, their own made instruments. Afterwards a common hoe was the only implement employed in the cultivation of the soil. They prepared their corn for use by beating it till the husks came off, then boiling it in large earthen pots. For pounding the corn, mortars were made by cautiously burning a large log to a proper level and length, then placing a fire on the top and wet clay around it in order to give the interior a proper shape. When the fire was extinguished, or occasion required, they chopped the inside with their stone instruments, patiently continuing the process until they finished the vessel for the intended purpose.

In certain localities on the Pedee, which appear to have been the centres† of their once extensive settlements, many tumuli were once to be seen.

---

*B. R. A., H. M.'s Philosophico-Historico-Hydrogeography of South Carolina, Georgia, and East Florida, 1751. Edited and republished by Plowden, C. J. Weston, 1856. P. 189.

†The plantation of the late James M'Call, Esq., in Darlington District, on the

They were similar to some of those described by Bartram* in East Florida, near the river St. Juan; "where," he observes, "I found the surface of the ground very uneven by means of little mounts and ridges. I had taken up my lodging on the border of an ancient burying-ground; sepulchres or tumuli of the Yamassees, who were here slain by the Creeks in their last decisive battle. These graves occupied the whole grove, consisting of two or three acres of ground."

During a visit of the author in 1859 to the upper part of Marlborough District, near the North Carolina line, a mound was pointed out to him which is related by tradition to have been the scene of an Indian battle. On a subsequent occasion it was visited for the purpose of exploration. It appears to have been raised originally but a few feet above the surface of the adjoining level, and had been almost entirely washed down. Its dimensions were about ten by fifteen feet. Many years before, a partial excavation had been made, and in digging down on this occasion for a short distance small pieces of bone were found mixed with the earth throughout, so that no opinion could be formed as to the depth of the first layer of bodies. Four feet below the surface a point was reached where the soil had not been disturbed, and a little below this were found from four to six skeletons, lying regularly, in a horizontal position, with the feet to the east, having evidently been placed in two layers. The larger bones were in a comparative state of preservation, and one of the jawbones with the teeth entire, apparently of a person about middle age. With the bones were found a stone hatchet, a beautiful arrow-head, and a pipe, and strange to relate, the smell of tobacco about the pipe was perceptible for several hours after the exhumation. The tradition relating to the battle and the burial was well founded, and carried them nearly a century back.

As to tobacco, the Indians affirmed, as some of the earliest travellers among them inform us, that the use of it

---

Pedee, is an instance of this, where many remains of the kind were once visible, though now for the most part levelled by the plough.

*Bartram's "Travels in the Carolinas, Georgia, East and West Florida," 1773-74.

was known to them before the Europeans discovered the continent. The skill of the Indians in medicine, in certain diseases, was remarkable, the process of cure being simple and expeditious. The knowledge of some of the most valuable plants not in use was derived from them.*

Some of the customs of the Indians of Carolina indicated a degree of kindness and social affection, as well as an appreciation of duty, of which they are not generally supposed to have been possessed. When, for example, one of their own nation had suffered any loss by fire, or otherwise, he was ordered to make a feast, to which all the tribe was invited. After they had partaken of the feast, one of their speakers, generally a grave old man, delivered a harangue, informing them of the particulars of the loss sustained, and of their duty under such circumstances. After which, every man, according to his quality, threw down some present upon the ground, of beads, skins, furs, or other valuables, which often amounted to treble the loss incurred.

So, if one wished to build a canoe, or make a cabin, they rendered him assistance, saying, "There were several works which one man could not effect, and that therefore they must help him; otherwise their society would fall, and they would be deprived of those urgent necessities which life requires." If a woman lost her husband, and had a large family of children to maintain, she was always assisted. The young men of the tribe were made to plant, reap, and do anything she was not capable of doing herself. At the same time they would not suffer any one to be idle, but compelled all to employ themselves in some work or other.†

As to religion, they believed generally that the world was round, and that there were two spirits, the one good and the other bad. The good spirit they reckoned to be the author and maker of everything. It was He, they said, who gave them the fruits of the earth; and taught them to hunt, fish, and be wise enough to overpower the beasts of the wilderness and all other creatures, that they might be assistant and beneficial to man. They did not believe

---
*Lawson, p. 172.
†Lawson, pp. 178, 179.

that the good Spirit punished any man in this life, or that to come, but that he delighted in doing good, and in making his creatures wise and happy. The bad Spirit (who lived, as they thought, separate from the good spirit) they made the author of sickness, disappointment, loss, hunger, travail, and all the misfortunes that human life is incident to. Some of our aborigines were found to have traditions of the great Deluge, and of this event they gave a curious description. Of some of their practices, and one in particular, Lawson gives a singular account. He says: "Several customs are found in some families, which others keep not; as, for example, the families of the Mach-a-pangas use the Jewish custom of circumcision, and the rest do not; neither did I ever know any other amongst the Indians that practised any such thing; and perhaps if you ask them what is the reason they do so, they will make you no manner of answer: which is as much as to say, I will not tell you."* They seemed to have been unwilling, for the most part, to give any account of their customs, particularly those of a religious character.

And so, the same writer remarks, that he knew them, for days together, to be amongst their idols and dead kings, though he could never get admittance to their sacred places to see what they were doing. The fact of their practising idolatry at all has been positively denied by other travellers, who profess to have informed themselves of all that relates to their habits and customs. It is likely that the different tribes, remote from each other, and possibly of different origin, differed much in their customs and traditional observances, and hence the conflicting accounts which have been given. Of one custom, remarkable as it is suggestive, which Lawson affirms to have prevailed among the Indians of Carolina, and of which no other writer is believed to give any account, it may gratify the curiosity of the reader to be informed. It is very certain that it must have nipped the risings of aboriginal Young Americanism in the bud, leaving to a far superior race to exhibit, in the management of their youth, much more indecision and weakness.

*Lawson, pp. 210, 211.

"There is one most abominable custom," says Lawson, "which they call husquenawing their young men, which I have not made any mention of yet.

"Most commonly once a year, at farthest, once in two years, these people take up so many of their young men as they think are able to undergo it, and husquenaugh them, which is to make them obedient and respective to their superiors, and (as they say) is the same to them, as it is to us to send our children to school, to be taught good breeding and letters. This house of correction is a strong, large cabin, made on purpose for the reception of the young men and boys, that have not passed this graduation already; and it is always at Christ-mas that they husquenaugh their youth, which is by bringing them into this house, and keeping them dark all the time, where they more than half starve them. Besides, they give them Pellitory bark, and several intoxicating plants that make them go driving mad as ever were any people in the world; you may hear them make the most dismal cries and howlings that ever human creatures expressed; all which continues about five or six weeks, and the little meat they eat, is the nastiest, loathsome stuff, and mixed with all manner of filth it's possible to get. After the time is expired, they are brought out of the cabin, which never is in the town, but always a distance off, and guarded by a jailer or two, who watch by turns. And, when they first come out, they are poor as ever any creatures were; for you must know several die under this diabolical purgation. Moreover, they really either are, or pretend to be drunk, and do not speak for several days; I think, twenty or thirty; and look so ghastly and are so changed, that it's next to an impossibility to know them again, although you was never so well acquainted with them before. I would fain have gone into the madhouse, and seen them in their time of purgatory; but the king would not suffer it, because he told me, that they would do me or any other white man an injury that ventured in amongst them; so I desisted. They play this prank with girls as well as boys, and I believe it is a miserable life they endure, because I have known several of them run away at that time to avoid it. Now, the savages say, if it was not for this, they could not keep their youth in subjection: besides that it hardens them after to the fatigues of war, hunting, and all manner of hardship, which their way of living exposes them to. Besides, they add, that it carries off those infirm, weak bodies, that would have been only a burden and disgrace to their nation, and saves the victuals and cloathing for better people, that would have been expended on such useless creatures."*

Lawson is the only one of the early Indian travellers in South Carolina, except Lederer, who passed through those parts of the State inhabited by the ancient dwellers on the Pedee. A large part of his book, however, is taken up with the natural history of North Carolina. He commenced a journey from Charlestown, December 28th, 1700, passed up the Santee and Wateree Rivers, and thence probably across to the Yadkin, and through North Carolina into Virginia. Among the Catawbas he must have met with the Cheraws and Pedees, if not in the parts higher up on our own river, though he does not mention them by name. In speaking therefore of the Carolina Indians generally, his remarks will apply to these, as well as others more particularly mentioned.

A few years after he was put to death in a most barbarous manner by the Indians in Eastern North Carolina; to which State he had rendered most important service as Surveyor-General, as well as by his interesting account of the Natural History of that region.

The author at one time cherished the hope of procuring some valuable traditional matter as to the Cheraws, through Wm. H. Thomas, Esq., of North Carolina, of whom mention has already been made. It was thought not unlikely that during his long and familiar intercourse with the Catawbas, Mr. Thomas might have gathered from their traditions something of the history of the Cheraws before the union of the tribes; but the hope was disappointed. The tradition of the Catawbas, already related, seems to be all

---

*Lawson, pp. 233-34.

4—H. O. C.

they have preserved. Every other source of information, now accessible, has been exhausted. And with the account here given, meagre and unsatisfactory as it is, we must be content, leaving these early occupants of the soil, proud and valiant and numerous as they once were, in that darkness and oblivion, to which the red man, as he has receded westward before the advancing tide of civilization, has ever been consigned.

CHAPTER II.

First settlements in the province—Establishment of counties—Craven County—Some account of it—The boundaries and extent—Difficulty as to dividing line between Craven and Berkeley—Province divided into ten parishes—First parochial organization in Craven County—St. James' Santee—Its extent—Prince George—Its boundaries—Prince Frederick next established—Settlement of line between Prince George and Prince Frederick—Letter of Col. Pawley—Petition and counter-petition to Council on the subject—Pedee not known in early history of province—History of dispute as to dividing line between North and South Carolina on the north-east and north—Some account of the survey—Conclusion.

MANY years passed away after the first settlements on the coast of Carolina before they began to extend very far into the interior. The country had not been explored, and the Indian, jealous of encroachment upon his hitherto uninterrupted domain, was hovering with murderous design upon the borders of civilization. It was necessary, therefore, for their own protection, that the whites should remain together, and cautiously advance, as accessions were made to their numbers, in search of richer lands towards the middle and upper parts of the province. In the meantime the people, who had hitherto lived under a kind of military government, now began to form a legislature for establishing civil regulation. Accordingly, the first parliament (as it was styled) held in South Carolina, was called together in 1674; and at this meeting acts were passed, which were ratified by the proprietors, and preserved in the records of the colony.*

In 1682, it was found necessary to divide the inhabited parts of the province into counties, of which three were laid out—Berkeley, embracing Charlestown, and the space around the capital, extended from Sewee on the north to Stono Creek on the south; beyond this to the northward was Craven county; and to the southward Colleton county, all extending within the land to a distance of thirty-five

---
*Hewitt's "History of S. C.," in 1st Carroll, p. 59.

miles from the sea-coast.* Shortly after, Carteret county was added to the number. These counties were subdivided into squares of 12,000 acres each, for the several shares of the proprietors, land-graves, and cassiques.†

Craven, formerly denominated Clarendon county, embraced in its subsequent extension a much larger territory than the other counties. From Berkeley, on the south, it reached towards Cape Fear on the north, and with North Carolina for one boundary on the north and northeast, and the Santee and its branches on the other sides, it extended through a wide belt of country from the sea-coast to the mountains.

At the time of the division into counties, Craven was so sparsely settled as not to be politically considered. But, twenty years afterwards, it was described as being pretty well inhabited, the Huguenots having settled on the Santee, about which time it sent ten members to the Assembly. It took its name from William, Earl of Craven, one of the first lord proprietors, and long retained it.

This county embraced the region of the Pedee throughout its course, from the North Carolina line southward. Some account, therefore, of its political divisions will be given, extending down to the period of those settlements in the upper parts of the Pedee country, to which attention is to be directed.

Not long after the division, some disputes appear to have arisen as to the dividing line between Berkeley and Craven counties, and an Act of Assembly‡ was passed in 1733 to settle the same.

The first parochial organization in Craven County was under an Act of Assembly of 1706, commonly called the Church Act, passed for the establishment of religious worship according to the Church of England, and for erecting churches.

It divided the Province into ten parishes, of which Craven County constituted one, by the name of St. James, Santee.§

*Rivers' "History S. C." p. 134.
†Oldmixon in Carroll's "Collection," vol. ii. p. 409.
‡"Public Laws of So. Ca.," p. 176.
§"Statutes at Large of S. C." vol. ii. p. 330.

By a further declaratory Act passed in 1708, the bounds of the several Parishes were defined, and those of St. James, Santee, were restricted as follows:—"To the N.E. by Santee River, to the S.E. by the Sea, and to the S.W. by Berkeley County." In 1721* the Parish of Prince George, Winyaw, was established,—bounded "on the S.W. by Santee River, on the N.E. by the Cape Fear River, on the East by the Ocean, and on the West as far as it shall be inhabited by his Majesty's subjects." Up to this time, however, the settlements had not extended far to the north and north-westward.

They were gradually going up along the line of the rivers, with their rich alluvial bottoms. The population of the Province receiving constant accessions from abroad, began at length to find its way into the interior; and the need of extending organizations was felt, with the privilege of representation and other facilities for progress which would be thereby afforded. In 1734, this need of a portion of the inhabitants of Craven County was recognized, and a further division took place; the Parish of Prince Frederick being established, and taken from that of Prince George, Winyaw, embracing, according to the terms of the Act, the region of the Upper Pedee on the West.†

It was soon after found, however, that this division was not sufficiently definite as to the Northern line. Accordingly in the following year, 1735, the Act was so changed as to make the said line extend due North over Pedee River to the utmost bounds of the Province, it being provided "that the tract of land to the East of the said line, between that and the Sea, should be deemed as part of the Parish of Prince George, Winyaw, and on the other side of the said line to the West, a part of the Parish of Prince Frederick."‡

Of the existence and operation of this amending Act, there appears to have been a singular oversight at a later period, as will be seen hereafter.

Dissatisfaction still continued to exist as to the dividing line between the two Parishes, on account of its extension

*3"Statutes," p. 171.
†3 "Statutes at Large," p. 374.
‡"Public Laws," p. 141.

across the Pedee. The following letter of Colonel George Pawley brought the matter to the notice of Council:—

"June 7th, 1739.

"Please your Honour,—I think it my duty to inform your Honour that the dividing line of Prince George and Prince Frederick's Parishes is not yet finished according to the additional Act made, which was to cross Pedee River, and continue a North course till it touch the Provincial line; which, if it is done, will, in my humble opinion, break that small company as is of late erected on that Neck lying between Great Pedee and Little Pedee rivers; also, it will cross some part of Queensborough Town-ship, which is a Parish of itself. Therefore, if your Honour pleases to think on it, I don't doubt but you will be of the opinion to have Great Pedee the boundary of the Parish upward from where the line is marked and strikes the said River; for as it now stands, there is a confusion among the Inhabitants, not knowing in what Parish they belong; also, the Surveyors now not how to certify their Plots, some for one Parish and some for the other. Therefore, if the river be the Bounds, the work is done, and no charge to the Publick; and that your Honour may have a better idea, I have drawn a small Draft of the Rivers in these Parts; so I beg your Honour will be so good as to forgive, if I have done amiss, for it is not my intent so to do, but the hearty desire for the good of the place. So beg leave to subscribe myself your Honour's most obedient, humble servant to command,

"GEORGE PAWLEY."*

"To the Hon. Wm. Bull."

Whereupon, it was "Ordered, that the Clerk do draw out two copies of Mr. George Pawley's letter, with the Draft of the Rivers, one of them to be sent to the Parish of Prince Frederick's, the other to be sent to the Parish of Prince George, to know whether they have any objection to make to the proposals contained in the said letter, for settling the Boundary of these Parishes, and to return an answer."

The matter having thus been referred to the inhabitants,

*"Council Journal," No. 7.

action was taken by them; and on the 25th of January, 1742, a Petition from sundry inhabitants of Prince George was laid before Council,* praying that the Great Pedee might be made the dividing line between the parishes; "because, as it was to be seen by the Act of 1734-35, it would divide the narrow strip of land between Great and Little Pedee rivers, and run alternately in the swamp of one or the other, which would be impracticable to run, and the branches of Little Pedee would sometimes make it difficult to distinguish that river, the lakes, &c." This petition was signed by George Pawley, John Woodbury, David Cherrey, and thirty-eight others.

A counter petition was at the same time presented by John Avant, and nineteen others, inhabitants of Prince Frederick's, praying the line should not be so run:

"1st. Because the Inhabitants residing between the said rivers are twelve miles and upwards nearer to our Parish Church than to George-town.

"2nd. The major part of the abovesaid inhabitants must go through our Parish and pass by our Church to public worship, and other religious duties, and other officers to George-town.

"3rd. Because the said inhabitants humbly pray to be included in the River.

"4th. Because the Town-ship of Queensborough is laid on both sides of Great Pedee river; and

"5th. That whenever the Legislature shall be pleased to erect the Town-ship of Queensborough and Williamsburg into separate Parishes, this of Prince Frederick's being the oldest Parish (from which Prince George was divided), will be confined to narrow limits, and consequently for ever remain one of the smallest, if not poorest, Parishes in the Province, if so valuable a branch as that of Pedee be taken from it.

"We further presume to acquaint your Hon^{rs} that the North line appointed by Act of Assembly to be run from John Bogg's plantation, on Black River, was supposed and intended (by our Representatives) to make Pedee River at or

---

*"Council Journal," No. 8, pp. 454, 455.

below the plantation, Euhaney, belonging to Mr. Percival Pawley about eighteen miles distant from said Bogg's plantation; but we now find that a North course excludes from this Parish sundry families residing on Pedee River, near the line as it is now marked, who constantly attend divine service in this Parish, being about twelve miles distant from our Church, and at least twenty-two miles from Georgetown.

"We therefore pray your Hon^{rs} to relieve the Inhabitants by ordering the dividing line to be run on a straight course, which shall be done on our own proper charges, from Bogg's plantation to Euhaney, that the Pedee River be the boundary to the mouth of Little Pedee, which is about fifteen miles above said Euhaney, and that Little Pedee river and the main branch thereof be the natural bounds up to the Provincial line."

The Petitions were ordered to lie on the table.

As, according to the original term of extension, when the Parish of Prince George, Winyaw, was created, so now Prince Frederick was made to embrace a large part of the hitherto uninhabited and valuable region stretching out to the North-westward.

More than twenty years after, in 1757, the Parish of Prince Frederick was divided; "the inhabitants of the upper parts of the same by their Petition to the General Assembly having represented many inconveniences they labored under, for the want of such a division." An Act was therefore passed, dividing Prince Frederick into two Parishes, "by continuing the North-westernmost line of Williamsburg Township to Pedee and Santee rivers; all the lands to the Southward of the said line, constituting a distinct Parish by itself, separate from the other part of Prince Frederick, and thereafter to be known as St. Mark's." The Parish of St. Mark's therefore embraced that portion of Craven County which was west of the Pedee and north of said line. But, returning to the Parochial organization as it was in 1734, and following up the valley of the Pedee through the then Parish of Prince Frederick's, a distance of about fifty miles, the traveller would have entered at what is now Marion District, with Darlington and Chesterfield above on the west, and Marlborough on the east of the Pedee, the territory, to the early settlement and subsequent progress of which attention is to be given.

Though more than seventy miles in length, from its southern bounds to the line of North Carolina above, and in width from thirty to fifty, abounding in every variety of soil, and presenting no mean facilities for transportation by water, this inviting region, until within a few years before, had remained entirely unexplored.

There is nothing to indicate that any settlements had been made previous to the year 1730.

Indeed, little was then known of this part of the Province. In some of the descriptions of Carolina, written not many years before the time referred to, the Pedee is not so much as mentioned by name. And in an account published as much as a half century later, after the mention of several rivers of importance, among which the Pedee is not classed, it is simply added, "There are many other Rivers and Creeks of lesser note."*

Before any settlements were made in the upper part of Craven County, some difficulty had occurred in determining the line between South and North Carolina, which line bounded Craven on the north and north-east. After the resignation of the Lords Proprietors, in July, 1729, and the consequent change of Government, the Province of Carolina, hitherto one, was divided, by order of the Council, into North and South Carolina.† That part of the Province, described generally as lying south and west of Cape Fear, became South Carolina. The exact limits of each were now to be defined, and, as was to be expected, disputes arose respecting the boundary line, before it was finally settled. In 1732 appeared the first public communications of a conflicting character between the Governors of the respective Provinces. This controversy led to instructions from the king to the Governor of North Carolina, in which it was said: "in order to prevent any disputes that may arise about the Southern boundaries of our Province under your Government, we are graciously pleased to signify our

*2 Carroll, p. 263.
†"Statutes," pp. 405-6.

pleasure that a line shall be run by Commissioners, appointed by each Province, beginning at the sea, thirty miles distant from the mouth of Cape Fear river, on the South-West thereof, keeping at the same distance from the said river, as the course thereof runs to the main source or head thereof, and from thence the said boundary line shall be continued due west as far as the South Seas."*

Agreeably to these instructions, the first survey was made in 1735, under the authority of the Royal Government. It commenced at the mouth of Little River, on the sea-shore; was extended in a north-west direction 64½ miles, to a point two miles north-west of one of the branches of Little Pedee. In 1737, the line was extended in the same direction 22 miles, to a stake in a meadow, which was erroneously supposed to be at the point of intersection with the 35th degree of north latitude. The entire length of the two lines is 86 miles 174 poles. In 1764, 24th September, James Moore, George Pawley, Samuel Wiley, and Arthur Mackay, under the direction of Governor Dobbs, of North Carolina, and Governor Bull, of South Carolina, extended the boundary due west from the stake at which the line of 1737 terminated, the distance of 62 miles; intersecting the Charles-town road at 61 miles, to a point near the Washaw Creek. In 1772 the line was extended from this point, under the authority of Governor Tryon, to the Tryon Mountain; and the controversy, which commenced with the formation of our constitution, and was unsettled until 1813, between North and South Carolina, grew out of it.†

Afterward, a part of the line of 1772 was re-run, and the line then extended to the westward until it reached a point of intersection with the boundary of Georgia.

In a description of South Carolina, supposed to have been written by Governor Glen about the year 1761, this subject is referred to, and certain reasons are there assigned for the continuance of the dispute. He says: "The Northern boundary of South Carolina is not so well agreed upon as

---

*1 Statutes, p. 406.

†Governor Swain's "Letter to Dr. Cooper, 27th March, 1835," 1 "Statutes at Large," p. 409.

might be expected, which is owing to the dishonest intentions of many lawless people, settled in those parts without legal titles, and not to any want of attention in Government, nor to any difficulty in the thing itself; but these people, by keeping up a dispute about the boundaries of North and South Carolina, evade paying quit-rents for their lands, &c.; and so long as they can enjoy the protection of Government without contributing their quotas towards the expenses of it, they will be keeping up the dispute about boundaries. This they have hitherto done in such manner as to defeat the good intentions of all the Orders and Instructions from time to time given for terminating these disputes and ascertaining the Boundary, which, in his Majesty's Instructions, is directed to be done by running a line thirty miles to the southward of Cape Fear River, parallel to, and observing the course of that River to its head, for the Boundary on that side; and though this order is not only too explicit to be mistaken, but hath been put in execution, or at least is said to have been so, the good intention of it nevertheless continues to be evaded."*

A part of the line on the north-east and north, constitutes that portion of the present boundaries of Marlborough and Chesterfield Districts, once embraced in Craven County. The tradition has been handed down, that the Commissioners appointed to make the survey, besides being ignorant of or inattentive to the difference between a statute and a geographical mile, were not at all times in a fit condition for the work, and that they took advantage of each other in behalf of their respective States, as opportunity offered, or over-excitment, on one side or the other, in the course of their gleeful expedition, happened to prevail. The truth of the matter, as those who have had occasion in later times, in surveying lands, to follow the track which the Commissioners pursued, agree in stating, appears to be this,—that its irregular, zigzag course indicates either gross carelessness in all the parties concerned, or, that the work was begun and ended in a common frolic, at the expense of both States.

*2 Carroll, pp. 178-9.

But thus it happened, that the dispute which took its rise prior to the year 1732, was not adjusted in all its details until near a century after; the Act for ratifying and confirming the joint work of the Convention of Commissioners, appointed for the establishment of the dividing line between the two States, not having been passed by the Legislature of South Carolina until the year 1815. In addition to the causes alluded to by Governor Glen, and which were doubtless operative in protracting the controversy; it is to be remarked, that there is a feeling of State pride likely to be excited by the continuance of such disputes, a feeling often as influential with States as with individuals. There are also peculiar difficulties in the way of adjusting such disputes, growing out of the extensive and somewhat unwieldy organization of States, and of the necessary agency of intermediate and often irresponsible parties.

Acting, too, at long intervals, it happens that errors, which might at first have been readily exposed, become deeply rooted with the lapse of time, and matters, trivial in themselves, are so magnified, that the controversies respecting them become in the end exceeding difficult of adjustment. It is to be hoped, that these States, originally but one Province, under the common name of "Carolina," and bound together by many affecting associations as well as local ties, will never again have their good understanding and harmony disturbed by conflicting claims or border difficulties; and with their last dispute buried along the line of the now established boundary, will remain one, and only one in every element of common peace and common prosperity hereafter.

Returning to the year 1734, when the Act was passed for establishing the parish of Prince Frederick, we find in that, and also Prince George, Winyaw previously embracing that part of Craven County to the northward, the parochial organizations within the bounds of which the first settlements were made in the upper parts of the Pedee.

It is a pleasing task, in tracing the early history of any region, to contemplate the change from a state of undeveloped resources in the hands of the wandering savage, to the first triumphs of civilization by a superior race, however feeble and unpretending their efforts. This, for a time, will be our employment. Of the early settlements on the Pedee, extending through a period of more than thirty years, some account will be given.

Through the aid of a few individuals, who having a taste for such inquiries, had gathered some information as to the history of families, and of valuable manuscript matter fortunately discovered here and there, with the more important light thrown upon the early emigration to this part of the State by its public records, the author succeeded beyond his most sanguine expectations at the first, in collecting material for his work.

If nothing more shall be accomplished, it will serve at least to rescue for those who cannot fail to cherish it, much that would otherwise have passed into oblivion.

CHAPTER III.

Inducements held out to Settlers in the Province—Progress of Population—The Plan of Townships—Its effect in inducing Immigration—Location of Township on the Pedee—Proceedings of the Council respecting it—Draft of Queensborough Township—The Welch Tract—Proceedings of Council on the subject—The Survey—Its Limits—Why enlarged—The Welch—Other Settlers—The Welch Neck—The Welch Colony—Church Organization—Continued Immigration—Names of Settlers—Term of Welch Grant extended—Immigration direct from Wales—Bounties offered by Government—Names of Grantees—Difficulties encountered by the Welch—Petition for Relief—Bounties continued—Notice of other early Settlers—Their Difficulties with the Welch—Exclusive Policy of the Welch—Accounts of different Families—The Welch Settlement—Its Progress—Welch Traits.

From the time of its first settlement, it was esteemed a matter of the utmost importance for the safety and prosperity of the Province that its population should increase as rapidly as possible.

To this end, every inducement was held out to immigration. The royal bounty was promised, in various forms, to the poor and oppressed of other lands to make America their home.

The unoccupied territory of the New World, fair and fertile, and teeming in boundless resources, was declared to be open to the over-burdened industry and fruitless enterprise of the densely populated States of Europe. Thus encouraged, large accessions were made, at successive periods, to our infant settlements.

From 1696 to 1730, although its population gradually increased, no large addition was made, at any one time, to the inhabitants of Carolina. About the latter year, a new scheme was adopted to promote the settlement of the province, which proved successful beyond the most sanguine expectations of Government. Governor Johnson was instructed "to mark out eleven Townships, in square plots, on the sides of rivers, consisting each of twenty thousand acres, and to divide the land within them into shares of fifty acres for each man, woman, and child that should come over to occupy and improve them. Each township was to form a Parish, and all the inhabitants were to have an equal right to the river. As soon as the Parish should increase to the number of a hundred families, they were to have the right to send two members of their own election to the Assembly, and to enjoy the same privileges as the Parishes already established. Each settler was to pay four shillings a year for every hundred acres of land, excepting the first ten years, during which term they were to be rent free. Governor Johnson issued a warrant to St. John, Surveyor-General of the Province, empowering him to go and mark out these townships; but he having demanded an exorbitant sum of money for his trouble, the members of the Council agreed among themselves to do this piece of service for their country. Accordingly, eleven townships were marked out by them in the following situations:—Two on the River Alatamaha, two on Savanna, two on Santee, one on Pedee, one on Waccamaw, one on Wateree, and one on Black River."*

The township on the Pedee was called Queensborough; and to the time of its being marked out—1731-32—or a period but little subsequent, it is to be assigned the date of our first settlements. There was no delay in the execution of this work (of marking out the townships), which had been committed to the Governor by his Majesty's Government, for building up its waste places, and the more speedy settlement of the Province.

The first proceedings with reference to the laying out of the townships was in meeting of the Council on Friday, March 16th, 1731, in Charles-town; his Excellency the Governor, the Hon. Lieutenant Governor, Messrs. Arthur Middleton, Robert Wright, Thomas Waring, John Fenwick, and William Bull, being present. It was resolved, "That the Hon. Mr. Chief Justice Wright and Alexander Skeene, Esq., do mark out three Townships, pursuant to his Majesty's instructions for that purpose, a copy of which is to be given them, with this resolution—one upon Black River, one upon Pedee River, and the other upon Waccamaw River—that

---

*1 Carroll: "Hewitt's History," p. 196.

they return Plots of the same to this Board, and that they be allowed £500 currency for each Township out of the Public Treasury for marking out the same."* Other persons were also appointed on this occasion to mark out townships on other rivers, according to instructions. In the following year—viz., March, 1732—the township on the Waccamaw appears to have been laid out, and called Kingston. "We are assured," said the Council, in reply to a message on the subject from the lower House, "that at the time of marking the said Township, there were no settlements made within the same, except one, then begun by Jennour, who claimed 700 acres, but by what title we could not learn, he then being in North Carolina; nor were there any other claims made to any lands within the Township, that we could hear of, save only by Mr. William Watties, of 500 acres, at a place called Pond Bluff, but not then settled."†

On the 2nd of June, of the same year, the Commissioners made full returns of the plans of the towns and townships, which they had marked out, pursuant to a resolution in Council, of the 20th of March previous, on Waccamaw, Pedee, and Black Rivers, and were ordered to be paid accordingly. From the annexed plot or draft, Queensborough Township appears to have been laid out on the Great Pedee, but a short distance above the mouth of Little Pedee River, embracing a part of what has since been known as Britton Neck (a narrow strip of land between the two rivers), and extending also on the west side of the Pedee. But for this Plot, most unexpectedly found,‡ the exact location of the Township of Queensborough could not have been determined. It was probably a part of the return made by the Commissioners, or may have been the "Draft of the Rivers," accompanying the letter of Colonel Pawley, to Council, of

---

*"Council Journal," No. 5.
†"Council Journal," No. 5, p. 202.
‡It was discovered by mere accident by the author, on a loose piece of paper, on turning over the leaves of what appeared to be the oldest record-book in the Secretary of State's office, Columbia, and which was being examined as a curious relic of the past. Its contents related to other matters of anterior date.

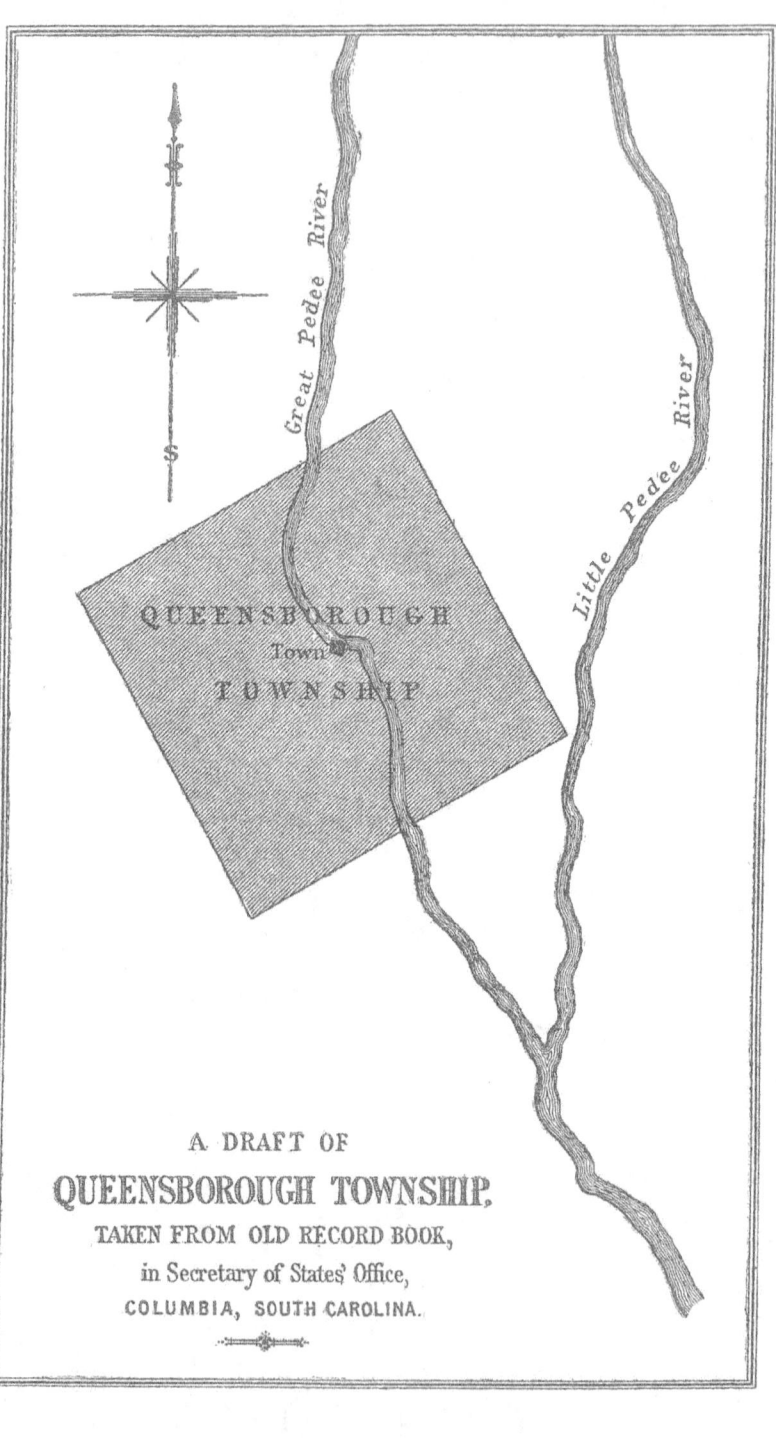

June 7th, 1793, in connexion with the dividing line between Prince George and Prince Frederick's, which has already been given.

No settlements appear to have been made up to this time within the limits of Queensborough Township. To encourage such settlements, generally, further action was taken by Council.

On the 14th of February, 1734, it was ordered, "That the several persons who have laid out the several Town-ships, do prepare a rough draft, or plan of a Town, to be layed out in each Township, containing about 800 acres, out of which a common of 300 acres, to be laid out in the back part, and the remaining 500 acres to be lay^d out in half-acre lots, to be at a convenient distance from the river, which rough Draft or Plan, is to be lay^d before this Board for their consideration."*

In accordance with these instructions, the draft or plan of a town in Queensborough Township† was made, as appears from a notice in the *Gazette,* as late as June 3rd-10th, 1751, advertising Lot No. 64, in Queensborough Town. There is, however, no evidence remaining to show that the town, as such, was ever settled. Its location appears to have been on the west bank of the river. The inducements held out in connexion with the townships appear to have led to a visit of some of the Welch from Pennsylvania for the purpose of exploration and settlement, and to the removal, very shortly after, of the colony, which was destined to form so important an element in the history and progress of the region of the Upper Pedee.

---

*"Council Journal," No. 6, pp. 41, 42.
†The Form of a Grant for Lots in the Townships, was as follows:—
So. Carolina.
    By his Excellency,   Esq., Governor, Captain-General and
      Commander in Chief, in and over the Province of So. Carolina.
   To   , Esq., Surveyor-General.
You are forthwith required to admeasure and lay out unto   ,
a lot in the town, as also   acres in the Township of Queensborough, on the Pedee River, in Craven County, observing to lay the same out agreeable to the Plan or Model thereof.
 Given under my hand and seal, the   day of   , Anno Domini   .
(Council Journal, No. 5, p. 257.)

The emigration from Wales to Pennsylvania, from which this to Pedee proceeded, "had its beginning," we are told, in the following manner. "In the spring of 1701, several Baptists in the counties of Pembroke and Cairmarthen, resolved to go to America; and as one of the company, Thomas Griffith, was a minister, they were advised to be constituted a Church. They took the advice, and the instrument of their confederation was in being in 1770, but is now lost or mislaid. The names of the confederates were as follows: viz., Thomas Griffith, Griffith Nicholas, Evan Edmond, John Edward, Elisha Thomas, Enoch Morgan, Richard David, James David, Elizabeth Griffith, Lewis Edmond, Mary John, Mary Thomas, Elizabeth Griffith, Tennet David, Margaret Matthias, Tennet Morris. These sixteen persons, which may be styled a Church emigrant, met at Milford Haven, in the month of June, 1701, embarked on board the good ship *William and Mary;* and on the 8th of September following, landed at Philadelphia. The brethren there treated them courteously, and advised them to settle about Pennepec; thither they went, and there continued about a year and a half, during which time their Church increased from sixteen to thirty-seven.

But, finding it inconvenient to tarry about Pennepec, they, in 1703, took up land in Newcastle County, from Messrs. Evans, Davis, and Willis, who had purchased said Welch tract from William Penn, containing upwards of 30,000 acres, and thither removed the same year, and built a little meeting-house on the spot where the present stands. This house was a neat brick building, forty feet by thirty.

The Welch tract was first in the province of Pennsylvania, afterwards, upon the change of boundaries, in the State of Delaware. This will account for the fact, that the Welch were sometimes spoken of as being come from Pennsylvania, at other times from Delaware.*

Some of those who were members of the colony on Pedee must have followed the first emigration from Wales to Pennsylvania, as their names do not appear in the foregoing list.

---

*Benedict's "History of the Baptist," p. 4.

The first visit of the Welch to Pedee appears to have been made in the latter part of 1735, or early in the following year. It led to a remarkable act of favour on the part of the Council, to induce the colony to come. Wishing, on their arrival, to settle in a body, and be possessed of ample and exclusive privileges as to the occupancy of the soil, they petitioned the Government that an extensive tract of land might be appropriated to their sole benefit for a certain period. This appears from a message of the Lieutenant-Governor to the Lower House of Assembly, 2nd February, 1737, in which he said:—"The late Lieutenant-Governor, with the advice of his Majesty's Council, thought it would greatly tend to the service and strengthening of this Province, to grant the petition of several natives of the principality of Wales, in behalf of themselves and others of their countrymen, who intended to settle in this Province from Great Britain and Pennsylvania, praying the lands near the Forks above the Township on Pedee River might be reserved and set apart for their use, and Mr. John Ouldfield, being thought a very proper person, was employed for that service."*

The petition here referred to bore date August 13th, 1736; and having been favourably received by the Council, his Majesty's Surveyor-General, James H. St. John, Esq., was instructed to have the said tract laid out. Accordingly, he directed a precept to John Ouldfield, bearing date Nov. 16th, 1736, "to admeasure and lay out, for the Welch families that were to be imported to this Province a tract of land, containing in the whole one hundred and seventy-three thousand eight hundred and forty acres, situated and being in Craven County. Ten thousand acres, being part thereof, lying within the limits of the Township of Queensborough, on the north side of Pedee River, the remainder of said tract lying on the south side of said river, and butting and bounding to the south-east on the reserved lands of the said Township of Queensborough, and all other sides on vacant lands as are supposed."

The survey was made, and a plot thereof returned 29th

---
*"Council Journal," No. 5, pp. 51, 52.

Nov. 1736, of which a copy is annexed.* With reference to this plot, the Lieutenant-Governor sent a message, 2nd February, 1737, to the Lower House, saying:—"I send it for your satisfaction and perusal, also his (Ouldfield's) acc^t which I think so very reasonable, hope you^1 make provision to pay the same, as the sinking fund is so far short of answering the engagements already entered into."†

The House replied the next day as follows:—"In answer to your Honour's message just now received, with the account of Mr. John Ouldfield, for surveying the Welch Tract of land on Pedee River, we beg leave to inform your Honour, that we have perused the said account, and we are very much concerned to find, as the acc^t is so very moderate and reasonable, that there should not be money sufficient in the Town-ship Fund to discharge it. But we hope your Honour will concur with us in opinion, that it is by no means necessary, nor would be justifiable in us to Tax our Constituents to pay any such expence, especially as it may be so much more justly and reasonably done by the duty on Negroes, should it be thought proper by your Hon^r, in conjunction with the two Houses of Assembly, to revise and continue that Duty, without which we cannot foresee any method by which this acc^t, or any other of the same sort, can, with justice to the People of this Province, be provided for.

"By order of the House,
"CHARLES PINCKNEY, Speaker.‡

"Feb. 3, 1737-8."

The tract thus surveyed, and extending up the river but a short distance above Mars Bluff, seems not to have been adapted to the wants of the Welch, or to have been a compliance by Council with their petition of the August previous, as was intended. They consequently petitioned again for such an extension of the tract as would answer all their purposes, and enable them to select their lands to advan-

---

*The original Plot was found, in a good state of preservation, among the old Township Plots, in the Office of the Secretary of State, Charleston.
†"Council Journal," No. 7, pp. 51, 52.
‡Ibid.

A PLOT OF THE
WELCH GRANT.
CONTAINING 173,840 ACRES.
November 16th 1736.

Scale of Original Plot 35 Chains per Inch.
Scale of Copy of Plot 320 Chains per Inch.

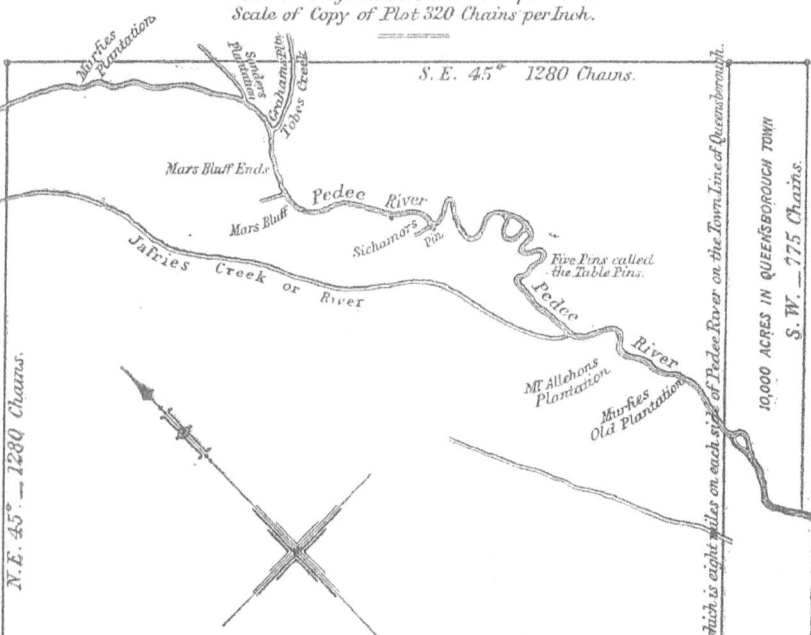

South Carolina, By virtue of Precept to me directed by James H. Johns, Esq'r. His Majestys Surveyor General, bearing date the Sixteenth of November, 1736. I have admeasured and laid out for the Welch familys that are to be Imported to this Province, a Tract of Land containing in the whole One Hundred and Seventy three Thousand, Eight Hundred and Forty Acrs, situated and being in Craven County, Ten Thousand Acrs, being part thereof Lying within the limits of the Township of Queensborough on the North side of Pedee River; the Remainder of Said Tract lying on both sides of said River, Butting & Bounding to the South East on the Reserved Lands of the said Township of Queensborough and all other sides on vacant Lands as is supposed, & hath such shape, form and marks as are Represented by this Delinated Plot, thereof given under my hand, 29th Day of November, 1736. per me, (Signed)

Deputy Surveyor

Note — This Copy made May 22nd, 1859, from Original Plot in Secretary of State's Office.
By *White & Ramsay*
Deputy Surveyors.

tage. Their request was favourably regarded, as appears from the following Proclamation: "By the Hon. Thomas Broughton, Esq., Lieut.-Governor, and Commander-in-Chief, in and over his Majesty's Province of South Carolina.

"Whereas, I have this day received information in Council, from Danl. James, that the Lands which David Lewis, Saml. Wild, and the said Danl James, prayed for in their petition of 13th August last, to be set apart for the Welch Families mentioned therein, were the vacant Lands they viewed, and desired might be reserved for them, lying on each side of Great Pedee River, and up to the two Main Branches thereof, and that the Lands set forth, and prescribed in the order of Council of the 21st January last, are not the Lands they desired, and were assigned them agreeable to the said Petition; nor will these Lands suit their intention of planting Hemp and Flax; and whereas I have also received information from the said Danl James, that several of the said Families, on the encouragement they had from the first Order of Council, have sold their Possessions in Pennsylvania, some being arrived, and others on their way to this Province, I have therefore thought fit, by and with the advice and consent of his Majesty's Hon. Council, to issue this, my Proclamation, to give Notice, that I have (with the advice and consent aforesaid) refused the said last order of Council of the 21st of January last, and confirmed the said first order of the 13th of August; and have ordered that the Lines be run parallel, as near as may be, with the course of Great Pedee River; and further to give Notice, that the Surveyor-General is ordered and directed to instruct his Deputies not to survey, (for any other Persons than the said Welch people) any more of the said Lands above Pedee Township, lying within eight miles on each side of the said River, and so up to the Branches aforesaid. Given under my hand and the Great Seal of this his Majesty's Province, this 8th day of February, in the 10th year of his Majesty's reign, Annoque Domini, 1737."[*]

This extension of the Welch Tract up the Pedee to the

---

[*] *Gazette*, Feb. 5-12, 1737.

two main branches thereof, gave the infant Colony exclusive privileges over a large territory, embracing for more than one hundred miles by the course of the river, its rich alluvial bottom, and a valuable class of lands in proximity to the swamp. The two main branches referred to, must have been the Yadkin and Uwhare, or Yadkin and Rocky Rivers—most probably the latter; in either case, a point (their junction) something considerably above the present boundary line between South and North Carolina,—the Rocky and Yadkin Rivers uniting twenty-five miles above the said State lines, and the Yadkin and Uwhare not less than fifty. With such inducements to emigrate to the Pedee, the Welch were not slow in making their way to the Province. The first visit of exploration by a few of their number was made not later than the spring of 1736. They appear, however, to have been preceded by some other settlers. The first name of which any record has been found, was Joseph Dopson. He was a grantee of 130 acres of land, in what was afterwards the Welch Tract, as early as 11th May, 1733.

This fact appears in a petition to Council by Jacob Kolb, in 1753, for the said land, the Petitioner stating therein that the said grant was still in the Surveyor-General's Office. The name of Dopson seems to have disappeared not long after from the country. He may have been a squatter, or merely in search of land, not making any permanent settlement. The earliest grants on the west side of the river, in the upper part of what is now Darlington District, go back to the year 1734.* Of the names of the Grantees no record perhaps remains. Lands were surveyed for Richard Barrow in what was called, soon after, the Welch Neck, as early as January, 1736.† Nothing is known of him, the name having soon after disappeared from this region. This was the case with many others of the first comers. They probably belonged to that class of people who live on the outskirts of civilization, leading the way as

---

*On the authority of the late Hon. Josiah J. Evans, in a letter to the Author. Judge Evans was proverbially accurate in his recollection of such matters.

†Of this fact the original evidence is in the Author's possession.

hunters, and keeping in the van of permanent settlers. They are not unfrequently men of enterprise, but with a roving disposition, and distaste for those wholesome restraints which society imposes on its members. Exploring the way that others may follow, they have often rendered essential service in the settlement of new regions, without being generally appreciated, however, or taking any place, as they have deserved, in the history of man. Thus it was with many, whose names appeared in the first record, only to be known for a short time afterward.*

In 1736, or early in the following year, a company of the Welch settled on Cat Fish, a stream in what is now Marion District, in the tract first assigned them. Among these were Jenkin and Owen David.† They remained there a short time, and then removed higher up the river to the neighbourhood of the Welch Neck. As appears from the petition which led to the extension of the Welch Tract much above its original boundary, the lands on the upper Pedee seem to have suited their agricultural purposes better, being well adapted also to settlements immediately contiguous to the river. To that rich and compact body of land, embraced in a bend of the river, opposite the present village of Society Hill, and called, from an early period, the "Welch Neck," the attention of these prudent settlers appears from the first to have been directed. And there they began to gather in a body. The "Welch Neck" extended from Crooked Creek above (on its outer line), to the "Red Bluff" below, a distance of about six miles, embracing the rich lands of the swamp, several miles across. During the Revolution, or about a

---

*In the letter of Judge Evans, already referred to, and written March 29, 1858, but a short time before his death, he remarks in confirmation of the fact stated above, "that of the 8 to 10 grants of which his plantations on Crooked Creek, Marlborough District, was made up, the name of not a single one of the original grantees was known, at a period long antecedent, in the country."

†Jenkin David died before the Revolution. He had three sons—Joshua, Josiah, and Benjamin. Of these, Joshua lived to take an active part in the Revolution. He died in 1822, and was the father of the late Captain Joshua David, of Marlborough.

Owen David had four sons—John, Azariah, Owen, and Jenkin. Of these, John was the only son who remained on the Pedee, the others having left the country at an early period. From these two progenitors the extensive and respectable connexion of the name in Marlborough has descended.

generation after the first settlement, the "Company which mustered at the M'Call old field," numbered from 130 to 140, all of them said to be Welch. Between the years 1736 and 1746, almost all the lands in the Welch Neck were granted.* By the latter part of 1737 most of the families from Pennsylvania had arrived, and the infant Colony began to assume an organized and permanent character. Under its leader, James James, Esq.,† were laid the foundations of future growth and prosperity. Mr. James was possessed of larger means than any of his companions, and the most prominent individual among them.

At this time a respectable portion of the Colony consisted of the following persons, viz., James James and wife, Philip James‡ and wife, Daniel Devonald and wife, Abel James and wife, Daniel James and wife, Thomas Evans and wife, John Jones and wife, Thomas Harry and wife, Daniel Harry and wife, John Harry and wife, Samuel Wild and wife,§ Samuel Evans|| and wife, Griffith Jones and wife, David Jones and wife, Thomas Jones and wife.

There were also others whose names appear at the same period, viz., Thomas James, Griffith John, William James,

---

*On the authority of Judge Evans's letter.

†Mr. James owned the lands on both sides of the river, at what is now known as Spark's Ferry. The first public Ferry in this region was established here in 1768. He died at Cat Fish, Nov. 21, 1769, where he had probably gone on a visit.

‡Philip James was a son of James James, Esq., and the first Pastor of the Welch Neck Church. He was born near Pennepec, in Pennsylvania, in 1701. He removed to Carolina, in 1735, and was ordained at the Welch Neck, April 4, 1743. His death took place in 1753. "In the latter part of his life," said a subsequent writer, "his mind was full of heavenly joys, and attentive only to spiritual concerns."—Wood Furman's "History of the Charleston Association," p. 70.

§Wild was a name ever after to be prominently connected with the history of the Pedee. The first settler appears to have had two sons, John and Abel. Abel was known afterwards and before the Revolution as Old Colonel Wild. His residence was on the east bank of the river, nearly opposite the Long Bluff. His widow was a lady noted in her day for excellence and strength of character. Colonel Wild had four sons—John, Samuel, Jesse, and George. John Wild, the other brother, was the father of John and Samuel. The latter of these became distinguished as Judge Wild, and was a man of very remarkable character. His brother John, who died prematurely, is said to have been even more talented.

||Evans, like Wild, was a name destined to become distinguished. From these first settlers, Thomas and Samuel, sprang the large and highly respectable connexion on the Pedee. The late Judge Evans was a descendant—being a great-grandson of Thomas Evans.

John Newberry, Evan Harry, Henry Oldacre, Hasker Newberry,[*] William Eynon, James Roger, David James, Daniel Dousnal, Samuel Sarance (Sorrency and De Sorrency as it was sometimes written), Evan Vaughn, William Tarell[†] (Terrell.)

The first-mentioned company[‡] were, in January, 1738, "organized into a society of the Baptist faith," and erected a house of worship on the east bank of the river, a short distance above the ferry.[§]

There they long continued to worship God after the manner of their fathers, and in that consecrated spot, where some monumental remains are yet to be seen, their dead repose, awaiting the last summons. This party, with others, appear to have moved in a body from the Welch Tract in Pennsylvania and Delaware to the Pedee during the previous year, if not a little earlier. Many sore lets and hindrances awaited the progress of their settlements.

Of one of these grievances complaint was made to Government, as appears from the following message, sent by the Upper House, or Council, January 26th, 1737, to the Commons House of Assembly:—

"Mr. Speaker and Gentlemen,—Some of the Welch Settlers on Pedee have lately complained to me that they have sufficient reason to believe that the Indians will molest and disturb them in settling the Lands run out for the Welch, intimating that one Thompson, a trader, has bought a great quantity of that Tract, and pretends to hold it by an Indian right, which, as I apprehend this practice may be attended

---

[*] In his "Annals of Newbury District," in attempting to trace the origin of the name, Judge O'Neall says: "Certain it is that a family of that name once lived beyond Pedee, in that section now called Marlborough District"—p. vii. It is not improbable that some member of this family may have removed to that part of the State, and hence the name, afterward given to the district.

[†] The grandfather of the late Captain John Terrell, of Marlborough, a worthy descendant of the old Welch stock, and one of the best men of his day and generation. Captain Terrell's father, William Terrell, was engaged in the public service before the Revolution, but did not survive that period.

[‡] This list of names was taken, with other information, from the records of the Welch Neck Church, the most of which, however, were unfortunately destroyed by fire or otherwise many years since. The earlier records now remaining are very meagre.

[§] Now known as Spark's—on the road leading from Society Hill to Bennetsville.

with fatal consequences, I desire you[1] appoint a Committee of your House, to join a Committee of his Majesty's Council, to consider of the most effectual method to prevent any private contracts with Indians for the land.

"WM. BULL."*

A few days after, Committees were appointed to consider the subject, and measures were adopted to prevent such difficulties in the future.

The tide of immigration had now set in, and constant additions were made to the population on the Pedee. "At a Council† held at Ashley Ferry, Sep^t 16th, 1738, the Hon. Wm Bull, President, signed the following grants for land in Queensborough Township, viz. :—

"Jacob Buckholt . . 250 acres.
Jeremiah Fickling . 450 "
Richard Thompson . 400 "
Joseph Jolly . . 600 acres."

The Government continued to manifest a due concern for fresh accessions to the Welch population.

In the Council Chamber, 11th May, 1739, it was ordered, "That the Term for reserving the Welch Tract upon Pedee River for the sole benefit of the Welch and Pennsylvanians, be prolonged for the space of two years from the expiration thereof, in the month of August next, and all Persons are required to take Notice thereof at their Peril. By order of his Honour the Lieu^t Governor, and his Majesty's Hon^l Council.

"ALEXR. CRAMAHE, C. C."‡

This was a liberal policy on the part of Government, and an act of great favour to the Welch.

The spirit of speculation began to show itself as to landed estate even at this early period. On the 25th of July, 1739, 1,000 acres were advertised in Queensborough Township, but by whom does not appear.

The removal of the Welch from Pennsylvania and Delaware, and the reports made to their countrymen in Wales, seem to have excited a spirit of emigration thither from that

---

*"Council Journal," No. 7, p. 38.
†*Gazette*, Oct. 5, 1738.
‡*Gazette*, May 12-19, 1739.

country. The colonial authorities, having received some tidings of this kind, held out additional inducements to them to come over. The following announcement was made in the *Gazette* of the 7th and 14th July, 1739:—"In council, the 7th day of July, 1739. There being great reason to believe that many poor People of the Principality of Wales would remove into this Province, provided they could be sure of having the same Bounty (over and above the Land allowed by his Majesty) as other poor Protestants have heretofore had who have become settlers in his Majesty's Townships,—Resolved, that the sum of Six Thousand Pounds shall be reserved out of the Township Fund, to be appropriated as a Bounty to the first two hundred People above twelve years of age (two under twelve years of age to be deemed as one) who shall arrive here from the Principality of Wales, and become settlers upon the Welch Tract upon Pedee, within the Space of Two Years from hence, the said Bounty to be proportioned as follows, viz.:—

"To each Head above twelve years of age, twelve bushels of Corn, one Barrel of Beef, Fifty w^t. of Pork, one hundred w^t. of rice, one Bushel of Salt.

"To each Male above twelve years of age, also, One Axe, one Broad Hoe, one Cow and Calf, and one Young Sow. And the charge of measuring out and the Fifty acres of Land per head allowed by his Majesty. A true copy.

"ALEXANDER CRAMAHE, C. C."

The inducements here offered are supposed to have encouraged and increased the emigration direct from Wales. By the year 1746, as already remarked, almost all the lands in the Welch Neck were granted, having been taken up exclusively by the Welch.

The number of settlers had largely increased between 1740 and 1743. The following list of names and of the quantities of land, respectively allotted, with the dates of entries, will convey some idea of the progress made down to the year 1734. The list did not embrace the names of all who had arrived, but only of those who had neglected to comply with the requirements of the law respecting the Township Settlers, and whose neglect operated to the prejudice of others who might wish to come in. It is taken from the *Gazette* of August, 1743.

"A list of Township Plots (on the Bounty) in the Surveyor-General's Office, August 15th, 1743:—

Queensborough Township.

Thomas James	650 acres	. .	October	3, 1738.
Griffith Jones	300 ,,	. .	,,	4, ,,
Griffith John	100 ,,	. .	September	1, ,,
William James	400 ,,	. .	,,	,, ,,
John Newberry	350 ,,	. .	,,	2, ,,
Henry Oldacre	50 ,,	. .	,,	4, ,,
Hasker Newberry	300 ,,	. .	,,	5, ,,
Evan Harry	100 ,,	. .	,,	30, ,,
William Eynon	500 ,,	. .	August	23, ,,
James Roger	50 ,,	. .	,,	26, ,,
David James	400 ,,	. .	,,	27, ,,
Thomas Evans	400 ,,	. .	,,	,, ,,
Daniel Dousnal	200 ,,	. .	,,	,, ,,
John Jones	250 ,,	. .	,,	28, ,,
Sam¹. Sarance	100 ,,	. .	,,	29, ,,
Richard Barrow	150 ,,	. .	,,	,, ,,
Evan Vaughn	350 ,,	. .	,,	30, ,,
Abel James	300 ,,	. .	,,	31, ,,
William Tarell	200 ,,	. .	,,	,, ,,
Thomas Walley	50 ,,	. .	May	18, 1740.
Philip James	250 ,,	. .	,,	21, ,,
Sampson Thomas	400 ,,	. .	,,	23, ,,
Jacob Buckles	250 ,,	. .	,,	24, ,,
Peter Kishley	400 ,,	. .	June	2, ,,
John Evans	200 ,,	. .	February	6, ,,
John Newberry	100 ,,	. .	November	22, 1741.
Wm. Tarell	100 ,,	. .	December	9, ,,
Thos. Evans	250 ,,	. .	,,	10, ,,
,, ,,	75 ,,	. .	,,	14, ,,
Abel Evans	100 ,,	. .	,,	11, ,,
John Evans	100 ,,	. .	,,	,, ,,
Mary Evans	300 ,,	. .	,,	13, ,,
John Jones	100 ,,	. .	,,	1, ,,
Jeremiah Rowell	150 ,,	. .	,,	16, ,,

HISTORY OF THE OLD CHERAWS. 57

Queensborough Township—(continued).

James Rowland	150 acres	December 14, 1741.
Evan Vaughn	100 „	„ 17, „
John Westfield	300 „	„ „ „
Thomas Elleby	250 „	„ „ „
Simon Parsons	100 „	„ 18, „
John Carter	100 „	„ 22, „
Wm. Evans	50 „	„ 23, „
Job Edwards	200 „	„ 28, „
Daniel James	350 „	„ 24, 1742.
John Jones	500 „	„ „ „
David Harry	125 „	„ 23, „
„ „	„ „	„ „ „
Philip James	100 „	„ 27, „
Philip Douglas	300 „	„ 29, „
William Carey	300 „	„ 31, „
Mary Evans	200 „	January 1, 1743.
David Malahan	150 „	„ 4, „
Thomas Moses	220 „	„ 5, „
William Jones	400 „	„ „ „
Nicholas Rogers	350 „	„ 6, „
Thomas Evans	100 „	„ 15, „
„ „	125 „	„ 28, „
William James	200 „	„ 29, „

"Upon perusing and considering the Memorial of George Hunter, Esq., Surveyor-General, relating to several Plots of land returned into and now lying in the Office of the said Surveyor-General, and which have remained in the said Office for many years, without any applications from the Persons in whose names the same are run, to have them taken out of the said Office, whereby other Persons are prevented from taking up the said Lands, and becoming Tenants to his Majesty for the same: It is Ordered that the said List be published in the *Gazette,* to the intent that the several Persons interested in or claiming the same may apply for, and take out the said Plots, on or before the 1st day of January next; and in case of their neglecting so to do, their failure therein will be taken as a Disclaimer of their Rights to the said Lands; and the same Lands may and shall be granted to any other persons who shall duly apply for the same. A true copy. "ALEXANDER GORDON, C.C."

The neglect of most or all of those mentioned in the foregoing list to take out their plots, &c., may doubtless be owing to the fact that they were too poor to do so, or that the lands first granted were in the lower part of the Welch Tract, and taken out before its extension; and having determined to go higher up the river, some of them may have abandoned their claims below, where their places were soon taken by others.

In common with other settlers, the Welch had many difficulties to contend against. The means of most of them were, no doubt, exhausted by the expense of the removal to Pedee. After their arrival, the distance from Charles-town, the seat of Government, where all public business had to be transacted, perplexed them no little. The following extracts from the Council Journals will show the mode of proceeding with reference to land, and the sore extremities to which these poor settlers were often driven.

"In Council Chamber, Jan. 26, 1742-43. Read the Petition of part of the Inhabitants of the Welch Tract, as also the Petition of Saml Sorrency, as follows, viz.: To the Hon. Wm. Bull, Lieu^t-Govr and Commander-in-Chief of his Majesty's Province of S. C., and to the rest of the Hon^l Members of his Majesty's Council.

"The petition of Samuel Sorrency Humbly sheweth, That your Petitioner at his first arrival in this Province obtained a Warrant for 100 acres of land, to be laid out in the Welch Tract, whereon I now live,—That your Petitioner hath since two children come from Pennsylvania to this place, which I have made oath of before Wm. James, Esq., who informs me that it will not do without my proving my right in the Council Chamber; but as I am but low in the world, and live at so great a distance from Charles-town, and not having a horse to ride nor money to bear my expenses, and the Bearer, Thomas Bowen, can prove, if need be, that I have such children—Your Petitioner therefore humbly prays your Honours to take my case into consideration, and grant me a warrant for 100 acres of his Majesty's land, to be laid out in the Welch Tract, and your Petitioner, as in duty bound, &c.

"The above and Samuel James swore to his family right before Wm. James, Esq., one of his Majesty's Justices assigned to keep the Peace in Craven County aforesaid. The Prayer of said Petition was granted, and it was ordered, that Mr. Secretary Hammerton do prepare a warrant accordingly.

"Read also the Petition of Daniel M'Daniel, for a warrant of 100 acres, for himself and wife, to be laid out in the Welch Tract, which was granted.

"Read also the Petition of several other Inhabitants of the Welch Tract, as follows:—

"The Petition of part of the Inhabitants of the Welch Tract humbly sheweth: That we have left Pennsylvania and have transported ourselves to this Province by the encouragement given to settle this aforesaid Tract of land; but as some of us had our lands run out, and the Plots put into the Surveyor-General's office 4 years ago, and as we are so poor that we cannot get money to pay the charge of surveying and granting it, has discouraged many from coming over; and we are afraid the discouragement being so great, we not being sure of our grants, by reason of our poverty, that some that have come over will return from us again. So we, your Humble Petitioners, hope your Hon^r and Hon^{ls} will take it into your serious consideration, what satisfaction it is to every man to have his titles to land secure, and will fulfill the encouragement given us that we should have our lands granted us free from all charge of surveying and granting; and, as we are in duty bound, we shall ever pray, &c.

"Philip James	Abel James	Peter Roblyn
Jeremiah Rowell	Thos Evans	Creen Vaughn
Philip Douglass	John Evans	Nicholas Rogers
Daniel Devonald	John Evans	Simon Parson
David Harry	John Carter	David Lewis
Thos Evans	Wm Kirby	Saml Sorrency
Thos Moses	Griffith John	Wm Terrell
Mary Evans	Danl Honehorn	John Jones
Jobe Edwards	Walter Downe	Abel Evans
Nathan^l Evans	David James	Wm James.

"Whereupon, it having been represented to his Hon^r the Lieu^t-Govr in Council, that several families of Welch that had intended to become settlers in the whole Tract on Pedee River, in this Province, have, as it was apprehended, been prevented from coming into this Province from the dangers arising from the present war with Spain, and that by the advices received from Pennsylvania, several of the said Welch families were expected to arrive here the next year; but as the time for reserving the Welch Tract would expire in the month of August next, it was prayed that the said Term might be further enlarged—the same was considered, and it was ordered by his Hon^r the Lieu^t-Govr, by the advice of his Majesty's Council, that the said Term be enlarged two years from the expiration of the said present Term; of which all persons concerned are to take notice.

"And upon reading and considering the Petition of Philip James, Abel James, Thos Evans, and others, settlers in the whole Tract, praying that the charge of surveying and granting their lands might be all defrayed to them; it was the opinion of the Board, upon considering the Prayer of the Petition, as it appeared to the Board that they had desired the lands only to be reserved for a Term to them, which was accordingly done, and which Term had been further enlarged for their benefit, but was not to have their survey of land carried through the offices at the publick expense, that being only for such Welch as should come from the Principality of Wales—that, as this Prayer of the Petitioners is what they had not before asked, nor had any reason to expect from this Government, it could not be regularly granted; but, for a further encouragement of the Settlers of the said Tract, it was the opinion of the Board, and so ordered, that for the first twenty barrels of good and merchantable white flour, of 200 lbs. weight neat each, which shall be made in the said Tract, and brought to the markets in Charles-town, there shall be paid to the makers thereof, upon proof of its being bona fide the produce of the said Tract, a bounty of 5 pounds currency for each barrel. Ordered, that the Clerk of this Board give a copy of the above minute to the Petitioners and the same to the Commissary."*

*"Council Journal," No. 8, pp. 455-458. There was then a great demand for

The exclusive privileges of the Welch in the large tract appropriated to them, led, in some instances, to difficulties either with those who came before them, thus acquiring the right of prior occupancy of the soil, though not having secured a legal title, or with others, who afterwards were allowed to settle among them, but subsequently objected to as neighbours by the Welch. The latter were doubtless clannish in their feelings, and unwilling to encourage strangers to come among them. Of the first class mentioned, was Francis Young, one of the earliest settlers within the limits of the upper portion of the Welch Tract of whom any record remains. He is supposed to have emigrated from Ireland. In the Council Journal, 9th November, 1743, is this entry: "Francis Young petitioned for 150 acres of land in the Welch Tract on the south side of the river, bounding between John Thomas's line and one Vaughn's land; and the Petitioner at the same time produced a certificate of his having lived there before the settlement of the Welch, signed by two Justices of the Peace, in that place. He appeared in person, and his petition was granted."

Another settler, about the same time, the first of a name which has since been well known on the Pedee, was James Galespy. He made a similar application, but was not so fortunate, for a time, at least, as to the result.

On the same day, 9th November, 1743, "was read the Petition of James Galespy, shewing that the Petitioner, having six persons in family, for whom, as yet, he has not had any lands assigned him, humbly prays that a warrant of survey for 300 acres be granted him in the Welch Tract. But, not appearing to swear to his family right, his petition was ordered to lie on the table."

---

flour, and it doubtless commanded high prices. Of other articles, the following table of prices appeared in the *Gazettes* of the day.

Charlestown, November 1, 1739.
Rice 32s. to 33s. per cwt.
Pitch, 40s.; Turpentine, 20s.
Tar, 30s.; Skins, 18s. to 19s.
Indian corn, 7s. 6d. to 10s. per bushel.

Charlestown, July 16, 1741.
Rice 3l. per cwt.; Skins, 16s. 6d. per lb.
Pitch, 55s. per barrel.
Tar, 45s.; Indian corn, 30s. per bushel.
Turpentine, 22s. 6d.
Indian peas, 30s. per bushel.

At the same time, Henry Roach made a similar application for 100 acres of land in the Welch Tract; but not appearing to be a Welchman, or of Welch extract, the consideration of his case was postponed. James Galespy came from the North of Ireland. He was a man of energy and enterprise. In connexion with General Christopher Gadsden, of Charlestown, he was engaged in boating on the Pedee many years before the Revolution, and is believed to have been the first person who ever brought a boat to Cheraw. The difficulty with the Welch doubtless led to his removal higher up the river, to the neighbourhood of the present town of Cheraw. He settled on the west side of the river, a short distance below the town, and entered on a successful career as a trader. He married a daughter of Francis Young. James Galespy died before the Revolution. He left two sons to inherit his name,* and two daughters.

The Welch did not extend their settlements much, if any, above the mouth of Crooked Creek, or the upper limits of the Welch Neck. Of those who were induced to enter upon the Welch Tract was Thomas Elerby, the first of that name who emigrated to the Pedee. He came soon after the first of the Welch, as appears from the following record of Council:† "July 5th, 1742. Read the Petition of Thomas Elerby, setting forth that he and his family, consisting of eleven persons, came from Virginia about five years past, and settled and cleared land near Pedee river, and obtained a warrant for his family right; but happened to be within the limits of the Welch Tract, and at a convenient place to fix a water-mill. When the Welch inhabi-

---

*The name was soon after changed to its present spelling, Gillespie. The sons of James Galespy were Francis and James. The former died before the Revolution. James was born in 1754, and was therefore of age when that stormy period commenced. He took an active part on the Pedee throughout the struggle, and was prominently connected with St. David's Parish. He settled on the east side of the river, on lands now owned by his son, General James Gillespie, of Marlborough. He married a Miss Wild, aunt of the late Judge Samuel Wild, of Darlington. The fruits of this marriage were Francis, Samuel, and James, and two daughters—Sarah and Mary.

James Galespy, senior, had also two daughters. Of these, one married John Westfield, one of the early emigrants from Virginia to Pedee. He lived on the west side of the river above Cheraw. John Westfield, with his wife, subsequently returned to Virginia and died there. Westfield Creek, in Chesterfield District, took its name from him. Obedience, the other daughter, married Thomas Elerby, from whom a numerous progeny sprung.

†"Council Journal," No. 8, p. 97.

tants came to settle, above four years past, one Daniel James persuaded the Petitioner to remove peaceably from that place by the run of water, and gave the Petitioner and his family liberty to settle and cultivate any other vacant land which he should find within the limits of the Welch Tract; and did also himself get a special warrant for 250 acres of land, which is run out for the Petitioner and returned: whereupon he begs for a grant for the same, having lived ever since thereon, and now wants more land in the same, or adjoining thereto, to cultivate and settle, his family being increased to 20 and 2 persons, he having six persons lately purchased or born, for which, as yet, he has had no warrant. He therefore prays for a warrant of survey for laying out 300 acres of vacant land, and a special warrant of survey for running out 550 acres of vacant land more, within the limits of the said Welch Tract, in the lieu of his common warrant. Resolved: that the consideration of the said Petition be deferred until the Petitioner appear personally before the Board." Mr. Elerby was doubtless successful in the end, as he remained in that neighborhood and became the owner of extensive landed possessions, a large portion of which has remained in the family to the present day.* John Elerby, a brother of Thomas, came with him to Pedee, and settled on the east side of the river. He either returned to Virginia or removed elsewhere at an early period. Thomas Elerby brought a good property with him, and was probably the first slaveholder on the Upper Pedee. Some years prior to the Revolution he had a large number—at least for that day. This family emigrated from England to Virginia.

The name is still known in England, and is spelt as it appears in our early records.

Not long afterwards, however, as was often the case, it was changed to its present form, Ellerbe.† Thomas Elerby,

---

*The mill site referred to in the petition of Thos. Elerby, was doubtless that on Juniper Creek, of which some signs yet remain near the road leading from Cheraw to Society Hill.

A grist and saw mill, at all events, were there, and in successful operation some time before the Revolution.

†This change, it is said, took place soon after Thos. Elerby's death, while his two sons were yet young, and was made by their teacher, the name not having yet become familiar.

who married, as already stated, Obedience Gillespie, had two sons, Thomas and William, from whom the extensive family connexion on the Pedee have descended.* Of the Evans, who were among the Welch settlers, a branch of the family went first, or soon after their arrival removed, to what is now Marion District. From Thomas and Samuel Evans, who were members of the Welch colony, the extensive connexion in Darlington and Chesterfield Districts descended.

With the main body of the Welch, or soon after came John Brown. He was born near Burlington, New Jersey, and brought up at Frankfort, in the neighbourhood of Philadelphia. Mr. Brown was ordained May 7th, 1750, and succeeded the Rev. Philip James in the charge of the Welch Neck Church, but did not continue long in that position. After this he continued to preach the gospel in different places until his death.

It is supposed that he was its founder, and gave name to the old Brownsville community, twenty miles lower down on the east side of the river.

About the years 1738-39, Robert Williams, then a young man, emigrated to Pedee. He was born at Northampton, North Carolina, in 1717. Mr. Williams settled on the west side of the river, opposite the lower part of the Welch Neck, and became, eventually, the owner of a large landed

---

*The widow of Thomas Elerby married Charles Bedingfield (called Bennyfield by the old people), a man of some note, but of unprincipled character. While his stepsons, William and Thomas Ellerbe, were yet young, he ran off with all the moveable property to Georgia, the West of that period, leaving them only the landed estate of their father with which, to make their way in the world. This was before the Revolution, and the name of Bedingfield was not known in this region afterwards.

The children of William Elerby were—Esther, who married Erasmus Powe; William F., who married Miss Ann Robinson (this lady subsequently married Clement Prince); Elizabeth, who married Joseph Ellerbe; Martha E., who married Thomas Powe; Zachariah, who married Obedience Ellerbe; and Thomas F., who married Rebecca Ellerbe.

The children of Thomas Ellerbe were—William E., who married a Miss Crawford; James, who also married a Miss Crawford; Thomas, who married Miss Leslie Prince; Jane, who married George Strother; Joseph, who married Elizabeth Ellerbe; Mary, who married Alexander McQueen; Rebecca, who married John M'Farland; and John Ellerbe, who married Martha Powe, and afterwards Mary, her sister. Of these large families there is now not one survivor.

William and Thomas Ellerbe were prominently connected with St. David's Parish, and worthy Whigs in the Revolution.

DAVID R. WILLIAMS,

Governor of South Carolina, Member of Congress, and General in the United States Army.

estate in this neighbourhood, most of which has remained in the family since.

In 1752, he was ordained at the Welch Neck, and became the pastor of that Church, retaining the position, however, but a short time afterwards. Robert Williams had two children—a daughter, who married Arthur Hart, and afterwards, Moses Murfee; and a son, David Williams. The latter was born on Pedee, February 1st, 1739, received his education in Charles-town, and after a brief but amiable and useful career, died January 1st, 1776.* He married a sister of Arthur Hart, and the fruits of this marriage were two children—a daughter, Mary Ann,† and a son, David Rogerson, who subsequently became distinguished as a member of Congress from the Pedee district, and Governor of South Carolina.

Robert Williams died April 8th, 1788, and had the following character given him: "He was kind to the poor, and remarkably so to the afflicted; a man of excellent natural parts, and a minister who preached the gospel to the edification and comfort of souls."‡

Another name which appears among the grantees of land in the Welch Neck, in 1743, was Nicholas Rogers. He was one of the Welch settlers, and died in 1759. He left a son, Benjamin,§ the father of the late Colonel Benjamin Rogers of Marlborough.

---

*The Rev. Evan Pugh officiated on the occasion of David Williams' funeral, preaching from John xi. 11, 12.

†Mary Ann, daughter of David Williams, was born April 16th, 1772, and married John M'Iver. The fruits of this marriage were four sons—John E., Alexander, David Rogerson Williams, and Thomas; and one daughter, Eliza, who married John Davis. Mrs. M'Iver died November 18th, 1834, having long survived her husband.

David Rogerson was born March 8th, 1776; and married, first, a Miss Powers, of Providence, Rhode Island, by whom he had one child, the late Col. John N. Williams, of Society Hill, a man of uncommon purity and excellence of character. His second wife was Elizabeth Witherspoon, who survived him many years. She was a lady of remarkable traits, and universally beloved.

General Williams, as he was afterwards known, was possessed of superior talents and extraordinary energy of character. After an active and useful life, both as a private citizen and public man, he came to his end November 17th, 1830, by the falling in of a bridge which he had had erected over Lynche's Creek, on the George-town road.

‡From the funeral discourse by Mr. Pugh, who performed the last rites for the father as he had done for the son.

§Benjamin Rogers lived on the hill below Juniper, on what has since been the

Allusion has been made to the course pursued by the Welch, with reference to others coming in among them. The feeling was a natural one, and under the circumstances, in such a chaotic state of society, when people of different nations, and many of them doubtless of bad character, were flocking in as squatters and traders, not to be condemned. The subsequent history of their colony, strongly and peculiarly marked as it was in all the elements of substantial growth and virtuous progress, will be found to have fully justified their exclusive policy. They planted themselves, in most instances, immediately on the river, and made locations of lands in small parcels.

The country being in a wilderness state, their position isolated, and their means limited, they selected such quantities of land as suited their present necessities, influenced also, to some extent, by the consideration of compactness, which gratified their social propensities, and enabled them besides to concentrate against the sudden incursions of the Indians, by whom they were surrounded. Here, on a virgin soil, they peacefully pursued their agricultural employments, being richly rewarded for the common toils and hardships endured.

In their new and yet wilderness home, drawn together more closely than by the common ties of friendship and of blood, surrounded by common dangers, against which they vigilantly guarded, with common wants and necessities sufficiently supplied, and meeting weekly around one consecrated altar to worship the God of their fathers, a more perfect unity, or virtuous and manly life can scarcely be conceived.

Such was the scene presented by this infant band of brothers in the early days of their history; with no court

---

main road leading from Cheraw to Long Bluff. He was a man of much excellence, and highly esteemed—an ardent Whig, but too old to take an active part in the Revolution. His name appears among the early records of St. David's parish. His son, the late Colonel Benjamin Rogers of Marlborough, was yet a mere youth in the Revolution; but, yielding to the impulses of his nature, and contrary to the more prudent counsels of his father, drew his sword on more than one occasion in the cause of liberty.

The sons of Col. Rogers are among the worthy and most respectable citizens of Marlborough and Darlington districts.

of justice in their midst to which conflicting claims and angry disputes might be referred, and no frowning gaol for the reception of the criminal. Nor were they needed. Few contentions, probably, were known, and the voice of society, though newly formed in this southern home, was potent enough to silence the voice of the blasphemer and make the evil-minded man pause in his ways.

Simplicity of character appears to have been one of the most marked traits of this people—a virtue which has been transmitted, through succeeding times, to their descendants. They were open and sincere, making no profession of feeling which did not exist.

For sobriety and moderation, also, with what was more essential as the foundation of all virtue, a deep religious feeling, they were distinguished. These virtues were strongly impressed upon the community they established, presenting in subsequent times a striking contrast to some other neighbourhoods on the Pedee, where dissipation and irreligion so much prevailed. The Welch brought with them to a new country those marked features for which their ancestors had been noted long before. The Welch are said to have been more jealous of their liberties than even the English, and far more irascible, though their jealousy soon abated. They were, from an early period, fond of carrying back their pedigrees to the most remote antiquity, and some of their manuscripts they make to be coeval with the Incarnation.*

But few relics† remain among the descendants of the early Welch settlers on the Pedee.

Intermingled, as they subsequently became with other races, their national peculiarities, except in a few instances of striking constitutional descent, gradually disappeared.

And of their names, as connected with the localities they inhabited, but a memorial is here and there left to tell of the first cultivators of the soil.

---

*Guthrie, p. 39.

†There is now, in the possession of a family descended from the Welch, and living in the neighbourhood of their first settlement, a Welch Bible, of the edition of 1676, which is supposed to have belonged to the leader of the colony, as it contains a record of the births, marriages, and deaths of the James family.

CHAPTER IV.

Settlements lower down on the river—One of the first comers—His family—History of the colony in Britton's Neck—The families composing it—Their history—The church building—Its subsequent history—The settlement at Sandy Bluff—The locality—Their church building—Accounts of the members of this community and their descendants—Incidents connected with different individuals—Irish Protestants—Who they were—Irish-town—Its locality—Other settlers in this region—Their history—Close of this period.

ABOUT the time of the Welch emigration to Pedee, settlements were made lower down the river in what was afterward Liberty Precinct, now Marion District. John Godbold was among the first who came to this region.

He was an Englishman, and had been long a sailor in the British service. Though advanced in years at the time of his arrival, such was his enterprising energy, that he succeeded in accumulating what, for that day, was a large property.

He settled in 1735 about a half mile below the site of the present village of Marion, being the first adventurer to that immediate locality.

The most profitable business at that time was stock raising, Charles-town* affording a good market for all the industrious settlers could carry thither. During the French and Indian wars, Mr. Godbold was plundered of almost all the personal property he had gathered. Of thirty negroes, twenty-two were taken from him and never recovered. A trunk of guineas, the fruits of many years' labour, was rifled.

He married, after his arrival on Pedee, Elizabeth M'Gurney, by whom he had three sons—John, James, and Thomas; and two daughters—Elizabeth and Anne; from whom the extensive connexion in Marion have descended.†

---

*Many of the early settlers drove their stock as far as Philadelphia.
†Of his sons, John, the eldest, married Priscilla Jones, and had three sons

John Godbold was a member of the Church of England and died in 1765, at the advanced age of more than one hundred years, in the faith of his fathers. About the time John Godbold came to Pedee, two important settlements were made in that region. One of these was in Britton's Neck, twenty miles below Mars Bluff,* and forty miles above George-town.

It was composed of the families of Britton, Graves, Fladger, Davis, Tyler, Giles, and others. They came directly from England, as one colony; and being members of the Established Church, one of their first acts was to erect a house† for the worship of God. Their minister, Dr. Robert Hunter, came with them, and is supposed to have died there. He was succeeded by the Rev. Mr. Allison.

—Zachariah, John, and Jesse. Of these, Zachariah was a captain in the Revolution.

James, the second son, married Mourning Elizabeth Baker, by whom he had six sons—John, James, Zachariah, Cade, Abram, and Thomas. Of these, John and Zachariah were lieutenants in the Revolution. Thomas, the youngest son, was the father of the late Hugh Godbold,* of Marion.

Thomas, the third son, married Martha Herron, and had four sons—Stephen, David, Thomas, and Ely. Of these, Thomas was the father of Asa Godbold, of Marion, and Ely, who left a son bearing his name.

*Mars Bluff took its name from an early settler, Maers (pronounced Mars). He left at an early period, and the name, except as marked by that locality, disappeared with him.

†This building was of black cypress, with a brick foundation, and is still to be seen, or was a few years since, in a good state of preservation, on the road leading from Port's Ferry to Potatoe Ferry, on Little Pedee. About the year 1780, the congregation having been long without a minister, and doubtless very much broken up by the troublous times of the Revolution, united with the Methodists, and the building passed into the hands of the latter, by whom it has since been retained. Charles Wesley is said to have once preached in it.

---

*To this gentleman, the late Hugh Godbold, the author was indebted for a large and valuable fund of information as to the early settlements on the Pedee and their subsequent history. To a memory of extraordinary tenacity (in genealogical details unequalled by any with which the author has ever met) was added a remarkable precision, and tender regard for truth, which gave his statements high authority, and made him always a witness of importance in courts of justice. He had, from early life, great fondness for everything connected with the local history of the region of his nativity, and having had intercourse with many of the old people of the second generation of those who first came to the Pedee, he collected a large fund of interesting matter, none of which seems ever to have escaped him. A man of general intelligence and sterling traits of character, his real worth was appreciated by few of his contemporaries. He died in 1859. Peace to his ashes.

The name of one of these families subsequently became distinguished in the person of Colonel Hugh Giles, who took a prominent part in this region during the Revolution. He was the son of Robert Giles. The other settlement referred to was made at a point on the east bank of the river, called Sandy Bluff,* two and a half miles above Mars Bluff. A few traces of it are yet to be seen at several points, immediately on the high bank of the river. The families of Crawford, Saunders, Murfee, Crosby, Keighly, Berry, and shortly after the Gibson's, made up this community. Sandy Bluff extended up the river about three miles. With the fertile uplands running out for some distance, and a rich swamp on the opposite side, and supplied, too, with numerous springs of good water, this locality was in many respects admirably adapted to the wants of the infant colony.

The chief drawback was its growing unhealthfulness, until the long process was passed through, of clearing the lands and draining the contiguous bottoms. These settlers built their houses, as did the Welch above, immediately on the river, and in close proximity to each other, for the convenience of water, of social intercourse, and their mutual protection against the Indian. It was also more healthy than locations further out from the river, as experience has proved.

They were from England and Ireland, and having landed at Charles-town, found their way to George-town, and thence up the river, attracted by the bounties which the Government had offered. Like their neighbours in Britton's Neck, they erected a building for public worship, according to the rites of the Established Church. Faint traces of this early structure were to be seen a few years since. The bricks used for the foundation were brought up the river in boats (the settlers thus transporting themselves and their stores), and were of a most superior quality.

The Rev. Wm. Turbeville came with this colony, and was their pastor. He was a well-educated man, and had a high reputation as a preacher.

---

*The Wilmington and Manchester R. R. crosses immediately below this point.

Eminent also for piety and devotion to his work, he retained the confidence and affection of the people in an extensive region of the country, to the close of a long life. One of the incidents related in connexion with him, is singularly illustrative of this feeling. Such was the general confidence in his piety and the efficacy of his prayers, that he was sent for from considerable distances, during the pressure of any general calamity, to make intercession to God in behalf of the people. On one occasion, about the year 1760, during the prevalence of a fearful drought, there was a general meeting at Bass's Mills to pray for rain. Mr. Turbeville was sent for. He answered the summons, and as tradition relates, before the sufferers had reached their homes, the heavens were opend and copious rains came down. Mr. Turbeville had no children. Several brothers came with him, of whom some descendants are now to be found in Marion.

He lived at Sandy Bluff until after the year 1800, then removed to the west side of the river, near Mars Bluff, where he married a second time, and died about 1810, at the advanced age of one hundred and three years.*

Of the settlers at Sandy Bluff, the Murfees, Saunders, Gibsons, and Crawfords accumulated the largest properties, and became most prominent. John Crawford, the first of that name, had three sons—James, John, and Hardy.

James, the eldest of them, amassed a large fortune for that day, and maintained through life a high character for integrity. He was a captain in the Revolution, and a valiant soldier in the cause of liberty.†

Of the Murfees‡ there were four brothers, Moses, Malachi, Maurice, and Michael.

---

*Mr. Turbeville was a poor man through life. It is said that Wm. Allston, grandfather of Govr. Allston, who lived at that time near the Warhees (a few miles below Mars Bluff) complained to Mr. T. on one occasion of his wearing such coarse garments. Mr. T. told him, he got but little for preaching, and could not afford to dress better.

Whereupon, Mr. Allston gave him a black suit and silk gown, on condition that he was not to use them except in preaching, and on other public official occasions.

†He was the grandfather of the late Chapman Crawford, of Marion.

‡Thus the name appears in the first records. It was afterwards changed to its present spelling, Murphy.

Of these, Malachi* became the wealthiest. He is said to have given one hundred slaves to each of three sons. He died before the Revolution.

Maurice had a son, bearing his name, who was destined to occupy a prominent place in the subsequent history of the Pedee.

Some notice of Michael Murfee appears in the records of Council:—"At a Meeting, 13th Ap^l, 1744, was read the Petition of Michael Murfee, an Inhabitant of the Welch Tract, shewing that about nine years ago, before the settling of the Welch, he purchased part of of a Warrant of one Howard, since dead, for 300 acres of land in the Welch Tract; but the said Warrant for running out the same being afterwards lost or mislaid, never was returned into the Office; notwithstanding which, he built a house on the same, settled there, and made other considerable improvements, and cleared above 400 acres thereof, and is well liked as a neighbour by all the Welch Famylies there. That the Petitioner, having since a considerable increase of fourteen persons in his family, for whom he has not as yet obtained any land, nor hath he any other land than as above said within the said Province, Prays a warrant of survey for seven hundred acres in a Tract or Tracts of vacant land, and then the said Tract of land whereupon the Petitioner is

---

*His *sons* were James, Malachi, and Moses. James the eldest, died young, leaving three daughters,—Hannah, who married Moses Saunders, of Darlington; Catharine, who married Nicholas Bedgegood, and afterwards J. B. Billingsby, of Marlboro'; and Mary, who married Jordan Saunders, *Malachi*, the second son, married first a Miss Knight, by whom he had two sons,—and afterward, Mary Hicks. The fruits of this marriage were Nathanael, Maurice, James, Elizabeth, and Sally. Elizabeth married a Rawls, and Sally married Wm. Johnson, of Sneedsboro, No. Ca. Malachi Murphy was a captain in the Revolution, and was killed at Bass's Mill. *Moses*, the third son, married a daughter of Robert Williams.

Of the daughters of Malachi Murfee, sen., Elizabeth married Wm. Pegues, of Chesterfield; another married the Rev. Nicholas Bedgegood, one of the early pastors of the Welch Neck Church; and Marcia married Claudius Pegues, of Marlborough.

Malachi Murfee, sen., married the widow of George Saunders. She was a sister of Gideon Gibson.

A female descendant, living a few years since in the neighbourhood of the original settlement, was the only representative left in that region,—such are the sad changes which time brings with it, causing the name of the most extensive family connexion, in a few generations, to pass entirely away, leaving scarce the memory of their former existence behind them.

settled as above, or so much thereof as shall appear, upon a re-survey, to be vacant, to be part of the same, which land is butting on or near Col. Pawley's land, and to the west of John Brown's.

"The Petitioner appearing in person, and swearing to the allegations of his said Petition, it was ordered, that 500 acres of land only be granted him, and the Secretary was accordingly ordered to prepare a warrant for the same."

The statement in the foregoing petition indicates a rapid increase of slave property for that early period. John, George, and William Saunders appear to have been the first of that name. In a list of grants in the Surveyor-General's Office (as to which notice was given to the parties to apply for and take out their plots), appear the names of George Saunders for 300 acres, May 24th, 1735; and John Saunders for 200 acres, May 12, 1736. They came from England. John Saunders had two sons, George and Thomas. George* was the father of Nathanael Saunders, who became a man of some note, and was the father of the late Moses and Jordan Saunders, of Darlington. The sons of Thomas Saunders removed at an early period to Tennessee.

Of the Gibsons, Gideon and Jordan were brothers. The latter went to the West as a companion of Daniel Boone. Gideon Gibson† came with his father from Virginia to Pedee. There is a public record of a grant to him for 550 acres of land as early as April, 1736. He settled at a place called Hickory Grove, five miles from Sandy Bluff, on a large and fertile body of land, long after noted as the most valuable in that region.

---

*George Saunders came to an untimely end, in connection with which a singular incident is related. He was engaged on a Sunday in cutting down a bee tree, a cypress, in the swamp on the opposite side of the river. As the cypress fell, the limb of an ash was broken off, and being thrown with violence on the head of Saunders, killed him instantly. An ash afterwards came up at the head of his grave and grew to a large tree, being regarded by the people as a standing monument of the judgment sent upon him for the violation of the Lord's Day, which led to his end.

It is but a few years since that the last vestige of this famous ash was to be seen. Near the spot are faint traces of the burial ground of the Sandy Bluff Settlement.

†He was the grand-uncle of the late Captain John Gibson, of Darlington.

He had three sons. Of these, Stephen* became wealthy, and removed to Georgia about the year 1800. Roger, another son, removed to the West before the Revolution. Gideon Gibson was a man of very marked character, of commanding influence, and prominently connected with the leading events of the region in which he lived. His death took place during the Revolution. Of the circumstances attending it some account will be given hereafter.

The settlement at Sandy Bluff was broken up at an early period, though some traces of it are yet to be seen.†

The following extract from the Council Journal of January 26th, 1737, is supposed to have related to a company of settlers on the west side of the river:—

"Read the Petition of several poor Irish Protestants, lately come in, setting forth that they had transported themselves and families into this Province, being induced thereto by the encouragement of having lands granted to them in Town-ships, which his Majesty has been graciously pleased to order to poor Protestants, importing themselves into this Province, and likewise the bounty of provisions, and therefore praying warrants of survey for the lands on either side of the Town-ships on Pedee River, and provisions, &c., according to the number of their families, as has been usually given to other poor Protestants. Recommended the same to the Commons House of Assembly."‡

The townships referred to here as being on the Pedee, were doubtless Queensborough and Kingston, the latter being on the Waccamaw. Who the petitioners were is not known. A notice of the first advertisement for the sale of lands in this region may throw some light on the locality of these poor Irish Protestants. This notice appeared in the *Gazette* of June 1, 1738, in these words: "To be sold,

---

*The Hon. Thomas Butler King, formerly of Georgia, married a daughter of Stephen Gibson.

†The author visited this interesting locality in company with the late Hugh Godbold, who took great pleasure in pointing out different points of interest. The visit was hurried and no careful examination made.

A more thorough exploration, particularly about the site of the old church, would doubtless bring some interesting relics to light. Mr. Godbold had an antiquarian taste, and an appreciation of the past which is seldom met with.

‡"Council Journal," No. 7, p. 37.

a Tract of land, of 100 acres; excellent good Land, fronting upon Pedee River, and back on Jeffrey's Creek; also, one Tract of 500 acres, in Irish-town." Of the locality of Irish-town, we are left to conjecture. It was probably on Jeffrey's Creek, and its inhabitants the Irish Protestants referred to.

A few other names appear in the records of this region. As early as 1735, Walter and Ralph Izard settled on the east side of the river, not far below Mars Bluff. They removed lower down a few years after. About the same time (1735), a family of Jamesons made a settlement at Little Bluff, in what is now Marion district.

In that, or the subsequent year, land was granted to a Colonel Jameson.

Nathan Evans[*] was a Welchman, and settled on Cat Fish. He either came from the Welch Neck above, soon after his arrival there, or was one of those who went first to the lower part of the Welch Tract, and remained there. Lands in the neighbourhood of Tart's Mill[†] were granted to Nathan Evans.

David Evans, a son of Nathan, was a captain in the Revolution, and a man of note. He died childless. About the same time, two families of James' and Lucas' came down the river, and settled on Cat Fish. With the latter of these, the Crawfords and Evans' intermarried.

Soon after, a family of Baker's came from Newbern, N. C., to Pedee. One of this name married a daughter of Nathan Evans. William Baker was prominent in the Revolution, and marked for his devotion to the cause of liberty.

The first settlements on Little Pedee were made a few years later (about 1740) by emigrants from Virginia and North Carolina—a lower class of people, many of whom became noted for their opposition to the cause of their country during its subsequent history.

The name of Buckholdt, known among the earlier settlers,

---

[*]Nathan Evans was the grandfather of the late Thomas Evans, and General Wm. Evans, of Marion. The father of General Evans was also named Nathan, and was a man of upright character through life.

[†]Tart's Mill is about six miles above Marion, C. H.

afterwards became prominent. Of this family were Abraham, Jacob and Peter. They settled on Cat Fish and in Cashway Neck. Major Abraham Buckholdt attained some distinction. This family were from Prussia. They were men of enterprise, but of a roving disposition, and left the Pedee at an early period.*

Thus closed the history of the first settlements on the Pedee. They were made between the years 1734 and 1740, the Welch element greatly preponderating. The river afforded facilities for transportation, of which advantage was taken. Stock raising was the most profitable business, and laid the foundation of fortunes, which rapidly increased. The Indian gradually retreated; Providence favoured the white man with good seasons and a fertile soil; and the tide of emigration thus begun, continued to flow in, until the troubles with the mother country, long gathering before the storm, at length burst upon the heads of a devoted people, put a temporary period to its progress.

---

*Soon after the Revolution the name disappeared. About that time Major Buckholdt removed to Georgia, and subsequently to Mississippi, from whence two of his grandsons found their way to Texas. They are the only representatives of the name surviving, and are now respectable citizens of Milam County, Texas—worthy descendants of a true Whig stock.

The only local trace of the name left in So. Ca. is in that of a Creek (Buckholdt's), four miles below the village of Society Hill in Darlington district.

CHAPTER V.

History of settlements contained—In neighborhood of Welch Neck, above and below on the river—Petitions of settlers—Their families and descendants—Certificates of character given—Battle of Culloden followed by transporation of rebels to America, and emigrations to Pedee—Valuable additions from this source—Settlers from No. Ca.—Huguenot element coming in—Braddock's defeat (1755) followed by emigrations from Pennsylvania and Virginia—Other settlers—Settlements on Lynche's Creek—Later additions—Continued to opening years of Revolution.

THE history of the settlements on the Pedee has been brought down through what may be termed its first period, viz., from 1734 to 1740. During these years only occurred the emigration of such bodies of persons to certain localities as could properly be termed colonies, as of the Welch above, and the Irish and English lower down on the river. There were also, as we have seen, individuals from different regions, who constituted valuable elements in the infant communities. From 1740 to 1760 large and important additions were made to the settlements, continuing, indeed, until the threatening difficulties with the Mother Country put a stop for the time to the increase of population from abroad.

About the year 1740, came the family of Lide. There were three brothers of this name—John, Thomas, and Robert. They were of Welch origin, and came to Carolina, from Roanoke, Virginia. After the emigration of this family from Wales, the name was Anglicized, and assumed eventually its present form. In Welch it was written Llhuyd,* in subsequent records, Loyd, which spelling was found in some branches of the family down to a comparatively recent period.

Of the three brothers, who came to Pedee, John, the eldest, left an only son, William, the father of John Wild Lide (who removed to and died in Tennessee), and of the late Mrs. Rebecca Punch, of Cheraw.

*Mill's "Statistics of S. C.," p. 618.

Thomas, the second son, settled on the river, at Cheraw Hill.* He was educated in the Church of England, and took an active part in the organization of St. David's Parish, having been a large contributor to the building of the church and the pecuniary resources of the parish afterwards. He married three times. By his first wife, who was a Miss Kimbrough, he had an only child, a daughter, the mother of the late Governor John Lyde Wilson, of So. Ca. By his second wife, a Miss Foster, he had five sons—John, Thomas, Charles Motte, Robert, and James; also a daughter.† Of these sons, Charles Motte was a man of remarkable parts. His name will appear hereafter. Col. Lide was a man of high character, and died in 1787, universally esteemed.

Robert, the youngest brother, was born in Roanoke, Va. in 1734, and brought to Pedee, by a maternal uncle, Crawford. He settled on the west side of the river‡ above, and afterwards near Cashway Ferry,§ in what is now Darlington district, and became the head of an extensive family connexion. He was a prominent actor in the subsequent history of that region, and took an influential part among the Whigs of Pedee in the Revolution. He was at one time a Major under Marion. Robert Lide married first Sarah Kolb, by whom he had three sons—James, Hugh, and Peter. He afterwards married Mrs. Fort, and subsequently contracted a third marriage.‖ The second son, the late Hugh Lide, of Darlington, was a man remarkable for

---

*Colonel Lide, as he was afterwards known, settled on the plain, between the site of St. David's Church and the river. He gave the land on which St. David's Church was built.

He subsequently became a prominent and influential Baptist, and donated the ground on which the first Baptist Church, at Cheraw Hill, was erected. This was between St. David's Church and the river, on the old road as it came up from the ferry.

Of the original deed, executed in 1785, the author has a copy.

†This lady became Mrs. Twitty, and afterwards Mrs. Burn.

‡The lands first settled by Major Lide, were in that large bend of the river below Sugar Loaf (a well-known point on Pedee), afterwards the property of the Saunders', and subsequently belonging to the late Colonel Bright Williamson, of Darlington.

§This ferry took its name from having been called by one of the first owners of it, "Cash-way," meaning that all persons who crossed were to pay cash.

‖The fruits of this marriage were the late Mrs. James Lide, Mrs. Cyms Bacot,

HUGH LIDE.

JAMES LIDE.

strength of character and solidity of understanding; of retiring disposition, however, he sought not publicity, and passed away, after a useful life, little known beyond the limits of his native district.

The name of Baxter appeared on the Pedee as early as 1740. About this time lands were granted to James Baxter on the west side of the river, on Poke Swamp, in what is now Marion district. He was probably the father of Colonel John Baxter, a man of note in civil and military life in that region.

After the Revolution the family moved lower down the river.

In September, 1743, 400 acres of land in the Welch Tract were granted to John Luke. The name continued to be known many years after on Pedee.

About this period William Colt and Abraham Colson settled on the east side of the river, below the Welch Neck. The name of Colson was long known, while that of Colt disappeared not many years afterward.

In 1744, John Wilks obtained a grant for 748 acres of land in Craven county. He was the ancestor of a worthy family, whose descendants are yet found in Darlington and Chesterfield districts. From 1747 onwards, the influx of population was more rapid, and continued to increase. In the latter part of the year previous came George Hicks, from Virginia. The family was of English descent. Being a man of means and influence, Mr. Hicks induced a number of his own relatives and others also to come with him. He became the head of a large connexion on the Pedee. The first record of his name is in a grant for land, in the Welch Tract, January 22nd, 1747. He had probably made a visit the year before. On the 18th of November, 1747, as appears from the records of Council, "was presented the humble Petition of George Hicks; setting forth, that

---

and Mrs. James Pugh, of Darlington; also John W. Lide, and Hannah, who married Thomas Hart.

After her husband's death, Mrs. Lide married a Mr. Holloway, of whom the late Jesse Holloway, of Darlington, was a son, a man of unassuming parts, but esteemed by all who knew him for his purity and excellence of character.

he lately arrived from Virginia, with a family consisting of nine whites and eleven blacks; that he is willing to settle and cultivate a part of his Majesty's lands,—Praying, that he may obtain grants in proportion to the said numbers; and being informed that a tract of land, containing 4,000 acres, was surveyed in the Welch Tract for James Griffith, by virtue of a warrant, dated December 6th, 1745, requiring the same to be returned into the Secretary's Office for a grant in 12 months, a Plot of which has passed the Surveyor-General's Office above a year ago, but no return made thereof into the Secretary's Office; and the said Griffith having some time ago left this Province, and as has been reported, and is generally believed, has since come to an untimely end. Wherefore, the Petitioner prays his Excellency & Hon^s, to direct the Surveyor-General to certify the said Plot in his name, and that he may obtain a grant thereof, though previously certified by him for the said Griffith; and also that the said Surveyor-General may be directed to certify for the Petitioner two Tracts of land in the Welch Tract,—one containing 200 acres, the other 100 acres,—surveyed for James Jones, by virtue of a Warrant, dated February 12th, 1745, requiring a return into the Secretary's Office in 12 months; which said Plots were returned into the Surveyor-General's Office, March 9th, 1746, where they now lie, no application having been made for the same. Your Petitioner further prays, that, in your order to the Surveyor, you may direct him to admeasure and lay out 300 acres of land in the Welch Tract, being in the whole 1000 acres.

"Upon examining the said Petition, and enquiring into his Family right, it appearing that three in whose right he had petitioned were not of his own family, being his Sister's children, and the third, his Overseer, it was Ordered, that the Surveyor-Genl do certify the Plots prayed for in the name of the Petitioner, and that 150 acres may also be surveyed for him in the Welch Tract."

Having thus secured a substantial landed estate, George Hicks began a successful career, and amassed a large fortune. He married a widow, Mrs. Sarah Gardiner (a daughter of the Rev. Philip James, first pastor of the

Welch Neck Church), and raised a large family, from whom a numerous progeny sprang.

Mrs. Gardiner, at the time of her marriage with Mr. Hicks, had a daughter, Sarah, who became the second wife of William Pegues, of Chesterfield. The fruits of her marriage with Mr. Hicks were five daughters and two sons. Of the latter, Benjamin died young; George married a Miss Hicks, and moved at an early period to the West. The daughters* were Mary, Elizabeth, Nancy, Lucy, and Charlotte. Colonel Hicks, as he was afterwards known, was a man of high character and extensive influence. His name will frequently appear in connexion with St. David's parish, and the opening scenes of the Revolution.

Of those who are known to have emigrated to the Pedee with Colonel Hicks, was a brother, William. He had three sons—Charles, Benjamin, and Daniel.

Daniel Hicks lived in Richmond County, N. C., near the State line, and was an active Whig in the Revolution. His family, after his death, removed to Georgia. The family of Benjamin Hicks also left Carolina at an early period.

In the year 1747, other names appear as grantees of land in the Welch Tract. Among these were John Powell, Alexander Staples, John Singleton, and Edward Boyakin.

In March, 1748, John Purvis petitioned Council for 150 acres of land on Thompson's Creek,† Pedee River, stating

---

*Mary married Malachi Murphy, and had several children, of whom account has been given.

Elizabeth married a cousin, Benjamin Hicks, who removed to the West.

Nancy married Thomas Godfrey. The children of this marriage were Sophia, Harriet (afterwards Mrs. Samuel Gillespie), Mary (Mrs. Saunders), Elizabeth, William, Samuel, Wilson, George, Richard, and Thomas.

Lucy married George Strother, and was the mother of Elizabeth (who married Robert Gregg), Mary (afterwards Mrs. Deer), Harriet (Mrs. Broughton), and a son, George. Charlotte, the youngest daughter, married John Wilson.

Of this marriage the sons, Benjamin and George, died young. The daughters were Eleanor, afterwards Mrs. James A. Harrington; Sarah J., who married Oliver H. Kollock; and Anne, who became the wife of James A. Hart. Of this large number, but few survive. And such have been the changes of time, that not one of the name of Hicks is now on the Pedee, though there are many descendants.

†The descendants of John Purvis, as has not very often been the case in this country of change, have continued in possession, as is supposed, of the land first granted, and remain there, some of them at least, to the present day.

that he had a wife and one child; that he came from Virginia the year previous, and had no land assigned him. His petition was granted.

About the same time was presented the petition of John Rushing, stating that he came from Virginia with a wife and one child, and had made a settlement in the Welch Tract on Thompson's Creek. A grant of 150 acres was made to him.

In 1749, Joshua Edwards emigrated to the Pedee. He was born in Pembrokeshire, South Wales, February 11th, 1703-4, and removed before his maturity to Pennsylvania, or the Welch Tract in Delaware, as it afterwards became. Here he remained about thirty years before following his countrymen to Carolina. He petitioned for land in 1751, stating that he was a settler in this Province, having come nearly two years since from Philadelphia, and that he had a wife and one child. His petition was granted. By his first wife, Joshua Edwards had two sons,* Thomas and Abel, and two daughters, Rachel and Phœbe. By his second wife, three sons,† Henry, Elijah, and John, and one daughter, Mary.

Joshua Edwards was ordained in 1751, and became the third pastor of the Welsh Neck Church. This connexion ceased after six years. He then took charge of the Mount Pleasant congregation, near Cashway Ferry, an off-shoot from the Welch Neck Church; and, resigning this, continued his work on Little Pedee, where he remained until 1768. Mr. Edwards was a man of ardent piety and great purity of character. He lived to see of his posterity eighty-two, and died August 22nd, 1784.‡

*Thomas, the first son, married Sarah Roblyn, the fruit of which marriage was but one child, Joshua Edwards, jun. Abel, the second son, married Sarah Harry; and afterward Sarah Douthel (Dousnel, as it appears in the earliest records). His children were Catharine, who married Thrashley Chapman; Edward, who married Mary Dewitt; and Sarah, who married John McDonald.

Rachel, the elder daughter, married Roderic McIver. Phœbe, the younger daughter, married Josiah Evans. Abel Edwards lived on the north side of Cedar Creek, near the crossing of the Cheraw and Darlington R. R.

†Of the sons of Joshua Edwards by his second marriage, John married Elizabeth Bevil, Henry married Elizabeth Oliver, Elijah———, and Mary, the daughter, John Rodgers. Henry Edwards is remembered by some persons of the present day as an old revolutionary soldier. He was a man of stout frame, and told of many a hard-fought battle through which he had passed.

‡Wood Furman's "History of Charleston Association," pp. 70, 71.

Abel, his second son, was a useful man, and a highly-esteemed member and deacon of the Welch Neck Church. He died in 1793. His son, the late Major Edward Edwards, of Chesterfield district, was the father of a large family, of which there are many descendants. Thomas Edwards received his education at the North. He died in Charlestown at an early age, January 1st, 1776.

In 1751, a name appeared for the first time in the history of settlements on the Pedee, which was destined to become distinguished in its future history. On the 2nd of April of that year, Henry Kolb petitioned Council for land, in or near the Welch Tract; stating that he was a settler in the same, with three in family, himself and two negroes, and that he was willing to cultivate the soil. He obtained a grant for 150 acres. Two years later, Peter Kolb also petitioned for land, stating that he had for some years been a settler in the Welch Tract; also Jacob Kolb, who appeared, from his petition, to have had then a plantation on the Pedee. He asked for more land. Martin Kolb was another settler of the name. They came from Pennsylvania. Peter Kolb married Ann, the eldest daughter of the Rev. Philip James. The fruits of this marriage were five children —Abel,* who became so distinguished, married Sarah James; Ann James, who married Joshua Edwards;† Hannah, who married Joseph Dabbs,‡ Benjamin,§ who married Elizabeth Murphy; and Sarah, who married Evander M'Iver.||

---

*The fruits of this marriage were Ann, who married the late Major James Pouncey, of Marlborough, of venerable memory, from whom a large connexion have descended; Sarah, who married first Benjamin David, and afterward Philip Pledger; and a son, James, who died young.

†Joshua, the grandson of Rev. Joshua Edwards, had four children—Sarah, who married James Hart, and afterwards John McIntosh; Thomas, who died at manhood; Peter, who married Jame Draughton; and Ann James, who married John Kirven, and afterwards Daniel Dubose.

‡The children of Joseph Dabbs were—Nancy, who married Benjamin Williams; Samuel, who married Sarah Grove; and William, who married Martha Elison.

§The children of this marriage were—Nancy, who married David Archer; Harriet, who married James Holloway; Abel, who married a Miss Meigs; Sarah, who remained single; Betsey, who married a Mr. McQuirt; and Mary, who married Thomas Meigs.

||Evander McIver had ten children—Catherine, who married Samuel Evans; Nancy J., who remained single; Rachel, who married Jesse Holloway; John Kolb, who married Sarah Marshall; Evander, who married Eliza Cowan; Abel,

The late Jehu Kolb, of Darlington, was a collateral relative of Abel Kolb,* probably the grandson of one of the first settlers of the name already mentioned. He was a man of unassuming character and retiring virtues, but bold and fearless when occasion demanded. He rendered effective service in the Revolution, carrying the marks of serious injuries received to his grave, and died some years since, universally respected.

In May, 1751, Anthony Pouncey obtained a grant for land in the Welch Tract. He petitioned for and obtained a grant for 800 acres on the Wateree, April 6th, 1749, where he probably settled first. In this petition he stated that he had a wife, six children, and eight slaves. The name of William Pouncey appears about the same time. The former was probably the father of William† and Roger.‡

In 1751, the name of John Todd appears as a grantee of

---

who married Ann Chapman, and subsequently Rachel Love; Peter Kolb, who married Elizabeth Chapman, and afterwards Mrs. Maria Nettles; Thomas A., who married Nancy Howard, of Alabama; Eliza, who married Thomas Griffin; and Mary Ann Williams, who married Horatio Cannon.

Mrs. Joshua Edwards, who survived her husband, married Enoch Evans. The fruits of this marriage were six children—Margaret James, who married William Kirven; Thomas, who married Mary Brooks; John, who married Mary Craig; Hannah Kolb, who married John F. Wilson; Enoch, who married Ann Pegues; and Benjamin, who died at an early age.

*Through his wife Abel Kolb became possessed of the plantation at the public ferry (Sparks') near Society Hill. His residence was a two-story brick building, immediately on the east bank of the river, a short distance above the ferry. The cellar-walls of this dwelling were brought to view a few years since by a freshet in the river breaking over the embankment, and interesting relics were obtained.

†William Pouncey died when quite young, leaving one son, the late Major James Pouncey—and a daughter, who married Alexander Peterkin, the father of Jesse and James Peterkin of Marlborough, well known to the present generation in that district. Major Pouncey married Ann Kolb, and reared a large family. His sons were William, who married Sarah Sparks; James, who married, first, Mary Pledger, and afterward, Mary Forniss; John A., who married Miss Armstrong, of N. C.; and Peter A. K., who married Miss Adelaide Hodge.

His daughters were Sarah, who married D. M. Crosland;
                Mary,   ,,   Dr. Robert S. Thomas;
                Eliza,   ,,   Wm. Crosland;
                Ann Jane,   ,,   John Smith, of N. C.

‡Roger Pouncey had two sons—Anthony and William—and three daughters—Mary, Lucy, and Delilah.

Anthony Pouncey died in Marlborough early in the present century. His widow afterwards married, and removed with her family to the West.

land on Pedee. This name continued to be known long after in Chesterfield District.

In 1752, an important addition was made to the settlement above the Welch Neck, on the east side of the river. Philip Pledger came from Virginia during that year, on a visit to the Pedee, as appears from the following certificate:—

"Amelia County: I, Charles Irby, one of his Majesty's Justices of the Peace of the said County, do hereby certify, that the Bearer, Philip Pledger, is and has been an Inhabitant of this County 12 years, and behaved well, and has published his intention of travelling into Carolina. Therefore I desire all Persons to permit the said Philip Pledger to pass and repass upon his lawful affairs, as he may have occasion. Given under my hand and seal, this 17th of March, 1752. CHARLES IRBY."

This interesting relic* indicates how closely the traveller was watched, and the importance attached to character at a time when any new comer was closely scrutinized by those among whom he was to settle. Having selected a valuable body of land on Pedee, Mr. Pledger returned for his family, with whom he also brought back other emigrants. Among these was a family of Councill, closely connected with the Pledgers; and afterwards numerous, but which, in name at least, has long since disappeared. Philip Pledger married a Miss Ellis, of Va. He had two sons, Joseph and John, and two daughters; one of these married James Hicks, the other married, first, a Councill, and afterward Wm. Terrill, a son of one of the Welch settlers. Joseph and John were old enough to take part with their father in the Revolution. Philip Pledger, though advanced in years when the war commenced, was active notwithstanding, and rendered efficient service. In 1754 he received a commission

---

*This document was found at the house of Philip Pledger, Esq., of Marlborough, a great-grandson of the first settler.

He resides at the old family seat on the lands originally purchased, and which have remained in the family ever since. Here the author found the largest and most valuable collection of early manuscript matter anywhere met with, to which Mr. Pledger kindly gave him free access to use as he might desire.

as Captain of Militia in his Majesty's service. Capt. Pledger was a man of high character and generous traits. Possessed of large means, he was able as he was willing to contribute to the public welfare.

In the beginning of the troubles with the Mother Country he received the highest marks of confidence from his fellow-citizens, and faithfully discharged the important trusts committed to him. He died at an advanced age.

About this time, valuable additions were made to the settlements on the Little Pedee in the upper part of what is now Marion District. Among these were the Betheas, of whom William Bethea was one of the first and most prominent. He was an active Whig. A large and respectable connexion of this name are yet found in Marion. Another settler at this period, still lower down on the Pedee, was Jacob Grice. He came from North Carolina. The family has been well known in Marion.

In 1752, the name of Gregg first appeared on the Pedee. This family was of Scottish origin. Not long after the time of Cromwell a part, if not all of them, removed from the North of Scotland to Londonderry, Ireland, from whence the emigration to America took place. On 3rd July, 1752, John Gregg petitioned Council, stating, that he was desirous of settling himself and family in this Province—that his family consisted of himself and wife, one Dutch servant, and five negroes, for whom no grant had been obtained,—and that he was desirous of getting two plots of 500 acres each, which had been surveyed for Mr. John Atkins about 1735-36, and were still lying in the Surveyor-General's office. He obtained grants for 1350 acres. At the same time Dr. John Gregg* petitioned for land lower down, in the fork of Black River and Pedee.

With John Gregg came a brother, Joseph. They were known, as were many others who came to the Province about the same time, as Scotch-Irish Presbyterians. Such was the Colony in Williamsburg. From these brothers, John and Joseph, descended the large connexion of the

---

*Dr. John Gregg was probably a near relative of John and Joseph, but of his subsequent history nothing is known.

name, most numerously represented in Marion. Branches of the family settled also in Massachusetts, Pennsylvania, and Virginia.

The children* of John Gregg and Eleanor, his wife, were James, John, Margaret, Robert, Mary, William, and Jennet. James, the eldest, married Mary Wilson, of the Presbyterian Colony in Williamsburg, and reared a large family. James Gregg lived on the west side of the river, on Poke Swamp. He was a captain in the Revolution, and with his brothers, who were of age, rendered efficient service in the cause of liberty. Joseph Gregg was also the father of a large family.† He was a brave and valiant Whig. John Gregg died about the latter part of the year 1775, having lived long enough to see the beginning of the troubles that were to come upon his children.

In Nov. 1753, John Stubbs obtained a grant for lands on Cat Fish. He was probably the ancestor of the large connexion of that name, since known in Marlborough District.

The battle of Culloden, which occurred in April 1746, led to the removal of many families to America. Among those who were ranked as rebels in that conflict and afterward, were several names which appeared about this time on the Pedee. Of these were M'Iver, M'Intosh, and Cusack.

The accounts of the battle were received in Charles-town, and published in the July following.

---

*The children of James Gregg, were Jennet, who married James Hudson; Mary, who married Adam Marshall; Sarah, who married a Mr. Jones, and removed to the west at an early period; Margaret, who married Samuel Hall, of No. Ca.; John, who married his cousin, Jennet Gregg; David, who married Athalinda Brocky; James, who married Cornelia Maxcy; Elizabeth, who married W. Davidson Hall, of No. Ca.; and Elias, who never married.

John Gregg married Eleanor McKnight, and had ten children—Jane, John, Alexander, Janet, William, Samuel, James, Margaret, Robert, and Elizabeth.

Margaret married a Mr. Scott. The fruits of this marriage were six children—Elizabeth, Rebecca, Mary, Samuel, John, and William.

Robert had but one child, a daughter.

Mary married Mr. Askins, and had four children—Samuel, John, Robert, and William.

William was the father of nine children—Robert James, William Gordon, Eliza, Gadsden, Levi, Wilds, Boyd, William, and Susannah.

Jennet married Mr. Bingham, and had several children.

†The children of Joseph Gregg were Alexander, Robert, Joseph, Jennet, Mary, Margaret, and Sarah. The descendants of most of these remain in Marion.

Among the ladies in custody, the Laird of M'Intosh's wife is mentioned, and Col. and Ensign M'Intosh were among the rebel officers slain. The names of Cusack and Murphy were among the prisoners.

A correspondent of the *Charles-town Gazette*, writing from London, May 10, said, "we are assured that his Majesty has been pleased to order such of the Rebel private men as his Royal Highness shall think proper objects of his clemency, to be transported to some of his Majesty's American Colonies."

Soon after this his Majesty's Council in this Province congratulated his Excellency, the Governor, on the glorious defeat of the rebels at Culloden. To some of these rebels and their children America was afterwards largely indebted for valiant services in the cause of freedom.

In 1756 the names of M'Iver and M'Intosh appear among our early records. In this year Sarah M'Iver was a grantee of land on Lynche's Creek. Roderick M'Iver was one of the first of this family. He came directly from Scotland. His first wife was Anne Rogerson. Soon after his arrival he married Rachel, daughter of Rev. Joshua Edwards, and had three children, Evander, John E., and Catharine. Evander M'Iver married Sarah Kolb, as already related, from whom a large family have descended. He was long and prominently connected with the Welch Neck Church. John E. married Mary Anne Williams.* Catharine married first Josiah Evans, and afterwards the Rev. Edmond Botsford,† a Baptist Minister of high standing and great excellence. Roderick M'Iver died in March, 1768; of that branch of the family (if they were connected) represented by Sarah M'Iver, nothing is known.

In the year 1756 John M'Intosh obtained a grant for land on Black River. He probably came soon after to the

---

*The fruits of this marriage were John E., who died at manhood; Ann Eliza, who married John W. Davis; Catharine, who died in infancy; David Rogerson Williams, who married Caroline Wilds, and afterwards Martha E. Grant; Thomas E., who married Eliza M'Intosh, and subsequently Sarah Bacot; and Alexander, who married Mary Hanford.

†Mr. Botsford's second wife was Catharine Evans, by whom he had one child, Catharine, who married Moses Fort. He contracted afterwards a third and fourth marriage. The children by his first marriage died in infancy.

neighborhood of the Welch Neck, on Pedee. John and Alexander, two brothers, were the first of this name. John, the elder of the two, settled about two miles below Long Bluff, on the west side of the river.* He married a Miss Mikell, and had five sons†—Alexander, John, Lochlin, William, and James. John M'Intosh died in 1774.

The name, in only two branches of his family, is now represented on the Pedee.

Alexander, the younger brother, settled on the east side of the river, a few miles below Long Bluff, in the Welch Neck. He married a Miss James, and had three children‡ —Catharine, John, and Eleanor.

Acquiring probably a good property by his marriage, he subsequently amassed a large fortune, and was prominently connected with the history of the Pedee in civil and military affairs. He was of handsome and commanding person, and possessed of a better education than was common in that day. His name will often appear in the following pages. He is said to have been the first of the early planters who brought the native African to this region.

The family of Mikell came about this time to Pedee. There were two brothers, John and William, and a sister. The latter, as has been stated, married John M'Intosh. John, the elder brother, settled on the west side of the river, a few miles above Long Bluff.§ He became a Major in the

---

*On the public highway, leading to George-town, just above Cock-run (a small swamp stream), where the traces of an ancient settlement are still to be seen.

†Of these Alexander, the eldest son, well known afterwards as Captain M'Intosh, served actively in the Revolution. John, the second son, married a Miss Mikell, and died early: Lochlin, a Miss Vereen, near George-town; William, a Miss Mikell, daughter of John Mikell (the late Mrs. F. C. Watson, of Chesterfield, was a child of this marriage); James, the youngest son, married a Miss Lucas, and was the father of the late James H. M'Intosh, of Society Hill. The father died early. His widow, a lady of advanced years, died in 1862. She was one of the few links left connecting the present with that generation.

‡Catharine married, and moved away at an early period.

John married, and died prematurely, leaving two children—Alexander and Eleanor. The latter became the wife of Alexander Norwood, formerly of Darlington.

Eleanor M'Intosh married a Mr. Bembridge, who removed to Maryland.

§This was on the first sand hill, near the river swamp, at what has in later years been known as the Falconer-place, on the old road from Cheraw Hill to Long Bluff.

Revolution, and was a man of decided character and influence. William, the younger brother, was killed by the Tories.

These settlers soon became thoroughly identified with the Welch. Intermarriages speedily took place, and religious differences were eventually laid aside for the bonds of a common faith, which were long after to unite them. The M'Intosh's and McIver's were Presbyterians in the Mother Country.

In May, 1761, a formal covenant and confession of faith was signed, and Alexander M'Intosh and Roderick M'Iver were received into union with the Welch Neck Church.

About this time (1756), the names of Joseph Brockington, John Kimbrough, Abraham Odam, John Holloway, James Sweeney, Charles Lowder,* (or Lowther), Samuel Windes, James and Alexander M'Kown, and (in the following year) George Nettles, are found among the records of our early settlements.

The most of these appear to have taken lands in the middle and lower parts of what is now Darlington District.

Joseph Brockington probably settled lower down on the river. This family was of English descent. The first of the name who came to the upper Pedee was Richard Brockington. He remained a short time in Charles-town, then purchased lands on the Pedee above George-town, and subsequently moved up the river. He had two sons and a daughter. William, the eldest, married Penelope Benton, who afterwards became Mrs. Bishop; Richard married Mary Hart;† and Rebecca, the daughter, married James Pawley.

John Kimbrough came from Wake County, N°. Cª. He settled about ten miles below Long Bluff, on the west side

---

*From this name came that of the lake (supposed to be the ancient bed of the river) so well known in Darlington. Charles Lowder probably settled in that neighborhood. The name, other than in this locality, disappeared at an early period.

†The late Mrs. Brockington, of Darlington District, whose mansion was for so many years the seat of the most generous hospitality. The chief delight of this excellent lady seemed to consist in ministering to the happiness of others.

of the river, and became a man of prominence in that region. He married Hannah Kolb, and had a daughter, Elizabeth, who became the wife of Lemuel Benton, a name destined to become distinguished in the history of the Pedee. Major Kimbrough was a staunch Whig, but too advanced in years when the war began to render active service.

His death took place in August, 1796. Of the other names mentioned as having appeared about this time, the Nettles' and M'Kown's have continued to be known in Darlington and Marion as large and respectable connexions. James Sweeney is supposed to have been the progenitor of the present family of Henegan.

It is known that this was called the Sweeney family at an early period. When or why the change took place, is not known to the present generation.

Barney, who was probably the son of James Sweeney, had two sons, Darby and John. Darby was the father of the late Dr. B. K. and Ephriam L. Henegan, of Marlborough. His daughters were Drusilla, who married L. E. Stubbs, and Lucretia, who married Alex. McCollum.

John Sweeney married a Miss Ridgel, and died young. John S. Henegan was the first of that name. The families became connected, and two generations back, took the name of Henegan. They lived first in Marion, where a portion of their descendants yet reside; the other, a highly respectable branch of the family, being in Marlborough.

About this period, came a family, in numbers and influence, prominently connected with Darlington District from an early period. John Du Bose was the first of the name who removed to this region. He was of Huguenot descent, and came from that settlement on Santee to Lynche's Creek. His sons were Isaac, Elias, Daniel, and Joseph. These brothers lived in the same neighborhood,* were men of property before the Revolution, and took an active part in that struggle. Daniel was a captain, and Isaac

---

*This settlement was on the east side of Lynche's Creek, at a point just above the crossing of the Wilmington and Manchester R. R.; a neighborhood in which a sanguinary struggle was carried on with the Tories, and in which the Du Bose's took a decisive part.

bore honorable office. Elias, the second son, was prominent for character and influence. He was a magistrate of note before and after the war. He married Lydia Cassels, of Sumpter, and reared a large family.* A sister, Rebecca, married her cousin, Andrew Du Bose,† whose name will appear in a prominent connexion in the history of the Revolution. Another sister, Margaret, married Wm. Dick.‡ Mr. Dick was an active Whig, and noted for strength and courage. He removed, after the war, to Darlington. Peter Du Bose, one of the earlier of the name, was of respectable revolutionary memory.

Soon after Braddock's defeat, the frontier inhabitants of Virginia and Pennsylvania began to move further south; and the region of the Pedee was settled by a few of them. The progress of population was slow previous to the Indian Treaty, in 1755; after which it began to increase.

John Donaldson was an early settler in what is now Marlborough District. He removed soon after to Richmond County, N. C., and there became a Col. of Militia. He died during the war.

Charles Irby came from Virginia, and settled in the neighborhood of Philip Pledger, on the east side of the river. In October, 1768, he married Mehitabel Kolb, and became a prominent and influential character. Col. Irby, as he was afterwards known, was the progenitor of a large family connexion.§ He died shortly after the Revolution. Edmond Irby, a brother or near relative of Charles Irby, took an active part as Captain in the revolutionary struggles.

In 1758, Thomas Ayer emigrated to Pedee. He came

---

*Jesse, Isaiah, and John Du Bose were sons of Elias.

†The sons of this marriage were Benjamin, Samuel, and Joshua, who lived on Lynche's Creek.

‡The mother of the late John D. Witherspoon, of Society Hill, was a Miss Dick.

§Of the children of Colonel Irby, Charles married Rebecca Evans, sister of the late Hon. Josiah J. Evans.

James married a Miss Wright, of Marlborough.

Elizabeth became the wife of William Pledger.

Anne married Thomas Lide, and another daughter married a Forniss.

The family of Charles Irby, after his death, removed to Alabama, and are well known in that State. The name was spelled Yerbey in some of the earlier records, and was thus pronounced by many for a long time after.

from Ireland to Virginia, and from thence to Carolina. He settled on the east side of the river, a few miles below Hunt's Bluff, set up a trading establishment, and amassed a comfortable property. Of an ardent temperament, and enthusiastic in his love of liberty, Thomas Ayer would cheerfully have sacrificed life and fortune had it been necessary for its advancement. Of his children, were Lewis Malone, born in 1769, the head of a large and respectable family in Barnwell District; and the late Hartwell Ayer, of Marlborough, from whom a most worthy family have descended.*

About this time came a family which was to contribute a large and valuable element to the population of Marlborough. Tristram Thomas, from whom this family is descended, emigrated from Wales to the Province of Maryland in the early part of the last century. He died February 11th, 1746, leaving a numerous family, of whom a portion remained in Maryland, and others emigrated, it is said, to Pennsylvania and Virginia. His eldest son, Stephen, emigrated to North Carolina, about the year 1750, and died there, leaving a large family. Several of his sons and daughters subsequently came to the Pedee, of whom a portion removed, soon after the Revolution, to the then Northwest Territory. This family was originally, and long continued to be, of the Society of Friends. While in Marlborough, they worshipped near Adamsville.†

Stephen's children were, Sarah, Robert, Stephen, Mary, William, John, Susan, Elizabeth, Lewis, Tristram, Philemon, Benjamin, and James, born between the years 1731 and 1758, inclusive.

Of these, Robert, the eldest son, married Mary Sands in

---

*To this venerable gentleman, through the kind assistance of his son, General L. M. Ayer, of Barnwell, the author is indebted for a thrilling narrative of scenes connected with the revolutionary struggle on the Pedee, and much other information of interest. Mr. Ayer, though quite a youth at the time to which his narrative refers, retained a distinct recollection of the most important events which fell under his observation. After his majority he left the Pedee, and settled in Barnwell. He died at his residence in Barnwell District in 1863, at the advanced age of 93, the last link which connected the present with the revolutionary era of the Pedee.

†Now known as Piney Grove. The original house of worship, having been purchased by Christians of different denominations, was long free to all, but ultimately fell into the hands of the Methodists, the Baptists building at Beaver-dam.

1756. They reared a large family.* The Rev. Robert Thomas was for fifty years a faithful minister of the gospel, laboring with his own hands for the support of his household. The old Churches at Beaver-dam and Salem, in Marlborough, were established through his instrumentality. He abandoned the faith of his fathers at an early period, and united himself with the Baptists. He was preaching when the Revolution began, and gave his eldest surviving son to the service of his country. He died at Britton's Neck, Marion District, at the advanced age of 84, while on a missionary tour to the destitute in that region.

Lewis, the second son, married a Miss Breeden, a name long known in Marlborough. Many of their descendants yet remain in that district.

Tristram, the seventh son, was born July 28th, 1752. He married a Miss Hollingsworth, of one of the Welch families. Though but a few years past his maturity when the Revolution commenced, he embarked actively in that trying contest, and became a prominent character.

William Thomas, of another branch of the same family, emigrated about this time from Maryland. He came as an adventurous youth, and found a kind friend in Col. George Hicks. While living with Col. Hicks, he married his niece, a Miss Little, who was possessed of a good property. He settled on the east side of the river, a few miles above Cheraw, and amassed a large fortune. He had one child, a son, William Little, who married Clarissa Benton. The fruits of this marriage, were two sons,† William L. and Alexander. The father, William L. Thomas, was a man of brilliant talents. The name of this branch of the family has become extinct.

About the year 1760, Claudius Pegues came to Pedee. He settled on the east side of the river not far below the State line. This family was of French descent. The father

---

*The children of Robert Thomas were Tristram, Elizabeth, Nathan, Sarah, John Sands, Lucy, Robert, H. Elijah, William, Jesse, Eli, and Benjamin.

The last of this large family, Eli, died in 1854. Many of their descendants are scattered through the West.

†Alexander died young. William L. married Jane M'Queen, of Chesterfield, and died childless. This lady afterwards married the late Hon. John Campbell, of Marlborough.

of Claudius Pegues is supposed to have left France after the Revocation of the Edict of Nantes, and with his wife, a Swiss lady, settled in London. Claudius, their son, emigrated to Carolina, and married a Miss Butler, in Charlestown in 1748-9. He removed thence to George-town, where his children were born. After his settlement on Pedee he was prominently connected with St. David's Parish. He died in 1790. Of his children, only two sons, William and Claudius, reached maturity. William married Elizabeth Murphy, and settled on the west side of the river above Cheraw, and near the N. C. line. The fruit of his first marriage was a daughter, Harriet, who married William Powe. His second wife was Sarah Gardiner, a step-daughter of Col. George Hicks. Wm. Pegues was a man of more cultivated tastes* than was usual at that day. He was a staunch Whig, and with others in this region, as will be seen hereafter, suffered severely from the depredations of the Tories.

Claudius, the younger son, married Marcia Murphy, and settled near his father, in the upper part of what is now Marlborough District.

A daughter, Henrietta, and other children died young. Of his four sons who grew up, William married Miss Speed (of N°· C^{a.}), and late in life Maria Punch of Cheraw; James married Jane, a daughter of Wm. Johnson, of Sneedsborough, N. C.; Malachi married Charlotte, another daughter; and Christopher married Eliza, a daughter of Col. Thomas Evans.† These brothers all reared large families, from whom a numerous and highly respectable connexion have descended.

Claudius Pegues, their father, was an active Whig, and a man of great usefulness in his day.

---

*The remains of a very excellent library were seen by the author a few years since in the neighborhood of Mr. Pegues's former residence.

†Colonel Evans was the father of the late Hon. Josiah J. Evans, of Darlington. He married Elizabeth Hodge, and had five children, viz.:—

Thomas, who married a daughter of Harris Evans; Josiah James, who married Dorothy Dewitt; Abel; Rebecca, who married Charles Irby; and Eliza, who married Christopher Pegues. Colonel Evans lived a little out from the Welch Neck, near the public road leading from Long Bluff to the Old Marlborough, C. H.

In 1759 the Rev. Nicholas Bedgegood came to Pedee, having been called to the charge of the Welch Neck Church. This charge was not assumed, however, until the following year. He succeeded Rev. Robert Williams. Mr. Bedgegood was born at Thornbury, in Gloucestershire, England, January 30, 1731.* He came to America in 1751, and was for some time connected with Mr. Whitfield, in the Georgia Orphan House. He became a Baptist in 1757, and not long after received the call to the Welch Neck. He returned in 1767 to the lower part of the Province, in the neighborhood of Charles-town, but having received a second call to the Welch Neck, came back and made a permanent settlement in this region. In 1769 he married a Miss Murphy. A son, the late Nicholas Bedgegood, of Marlborough, was his only child.

The Rev. Mr. Bedgegood was a good classical scholar,† and is said to have been an accomplished speaker. "Calm, however, and didactic, rather than impassioned in his style of preaching, his efforts were calculated to instruct rather than to move the feelings. But few were added to the church during his Ministry."‡ His death took place in 1774, and on 1st February following, this entry was made on the records of the Welch Neck Church: "The Rev. Mr. Nicholas Bedgegood died near fifteen years after his first call to this place; and almost seven years after his return, from which time he ministered here until his death. He was regarded a good scholar and a sound divine, an eloquent preacher, and a polite gentleman; and well beloved by his acquaintance: yet, notwithstanding all his ability and endowments, he was never very successful, especially in the latter part of his life; none being baptized after his return."

---

*The following is a copy, as preserved by himself, of the original record of his baptism:—
"Nicholas, Son of Nicholas and Anne Bedgegood, Gent., Baptized Feby. ye 22nd, 1731.
"This is a true Copy of ye Register at Thornbury.
                                         JAS. RUTTER, Curate.
"Born January ye 30th, 1731."
†He owned a large and valuable library. A few volumes from this library, with a private journal of Mr. Bedgegood, were presented to the author some years since by the late Mrs. Catharine Billingsly, of Marlborough.
‡Wood Furman's "History," pp. 75, 76.

To this statement it ought to be added, that from 1767 to 1774, when Mr. Bedgegood finished his course, the spirit of the time and disturbed state of the country were most unfavorable to general religious progress or the growth of any congregation.

Not later than 1760, Martin Dewitt emigrated to the Pedee from Fredericksburgh, Virginia. He settled on the lower part of Black Creek, in what is now Darlington District. He married Ellen Douthel. His sons, who came with him, were William, Harris, Thomas, and John. He took part in the Revolution, though advanced in years, and died in the place of his first settlement. William, the eldest son, married Mary, the daughter and only child of Daniel Devonald, one of the Welch settlers.* Harris married Elizabeth, a daughter of Richard Brockington, and afterwards a Miss Pawley, and removed to the West at an early period. Thomas married and died early. John was the father of the late Martin Dewitt, of Darlington; a man who maintained a most unblemished character through life.

William Dewitt, afterwards well known as Cap$^{n.}$ Dewitt, settled in the upper part of the present district of Darlington.† His sons were John, Charles M., and Daniel, who died when a boy. John, the late Major Dewitt of Society Hill, married Nancy, daughter of Thomas Powe. Charles never married. He was a man of superior talents. The daughters of William Dewitt were Mary, who married Edward Edwards; Sarah, who married a Mr. James, and subsequently Sam$^{l.}$ Ervin; Eleanor,‡ who married Allen Chapman; Elizabeth, who married Sam$^{l.}$ Wilds, and afterwards Dr. Thomas Smith; Margaret, who married Enoch Hanford, and Dorothea, who married Josiah J. Evans. Harriet, another daughter, died at an early age. Cap. Dewitt was a man of strongly marked character, and an

---

*Her mother was long a widow, of good property for that day, and lived a short distance above the old Welch Neck Church, on the east side of the river.

†On Cedar Creek, near the village of Society Hill, where the late Judge Evans resided.

‡This excellent lady, the last of her father's family, and almost of her own, died in 1860. The writer was indebted to her for much interesting information.

active and devoted Whig. He survived his wife, and died about 1812.

Another branch of the family came from Virginia about the same time, and settled lower down on the river, in what is now Marion District.* Thomas Dewitt, the father of this connexion, was probably a brother, or other near relative of Martin Dewitt. His sons were Thomas, William, and Charles. Charles married a Miss M'Call in 1771. The name is yet known in Marion. Many other settlers came about this time to Pedee. Among these was Elisha Parker. He purchased lands on the east side of the river, just below the State line. Here a public ferry was established soon after, known as Parker's Ferry. Elisha Parker died at an advanced age. His son, Stephen, who came with him, was a ship-builder, and before the Revolution built boats for the navigation of the river. Stephen Parker accumulated a good property, and died about 1810. Some of his descendants are now living in Chesterfield District.

Hewstiss was another name early known. This family contributed its quota to the cause of liberty. Of the Turnages, who emigrated to what is now Chesterfield District, William served his country faithfully. He died at an advanced age about 1823. A son, John Turnage, yet survives, a worthy citizen of Chesterfield. With the Turnages came the Ruthvens, some of whom are yet found in Chesterfield.

The name of Sparks goes back to this period, on the Pedee. There were four brothers who came from Virginia, viz., Daniel, Charles, Samuel, and Harry. Of these, Charles and Samuel went to sea. Harry, a noted Whig, was killed by the Tories. Daniel, the eldest brother, settled first at what has long been known as the Beauty Spot, in Marlborough District. The family afterwards resided at the "Red Bluff," in the Welch Neck.

Daniel Sparks married Martha Pearce,† and had three sons—Alexander, Samuel, and Daniel. Alexander married

---

*This place of settlement was called afterwards Dewitt's Bluff, and is still known by this name on the river.
†This excellent and venerable lady died a few years since, near Society Hill, at a very advanced age. She retained her physical vigour and mental faculties to the last to a very remarkable degree. Her life was one of many trials, having embraced the stormy years of the Revolution.

Jeanette M'Kearly; Samuel married Ann Hurry; and Daniel, a French lady in Louisiana. The daughters were— Martha, who died single; Polly, who married John Crosland; Lucy, who married Alexander Stubbs, and subsequently Thomas Stubbs; and Sarah, who married William Pouncey.

Daniel Sparks, the father, was a noted Captain of Militia in the Revolution, and rendered valuable service to his country.

Edward Crosland, who was thrown upon his own resources as an orphan boy, came about the year 1760 from Virginia to Carolina.

The tradition has been handed down in the family, that he joined a company of adventurers of about thirty persons, near the middle of the Province, some time before the Revolution, for the purpose of exploring and hunting in the South-West. The company, it is said, went through North Carolina, Tennessee, and Kentucky, to the Ohio River, thence to the Mississippi; and after exploring that stream to the mouth of the Missouri, retraced their steps, and descended the Mississippi to New Orleans. A part of the company returned, leaving their companions behind.

After returning to North Carolina, Edward Crosland married a daughter of Samuel Sneed, of that State, and settled near the boundary line; acting chiefly in South Carolina during the Revolution. Subsequently, he removed to Santee, and after a few years, settled on the Pedee, near Gardiner's Bluff, in what is now Marlborough District, where he reared a large family. His sons were, John, Samuel, Daniel M., Israel, David, George, Philip, and William. His daughters were, Temperance, Mary, Sarah, Elizabeth, Rebecca, and Ann. Not a few of the descendants of this family are now numbered among the respected citizens of Marlborough.

The Websters, Adams, and Fletchers, came about this time from Virginia and Maryland to Pedee.

These families have extensive connexions in Marlborough. Emanuel Coxe settled lower down on the river. He reared a large family, from which many of the citizens of Marlborough have descended. Several of this name were among the soldiers of the Revolution. William Coxe was particularly noted.

Settlements were made about this time on Lynche's Creek, in what is now Chesterfield District.

Among the first who came here, were Charles and George Evans, of the Welch stock on Pedee; and John Blakeney. The latter came from Ireland, and established himself as a trader. He had two sons—William and John. William was the father of the late Gen[l] J. W. Blakeney of Chesterfield; and from these brothers, the large connexion in that District have descended. John Blakeney was an active Whig in the Revolution. His name appears in the records of St. David's Parish. Lower down on Lynche's Creek, in what is now Darlington District, were the Huggins, Carters, and others, well known since in that region. This settlement extended from the Effingham Mills, a point of note in those days, towards the Fork of Lynche's Creek.

The names of Cannon, Hunter, Williamson, Coker, and Pawley, appear here. They settled on Black Creek, in Darlington, and were active Whigs.

Colonel George Pawley was prominent in the neighbourhood of George-town at an earlier period. He is supposed to have removed subsequently higher up the river, having become the owner of lands on the east of the Pedee, above Mars Bluff. James Pawley was probably a son or collateral relative. He married Rebecca Brockington, and afterwards a Miss Hunter. Cusack was also a name of a still earlier settler, and destined to become sadly noted in the trials that awaited these infant settlements. Lower down on Jeffrey's Creek, was Wm. McDowell. He emigrated from Ireland to North Carolina, and subsequently to this region, bringing a family with him.* He was a stanch friend of his country, and suffered much from the Tories, who made frequent forays in this neighbourhood. Simon Connell was one of his companions, and a name which appears in favourable connexion with the struggles which shortly followed. He was killed by the Tories.

On Cat Fish, in what is now Marion District, were the

---

*Mary, a daughter of William McDowell, born in 1769, was surviving in 1859, near Florence (Wilmington and Manchester R. R.). She married Wm. Britt soon after the Revolution. Her husband was in the battle of Guilford Court House. He died at an advanced age.

Cherrys. George Cherry was noted in the revolutionary struggle.

Higher up were the Hodges, than whom few families gave a larger number of soldiers to the cause of liberty. The late Cap^n Geo. Hodge,* of Marlborough, was the last connecting link with that generation. He married a daughter of George Cherry. Townsend was another family known at this period. The name of Light Townsend appears among the records of the Revolution. The family has become extensively connected in Marlborough. William Forniss was advanced in years when the war began, and an ardent Whig. The late venerable James Forniss, of Marlborough, was a lineal descendant. This family settled in the upper part of the Welch Neck, on the river. In the same neighbourhood were the Downes;† and farther out, on Crooked Creek, were Samuel and Joseph Dabbs, the first of that name on Pedee. Joseph Dabbs married Hannah Kolb. His devotion to liberty was sealed with his blood. His descendants are found now in Darlington. In the neighbourhood of Hunt's Bluff, on the east side of the river, were the Sweats, a worthy family, and devoted Whigs.

Wm. Sweat, the father, was an old man when the Revolution began. His sons, James and Nathan, were young men at that time. This was probably a branch of the family which came with Gideon Gibson from Virginia.

The Quicks, higher up the river, are worthy of mention among the early settlers of that region. They came from Bertie County, North Carolina, where the family resided in 1742.‡ Thomas Quick was one of the brave Whigs of the Upper Pedee.

---

*Captain Hodge was the maternal uncle of the late Judge Evans.
†This name has long since disappeared.
‡The following is a copy of one of the relics of those days:—
"North Carolina,   At a Court begun and held for said County at the Bertie County.   House of John Collins, near Red Bird, on tuesday, the 9th Day of November, Anno Domi 1742;

"Present, His Majesty's Justices of the Peace &c. Personally came Thomas Quick of this County, and in open Court made oath on the Holy Evangelists, that his family consists of six persons;—viz., Thomas Quick, Ruth Quick, Bertha Quick, Anne Quick, Willis Quick, & Rachel Quick: which is Ordered to be Certified.

"Witness George Gould Esqr, Chairman of the said Court at Bertie, the 20th Day of November, Anno Domi, 1742.

"Dated at the Clerk's Office the 20th   "GEO. GOULD.
Day of November, Anno Domi, 1742.   "HENRY DE LA CLASPER."

In 1762, Evan Pugh emigrated to the Pedee. His ancestors came from Wales to Pennsylvania, where he was born. They were associated with the Quakers, and probably constituted a part of the colony of William Penn. While he was yet a boy, his father removed to Winchester, Virginia. Upon arriving at manhood, Mr. Pugh became a teacher, and acted in that capacity on the Yadkin River, North Carolina. While there he became a Baptist. In 1762 he pursued his studies at Long Bluff, and was ordained two years afterwards.

Subsequently he removed to Cashway, and took charge of the Mount Pleasant congregation in that neighbourhood. Mr. Pugh married Martha McGee.

By this marriage he had two sons and a daughter. James, the elder son, was the father of the family in Darlington. Ezra, the younger son, died prematurely just after commencing life as a lawyer at George-town. Elizabeth, the daughter, married Hugh Lide, of Darlington. Of the life and character of Rev. Evan Pugh, account will be given hereafter. He died in 1802.

About this time, Dr. James P. Wilson came to Pedee, and settled at Long Bluff. He was a native of Buck's County, Pennsylvania, and educated at Carlisle, in that State.

He settled first as a physician at Winchester, Virginia, and remained there several years. During his residence at that place, he married Martha Jamison.

His children were the late John F. Wilson, of Society Hill, who married Hannah Evans; Mary, who married Edward Burch; and Martha, who married John Sweeney. Dr. Wilson, for many years, had a large practice on the Pedee, and was surgeon in Marion's Brigade.

Virginia continued to furnish valuable elements to the growing population on the Pedee. Thomas Powe emigrated from that State about this period. He married a Miss Allen, of Virginia. His children were William, who married Harriet Pegues; Erasmus, who married Esther Ellerbe; Mary, who married William Falconer; Rachel, who married Allen Chapman; Nancy, who married John Dewitt; Alexander, who married Miss Spencer; and Thomas, who married Martha Ellerbe.

Mr. Powe first settled on Cedar Creek, near the present village of Society Hill, and afterwards removed to the neighbourhood just above Cheraw Hill, where he lived and died. Thomas Powe was a magistrate of note after the Revolution, and was an active and useful man on the Pedee. His second son, Genl Erasmus Powe, of Chesterfield, was also a man of much excellence and usefulness in his day. The widow of Thomas Powe married Calvin Spencer, whom she survived many years.

The Godfreys were of English descent. This name appears in the early history of Carolina.

Richard Godfrey died some years before the Revolution, in the neighbourhood of Cheraw. He probably removed to that locality late in life. His sons were, William, Wilson, Richard, and Thomas, all of whom were old enough to take part in the struggle for liberty. William married a Miss Britton, in what is now Marion district; Richard, a Miss Davis; Wilson also married, and died in Marion; Richard lived on the river, at the place since known as Godfrey's Ferry. He was active in the Revolution. He held several public offices in Marion, and died about 1821.

Thomas lived in the neighbourhood of Cheraw. He married Nancy, a daughter of Col. Geo. Hicks, from whom a large family descended, and of which account has been given. Thomas Godfrey was long connected with St. David's parish.

John Wilson emigrated from Maryland to Pedee when quite a young man. He settled on the east side of the river, opposite Cheraw, and entered upon a successful career as a planter. His first wife was a daughter of Col. Thomas Lide. The only surviving child of this marriage was the late Governor John Lide Wilson.* The other children died young. Of Mr. Wilson's family by his second wife, Charlotte Hicks, account has been given. He was an active Whig, and prominently connected with St. David's Parish. His death took place in January, 1823, Mrs. Wilson following him in August of the same year.

---

*Governor Wilson married, first, Charlotte, a sister of Governor Joseph Allston. His second wife was a Miss Eden, of Philadelphia, a ward of Aaron Burr.

Lemuel Benton emigrated from Granville County, North Carolina, to Pedee. He settled in the neighbourhood of Major Kimbrough, and soon after married his daughter, an only child. The fruits of this marriage were four sons—John, Lemuel, Buckley, and Alfred. The daughters were, Clarissa, who married William L. Thomas; Charlotte, who married Laurence Prince; Gilly, who married Isaiah Du Bose; and Elizabeth, who married George Bruce. Of the sons, John and Alfred died young. Lemuel came also to an untimely end. Buckley reared a family. The father, afterwards known as Colonel Benton, was a man of very strongly marked character, and will appear prominently hereafter.

In 1766, the lands on which the present Town of Cheraw was built, were granted to Eli Kershaw. With a brother, Joseph, he set up a large trading establishment at this place. They removed, a few years afterwards, to Camden, where the name has been well known since.

William Henry Mills, an Englishman, came, about this time, to Pedee, and settled in the neighbourhood of Long Bluff. He was a physician, and a well-educated man, and for a time a prominent citizen.

John Manderson lived in the lower part of what is now Chesterfield District, and was a man of large means. He left soon after this period.

About this time came Samuel Wise. He emigrated from England to Charles-town, where he was residing as a merchant in 1766. A year or two after, he settled on the Pedee, on the east side of the river, a short distance below the State line. Mrs. Wise, who came with him, was a woman of marked traits. Their only child, a daughter, married Joseph Ball, from the lower part of Carolina. Samuel Wise was a man of high character, and took a prominent place in the public service. He removed, during the Revolution, to the Wateree, where he owned a valuable property. His career ended during the war.

Henry William Harrington emigrated from England to the West Indies. After remaining a short time at Jamaica, he came to South Carolina, and settled on the Pedee. He took up his residence first on the river, opposite Cheraw Hill, but soon after went down to the Welch Neck. While living there, he married Rosanna, daughter of Major James Auld, of Anson County, North Carolina. The fruits of this marriage were, Rosanna, who married Robert Troy; Henry William;* James Auld, who married Eleanor Wilson; and Harriet, who married Belah Strong. In 1776, Mr. Harrington removed to Richmond County, North Carolina, where he continued to reside through life. Of his name frequent mention will be made in connexion with his eminent public service, and devotion to his country.†

Arthur Hart, a relative of General Harrington, emigrated, about the same time with the former, from England. He settled first in Virginia, and there married, remaining, however, but a short time. From Virginia he came to Pedee, and settled on lands on the east side of the river, in the neighbourhood of the Welch Neck. His second wife was Elizabeth, a daughter of Rev. Robert Williams. This marriage took place in 1771. His third wife was Miss Irby, a sister of Colonel Charles Irby. The fruits of this marriage were three children, James, Mary, and Sarah.

James Hart married Sarah Edwards, of whom were born two sons, James and Thomas. Mary, the eldest daughter, married Richard Brockington. Sarah married Nicholas Rogers. James Hart died in 1797.

Arthur Hart was a man of good property and high respectability. He was an ardent Whig, but died before the thickest of the strife, in 1777.‡

Samuel Bacot came to the neighbourhood of what is now Darlington District in 1769. His grandfather, Pierre Bacot, was a native of Rochelle, France, from whence he fled, with other Huguenots, in 1694, to Charles-town. Samuel Bacot married a Miss Allston, and with her brother, Peter Allston, came to the Pedee, settling himself on Black Creek, not far

---

*To Colonel H. W. Harrington, of Richmond County, the author is indebted for much interesting traditional matter, and for valuable manuscripts in connexion with the family and the Revolutionary era.

†The larger part of the private journal and other papers of General Harrington were unfortunately destroyed by the Tories in one of their plundering forays to the neighborhood of his residence. A few manuscripts of interest were preserved.

‡Arthur Hart owned the site of the factory near Society Hill, and was residing there at the time of his death.

from the present village of Darlington. Mr. Allston soon removed to Waccamaw Lake, North Carolina.

Samuel Bacot was a man of energy, a useful citizen, and ardent patriot. The late Samuel Bacot and Cyrus Bacot, of Darlington, were his sons.

William and Calvin Spencer emigrated from Connecticut to the Pedee a few years before the Revolution. William settled in Anson County, North Carolina, and rose to distinction in that State.

Calvin Spencer was an active Whig and useful man. Chesterfield was his permanent residence.

About the year 1770, the name of Charles Augustus Steward, appeared on the Pedee. He married* a daughter of George Gabriell Powell, a name destined to become prominently connected with the early history of the Pedee. Captain Steward removed to the neighbourhood† of Cheraw, where he became a prominent character, and continued to reside.

John Mitchell was another name familiar at this period. He was a successful trader at Meldrum,‡ near Cheraw, but left soon after, and the name disappeared with him. His sympathies were not with his adopted country, and the difficulty growing out of this fact led to his removal.

The tide of emigration was stopped by the troublous times immediately preceding the Revolution, and the trials of that struggle. Additions were made to the population on the Pedee after the establishment of peace, of which some account will be given.

The history of our settlements has been brought down

---

*This announcement appeared in the *Gazette*, Charles-town, June 27, 1769:—"On the 15th inst., was married, Charles Augustus Steward, Esq., first Captain in his Majesty's 21st Regiment, to Miss Sally Powell, Daughter of George Gabriell Powell, Esq., of Prince George Parish."

†This was the plantation immediately below the town of Cheraw, and called Fairy Hill.

‡Of the locality of Meldrum, mentioned in the papers of the day as being "near the Cheraws," the author, after every effort, has been unable to obtain any information whatever.

Mr. Mitchell is known to have owned lands and a plantation on Thompson's Creek. Meldrum was probably in this neighbourhood, and the name given to his place of residence.

through a period of about thirty-five years, during which, with very varied and valuable elements, were laid the foundations of future growth and progress. The reader will now be carried back to take a survey of other matters of interest connected with this stage in the history of the Pedee.

CHAPTER VI.

Caucasian race progressive—Varied elements of population on Pedee—Anglo-Saxon predominant—First wants of settlers—Stock raising—Wild Stock—First markets—How reached—Other articles exported—Products of the soil—Indigo—Its culture and history—Trading establishments—Navigation of the river—Roads and early conveyances—Road districts established—Public ferry and its regulations—First grants of land—Reservations and taxes—Progress of the Province—Of this portion of it—Increase of slaves—First settlements—Where made—Diseases—Long Bluff—Its history—Cheraw Hill—Its settlement—Planters' Club—Militia of Craven County—Justices of Peace—Social life—Religious element on Pedee—Growth of spirit of independence—Causes of it—Feeling towards Earl of Chatham by the colonies—His statue—Old medal—Its history—A Parochial organization at hand—The dawn of a brighter day for the Pedee.

The history of the Caucasian or white race has been one of progress.

Unlike other ancient and populous divisions of the family of man, which have never advanced beyond a certain point of improvement, not always remaining at that, this has never continued stationary.

Much of course depends on the peculiar combination of the elements of which the white race is composed—leading either to a general deterioration, or to a people, in their diversity singularly fitted to advance in every department of human progress. Such is the Anglo-Saxon, which has been most remarkable in its developments, and is destined to fill so large and commanding a place in the latter stages of the world's history.

In the first settlements on the Pedee, extending through about one-third of a century, various types of race and character were represented. France, England, Wales, Ireland, Scotland, Germany, and the more northern provinces of America, whose inhabitants had been chiefly drawn from the same sources, all contributed in their measure—the Welch element preponderating in the central locality, and destined, as will be found, to give character to the communities around it.

With our early settlers there was every stimulus to exertion. Their fortunes were yet to be built up, but little means, for the most part, having been brought with them. They found in the fertile lands to which they came, with rich pasturage and luxuriant forests, all that nature could provide for the supply of their first necessities, and on the bosom of the river was presented an outlet for their multiplying productions, as well as a channel of conveyance for ministering in turn to their increasing wants. Attention was first to be turned to their immediate necessities, and to the means of intercommunication with each other, and facilities for trade. Lands were to be cleared, enclosures made, and the soil developed. Already premiums had been offered by Government to encourage the cultivation of certain crops, and a ready market on the coast awaited their superabundant stores. Some of those who came from the more northern provinces drove their horses, cattle, and hogs, over land with them.*

Large numbers of wild horses and cattle in addition were found by the first settlers in the woods of Carolina. Many were caught and domesticated, and stock-raising at once became a prolific source of wealth. Most of the early fortunes on the Pedee were made in this way. Energy, rather than capital, was required in the first instance, and but little labour demanded afterward. Everywhere in those days, on the hills and in the valleys, the best ranges were found, and it was only necessary to drive the stock from place to place in search of fresh pasturage, as the supply became exhausted. The numbers owned by single individuals, and thus driven about, were very large, almost incredibly so to those accustomed to the condition of things in this respect now exising in the older States. It was in this kind of life, habituated to the use of the saddle in the woods for days and weeks together, often in the dangerous adventures of the chase, that our early settlers became such expert horsemen, and so inured to exposure

*Ramsay's "History of So. Ca.," vol. ii. p. 274.

and hardship as to meet successfully the extraordinary demands of that protracted struggle which was soon to overtake them.

The wild stock was captured by the simple contrivance of a large and well-secured pen in the fork of two branches, or larger streams, into which the frightened and overpowered animal was driven. In some cases, where the branches were boggy, and could not be entered, a fence was built across, some distance above the point of junction, and this was the only enclosure required. Some of our smaller streams are yet found to retain the name, "horsepen," indicating that they were made to subserve the purpose mentioned. The stock was driven to Charles-town and other places on the coast, as well as to more distant markets. Large numbers of cattle were sent from Pedee to Philadelphia.*

Pork soon became a valuable article of export. In the course of time, "Cheraw bacon" was destined to be famous in distant parts of the country. Lumber was also sent off in large quantities, saw-mills having been erected at different points soon after the first settlements.†

The "Effingham Mills," in what is now Darlington District, are mentioned early, as well as others more immediately contiguous to the river.‡

---

*It is related of Malachi Murphy, who drove many beeves annually to Philadelphia, that on one occasion was a famous beast, called "Blaze Face," of great size and unusual sagacity, which he sold in Philadelphia.

On the night of his return home to Pedee, and soon after his arrival, he heard the low of Blaze Face. He had escaped and followed close upon the track of his owner, swimming rivers and distancing all pursuers. Mr. Murphy drove him a second time to Philadelphia, and again he returned. Such a spirit was worthy of a better fate, but did not shield the bold rover. He was taken a third time to Philadelphia, and came back no more. This was related to the author by the late John D. Withirspoon, of Society Hill.

†The prices of some leading articles of trade in Charles-town at this period will give some idea of the remuneration received by the settlers:—

(From *Gazette* of the day.) *Nov.* 1, 1739.

Rice, 32s. to 33s. 9d. per cwt. Pitch, 40s. per cwt.
Turpentine, 20s. per cwt. Tar, 30s. per cwt. Skins, 18s. per cwt.
Indian corn, 7s. 6d. to 10s. per cwt.

July 16, 1741.

Rice, 3l. per cwt. Skins, 16s. 6d. per lb. Pitch, 55s. per barrel.
Tar, 45s. per barrel. Indian corn, 30s. per bushel.
Turpentine, 22s. 6d. per bushel. Indian peas, 30s. per bushel.

‡The following notices, which appeared in the *Gazette*, Charles-town, a few

Hemp and flax did not prove to be such profitable crops as the Welch at first anticipated, and were not much raised. Neither the soil nor climate were well adapted to their production. For hemp, particularly, very rich land, of a peculiar quality, was required. Wheat and corn were found more valuable, especially the latter. Indigo, however, proved to be the most lucrative crop. The rich lands on the river were admirably adapted to its production, more so than those in the lower parts of the Province near the coast.

"About the year 1745," we are informed, "the fortunate discovery was made that this plant (indigo) grew spontaneously in the Province, and was found almost everywhere among the wild weeds of the forest."

As the soil naturally yielded a weed which furnished the world with so useful and valuable a dye, it loudly called for cultivation and improvement.

For this purpose, some indigo seed was imported from the French West Indies, where it had been cultivated with great success, and yielded the planters immense profit. At first the seed was planted by way of experiment, and it was found to answer the most sanguine expectations. In consequence of which, several planters turned their attention to its culture, and studied the art of extracting the dye from it. Every trial brought them fresh encouragement. In the year 1747, a considerable quantity of it was sent to England,

---

years after, will give some idea of the progress which had been made in this department of industrial enterprise:—

"*Notice by John Manderson.*

"To be sold at Private Sale, the Subscriber's three saw-mills and grist mill on Big and Little Cedar Creek. 60,000 feet lumber have been carried by 2 hands on one raft to George-town—most populous part Cheraws District—15 hands of the Chickasaw and English breed.

"*Sept. 11th, 1777.*"

"*May 6th,* 1778. Valuable Saw and Grist Mills on Juniper Creek, 4 miles below Cheraw Hill, with a bolting mill—also a bolting mill, distance 2 or 3 miles to Cheraw, where the Church is.

"Timber may be rafted from pier head of lowest mill in small Rafts to the River, it being not more than 4 miles from the mill to the River down the Creek, and 3 by land,—where the rafts are joined to carry down to George-town, and has generally been done in Rafts containing from 30 to 40,000 feet in 5 days, the distance from George-town by land is 90 miles,—by JACOB VALK, Charles-Town."

which induced the merchants trading to Carolina to petition Parliament for a bounty on Carolina indigo. This petition from the merchants was followed by another from the planters and inhabitants of Carolina. Accordingly an Act of Parliament was passed, about the beginning of the year 1748, for allowing a bounty of sixpence per pound on all indigo raised in the British American plantations, and imported directly into Britain from the place of its growth.* It was sent by our farmers to Charles-town, and sometimes to London,† and occasionally to markets in the neighbouring colonies. The amount of indigo exported from South Carolina, in 1754, was 216,924 pounds.‡

Fortunes were made rapidly by its cultivation.§ It brought at one time from four to five dollars per pound. Traces of the old indigo vats are to be seen here and there on the Pedee. Its cultivation ceased about the close of the century, or soon after.

Higher up the river, in North Carolina, it was followed by tobacco, which became the principal export, and, for a time, the chief circulating medium.||

Some of the first settlers established themselves as traders, chiefly on the river. Cheraw Hill, Long Bluff, and Hunt's Bluff were points of note for trade. The navigation of the river commenced with the arrival of the colonists, as at Sandy Bluff, who are said to have come up in boats. As early as 1740, the navigation was open from Cheraw down. There were serious obstructions, however, which became the subject of legislation in after years, and with the aid of individual energy and enterprise, were gradually removed. The subject of roads, bridges, and ferries claimed the early

---

*Ramsay's "History S. C." vol. ii. pp. 138, 139.

†The account sales of one cask indigo shipped to London from the Pedee in 1766, shows that it commanded 2s. 3d. per pound, amounting to 37l. 4s. 3d. The bounty on it was 3l. 12s. 4d. The total expense of the shipment from Charlestown was 3l. 6s. 4d.

‡Ramsay's "History," p. 191.

§As an illustration of the value of the crop, it may be mentioned that General Harrington sent three four-horse waggon loads to Virginia, and with the proceeds of the sale bought from fifteen to twenty negroes.

||Where it was raised above the head of navigation on the river, tobacco was carried off to market in hogsheads, weighing from 1000 to 1400 lbs. The hogsheads were strongly hooped, and with an axle and felloes of pine to prevent the middle from being injured, drawn by two horses.

attention of the settlers. Highways were to be established for travel and transportation. The first roads, rough corduroys, were just wide enough to admit the passage of a kind of vehicle common then, called a sled. It was of simple construction, but indispensable at that early day, when something better was not to be had. It required but two side pieces of oak, with the ends turned up in front, and confined together, about four feet apart, by cross pieces securely tenanted into them. Thus, rough-hewn and expeditiously put together, this simple conveyance was ready for use. With it, rails were hauled for fencing, wood for fuel, and logs and other materials for cabins. By the addition of a box for a body, the corn and other products of the field were carried to the barn, and families often to places of gathering. But these could not long continue to supply the growing demands of an advancing population. Better roads and better conveyances were to be provided. Accordingly, in 1747, we find the first effort made in this direction.* An Act was passed in that year by the Commons House of Assembly, of which the preamble was in these words:—
"Whereas the Upper Settlements on Pedee, Waccamaw, and Black Rivers are very extensive and remote from each other, by reason whereof it will be convenient to divide the same into several districts, under several sets of Commissioners, to the end that the making and repairing of highways and causeways in those parts may be better attended to and performed," &c.

It was accordingly enacted, "That the Parts situate upon or near to Pedee, Waccamaw, and Black Rivers," should be divided into five districts. Of these, the third district was to embrace the settlements on the eastern side of Great Pedee River, extending from the Province line south-eastward to Cat Fish Creek; and William Colt, William James, Abraham Colson, Malachi Murphy, and Jacob Buckholt, were appointed Commissioners of Highways for the said district. The fourth district embraced the lands "situate on the south-west side of Great Pedee River, from Lynche's Creek south-westward to the bounds of the Province; and

---

*"Statutes at Large of So. Ca.," vol. ix. p. 144.

James Gillespie, Francis Young, John Dexter, Samuel De Sorrency, and Thomas Elleby, were appointed Commissioners."

By the same Act, the Commissioners were directed to meet at such places in their respective districts as the majority should appoint, twice a year—viz., on Easter Monday and the first Monday in August, for the despatch of business.

They were to establish ferries as well as highways. For some years after this, no further legislation was needed. It was not until 1768 that another Act was passed, establishing a public ferry "at the lands of James James, in the Welch Tract, on the South East side of Great Pedee River, in the Parish of Prince George, opposite to Cedar Creek, which is on the South West side of the said river, in the Parish of St. Mark, on the lands of the said James James, and to land on either side of the said creek;" "the said ferry to be vested in the said James James, his heirs, &c., for the term of fourteen years." The rates of ferriage were: "For every single person, one shilling and three pence; for a horse and chair, or a horse and cart, five shillings; for a four wheel carriage, with five horses, twenty shillings; for neat cattle, ferried or swum, seven pence half penny in the current money of the Province."

"All Ministers of the Gospel, all persons going to and from Church Service, and muster of Militia, and all persons in time of alarm, and all Expresses or Messengers sent in the service of the Government, and free Indians in amity with the Government," were to be free from toll.

"Abel Wilds, David Evans, James James, Alexander Mackintosh, John Kimbrough, Thomas Evans, George Hicks, Thomas James, and John Mackintosh, were appointed Commissioners for laying out, making and keeping in repair, a road from the North-east side of the above-mentioned ferry, to lead down the country into the public road; and likewise a road to lead from the upper side of the above-mentioned creek; and also a road to lead from the lower side of the above-mentioned creek, into the public road which leads down the country."

This was the second Act passed on the subject of roads

and ferries for this part of the Province, and no other appears for sixteen years following.

Some of the earlier land grants contained several curious privileges, reservations, and conditions.

In a grant of land in the Welch Tract, dated 1750, after the usual form, &c., it is added; "together with privilege of hunting, Hawking, and Fowling, in and upon the same, and all Mines and Minerals whatsoever; Saving and Reserving, nevertheless, to us, our Heirs and Successors, all white Pine Trees, if any there should be found growing thereon: and also Saving and Reserving to us, our Heirs and Successors, one-tenth part of Mines of Silver and Gold only." Also it was provided, that the grantees "should clear and cultivate at the rate of one acre for every Five Hundred Acres of Land, and so in proportion according to the quantity of Acres contained therein; or, build a Dwelling House thereon, and keep a stock of Five Head of Cattle for every Five Hundred Acres, upon the same, and in Proportion for a greater or lesser quantity."

It was also provided, that "on every Twenty Fifth Day of March, the said Grantee, his Heirs, &c., should pay to the Receiver-General of the Province, or to his Deputy, or Deputies, for the time being, at the Rate of Three Shillings Sterling, or Four Shillings Proclamation Money, for every Hundred Acres, &c."

This was one of the tokens and acknowledgements of a subjection under which the Colonists had even now become restive. As a source of revenue to the Crown* simply, it was less objectionable.

"Few countries," it is said, "have at any time exhibited so striking an instance of public and private prosperity as appeared in South Carolina between the years 1763 and 1775.

---

*The following is a specimen of the payment, by way of crown tax, thus required:—
"South Carolina.
"Received, the Thirteenth Day of August, in the year of our Lord one Thousand seven Hundred and Sixty four, of Philip Pledger and Jesse Councill, the sum of Ten pounds, sixteen shillings, Proclamation money; being for Eighteen years quit-rent due to the Crown, the Twenty Fifth Day of March last, for Three hundred Acres of Land held by them, and situated in Craven County. I say, received for the use of his Majesty, by
"ALEX. MACKINTOSH;
"£10 16s. 0d." "Deputy Receiver.

The inhabitants of the Province were in that short space of time more than doubled. Wealth poured in upon them from a thousand channels. The fertility of the soil generally repaid the labour of the husbandman, making the poor to sing, and industry to smile through every corner of the land. None were indigent but the idle and unfortunate. Personal independence was fully within the reach of every man who was healthy and industrious. The inhabitants, at peace with all the world, enjoyed domestic tranquillity, and were secure in their persons and property. They were also completely satisfied with their Government, and wished not for the smallest change in their political constitution."* This glowing account of the general condition of the Province was literally true of the upper parts of the Pedee. Nowhere else were the leading elements of prosperity more vigorously operative. As an illustration of the progress made by the settlers in these parts in manufactures, the following extract will suffice. It appeared in the *Gazette,* Charles-town, Dec. 22, 1768.

"A gentleman of St. David's Parish, in this Province, writes to his correspondent in Charles-town: 'I expect to see our own manufactures much promoted in this part of the Province. I send you some samples of what hath been already done upon this River and in this Parish. The sample of white cotton was made in the proportion of twelve yards to one pound of cotton. Hemp, Flax, and Cotton may be raised here in any quantity; as to wool, one cannot have much of it.'"

To this, the Editor of the *Gazette* added:—"The number of samples mentioned above is eleven, which the curious may have an opportunity of seeing, by enquiring of any one of the young men, at the Great Stationery and Book Shop." Where, or by whom, these samples were produced, is not known. Cotton was not much cultivated for many years after this. Another notice appeared in the *Gazette* of March 2, 1769, to this effect:—"Many of the Inhabitants of the North and Eastern Parts of this Province have this winter clothed themselves in their own manufactures; many more would purchase them if they could be got, &c."

*Ramsay's "History Revolution in So. Ca.," vol. 1. p. 7.

One of the drawbacks experienced, was in the droughts which sometimes prevailed for months together, and with great severity. This was the case in 1752, and again in 1769, as was stated in the *Gazette* of July 5th of that year, viz. :—"That there was a great drought in the Province, and to the North-Eastward, as far as Virginia—none such having been known since that of 1752. Drivers of cattle to Charles-town have to dig fifteen feet for water." Mention has been made of the increasing number of slaves. This began to be the case almost immediately after the first settlements. The prices paid about this time indicate the extent of the demand. In 1762, a woman, with two children, a girl and boy, sold for 477 pounds current money. In the following year, the same prices were given. Some of the first settlers brought their slaves with them. The labour of the negro was found to be indispensable on the river low-lands to which the first clearings for a time were almost exclusively confined. The first settlements were for the most part made immediately on the banks of the river, at elevated points, where good springs of water were to be found. Such a position experience has proved to be healthier than the intermediate swamps between the river and the high land, or even than the latter, when contiguous to the swamps. At first the emigrant from more northern latitudes, or healthier climes, did not experience any serious effects from a residence in the miasmatic regions of the south. It was only after the clearings began, that diseases appeared, except the fever and ague, which were known from the first. This, however, was more troublesome and enervating than dangerous. When openings were made, and the rich alluvial soils and stagnant waters became exposed to the sun, the inhabitants began to suffer more severely from bilious and other more fatal forms of fever. The planters were consequently driven from their swamp homes to healthier localities.

In addition to all this, it is a well-established fact in the history of the diseases incident to rich alluvial bottoms, that a season marked by certain atmospherical changes, or other unusual atmospheric phenomena, may give rise to types of fever of the most malignant character. During the months of June, July, and August, 1752, the heat in Carolina is said to have been oppressive to a degree never felt before.* Such seasons, doubtless, had much to do, when recurring, with changes of residence. The removal of the planters from the east side of the river in the Welch Neck formed the germ of a settlement at the Long Bluff† on the west, in what is now the District of Darlington. As early as 20th Dec., 1748, Saml. Wilds, who had settled a little below on the opposite side of the river, petitioned Council "for 100 acres of land across Pedee, stating he was a settler in the Welch Tract, on lands he purchased about five years ago, which is low and often overflowed—that there was a Plot of vacant land opposite his across the River Pedee, which was high land, and which, for the health of his family, he desired to settle." His petition was granted. The land here referred to is situated a little below the Long Bluff. To this period we may refer the beginning of the community at the latter point, which continued to increase, with accessions to its population from other quarters. In a few years it became a place of some importance. It had the advantage of being central and accessible. It was immediately on the river, and though exposed to the miasma from the extensive swamp across, continued for many years to be comparatively healthy. The public highway leading from Cheraw Hill to George-town passed near it.‡

The settlement at Cheraw Hill also continued to advance for the like reasons in part, but chiefly because of its note as a point for trade. Being at the head of navigation on the river, with an extensive and fertile country to be developed, and mainly dependent on it for supplies, its location was peculiarly advantageous. The land on which the town is built was granted to Eli Kershaw in 1766.

About the same time it was laid out by the Kershaws,§

---

*"Ramsay," ii. p. 179.
†So called from its being one of the longest bluffs on the river, extending without break for about three miles.
‡The Cheraw and Darlington R. R. runs for a short distance along this old track, from a point opposite Long Bluff, up.
§The following notice, which appeared in the *Gazette*, Charles-town, shows that the Kershaws left a few years after this:—

Eli and Joseph, with others. It was a few years after, probably in 1775 for the first time, called Chatham, in honour of the first Earl of that name, which it bore until its incorporation long afterward. It did not advance much in growth, but few families being attracted to it as a place of residence. As late as 1792 it is said to have contained not more than a dozen dwelling-houses.

Among other signs of progress was the formation, as early at least as 1768, of the "Planter's Club," or "Society," as it was otherwise called. It was often alluded to in a private journal of the time, and is supposed to have embraced the principal planters on the river above the Welch Neck.

It was probably formed for social purposes chiefly, after the manner of the "Clubs" which had been in exsistence before, and were then so well-known in the lower parts of the Province. Committees were appointed for the transaction of business, and meetings frequently held. On one occasion—an anniversary, perhaps—a sermon was preached before it by the Rev. Nicholas Bedgegood. It continued in existence until the Revolution.

Not much attention had yet been paid to military matters in the interior of the Province. A small banding together of neighbourhoods against the Indians, appears to have been all that was demanded. George Pawley was Colonel of the Craven County Regiment in 1744. Soon after this militia companies were formed in the upper parts of the Pedee. Philip Pledger was commissioned Captain

"Sale.

"1774. On wednesday, the 16th day of Nov. next, and the following days, at the Court House, at Long Bluff, will be sold,

"That valuable Plantation, called Liberty Hill, and all their other Lands, at and near Cheraw Hill, on Pedee River, together with their Store Houses, Mills, remaining stock of store goods, and about fifty valuable negroes, employed in carrying on their business at Chatham, under the firm of Eli Kershaw and Co. The whole being to be sold in order to make a final settlement of the copartnership which lately subsisted between the subscribers. Twelve months credit will be given, if required, upon all sums above one hundred pounds, on paying interest from the day of sale, giving such security as shall be approved of by

"Joseph Kershaw,
"John Chesnut,
"Eli Kershaw,
"William Ancrum,
"Aaron Loocock."

in his Majesty's Service in 1756. George Hicks and Thomas Loyd were Captains in 1762, and Alexander Mackintosh in 1765. In January 1748 the Craven County Regiment consisted of 1200 men. The first General Militia Review for the upper Pedee was ordered in 1759 by George Pawley, Adj$^{t.}$ Gen$^{l.}$, beginning with George-town, Oct. 4th; Mars Bluff, Oct. 11th, and Westfield on Pedee* Saturday, October 15th. The only military organization in the Province prior to this time, and going back as far as 1703, consisted of companies, battalions, and regiments. The Act of 1747, which was continued by Act of 1753 for two years, and revived and continued by Act of 1759, provided for the calling and assembling of all persons from sixteen to sixty years of age, and to be formed into companies, troops, and regiments. It was not until 1778 that brigades were established.

The earliest list of Justices of the Peace, embracing the upper part of Craven County, appeared in 1756, when George Hicks and Abraham Buckholts were appointed. In 1761 Alexander Mackintosh was added, and in 1767 Claudius Pegues.

A generous hospitality and unrestrained social intercourse were strikingly characteristic of this period. The sparseness of the population and the few public occasions which there were to bring the people together, made our early settlers more dependent on each other for whatever of pleasure and excitement social intercourse could afford. Hence, every house was open. A cordial greeting awaited the visitor. He might prolong his stay without danger of becoming an annoyance. A social bore was scarcely known. The news, from whatever quarter, when it reached the settlements, was thoroughly discussed and well digested. As we look back upon them from a more conventional age, we are tempted to exclaim, Happy were the days of which so much in this respect could be said. It was fortunate for the healthy progress of the settlements on the Pedee, that in the central and most important of them all, the religious element so largely prevailed.

---

*This was near Cheraw Hill.

There the simple and unobtrusive, yet sturdy and manly virtues which the Welch Christians brought with them, were found in active operation. How much, in the end, other neighbouring communities were indebted to their salutary influence, it would be difficult to estimate.

That they continued to operate, and to form a public sentiment of a sound and elevated character, there is abundant evidence. And in this, as in the virtuous influence brought to bear upon the mingled elements of population from whatever sources entering in, was found the germ of that steady intellectual and moral advancement, of which the happiest indications afterward appeared.

Even the troublous times of the Revolution could not altogether repress this spirit, as will be found in tracing the subsequent marks of its progress.

Another feeling, however, was now beginning to take possession of the hitherto peaceful dwellers on the Pedee. Attached as the people of the Province had ever been to the Crown, they still rejoiced in their connexion with the Mother Country, and in being subjects of the same king.

Up to this time there had been no special cause, except the want of courts of their own, for dissatisfaction with the Royal Government on the part of the people of Carolina, as was the case in some other of the colonies. Though essential changes had been made in the commercial system of the colonies for preventing a contraband trade with the French and Spaniards, and for enlarging the powers of the Courts of Admiralty, creating great uneasiness in some parts of the continent; the Carolinas, whose commerce was carried on agreeably to the British laws of trade and navigation, were very little affected by these innovations. Until the accession of George III., Great Britain, in time of war, had been in the habit of making requisitions for supplies to the Provincial Assemblies. These were so liberally granted by many of them, and particularly by that of South Carolina, that the Parliament of Great Britain had sometimes reimbursed them for their extraordinary expenses.*

Some of our wealthier planters had been in the habit of

---

*Ramsay's "History Revolution in So. Ca.," vol. i. p. 9.

sending their sons abroad to be educated. As a whole, the colonists were as loyal as any of the subjects of the Crown at home. But, in 1763, when the scheme of an American revenue was laid before Parliament, to be collected in the colonies without the consent of their local legislatures, the first shock was given to that loyalty which had never before been seriously disturbed. How that first shock soon after settled down into a feeling of dissatisfaction, which continued to increase, with an occasional struggle of the old attachments of birth and association, and at length attained complete ascendancy, are among the records of history. The people on the Pedee, from the first, participated deeply in the feeling of resistance against that, which in common with their countrymen elsewhere, they regarded as the encroachments of oppression at the expense of that well-regulated liberty which they had been accustomed to enjoy. They were, moreover, active and steadfast throughout the great controversy and struggle which were at hand.

As yet, they could scarcely be said to have a voice of their own in the Provincial Assembly, where the first notes of opposition were to be heard. Though nominally embraced in parochial organizations, which were influential, they were virtually unrepresented. But little intercourse had yet been established with the parishes lower down; and no member of Assembly had appeared from the Upper Pedee. For this and other reasons, much anxiety was felt to have a distinct organization of their own, through which their sentiments might become known, and their influence be felt beyond the boundaries of their settlements, which were remote, and, as yet, comparatively unknown. One relic remains, identifying them with the general feeling which pervaded the people of the Province at this period—a relic connected with the immortal Pitt. It was after the repeal of the "Stamp Act," when the difficulty with the Mother Country was thought for a time to have been happily adjusted, that so large a debt of gratitude was felt by the colonists to be due to Lord Chatham, the fearless and eloquent defender of the oppressed people of America. In Great Britain, the repeal of the "Cider Act" helped also to swell the feeling of enthusiasm which moved the hearts of that great people.

In the *South Carolina Gazette and Country Journal,* of Charles-town, July 22nd, 1766, appeared this item of news from the British correspondent:—"There is a handsome medal struck and distributed, about the size of a crown-piece, on which is the head of Mr. Pitt, with his name; and for the reverse, the following inscription: 'The Man, who, having saved the Parent, pleaded with success for her children.'" It was also added: "A great number of rings, set with the head of Mr. Pitt, is intended to be sent, as presents, to some of the principal merchants in America, by their correspondents in the country." One of these medals was found a few years since in an ancient clearing* at Cheraw Hill, in a good state of preservation. It is a handsome piece of work, the face being well executed, with the inscription, "Gulielmus Pitt;" and on the reverse the words already quoted.

The repeal of the Cider and Stamp Acts, in which Pitt took so prominent a part, produced a general and extraordinary outburst of enthusiasm. "The Irish," it was said, in the Account already noticed, "are going to erect his Statue in every City in the Kingdom, as the Man who first saved the Mother, and after that her children, from ruin!" alluding to Great Britain and the colonies. Statues were ordered

---

*It was picked up by a child on the surface in an old field near St. David's Church, and given to the author. No clue was found as to its history, until the account of it was met with in the old *Gazette.*

The woodcut annexed represents it correctly.

this year by the Commons House of Assembly of Maryland to the honour of this noble defender of the rights of man. The Assembly of New York also ordered an elegant statue of brass from England. "They have also ordered," it was said, "that a piece of Plate, value 100 pounds sterling, be presented to John Sergeant, Esq., of the City of London, with the thanks of the House, for his having cheerfully undertaken at their request, and to their great satisfaction faithfully discharged, the trust of special agent, and liberally declined any allowance for his trouble. June 30th, 1766."

The language inscribed on the medal appears to have been quite in vogue at the time.

In the *Gazette* of July 8th, of the same year, it was said: "In the House of Commons, the entire illegality of General Warrants, was determined 25th April, even without a Division; upon which occasion, that great Man, 'who saved the Parent, and pleaded with success for her children,' exerted himself in a remarkable manner." Occasionally the British papers contained happy hits at the opponents of American Rights, of which the following was a specimen:—

"London, March 1.
"Intelligence extraordinary.

"A person of considerable eminence is said to be preparing the heads of a bill, to be laid before a great, august Assembly, in which, among other things, it will be proposed to be enacted, that no American shall presume to eat, drink, or sleep for the space of one whole year."

The feeling in Carolina, after the repeal of the Stamp Act, was intense. A marble statue of Pitt was ordered from England, to be executed in the highest style of art. When received in Charles-town, the enthusiasm of the people knew no bounds. The principal men of the city, unwilling for the precious burden to be borne by other hands, drew it themselves, amid the firing of cannon and other demonstrations of admiring affection, to the spot selected for its erection, the intersection of Broad and Meeting streets. The subsequent history of this statue was remarkable. The right arm, raised in eloquent attitude, was shot off by a cannon-ball discharged from a British Fort on James Island, during the siege of Charles-town, in 1780. And such is the fickleness of popular feeling, that a few years after, the excitement against the son of Mr. Pitt, who was then directing the war against France, was as great with some at the South as it had been enthusiastically warm for the father. In consequence of which, it is said that the statue in being taken down for a change of place, was allowed to fall, and in its broken and mutilated state put away among some old rubbish, where it remained for years uncared for and forgotten.* Until, at length, the noble impulse that had prompted its execution in the first instance, once more attained the ascendancy, and the valuable relic was carefully placed where it now stands, in front of the Orphan House in Charleston, an ornament to the city which should hold it dear to the latest generation.

Such had been the progress of the settlements on the Pedee in all the elements of prosperity, that a distinct organization of their own, the want of which had been long felt, was now imperatively demanded. And happily for them, their claims in this behalf, could no longer be overlooked. It will be seen how a new impetus was thereby given to their hitherto steady progress, and an opportunity afforded them of taking their proper place in the affairs of the Province, to the advancement of which, in their measure, as good citizens, they had faithfully contributed.

The time withal was at hand, when *their* voice was of right to be heard; and their efforts, as an organized body, to be acknowledged, who, having once been as loyal as any other subjects of the British Crown, were now to be as prompt and decided in throwing off the yoke which a misguided government, as an unnatural parent, would fain have put upon them.

---

*Drayton's "Memoirs," v. 1, p. 60, and note, giving an interesting account of this statue.

CHAPTER VII.

Judicial history—Only Courts held in Charles-town—Evils resulting—Lynch law—Disturbances in North Carolina—Similar troubles in this Province—How remedied by the people—Regulation movement—First expression of the popular voice by petition for Circuit Courts—Action of Council thereon, and of Commons House of Assembly—Nothing done—People discouraged and disaffected—Acts of Regulators—Government alarmed—Accounts from Back Country—Proclamations of Governor to quiet disturbances—Further accounts from interior—Action of Council—Legal proceedings instituted—Disturbances continue—People await the fate of Circuit Court Act—Disturbances in neighbourhood of Mars Bluff—Colonel Powell—Companies from Long Bluff—Accounts of the conflict—Its end—Government alive from the first to the serious nature of the troubles—Regulators meet—Account of them—New election of Members of Assembly ordered—General meeting of Regulators—Precautions to preserve quiet at elections—Assembly meets—His Excellency's address—Assembly's reply—Domestic manufactures—Efforts to promote them—Subscription in St. David's—Assembly espouses cause of colonists—Concluding reflections.

TOWARD the close of the period of which some account has been given, events were transpiring, important beyond all others in their bearing upon that decisive change which the conflict with the Mother Country was soon to bring about. An alarming state of affairs had existed in the interior and more remote parts of the Province. Prior to the year 1769, the General Court was holden in Charles-town. This had supplanted the County and Precinct Courts which were appointed in 1725; and being the only Court of Criminal and Civil jurisdiction in the Province (except the Courts of Justices of the Peace, which had jurisdiction in all civil causes as high as twenty pounds current money), great oppression and inconvenience were felt by the people living remote from the seat of justice—by parties, witnesses, and jurors, who were obliged to attend the court; and especially by suitors and prosecutors, who were often worn out by the law's delay, insulted by the insolence of office, and ruined by costs and expenses, most unreasonably incurred and cruelly exacted.* The delay of suits, in many cases, in consequence of the distance from Charles-town, was very great, and the cost and inconvenience of such attendance exceedingly burdensome and detrimental. The business of the Provost Marshal was much too extensive to be duly executed, and his fees, by reason of the extent of his office throughout the Province, often more than half the amounts sued for. The expense of recovering small debts frequently exceeded their whole sum. In consequence of this state of things, numbers of people, it is said, were deterred from becoming inhabitants of the Province, and many large and valuable tracts of land continued to lie uncultivated, to the injury of the public revenue and the trade with Great Britain. And yet greater evils prevailed, so as seriously to affect the inhabitants of the interior, because unprotected to a great extent in their persons and property by the strong arm of the law. They were too remote to think of carrying thieves and other offenders, except in extraordinary cases, to Charles-town. Hence the most unhappy facilities were afforded to the worst classes of people to escape the punishment due to their crimes, and the payment of their just debts. This state of things drove the inhabitants of the middle and parts of the upper county, then the frontier settlements, into the most disorderly and violent measures. The laws, which were found ineffectual to restrain and punish horse thieves and other notorious offenders, were also disregarded by good and honest men, who undertook to do themselves justice, and to punish the guilty by arbitrary measures. The authority of the civil magistrate was held in contempt, because insufficient for the maintenance of order and the regular execution of the laws. Some efforts were made to repress these disturbances, but they were found unavailing.†

The evil, which had been of long standing and grown with the increase of population, at length became intolerable.

---

*Introduction to Brevard's "Digest," vol. i. p. 14. This introductoin is of great value in connexion with the Judicial History of this period. Though brief, it is a very able and comprehensive exposition of those evils which drove the people to desperation, and of the changes imperatively demanded.
†Brevard, vol. i. p. 14.

Such was the distance to Charles-town, the seat of justice; such the difficulty, nay, the impossibility in most instances, of securing the attendance of necessary parties, and the great expense withal, that redress was literally out of the question—redress according to the forms of law. This, indeed, has been the case in the first settlement of all our western states at later periods.* To increase the difficulty in Carolina, a certain class of offenders now abounded. There was a floating element—men of lawless character, who lived by their wits, and infested every community. Horse thieves and negro stealers, highway-robbers and abandoned trespassers had to be dealt with. Signal and summary punishment, though often demanded by the atrocious circumstances attending peculiar cases, was not to be had according to the established course of justice. However heinous their offences had been, criminals could not ordinarily be brought to a legal condemnation. They came in strongly organized bands, and by their mutual support, false swearing, and intimidation of prosecutors, either caused the law to be ineffectual, or the guilty entirely to escape. Having in vain sought relief from the Government, the virtuous inhabitants had but one alternative left—to take the administration of remedial measures into their own hands.

They called themselves "Regulators;" and thus "Lynch law" had its origin at this period.

The Regulators consisted of respectable planters and others, who demanded a better system for the more regular, equal, and vigorous, as well as prompt administration of justice.† Such was the character of the actors, and of the movement made on the Pedee. The Regulators maintained for some time a vigorous and effective organization, not abusing the powers they assumed, or exercising them beyond the exigencies of their unhappy condition. On the other hand, the Government, instead of giving ear to their timely and respectful complaints, and providing some redress, employed as instruments to subdue the spirit of rebellion, as it

---

*Remarkably so in Texas, where the history of Lynch Law, or the Regulators, has been one of a peculiar and most instructive character.
†Brevard's "Introduction," p. 14.

was called, and enforce the existing system, men of little or no character or respectability, the obsequious tools of those in power, who abused their authority and fattened on the general distress. This was more or less the case in all the interior parts of the Province, and especially in the western district, where a man of low character, named Scovill, was employed to enforce the law among the self-constituted Regulators.* In executing his commission he adopted very severe measures, and came into serious collision with numbers of the better classes among the people, involving multitudes in great distress. All this led, in that part of the Province, to very grave difficulties and disturbances at the commencement of the Revolution.

In North Carolina also serious troubles now existed. The first complaints there arose from oppressive exactions laid by government officials in the shape of exorbitant fees and otherwise upon the people.

As early as 1766, these disturbances, beginning in Granville, extended into Orange and Anson Counties. Up to April, 1768, those who had taken part in these proceedings in North Carolina were designated by the appellation of the "Mob," and seem to have adopted it themselves. On the 4th of April they changed it to that of "Regulators."† Oppressed with the malpractices of some avaricious individuals, they forcibly opposed the administration of civil government under the officers of the Crown. These insurgents, though numerous, being undisciplined, and for the most part without arms, were easily dispersed by Govr· Tryon at the head of the incorporated militia of the country. Some of their leaders were killed in action, others were hanged, and all of them were involved in distress.‡ Three hundred of their number were left dead upon the field. It might have been expected that those in either Province, who were thus ready to resist the constituted authorities, on account of oppressions, or to take the law into their own hands in order to bring the guilty to condemnation, would

---

*Ramsay's "History of Revolution in So. Ca.," vol. i. p. 63.
†Martin's "History of No. Ca.," pp. 215-217.
‡"Ramsay," vol. i. p. 213.

be true to their country in the great conflict then approaching. These were in reality the first revolutions in America,* and those who assumed therein the attitude of open resistance were the first rebels. But, disappointing public expectation, many in North Carolina afterwards joined the royal party.

As it was with those between the Broad and Saluda Rivers in S$^o.$ C$^a.$ who came in conflict with Scovill, having suffered so severely for opposing regular government, they could not be persuaded afterward to co-operate with their countrymen in the support of congresses and committees raised for purposes of resistance.† And thus, a spirit true to the instincts of liberty in the inception of the struggle, though to some extent misguided, was crushed by the disasters it encountered, and turned at last against that cause which it might so nobly have sustained. Such, however, was not the history of the Regulation Movement on the Pedee. It began not so much in the shape of open resistance or opposition to Government, as in the assumption of authority within certain limits, which the best citizens deemed essential to the public welfare and to individual safety. The most respectable and influential inhabitants were found chiefly on the river, where the first settlements were made, and these were all united in their respective neighbourhoods, as committees of vigilance, for the detection and punishment of offenders. With them no stigma attached to the name of Regulator. They were actuated by good motives, and only sought to effect, by a summary process of their own, what the law, as then administered, had signally failed to accomplish. Violent measures were only resorted to as a temporary expedient. Under the extraordinary circumstances of the time, the course of these Regulators cannot be condemned. It furnishes, however, no precedent for a similar line of conduct in others who live in a more advanced and better regulated state of society, with the important privilege, moreover, of courts of their own, which to our early settlers was denied.

---

*Sabine's "American Loyalists," p. 27.
†Ramsay's "Revolution in So. Ca.," vol. i. p. 64.

The position taken by the Regulators on the Pedee, and the conflicts to which it led with the royal authority, undoubtedly nursed the spirit of liberty, preparing the way for that early and bold declaration of their rights, as well as for those heroic sacrifices and unflinching struggles in the cause of independence, for which the Whigs of the Old Cheraws were to be afterward distinguished.

The first expression of the popular voice, with reference to the evils of which we have spoken, is found in the records of the Upper House of Assembly, or Council, March 16th, 1752. On that day, this entry was made:—"Read the petition of the Inhabitants on Pedee River, about the mouth of Lynche's Creek, Humbly setting forth: That the Humble Petitioners reside in the remotest parts of this Province, having 200 miles to travel to the seat of Government; and that trade and commerce among us are greatly obstructed for want of a County Court appointed to hear and determine all causes, as well civil as criminal, in the same manner as every Court in each Province to the Northward, has power to hear and determine all such causes. We find the frontier here to be a place of refuge for many evil-disposed people and those of the meanest principles, crowding in amongst us—such as Horse Stealers and other Felons, having made their escape from North Carolina, and other parts—others cohabiting with their neighbour's wives, and living in a most lascivious manner, while we have no way or means to suppress them. We therefore humbly pray, that an Act be passed, dividing Craven County; and that that part from the mouth of Lynche's Creek upward, to the extent of this Province, on both sides of Great Pedee River, bounding Southwardly by Lynche's Creek, Northwardly by the Province line, which we pray may be further extended; and likewise by a North line from opposite to the mouth of Lynche's Creek to the Province line—be one distinct County, in which we may have twelve or more Justices appointed and authorized, without fee or reward, to hear and determine all causes, as well civil as criminal, without having their jurisdiction limited—any person supposing himself aggrieved, to be redressed by appealing to a Superior Court in Charles-town. We likewise humbly pray, that in consequence of the great expense which our County will be at in building a Court House, prison, pillory, and stocks, we may be exempt from paying such public taxes for some few years, as in your wisdom you shall think fit. And your Petitioners, as in duty bound, &c.,

"JOHN CRAWFORD,
"OWEN DAVID,
"WM. SUMMER,
"And about 60 more subscribers."*

This timely and earnest appeal could not be altogether slighted. The better classes of people were groaning under the evils of which they here complained.

"The said Petition," as the Records of Council further inform us, "being considered; it was Ordered, that the same be sent down to the Commons House of Assembly by the Master in Chancery." On the following day, the House "Resolved to appoint a Committee to take the same into consideration, consisting of Mr. Trapier, Mr. Powell,† Mr. Lynch, Mr. Dart, and Captain Buchanan."

On the 22nd of April, the Committee reported, "That they have, pursuant to the Order of the House, examined the matter of the said Petition; and are of opinion, that it will be no wise to the advantage of the Petitioners to have the County of Craven divided, as prayed for by their Petition,—because there is no town or other place proper for holding Courts of Judicature in that part of the Country which the Petitioners pray may be established a separate and distinct County. But the Committee are of opinion, that it is absolutely necessary that a Court be established, to be holden at George-town, Winyaw, in the

---

*From two of the names subscribed to this petition—viz., John Crawford and Owen David, it is manifest that the petitioners were not confined to the country about the mouth of Lynche's Creek, but extended much higher up the river. The distance stated to the seat of Government (Charles-town) being double the distance from Lynche's Creek, would also indicate that the more remote parts of Craven County were actually embraced in those taking an active part in the movement.

†This was George Gabriell Powell, a member from Prince George, Winyaw, with whose name we are to become so familiar, as connected with the region above.

said County, for hearing, trying, and determining all actions, causes, and crimes whatever (capital crimes excepted), that may arise or happen in the said County; And humbly recommend that a bill be brought in for that purpose, and that a Message be sent to the Governor by this House, to desire that his Excellency will be pleased to appoint Justices of the Peace in that Part of the Province, agreeably to the prayer of the said Petition." This Report was read, considered, and duly agreed to by the House; and a Committee appointed to prepare and bring in a Bill for establishing Courts of Justice at George-town, in Craven County, and at Beaufort, in Granville County. A Message was also Ordered to be sent to his Excellency, requesting him to appoint Justices of the Peace in the distant Parts of the Province.

And thus the matter ended, except that additional Justices of the Peace were appointed. But their powers were too limited to afford such relief as the inhabitants demanded. No distinct county organization, such as was prayed for, being provided, the consequence was they were deprived of whatever benefit even a County Court of inferior jurisdiction would have brought with it. No court was established at George-town, as recommended by the Committee. The Representatives of the people felt the necessity of such measures, but the Government, actuated by a most mistaken policy, was unwilling to lend any encouragement.

The inhabitants were consequently forced, either to submit to the grievous delay and ruinous expense of prosecuting their claims there, and carrying criminals to Charles-town, or to take the redress of their grievances into their own hands. Finding their efforts for relief ineffectual, they appear to have made no further attempt in that direction for years to come. In the meantime the evils of which they had complained continued to increase, and at length became insupportable. The Provincial Government, reflecting the wishes of that of the Mother Country, was unwilling, as will be found in the sequel, to establish Courts in the interior. These once secured, other privileges, it was thought, would be demanded, gradual encroachments be made on the established order of things, the influence of the Government in Charles-town lessened, and by degrees the way prepared for the spirit of liberty, and the assertion of their rights by the people of Carolina. It was a short-sighted and fatal policy. For the people who were thus aggrieved began to feel at length, that those who ought to have been most deeply alive to their sufferings, and who had the power to give redress, were willing to sacrifice them, if need be, to the interests of the Crown.

Of the history of the efforts made by the back settlers, during the nearly quarter of a century which followed before they became their own masters, to rid themselves of the evils mentioned, no record remains. The earliest account left to us was of a similar state of things in another part of the Province. In the *Gazette* of May 26th, 1767, appeared the following extract of a letter from Pine Tree Hill (Camden), dated May 14th, 1767:—"On the 6th inst, a number of armed men, being in search of Horse Stealers, robbers, &c., discovered a parcel of them in camp on Broad River, where an engagement soon ensued, and the Thieves were put to flight; and though none of them were taken, it is reasonable to suppose, from the quantity of blood on the ground, that some of them were killed. They left behind them ten horses, thirteen saddles, some guns, &c."

This was but the commencement of troubles. The great evils complained of began to appear in a thoroughly organized, and, to the Government, very alarming form. The *Gazette* of July 27th—August 3rd following, made this statement:—"The gang of Villains from Virginia and North Carolina, who have for some years past, in small parties, under particular leaders, infested the back parts of the Southern Provinces, stealing horses from one, and selling them in the next, notwithstanding the late public examples made of several of them, we hear are more formidable than ever as to numbers, and more audacious and cruel in their thefts and outrages. 'Tis reported that they consist of more than 200, form a chain of communication with each other, and have places of general meeting; where (in imitation of Councils of War) they form plans of operation and defence, and (alluding to their secrecy and fidelity to each other), call their places Free Mason Lodges. Instances of their cruelty to the people in the back settlements, where they rob or otherwise abuse, are so numerous and shocking, that a narrative of them would fill a whole *Gazette,* and every reader with horror. They at present range in the Forks between Broad, Saludy, and Savannah Rivers. Two of the gang were hanged last week at Savannah, viz., Lundy Hart and Obadiah Greenage. Two others, James Ferguson and Jesse Hambersam, were killed when these were taken." Soon after this, other alarming accounts reached Charles-town from the interior, for the back settlements were now in a stage of general commotion. At a Meeting of Council, October 5th, 1767, "His Excellency informed the Board that he had received information that a considerable number of the Inhabitants between Santee and Wateree rivers had assembled, and in a riotous manner gone up and down the country, committing riots and disturbances, and that they had burnt the houses of some persons who were reported to be Harbourers of Horse Thieves, and talk of coming to Charles-town to make some complaints. The Board gave it as their opinion to his Excellency that to prevent the mischief such commotions would be attended with, it would be proper for his Excellency to issue a Proclamation, commanding them to disperse, and enjoining all officers to take care to preserve the public peace." How unfeeling must have been a Government which had no sympathies for the troubles of its unoffending subjects! and how blind to imagine that proclamations could quiet the public mind, and restore tranquility among those whose persons and property were endangered by outlaws, who were running at large, the enemies of mankind!

In November following, a petition* from the upper and interior parts of Craven County, for the redress of grievances, was presented to Government.

In reply to this, and as touching the fearful state of things of which accounts were now frequently coming in, his

---

*It is a source of much regret to the author that he was unable, after diligent search, to discover any further trace of this petition. It was not copied, as was usual in the proceedings of Council, and was nowhere else to be found among the public records of the time. It came from the Upper Pedee.

Excellency Lord Charles Grevill Montagu, on 5th of November, made the following address to both Houses of Assembly:—

"Hon. Gen^{tn}: I should think myself equally negligent in the duty I owe to my King and this Province, if I did not recommend to you an early and serious consideration of the unhappy situation of the Back Parts of this Country. The various acts of villainy committed there, in contempt of all laws, human and divine, we have too frequent accounts of, and too recent proofs of, in the late trials of the unhappy convicts now under sentence of death. Far remote from the seat of Justice, they are daily exposed to misery and distress. These are objects that require redress, and are worthy the care of the Legislature. Tumultuous risings of any people, if not properly attended to, are of dangerous tendency, and they are a disgrace to a country, and particularly pernicious to a commercial and newly settled colony. The means to suppress those licentious spirits that have so lately appeared in the distant parts of the Province, and, assuming the name of Regulators, have, in defiance of Government, and to the subversion of good order, illegally tried, condemned, and punished many persons, require an attentive deliberation."

To this the Upper House of Assembly made the following reply:—

"The Humble Address of his Majesty's Council. We, his Majesty's dutiful and loving subjects, the Council of this Province, beg leave to return our thanks to your Excellency for your speech delivered yesterday to both Houses of Assembly. It is with the utmost concern that we behold the distracted state of the Frontier Settlements of this Province, where force and rapine, riot and disorder, supersede the temperate provisions of law and justice; but, tumultuous examples never fail to multiply those evils which it is the policy of well-regulated States to prevent by proper laws. The great objects proposed to our consideration deserve the most serious and deliberate attention, and we assure your Excellency that we shall, on our part, most heartily concur in every measure calculated to advance the public good, to compose the minds and remove the distresses of our fellow subjects."

The Government, as is here manifest, did not comprehend the real nature of existing evils, or the remedies necessary to be applied. It is also evident from the Governor's language, that there was not only no sympathy with them, but that a feeling of very decided opposition had been excited against the Regulators.

As an evidence of the feeling entertained by the Government, the fact may be mentioned that in March following (1768), a Petition from the Back Settlers for a Circuit Court Bill, as a measure of relief, was disposed of by Council, "after mature deliberation, by determining 'that it would not be necessary to take any notice of the same.'" This, of course, only led to more desperate measures on the part of the sufferers.

In less than a month, however, the authorities in Charles-town were induced to change their minds, and pursue a different policy, such were the indications of approaching difficulties, threatening to bring the people at once into an attitude of open rebellion, and perchance to overthrow the Government itself. On the 18th of April, a Circuit Court Act was passed, but afterwards failed to become a law. On the next day, April 19th, at a Meeting of Council, "His Hon^r the Lieut.-Govr observed to his Excellency, that a great number of Prosecutions were now being carried on against the people who had committed several outrages in the Back Country, and went by the name of Regulators, that several of the delinquents were very poor, and would be much harassed by them, and they had been unhappily deluded by some, who were ring-leaders in these riots, the punishment of whom, he apprehended, would answer the end of public justice, and vindicate the honor of Government; and therefore mentioned it as his opinion, that it would be proper to give directions to the Attorney-General, after a sufficient number of the most considerable were convicted, to enter Nolle Prosequis on the remaining prosecutions. The Board agreeing in opinion with his Honor, his Excellency was pleased to direct, that the

Attorney-General, after such a number as he should think convenient, not to exceed eight of the Principal Rioters, were convicted, to stop further proceedings against the rest."* Little did his Excellency, his Honor, and the Council understand the real state of the case. United as the sturdy yeomen of the Back Country were, and far removed from the coast, what cared they for prosecutions commenced in Charles-town? Having in vain petitioned for redress, no alternative was left them but to enter boldly upon the conflict now at hand. In less than three months they were found at work, as appears from the following remarks in the *Gazette* of June 13th. "It seems hardly probable that the disturbances in our back settlements will entirely subside, notwithstanding all the prudent steps that have been taken, or can be taken, by the Government to suppress them, until the late Act of the General Assembly of this Province for establishing Circuit Courts, takes effect: for we daily hear of new irregularities committed by the people called Regulators, who, seeming to despair of rooting out those desperate villains that remain among them any other way, still take upon themselves to punish such offenders as they can catch. We hear, that within this month, one Watts and one Distoe, have received 500 lashes each by their direction; and that an infamous woman has also received corporal punishment. We hear, also, that one John Bowles has lately lost his life in attempting to take Mr. Woodward, one of the leaders of the people called Regulators. According to our account, Woodward, refusing to surrender himself, Bowles fired at, and would have killed him, but the ball struck the barrel of a gun which he held across his breast, upon which, some people in company with Woodward, fired, and killed Bowles."

It seems that up to this time, the authorities in Charles-town were not apprized of the fact that the regulation movement embraced the most respectable and influential element in the Back Country. At a later period even, a most singular misapprehension will be found to have prevailed on the subject. The crisis on the Pedee was now

---

*"Council Journal," No. 34, pp. 118, 119.

rapidly approaching. The next intelligence of which any account remains, though not directly from that quarter, indicates what was going on there.

"At a Meeting of Council, July 5th, 1768, his Honor communicated to the Board a letter he had rec$^{d.}$ from Tacitus Galliard, Esq., to whom he had sent an express, desiring him to use his endeavours to apprehend the Deserters from the Regulars in Charles-town, in which Mr. Galliard informed his Honor, that the Back parts of the Country were far from being quiet, and that those people called Regulators, continued still to assemble together; but, as few members were present, the further consideration of what might be proper to be done, was adjourned over till next Friday morning."*

At that meeting, however, no action appears to have been taken. On 25th July, the following intelligence was given in the So. Ca. *Gazette*. "The last accounts from the Back Settlements say, that the People called the Regulators were to have a meeting at Lynche's Creek, on last Friday, where it was expected 1200 would be assembled. The occasion of this meeting is said to be, a Party of them lately having been roughly used by a Gang of Banditti, consisting of Mulattoes, Free Negroes, &c., notorious Harborers of runaway slaves, at a place called Thompson's Creek, whom they ordered to remove. It is added, they anxiously wait to hear the fate of the Act for establishing Circuit Courts in this Province, sent home for the Royal approbation, which, if it obtains, will restore good order in those parts." It may surprise the reader to find that so large a number of the classes here mentioned, Mulattoes, Free Negroes, &c., had collected at this early period in the settlement of the Province. Such a meeting of the inhabitants would indicate a formidable band of desperadoes. A more serious conflict was now to begin on the River. In Council, August 2nd, "His Honor communicated to the Board a letter from Col. Powell, and another from Robert Weaver, Esq., a magistrate for Craven County, and an affidavit taken by Mr. Weaver from some of the people who

---

*"Council Journal," No. 34, pp. 174, 175.

live upon the Pedee; from which it appeared that a Constable having a Warrant of Distress to execute on the Chattels of some of the Regulators, had called to his assistance 13 other men; that this party had fallen in with a considerable number of the Regulators, under Gideon Gibson, an Inhabitant of those Parts, when a skirmish was begun by the Regulators, in which one of the Constable's party was killed; that the Regulators then overpowered the Constable's party, and whipt some of them in a most cruel manner, and threatened to hang one of them, in case one of their party, a brother of the said Gibson, who was wounded in the affray, should die. It also appeared that Mr. Weaver, the Magistrate who had issued the warrant, and was obnoxious to them because he declared his disapprobation of their proceedings, lived in the greatest terror and danger of his life and property, and that all that part of the Country was a scene of riot and disorder."

"His Honor, by the advice of the Board, sent for Mr. Campbell, the Clerk of the Crown and Peace, and directed him to lay those papers before the Judges, and to inform them that he earnestly recommended to them to take such steps as would enforce obedience to the laws, quell the disorders in the Back Country, and bring some of these atrocious offenders to condign punishment; and to assure them of his readiness to give all assistance in his power to accomplish these ends."*

This disturbance near Mars Bluff thus begun, proved to be of most important consequence in alarming the Government on the one hand, and rousing and uniting the better class of inhabitants in the interior on the other. Gideon Gibson, though of violent and perhaps turbulent character, was a man of property and influence, an acknowledged leader in that part of the Country, and as bold as he was intent upon vindicating the rights of the people. It was necessary, therefore, if a Government whose authority was now on the wane, was to be supported, that prompt and stringent measures should be adopted. In Council, August 3rd, "His Honor observed to the Board, that his Majesty had

---

*"Council Journal," No. 34, pp. 194, 195.

published a very strong Proclamation in England on account of the late riots near London, and desired the opinion of the Board if it might not be proper to issue something similiar to it here, on account of the Riots in some of the Back Settlements. The Board were of opinion that it would be proper; and the following draught of a Proclamation being approved of, it was ordered to be prepared."

"South Carolina.
"By the Hon^{l.} Wm. Bull, Esq., Govr. and Commander-in-Chief in and over the said Province.

"A Proclamation.

"Whereas, it has been represented to me, that divers dissolute and disorderly persons have of late frequently assembled themselves together in the North-Western Parts of this Province, in a riotous and unlawful manner, to the disturbance of the public Peace, and in particular have, in the most illegal manner, taken upon them to whip and confine several persons, under the pretence of punishing them for crimes which they have charged against them, instead of delivering them into the hands of public Justice, and have daringly resisted the execution of the King's Process; and that these acts of violence have been accompanied with threats of still greater outrages, which have spread terror and alarm amongst those most likely to be affected thereby; and that some of those dissolute and disorderly persons have audaciously attempted to deter and intimidate the Civil Magistrates from doing their duty—I have taken the same into serious consideration, and being duly sensible of the mischievous consequences that may ensue from the continuance and repetition of such disorders, have thought fit, by and with the advice of his Majesty's Hon^{l.} Council, to issue this my Proclamation, hereby strictly requiring and commanding all the Justices, the Provost Marshal, and all other the Peace Officers of this Province, that they do severally use their utmost endeavours, by every legal means in their power, effectually to prevent and suppress all such tumults and unlawful assemblies, and to that end to put in due execution the laws for preventing, suppressing, and punishing the same, and that all his Majesty's dutiful and loyal subjects be aiding and assisting therein: And further, that the Magistrates and all others acting in obedience to this my Proclamation, may rely on the protection and support of the law in so doing, as they shall answer at their peril for the neglect thereof. Given under my hand and the great seal of his Majesty's said Province, at Charles-town, this third Day of August, 1768, and in the eighth year of his Majesty's reign. "WILLIAM BULL.

"By his Honor's command,
"Thos. Skettowe, Secty.

"God save the King."*

This measure, however, being deemed insufficient, further action was taken. In Council, August 5th, "His Honor the Lieut. Govr. observed, that several of the People who had associated with the Regulators had been unwarily led into the tumultous proceedings they had been engaged in, and had also been greatly provoked thereto by the repeated losses they had sustained from the villainous gangs of Horse-Thieves that infested those parts; and that he was of opinion that if a promise of a free pardon was to be offered to them for outrages already committed, it would probably disperse them and restore peace and tranquility to the Back parts of this Province; and a majority of the Board agreeing with his Honor in opinion that the effect of such a Proclamation should be tried; the following draught of a Proclamation being approved of, it was ordered to be published.

"A PROCLAMATION.

"South Carolina,
"By the Honl. Wm. Bull, &c.

"Whereas, by the advice of his Majesty's Honl. Council, I did, on the 3rd day of August inst. issue my Proclamation, reciting, that it having been represented to me that divers dissolute and disorderly persons had of late frequently assembled themselves together in the North-Western parts of this Province, in a riotous and unlawful manner, to the disturbance of the public Peace; and particularly had, in

*"Council Journal," No. 24, pp. 203-204.

the most illegal manner, taken upon themselves to whip and confine several persons, under pretence of punishing them for crimes which they had charged against them, instead of delivering them into the hands of Public Justice, and had daringly resisted the King's Process, and that their acts of violence had been accompanied with threats of still greater outrages, which had spread terror and alarm amongst those most likely to be immediately affected thereby; and that the said disorderly persons had audaciously attempted to deter and intimidate the Civil Magistrate from doing his duty; and I, having taken the same into my serious consideration, did think proper thereby strictly to enjoin and command the Justices, Provost Marshal, and all other the Peace Officers of this Province, to use their utmost endeavours, by every legal means in their power, to prevent and suppress all such tumults and unlawful assemblies; and to that end to put in due execution the laws for preventing, suppressing, and punishing the same, assuring them and all others acting in obedience thereto, of the protection and support of the law in so doing: But forasmuch at it has also been further represented, and appears unto me, that very many of the persons concerned in the said acts of violence, have unwarily been drawn in, and even provoked thereto by the great and repeated losses they have sustained from the gangs of Robbers and Banditti who infested those parts, and who were become the more dangerous and daring by being confederated in numerous bodies, and it was thereby rendered difficult to bring them to Public Justice: I, therefore, taking the same into my serious consideration, and being willing, under such circumstances, rather to prevent than to inflict the punishment due to such outrageous and illegal proceedings, do, by and with the advice of his Majesty's Hon[l.] Council, issue this my Proclamation, hereby strictly commanding and requiring all persons so unlawfully assembled to disperse themselves and repair peaceably to their respective homes and occupations, and forbidding them and all persons hereafter, at their utmost peril, so to assemble again; and I do promise his Majesty's most gracious Pardon for the misdemeanors by them committed at any time before the date hereof in so unlawfully assembling, whipping or confining any person or persons as aforesaid, to all such as shall forthwith pay due obedience to this my Proclamation, excepting to those persons concerned in the outrages and daring violences committed by Gideon Gibson and others upon George Thompson, a lawful constable, and his party, in the actual execution of a legal warrant, at or near Mars Bluff, in Craven County, upon the 25th day of July last. Given under my hand, and the Great Seal of the Province, &c., this 6th August, 1768.

"WM. BULL."*

This was followed, two days after, by the following statement in the *South Carolina Gazette*:—"Tuesday last, the Proclamation inserted in the first page of this paper was published in the usual manner; and on Saturday there was another, which is not come into our hands. A variety of reports continue to be circulated in different ways, and no doubt with different views, of the Proceedings and Intentions of the People called Regulators, in the North Western† part of this Province, some of them very alarming: amongst others, that 2 or 3000 of them were to assemble on Thursday, at the Congarees, for very unjustifiable purposes; but we are assured, that the People so met, or to meet, are not so considerable a body, and have only in view to be informed of the Bounds of the Respective Parishes to which they belong (the lines of which have been but lately run), that they may not lose the right of voting for Representatives of their own nomination, at their next general election, whenever the law gives it them."

August 15th, the *Gazette* said:—"The outrageous opposition lately offered to the Civil authority near Mars Bluff, on Pedee River, being at present a general subject of conversation, and by many attributed to the People called Regulators, it may not be amiss to lay before the public the following information, viz.: That there are two parties so called, and the proceedings of the one frequently confounded with those of the other. That the first (called the Honest party) consists in general of people of good prin-

---

*"Council Journal," No. 34, pp. 208-211.
†It should rather have been "North Eastern," &c.

ciples and property, who have assembled chiefly about the Congarees, the Ridge, &c., professedly with the view of driving all horse thieves, with their harbourers, abettors, and other vagabonds, from amongst them; and that the other (called the Rogues' party) are a gang of banditti, a numerous collection of outcast Mulattoes, Mustees, Free Negroes, &c., all horse thieves from the borders of Virginia and other Northern Colonies (the very people whom the Regulators would have expelled the Province, or brought to Justice), and have taken up arms to carry on their villainy with impunity. The last accounts we have received of both are, That the former, on the 16th past, took up one Charles Sparks, of infamous character, on Pedee, and ordered him to receive 500 lashes and quit the Province: and of the latter, that an armed company of them, headed by one Gideon Gibson, on the 25th past, near Mars-bluff, surrounded a Constable and 12 men, who were sent to bring one of the villains before a magistrate, and after a smart skirmish, wherein two of the Constable's party were mortally wounded, and one shot through the shoulder, took the rest Prisoners, whom he discharged, after ordering them 50 lashes each. In the skirmish, Gibson had one of his sons killed, and another wounded in the neck. Proper measures are taken to bring the principals of this desperate gang to Justice."

On the 22nd August, the *Gazette* said:—"We are sorry that we cannot have the pleasure of informing the public, that either of the Proclamations issued by his Honor the Lieu^t Govr on the 3rd and 6th ins^{ts}, are likely to produce the desired effects; Gideon Gibson declining to surrender on any terms; having put himself under the protection of people that do not at present seemed disposed to give him up. This man's character, we are told, always stood fair, till he lately became the tool of a Party, who committed the outrages near Mars-Bluff, mentioned in our last."

The *Gazette*, from which the preceding extracts are taken, was in the interest of the Government, and therefore disposed to cast as much odium as possible on every proceeding in which the people arrayed themselves against the constituted authorities of the Province. At first the Regulators were spoken of in terms of unmeasured condemnation; but, as the fact became known that they embraced the best people in the interior settlements, the tone of the press, as well as of the Government, became very much softened. To Gibson, however, no mercy was to be shown. He was made to appear as one of the Rogues' party. How far this was from being the case will appear in the sequel.

Immediately after the receipt of the intelligence in Charles-town, Col. Powell, of the Pedee Regiment, with the Provost Marshal, was despatched to the interior to quell the disturbance. In Council, 26th August, His Honor, Wm. Bull, informed the Board, that Roger Pinckney, Esq., the Provost Marshal, had returned from the Northward, for which place he had set out with warrants against Gibson, one of the Regulators, and that he had, by him, received the following letter from Col. Powell:—

"To the Hon^l Wm Bull, &c.
"Hon^l Sir,

"On the 9th ins^t I set out with Mr. Pinckney for Mars-bluff, and reached Lynche's Creek, distance 42 miles, that night, where we were joined by about 25 of the Posse Comitatus; and the following evening arrived at Mars-bluff, distance 30 miles; at which place we found 15 men of Capt. Weaver's company, and were the day following reinforced by 20 men of Capt. Thomson's company. It appeared to us, by all accounts, that Gibson was guarded by a large body of men, and could in an hour raise 300 more. Mr. Pinckney and myself thought it prudent that I should send orders to the Captains, Pledger, Hicks, and M'Intosh, and to the Lieutenants, Clary and Michael, to join us with 20 men of each of their Companys,* at Mars-bluff, the 15th ins^t, under the hopeful expectation of being able to prevail on these gentlemen to assist us readily in

---

*In the private journal of Rev. Nicholas Bedgegood, then pastor of the Welch Neck Church at Long Bluff, this entry appears during the year 1768:— "Sunday, 14th August. No sermon, on acct. of march of ye Companies to Mars-bluff."

Until the letter of Colonel Powell was found, the author had no clue to the purport of this entry, and was for a time wholly at a loss to explain it, not having heard of the tradition which had come down in the neighborhood, of Gibson's fight at Bass's Mills, &c.

taking Gibson, Lance, &c. Mr. Pinckney being informed that Gibson would surrender himself, and desirous of accomplishing his purpose in the most prudent manner, nor willing to risk the lives of those of the King's subjects he had with him, by opposing them against such unequal numbers, agreed with me in opinion, that my inviting Gibson to meet me in a certain place in the woods, where he and I might be alone, and there talking the matter calmly over with him, might perhaps have a good effect. I wrote to Mr. Gibson, and met him accordingly, on Sunday, the 14th, where, after an hour and a half's conversation, he solemnly promised to deliver himself up to Mr. Pinckney the following Monday, 8 o'clock in the forenoon; and, indeed, I had not the least doubt but that the man would have fulfilled his promise. However, when the time came about, I found myself egregiously mistaken; for, instead of coming, he wrote me a letter, signifying that he had altered his resolution, and would not surrender himself. About 10 o'clock, that day, Monday the 15th, Mr. Claudius Pegues came to Mars-bluff, and assured me he would render all the service in his power, seemed to know nothing of Gibson's measures, nor the intentions of the Captains,* Pledger, Hicks and M'Intosh, and Lieutenants Clary and Michael, who arrived about noon; drawing up their company in the woods at half a mile's distance from Weaver's house. Mr. Pegues then told us, they did not intend to advance any further. Whereupon, Mr. Pinckney and myself, together with Pegues, went to meet them; where, to our surprise, we found, instead of 100, 300 men and upwards. I acquainted the officers with the occasion of my calling upon them, and the service expected from them.

"Mr. Pinckney also acquainted them with his errand in these parts, read to them his authority, and your Honor's Proclamation, and demanded their aid accordingly. Which, instead of paying any regard to, they absolutely refused, as

---

*These were John Pledger, George Hicks, and Alexander M'Intosh, among the most prominent and influential men on Pedee, in the neighbourhood of Long Bluff, as was John Mikell—and all distinguished afterwards in the Revolution. Mr. Pegues was the first member elect to the Assembly, from St. David's, showing the estimation in which he was deservedly held.

Gibson, they said, was one of them (Regulators), and had applied to them for protection.

"They said much about certain grievances which they conceived themselves labouring under, for the want of County Courts, and the exorbitant expense of the Law, as it now stands. It was with the greatest difficulty we could persuade them to march to Weaver's, against whom they express much resentment. However, as victuals were provided for them there, and I was in hopes of bringing them into better temper, by taking opportunity of conversing with the leading men singly, I put myself at the head, as their Colonel, and marched them to Weaver's house, where both Mr. Pinckney and myself took great pains to point out to them the mistakes they were running into, prompted, as it appears evidently to us they were, by some turbulent, designing persons. Mr. Pegues seemed to be an active man amongst them, and is a person pitched upon to represent them in the next General Assembly; for which purpose, a subscription is already set on foot to bear his expenses. To enter into a detail of their unprecedented behaviour, would be drawing this letter to too great a length, and I must beg leave to refer your Honour to Mr. Pinckney.

"Only I would observe that, notwithstanding I had heard much of the notorious behaviour of the Regulators in general, yet, as several of them are men of good property, I flattered myself they might be open to conviction, and induced to admit that the method they were pursuing was not the proper mode to bring about their wished-for purpose; but, to my astonishment, I found all arguments lost upon them, and I am ashamed to tell your Honor, that if there had not been left amongst them some faint regard for their Colonel, the Provost Marshal would have been grossly abused, a scheme having been laid for that purpose.

"These people proposed to Alran,* his releasement; and

---

*Of Alran, to whom Colonel Powell here refers, nothing is known. In the journal of Mr. Bedgegood, this entry is found:—
[1768.] "Sunday, 5th June, Mr. Alran taken by the Regulators."
If he had, prior to this time, made himself obnoxious to the civil authorities, and been rescued by the Regulators, it would seem that he was seized a second time, and would have been released again had he desired it.

it was only owing to himself, the Provost Marshal could bring him to town.

"Upon the whole, Sir, these disturbances seem to have so dismal a tendency, that I am at a loss to guess where they may terminate, and I think I may now say with safety, that unless some speedy measures are fallen upon to put a stop to them, the consequences will be very shocking. I cannot, with any propriety, continue to be Colonel of a Regiment of Militia, amongst whom I have the mortification to find myself of so little weight as not to have been able to persuade them to do the duty they owe to their King and Country. I must therefore beg leave to resign my commission, and I would have enclosed it to your Honor, but that I lost it on my return from Keeowee, in fording Broad River. In consequence of my promise, I enclose to your Honor a letter from the Officers of the Regiment respecting Captain Weaver.

"I am, with great respect,
"Honorable Sir,
"Your most obedient, humble Servant,
"G. G. POWELL.

"Weymouth, 19th August, 1768."

"His Honor also informed the Board that he had received a copy of a letter, directed to the Provost Marshal, which was delivered him by a waggoner in the Back Country, threatening his Deputies, if they offered to serve any process in those parts, and advising them not to send them up, as they were determined to pay no obedience to any process issued from Charles-town. His Honor informed the Board that he had written an account of these matters to his Excellency, the Governor, and that he proposed, in a week or ten days' time, to dissolve the Assembly, and to call a new one, which would be ready to meet about the time his Lordship might be expected to return into the Province."*

The interesting letter of Colonel Powell discloses the fact, how much deceived and disappointed he was as to the feel-

---

*"Council Journal," No. 34, pp. 219-225.

ing of the officers and companies from Long Bluff, with respect to Gibson and his proceedings, as well as to the course of the Government in general. Loyal yet in his own sentiments, and not having felt, perhaps, as others had done, the grievances of which they so justly complained, he was at a loss to account for their conduct. His visit to Broad River was probably made in the service of the Government, to assist in quieting disturbances in that region. He appears, after all, to have retained his commission; and what is more remarkable still, not to have forfeited the confidence and affection of the people on the Pedee, having been afterwards, for several years in succession, the Representative from St. David's Parish* in the Commons House of Assembly, and cherishing himself, to the close of his useful life, the deepest interest in all that related to the welfare of that Parish.

Colonel Powell's letter also corrects the tradition,† as it has come down in a most distorted shape, in the immediate neighborhood of the fight, in which Gibson bore so prominent a part.

The result, upon the whole, as the affair ended, was of much importance. The popular feeling became deeper and more determined than ever. The line was now, as it was henceforth to be, distinctly drawn. And the Government

---

*St. David's Parish had been established in April of this year (1768).

†The tradition was related to the author by the late Hugh Godbold, of Marion District, as he had heard it in his younger days from some aged persons who were cotemporaries of Gibson. According to that account, the Regulators came down from North Carolina, increasing in numbers as they came, and headed by Weaver, White, and Gurley. Crossing the river at Mars Bluff, they went up to what has since been known as Bass's Mill, on Naked Creek, where an island was formed by a bend in the Creek, and a channel cut across the mouth of the bend for mill purposes.

On the island they found Gibson strongly posted, at the head of the citizens. He defeated them, killing several, taking the rest prisoners, and giving them fifty lashes apiece. There is no doubt but that a conflict took place at the point described, which was not far from Gibson's residence; but it was that between Gibson's party and the Constable's, confounded by the tradition with the march of the companies afterward to Mars Bluff, as it was also erroneously related that the companies had come down from above under Weaver, Gurley, &c. This spot was but a few years after the scene of a bloody conflict between the Whigs and Tories in the Revolution, of which some account will be given. The author visited the locality in company with Mr. Godbold. The facts above related show how, even in a generation or two, past events may be perverted by tradition.

was from the first, perhaps, fully aroused to the magnitude of the issues involved, as well as the futility of the measures which had been adopted to quell the rising spirit of opposition throughout the back parts of the Province.

His Honor and his Majesty's Council must have felt grave apprehensions now, if never before, that Proclamations, prosecutions, and official action of whatever kind, would be unavailing, if timely concessions were not made to the just and long-continued demands of the people. The necessity for Circuit Courts could no longer be denied. The Government at home, yielding to the pressure which it had been unable to resist, lent its active aid in effecting so desirable an object, and in less than a year, a Bill to that effect became law. In the meantime, the Regulators continued to meet, and to keep up their organization.* On the 2nd of September, there appeared in the *Gazette,* the following "extract of a letter from a Gentleman at Pedee, to his friend in Town":—"I wish you would inform me what is generally thought in town of the Regulators, who now reign uncontrolled in all the remote parts of the Province. In June, they held a Congress at the Congarees, where a vast number of people assembled; several of the principal settlers on this River, men of property, among them. When these returned, they requested the most respectable people in these parts to meet on a certain day; they did so, and, upon the report made to them, they unanimously adopted the Plan of Regulation, and are now executing it with indefatigable ardour. Their resolution is, in general, effectually to deny the Jurisdiction of the Courts holden in Charles-town over those parts of the Province that ought to be by right out of it; to purge, by methods of their own, the country of all idle persons, all that have not a visible way of getting an honest living, all that are suspected or known to be guilty of malpractices, and also to prevent the service of any writ or warrant from Charles-town; so that a Deputy Marshal would be handled by them with severity. Against those they breathe high

---

*In Mr. Pugh's journal the following and like entries are found:—"Aug. 16th. Went over the Marsh to a meeting of the Regulators." "Septr. 12. Went to Murphee's. Regulators met there."

indignation. They are every day, expecting Sundays, employed in this Regulation work, as they term it. They have brought many under the lash, and are scourging and banishing the baser sort of people, such as the above, with universal diligence.

"Such as they think reclaimable, they are a little tender of; and those they task, giving them so many acres to tend in so many days, on pain of flagellation, that they may not be reduced to poverty, and by that be led to steal from their industrious neighbours. This course, they say, they are determined to pursue, with every other effectual measure, that will answer their purpose; and that they will defend themselves in it to the last extremity. They hold correspondence with others in the same plan, and are engaged to abide by and support each other whenever they may be called upon for that purpose. This, it seems, they are to continue till County Courts, as well as Circuit Courts, shall be rightly established, that they may enjoy, by that means, the rights and privileges of British subjects, which they think themselves now deprived of. They imagine that, as the Jurisdiction of the Courts in Charles-town extends all over the Province, Government is not a protection, but an oppression; that they are not tried there by their Peers; and that the accumulated expenses of a law-suit, or prosecution, puts justice out of their power; by which means the honest man is not secure in his property, and villainy becomes rampant with impunity.

"Indeed, the grievances they complain of are many, and the spirit of Regulation rises higher and spreads wider every day. What this is to end in, I know not; but thus matters are situated; an account of which, I imagine, is not unacceptable, though perhaps disagreeable to hear."*

This letter, singularly calm in its tone for a time of such general and intense excitement, appears to have been written by some one who was yet loyal in his feelings toward the Mother Country.

It may be regarded, upon the whole, as an impartial account of the Regulation movement, and exhibits the

*Gazette, August 26, September 2, 1768.

character of those who were taking the lead in the matter, as well as the laudable objects they proposed to accomplish.

A few days after, September 12th, we find this account in the *Gazette*:—"On Thursday last, the General Assembly of this Province was dissolved by Proclamation, and writs for the General Election of new Representatives, we hear, will be signed and issued on Thursday next: so that it is probable the election days may be fixed for Tuesday and Wednesday, the 4th and 5th, and the day for the meeting of the next General Assembly, for Monday, the 25th of next month. The People called Regulators have lately severely chastised one Lum, who is come to Town; but we have not yet learnt the real cause for this severity to him. A letter from Pine Tree Hill (Camden), dated the 6th inst, contains the following intelligence, viz.: The Regulators have fixed upon the 5th of next month to have a meeting here, to draw up their grievances, in order to be laid before the new Assembly. 2500 or 3000 of them, from St. Mark's and St. David's Parishes, are to rendezvous, on the 10th, at Eutaw, and thence proceed to Charles-town, to pursue the proper measures for Redress. The Regulators from the Congaree, Broad and Saludy Rivers, are not to proceed to Town, unless sent for by their brethren; but 1500 of them are to hold themselves in readiness, in case they should be wanted. They do not intend the least injury to any person in Town, desiring only provision and quarter till their complaints shall be heard. The confusion in North Carolina is still greater than in this Province; where the People of Orange County again threaten Col. Fanning, and refuse paying any Taxes, till an Act, granting an enormous sum for building a House for the Governor, be repealed; so that Govr Tryon has been obliged to draught 2000 men from Mecklenburgh and Dobbs Counties, to overawe them, who are to march from the Town of Mecklenburgh the 12th inst. Two of their Leaders have been secured, but it's apprehended they will be released before they can be brought to Trial, as the People in general complain loudly of the above-mentioned Act, as a Great Grievance, as well as of that laying a Duty on Paper, Glass, &c., which will soon drain from them what little specie they have. Their paper Currency being mostly sunk, and a Poll

Tax of eleven shillings Proclamation money, does not fail to add to the distresses of that Country."

The next intelligence from the interior was of a more cheering character. The *Gazette* of September 26th says: "The People in the Back Settlements of this Country, we hear, are now perfectly quiet, having almost thoroughly expelled the dangerous set of Horse Thieves and Vagrants that were becoming formidable amongst them; and they will probably continue so (his Honor the Lieutenant Governor's Proclamation of the 3rd ult^{o}, having had a very good effect), until the important crisis of the next General Election, which takes place throughout the Province on Tuesday and Wednesday next week; or, until the Meeting of the General Assembly, when, they say, they will, in a Constitutional way, not only have their Grievances heard, but also redress, so far as it may appear to be in the Power of the Legislature. But, the Disturbances in North Carolina have not subsided, according to our last accounts from the Back Counties in that Province, dated the 16th ins^{t}, his Excellency, Govr Tryon, was then there, and to proceed from Salisbury to Orange County, the 22nd ins^{t}, but not likely to succeed, the People seeming almost unanimous in refusing to submit to any Laws that seemed to them oppressive or unconstitutional. Further particulars must be deferred till our next."

The election for General Assembly was now drawing near, and much trouble apprehended by the authorities. But, the opportunity being therein presented to the people of expressing their own will, such apprehensions proved to be groundless. The *Gazette* of October 10th, said, as to this matter:—"Great disorder was apprehended in several Country Parishes, at the General Election of Representatives on Tuesday and Wednesday last, from numbers of the People called Regulators coming down from the Back Settlements to vote, where it appeared to them they had a right; but, we are informed, that they behaved everywhere with decency and propriety.

"They mentioned many intolerable grievances they had long laboured under, and seemed to have most immediately in view, a more equal Representation in Assembly; the obtaining, without loss of time, an Act for ascertaining and better regulating public officers' fees, especially in law matters; and, another for establishing County Courts, if the Precinct Court law lately sent home, should fail to receive the royal approbation."

The real objects of the Regulators were now understood, and justice was at length to be meted out to their motives and conduct. The elections had passed off quietly, notwithstanding the fears of disorder and violence.

In the Parish of St. David's, recently organized, and where the polls were opened for the first time, militia companies were detailed for each election precinct, to preserve the peace, and other precautions used to prevent disturbance. But, no disposition was evinced by the people to resort to any improper measures.

The elective franchise was one of those rights which they were most anxious to exercise. They were satisfied it would result in still more favourable changes. The struggle for constitutional liberty thus commenced, was destined, however, to continue, and to encounter, at every step of its progress, the most determined opposition.

The news now on the way from England, was to be by no means cheering, so misguided was the policy persisted in by the Mother Country towards her aggrieved and petitioning Colonists.

The *Gazette* of October 10th, gave the following information to the public:—"Last Thursday, arrived here the ship *Beaufain*, Cap^n David Curling, in 45 days from the Downs, by whom we have not received a single article of agreeable news for North America. Our Circuit Bill, passed the 12th of April last, was not likely to receive the Royal assent; so that the Back Settlers, or People called Regulators, in this Province, may, in all probability, obtain what they seem more anxious to obtain, a Bill for establishing County Courts."

"We are informed that the People called Regulators, have lately brought back five mortgaged Negroes from North Carolina, which were carried off by an absconding debtor from Pedee: that, if any creditor is doubtful of a debt due there, and will come amongst them, they have offered to protect and assist him in procuring good security for whatever may be owing; and, if that cannot be obtained (provided he brings a blank writ up), to deliver the debtor into the common Gaol: that the affair of Gibson's party in July last, has been grossly misrepresented: and that they did not rendezvous, as it was proposed, at Eutaw, on the 10th inst."

Having elected Representatives of their own choice, the Regulators were satisfied to leave the redress of grievances to them in Assembly, and hence the failure to meet at Eutaw, as was intended. The public statement, that the affair of Gibson had been grossly misrepresented led to the following account in the *Gazette* of October 24th: "If we are to credit the Depositions of George Thompson, William Loving, James White, Stephen Sebastian, Godfrey Kerfey, John Holloway, Reuben White, and William White, produced to us by Robert Weaver, Esq. of Mars-Bluff, the conduct of Gideon Gibson was not misrepresented in this Paper of 15th August last, unless by the omission of some aggravating circumstances."

So well had the facts of the case been established, however, that Gibson and his friends deemed it unnecessary to reply to this. Comparative quiet was at length restored. The claims of the Regulators were respected and their power acknowledged. A general desire was now felt to comply with their just demands, which had been so long urged in vain.

On the 15th November, the General Assembly met, and the inhabitants of St. David's Parish were represented for the first time by one of their own choice, in the person of Claudius Pegues, Esq. On 17th Novr his Excellency, C. G. Montague, made an address to the Commons House of Assembly, of which the following is an extract:—"I shall now only recommend to your attention, the falling upon some method to retrieve the distresses of your fellow subjects in the remote parts of this Province, and, at the same time, to discharge, and, if possible, entirely to prevent, for the future, such illegal insurrections as have for some months past appeared in those parts. In every constitutional measure to promote these purposes, I shall cheerfully concur, and will strenuously exert myself."

In the conclusion of their address, the Assembly made this reply:—"Your Excellency may depend on our doing everything in our power, to relieve the distresses of our fellow-subjects, in the remote parts of this Province, and thereby prevent future insurrections; not doubting of your Excellency's cheerful concurrence in every constitutional measure that may be thought necessary to answer these good purposes; though, at the same time, the House cannot but lament, the very little power that is left, by ministerial instructions, in the Legislature of this Province, to remedy the capital grievances which these people labour under; particularly, the want of Courts of Justice amongst them, the want of an equal representation in Assembly, and the excessive fees of office, and charges of the law."

This portion of the Assembly's address, while respectful in tone, was decided in sentiment, and gave token of the last days of Royalty in Carolina. Here was to be seen the germ of a spirit which continued to grow, until, a few years later, it assumed the form of open opposition and revolutionary conflict—the Assembly of the Province having boldly espoused the cause of his Majesty's injured subjects.

"The little power left in the Legislature, in consequence of ministerial instructions, to remedy the capital grievances of the People," was felt more and more, until these instructions ceased to be regarded, and the governor himself, the last vestige of the power of the throne, was forced to fly from the City, to a British Man-of-War in the harbour of Charles-town.

The people were not only determined to be independent as to Courts of their own. There was a general disposition to throw off the yoke, and cherish the spirit of a timely self-reliance. This was the case as to many articles of manufacture which had been supplied to the Colonies from the Mother Country. It will be remembered, that as early as December 22nd, 1768, the letter from a gentleman on Pedee, to his correspondent in Charles-town, related to this matter. He said, "I expect to see our own manufactures much promoted in this part of the Province," and samples of white cotton cloth, which had been produced in that region, were sent to Town for inspection.

It was stated in the *Gazette* of March 2nd, 1769, that "Many of the Inhabitants of the North, and Eastern parts of this Province have this winter clothed themselves in their own manufactures; many more would purchase them if they could be got; and a great reform is intended in the enormous expense attending funerals, for mourning, &c., from the patriotic example lately set by Christopher Gadsden, Esq., when he buried one of the best of wives, and most excellent of women. In short, the generality of the People now seem deeply impressed with an idea of the necessity, and most heartily disposed, to use every means to promote industry, economy, and American Manufactures, and to keep as much money amongst us as possible."

The next allusion to the subject is found in December of the following year (1770), when a most important plan was set on foot for promoting the objects just referred to. The *Gazette* of the 29th of Decr contained this intelligence: "The Committee to consider the ways and means for establishing and promoting such manufactures as this Province is capable of producing, have already had several meetings. It consists of fifteen gentlemen, who have determined to begin, by setting forward a General Subscription to raise a Fund of Money, towards which themselves have collectively subscribed upwards of 2200*l*. They have chosen Henry Laurens, Esq., for their Chairman and Treasurer: and Subscription Papers are forthwith to be printed, which, with a Circular Letter, are to be despatched to all Parts of the Province. This is one of the measures which an unkind mother and false brethren have given rise to."

A non-important agreement had very generally been entered into, and pledges or articles signed, and great dissatisfaction was felt now towards the Northern Colonies, in departing from their non-importation agreement—hence the action above.

A meeting was held in Charles-town on the 13th inst. (Dec.) and a sub-committee appointed, by the General Committee of the friends of liberty, to consider of every means for the encouragement of domestic Manufactures and non-importation of tea and various articles of luxury.

Of the Circular Letter, to be despatched to the different parts of the Province, no trace has been found. But, of the Subscription Papers, which were also to be printed and sent with the Letter, the following relic appears in a memorandum book* of the day, viz.:—

"*Subscribed for the Papers*:

	£	s.
Thomas Evans	15	0
*James Hicks	10	0
William Coward (paid £3 5s.)	5	0
James Shields	10	0
John Adam	10	0
*Daniel Walsh	5	0
*John Hodges	5	0
Philip Singleton	10	0
Claudius Pegues, jun^r.	10	0
Benjn. Rogers	12	0
William Thomas, paid	20	13
Charles Sparkes	10	0
Fran^s. Gillespie	5	0
John David	5	0
*Charles Mason	15	0
*Thomas Ellerbe	12	0
William Ellerbe	7	10
Isham Hodges	5	0
Joseph Dabbs	5	0
James Gregg	5	0
Moses Murphy	10	0
Duke Glen	10	0
John Brown	5	0
John Hodge (Cashway) (paid £4 17s. 6d.)	10	0
Daniel Sparks	7	0

---

*This old book was found, containing also other valuable matter, among the collection of papers in the possession of Philip Pledger, Esq., in Marlborough District, already referred to.

	£	s.
*Thomas Powe	5	0
George King	5	0
John Hire	5	0
Tristram Thomas	5	0
*Ben[n.] James, Cons[ble.]	10	0
Nathaniel Saunders (paid £9 15s.)	15	0
*John Thomson	10	0
*John O'Neal, paid	10	0
Aaron Daniel	10	0
Auth[o.] Pouncy	10	0
Rob[t.] Witherspoon	10	0
Thos[s.] North	5	0
Stephen Ford, Jun[r.]	20	0."*

This was, doubtless, but one of the lists of subscriptions in the Parish of St. David.

The prompt and liberal response of the inhabitants in this matter was only one of the many indications of that determined spirit by which they were now actuated in the struggle for independence.

Defensive, not less than offensive, measures were thus set on foot for their protection and support. To the latter they had become accustomed, and were ready for any further conflict which time might bring about.

We have seen how the years 1767 and 1768 were among the most eventful in preparing the minds of the people for Revolution. In bringing this result to pass, the regulation movement and the conflict to which it led, were largely instrumental. Though an extreme measure, it must be sanctioned by the verdict of history, inasmuch as those, who, in the character of humble and loyal subjects of the Crown, began to petition as early as 1752 for the redress of their grievances, but in vain, were justified in the use of the means to which they were driven by necessity.

---

*For some time after the discovery of this interesting record, the author was greatly at a loss to explain it, the simple heading, "Subscribed for the papers" furnishing the only clue to its history. Upon the subsequent discovery, in the old *Gazette* of the day, of the plan of the "Circular Letter and Subscription Papers," &c., the difficulty was at once removed.

It was not until every constitutional method was exhausted, that they were induced to fall back upon those rights of man which are inalienable.

The descendants of the Regulators on the Pedee may revert, with honest pride, to this unequal, but finally successful struggle of their fathers.

CHAPTER VIII.

The name of St. David—Some account of it—Welch names—Necessity for a parochial organization—Provisions of the Act establishing the Parish of St. David—What it contemplated—The first records of the parish—Proceedings of Commissioners—Names of voters for parish officers—Election of Representative to Assembly—Names of voters—Previous Proceedings—Second election—Names of voters—Colonel G. G. Powell—Account of him—Appointment as Judge—Proceedings of Commissioners for building a church—Church officers—Efforts to procure a clergyman—Progress of Church building—History of it afterward—Successive elections for Representative to Assembly—Church officers and other officers from year to year—Proceedings of vestry—Notice of individuals—The close of the parish history—Concluding reflections.

IN the year 1768, a name appears for the first time among its records, which was ever after to be identified with the history of the Pedee. This was St. David,* the Tutelar Saint of the Welch, given to the first parochial organization which was here established. The "Welch Neck" is the only other name remaining, to indicate the origin of the Colony that led the way in the settlement of this region. Unlike the English, French, and Spaniards, who, in their first discoveries and settlements in the West, failed not to leave many of their distinctive national appellations behind them, the Welch were satisfied to give to one locality a name that would link it perpetually with the land of their

---

*St. David was the most famous of all the Welch names. He was a Bishop of Wales in the sixth century, celebrated for his learning and piety, and a patron of those schools of literature which flourished there at an early period. He is supposed to have been, by the mother's side, of regal descent. His consecration took place at Jerusalem, it being a distracted time at home, and the Britons, who were most inclined to devotion, preferring to go thither. His domestic education is said to have been under Paulinus, a disciple of St. German, in Whiteland, Caermarthenshire. Soon after his return from Jerusalem, he attended a famous synod of bishops, abbots, and others, held at a place called "Llandein-Brevi," the church of St. David at Brevi; and here, by his authority and eloquence, put an effectual stop to Pelagianism, and before the end of the synod, it is said, was chosen, by general consent, Archbishop of Caerleon, and so continued in the exercise of his episcopal functions to the close of an honoured life. His day, as a tutelar saint of the Welch, is 1st March.—Stillingfleet's "Antiquities," vol. ii. pp. 515-523.

fathers. They left, however, a better memorial in those virtuous principles and sturdy traits of character which were transmitted to their descendants.

The population of the upper parts of the Parishes of Prince George and St. Mark's, extending on both sides of the river to the line of North Carolina, had now reached a point demanding a distinct organization of its own. The inhabitants of these parts, remote from the parochial centres below, could no longer endure the disadvantages and hardships which their present condition involved, without being seriously affected. Application was accordingly made to the Assembly, and an Act passed, April 12th, 1768, "for establishing a Parish in Craven County, by the name of St. David, and for appointing Commissioners for the High Roads in the said Parish."

The Preamble to the Act was in these words: "Whereas, the inhabitants residing on Pedee River, in the Parishes of St. Mark's and Prince George, in Craven County, have represented many inconveniences which they are under for want of having a parish laid out and established in the said County, and prayed that a law may be passed for that purpose:" it was therefore enacted—

"I. That a Parish shall be laid out and established in Craven County aforesaid, bounded in the following manner (that is to say) by a North-West line to be run from the northward-most corner of Williamsburg Township to Lynche's Creek, and from thence by that Creek to the provincial line; and that the line dividing St. Mark's from Prince Frederick's Parish, be carried on in the same course from the Great Pedee, where it now ends, to the provincial line aforesaid; by which, together with lines aforesaid, and Lynche's Creek, the new Parish shall be bounded, and that the said Parish shall hereafter be called and known by the name of St. David.

"II. That a Church, Chapel, and Parsonage house shall be built at such places, within the bounds of the said Parish, as the major part of the Commissioners hereafter named shall order and direct.

"III. That the Rector or Minister of the said Parish, for the time being, shall officiate in the said Church and

Chapel alternately, and shall be elected and chosen in the same manner as the Rectors or Ministers of the several other parishes in the Province are elected and chosen, and shall have yearly paid to him and his successors for ever, the same salary as is appointed for the Rector or Minister of any other Parish in this Province, (the Parishes of St. Philip and St. Michael excepted,) out of the fund appropriated, or to be appropriated for payment of the salaries of the Clergy of this Province; and the public Treasurer, for the time being, is hereby authorized and required to pay the same, under the like penalties and forfeitures as for not paying the salaries due to the other Rectors or Ministers of the several other parishes in the Province; and the said rector or minister of the said Parish shall have and enjoy all and every such privileges and advantages, and to be under such rules, laws, and restrictions as the rectors or ministers of the other parishes in this Province have and enjoy, or are subject and liable unto.

"IV. That Claudius Pegues, Philip Pledger, Alexander M'Intosh, George Hicks, Thomas Ellerbe, Robert Allison, Thomas Lide, Charles Bedingfield, James James, Robert Weaver, Thomas Crawford, James Thompson, Thomas Port, and Benjamin Rogers, be, and they are hereby appointed, Commissioners, or supervisors, for the building of the said Church and Chapel, and parsonage-house in the parish of St. David; and they, or a majority of them, are fully authorized and empowered to purchase a glebe for the said parish, and to take subscriptions, and to receive and gather, collect and sue for all such sum or sums of money, as any pious or well-disposed person or persons shall give and contribute for the purposes aforesaid; and, in case of the death, absence, or refusing to act of any of the said Commissioners, the Church wardens and Vestry of the said Parish of St. David, for the time being, shall and may nominate and appoint another person or persons to be Commissioner or Commissioners, in the place of such so dead, absent, or refusing to act, as to the said Church wardens and Vestry shall seem meet, which Commissioner or Commissioners, so to be nominated and appointed, shall have the same powers and authorities for putting this Act into execution, to all intents and purposes, as the Commissioners herein named.

"V. That from and immediately after the passing of this Act, the Commissioners herein appointed, &c., do call the inhabitants, &c., together, to choose parish officers, and fix on the most proper places for building the Church and Chapel.

"VI. That from and after the dissolution of the present General Assembly, the inhabitants of the parish of St. Mark's (which heretofore chose two members of Assembly), and the inhabitants of the Parish of St. David, qualified by law for that purpose, shall choose and elect one member each, and no more, to represent the said parishes respectively in General Assembly; any law, usage, or custom, to the contrary in any wise notwithstanding; and that writs for electing members to serve in General Assembly for the said parishes, shall be issued at the same time, and in the same manner as for the several other parishes in this Province, according to the directions of the Act of the General Assembly in that case made and provided.

"VII. That Claudius Pegues, Philip Pledger, Alexander M'Intosh, George Hicks, Thomas Ellerbe, Robert Allison, Thomas Lide, Charles Bedingfield, James James, Robert Weaver, Thomas Crawford, James Thompson, Thomas Port, and Benjamin Rogers, shall be, and they are hereby appointed Commissioners for the high roads in the said parish of St. David; and the said Commissioners, or a majority of them, shall have the same power and authorities for laying out, and making and keeping in repair, the roads in the said parish, and shall be subject and liable to the like penalties and forfeitures as the Commissioners for the high roads in the other parts of this Province have, or are subject and liable unto the laws of this Province; and in case any of the Commissioners appointed by this Act, shall happen to die, depart the Province, or refuse to act, it shall and may be lawful for the remainder of the Commissioners, or a major part of them, to nominate or appoint another Commissioner or Comissioners, in the room of him or them, so dying, departing the Province, or refusing to act, and the Commissioner or Commissioners, so nominated and appointed, shall have the same power and authorities, and be subject to the same penalties and forfeitures as the Commissioners appointed by this Act."*

The organization here contemplated, was ecclesiastical, according to the Act of 1706, commonly called the Church Act, for the establishment of religious worship, according to the Church of England, and for erecting Churches, supporting ministers, &c. It also embraced, in part, the management of the civil affairs of the Parish, as it was made the duty of the Vestry, by Act of 1712,† to nominate yearly Overseers of the poor of the Parish, as well as to exercise other functions strictly civil. The Overseers of the poor, with the Churchwardens, were to have the ordering and relieving of the poor committed to them, out of such monies as might be given for that purpose, or raised by assessments laid on the inhabitants of the Parish. The Vestry was also to bind out orphan children as apprentices; and by Act of 1721,‡ it was made the duty of Churchwardens to provide for the election of Members of Assembly.

This was the only parochial organization known at the time, and was therefore so ordered as to provide for all the wants and exigencies of the Parish.

The first record following the passage of the Act, establishing the parish of St. David, opens the journal§ of the proceedings of the Vestry, and is in these words: "The General Assembly of the Province of South Carolina having passed an Act, bearing date   day of   , for making a new Parish out of part of the parishes of St. Mark, Prince Frederick, and Prince George;‖ the following gentle-

---

*"Statutes at Large," vol. iv. p. 300.
†"Public Laws," p. 104.
‡"Public Laws," p. 113.
§The old Parish Book, of later years among the records in possession of the vestry, was found by the late Rev. Andrew Fowler at the residence of Mrs. Sarah Pegues, of Chesterfield District, whose husband was a son of one of the first vestrymen.
Mr. Fowler made a visit to St. David's as a missionary, in December, 1819, and was afterwards appointed for a longer period. On one occasion, while searching among the old books and papers at Mrs. Pegues's this interesting and valuable record was found. Mr. Fowler was a faithful and devoted minister of Christ, planting the Church and building it up in not a few places where it had gone to decay. He died at a very advanced age, a few years since.
‖It will be observed, that the Act is here said to have been passed for making a new parish out of part of the parishes of St. Mark, Prince Frederick, and

men were, by the said Act, appointed as Commissioners for the said Parish, which, by the Act, is appointed to go by the Name of the Parish of St. David"—and the list of names is then given.

On Monday, August 1st, the Commissioners met, according to public notice, at the house of Charles Bedingfield;* when Alexander M'Intosh, James James, and Robert Allison, declined acting in the affairs of the Church.† The following parish officers were elected, viz.: Claudius Pegues, Philip Pledger, William Godfrey, Charles Bedingfield, Thomas Lide, Thomas Ellerbe, and Thomas Bingham, Vestrymen; Alexander Gordon and Benjamin Rogers, Churchwardens; Durham Hitts was appointed Clerk. The oath of office was administered the next day.

The names of those who voted for Vestrymen and Wardens were as follows, viz.: "William Hardwick, Duke Glen, John Mackintosh, John Jenkins, Edward Ellerbe, John Husbands, Thomas Boatwright, Sen., John Pledger, Robert Anderson, Robert Clary, Benjamin Jackson, James Knight, Samuel Wise, James Thorsby, Thomas Williams, Thomas Wade, and Leonard Dozier—in all 18."

The next matter which engaged attention was the election of a Member to the Commons House of Assembly, as to which the following entries appear upon the Journal of the Vestry:—

"Monday, September 26th, 1768.

"The writs of election of a Member of Assembly for the Parish of St. David having been sent up from Charlestown, twenty-six advertisements were sent to the different parts of the Parish, requiring the appearance of the inhabitants of the said Parish at Mr. John Mackintosh's,‡ on

---

Prince George. From this it would appear that, according to the understanding of the inhabitants at the time, "Prince Ferederick" did extend over, forming a part of the territory east of the Pedee. The confusion on this subject in the Acts of Assembly has been mentioned.

*This was at what is now known as Irby's Mills, in Marlborough District, on the public road from Cheraw to Bennettsville, and three miles from the former place.

†These gentlemen lived some distance below on the river, and two of them were of other religious connexions.

‡This was just above Cock Run, about two miles below Long Bluff, on the public road leading thence to George-town, called long afterward the "Old River Road," where the traces of the first settlement are still to be seen.

Tuesday; and at Mr. Charles Bedingfield's, on Wednesday, the fourth and fifth days of October, ensuing; Being the Days appointed for the Election of a Member to represent the Parish in the Commons House of Assembly.

"Likewise, Circular Letters were writ to the Captains, James Knight, James Thomas, Thomas Conner, and Benjamin Jackson; and to Messrs. John Kimbrough, William Watkins, Robert Lide, and Gideon Gibson, with two or three of the Advertisements of the Election enclosed in each, to put up at the most Public Places in their respective Districts, and a desire to bring their Companies, under their proper leaders, to the Places of Election, to prevent confusion."*

The Advertisement was as follows:

"The Inhabitants of the Parish of St. David are required to meet on Tuesday, the Fourth Day of October, ensuing, at the House of Mr. John Mackintosh, and on Wednesday, the fifth day of the same month, at the House of Mr. Charles Bedingfield, in order to Elect a Member of Assembly for the said Parish. The Hours of Election to be from ten in the forenoon to four in the afternoon.

"By Order of the Church wardens,
"DURHAM HITTS, C.P.

"September 26th, 1768."

The Circular Letter was as follows:

"Sir,—You have Enclosed Advertisements, for Electing a Member of Assembly for this Parish. Please to circulate them to the most convenient Places. You are desired by the Captains, Pledger, Hicks, Lide, &c., for the Honor of the Parish, to bring as many Voters as you possibly can to the Place of Election, where they will meet you with each of their Companies.

"They also desire that you will keep and bring up the People under their proper Leaders, in order to prevent con-

---

*This precaution, it will be remembered, resulted from the apprehension on the part of the Government that disturbances might ensue in consequence of the previous action of the Regulators, and *the fear*, in particular, that numbers of them might come down from North Carolina to overawe the law-abiding citizens, as these last were esteemed, and thus the general state of alarm and confusion be increased.

fusion. They hope that you will, on this occasion, exert yourself to the utmost of your power.

"I am, Sir,
"Your humble Servant,
"DURHAM HITTS, C.P.

"September 26th, 1768."

The foregoing Circular Letters were directed for forwarding to Mr. John Kimbrough, as follows:

"Sir,—As the time is so short between our receiving the writs of Election, and the time for Electing of a Member for this Parish (as you will see in the Letter directed to you), you will do a good piece of service to the Public, in causing the Letters enclosed, directed to the Captains, Thomson and Knight, and to Mr. Watkins and Mr. Gibson, to be conveyed to them as speedily as possible.

"I am, Sir,
"Your humble Servant,
"DURHAM HITTS, C.P.

"September 26th, 1768."

"Tuesday, October the Fourth, 1768. The Poll for the Election of a Member of Assembly for the Parish of St. David, in Craven County, South Carolina, was opened at the House of Mr. Mackintosh, and the following Persons voted, viz.:

"Bartholomew Ball
Simon Holmes
John Renynolds
William Reeves
John Holley
William Lucas
John Jamieson
Robert Clary
Samuel Sparks
Lewis Rowan
Charles Strother
John Davis
John Courtney
Malachi Newberry
Thomas Evans

Richard Pouder
Francis M'Call, Jun.
Thomas Harry
John Mackintosh
Charles M'Call
Roderick M'Iver
John Evans
Daniel Devonald
Thomas James
Alexander Mackintosh
Philip Howell
Edward Lowther
Francis M'Call
Gideon Parish
William Edwards

John M'Call
John Cheeseborough
Richard Blizard
Nathaniel Douglass
Thomas Davidson
John Prothero
Evans Prothero
James Knight
James Rogers
Joseph Dabbs
Peter Kolb
John Kimbrough
John Cooper
David Harry
William Dewitt
William Allen
Andrew Hunter
John M'Call
Christopher Teal
George King
Josiah Evans
Joseph Luke
Samuel Wilds
John Rowell
Dennis Galphin
Benjamin Pruiel
Thomas Edwards
John Griffith
John Knight
Philip Pledger
James James
Daniel Man
Magnus Corgill
William James
John Dyer
John Marsha
Thomas Levy
Robert Blair
Lewis Blalock

Daniel Luke
David Harry
Joshua Douglass
Jacob Lamplugh
Howel James
Joseph Barker
Isam Ellis
William Tyrrell
Abel Edwards
James Bruce
William Pouncey
John Jackson
Joshua Edwards
John Brown
Enoch Luke
Jenkin David
Richard Allen
Philip Robland
Abel Wilds
Edward Jones
Benjamin Wright
Gilbert Moody
Thomas Lane
William Megee
Samuel Evans
Martin Kolb
Robert Lide
Joseph Alison
John Alran
John Brown
John Flanagan
Job Edwards
Richard Mc La More
Anthony Pouncey
Duke Glen
Joshua Hickman
David Evans
Walter Downes
Aaron Daniel

John Bruce	Martin Dewitt
James Dozier	John Darby.
"Number of Voters this Day, 113."

"Wednesday, October 5th, 1768. The Poll for Electing of a Member of Assembly for the Parish of St. David, in Craven County, South Carolina, was opened at the House of Mr. Charles Bedingfield, and the following Persons voted, viz. :—

"Thomas Boatright	Samuel Hatfield
Lewis Gardiner	John Jones
William Carter	William Johnson
Benjamin James	Thomas Williams
John Purvis	William Hicks
Charles Bedingfield	John Beverly
Enoch James	George Hicks
Jesse Counsell	John Lyons
William Gardiner	John Sutton
John Pledger	Edward Bryan
John Williams	Benjamin Rogers
John Jenkins	Thomas Bingham
Abraham Colt	William James
William Ellerbe	Thomas Conner
Thomas Ellerbe	Kedar Keaton
Enoch Thomson	William Godfrey
Edward Ellerbe	George Sweeting
Charles Irby	John Moffatt
Alexander Gordon	John Westfield
Peter Heathy	Jonathan Wise
John Frazier	John Shumake
Thomas Sommerlin	John Hicks
John Williams	Thomas Rogers
William Hardwicke	Samuel Williams
Thomas Lide	John Pow
John Husbands	William Hernsworth
Jonathan Williams

"Number of Voters this Day, 53."

"Claudius Pegues, Esqr., was unanimously elected a

Member of Assembly for the Parish of St. David's, all the Votes for both Days being for him.

"The Votes for the first Day were . . . 113
 "   the second Day   . . . 53
                                     ———
"The full number of votes were . . . . 166"

To have been elected their first representative by a unanimous vote, was a singular mark of the esteem and confidence entertained for Mr. Pegues by his fellow-citizens, and more particularly so as he had not been very long a resident among them. He came to Pedee about eight years before, and was now in his forty-ninth year—an active, prudent, and useful man. Retiring in his disposition and habits, he withdrew, after serving one term in Assembly, to the more congenial pursuits of private life—continuing, however, as he had ever been, faithful and untiring in his devotion to the public good and the rights of the people.

With the account of this election closes the Parish record for 1768. The proportionate numbers, voting respectively at the two polls, indicate a large preponderance of population in the lower parts of the Parish. These embraced the two principal settlements of the Welch, near Long Bluff, and the Sandy Bluff neighbourhood below, which continued for many years after, to maintain the ascendancy. The record of the year 1769 opens with the order for the election of a new Member of Assembly, "the last Assembly," it was said, "having been dissolved by his Excellency, the Governor of South Carolina, almost as soon as called."

New writs of election were sent up to the churchwardens, February 25th, and the election ordered for the 7th and 8th of March, at the same places as in the former year. At the lower poll, 98 votes were cast, and among them were the following names which did not appear at the former election, viz.:—

Daniel Saunders
— Saunders
John Rothmahler
Nicholas Bedgegood
Daniel Monahan
John Crawford
Jordan Gibson, jun.
Reuben Gibson
Nathaniel Hunt
Daniel Sparks
Thomas Avery
Charles Sparks

James Mikell
Solomon Staples
Robert Moody
Moses Bass
Joshua Lucas
Malachi Murphy
Arthur Hart
William McTierre
Stephen Sebastian
Edward Owens
Samuel Haselton
Walter Owens
Harrison Lucas
Charles Lisenby
John Hitchcock
John Crews
Blundell Curtis
John Mikell
William Floyd
George Booth
Jacob Baxter

At the upper poll 59 votes were cast, and among them, certain names for the first, viz.:—

Rebecca Lide
Catharine Little
Francis Benton
Simon Lundy
Cornelius Acmens
Robert Westfield
John Perkins
Elizabeth Counsell
Michael Griffith
Samuel Hards
Wm Gardiner, jun.
Silas Harandine
Francis Gillespie
James Salmons
James Lundy
Jacob Johnson
Richard George
Daniel Lundy
Benjamin Ladd
William Lankford
Sarah Booth
Abel Wilds
William Crowley
Thomas Wade
William Prestwood
Soloman Holmes
Frederick Kimbell
Joel Yarborough
William Jackson
Thomas Tomkins
David Davidson
Joseph Parsons
Thomas Williamson
William Hayes.

At this election, Col. George Gabriel Powell received 154 of the 157 votes cast, and was consequently returned as the new member for St. David's. It is the first time that the name of Col. Powell appears in connexion with the Parish of St. David, though shortly afterwards to become so prominent in all the leading events of its history. He had been for some time in command of the Craven County Regiment.

On the 10th of August, of this year, he was appointed one of his Majesty's Judges for the Courts of General Sessions and Common Pleas, and took his seat on the Bench the 16th

October following, retaining it until 1772, when he was superseded.

The change was then doubtless made in consequence of his manly independence and unflinching devotion to the rights of the Colonists. He did not sympathize sufficiently with the Crown, though a loyal subject, as his course with reference to the difficulty at Mars Bluff, of the previous year, very clearly indicated, as did also a want of cooperation on his part with the Regulators and a misunderstanding of their movement.

His first charge from the Bench was spoken of in the public Prints of the day, as having given universal satisfaction.

On Easter Monday, March 27th, at at meeting of the freeholders of the Parish, at the house of Charles Bedingfield, the church officers of the previous year were re-elected. It was not until the 23rd of September following (1769) that the Commissioners appointed under the Act of Incorporation, for that purpose, held a meeting with reference to the erection of a Church Building. In consequence, however, of some informality in the notice calling them together, there was not a full attendance, and nothing was done. It was agreed by those present, viz., Claudius Pegues, Robert Allison, Benjamin Rogers, Philip Pledger, Thomas Lide, Thomas Ellerbe, and Charles Bedingfield, that the Commissioners should meet again on the 25th of October ensuing; but, owing probably to the engrossing events of the time, or differences of opinion as to the location of the Church, no meeting was held, or at least no further entry appears on the records of the Parish, until Feb. 1st, 1770.

On that day, at a meeting of the Vestry and Wardens, Ely Kershaw was appointed a Commissioner in the place of Robt. Allison, deceased. And on the 22nd of the same month, an agreement was executed in due form, between Thomas Bingham, of the one part, and Ely Kershaw, Philip Pledger, George Hicks, Thomas Lide, Benjamin Rogers, Charles Bedingfield, Thomas Ellerbe, and Claudius Pegues, Commissioners, of the other part, for the building of the Parish Church. It was to be erected on the south-west side of Pedee River (at Cheraw Hill), upon land given for that purpose by

Ely Kershaw, and completed on or before the first day of March, 1772. In consideration whereof, the said Commissioners agreed to pay the sum of Two thousand six hundred pounds currency, one half when the building should be raised, enclosed, and covered; and the other half upon its completion.

It was also provided, by additional agreement, that alterations might be made in the stipulated plan, if agreeable to both parties.

It does not appear that a Glebe was ever set apart, or any steps taken towards the erection of a Parsonage. This was doubtless owing to the failure to procure a settled clergyman.

On the 30th of April, of this year (1770), at a meeting of the Freeholders of the Parish, the following gentlemen were elected Church officers, viz.:—John Kimbrough, Ely Kershaw, Jesse Counsell, Samuel Wise, Henry William Harrington, John Pledger, and William Ellerbe, Vestrymen: William Godfrey and William Pegues, Wardens.

The important subject of procuring a Parish Clergyman had already engaged attention.

During a part of this year, the Rev. James Foulis* officiated, but remained a short time only in the Parish. "The Rev. Mr. Hogart, of England, was next invited to this Cure; but not accepting it, application was made, in 1772, to the Rev. Mr. Robinson to officiate, and if approved of, the Vestry would recommend him for Holy Orders." It is probable that this gentleman was a minister of some other communion. The Journals are silent as to the result.†

The church building was not completed until some time subsequent to the spring of 1774, as appears from the fact that its unfinished state was made the subject of presentment by the grand jury of Cheraw District, as will be seen hereafter.

It was opened, however, for public worship as early as December 1772,‡ and continued to be used in common by

---

*Mr. Foulis had charge of St. Helena parish, Beaufort, during the latter part of 1778. It is not known how long he remained, or what became of him afterwards.

†Dalcho's "Church of So. Ca." p. 327.

‡The Rev. Evan Pugh speaks in his private journal of having officiated there in the parish church.

the denominations around, as religious ministrations could be had at that early period.

It was almost a half century afterward before it was restored to its original use and design as an Episcopal Church. During its common occupancy the burden of its repairs was borne by the inhabitants generally; and as a consequence, when an exclusive claim was set up in the year 1819 to its possession, no little feeling was aroused, and there was for a time a determination to resist it. The original Act for the Organization of the Parish and the proceedings under it, were either unknown or lost sight of, and having been so long occupied and repaired in common, it is not surprising that a feeling of strong opposition was excited. The discovery, however, of the old Parish records and subsequent investigation, cleared the whole matter up, and the claim was fully established. It was described many years after as a neat church, "a frame building, on a brick foundation, 53 feet long, 30 wide, and 16 high in the clear, with a cove ceiling, and arched windows. The chancel 10 feet by 6." Subsequently to the year 1819 the interior arrangements were materially altered, the chancel being removed from the side, as it was at first, to the east end, and other changes made. A porch was also added, with a beautifully proportioned steeple.

For a short time, during the summer of 1781, it was occupied by British soldiers, and not a few of them, it is said, who fell victims to the climate, lie buried in one common grave under the shadow of its portals.

Unharmed by the ravages of time, the venerable building still remains, one of the few material relics left us of that era. It was erected by the sturdy men of that day with the care befitting such a work, and upon a sure foundation. There has been wonderful progress since in every department of human labour—but a progress rather in matters of outward adornment than in those durable elements and that thorough finish which are calculated for lasting use.

The affairs of the Parish continued to be administered with regularity, though becoming more local and circumscribed than was anticipated at the time of its organization. After the appointment of Col. Powell as one of the Assistant

Judges, there appears to have been no further election for Members of Assembly until March, 1772, when Col. Charles Augustus Steward was returned. A new election having been ordered in September following, for the Assembly, which was to meet in Beaufort, 8th Oct., Col. Stewart was again successful, after an exciting contest. There was now a deepening conviction in the minds of the people, that their representatives would shortly be called to contend in a decisive struggle for every constitutional right. The powers of Royalty and of popular sovereignty were being rapidly arrayed. There was a premonitory feeling, in short, though with no clear conception as to the course events would take, that momentous changes were approaching.

Col. Stewart retained his seat but for one session. In December Col. Powell was again returned. He was reelected the following February. Up to this time, and for a year later, the Commons House of Assembly consisted of 48 members. It was summoned to meet, February 23rd, 1773, and dissolved for the last time by Royal authority 1st Sept. 1775. During the intervening period Col. Powell continued to represent the Parish of St. David, and was the able and faithful guardian of its rights. He is supposed to have practised at the Bar of Cheraw District; but, though owning property in it, never had his residence within its limits. With his name closed the list of Representatives of St. David under the old regime.*

At a meeting of the Freeholders of the Parish, April, 1771, the following officers were elected, viz.: Jesse Counsell, Ely Kershaw, Charles Bedingfield, Samuel Wise, Thomas Wade, William Godfrey, and John Westfield, Vestrymen: Thomas Lide and Thomas Ellerbe, Wardens: George Hicks, Daniel Lundy, and John Mitchell, Overseers of the poor. The list of paupers was increasing, and their support formed the chief burden of the Parish. At a meeting of the wardens and vestry, Feby. 18th, 1772, it was agreed that the inhabitants should be taxed 2s. 6d. for every 100 acres of land, and the same amount for all negro slaves, free-negroes,

*Drayton's "Memoirs," vol. i. p. 162.

Mulattoes, and Mestizoes, to defray the expense of maintaining the poor of the Parish. William Godfrey and Charles Bedingfield were appointed to collect the same. The surplus, if any, was to be paid into the hands of the churchwardens. The following Church Officers were elected, April 20th, 1772, viz.: James Kelly, Daniel Lundy, Jacob Johnson, John Kimbrough, William White, William Dewitt, and John Jackson, Vestrymen: Thomas Wade and Wm. Henry Mills, Wardens: George Hicks, Malachi Murphy, and Robert Anderson, Overseers of the poor. Nothing of special interest appears among the Parish records of this year. Public affairs were becoming more and more the engrossing topic of thought and conversation, the Parochial Officers giving their attention only to the care of the poor, and the appointment of assessors and collectors of the Parish taxes.

On Easter Monday, April 12th, 1773, were elected, Charles Augustus Steward, Claudius Pegues, Ely Kershaw, Jesse Counsell, Thomas Lide, Thomas Ellerbe, and William Dewitt, Vestrymen: Philip Pledger and Samuel Wise, Wardens: Alexander Gordon, Malachi Murphy, and John Blakeney, Overseers of the poor. The meetings of the vestry were more frequent than during the previous year, the care of the poor increasing upon them. The sum of 357*l.* 13*s.* was expended in 1772; and in more than one instance 60*l.* had been appropriated to a single individual—a liberal amount for a sparse population, with limited means at their command.

On Easter Monday, April 4th, 1774, the Church Officers elected were as follows, viz.: Henry Counsell, John Andrew, Thomas Bingham, Burwell Boyakin, Aaron Daniel, John Hewstess, and William Henry Harrington, Vestrymen: Claudius Pegues and Ely Kershaw, Wardens; John Kimbrough, Charles Evans, jun., and Thomas Conner, sen., Overseers of the poor.

Thomas Williams, George Hicks, and William Ellerbe, were appointed Parish Assessors, to defray the expenses of the preceding year. The name of Thomas Lide was subsequently inserted in the place of George Hicks. A tax of 3*s.*, current money, was laid on every 100 acres of land; also, for all negro slaves, free negroes, Mulattoes and Mestizoes. Philip Pledger and Samuel Wise were appointed to collect the same.

The same tax was levied the next year, and Claudius Pegues and Ely Kershaw were appointed Collectors. At a meeting of the Vestry on this occasion (April, 1775), the name of Chatham, instead of "Cheraw" and "Charraws," as heretofore, appears for the first time in the Parish records. The change was made in honour of the Earl of Chatham, the eloquent advocate of American rights.

The following Church Officers were elected April 24th, 1775, viz.: Aaron Pearson,* William Dewitt, William Ellerbe, William Strother,† John Westfield, John Jackson, and Charles Irby, Vestrymen: Henry William Harrington and William Pegues, Wardens: Daniel Sparks, Robert Lowry,‡ and William Allen, Overseers of the poor.

After this time, scarcely anything more than the annual election of officers, the provision for the Parish taxes, and the care of orphans, appears in the records.

In 1776, the officers elected were, William Ellerbe, Francis Gillespie, Capt. John Blakeney, Thomas Powe, Matthew Saunders, Capt. Lafayette Benton, and Buckley Kimbrough. Vestrymen: Col. George Pawley and Claudius Pegues, Wardens: Alexander Deau Bois and Peter Roach, Overseers of the poor.

For 1777, the following: John Kimbrough, Thomas Lide, James Hicks, Thomas Powe, William Pegues, Joseph Griffith, and Robert Lowry, Vestrymen: John Andrews and Charles Irby, Wardens: Benjamin Jackson, John Pledger, and John Jackson, Overseers of the poor.

At a meeting of the Wardens and Vestry, 21st June, 1777, it was resolved, "That a letter should be written to

---

*The Pearsons settled on the east side of the river, in what is now Marlborough District, on a valuable tract of land, known afterwards and from an early day as the "Big Plantation." Moses Pearson was a noted captain in the Revolution.

†William Strother, whose name appears here for the first time, was a son of Charles Strother, who emigrated from Virginia to Charles-town, and died there. William Strother moved to Cheraw not long before this period. He married, first, a Miss Rogers, daughter of Benjamin Rogers, and afterwards, Lucy Hicks, a daughter of Colonel George Hicks.

‡The Lowrys settled in the upper part of what is now Chesterfield District,—a name long and respectably known in its history.

the Rev. Mr. Winchester,* to preach a sermon, on Saturday, the 28th instant, on the happy deliverance of the State from our cruel and oppressive enemies, 28th June, 1776."

It was the first anniversary of that auspicious event, and the hearts of the people were full of gratitude to Him, who ruled the destinies of nations, and in the hour of their first great conflict had given them the victory.

In the spring of the following year, the same tax as before was laid, and Charles Irby and William Pegues were appointed Collectors.

The Church Officers for 1778 were, Benjamin Hicks, sen., Claudius Pegues, jun., William Thomas, Francis Gillespie, Thomas Ellerbe, William Ellerbe, and John Speed, Vestrymen: Benjam'n Hicks, jun., and William Lide, Wardens: Benjamin Rogers, Tristram Thomas and William Blassingame, were appointed Overseers of the Poor. The foregoing continued in office until the spring of 1780.

The following was the record of Parish Officers until 1785:—

For 1780.

Wm. Pegues and Benj. Hicks, Sen. . Wardens.
Claudius Pegues, Jr., Thos. Powe, Charles Irby, John Westfield, John Andrews, John Wilson, and Holden Wade . . . . } Vestrymen.
John Husbands, Guthridge Lyons, and Benjamin Jackson . . } Overseers of Poor.
Jesse Baggette . . . . Clerk.

1781.

Wm. Pegues, and Benj. Hicks, Sen. . Wardens.
Charles Irby, Claudius Pegues, Jr., John Westfield, Holden Wade, and John Wilson . . . } Vestrymen.
Guthridge Lyons . . . . Overseer of Poor.

1782.

Thos. Ellerbe and Wm Strother . Wardens.

---

*Mr. Winchester was the pastor of the Welch Neck Church, and an ardent friend of his country.

Charles Irby, Claudius Pegues, Jr., John Westfield, John Wilson, Wm. Lide, Wm. Dewitt, and Wm. Pegues . . . . . } Vestrymen.

1783.

Thomas Powe, and Claudius Pegues, Jr., Wardens.
Charles Irby, John Andrews, Thos. Ellerbe, Benj. Hicks, Jr., Robert Pasley, James Gillespie, and Lemuel Benton . . . . } Vestrymen.

1784.

Benj. Hicks, Sen., and Wm. Pegues . , Wardens.
Thos. Ellerbe, Wm. Strother, John Westfield, Claudius Pegues, Jr., John Wilson, Benj. Hicks, Jr., and Wm. Ligate. . . . } Vestrymen.

1785.

Col. Lemuel Benton, and Capt. Calvin Spencer . . . . } Wardens.
Thos. Powe, Wm. Ellerbe, Sen., John Andrews, Holden Wade, Wm. Pegues, and Morgan Brown . } Vestrymen.

With this year (1785), upon the division of the Parish into Counties, and the establishment of County Courts, the parochial organization ceased to exist. No further records appear until after the year 1819, when the Parish was revived as before mentioned, under Rev. Mr. Fowler. Upon the prorogation of the Assembly in April, 1770, a Bill was under consideration for altering the bounds of St. David's Parish. It appears to have been subsequently abandoned, and of its provisions nothing is known.

Amid the changes of time and civil rule, only the old Parish Church remained to tell its tale in the associations and traditions connected with its earlier days. It had been polluted by the tread of invading foes, and resounded with the shock of arms. Around it lie the dead of successive generations. But a year or two more, and its first century will be completed.

Long may it stand, a touching relic of the past, the spiritual home and joy of many in the present, and to be open, as of old, to others yet to come!

CHAPTER IX.

Parochial organization inadequate—Disturbances continue—The Moderators and Regulators—Circuit Courts growing in favour—Governor's address on the subject—Circuit Court Bill passed by Assembly—Governor refuses his sanction—Again passed and made a law—Its provisions—Boundaries of Cheraw District—Times for holding courts—Commissioners for building court house and gaol—Their proceedings—Cheraw Hill selected—Petition of Freeholders, &c., against it, and in favour of Long Bluff—Counter petition—Memorial of commissioners to Assembly sustaining their action—Assembly decides for Long Bluff—Lieutenant Governor's order to Commissioners—Their error—Effect of Courts—The buildings progress—Disturbances revived—Last affair of the kind on Pedee—Court house finished—Account of it—Officers, how appointed—Persons selected—Opening of Court at Long Bluff—Presentments of grand jury, November 1772—Presentments in April, 1773—Reflections on same—Presentments in November, 1773—Published accounts—Presentments April, 1774—Early history of Bar of the Old Cheraws.

Going back to the beginning of the year 1769, it will be found that the parochial organization, established a short time before, did not meet, in some very important respects, the wants of the people. Though affording partial relief in the provision made for a Representative of their own in Assembly, and the care of the poor, it left one of the chief grievances, of which they had long complained, remaining in full force. They were yet without a Court of their own, easy of access, and in which rights could be enforced, and crime punished, without the intolerable burden of long delays and ruinous expenses. Comparative quiet, indeed, had been restored through the effective measures of the Regulators, and yet the disturbances continued to threaten the public peace and safety. In the *South Carolina and American General Gazette* of 27th March, 1769, it was said:—"Various accounts continue to be received from the back country. A new set of people, who call themselves Moderators, have appeared against the Regulators. These two parties mutually accuse each other. What justice they have on either side, time will discover."

The plan of a Circuit Court Act was gaining ground

daily. On the 29th June, the Governor, in his address to the Assembly, said: "Although there are several matters that well deserve your serious consideration, I cannot help mentioning to you the grievances that your fellow-subjects suffer in the interior parts of this Province, from the want of an equal distribution of justice, as a matter that claims your immediate attention and regard. As I have lately been an eye-witness to the distresses they labour under, I earnestly recommend to you, to pursue such measures as will tend to relieve them; and, in order to ease your deliberations on this point, I will lay before you copies of the Report of the Lords Commissioners for Trade and Plantations, on the Bill for establishing Circuit Courts in this Province; passed some time since, wherein you will see stated, the reasons that operate against that Act's receiving the Royal approbation."

This timely and urgent recommendation of his Excellency had the desired effect, though the Assembly needed not any new arguments to lead them to speedy action on the subject.

The result was, that on the 5th of July following, a Circuit Court Bill was brought into Assembly, and passed its first reading. It was also stated in the public prints of the day, "that, in consideration of the great inconveniences and grievances to which the back settlers are subject, as soon as the Circuit Court Bill is gone through, another Bill will be presented to the House for establishing temporary County Courts." On 27th July, the Circuit Court Bill, having been passed, was presented to the Governor, who refused his sanction. On what ground, after his own urgent recommendation for some measure of relief, does not appear.

There may have been, in his view, some particular feature of the Bill of an objectionable character. It passed the House again, and on the 2nd of August received the Governor's approbation.

And thus, the long-fought battle ended in victory for the people. Popular rights, enforced by the strong arm of popular sovereignty, came out of the conflict triumphant.

It was thought advisable by the Government at this critical juncture, to adopt, in addition, a precautionary measure for preserving the public peace on the Pedee and in neighbouring parts of the Province. The *Gazette* of August 10-17th, said: "His Honor the Lieut.-Gov. has been pleased to appoint George Gabriel Powell, Esq., Colonel of the Militia in the North Eastern parts of this Province, to be one of his Majesty's assistant Judges; an appointment, which, it is thought, will give general satisfaction, particularly to the back settlers, by whom that gentleman is much and deservedly respected."

The Circuit Court Act was passed, "for laying off several Districts or Circuits, and authorizing the holding of Courts of General Sessions and Common Pleas twice a year, for the trial of causes criminal and civil, arising within the same respectively, as nearly as may be, as the Justices of Assize and Nisi Prius do in Great Britain. Circuit Courts were, by this Act, to be held at Orangeburg, Ninety-Six, the Cheraws, George-town, Beaufort, and Charles-town"—to sit six days each. The Courts to be held in Charles-town, however, were not strictly speaking Circuit Courts; but, like those of Westminster Hall, in England, alone possessed of complete original and final jurisdiction, all writs and other civil processes issuing therefrom and being made returnable thereto.

The provision made for the interior Districts, was not, for this reason, altogether complete, though a signal advance for them, on their previous condition. Henceforth, Government became more efficient, and justice was brought nearer the habitation of each individual.*

And withal, as their own rights would thus be made to pass in review before them, as also the wrongs and oppressions of Government, if any there were, a decided impetus would thereby be given to the progress of enlightened sentiments, and the expression of them, in a bold and independent manner by the people.

"By the Circuit Court Act, the Judges were authorized to determine, without a Jury, in a summary way, on petition, all causes cognizable in the Circuit Courts for any sum not exceeding twenty pounds sterling; except when the title of land should be in question. But each party might claim

---

*Brevard's "Digest," vol. i. p. 14.

to have the benefit of a Jury trial. The office of Provost Marshal was abolished, and Sheriffs and Clerks were appointed."*

The Judicial District of Cheraws "was to be bounded by the course of Lynche's Creek north from the point where a north-west line from the northernmost corner of Williamburg Township reached the said Creek, to the Provincial line, by the Provincial boundary, and the line dividing St. Mark's and Prince Frederick's Parish, which shall be continued till it intersects the northern Provincial line."†

These boundaries were identical with those of the Parish of St. David, created by Act of the previous year. The Courts were to be holden "on every 15th day of April and November, at the Cheraws, for the District of Cheraws." And, by the Act, the Judges of the Courts of Common Pleas were authorized and directed, "to contract and agree with proper persons, for the building and erecting Court Houses and Gaols, in places most convenient for holding the said Courts, and to purchase land for that purpose."

George Hicks, Thomas Lide, Jonathan Wise, Benjamin Rogers, and Eli Kershaw, were appointed Commissioners for building the Court House and Gaol in the Cheraw Precinct.

Agreeably to the instructions sent them by the Lieutenant-Governor, 22nd March, 1770, they met on 13th April, and contracted for one and a half acres of land on Cheraw Hill, whereon they proposed to have the said buildings erected; as they judged that the most convenient and proper place, from its being the most public and healthy situation on the Pedee.

Active steps were taken to carry their resolution into effect. It excited, however, very decided opposition on the part of many, who thought the neighbourhood of Long Bluff a better location for the Court House.

The result was, that a petition for the change, and a counter-petition were sent up to the Assembly, and action taken thereon.

---

*Brevard's "Digest," vol. i. p. 15.
†"Statutes at Large," vol. vii. p. 199.

The following extracts, from the Journal of the House, will explain the whole proceeding:

"August 17th, 1770.

"A Petition of the Freeholders and Electors of the Parish of St. David's and the Cheraw District, was presented to the House and read, in the words following, viz.: 'That, whereas an Act of Assembly, passed the 29th July, 1769, for establishing Courts, &c., for the more convenient administration of Justice in this Province, and for the ease and advantage of the Inhabitants thereof; And, whereas, there is another Act passed at the last Session of Assembly, nominating the Long Bluff as the place for building the Court House and Gaol for the Cheraw District; which Acts your Petitioners humbly conceive perfectly answer and confirm the purposes of the first (to wit), the convenience, ease, and advantage of the Inhabitants; for your Petitioners think the Long Bluff not far from the real centre of the District; at least the nearest to it of any place they know suitable for the Court House on Pedee River. These Acts, so wisely calculated to answer many of the greatest and best purposes, must, under the present House of Representatives, ever dear to their constituents, and especially to the grateful Inhabitants of St. David, be enforced. Nevertheless, it is with the deepest concern, your Petitioners find themselves under the disagreeable necessity of remonstrating to this Honorable House against the proceedings of a majority of the Commissioners relative to the Court House, they being acquaintances and neighbours of your Petitioners, a conduct your Petitioners apprehend, tending altogether (as far as in them lies), to defeat the good intention of the Legislature, they having appointed the Cheraw Hill (as it is lately called), or a place at or near Mr. Kershaw's Store, for the Court House, in direct opposition, as your Petitioners apprehend, to the Act of Assembly: Because, a very worthy Member of the House, of the first character, Thomas Lynch, Esq., informed them there was an Act for having the Court House and Gaol at the Long Bluff, which information was given before they had contracted for any part of the materials; and soon afterwards, our own worthy and honorable Representative also acquainted them with the certainty of the Act, and even sent them a copy thereof, before it was printed, certified by the Secretary, to convince the Commissioners they were acting wrong: Yet they have contracted for, drawn on and received from the Public Treasurer, three thousand pounds, in order to build a Court House at Cheraw Hill. This appropriation of the public money is, your Petitioners humbly conceive, altogether contrary to the intention of the Legislature, and tending to retard the work, which will be a prejudice to the whole Province, if, as your Petitioners are told, the Judges do not ride the Circuit till the Court Houses are all finished according to law. If the proceedings of the Commissioners were not contrary to the Act of Assembly, yet, the ill consequences of their conduct to the inhabitants of this Parish, will be obvious to all who consider, that Mr. Kershaw's store is seventeen or eighteen miles from the Long Bluff, which consequently enhances the cost of every precept, as well as the expense and fatigue of travelling an unnecessary distance; all which, your Petitioners conceive, the poor people will be the likeliest to suffer, as, in all probability, they will be the most liable to actions of debt. If the intention of the Legislature, in passing the Act, was partly to encourage trade, as some of the Commissioners say, yet, their wanting the Court House at Mr. Kershaw's store, within eight or nine miles of the Province line, would, we think, only encourage the inland trade of that part of North Carolina next to the Court House. There is not an argument which your Petitioners ever heard advanced in favor of Cheraw Hill, nor, any produced against the Long Bluff, why (for convenience, agreeableness of the place, as well as its central situation) it should not answer all the salutary purposes intended by the Act, but what your Petitioners are willing, if called upon, and think themselves perfectly able to confute: and, although two of the Commissioners very candidly confessed they are interested in having the Court House at Cheraw Hill, viz., Messrs. Eli Kershaw and Thomas Lide, —'for then we will sell grog and osnaburgs,' as Mr. Kershaw expressed it; yet, your Petitioners with confidence hope, this Honorable House will always protect the public welfare of this Province against all private interests, and we think we have reason to suspect, that the Commissioners concerned in the Draft upon the Table, intend to use their own and their friends' interest to have the Act repealed at the next meeting of Assembly, in order to carry their point of having the Court House at Cheraw Hill; but, should such a motion be made in the House by Petition or otherwise, your Petitioners humbly pray this Honorable House maturely to consider of it, and to repeal or continue the Act, as to you in your great wisdom, shall seem meet'."*

"21st August, 1770.

"A Petition of a considerable part of the Free-holders and Inhabitants of the Cheraw Precinct, in the Parish of St. David, was presented to the House, and read in the words following, viz.: 'That your Petitioners have always entertained the highest regard for the Legislature, and were never so sensible of its wisdom and equity as when an Act was passed for the more easy and convenient administration of justice; nor, did your Petitioners fail of paying due respect to that impartial regard to the general good which appointed this populous part of the country to be a Precinct, by which salutary measure, your Petitioners will be delivered from innumerable grievances and enjoy one of the best privileges of the British Constitution. That your Petitioners had an additional prospect of felicity by the Commissioners having appointed the Cheraw Hill as the most proper place for the Court House and Gaol to be built on, agreeably to the trust reposed in them, before they were informed of a different appointment made by the Legislature. That your Petitioners (paying the greatest deference to the wisdom which originated the choice of the Long Bluff, in preference to the said Cheraw Hill, on account of the former being nearer to the centre of this Precinct), pray for leave to represent, that, from a personal knowledge of both places, they humbly conceive it would better answer the beneficent intention of the Legislature, if the Courts of Justice should be held at the place nominated by the Commissioners; because your Petitioners apprehend, that the

*"Journal of House of Assembly," No. 38, pp. 407-409.

centre will certainly be removed a considerable distance higher up, when the error which was made in removing the Provincial line shall be rectified: and, more especially, because your Petitioners conceive from the situation of the Cheraw Hill, with respect to the country round about it, and also from the apparent circumstances of trade now existing, and very likely to flourish, that place will always undoubtedly be the Capitol of the Precinct, and therefore, every encouragement given to it, will, in the same proportion as it promotes commerce, encourage industry in general, but particularly the poor families on the frontier of this Province, who are now very numerous, and daily increasing by emigrations from the Northern Colonies, and whose lands are capable of the best improvements; but, were it not for the encouragement given them by the Stores at the Cheraws, their valuable lands would be in a manner lost, on account of the great distance they are situated from market, which circumstance alone has been introductory of some of the worst consequences. Your Petitioners therefore humbly pray, that such instructions may be given to the Commissioners as in your wisdom you shall deem most proper.'

"Ordered to be taken into consideration to-morrow."*

"22nd August, 1770.

"When the House (according to order), proceeded to take into consideration the Petitions of the Free-holders and Electors of the Parish of St. David's and Cheraw District, which was presented to this House on the 17th inst., and also the Petition of a considerable part of the Free-holders and Inhabitants of the Cheraw Precinct, in the Parish of St. David, which was presented to this House yesterday, and the Petitions were severally read, and a memorial of George Hicks, Thomas Lide, Jonathan Wise, Benjamin Rogers, and Ely Kershaw, commissioners appointed for building the Court House and Gaol in the Cheraw Precinct, presented to the House, and read in the words following, viz.: 'That they, the subscribers, being appointed commissioners to contract for, and superintend the building a Circuit Court House and Gaol at Cheraw, in the Parish of

*"Journal of the House," No. 38, pp. 415, 416.

St. David, by an Act of the General Assembly, passed the 29th July, 1769, did agreeably to the instructions sent them by the Lieut.-Gov., the 22nd March last, in obedience thereto, meet on the 13th April, and contracted for one and a half acres of land on Cheraw Hill, whereon they proposed to have the said buildings erected, as they judged that the most convenient and proper place, from its being the most public and healthy situation on Pedee River; Public notice was also given, that they proposed to meet again at Cheraw on the 10th of May, at which meeting they received a letter from George Gabriell Powell, Esq., wherein he informed them, that a bill for removing the Court House and Gaol to Long Bluff had been framed, but had not passed; that, therefore, the commissioners were left at liberty to have the said buildings carried on with all possible despatch, at any place they thought proper: they, therefore, agreeably to this letter, and the instructions sent them formerly, contracted for the materials, the chief of which are now ready upon the land above mentioned.

" 'But, since our agreeing for the said materials, your memorialists have been informed that the General Assembly had thought proper to have the said buildings at Long Bluff —a place which, they humbly conceive, is not so convenient as the above, being a low situation, surrounded with low, flat land, and subject at some seasons of the year to be in a manner surrounded with water, and not likely ever to be a town, or place of trade.

" 'They would also beg leave to observe, that though the Long Bluff, as the Provincial line now runs, is nearer to the centre of the Cheraw District, yet they are informed the north Provincial line is likely to be extended higher up; but, even if it never should, 'tis their opinion that the Cheraw Hill will be as central to the majority of the people, and they conceive it would have been as convenient to have placed the Court House and Gaol for George-town District in the centre of that Precinct, as to place the Court House and Gaol for Cheraw District at Long Bluff. And they further beg leave to observe, that the Cheraw Hill is at present, and has been for many years past, the most public and the greatest place of trade upon Pedee

River. They, therefore, hope this Honorable House will take the premises into consideration, and get such information of the situation of both places as to your Honors shall seem meet; and they have agreed, in order that the public may not be disappointed, to continue to forward the work already contracted for, at Cheraw Hill, with all expedition, so as to have them ready as soon as the other Court Houses and Gaols. And, after this Honorable House hath considered the matter, and obtained such information of both places as you may judge necessary, should it then be determined by your Honors to have the said buildings erected at Long Bluff, the frame and other materials might be removed thither by water, though at a very considerable expense. Your memorialists, therefore, thought it necessary to lay their proceedings before this Honble. House for their inspection, and at the same time to give their opinion respecting both places, in order that they might not be reflected upon hereafter, should this Honorable House be imposed on and persuaded to place the buildings at an improper place.

"'And it is not their intention to contract for anything further, until they receive positive orders at which place they can with safety have the said buildings erected.'

"And a debate arising thereon, a motion was made, and the question being put, that the said Petition and Memorial be referred to a committee, the House divided, and the yeas went forth.

Teller for the Yeas, } 17   Teller for the Noes, } 19
   Mr. M'Kenzie.   Mr. Lowndes.

"So it passed in the negative.

"Ordered,

"That a Message be prepared to be sent to the Lieut.-Gov., to desire, that his Honor will be pleased to give positive directions to the Commissioners appointed for building the Court House and Gaol at the Cheraws District, to cause the said Court House and Gaol to be erected and built at the Long Bluff.

"According to Order, the following Message was prepared, to be sent to the Lieut.-Gov.; which, being read a second time, was agreed to, and Mr. Speaker ordered to sign the same, viz. :—

"May it please your Honor,
"It appearing to this House, that some doubts have arisen with the Commissioners for building the Gaol and Court House in the Cheraw District, about the proper place for erecting the same, and the House being of opinion that it is clearly fixed by an Act passed, the 7th of April last, to be at a place called the Long Bluff: we humbly desire that your Honor will be pleased to give positive directions to the Commissioners, appointed for that purpose, to cause the said Gaol and Court House to be immediately erected on the spot appointed by the said Act, that there may be no delay in carrying into execution the good purposes intended by the Circuit Court law.
"By order of the House,
"PETER MANIGAULT, Speaker."*

"A Message from the Lieut.-Gov., by the Clerk of the Council :—

"Mr. Speaker and Gentlemen,
"According to your desire, I have given positive orders to the Commissioners for building the Gaol and Court-house in the Cheraws District, to erect the same at the Long Bluff, and to proceed in the finishing these buildings with the utmost expedition.
"WM. BULL.†
"August 23rd, 1770."

The subject was thus very properly disposed of by the House without debate. And though the Act in favour of Long Bluff had not been previously passed, the fact would yet have remained obvious, that the reasons in favour of that location greatly preponderated. The counter petition in support of Cheraw Hill, sounds very much like the production of a Lawyer paid for the work, and the Memorial signally failed to establish its case. The interest of a portion

*"House Journal," No. 38, pp. 417-420.
†Ibid, pp. 421, 422.

of the Commissioners, who were influential, doubtless, gave shape to the proceedings of the Board; and the struggle was between the interests of a few and the convenience of many. It is a sad illustration, often furnished in the history of human affairs, how men of probity may thus be unconsciously biased. Long Bluff itself was almost too high up, could an eligible location below have been made available. Under all the circumstances, it was by far the best point that could have been selected, and there ought not to have been a moment's hesitation on the part of those entrusted with the work. In the subsequent division of Cheraw District into Counties, this was the point most central to them all. It never, indeed, became a place of any commercial note, and was eventually abandoned, or its immediate site, at least, as a place of residence. And yet it was at that time the most central and accessible point for the District generally, and withal, a place of some importance, as it continued to be for many years afterward.

Henceforth, Long Bluff was to become the resort of judges and lawyers. There, deeds of blood were to meet with their reward, and rigid justice was to be meted out. There, a people, hitherto practically debarred by the circumstances of their position from the exercise of some of the dearest privileges of free-men, were no longer to look upon the administration of justice and the adjudication of their rights from afar. The law was now to come nigh them, and trial by jury to be their immediate prerogative.

Public wrongs, as well as private grievances, were to be the subjects of their investigation and complaint. Answerable themselves to the Government under which they had been reared, that power, venerable and august as it was, was to become amenable to them in turn for its abuses.

And but a few short years were to pass away ere Long Bluff was to become a name, indissolubly associated with all that was lofty and ennobling in the first developments and commanding power of the spirit of independence on the Pedee.

The dispute about the location, and the transportation of the materials from Cheraw Hill, caused some delay in the prosecution of the work. It became necessary therefore to use all possible despatch, so as not to be behind the other Judicial Districts in the erection of their Court Houses and Gaols. As early as April 12th, 1770, it was said in the *Gazette*, "We are advised, from different parts of the country, that the utmost despatch is used by the several Boards of Commissioners for building Precinct Court Houses and Gaols, to complete the same during the course of the present year; especially in the frontier Districts, which again begin to be infested with great numbers of Horse Thieves and other Vagabonds, from whose depredations and outrages they fear they can never be completely relieved till a Vagrant Act is passed."

The partial calm which followed the determined action of the Regulators during the previous year, was seriously disturbed again. Old offenders, who had been driven off, returned once more.

The *Gazette* of April 5th said: "We are informed that a great number of Horse Thieves, and other Banditti, who fled from the back parts of this and the neighboring Provinces quite to West Florida, while the regulating scheme prevailed, after having sold the horses they rode off, are returned and returning, in small parties, by sea, to different sea-ports on this continent, perhaps to play their old game over again; but they will be narrowly watched, and 'tis not very unlikely that some of these gentry may furnish the first business of our new Circuit Courts."

More than a year subsequent to this time, a serious disturbance occurred on the Pedee.

Of the last notable affair of the kind, the *Gazette* of October 3rd, 1771, contained the following account:—"Winsler Driggers, a notorious villain, who escaped out of Savannah Gaol about thirteen months ago, under sentence of death, and for the taking of whom a reward of fifty pounds sterling was offered, has at length met with his deserts. He was taken about a month ago, near Drowning Creek, in the Charraw Settlement, proved to be a Mulatto, tried under the Negro Act, and hanged. It seems he had been in those parts some months, collected a gang of other desperate villains, in number near fifty, who committed all manner of depredations. Capt. Philip Pledger, with a number of his neighbors, at length made an attempt to take or drive them out of the settlement. As soon as Capt. Pledger's party appeared, the villains fired, and Driggers wounded Capt. Pledger in one of his arms, so that he has since lost it (it was amputated). Pledger's party returned the fire, killed one William Hodge and one Johnston, wounded Driggers in one arm and the back, who nevertheless escaped, but was afterwards taken."*

Depredations were committed after this, but by smaller parties and by stealth, until the troubles of the Revolution came on, when this class of people, under the wing of the Tories, renewed their outrages more boldly than ever.

The Court House and Gaol at Long Bluff, now rapidly approaching completion, were built after the substantial manner of those days, when appearance was less consulted than strength and durability. With massive walls and heavy oak frames, carefully selected and well put together, the Court House continued to stand for many years, and until the ancient village, in the next century, had become deserted. It stood on the right of the main street, or road, as it approached the river, and about three hundred yards from the latter. It was taken down about the year 1817.

The Parish of St. David, except as to the elective franchise, was henceforth to be overshadowed by the more imposing judicial organization now established, and the story of the "Old Cheraws" to become the subject of historic renown.

The offices created by the Circuit Court Act, of Sheriff, Clerk, &c., were to be filled by appointment of the Crown. The only popular election yet provided for, in addition to Parish officers, was the Member of Assembly. The Sheriff was to be appointed every second year, the Court nominating three proper persons, freeholders, and residents of the District or Precinct, whose names were to be presented to

*The tradition of this fight was handed down in the neighborhood, and in a correct shape as to many of the particulars, except, that it purported to have been an affair between Captain Pledger and the Tories.

It was related to the author by the late Captain John Terrell, of Marlborough, a grandson of Captain Pledger. The fight occurred near the place where Captain Terrell lived and died. Driggers was hung near Muddy Creek, on the Old River Road, six miles below Cheraw. The spot is yet pointed out.

the Governor, Lieutenant-Governor, or Commander-in-Chief for the time being, and from whom one was to be selected and commissioned.

The names of Charles Augustus Steward, Alexander M'Intosh, and William Henry Mills, were presented to his Excellency the Governor in June 1772, as suitable persons for Sheriff of Cheraw District. As was to be expected, from what was already well known of these gentlemen in connexion with their political sympathies, the latter was selected and commissioned. He retained his place until a change of Government in 1776. On the 3rd of November (1772), the *Gazette* said: "Since our last, their Honors, the Judges, set out to open and hold the Circuit Courts for the several Districts in this Province, which began the 5th inst., and is the first since the passing of that Act." Chief Justice Gordon and Justice Murray took the "North-Circuit," as it was then called. They were to sit first in George-town. On Monday, the 16th November, henceforth to be a day memorable in the history of the Pedee, the Court was to open at Long Bluff.

Imagination may picture to itself the interest with which the people looked forward to the consummation of their long-cherished wishes, and the triumph of the hard-fought battle for their rights.

Happily for them and for their children, the administration of justice in their midst on so august an occasion was not to commence without invoking first the blessing of Heaven, and recalling the sanctions of that Holy Religion, established by Him who is the Lord and Judge of all the earth. In accordance, therefore, with the pious custom of the time, a "Sessions Sermon" was preached on the morning of the 16th, before the opening of the Court, by the Rev. Nicholas Bedgegood, Pastor of the Welch Neck Church. The duties and responsibilities of those in authority, as well as of the subjects of the state of every degree, were doubtless enforced, and the thoughts of all alike directed to a judgment in the end of the world, from which there is to be no appeal.

The Presentments of the Grand Jury for Cheraws District, made on Monday the 16th, were ordered to be published in the general *Gazette* of the Province, and were as follows: —

"I. We present, as a grievance, the want of a Law to cleanse the River of the great number of trees and logs which interrupt the navigation.

"II. We present, as a grievance, the want of a Bridge over Thompson's Creek, near Yorkshire Mills; and another over Black Creek, a small distance above the Ferry, known by the name of Douglass Ferry.

"III. We present, as a grievance, the want of a Free-school in the District.

"IV. We present, as a grievance, that neither the Laws of this Province, nor the Statutes of Great Britain, now in force, are printed or published in such a manner as to be procured by the inhabitants of this District.

"V. We present Edward Williams, late a constable, for suffering Ralph Sutton, charged with Felony, and John Williams, the Prosecutor, to escape from him,—by the information of Col. Charles Augustus Steward.

"Charles A. Steward, *Foreman.*	L.S.
Abel Edwards.	L.S.
Thomas Edwards.	L.S.
Henry William Harrington.	L.S.
Robert Blair.	L.S.
William Godfrey.	L.S.
Richard Carter.	L.S.
Samuel Chandler.	L.S.
Peter Kolb.	L.S.
John Hodges.	L.S.
William Dewitt.	L.S.
George Hicks.	L.S.
Benjamin Rogers.	L.S.
Arthur Hart.	L.S.
Thomas Evans.	L.S.
Robert Clary.	L.S.
William Pegues.	L.S.
John Perkins.	L.S."

The attention given by the Grand Jury on this occasion to the important subjects of internal improvements, Education, and the Publication of the Laws of the Province, was timely. They were matters of serious regard, and failed not afterward to be brought to public notice as occasion demanded. In the *Gazette* of 15th December following this account appeared, viz.: "At Cheraws seven Bills were given out, and four found. Jacob Tilley, convicted of Horse-stealing, was sentenced to receive thirty-nine lashes, and to have his right ear cut off; Randall Johnson, convicted of Larceny, was burnt in the hand."

On the approach of the April Assizes, 1773, Justices Savage and Fewtrell chose the Northern Circuit. The Court opened for Cheraws, April 15th. The Presentments of the Grand Jury, ordered to be printed, were as follows:—

"I. We present, as a grievance, the want of a Law for cleansing Pedee River.

"II. We present, as a grievance, the want of a Bridge over Thompson's Creek,* and also over Black Creek, on the road between the Cheraws and George-town.

"III. We present, as a grievance, the want of a Free-school in the District.

"IV. We present, as a grievance, the general neglect of the Militia and Patrol Acts, and recommend that they may be amended.

"V. We present, as a grievance, the want of a Vagrant Act, the District being infested with many idle and disorderly persons, who having no visible means of subsistence, either plunder the industrious inhabitants, or become chargeable to the Parish.

"VI. We present, as a grievance, the want of a Chapel of Ease in the lower part of the District.

"VII. We present, as a grievance, that the lines of the District are not now ascertained.

"VIII. We recommend that a Law be passed, obliging Persons not resident in the Province, or their agents, to give security, upon commencing any Suit in the Courts of Common Law, to pay the costs thereof, if a verdict shall pass for the defendant; and also obliging Prosecutors,

---

*This was doubtless at the point referred to in the former Presentment as near Yorkshire Mills; and was on the road from Cheraw to Long Bluff.

on behalf of the Crown, for misdemeanor, to pay the costs where the defendant shall be acquitted, or not prosecuted to trial.

"IX. We present, as a grievance, that witnesses attending the Sessions on behalf of the Crown are not allowed their expences.

"X. We present, as a grievance, that neither the Laws of this Province, nor the Statutes of Great Britain, made of force therein, are printed or published.

"XI. We present Edward Jones, Constable, for a wilful neglect of his duty, on the information of Unity Hunter.

"XII. We present Joseph Gourly, Esq., one of the Justices for the District, as a common drunkard, a profane swearer, and disturber of the peace, on the information of Robert Dowling.

"XIII. We present, as a grievance, the want of a wall to enclose the Gaol and the yard round the same, it being at present entirely open, by which means, persons from without can reach instruments to the prisoners within, to facilitate their escape; and also the want of a well for the use of the same.

Alexander Mackintosh, *Foreman*.	L.S.
Claudius Pegues.	L.S.
William Johnston.	L.S.
Samuel Wise.	L.S.
Thomas Lide.	L.S.
Thomas James.	L.S.
Robert Lide.	L.S.
John Kimbrough.	L.S.
Martin Kolb.	L.S.
John Mikell.	L.S.
Thomas Burton.	L.S.
Thomas Ayer.	L.S.
John Hewstess.	L.S.
Malachi Murfee.	L.S.
William Dewitt.	L.S.
Thomas Ellerbe.	L.S.
Martin Dewitt.	L.S.
John Hitchcock.	L.S.
John Wilds.	L.S.

Aaron Daniel. L.S.
Magnus Corgill. L.S.
Abel Wilds. L.S."

The effect upon the minds of the people of having Courts of their own, holden among them, was now becoming apparent. Respect for the constituted authorities of the Province was partially restored, and the majesty of the law vindicated.

Secure in the feeling that the guilty would not go unpunished, attention was naturally turned to those important subjects connected with the general welfare and progress of society, and hence the several matters brought to public notice by the Grand Juries, both for Legislative action, and district regulation and control.

It is somewhat singular, as appears from Presentment fourth, that after such recent disturbances and in so unsettled a state of the country, there should have been a general neglect in enforcing the Militia and Patrol Acts. It was doubtless attributable in part to the sparsity of the population, as well as to the difficulty ever existing in the early stages of society, of securing thoroughly organized and constant effort for the removal of public evils, or the enforcement of the laws of the land. A Vagrant Act was now imperatively demanded. The public expression by a Grand Jury of the want of a Chapel of Ease (as it was called in the language of the time, being an adjunct of the parish church), was a happy omen for the religious sentiment and public opinion of the day. The country was very scantily supplied with religious services, and the want of additional facilities for public worship was sorely felt. In this connexion, the presentment of a Justice of the Peace, as a drunkard and profane swearer, is worthy of notice, and is an example which their posterity might well follow more sedulously than they do, as to the high standard of character which ought ever to be required in those who aspire to offices of public trust. The functions of a Grand Jury, as the high inquest of the State, and as here faithfully discharged, have been too much ignored in later times. To such a body the most solemn trust is committed; and boldly brought to bear upon society, its influence would be largely felt. The conduct of the Grand Juries of the Cheraws District in the early days of its history is worthy of perpetual remembrance.

At the November Term, 1773, Chief Justice Gordon and Justice Savage presided. Up to this time, the name of Thomas Turner appears as Clerk for Cheraw District, and James Johnston deputy-Clerk. The latter place was filled on this occasion by Henry Wm. Harrington.

The Presentments of the Grand Jury were as follows:—

"I. We present, as a grievance, the want of a Vagrant Act in this Province, this District in particular being infested with many Vagrants, who do great damage, particularly by fire hunting.

"II. We present, as a grievance, that the division line lately run between this District and the District of Georgetown, does not extend lower down Pedee River than sixteen or seventeen miles from the Court House: which, we humbly apprehend, was not originally intended in the division of the Districts in this Province, and therefore do recommend that this matter be taken into consideration by the Legislature.

"III We present, as a very great grievance, the want of a Free School in this District.

"IV. We present, as a grievance, the want of a Law for cleansing Pedee River, its navigation at present being very unsafe.

"V. We present, as a grievance, the want of a Bridge over Thompson's Creek, near Col. Steward's Mill, and another over Black Creek, near the present Ferry.

"VI. We present, as a grievance, the present insufficiency of the Gaol of this District, by which persons confined therein are enabled to make their escape; and we do recommend that it be surrounded by a sufficient wall, at a convenient distance therefrom, to prevent the confederates of the Prisoners from furnishing them with implements for breaking the same.

"VII. We present, as a grievance, the want of a new Jury list in this District.

"We recommend that these our Presentments be published in the several *Gazettes* of this Province.

"John Kimbrough, *Foreman*.	L.S.
George Hicks.	L.S.
William Pegues.	L.S.
Malachi Murfee, Sen.	L.S.
Robert Lide.	L.S.
Thomas Ayer.	L.S.
John Hodge.	L.S.
Abel Wilds.	L.S.
Thomas Ellerbe.	L.S.
Joshua Hickman.	L.S.
Robert Blair.	L.S.
Arthur Hart.	L.S.
William Godfrey.	L.S.
Alexander Mackintosh.	L.S.
Martin Dewitt.	L.S.
Robert Clary.	L.S.
Elias DuBose.	L.S.
John Mikell.	L.S.
James Kelly.	L.S.
Thomas James.	L.S."

On 21st December, the following notice appeared in the *Gazette,* viz.: "At Cheraws, twelve bills of Indictment were given out, of which nine were found. Samuel Winds, convicted of Horse-stealing, was sentenced to lose his right ear, and be publickly whipt. John Odom, Sen., Alexander Purvis, and James Wright, convicted of Petit Larceny, were sentenced to be whipt. William Lewis, alias John Macallister, found guilty of Forgery, was sentenced to stand in the Pillory, and be publickly whipt. Samuel Winds, Alexander Purvis, and James Wright have been pardoned by his Honor, the Lieutenant-Governor."

Notwithstanding the urgent recommendations of the Grand Juries from time to time, nothing was done by the Legislature to improve the navigation of the river. The matter was not acted upon until some years subsequent to the Revolution. Nor were any steps taken for the establishment of Free Schools. Difficult as it has been since to make any adequate provision of the kind, the difficulty was much greater then in consequence of the low state of the public funds and the sparseness of the population.

On Friday, April 14th, 1774, the following Presentments were made by the Grand Jury of Cheraws, and ordered to be published, viz.:—

"I. We present, as a grievance, the want of a new Jury list.

"II. We present the Commissioners appointed for building the parish church of St. David, for not having it completed in proper time, the money having been granted by the Commons House of Assembly near four years, for that purpose,—by the information of Charles Augustus Steward, Esq.

"Alexander M'Intosh, *Foreman*.	L.S.
John Hodges.	L.S.
William Hardwick.	L.S.
Wm. Henry Harrington.	L.S.
Malachi Murfee.	L.S.
Joshua Hickman.	L.S.
Thomas James.	L.S.
John Wilds.	L.S.
Robert Clary.	L.S.
Robert Blair.	L.S.
Abel Wilds.	L.S.
Thomas Ayer.	L.S.
Moses Speight.	L.S.
Robert Lide.	L.S.
William Godfrey.	L.S.
Martin Dewitt.	L.S.
William Pegues.	L.S.
Elias DuBose.	L.S.
Martin Kolb.	L.S.
Alexander Gordon.	L.S."

Calvin Spencer was deputy Clerk at this term of the Court.

The parish church had been used in December, 1772, as

already stated, though doubtless in an unfinished state, as this Presentment would indicate. Of the early history of the Bar of the Old Cheraws very little is known.

Of its learned arguments, its eloquent appeals, and brilliant conflicts, no tradition even remains. Up to this time and for years subsequent, there was no resident lawyer in the District. Colonel Powell was doubtless a regular attendant and leading advocate there from the first, as were some of the eminent members of the Bar of Charles-town, with Judges Waites and Brevard, before their promotion to the Bench.

The records which remain are silent on the subject, and no tongue is left to tell the stirring scenes which were enacted there. For many years past every material vestige, except a few scattered bricks, has disappeared.

The plough, for more than a generation, has made deep furrows over the ground on which the old Court House stood. We can only wander back in imagination to its earlier days, and sadly muse on the past.

Another chapter will open, and burning words come back—the opening chapter of the manly declaration of their rights and of their country's wrongs, by the sturdy patriots of the Old Cheraws.

CHAPTER X.

A general Congress of the colonies proposed—Scene thereupon in Assembly of South Carolina—Action of the Assembly—South Carolina takes the lead—Repeal of the Stamp Act—Declaratory Act—Claim of taxing the colonies asserted—East India Company imports tea—Course of South Carolina—Cargo restrained from sale—Course of other colonies—Town meetings called—Circular letter from Massachusetts—Arrival of it in Charles-town—Excitement—Circular letters sent through the Province—General meeting in Charles-town—St. David's represented—Action of meeting—Provincial Congress called—Deputies from St. David's—Action of the Congress—November courts—William Henry Drayton appointed judge—Account of him and his appointment—Presides at Long Bluff—His charge to the grand jury—Address of petit jury in reply—Presentments of the grand jury—Reflections—Account of Judge Drayton—Subsequent career and death—Action of general meeting in Charles-town as to the poor of Boston—Province sends relief—Subscription in St. David's parish—Reflections—Close of year 1774—Concluding remarks.

As early as 1765, the passage of the memorable Stamp Act by the British Parliament roused the American Colonists generally to opposition. To make this feeling effective, it was necessary that some common plan of co-operation should be adopted. Among other propositions offered to secure such a uniform line of conduct in the several colonies, was that of a general Congress of Deputies to be elected from each. When this measure was first proposed in the Assembly of South Carolina, there were not wanting, as in all revolutions, those who were disposed to frown it down. It was ridiculed by a humorous member, on that occasion, in words to the following effect, viz.: "If you agree to the proposition of composing a Congress of Deputies from the different British Colonies, what sort of a dish will you make? New England will throw in fish and onions. The Middle States, flax-seed and flour. Maryland and Virginia will add tobacco. North Carolina, pitch, tar, and turpentine. South Carolina, rice and indigo; and Georgia will sprinkle the whole composition with saw-dust. Such an absurd jumble will you make, if you attempt to form a union among such discordant materials as the thirteen British Provinces." To which, a shrewd country member replied: "He would not choose the gentleman who made the objection for his cook; but, nevertheless, he would venture to assert, that if the Colonies proceeded judiciously in the appointment of Deputies to a Continental Congress, they would prepare a dish fit to be presented to any crowned head in Europe."*

This reply was worthy of Carolina, and equal to the occasion that called it forth. The Commons House of Assembly was prepared for decided action; and having passed resolutions, strongly affirming their rights as British subjects, proceeded to the election of Deputies to the Congress which was to meet the following October. South Carolina was the first of the colonies, out of New England, to take this step toward a Continental union. The effect of the meeting of the Congress, and of the decided stand taken by the Colonies, was a repeal of the Stamp Act. The repeal was accompanied, however, by an Act, commonly called the Declaratory Act, which affirmed, "that the Parliament of Great Britain had a right to bind the colonies in all cases whatsoever." In pursuance of this right, thus unconstitutionally claimed, the experiment of taxation was renewed in 1767, though more artfully than before, in the shape of small duties on glass, paper, tea, painters' colors, &c. Again the Colonies petitioned, and agreed, moreover, among themselves, to import no more British manufactures.

The Government, alarmed once more at this general and decided manifestation of the spirit of intelligent resistance and revolt, repealed all the odious duties except that of threepence a pound on tea.

In the mean time, the East India Company, in order to take advantage of this state of things, adopted the scheme of exporting large quantities of tea, to be sold on their account in the several capitols of the British Colonies. This increased the jealousy of the Colonies, and made them more determined than before to resist the encroachment on their rights. Accordingly, combinations were entered into to obstruct the sales of tea thus sent out by the East India

---

*Ramsay's "Revolution in So. Ca." vol. i. p. 13.

Company. A cargo sent to South Carolina was stored, the consignees being restrained from exposing it to sale. In other colonies similar measures were adopted. In Boston a few men in disguise threw overboard 340 chests of tea, the proportion sent by the East India Company to that Province. This led to a retaliatory Act by Parliament, blocking up the Port of Boston, and was followed by other Acts of a similar kind. One of these was called an "Act for the better regulating the Government of Massachusetts," the effect of which was to alter essentially the Charter of that Province, taking the executive control out of the hands of the people, and vesting it in the King or his Governor. Other abuses of the most offensive and alarming character speedily followed.

The colonists generally took the alarm. The inhabitants of Boston were thrown into the utmost consternation. Town-meetings were called; and at one of them, May 13th, 1774, a resolution was passed, calling upon the other Colonies in the most earnest manner to put a stop at once to all importations from Great Britain and the West Indies until the Act for blocking up Boston Harbor should be repealed, or else there would be reason to fear "that fraud, power, and the most odious oppressions would rise triumphant over justice, right, social happiness, and freedom." A copy of this vote was immediately forwarded to the other Colonies. On its arrival in Charles-town, intense feeling was excited; and in order that it might be submitted to the general voice of the people, some of the principal gentlemen of the town caused circular letters to be sent out by express, to every Parish and District in the Province, calling a general meeting of the inhabitants. The summons was urgent, and met with a hearty response.

Everywhere the people assembled, and appointed Deputies to meet in Charles-town on the 6th of July ensuing. When that day arrived, "Charles-town was filled with persons from the country. One hundred and four Deputies represented all parts of the Province, except Greenville County, St. John's, Colleton, and Christ Church Parish, which were without delegations. In behalf of Charles-town, the General Committee appeared."* Col. George Gabriel Powell was one of the Deputies from St. David's Parish, and took a conspicuous part in the proceedings of the meeting.

Of the names of the other deputies from this Parish no record remains. No complete list, indeed, of all those in attendance, appears in the published accounts of the time.

The meeting was held under the Exchange, July 6th, and a crowded assemblage it was.

At 9 o'clock in the morning, Col. Powell took the chair; and it was carried, "that votes should be given by each person present, and not by Parishes"—and also, "that whoever came there might give his vote." The business of the day then opened with the reading of the communication from the Colony of Massachusetts. Afterwards resolutions were considered, touching American rights and grievances. A resolution was passed, providing for the safety and welfare of the Province, by the appointment of a Committee of ninety-nine persons, to act as a General Committee, to correspond with the Committees of the other Colonies, and to do all matters and things necessary to carry these resolutions into execution; and that any twenty-one of them, met together, may proceed in business, their power to continue till the next general meeting."†

The General Committee was accordingly appointed by the meeting, and consisted of fifteen merchants and fifteen mechanics to represent Charles-town; and sixty-nine planters to represent the other parts of the Province.‡

This proceeding, though not strictly authorized by the people in the action taken at their primary meetings, was acquiesced in, as being demanded by the extraordinary circumstances of the time, and manifestly intended for the public good.

After a session of three days the meeting adjourned. Thus matters went on, the members of the General Committee attending to their several duties throughout the Province. In the fall, it was determined by the Committee to convene a Provincial Congress, by the election of

*Drayton's "Memoirs," p. 126.
†Ramsay's "Revolution in So. Ca." vol. i. p. 22.
‡Drayton's "Memoirs," vol. i. p. 131.

Representatives from every District and Parish in the Province, to meet in Charles-town early in the ensuing year. The designs of the British Government, in the meantime, had been more fully developed, and the necessity for increased energy and more perfect union among the colonists was most apparent.

By means of the Congress of delegates it was thought the public arm would be strengthened, and the sentiments of the people better known and more firmly established. For this purpose, on the 9th of November, the Committee issued Resolutions, providing for the general election of Deputies throughout the Province, by appointing the time, describing the Districts and Provinces, and fixing the number of Representatives for each. As before, in fixing the ratio of the General Committee, thirty were allowed for Charles-town, ten to each of the four large Districts of Ninety-six, of those between the Broad and Saluda, the Broad and Catawba rivers, and that eastward of the Wateree; and six Representatives to each of the Parishes,—making in all one hundred and eighty-four, nearly four times as many as constituted the Commons House of Assembly.

The Resolutions required the Representatives elected to assemble in Charles-town on the 11th of January, 1775; and also set forth the objects of the meeting, viz., to receive an account of the proceedings of the late Continental Congress, to elect delegates for another Congress, to be held in the ensuing May, to elect a new General Committee, and to establish such regulations as the exigencies of the times might render necessary.

The following gentlemen were elected from St. David's Parish, viz., Honorable George Gabriel Powell, Claudius Pegues, Henry Wm. Harrington, Alexander M'Intosh, Samuel Wise, Esq., and Col. George Pawley.

In the meantime, the people on the Pedee, fully alive to the critical state of affairs and prepared for every emergency, had spoken in language of no doubtful import on those exciting topics which now agitated the public mind. The November Courts (1774) having come on, the Honorable Wm. Henry Drayton, one of his Majesty's Assistant-

Judges, and Mr. Justice Fewtrell, took the Northern Circuit, embracing the Districts of Camden, Cheraws, and George-town. Of all the public men of the Province at that time, no one was better qualified, in every respect, than Judge Drayton, to stir up the minds of the people and keep alive in them the spirit of liberty.

He had been appointed to the Bench the previous winter in the place of Mr. Justice Murray, deceased. Prior to this time the Bench seems to have been filled with Assistant-Judges of independence and property in the Colony, who served the public in that capacity without fee or reward. Upon the death of Justice Murray, his Majesty's Council found some difficulty in getting a gentleman of proper mark and character to take his place, in consequence of the inadequate inducement, and the probability, moreover, that the appointee would be superseded by a Barrister sent from England. The case seemed difficult to the Council, yet a Judge must of necessity be appointed. After some time spent in agitating the subject, Mr. Drayton (being one of the Council) offered his services until some one should be selected by the King; which public-spirited behavior was very readily and unanimously approved by the Lieut.-Governor and Council. This was in January, 1774. Not long after a Pamphlet appeared, under the signature of "Freeman," stating the grievances of America, and presenting a bill of American rights. It was addressed to the Congress at Philadelphia, and excited general attention. Being understood to have come from the pen of Mr. Drayton, it gave great offence to the Royal officers and friends of the Crown.

Some strictures were also made in it, respecting the writs of assistance to the Customs, granted by the Judges. These last fancied the thrust was aimed at them.

Whereupon, the Chief Justice, Thomas Knox Gordon, and one of the Assistant-Judges, Charles Matthew Cosslet, presented a remonstrance to the Lieut.-Govr., complaining of the publication of "Freeman," charging it to Mr. Drayton, and submitting, whether such a person was fit to hold the office of Assistant-Judge. To this Judge Drayton replied, and before the dispute was settled, the November Circuits came on. Judge Drayton had scarcely left Charles-town when Mr. Gregory arrived from England to take his place on the Bench.* It would have been a signal gain for the Crown, and as great a loss to the cause of Independence, if the last circuit of this illustrious patriot had been prestalled.

He appeared at Long Bluff upon the opening of the Court, on Tuesday, November 15th, and delivered the following charge:—

"Gentlemen of the Grand Jury,

"You are now met to discharge one of the most important duties in society, for you are assembled arbiters of the innocence or guilt of those of your fellow-citizens who are so unfortunate as to have afforded occasion, however slight, for the laws to take cognizance of their conduct.

"You are authorized to pass judgment, in the first instance, upon the apparently guilty wretch, and by your acquitting voice, to shield apparent innocence from a malicious prosecution. Such powers have the constitution of your country vested in you; powers no less important than truly honorable, when exercised with a fearless integrity.

"It is your indispensable duty to endeavour to exercise those powers with propriety; it is mine, concisely to point out to you the line of your conduct—a conduct, which the venerable constitution of your country intends, by protecting the innocent and by delivering the guilty over to the course of law, should operate to nourish, in its native vigour, even that constitution itself, from whose generous spirit we have a title to call ourselves free-men, an appellation which peculiarly distinguishes the English subject (those unfortunately disappointed fellow-citizens in Quebec excepted), and ranks them above all the civilized nations of the earth. By as much as you prefer freedom to slavery, by so much ought you to prefer a generous death to servitude, and to hazard everything to endeavour to maintain that rank which is so gloriously pre-eminent above all other nations. You

---

*Drayton's "Memoirs," vol. i. pp. 151-161.

ought to endeavour to preserve it, not only for its inestimable value, but from a reverence to our ancestry from whom we received it, and from a love of our children, to whom we are bound, by every consideration, to deliver down this legacy, the most valuable that ever was or ever can be delivered to posterity. It is compounded of the most generous civil liberty that ever existed, and the sacred Christian Religion, released from the absurdities which are inculcated, the shackles which are imposed, the tortures which are inflicted, and the flames which are lighted, blown up and fed with blood, by the Roman Catholic doctrines, which tend to establish a most cruel tyranny in Church and State—a tyranny under which all Europe groaned for many ages.

"And such are the distinguished characters of this legacy, which may God, of His infinite goodness and mercy, long preserve to us, and graciously continue to our posterity; but, without our pious and unwearied endeavours to preserve these blessings, it is folly and presumption to hope for a continuance of them; hence, in order to stimulate your exertions in favour of your civil liberties, which protect your religious rights, instead of discoursing to you of the laws of other States, and comparing them to our own, allow me to tell you what your civil liberties are, and to charge you, which I do in the most solemn manner, to hold them dearer than your lives; a lesson and charge at all times proper from a Judge, but particularly so at this crisis, when America is in one general and generous commotion touching this truly important point. It is unnecessary for me to draw any other character of those liberties, than that great line by which they are distinguished; and happy is it for the subject, that those liberties can be marked in so easy and in so distinguishing a manner. And this is the distinguishing character: English people cannot be taxed, nay, they cannot be bound by any law, unless by their consent, expressed by themselves, or their Representatives of their own election. This Colony was settled by English subjects; by a people from England herself; a people who brought over with them, who planted in this Colony, and who transmitted to posterity the invaluable rights of Englishmen—

rights which no time, no contract, no climate, can diminish. Thus, possessed of such rights, it is of the most serious importance that you strictly execute those regulations which have arisen from such a parentage, and to which you have given the authority of laws, by having given your constitutional consent that they should operate as laws; for by your not executing what those laws require, you would weaken the force, and would show, I may almost say, a treasonable contempt of those constitutional rights out of which your laws arise, and which you ought to defend and support at the hazard of your lives. Hence, by all the ties which mankind hold most dear and sacred; your reverence to your ancestors; your love to your own interests; your tenderness to your posterity; by the lawful obligations of your oath; I charge you to do your duty; to maintain the laws, the rights, the constitution of your country, even at the hazard of your lives and fortunes.

"Some courtly judges style themselves the king's servants —a style which sounds harshly in my ears, inasmuch as the being a servant implies obedience to the orders of the master; and such judges might possibly think that, in the present situation of American affairs, this charge is inconsistent with my duty to the king. But, for my part, in my judicial character, I know no master but the law; I am a servant, not to the king, but to the constitution; and, in my estimation, I shall best discharge my duty as a good subject to the king, and a trusty officer under the constitution, when I boldly declare the law to the people, and instruct them in their civil rights.

"Indeed, you, gentlemen of the Grand Jury, cannot properly comprehend your duty, and your great obligation to perform it, unless you know those civil rights from which these duties spring, and by knowing the value of these rights, thence learn your obligation to perform these duties.

"Having thus generally touched upon the nature and importance of your civil rights, in order to excite you to execute those laws to which they have given birth, I will now point out to you the particular duties which the laws of your country require at your hands.

"Unbiassed by affection to, and unmoved by fear of, any man, or set of men, you are to make presentment of every person, and of every proceeding militating against the public good. The law orders me particularly to give in charge, to watch carefully over our Negro Act, and our Jury Law—a law which cannot be too highly valued, whether we regard the excellency of its nature, or the importance of its object. This law carries in itself an indelible mark of what high importance the Legislature thought it, when they enacted it; and it carries in itself, also, a kind of prophecy, that its existence, in its native vigour, would in after times be endangered, and therefore it is that the law orders the Judge ever to charge the Grand Juries to watch over it with care; indeed, you ought to do so with the most zealous circumspection. A learned judge says: 'Every new tribunal erected for the decision of facts, without the intervention of a jury, is a step towards aristocracy, the most oppressive of absolute governments; and it is therefore a duty which every man owes to his country, his friends, to posterity, and himself, to maintain to the utmost of his power this valuable constitution in all its rights; to restore it to its ancient dignity, if at all impaired; to amend it wherever it is defective; and, above all, to guard with the most zealous circumspection against the introduction of new and arbitrary methods of trial, which, under a variety of plausible pretences, may in time imperceptibly undermine this best preservative of English liberty.'

"Mr. Justice Blackstone terms the English Trial by Jury, the glory of the English law. Let me tell you, our trial by jury is that kind of glory in full meridian lustre, in comparison of which the English mode appears only with diminished splendor. But let not your care of this great object occupy all your attention. You are to find all such Bills of indictment, as the examination of witnesses in support of them, may induce you to think there is a probability that the fact charged is true; for you are not to exact such circumstantial and positive evidence as would be necessary to support the indictment before a Petit Jury.

"To make these Presentments, and to find these Bills, it is not necessary that you all agree in opinion, twelve united voices among you are sufficient to discharge the duties of a Grand Jury; but it is absolutely necessary that twelve of you agree in opinion upon every point under your consideration; and happy, happy, thrice happy are that people who cannot be made to suffer under any construction of the law, but by the united voices of twenty-four impartial men, having no interest in the cause, but that the laws be executed and justice administered. In short, that you may discharge your duty with propriety, and that you may pursue that course of conduct which the law requires, let me, in the strongest terms, recommend to you, that you keep constantly in your mind the nature and particulars of the oath which you have just taken. To you, this oath is of as much importance as the mariner's compass is to those who sail on the ocean; this points out the course of their voyage; your oath as clearly points out to you the course of your conduct. I dare say you are willing to discharge that duty which you owe to society. I make no doubt but that you will discharge it with advantage to the public, and therefore with honor to yourselves."*

This able and eloquent vindication of their rights, and spirited appeal to his fellow-citizens, both as Americans and British subjects, appears to have been carefully prepared for the occasion, and delivered by the Judge at the other Courts on the Circuit. It was a most critical juncture in the affairs of the Colonies. The lines were being drawn, and the people were ranging themselves on one side or the other, for the rapidly approaching struggle. And then it was, that no more timely or influential voice was heard among them than that of William Henry Drayton. Whether here, or during his subsequent mission, with Rev. Mr. Tennent, among the disaffected in the Ninety-Six District,— or in his charges afterwards to the Grand Juries of Charlestown, as Chief Justice, or in the Continental Congress— wherever he appeared, the same thrilling tones were heard in behalf of liberty.

The Petit Jury were so much roused by the charge on

*"American Archives," vol. i. pp. 959-962; also, *So. Ca. and American General Gazette*, December 16-23, 1774.

this occasion that they were induced to present (though a most unusual course for such a body), a formal address in reply, breathing throughout the lofty spirit of constitutional obligation and patriotic devotion to liberty, which his Honor had impressed upon them. It was in these words:

"May it please your Honor,

"As your Charge at the opening of the Sessions contained matters of the highest importance to every individual in this Colony, as well as to the Grand Jury, to whom in particular it was delivered, we, the Petit Jury for the District of Cheraw, beg leave to testify our great satisfaction, and to return your Honor our warmest acknowledgements for so constitutional a charge at this alarming crisis, when our liberties are attacked, and our properties invaded by the claim and attempt of the British Parliament to tax us, and by their edicts to bind us in all cases they deem proper; a claim to which we will never submit, and an attempt which we are determined to oppose at the hazard of our lives and property; being fully convinced, that by the Constitution of this Country, we owe obedience to no human laws but such as are enacted with the consent of our Representatives in General Assembly. These being our fixed sentiments, we take this opportunity of publicly declaring them; and we would esteem it a particular favor conferred on us, if your Honor would direct your Charge to be printed, that the benefit arising from it may be as diffusive as possible, and that it may remain as a pattern of that constitutional language which a Judge should deliver, who is above Ministerial influence, and knows no *Master* but the *Law*.*

"Claudius Pegues, *Foreman*.
William White.
William Hardwick.
Zachariah Nettles.
Benjamin Williamson.
Benjamin Rogers.

---

*"American Archives," vol. i. p. 959. This invaluable collection of the records of the few years preceding the Revolution is to be found in the Charleston Library. *S. C. Gazette*, December 16-23, 1774.

Enoch James.
William Hickman.
Jacob Bruce.
Benjamin Davis.
Stephen Jackson.
Joseph Parsons."

This early declaration of their rights, as American freemen, and of determined resistance to the encroachments of the British Crown to the last extremity, reflected immortal honor upon the bold and inflexible patriots of the Old Cheraws! Carolina sent forth no timelier or more fearless voice from her borders. Nor were the Grand Jury, to whom the charge of his Honor was more specially directed, wanting in the spirit befitting such a crisis. They took the matter into anxious consideration, and on the 19th of November, the day following the address of the Petit Jury, made their Presentments in these words (relating first to local matters) :—

"I. We present, as a grievance, the want of a Law for clearing Pedee River, and to prevent trees being felled therein, its navigation at present being unsafe.

"II. We present, as a grievance, the want of a Law to prevent the hunting of deer by fire in the night time, by which means many horses and neat cattle are destroyed, to the great damage of the owners.

"III. We present Andrew Gibson for wilful and deliberate perjury; by the information of George Cusack.

"IV. We present, as a grievance of the first magnitude, the right claimed by the British Parliament to tax us, and by their acts to bind us in all cases whatsoever. When we reflect on our other grievances, they all appear trifling in comparison with this; for if we may be taxed, imprisoned, and deprived of life, by the force of edicts to which neither we or our Constitutional Representatives have ever assented no slavery can be more abject than ours.

"We are, however, sensible that we have a better security for our lives, our liberties, and fortunes, than the mere will of the Parliament of Great Britain; and are fully convinced that we cannot be constitutionally taxed but by

Representatives of our own election, or bound by any laws than those to which they have assented.

"This right of being exempted from all laws but those enacted with the consent of Representatives of our own election, we deem so essential to our freedom, and so engrafted in our Constitution, that we are determined to defend it at the hazard of our lives and fortunes; and we earnestly request that this Presentment may be laid before our Constitutional Representatives, the Commons House of Assembly of this Colony, that it may be known how much we prize our freedom, and how resolved we are to preserve it.

"We recommend that these Presentments be published in the several *Gazettes* of this Province.*

Alexander M'Intosh, *Foreman*.	L.S.
Henry W. Harrington.	L.S.
Thomas Ayres.	L.S.
Robert Blair.	L.S.
William Pegues.	L.S.
Robert Lide.	L.S.
George Hicks.	L.S.
John Hodges.	L.S.
Arthur Hart.	L.S.
Elias Du Bois.	L.S.
Robert Clary.	L.S.
Martin Dewitt.	L.S.
Thomas Ellerbe.	L.S.
Martin Kolb.	L.S.
John Kimbrough.	L.S.
Moses Speight.	L.S.
Thomas Lide.	L.S.
Thomas James.	L.S.
John Wilds.	L.S.
Thomas Edwards.	L.S.

"Whereupon the following order was passed, viz.:—
"South Carolina,
"Cheraws District.
"At a Court of General Sessions of the Peace, Oyer and

---

* "American Archives," vol. i. p. 959; *S. C. Gazette*, Dec. 16-23, 1774.

Terminer, Assize and General Jail Delivery, begun and holden at Cheraws, on the 15th day of November, in the year of our Lord, 1774, before the Honorable William Henry Drayton, Esq., one of the Justices of our Sovereign Lord the King, Ordered, that the Charge of his Honor, the Judge, together with the address presented to his Honor by the Petit Jury, immediately before their discharge on the 18th inst., and the Presentments of the Grand Jury, the next day, at the present Sessions, be published in the several *Gazettes* of this Province.

"By the Court,
"CALVIN SPENCER,
"D.C.C. & P."

Thus, in language as manly as had been previously uttered, did the Grand Jury give expression to those lofty sentiments which had taken deep hold of the hearts of the people. In doing so, they gave utterance to those convictions which repeated acts of oppression had only served to strengthen. The idea of a true constitutional representation was now as thoroughly comprehended, as the determination was fixed to secure it, or perish in the attempt.

It is questionable, whether any earlier or bolder declaration of rights is to be found in our Provincial records.

The Charge of Judge Drayton, delivered at the Cheraws, and other Courts of the Circuit, with the Presentments of the several Grand Juries, was laid by the Ministers before the two Houses of Parliament, and made the subject of exciting and indignant comment.*

In his celebrated Charge to the Grand Jury of Charlestown, in April, 1776— a charge "replete with patriotism, reasoning, and learning"—Judge Drayton, then Chief Justice, alluded to this subject, saying: "The British Ministers already have presented a Charge of mine to the notice of the Lords and Commons in Parliament; and I am nothing loath that they take equal resentment against this Charge. For, supported by the fundamental laws of the Constitution, and engaged as I am in the cause of virtue, I fear no consequences from their machinations."†

*Drayton's "Memoirs," vol. i. p. 216.   †Preface to ditto, p. xvi.

It was to be expected, that a Judge, who could speak in tones of such eloquent defiance, would be speedily removed from the Bench; and accordingly, he was superseded the next month (December), by a more subservient successor.

The important part performed by Judge Drayton in preparing the way for Independence, has not in later times been fully estimated.

He left a kingly bench only to shine with more brilliant lustre, if possible, as Chief Justice of a Republican Court; and from that high position to be transferred to the Continental Congress by the united voice of his countrymen. While engaged in the active labors of that body in Philadelphia, in Sept. 1779, his honored life was prematurely brought to a close, not having completed by a few days his thirty-seventh year. Seldom indeed has such a man, at so early an age, gone down to the grave, after a career of labour and a reputation like his. The sounds of universal mourning were heard, and Carolina grieved as a mother for her favorite son!

In the midst of the excitement to which the discussion of the momentous questions of political rights and constitutional liberty gave birth, the debt of charity which common sufferings in a common cause created, was not overlooked.

One of the resolutions passed at the General Provincial Meeting in Charles-town, in July (1774), was in these words, viz. :—

"Resolved, That while the oppressive acts relative to Boston are enforced, we will cheerfully, from time to time, contribute towards the relief of those poor persons there, whose unfortunate circumstances may be thought to stand in need of most assistance."

Before this time, indeed, subscriptions had been opened in Charles-town to relieve the suffering poor of Boston, who had been usually employed in the trade of that town, and were now by the acts of the British Government deprived of employment. On the 29th of June, 204 barrels of rice were sent from Charles-town for their support, while the subscription was still promoted, as a source of future supply.* There was a general response throughout the Province.

The following interesting record remains to do honor to the patriotic sympathies of the people of the Pedee. The list embraces the names chiefly of persons in the middle and upper parts of St. David's Parish. Other similar subscriptions were doubtless circulated.

Account of Cash received for the Poor of Boston, by Henry W. Harrington.

			£	s.	d.
1774. Dec. 27.					
Of Philip Pledger			13	0	0
Of Arthur Hart			7	7	0
Of H. W. Harrington			13	0	0
Of John Warden,	by Mr. Hart		1	15	0
Of Abraham Parks,	by	ditto	3	10	0
Of Noble Barnard,	by	ditto	1	12	6
Of George Wright,	by	ditto	1	12	6
Of Ethelred Rogers,	by	ditto	1	12	6
1774. Dec. 30.					
Of Walter Downs			1	12	6
1775. Jan. 2.					
Of Henry Councel			1	12	6
Of Claudius Pegues,	by Mr. Hicks		13	0	0
Of Thomas Lide,	by	ditto	13	0	0
Of Nathanael Saunders,	by	ditto	8	5	0
Of Malachi Murfee, Jun.,	by	ditto	8	2	6
Of James Reed,	by	ditto	1	12	6
Of Thomas Williams,	by	ditto	1	12	6
Of John Andrews,	by	ditto	1	0	0
Of Burrell Boykin,	by	ditto	3	5	0
Of William Pegues,	by	ditto	7	7	0
Of James Sanders,	by	ditto	10	0	0
Of David Roche,	by	Self	1	12	6
Of George Hicks,	by	ditto	10	0	0
			£125	11	6

Paid this sum to Col. G. G. Powell.

*Drayton's "Memoirs," vol. i. p. 113.

1775. Jan. 27.   £   s. d.
   Of Daniel Sparks, by self 1 12 6
1775. Feb. 7.
   Of Thomas Ellerbe 6   0 0
   Of William Hardick 1 12 6
   Of Thomas Bingham 1 12 6
   Of Francis Gillespie 3   5 0
   Of John Donaldson 5   0 0
   Of Magnus Corgill, 5 bush. corn, at 12s. 6d. 3 2 6
1775. May 23.
   Of Abel Edwards 2 10 0
                                                   24 15 0
  Of the Council of Safety, agreeably to an order
    of the Committee 27 0 0
                                                   £51 15 0

                            Cr.
1775. May 20.   £   s. d.
  By cash paid by H. W. Harrington
    to Pike Johnson, for bringing an
    express 27 0 0
1776. Nov. 2.
  By cash paid to the Committee by
    H. W. Harrington 24 15 0
                                          51 15 0*

Thus the year, 1774, in its eventful progress, drew to a close—a year for ever memorable in the history of St. David's Parish and the "Old Cheraws."

To the first appeals in behalf of liberty, a hearty response was made by their inhabitants.

---

*The original book of entry, with this subscription and other interesting and very valuable matter, was found among the papers of Philip Pledger, Esq., of Marlborough, already referred to, and though subsequently used for common purposes of memorandum and account, happily escaped the ravages of time, and remains, in all probability, the only relic of the kind connected with the efforts made by the patriots of Carolina, under the action of the Provincial Congress, for raising funds for the suffering poor of Boston—the saddest commentary, it may also be added, furnished by the history of that era, on the changes that have taken place since!

The approaching crisis found them ready, intelligent, watchful, and unyielding defenders of every sacred right. Among the first to make known their political sentiments to the world, they were not behind the foremost in the vigor and boldness of style in which those sentiments were expressed. The documents which have been given, will compare favorably with any of a similar kind to which this eventful era gave birth; and were only surpassed, if at all, as to a spirit of lofty defiance, by sentiments subsequently uttered by the patriots of the Pedee themselves.

And yet, so slow are mankind to relinquish long-existing habits of thought and feeling, and so deeply rooted is the attachment to forms of Government immemorially established, that even at this point, far as they had gone, any reasonable concessions on the part of the Crown and the repeal of a few odious acts of Parliament, with the exhibition of a spirit of justice and consideration for the Colonies, might have turned back the rising tide of rebellion, and secured for the king once more the affection of his faithful subjects.

But such concessions were not to be made. The suicidal policy of the Government was pursued with a strange infatuation. The die had been cast. The hand of Providence was in the work; and many tribes and tongues who looked from afar upon the unnatural conflict, deeply interested in its issues, anxiously waited for their final deliverance, and rejoiced as the end came, to call the patriots of America blessed!

CHAPTER XI.

Last days of Royalty in So. Ca.—List of appointees of the Crown published—Object of publication—Magistrates for Cheraws District—Regimental officers of militia for Cheraws—Meeting of Provincial Congress—Account of it—Members for St. David's—District committees appointed—Committee of St. David's—Duties of committees—Their powers—Additional power given—Inhabitants to arm themselves—Circuit Court for Cheraws—His Majesty's Justices appear for last time—Presentment of grand jury of Cheraws—Attempt of Court to quash chief presentment—It appears in the papers—Reflections on these proceedings—Grand jury exponent of popular sentiment—Congress called together before time fixed for meeting—Circular letter on subject—Articles of Association adopted—Other resolves—Military ardor of people—Provincial officers elected by Congress from St. David's—Names of persons added to Committee of Observation for St. David's—Action of committee as to Colonel Steward and John Mitchell—New election for Congress ordered—Spirit of volunteering—William Henry Harrington commissioned Captain—Stockade Fort at Cheraws—History of it—Volunteering increases—Commissions issued for St. David's parish—Dissatisfactions—Captain Wise resigns—His character—Congress meets—Its action as to St. David's—Detachment from Colonel Powell's regiment ordered to join Colonel Richardson—Major Thomas marches—Colonel Hicks stopped—Conflict with Tories on Pedee—Concluding remarks.

WITH the opening of the year 1775, everything indicated the approach of the last days of Royalty in South Carolina. There was an evident effort on the part of the officers of the Crown, if not to assume more authority, at least to make the most, by public demonstrations, of what they had. Their object was to impress and overawe the people. The time, however, for effect, by means like these, had passed. The charm which Majesty had carried with it was gone. The insignia of office did not attract as heretofore, while promises and threats, though in the name of the King, were stript of their ancient powers.

There was in the popular mind a growing consciousness of right, and of the strength which a righteous cause imparts. Names now passed for what they were worth, and things were rated according to their intrinsic value.

So it has ever been in the history of those great revolutions in human opinion which have overthrown successive dynasties, or hurled the mightiest monarchs from their thrones. Once the veil is taken away and the bonds are cast asunder, the progress of liberal thought becomes henceforth as rapid as it had been fixed, or even retrograde in its state of unnatural bondage. Men wonder then that they did not discover the right or see the wrong before, and wondering thus, are not unfrequently impelled to hasty, and as a consequence, unhealthy action. The decline of royalty from what it had been in the American Colonies before the opening stages of the Revolution, is in some respects a sadly touching story. So much was there on the one hand to be lost and such wondrous pomp to be brought low, with so many long-existing ties on the other to be rudely severed, that the heart cannot remain unmoved at the recital.

The year 1775 opened with an order on the part of Government, the object of which seems to have been, in part at least, to recall the leading inhabitants, by the very fact and public declaration of official position, to a sense of their allegiance to the king; and also to impress the people, by such an exhibition of royal prerogative, with the vigor and determination of the existing rule.

This action was as follows, viz. :—

"South Carolina, Jan. 9th, 1775.

"It is ordered by his Honor, the Lieutenant-Governor, in Council, that the names of the Magistrates for the several districts in this Province be printed in the several *Gazettes*."*

The names of the Magistrates for Cheraw District, as published, were these, viz.: "William Arthur, Thomas Wade, James Lindlay, Henry Patrick, Claudius Pegues, Charles Augustus Steward, Thomas Turner, John Perkins, Arthur Hart, Alexander M'Intosh, Philip Pledger, and Wm. Henry Harrington." In this list of his Majesty's Justices for Cheraws, are found the names of some who had already become conspicuous from their opposition to the encroachments of the Crown. It may have been a stroke of policy as to them; but if so, it seems to little purpose that the

*So. Ca. Gazette, January 6-13, 1775.

effort was made. These devoted friends of liberty never faltered in the course they had begun. They were true indeed to their king, as far as he would allow them to be, but not less true to themselves, as the first instincts of nature prompted them.

The names of the officers of the Provincial Militia were likewise published in the early part of this year. The militia at this time consisted of twelve regiments of foot and one of horse. The Regiment of Cheraws District was the 7th of Foot, with the following officers, viz.: George Gabriel Powell, Colonel; Charles Augustus Steward, Lieut.-Col., and Abraham Buckholdts, Major.* These officers were all of royal appointment, and hence the appeal to their fidelity, and the stigma, as it was thought, which might thus be made to attach to their desertion from their sovereign's cause. If the Government, long established, was to continue undisturbed in the exercise of its authority, the increasing pressure of the time called for redoubled efforts, and made it necessary for the prerogatives of the king to be stretched to their utmost bounds.

The delegates elected by the several districts and parishes in November, were to meet in Charles-town on the 11th of January of this year.

This new representative body was destined to give shape and effectiveness to the rising spirit of discontent throughout the colony, and to mark an era in its history.

The following notice of its first assembling appeared in the papers of the day.

"Charles-town, Jan. 13th, 1775.

"On Wednesday last the gentlemen chosen by the several parishes, &c., in this Province, convened here in a general meeting, and elected Charles Pinckney, Esq., Chairman. The meeting has been continued every day since, and is now sitting. We have been favored with the following list of the gentlemen elected."† Of these, the names for St. David were those already given, viz.: Hon. George Gabriel Powell, Samuel Wise, Claudius Pegues,

---
*Drayton's "Memoirs," vol. i. p. 352.
†*Gazette,* January 13, 1775.

Alexander M'Intosh, Henry William Harrington, Esqrs., and Col. George Pawley. During the session the members resolved themselves into "a Provincial Congress," and the body was thus designated afterward. The proceedings of the Continental Congress, which had adjourned in October previous, were submitted to its consideration. One of the Articles of Association, adopted by the Continental Congress on the 26th October, was in these words, viz.: "Eleventh— That a Committee be chosen in every county, city, and town by those who are qualified to vote for Representatives in the Legislature, whose business it shall be attentively to observe the conduct of all persons touching this association; and when it shall be made to appear to the satisfaction of a majority of any such Committee, that any person within the limits of their appointment has violated this association, that such majority do forthwith cause the truth of the case to be published in the *Gazettes,* to the end that all such foes to the rights of British America may be publicly known and universally contemned as the enemies of American liberty; and thenceforth we respectively will break off all dealings with him or her."* In accordance with this recommendation, it was resolved by the Privincial Congress, on the first day of its sitting, that the following gentlemen be the committees for the several districts and parishes hereinafter mentioned, for effectually carrying into execution the Continental Association, and for receiving and determining upon applications relative to the law processes, &c. The committee under this resolution for the Parish of St. David consisted of the following gentlemen, viz.: Henry William Harrington, George Pawley, Alexander M'Intosh, Claudius Pegues, Burwell Boyakin, George Hicks, Philip Pledger, and John Donaldson. According to the system of Government and its subordinate authorities for the Colony, established by the Congress, the representatives of the parishes and districts respectively composed their local committees; and they were also assisted by Committees of Inspection. The Provincial Congress made all these appointments in the first instance; and even filled up the

*Ramsay's "Revolution in So. Ca.," vol. i. p. 258.

double returns of representatives, in order that no time should be lost in giving a complete appearance to the body politic and the greatest energy to their operations; but all future vacancies were to be filled up by the respective districts and parishes in which they should occur.

By these arrangements an independent authority virtually arose; while the Royal Government retained little else than public officers without power, and a show of government without the means of supporting it.* This plan seems not to have been carried out fully as to St. David's Parish, so far as the committee being identical with its delegates in the Congress.

The Committees of Inspection were distributed throughout the district or parish, so as to secure a thorough oversight in every part. The central or executive committee was to meet twice a month for consultation and despatch of business. The system was admirably arranged, and gave unity and efficiency to the general efforts to prepare the way for revolution and a change of government.

It was further resolved, "That it is the unanimous opinion of this Congress, that no action for any debt shall be commenced in the Court of Common Pleas of this colony, nor any such action pending there, which was commenced since last September return, be proceeded in, without the consent of the committee of the parish or district in which the defendant resides, until it shall be otherwise determined in Provincial Congress—That the said committees respectively, or a majority of such of them as shall meet (provided they are not less than three, in the country parishes and districts), do, upon application, give permission for the bringing or proceeding in such suits, in the following cases—that is to say, where the debtors refused to renew their obligations, or to give reasonable security, or are justly suspected of intending to leave the Province, or to defraud their creditors, or where there shall appear to the majority of such committees, as aforesaid, any other reasonable cause for the granting such permission; which committees shall meet and sit on the first and

---
*Drayton's "Memoirs," vol. i. p. 175.

third Saturdays in every month, at twelve o'clock at noon, or oftener, as it shall be found necessary, for the purposes of hearing and determining on such applications. That seizures and sales upon mortgages shall be considered on the same footing as actions for debt. That it be recommended to the committees for each parish and district, that they use their best endeavours to prevent any debtors from removing their effects out of the colony, without the knowledge and consent of their creditors. That the Congress will indemnify the committees for so doing. And that no summons shall be issued by any magistrate in small and mean causes, without the like consent."*

A resolution passed at a subsequent meeting of the Congress in June, conferred additional powers on the committees, and was in these words:—"Resolved, that any person having violated, or refused obedience to the authority of the Provincial Congress, shall, by the committee of the district or parish in which such offender resides, be questioned relative thereto; and upon due conviction of either of the offences aforesaid, and continuing contumacious, such person shall, by such committee, be declared and advertised as an enemy to the liberties of America, and an object of the resentment of the public; and that the said committee shall be supported in so doing."†

The committees were requested to use their utmost endeavors to obtain liberal subscriptions for the suffering people of Boston.

Resolutions were also passed, recommending that all the inhabitants of the colony should be attentive in learning the use of arms; and that their officers should train and exercise them at least once a fortnight.

The Congress then adjourned, January 17th, until it should be called together by the Charles-town General Committee.

Such was the state of things now, that those who were not well affected began to be seriously alarmed, and, doubtless, to organize as well as they could for the approaching

---

*"American Archives," vol. i. p. 1109.
†Ibid., p. 953, and "Journal of the Congress."

conflict. Some evidences of this will be found towards the close of the year. Others, not willing to take up arms against their adopted country, arranged their affairs so as to go abroad. Events were transpiring in rapid succession, startling to the officers of the Crown, and committing the rising sons of liberty more unchangeably to the lofty and unyielding position they had taken.

Once more were the people of Cheraws District, in the highest capacity known to the law, to make a public declaration of their sentiments, but not, as before, in the presence of one who had encouraged them, by his own fearless bearing and eloquent tones, to resistance.

His Majesty's Justices made their last circuit in the spring of 1775. The successor of Judge Drayton, Justice Gregory, with Justice Savage, appeared on the Northern Circuit. The course of Judge Drayton had equally alarmed and offended the Royal Government, and it was doubtless arranged for his successor to preside in this part of the Province for the first time, so as to efface to some extent, if possible, the impression which had been made, and stem at the outset the tide of independence.

Some evidences of such an attempt, though worse than fruitless, will be found in the conduct of the King's Judges on this occasion.

The action of the Grand Jury, so far as it was published by order of the Court, was as follows, viz.:—

"The Presentments of the Grand Jurors for the District of Cheraws, &c., at Long Bluff, Saturday, the 15th day of April, 1775.

"I. We present, as a grievance, the want of a new Jury list in this district.

"II. We present, as a grievance, the want of a Law for cleansing Pedee River, and to prevent trees being felled therein, its navigation at present being extremely dangerous.

"III. We present, as a grievance, the want of a Bridge over Thompson's Creek, on the road from the Cheraw Hill to the Court House; and another over Black Creek, at or near the present ferry.

"IV. We present, as a very great grievance, the want of

a Vagrant Act in this Province; this District in particular being much infested by many idle people, who have no visible way of obtaining an honest livelihood.

"We present, as a grievance, the little notice generally taken of the Presentments of the Grand Juries of this district.

"Lastly. We recommend that these, our Presentments, may, by order of the Court, be laid before the Commons House of Assembly of this Colony, and be made public in the *Gazettes*.

"Thomas Lide, *Foreman*.	L.S.
Samuel Wise.	L.S.
John Kimbrough.	L.S.
John Ellerbe.	L.S.
Charles M'Call.	L.S.
Wiliiam Dewitt.	L.S.
Peter Kolb.	L.S.
Moses Speight.	L.S.
Aaron Daniel.	L.S.
Magnus Corgill.	L.S.
Zachariah Nettles.	L.S.
Benjamin Jackson.	L.S.
Claudius Pegues.	L.S.
William Pouncey.	L.S.
Benjamin Rogers.	L.S.
Thomas Bingham.	L.S."

Unfortunately for the cause of royalty, the additional matter was published, viz.:—

"The Grand Jury likewise offered the following as a Presentment, but it was quashed by the Court: 'We present, as an enormous grievance, the power exercised by the British Parliament of taxing and making laws, binding upon the American Colonies in all cases whatsoever, such power being subversive of the most inestimable rights of British subjects—that of being taxed by their consent only, given by their Representatives in General Assembly, and that of trial by jury—both which are evidently inherent in every British American, and of which no power on earth can legally deprive them: We, well knowing the importance of these rights, in securing to us our liberties, lives, and estates, and conceiving it to be every man's indispensable duty to transmit them to his posterity, are fully determined to defend them at the hazard of our lives and fortunes.

"'At the same time that we thus openly declare how highly we prize our rights, we beg leave to assure your Honor that we have a due sense of that allegiance, so strongly recommended to us by your Honor in your charge; and that while our Sovereign adheres to his part of that original and reciprocal contract made with his people, and expressed in his Coronation Oath, none of his subjects shall exceed us in constitutional submission and fidelity.

"'As your Honor, on the second day of the Sessions, was pleased, not only to acquaint us your Honor had been informed, "that some of the magistrates of this district had declared to the people that there was no law," but also to recommend to us, "to make strict inquiry, and to present all such magistrates, that they might be deservedly struck out of the commission of the peace:" we think it incumbent on us to assure your Honor that, notwithstanding we have made all possible enquiry, we have not received the least information, except from your Honor, in the general terms above expressed, of any of the magistrates having acted so exceedingly indiscreetly; and therefore, we cannot but conceive, that some wicked, malicious persons, enemies to the happiness and prosperity of this country, have endeavored, by false and secret accusations, to prejudice your Honor against some of the magistrates in this district; but, as the informers have not thought proper to support their accusations in public, which they venture to advance in private, we trust that your Honor will transfer your displeasure from the innocent accused, to the base accusers.'"*

It is manifest, from this bold and spirited document, which the Court very unwisely and vainly attempted to suppress, that the people of Cheraws District, instead of receding from the position taken the year before, had gone further in the fearless expression of their sentiments, and in commenting on the remissness of the Government. It

*Gazette, June 9-16, 1775.

had not yet become customary to call public meetings, except in the larger towns, as a means of giving expression to the opinions of the people on questions of political moment. The settlements in the interior were too remote from each other to render it practicable. The Grand Jury was therefore made the exponent of the popular sentiment, as the most authoritative and imposing organ by which the feelings of a people, under such circumstances, could be expressed. Though the Court could quash, the Press could not be silenced. And what his Majesty's Justice would not allow to be entered on the records, was given shortly after, in a more public form, to the world. The Grand Jury of Cheraws is believed to have been the only one in the Province which made the wrongs inflicted by the Crown the subject of presentment during the Spring Assizes.*

Their vindication of the magistrates,† upon whom the Court reflected with so much severity, was as bold as the calling attention to the fact "of the little notice generally taken of the Presentments of the Grand Juries of this District."

The issue was now made with the King by his loyal subjects, on the ground of his own solemn coronation oath, the principle being, "that protection and subjection are reciprocal; and that these reciprocal duties form the original contract between King and people"‡—a contract which is broken if the Sovereign oppresses on the one hand, or fails, through any fault of his, on the other, to afford due protection.

The tide of events was rolling on. The Provincial Congress had adjourned to meet on the 20th of June.

But intelligence of the battle of Lexington, which had taken place on the 19th of April, reached Charles-town, and was laid before the General Committee on the 8th of May. Upon which a vote was passed to summon the Congress to meet on the first day of June. For now that hostilities had

---

*The Courts of Charles-town, George-town, and Beaufort, at least, were silent, and the silence of the press leads to the inference that others were also.

†The list of magistrates, as given on a foregoing page, embraced some of the most prominent and influential men in the district. They had doubtless made themselves obnoxious to the Crown.

‡Judge Drayton's charge to Grand Jury of Charles-town, "Ramsay," vol. i. p. 114.

actually commenced, immediate and decided measures were deemed necessary for promoting the public welfare. One of the Circular Letters sent out to call the Congress together, was as follows, viz.:—

"To the Committee for the Parish of St. David.
"To the care of Henry Wm. Harrington, Esqr.
"On the Public Service.

"Charles-town, May 8th, 1775.

"Gentlemen,—We enclose you a newspaper, giving an important account of an action between the British Troops and the Bostonians. Upon this interesting event, the General Committee have thought it absolutely necessary to call the Provincial Congress to meet at an earlier day than the 20th of June. They have therefore resolved that the Congress shall meet in Charles-town on the 1st of June.

We hereby transmit a proper notice of this new appointment, and hope you will punctually attend at the appointed time. The General Committee have also given in charge to us, to recommend in the strongest terms to you, to cause the patrols to ride often and diligently, as we have intelligence of exciting the slaves to revolt has been laid before Administration; and you are desired to keep this intelligence relating to the slaves as secret as may be.

"We are Gentlemen,
"Your most obedient servants,
WM. HENRY DRAYTON.
CHARLES COTESWORTH PINCKNEY.
WM. TENNENT.
ARTHUR MIDDLETON.
JOHN LEWIS GERVAIS.

"P.S.—You will give as general notice to the Members of the Congress as you possibly can."

Of the diabolical plan here alluded to, for exciting the slaves to revolt, no further notice appears in the histories of the day. If conceived at all, it was doubtless found to be either impracticable, or calculated to drive the inhabitants to desperate measures of revenge, and hence abandoned.

On the 1st of June, one hundred and seventy-two members of the Congress met, and such was the zeal of the people and alarm felt throughout the Province, that on the second day, an Association was considered and passed, to be entered into by the inhabitants of the colony, to which the members forthwith affixed their names. It was in these words, viz. :—

"South Carolina.

"The actual commencement of hostilities against this continent by the British Troops, in the bloody scene on the 19th of April last, near Boston, the increase of arbitrary impositions from a wicked and despotic ministry, and the dread of insurrection in the colonies—are causes sufficient to drive an oppressed people to the use of arms. We, therefore, the Subscribers, inhabitants of South Carolina, holding ourselves bound by that most sacred of all obligations, the duty of good citizens towards an injured country, and thoroughly convinced, that under our present distressed circumstances, we shall be justified before God and man in resisting force by force; do unite ourselves, under every tie of religion and honor, and associate as a band in her defence against every foe; hereby solemnly engaging that, whenever our Continental or Provincial Councils shall decree it necessary, we will go forth and be ready to sacrifice our lives and fortunes to secure her freedom and support. This obligation to continue in full force until a reconciliation shall take place between Great Britain and America, upon Constitutional principles, an event which we most ardently desire. And we will hold all those persons inimical to the liberties of the colonies who shall refuse to subscribe this association."

Non-subscribers were made amendable to the General Committee and by them punishable, according to sound policy.

It was also resolved, "That all absentees holding estates in the colony, except those who were abroad on account of their health, and those above 60 years, and those under 21, ought forthwith to return; and that no persons holding estates in this colony ought to withdraw from its service, without giving good and sufficient reason for so doing, to the Provincial Congress; or, during its recess, to the General Committee."* On the 5th day of the session, the Congress resolved to raise 1500 Infantry, rank and file, in two regiments; and 450 Horse Rangers, constituting another regiment. Proper pay, clothing, and provisions were assigned them; and the troops so raised were to be subjected to military discipline and the articles of war, in like manner as the British troops were governed.

So great, we are told, was the military ardor among the gentlemen of the Province, that the candidates for commissions in the proposed regiments were four times as numerous as could be employed; and in their number were many of the first families and fortune. In making a selection among the numerous candidates that offered, care was taken to choose men of influence, decision and spirit, residing in different parts of the Province, so as to unite all its energies in the common cause.

Four or five had the recommendation of having served in the war of 1756; but the other candidates were preferred solely on the ground of their possessing the natural qualifications requisite for making good officers, in addition to their holding an influential rank among their fellow citizens.†

Soon after the resolution passed for raising the regiments, a ballot for officers was held. Of these, Alexander M'Intosh, of Cheraws, was elected Major of the 2nd Regiment. He had held the commission of captain some years before. His decision and energy, with a commanding person and ample fortune, gave him a peculiar fitness for the position. Of the Regiment of Rangers, Samuel Wise and Eli Kershaw, from the Cheraw District, were elected Captains, and John Donaldson, a First Lieutenant. On the 18th of June, Isaac DuBose received the commission of Second Lieut. in the 2nd Regiment of Foot. Major M'Intosh was soon after promoted, and continued in active service. Captain Wise was also promoted to the rank of Major in the same Regiment.

---

*Drayton's "Memoirs," vol. i. pp. 255, 256.
†"Ramsay," new edition, p. 135.

In meeting of the Council of Safety in Charles-town, 23rd June, 1775, it was resolved, "That, in prosecution of the Resolution of the Provincial Congress of the 19th inst., the Committee of Observation for the Parish of St. David, do allow Mr. John Mitchell, of Meldrum, the sum of seventeen shillings, sixpence, per pound, for three hundred and ninety-two pounds weight of gunpowder, bought of him, and that they do draw for payment thereof, upon this Council.

"Resolved, That the said gunpowder do remain in the hands of the said committee, for the public service, and that they do account for the same with this Council."*

On the 22nd of June, the Provincial Congress Resolved, "That the following gentlemen be added to the Committee of Observation for the Parish of St. David, viz., Messrs. David Williams, Ely Kershaw, William Dewitt, Thomas Ellerbe, John Alran, John Kimbrough, William Pegues, Elias Du Bois, Charles Evans, Junr., Benjamin Rogers, Arthur Hart, Robert Lide, Aaron Daniel, Francis Gillespie, Thomas Powe, Thomas Lide, Henry Counsel, Thomas Edwards, Benjamin Jackson, and Abel Kolb."†

The duties of the committee were most responsible and arduous, and the number first appointed, doubtless, proved too small to take due oversight of the extensive territory embraced within the limits of St. David's. Of those here added, there was about an equal distribution among the different sections of the parish.

It was not long before they were called to take decisive action as to two of their fellow-citizens, who had hitherto maintained a highly respectable position as neighbors and friends.

The following record of their proceedings remains.‡

"In Committee of Observation.
"St. David's Parish, August 7th, 1775.

"Charles Augustus Steward, Esq., having counteracted the Resolves of the Provincial Congress in frequently issuing

---

*"Collections of Historical Society of So. Ca.," vol. ii. p. 27.
†Supplement to *Carolina Gazette* of September 7th, 1775.
‡*So. Ca. Gazette*, October 3, 1775.

summons for debt, was this day caused to appear before the committee for said Parish, and being questioned relative thereto, acknowledged that he had done so, and, if applied to, should again.

"Resolved, thereupon, that the said Charles Augustus Steward, Esq., is an enemy to the liberties of America, and an object of the resentment of the public. Ordered, that the same be publicly advertised on the morrow.

"By order of the Committee,
"GEORGE HICKS,
"Chairman."

Colonel Steward appears not to have receded from the position thus rashly and boldly taken; and from that moment, advertised and regarded as an enemy to the liberties of America, his career was decided, and took a downward turn, ending a few years after in a decline of fortune, a broken spirit, the confiscation of his estate,* and a premature close of his life.

Another case also engaged the attention of the Committee, and seemed for the time at least to have been happily disposed of.

"In Committee of Observation.

"St. David's Parish, August 8th, 1775.

"Mr. John Mitchell having signed the under-written advertisement, it was ordered that the same be immediately published in the several *Gazettes* of this Province.

"By order of the Committee,
"HENRY WILLIAM HARRINGTON,
"Chairman."

"St. David's Parish, August 8th, 1775.

"Whereas, I, John Mitchell, of Meldrum, in the said parish, merchant, having sent three judgment bonds to Thomas Phepoe, Esq., to be by him entered up, and having received three executions of the said gentleman in May last, one of which has been since personally served by the Sheriff on John and Bartholomew Hodges, and one other

---

*His estate was relieved from the penalties of confiscation, as will be seen hereafter.

on Enoch James, contrary to the Resolves of the first session of the Provincial Congress, for which I am truly sorry, and humbly ask pardon of the said Congress, and of their constituents, sincerely promising never to act in the least contrary to the Resolves or orders of the Honorable Continental Congress, or of our Provincial Congress, being fully convinced that every friend to America ought religiously to observed the Resolves and Orders of the said Congress and Councils.

"Given under my hand, the day and year above written.
"JOHN MITCHELL."*

Notwithstanding this timely warning and seemingly penitent resolve, Mr. Mitchell, though never in arms, took sides against his country, in the contest which soon came on. His estate was afterwards confiscated. It will be remembered, that the notice of his departure from the Province, already given, was in March of this year.

A new general election for members of the Provincial Congress was appointed to take place in the Country Districts and Parishes on the 8th of August, after which the Congress adjourned.

Much of its authority was delegated to the Council of Safety and General Committee.

The most effectual methods were adopted to have the Association generally signed throughout the colony, and to require from non-subscribers the reasons of their refusal. Every effort was also made to put the Province, exposed as it was, in such a state of defence as the exigencies of the times demanded. The more effectively to carry out the recommendations of the Congress, volunteer companies were formed, and the whole Province presented one unbroken scene of military preparation.†

On the 3rd of August, Wm. Henry Harrington received a commission‡ as Captain of a Volunteer Company in St. David's Parish.

---

*Gazette, October 3, 1775.
†S. C. Gazette, June 23-30.
‡The commission ran as follows, viz :—
  "South Carolina.
           "In the Council of Safety.
"In pursuance of the power in us vested by the Provincial Congress, begun

In the mean time, the several committees in the interior were actively engaged in the discharge of their responsible duties. In August, the elections took place for members of the second Provincial Congress.

In September, matters having become so threatening in Charles-town as to make it hazardous for the Royal Governor, Lord William Campbell, any longer to remain, he took flight, precipitately, on 15th Sept., on board the *Tamer* sloop of war, and dissolved, for the last time, the Commons House of Assembly of South Carolina. George Gabriel Powell was then the member for St. David's. Col. Powell had taken an active and prominent part in the proceedings of the Council of Safety, and as one of the Commissioners appointed to supervise the military works then in progress about Charles-town. Attention had also been directed to other points which were likely to be exposed to the assaults of the enemy, from whatever quarter. The neighborhood of the upper Pedee was not overlooked.

The stand early taken by the inhabitants in this region, seems to have developed a spirit of opposition in places not very remote, and to have led to the opinion that they would be much exposed to hostile demonstrations from the Tories and others on their borders. The feeling already prevailing in some of the neighboring communities of North Carolina, along the line of Little Pedee, was well known, and led to the apprehension of the bloody struggle which actually ensued during the progress of the Revolution, and deluged the valley of the Pedee with blood. Hence it was, that some time about the latter part of October of this year, "at the request of Col. Powell and others, a detachment of fifty men was sent to the Cheraws, to garrison a fort that was to be built there, for the protection of the families of the well-

to be holden on the first day of June last, we do hereby appoint Henry William Harrington, Esq., to be Captain of a Volunteer Company of Foot, in the militia of St. David's Parish, Craven County. Dated in the Council of Safety, the third day of August, 1775.

THOMAS HEYWARD, JUN.,	RAWS. LOWNDES,
THOS. FERGUSON,	BEN. ELLIOTT,
THO. BEE,	HENRY LAURENS,
CHARLES C. PINCKNEY,	M. BREWSTER,
J. A. HUGER,	JAS. PARSONS,
WM. WILLIAMSON,	ARTHUR MIDDLETON."

affected, against the Tories, who were very numerous in that part of the country; this was an expensive work and of very little consequence."*

The history of this matter, to which Moultrie thus refers, will be fully explained by the following extracts from the Journal of the Commons House of Assembly. No allusion is made to it in any other history of the time.

"Stockade Fort at Cheraw, 23rd September, 1776.

"Message from the President by the Clerk of the Legislative Council:

"Mr. Speaker and Gentlemen,
"Col. Powell having represented the necessity of a Stockade Fort at the Cheraw Hill, I gave him directions some time ago (by advice of the Privy Council) to have one built there. But, on receiving from him the petitions and estimates herewith laid before you, some of which petitions prayed that it might be built at that place, and others at Long Bluff; and being informed by several inhabitants of St. David's Parish, that a fort at either of those places was altogether unnecessary, I thought it proper (the time of your meeting being then not very distant) to suspend the matter till I could have your opinion respecting it, and I now refer this subject to your consideration.

"JOHN RUTLEDGE.

"The petitions &c. being read, it was
"Ordered that the message, with the papers accompanying the same, be referred to a committee. And they are referred to Mr. Harrington, Major Hicks, Mr. Pegues, Capt. Withers, Capt. White, Mr. Young, and Capt. Trapier."†

"25th September, 1776.
"Mr. Speaker and Gentlemen,
"I send you some other petitions which have

---

*Moultrie's "Memoirs of the Revolution," vol. i. p. 92.
†"House Journal." No. 40, p. 145.

been lately presented to me relative to a fort at the Cheraw Hill.

"JOHN RUTLEDGE.

"The petitions were read and referred to the same committee."

On the following day, Mr. Harrington, from the committee, reported: "That they, having examined the petitions for and against building a Stockade Fort at the Cheraws, are of opinion, that a fort in that secure part of the country is entirely useless.

"And are further of opinion, that the keeping a guard of 300 men in June and July last, and of 50 men in August and the present month, at the said place, was a measure not only unnecessary and expensive to the State, but detrimental and destructive to the crops of many of the poor inhabitants. They therefore recommend, that the said guard of 50 men be immediately discharged.

"And whereas a quantity of gunpowder and lead was, by order of Congress, lodged in the hands of the Committee for St. David's Parish, for the use of the militia, part of which powder and lead has been drawn out of their hands by order of the Commanding Officer:

"Your Committee therefore recommend, that orders be given to the said Commanding Officer, to return the said powder and lead to the aforesaid Committee."*

The report was ordered to be taken into consideration on the morrow, but postponed to the following day, Sept. 28th, when it was taken up, and being read, the first clause was agreed to by the House.

A motion was then made and seconded, "That the further consideration of the report be postponed, and that a message be sent to the President, requesting that his Excellency will be pleased to lay before this House, the reasons for ordering and keeping a guard of 300 men at the Cheraws in June and July last, and of 50 men in August and the present month, at the same place."†

---

*"House Journal," No. 40, pp. 164, 165.
†*Ibid.*, pp. 172, 173.

The message was accordingly sent to his Excellency, and the following reply made, October 1st, viz.:—

"Mr. Speaker and Gentlemen,
"On the 17th of May, I was informed by a letter from the Committee of Secrecy, War, and Intelligence in North Carolina, of their having received advices that the enemy, who then lay on Cape Fear River, had planned a descent at the mouth of Little River, near the borders of this colony, in order to attempt a passage into the back country of that by the Lake of Waccamaw. Having occasion to confer with the Hon. Col. Powell on this subject, he urged very strongly the absolute necessity of building a Stockade Fort and keeping a garrison at the Cheraw Hill, as a security against incursions of the disaffected about Cross Creek, and for preventing or suppressing insurrections which they might occasion amongst our own people, near the North Carolina line—events which might be feared, especially if the intended junction between the British forces and the malcontents in that Province, had taken place.

"I thought so much attention and respect due to the representation of a gentleman in his station, who was well acquainted with that part of the country, and had the command of a large regiment there, as to lay it before the council for their advice, which I did.

"He attended them, and, on considering what he offered on this head, they were unanimously of opinion, that it was necessary to erect such a fort and keep such a garrison, in consequence of which, I gave orders for that purpose.
"JOHN RUTLEDGE.
"Sept. 30th, 1776."

On the next day, it was ordered, "That the Report of the Committee to whom the President's Message and other papers, relative to the building of a Fort on Cheraw Hill, were referred, be recommitted; that the President's Message of yesterday, upon the same subject, and Col. Powell's Letter, be referred to the same Committee; and that Major Huger, Major Simmons, Mr. Cantey, and Capt. Roger Smith, be added to the said Committee."

On the 4th of October, Mr. Harrington made a report, which, having been amended and agreed to, was as follows, viz. :—"That they, having examined the petitions for and against building a Stockade Fort on Cheraw Hill, are of opinion that a fort in that secure part of the country is entirely useless. That they have heard Col. Powell on the subject of keeping a garrison at Cheraw, and on full consideration of the matter, are of opinion, that a garrison in that part of the country is unnecessary.

"And whereas, a quantity of gunpowder and lead, was, by order of Congress, lodged in the hands of the Committee of St. David's, for the use of the militia, part of which powder and lead has been drawn out of their hands by order of the Commanding Officer, the Committee do therefore recommend, that orders be given to the Commanding Officer to return such part of the said powder and lead as remains unused, to the aforesaid Committee."*

Whereupon, the following message was sent to the President, a few days after, October 18th, viz. :—

"May it please your Excellency,
    "This House, having resolved that a fort and guard at the Cheraws are unnecessary, request that your Excellency will be pleased to give orders to discontinue the building of the said fort, and for the discharge of the guard now there; and that such part of the powder and lead which the colonel of the regiment of that district had received for the use of said guard as remains unused, be delivered to the care and custody of the Committee for St. David's Parish."†

Of the exact locality of the fort, nothing is known; even the knowledge of the fact that such a work was once begun, appears to have passed away, no tradition of it having been handed down.

Many volunteer companies of militia were organized about this time throughout the Province.

In St. David's Parish were the following, in September and October of this year, as shown by the date of the com-

---
*"House Journal," No. 40, pp. 193, 194.
†*Ibid.*, p. 221.

missions, though these were subsequently made out. The number indicates the alacrity with which the inhabitants on the Pedee responded to the call to arms.

"Council of Safety, Feb. 20th, 1776.

"The following commissions were made out, signed and dated as here entered, for officers in Col. Powell's Regiment of Militia, St. David's Parish:—

	Captain Abel Kolb, Ensign Aaron Daniel,	25th Sept., 1775.
Volunteer Corps.	Capt. John Dozier, 1st Lieut. Henry Britton, 2nd " Joseph Graves,	"
"	Capt. Luke Prior, 1st Lieut. David Davis, 2nd " Samuel Smith,	26th Sept., 1775.
"	Capt. James Ford, 1st Lieut. Benjamin Harlow, 2nd " Charles Moody,	"
"	Capt. Luke Whitfield, Ist Lieut. Isaac Neavill, Ensign William Johnson,	"
"	Capt. William Davis, 1st Lieut. Henry Davis, 2nd " Wright Wall,	"
"	Capt. George King, 1st Lieut. Amos Windham, 2nd " George Spivey,	28th Sept., 1775.
"	Capt. Thomas Hardyman, 2nd Lieut. James Galloway, Ensign Joseph Hardyman,	"
"	Lieut. Duncan McRae, Ensign John Sutton,	Capt. Thos. Lide's Company. 2nd Oct., 1775.
"	Captain Charles Evans, jun., 1st Lieut Matthew Holding, 2nd " Elisha Magee,	" "

Additional companies having soon after been formed in St. David's Parish, their officers were nominated and appointed by the Provincial Congress on 16th of November; and on the 30th their commissions were applied for and granted, as follows, viz.:

"Daniel Britton, 1st Lieut.,
Richard Reynolds, 2nd Lieut.,
John Witherspoon, Ensign,
} Of Capt. Thos. Port's Company of Volunteers in St. David's Parish.

John Kimbrough, Esq., Capt.,
Samuel Benton, 1st Lieut.,
James Knight, 2nd Lieut.,
William Standard, Ensign,
} Of another Company of Volunteers in the said Parish.

John Blakeney, Esq., Capt.,
John Reynolds, 1st Lieut.,
Thomas McManess, 2nd Lieut.,
John Ewbank, Ensign,
} Of another Company of Volunteers in said Parish."

On the 23rd of January following, Thomas Williamson was Commissioned Captain in Colonel Powell's Regiment; and on 2nd February, Maurice Murphy was also Commissioned Captain in the same Regiment.*

Thus thoroughly and extensively organized were the inhabitants of St. David's Parish at this early period for military service. Along the river, and from the extreme upper parts of Lynche's Creek to the neighborhood of its mouth, did the spirit of volunteering extend. The people were roused to the highest pitch of patriotic ardor.

Some dissatisfaction, however, had existed among the volunteer companies soon after their organization in September, owing probably to the fact, that their services were not at once accepted, and their officers commissioned. And hence, doubtless, the action of the Council of Safety, as it has been given. About this time, Captain Samuel Wise, of the Regiment of Rangers, was induced, for some reason, to resign his commission, as appears from the following letter:—

"To the Honorable, the Council of Saftey.
"Honorable Gentlemen,—I am extremely sorry any in-

---

*The lists of Commissions here given, were taken from manuscript papers of the Council of Safety, known as the "Laurens Papers," now in possession of the Historical Society of South Carolina, and kindly shown to the author by F. A. Porcher, Esq., corresponding secretary.

cident should have arisen that would oblige me to send the commission you were pleased to honor me with unto Mr. Drayton; for, having entered into the service with a heart full of zeal for the legal freedom of myself and fellow subjects of this Province in particular, and the constitutional rights of America in general; so, nothing less than being dishonored by a suspicion of want of integrity to the great cause of constitutional liberty, would have induced me to have taken this step; and I hope your Honors will be pleased to consider the bitterness of my feelings, when Mr. Drayton refused to tell me the name of the man who had thus disgraced me. But, as my friends here seem to think that I have been rather hasty, if your Honors, too, should be of that opinion, I shall be exceedingly grieved; for it was never my intention to give the least offence, and do beg leave to submit myself and cause to your Honors' judgment.

"I am, with great respect,
"Your Honors' most obedient,
"humble Servant,
"SAMUEL WISE.*

"Charles-town, Sept. 30th, 1775."

Captain Wise was a man of the nicest sense of honor, and doubtless betrayed a morbid sensibility under the wound which had been unjustly inflicted on his reputation. He was induced to withdraw his resignation, probably by the Council of Safety, as well as his immediate friends, and continued in the active service of his country, for which he was eminently fitted. The Provincial Congress was called together on the 1st of November. The former members for St. David's were re-elected, and with the exception of Claudius Pegues, Esq., appeared and took their seats.

Col. Powell was also elected a member for St. Philip's and St. Michael's, but declined that position in favour of St. David's Parish. Mr. Harrington was one of a committee appointed to report upon the state of the colony, and the proper measures which ought to be pursued for putting the

*Manuscript papers of Council of Safety.

same into the best posture of defence. On Monday, Nov. 6th, it was ordered, "That Mr. President be requested to direct Lieut.-Col. Thompson, of the Rangers, to send Isaac Jordan, a private in his Regiment, charged with horse-stealing and breaking gaol at Cheraws, and cause him to be delivered to the Sheriff of Cheraws District, or his deputy, or to the keeper of the Common Gaol."

A new Council of Safety having been elected on 16th Nov., a committee was appointed the following day, of which Mr. Harrington was one, to "consider of, and bring into one view, the powers and authorities proper to be vested in the Council of Safety."* On the 28th of Nov., it was resolved, "That the Committee of St. David's Parish be authorized to purchase what lead they can get, on the public account." On the same day it was also resolved, "That 600 men from Col. Powell's Regiment should forthwith be detached, and directed to rendezvous at the Congarees." And the following letter was thereupon written:—

"By authority of the Congress.

"Charles-town, Nov. 25th, 1775.

"Sir,—You are hereby ordered, with all possible despatch, to detach six hundred men of your Regiment, to rendezvous at the Congarees, to act under the orders of Col. Richardson.

"I am, Sir,
"Your most humble servant,
"WM. HENRY DRAYTON,
"President.

"To Col. Powell."

This action was taken in consequence of difficulties at Ninety-six. There had been a recent skirmish between Patrick Cunningham, Jacob Bowman, and others, on the one side, and a body of militia under the charge of Andrew Williamson, on the other.

On the 27th of Nov., Col. Richardson was in camp at the Congarees, and about 1st Dec. crossed Saluda river into the Dutch Fork. A few days later, he was joined by several

*Drayton's "Memoirs," vol. ii. pp. 61-77; and "Journal of the Congress."

detachments. After advancing southward and effecting the object of the expedition, the troops were disbanded the latter end of December, and returned to their respective homes. A detachment had started from Pedee under Major George Hicks, but was stopped by the following order from the Council of Safety:—

"Wednesday evening, Dec. 20th, 1775.

"Gent.,—Intelligence which we have just received from Col. Richardson, induces us to believe that he will be able to accomplish the business upon which he was ordered by the Congress, without further aid; and as Col. Powell has intimated, that the detachment from his regiment was either not marched, or if marched, might soon be overtaken by orders: We desire you will take the proper steps for recalling or stopping the detachment, and directing the officer in command to dismiss the men until further orders—after which, he will transmit a proper account of the time of actual service performed by that detachment.

"By Order of the Council of Safety,
"HENRY LAURENS,
"President.*

"On Colony Service.—Recommended to the Committee of George-town to be forwarded if needful by express. The expense will be paid by the Council of Safety.

"To the Committee of the Parish of St. David."

On the 29th of Nov. it was ordered by the Congress, "That three hundred pounds weight of gunpowder be delivered out of the public stock, reserved for the aid and defence of this colony, to the order of the Committee of St. David's Parish, to be distributed among such of the men in Col. Powell's Regiment as are unprovided, to be by them reserved for public uses only."

One of the chief difficulties now was to get ammunition as it was wanted, such was the limited supply. After a Session of the most important and decided character, the Congress adjourned, November 29th. The die was cast. The struggle had begun. The people were everywhere in

---

*"Laurens Papers" of Historical Society of So. Ca.

arms. The selfish, it is said, among the merchants and planters, whose gains were lessened by the cessation of trade, wished for the return of business; but the main body of both classes most heartily concurred in the popular measures. No revolution was ever effected with greater unanimity, or with more order and regularity.

A great majority of the people determined to sacrifice ease, pleasure, and fortune, and to risk life itself to obtain permanent security for American rights.

They believed their liberties to be in danger. Roused by this apprehension, they were animated to the most self-denying exertions.* Such was the feeling on the Pedee.

With very few exceptions, the intelligent and influential inhabitants were the ardent friends of their country. They had already taken a conspicuous stand, and to every appeal in behalf of liberty had made a hearty response.

Peculiarly exposed to the worst of enemies, they were called, from the first, to bear the heat and burden of a sanguinary conflict with the Tories on Lynche's Creek and the Little Pedee. But tried to the uttermost, they never despaired. Among the first to make a public declaration of their rights, they were among the last to lay down their arms, when further resistance seemed more than futile, and for a time overpowered, not conquered, they were forced to take protection, but only to throw off every vestige of submission, and, with the returning hope of liberty, to submit to the oppressor no more.

*"Ramsay," vol. i. p. 79.

CHAPTER XII.

Opening of the year 1776—Charles-town threatened—Council of Safety writes to Major M'Intosh—Response from Pedee—Difficulties in Civil Administration—William Strother writes to Council of Safety—The Council provides ammunition for St. David's—The Congress meets—Mr. Harrington's return as to member in place of Claudius Pegues—Action of Congress—Payments ordered to certain persons in St. David's—Congress takes action as to a "form of government"—Other proceedings—Pay to Major Hicks refused—Additional forces raised—Major M'Intosh elected Lieutenant-Colonel—"Form of government" adopted—Officers elected, and appointments for St. David's—Colonel Powell and Speaker Parsons' address to the President—Colonel Powell elected assistant-judge—Declines—Address of Baptist Churches, by Rev. Messrs. Hart and Winchester to Vice-President Laurens—His reply—Courts opened—Presentments of grand jury of Cheraws—Whigs and Tories—Latter compared with Loyalists—Conflict with Tories on Pedee—Committee of St. David's continues to meet—Abel Kolb—His character—David Williams dies—Major Wise on Sullivan's Island—Letters to Henry William Harrington—Captain Harrington at Haddrell's Point—Prisoners sent to gaol of Cheraws District—Election of two members from St. David's to Assembly—Charges against Colonel Powell—His letter on subject—Action of Assembly—Affair dropped—Salt provided for St. David's—Act passed as to places of election for the parish—First courts after Declaration of Independence—Chief Justice Drayton's charge in Charles-town—Presentments of grand jury of Cheraws—Reflections on same—Quiet restored—Commerce revives—Death of Arthur Hart—Letter of Major Wise—Member elected for St. David's—Educational wants sorely felt.

THE year 1776 was ushered in under the most threatening aspects for the Province. In the early part of January, the inhabitants of Charles-town apprehended an attack by sea. The Council of Safety acted with the utmost decision. Having made arrangements with Colonel Moultrie for protecting the town, attention was turned to the subject of collecting an adequate militia force from the country. Though the enemy soon after withdrew, the apprehension of an attack still continued, and the more solicitude was felt as the militia came in slowly. The following letter from the Council of Safety to Major Alexander M'Intosh, at this alarming juncture, shows the state of feeling in Charles-town.

"In Council of Safety.
"Charles-town, Jan. 13th, 1776.

"Sir,—Three ships of war appear at anchor near our Bar, and will probably come within tomorrow.

"One, said by a lieutenant who has been in a 10 oar'd barge as high as Rebellion Road, and spoke from Fort Johnson, the crew of which passed upon him for simple fishermen, to be of 50 guns—but, we believe only 36—the other two of 20. They have detached a sloop, probably for the Tamar and Cherokee. The lieutenant was greatly mortified at finding they were not here. The alarm will be fired through the colony to-morrow (Monday). Your presence, and the presence of every provincial officer, is required here. You will therefore repair to your regiment with all possible despatch, after giving pressing orders to the commanding officer of Col. Powell's Regiment of militia, to detach to our assistance with all possible expedition, as many officers and men as will voluntarily come, in small parties of 20 or 50, as they can be collected.

"This is the time for evincing our professions and declarations of love of liberty and the righteous cause of America. Words are not necessary to influence those who are sincere, to fly to the banner of their country. Order all provincial officers you may meet with, to their duty here immediately.

"By Order of the Council of Safety,
"HENRY LAURENS, President.*
"Major M'Intosh."

To this spirited appeal, Major M'Intosh, with other officers, and many of the militia from the Pedee, responded. Major George Hicks went down in command of a detachment, and Captain Samuel Wise also commanded a company. On the 6th of February, it was said, three hundred volunteers of Richardson's and Powell's Regiments, who had been down on duty, being willing to remain, were kept until the 1st of March, the rest of the country militia being discharged. This was the first important military service rendered to the Province by the inhabitants of the Upper Pedee.

In the present unsettled state of affairs, serious difficulty was experienced in matters of ordinary civil transaction and

---

*Manuscript papers of Council of Safety.

adjudication. The want of some established authority was sorely felt, as in the management of estates and the case of orphans.

The following letter was addressed to the Committee in Charles-town on this subject, from St. David's Parish:—

"January 11th, 1776.

"Gentlemen,

"On the death of sundry persons in the district where I live, application has been made to me to know how to proceed, or how they should obtain Letters of Administration; and not knowing what has been resolved by the Congress on such occasion, I beg to be informed, as some of the orphans must suffer greatly in their estates if not shortly secured.

"Your answer will much oblige,

"Your humble servt.,

"Wm. Strother.*

"To the Honorable Council of Safety,
Charles-town."

The Parish of St. David's was not yet adequately supplied with war stores, and the Council took further action, as follows:—

"Wednesday, January 24th, 1776.

"The Congress at the late session, ordered three hundred weight of gunpowder to be issued for the use of St. David's. The order was brought to us yesterday under many indorsements; as we think it will save trouble, expense, and risk, we desire you will, upon sight of the order which we have referred to you for that purpose, direct a compliance with the contents from the public store of gunpowder under your care, and transmit the order to us.

"By order of the Council of Safety,

"Henry Laurens, President.

"The Committee for George-town."

No time was lost in complying with this direction, as appears from the following receipt:—"Received of the Committee at George-town three hundred pounds weight of

---

*Manuscript papers of Council of Safety.

gunpowder, from the public stock, by direction of the Council of Safety, for St. David's.

"AARON DANIEL."*

"George-town, Jany. 26th, 1776."

On the 1st February, the Congress, which had adjourned 29th of Nov. previous, met again in Charles-town.

On the 3rd, Mr. Harrington made this special return, addressed to the President: —

"Charles-town, Feby. 2, 1776.

"Sir,

"Claudius Pegues, Esq., one of the six deputies duly elected to represent the Parish of St. David's in Congress, signified by letter, addressed to the Committee of the said Parish, that he declined serving the said Parish in Congress. He delivered the letter to me to lay before the Committee, who were not to meet till the 19th of last month; and as the Congress was to sit on the 1st instant, I, as church warden, and not recollecting the resolve of the last Congress relative to election, advertised the 23rd of January as a day of election for a deputy to Congress instead of Mr. Pegues, when it appeared that Willian Henry Mills had a majority of votes, of which I acquainted him by letter.

"I am, Sir, your most obedient, humble servant,

"HENRY WILLIAM HARRINGTON."

"Whereupon, it was resolved, That a Member of Congress cannot resign his seat during the continuance of the Congress in which he took his seat as a member; and, therefore, as Claudius Pegues, Esq., could not decline his seat in the present Congress, the election of William Henry Mills, Esq., as a member of Congress in the room of Claudius Pegues, Esq., was null and void."†

On Tuesday the 6th of February, the Council issued orders on the Treasury for the payment of the following sums, among others, viz. :—

---

*Manuscript papers of Council of Safety.
†"American Archives," vol. v. p. 566.

	£	s.	d.
"To Major George Hicks, for pay and rations to the detachment from Col. Powell's Regiment of Militia, ordered to join Col. Richardson, to be placed to account of Col. Richardson's expedition	8567	12	6
"To H. W. Harrington, Esq., so much advanced by him for two expresses,* from Charles-town	43	0	0
"To Calvin Spencer's order for his service as messenger to the Committee of St. David's	50	0	0
"For ferriage of Capt. Wise's Company over Pedee, to John Eddens	10	0	0"

On the 8th of February, a Committee was appointed by the Congress, consisting of the Council of Safety, together with others, of whom Col. Powell was one, "to take into consideration the following resolution of the Continental Congress, passed the 4th of Nov. last, viz.: 'Resolved, that if the Convention of South Carolina shall find it necessary to establish a form of government in that colony, it be recommended to said Convention to call a full and free representation of the people; and that the said representatives, if they think it necessary, establish such form of government as, in their judgment, will best promote the happiness of the people, and most effectually secure peace and good order in the colony during the continuance of the present dispute between Great Britain and the colonies.' "†

A few days after, a Committee of eleven was appointed to prepare and report such a plan or form of government as would best promote the happiness of the people.

On the 12th, a committee, of which Mr. Harrington was one, "was appointed to consider and report upon the best method for promoting the manufacture of saltpetre in the colony."‡

The want of ammunition began to be sorely felt, and the

---

*This was the item, as a credit, in the account of Mr. Harrington, of receipt for poor of Boston.
†Drayton's "Memoirs," vol. ii. p. 171.
‡"American Archives," vol. v. pp. 569, 570.

necessity became more apparent daily for relying upon themselves for its production.

On the 14th of February, a motion was made, "that the Congress do order payment of certain expenses, amounting to 234*l.*, incurred by a detachment of militia under the command of Major Hicks, lately marched to this town, for camp utensils and other articles. A debate ensued, and the question being put, it was carried in the negative."*

On the 18th, Col. Powell and Cap. Harrington, with others, were placed on a committee to report upon the militia, its division, regulations, &c. This important subject urgently demanded attention. The haste with which it had been necessary to devise certain measures for defence, had involved the military affairs of the colony in more or less confusion.

The situation of Charles-town, as was now most apparent, demanded immediate aid from the country for its protection. And notwithstanding the difficulties attending such a step, the Congress voted on the 19th of February, that 1050 men of the country militia should be immediately drafted and marched down. And three days after, the military establishment was augmented by the resolution to raise two Rifle Regiments, one of seven, and the other of five hundred men.

The field officers were to be elected by a majority of the ballots of the whole number of members present in the Congress. Of the first Regiment, Alexander M'Intosh was elected Lieut.-Colonel.

From this time Col. M'Intosh was engaged in constant service.

On the 5th of March the Committee on "a form of Government" reported. On the 8th the Congress resolved itself into a committee of the whole, to take the same into consideration. After several days' deliberation it was turned over to the Congress for final disposal; and from the 15th to the 26th of March, carefully weighed in its details, well adjusted in every part, and on the latter day, under the title "of a Constitution or Form of Government," adopted.

A Legislative Council of thirteen, to be elected by ballot

---

*"American Archives," vol. v. pp. 569, 570.

from the members of Assembly, for two years, was substituted in the place of the "King's Privy Council," as formerly, the Vice-President being *ex-officio* a member and President of the same. The legislative authority was vested in the General Assembly and Legislative Council; both of which were to be elected every two years. The General Assembly was to consist of the like number of members as the Congress had done, each district and parish having the same representation as was then present.

This gave to St. David's six members. Justices of the Peace were to be nominated by the General Assembly, and commissioned by the President and Commander-in-Chief, during pleasure. All other judicial officers were to be elected by joint ballot of the Assembly and Council.

All persons chosen and appointed to any office, or place of trust, before entering upon the execution of the same, were to take the following oath, viz.: "I, A.B., do swear that I will to the utmost of my power, support, maintain, and defend the Constitution of South Carolina, as established by Congress on the 26th day of March, One Thousand Seven Hundred and Seventy-six, until an accommodation of the difficulties between Great Britain and America shall take place, or I shall be released from this oath by the Legislative authority of the said colony, so help me God." Such were some of the features of the "Constitution, or Form of Government," thus adopted. An accommodation of the difficulties with the Mother Country seemed yet to be looked forward to as an event not impossible; and therefore this provision made for regulating the affairs and promoting the welfare of the Province was so far only temporary. On the day of its adoption, the election of officers took place under the Constitution. George Gabriel Powell, one of the members for St. David's, was made Speaker of the Legislative Council. Henry William Harrington was elected Sheriff for Cheraws District, and the following gentlemen were nominated as suitable persons to fill the office of Justices of the Peace for the same, viz.:

John Alran, Henry Wm. Harrington, George Pawley, William Dewitt, Arthur Hart, Claudius Pegues, Elias Du Bose, John Kimbrough, William Pegues, Charles Evans,

Thomas Lide, Philip Pledger, Robert Gray, Wm. Henry Mills, and George Hicks.*

In the present critical state of public affairs, this office was one of much importance, and hence men of intelligence, influence, and well-known principle were selected for the post.

On the 3rd of April, Mr. Speaker Powell and James Parsons, Esq., Speaker of Assembly, made the following address to the President, John Rutledge, Esq.

"May it please your Excellency:

"We, the Legislative Council and General Assembly of South Carolina, convened under the authority of the equitable Constitution of Government established by a free people, in Congress, on the 26th ult., beg leave, most respectfully, to address your Excellency. Nothing is better known to your Excellency than the unavoidable necessity which induced us, as members of Congress, on the part of the people, to resume the powers of Government; and to establish some mode for regulating the internal polity of this colony; and, as members of the Legislative Council and General Assembly, to vest you, for a time limited, with the executive authority. Such constitutional proceedings on our own part we make no doubt will be misconstrued into acts of the greatest criminality by that despotism which, lost to all sense of justice and humanity, has already pretended that we are in actual rebellion. But, Sir, when we reflect upon the unprovoked, cruel, and accumulated oppressions under which America in general, and this country in particular, has long continued; oppressions, which gradually increasing in injustice and violence, are now by an inexorable tyranny perpetuated against the United Colonies, under the various forms of robbery, conflagration, massacre, breach of the public faith, and open war—conscious of our natural and inalienable rights, and determined to make every effort in our power to retain them; we see your Excellency's elevation, from the midst of us, to govern this country, as the natural consequence of such outrages.

---

*"American Archives," vol. v. p. 620.

"By the suffrages of a free people, you, Sir, have been chosen to hold the reins of Government; an event, as honorable to yourself, as it is beneficial to the public.

"We firmly trust, that you will make the Constitution the great rule of your conduct, and, in the most solemn manner, we do assure your Excellency, that, in the discharge of your duties under that Constitution, which looks forward to an accommodation with Great Britain (an event which, though traduced and treated as rebels, we still earnestly desire), we will support you with our lives and fortunes."*

To this address the President made a brief and happy reply. After putting the Government in operation and transacting other important business, the General Assembly adjourned, to meet the first of October following, leaving the administration of affairs in the mean time to President and Council.

On the 27th of March, the day after the adoption of the Constitution, Col. Powell was elected one of the Assistant Judges, but requested leave to resign, and giving such reasons as were satisfactory to the House, his request was granted. It was the second time this honor had been conferred upon him, the Royal Government having previously elected him to the same position.

Col. Powell was highly esteemed, and had been for years prominent in the affairs of the Province.

That he should have persistently retained his connexion with St. David's Parish, though not a resident, and declined the representation of such Parishes as St. Philip's and St. Michael's, is a fact of which we can give no explanation; unless it was, that having become interested in the Upper Pedee by his attendance at the Bar of Cheraw, and the purchase of lands, and honored with the confidence of the people from the first, a feeling of gratitude prompted him to remain in their service to the close of his career.

The rising spirit of liberty and the present alarming crisis affected all classes.

Religious bodies were roused to take a decided stand, and

---

*"Drayton," vol. ii. p. 264.

by their encouraging tones of approval, to stimulate the public men of the day in their efforts for the country.

The following address is expressive of the feeling that prevailed:—

> "To the Honorable Henry Laurens, Esquire, Vice-President of the Province of South Carolina.
>
> "The address of the Baptist Congregations in said Province.

"May it please your Honor,

"We can truly say, we rejoice in the present happy form of government established among us; and beg leave to assure you, Sir, that we are filled with the most sensible pleasure on your Honor being chosen Vice-President, as it is well known that you are a most hearty friend to liberty, and have managed the many important trusts committed to you with fidelity. It gives us joy, that you, Sir, are still continued in the important service of your country at this critical juncture; and we do most heartily congratulate you on this happy occasion. We hope yet to see hunted Liberty sit Regent on the Throne, and flourish more than ever under the administration of such worthy patriots; may we not hope that the time is come, in which our rulers may be men fearing God, and hating covetousness, a terror to evil-doers, and a praise to them who do well! We bless God that he hath begun our deliverance; and that he will complete it, shall be our constant prayer.

"And now, wishing your Honor all peace, happiness, and prosperity upon earth, and everlasting happiness above, we subscribe ourselves, your Honor's most obedient and most humble servants,

> "OLIVER HART, *Pastor of the Baptist Church, in Charles-town.*
>
> "ELHANAN WINCHESTER, *Pastor of the Baptist Church, at the Welch Neck, on Pedee.*

"Signed in behalf of the Baptist Congregations in general, this 30th day of March, 1776."

To this Mr. Laurens replied as follows:—

"Gentlemen,
"I receive your address on behalf of the Baptist Congregations with the same cordiality of affection in which, I am persuaded, it was made, although it becomes me to acknowledge, that you have done me an honor which I had no ground to expect.

"The persecution against the liberties of American subjects, which, immediately after the death of his late Majesty, of glorious memory, was devised at the Court of St. James, and which, at different periods, has been revived, rendered it necessary to make occasional and suitable opposition.

"Hence the appointment of Committees in every town and district from New England to Georgia; hence the assembling of that august body, the Representatives of the Thirteen United Colonies, in Congress, at Philadelphia, and of the Congress and Council of Safety in this colony; hence also those numberless humble Petitions and Addresses to the Throne, and to both Houses of Parliament, which have in every instance been most ungraciously spurned, and treated with disdain by the King and his Ministers.

"The high hand with which that persecution hath lately been carried on by imprisonments, bloodshed, confiscations, plunder, and barbarous devastation of cities and towns by fire, hath at length impelled the colonists to make a solemn appeal to the King of kings, and to resist by force and arms. One obvious measure in the plan of our enemies and cruel persecutors, was to drive the peaceable and defenceless inhabitants of the Colonies into a state of confusion, by depriving them of the benefit of legislation, and the ordinary mode of representation by assemblies. This fact is incontestably proved by those repeated prorogations and dissolutions which blot the pages of every journal where the King's ministers could extend and exercise their master's prerogative.

"South Carolina had in an eminent degree suffered by this species of revenge, which has been aggravated of late by daily menaces of attacks by British soldiers and ships of war, by instigated insurrections of negroes and inroads by savage Indians; and by what was more to be dreaded, fire and sword in our very bowels, by the hands of false brethren; in a word, 'the sword without and terror within, threatened to destroy both the young man and the virgin, the suckling also, with the man of grey hairs.' But, through the special protection of Divine Providence, a happy union of the principal inhabitants was formed, and we have hitherto miraculously escaped. This metropolis, since the late Governor's desertion, has been kept in a state of quietness and good order unknown in almost every former period. After long suffering and forbearance, the people of this country, seeing the noble lord who had been sent to be their Governor, although he had abandoned his post, still continuing in this and the next neighboring colony, exercising and encouraging every hostile and injurious act against them, judged it indispensably necessary to resolve upon the present form, as a temporary expedient for government, until an accommodation of our disputes with Great Britain and a redress of grievances can be obtained.

"I had the honor of being one among many who framed that Constitution. It therefore makes me happy to learn that those respectable bodies, the Baptist Congregations, are satisfied and pleased with the important event. I esteem, as equally friendly and obliging, their particular gratulations upon my being called by my country to act in the honorable station of Vice-President of the Colony, and I accept them with thankfulness.

"Let each man among us, whether in the State or in the Church, whether in public or in private life, by example, by precept, by every becoming act, presevere, and be ready with his life and fortune to defend the just cause in which God has been pleased to engage us.

"We shall, weak as we are, succeed against those who have assumed to themselves the powers of Omnipotence, who trust in fleets and armies to determine the fight. We shall be the happy instruments of establishing liberty, civil and religious, in a wilderness, where towns and cities shall grow, whose inhabitants to the latest posterity will look back to this happy epoch, and celebrate and bless the memory of this generation. In order effectually to accomplish these great ends, it is incumbent upon us to begin wisely, and to proceed in the fear of God; and it is especially the duty of those who bear rule, to promote and encourage piety and virtue, and to discountenance every degree of vice and immorality.

> "I have the honor to be, Reverend Sirs,
> "Your faithful, affectionate,
> "and obliged humble servant,
> "HENRY LAURENS.*

"March 30th, 1776.

"To the Rev. Oliver Hart, M.A., Pastor of the Baptist Church in Charles-town, and the Rev. Elhanan Winchester, Pastor of the Baptist Church at Pedee, on behalf of the Baptist Church Congregations in South Carolina."

The establishment of the new Government, the first organized in any of the colonies, inspired fresh confidence and gave increased strength to the union of the people for the defence of their liberties.

Order followed confusion, and a uniform conduct in those who governed took the place of the uncertainty and capriciousness that had prevailed before. The State and District officers entered upon the discharge of their respective duties, and the courts of law, which had been suspended for nearly twelve months, were opened on the 23rd of April (1776), "with great solemnity; to the infinite joy of the well-disposed, and the discomfiture of those whose offences called for punishment."†

It was on this occasion that Chief Justice Drayton, in language similar to that he had held eighteen months before, delivered his first charge to the Grand Jury of Charles-town District.

And again did the Grand Jury of Cheraw District, partaking in the general feeling of enthusiasm which now prevailed, give expression to their deep convictions as to the just and righteous cause of their oppressed and bleeding country.

---

*So. Ca. Gazette. †"Drayton," vol. ii. p. 253.

At a Court for said district, holden at Long Bluff, on Monday, May 20th, Mr. Justice Matthews presiding, the following presentments were made: —

"I. When a people born and bred in a land of freedom and virtue, uncorrupted by those refinements which effeminate and debase the mind, manly and generous in their sentiments, bold and hardy in their nature, and actuated by every principle of liberality, from too sad experience are convinced of the wicked schemes of their treacherous rulers to fetter them with the chains of servitude, and rob them of every noble and desirable privilege which distinguishes them as freemen; justice, humanity, and the immutable laws of God, justify and support them in revoking those sacred trusts which are so impiously violated, and placing them in such hands as are most likely to execute them in the manner and for the important ends for which they were first given.

"II. The good people of this colony, with the rest of her sister colonies, confiding in the justice and merited protection of the King and Parliament of Great Britain, ever signalized themselves by every mark of duty and affection towards them; and esteemed such a bond of union and harmony as the greatest happiness. But, when that protection was wantonly withdrawn, and every mark of cruelty and oppression substituted; when tyranny, violence, and injustice took the place of equity, mildness, and affection; and bloodshed, murder, robbery, and conflagration, and the most deadly persecution stamped the malignity of their intentions; self preservation, and a regard to our own welfare and security became a consideration both important and necessary. The Parliament and Ministry of Great Britain, by their wanton and undeserved persecutions, have reduced this colony to a state of separation from them, unsought for and undesired by her: a separation which now proves its own utility, as the only lasting means of future happiness and safety. What every one once dreaded as the greatest misery, they now unexpectedly find their greatest advantage. Amidst all her sufferings, and the manifold injuries which have been done her, this colony was ever ready, with her sister colonies, to ask for that reconciliation which showed every mark of forgiveness and promise of future harmony. But how were they treated? Each token of submission was aggravated into usurpation; humble petitions styled insults; and every dutiful desire of accommodation treated with the most implacable contempt. Cast off, persecuted, defamed, given up as a prey to every violence and injury, a righteous and much-injured people have at length appealed to God; and trusting to His divine justice, and their own virtuous perseverance, taken the only and last means of securing their own honor, safety, and happiness.

"III. We now feel every joyful and comfortable hope that a people could desire in the present Constitution and form of Government established in this colony: a Constitution founded on the strictest principles of justice and humanity; where the rights and happiness of the whole, the poor and the rich, are equally secured; and to secure and defend which, it is the particular interest of every individual, who regards his own safety and advantage.

"IV. When we consider the public officers of our present form of Government now appointed, as well as the method and duration of their appointment, we cannot but declare our entire satisfaction and comfort, as well in the character of such men, who are justly esteemed for every virtue, as in their well-known abilities to execute the important trusts which they now hold.

"V. Under these convictions, and filled with these hopes, we cannot but most earnestly recommend it to every man, as essential to his own liberty and happiness, as well as that of his posterity, to secure and defend with his life and fortune, a form of government so just, so equitable, and promising; to inculcate its principles upon his children, and hand it down to them unimpaired, that the latest posterity may enjoy the virtuous fruits of that work, which the integrity and fortitude of the present age had, at the expense of their blood and treasure, at length happily effected.

"VI. We cannot but declare how great is the pleasure, the harmony and political union which now exist in this district affords; and having no grievances to complain of, only beg leave to recommend that a new 'jury list' be made for this district, the present being insufficient.

"And lastly, we beg leave to return our most sincere thanks to Mr. Justice Matthews for his spirited and patriotic charge; at the same time requesting, that these our Presentments may be printed in the public papers.

"Philip Pledger, *Foreman.*
Abel Edwards.
John Hewstis.
Charles M'Call.
John Wilds.
Thomas Lide.
Martin Dewitt.
John Mikell.
Benjamin James.
Magnus Corgill.
Thomas Bingham.
Peter Kolb.
Benjamin Rogers.
Thomas Ellerbe.
Moses Speight."

These spirited Presentments,* not unmeet to be placed side by side with those which had been made before by the Grand Juries of Cheraw District, were republished in full in England the following winter.

The "harmony and political union" referred to as existing in the district, continued throughout the Revolution to be strikingly characteristic of its inhabitants, except in the outskirts, and in the case of a few individuals here and there on the river.

No other part of the Province was more united in patriotic feeling.

The distinction of Whig and Tory took its rise during

---

*They appeared in the "Remembrancer; or, Impartial Repository of Public Events. Part iii. for the year 1776. London, 1777." A copy was first placed in the hands of the author by Mr. Hugh Godbold, of Marion, already referred to; and the volume containing them, with others of the series, a valuable collection, was afterwards presented to the author by Mr. G.

the previous year. Both parties in the interior country were then embodied, and were obliged to impress provisions for their respective support. The advocates for Congress prevailing, they paid for articles consumed in their camps; but as no funds were provided for discharging the expenses incurred by the Royalists, all that was consumed by them was considered as a robbery. This laid the foundation of a piratical war between Whigs and Tories, which was productive of great distress, and deluged the country with blood. In the interval between the Insurrection of 1775 and the year 1780, the Whigs were occasionally plundered by parties who had attempted insurrections in favor of Royal Government.[*]

This testimony of a contemporary writer was emphatically true of the struggle on the Pedee, but was far from representing all that marked the conflict in this region. The Whigs of Cheraw District were subjected to frequent predatory incursions by the Tories from the neighboring parts of North Carolina towards Drowning Creek and Little Pedee. These were Scotch settlements chiefly, and were capable of sending out large parties to plunder the patriotic inhabitants along the valley of the Pedee.

There were undoubtedly many worthy persons among the loyalists—men who were actuated by noble feelings and generous sentiments, and who would have sacrificed themselves and all that they had in the cause of the King. With the mass of the Tories it was very different. They acted a despicable part, being influenced chiefly by motives of interest or fear. The bloodiest and most relentless characters of the Revolution were found in their ranks. The best illustration, indeed, of their character was furnished in the desperate means used, by way of retaliation, to which the Whigs were not unfrequently driven.

On the 31st of December, 1775, the Rev. Evan Pugh made this entry in his private journal: "Called at Mr. Lide's,[†] who was just come home from the camp, having been against the Tories."

---

[*] "Ramsay's Revolution," vol. ii. p. 269.
[†] Robert Lide, afterwards known as Major Lide.

It was a record of the time which might have been often made.

The Committee of Observation for St. David's Parish continued to meet. On the 4th of May, Mr. Pugh says:—"Went to Abel Kolb's* to the committee." Similar entries are found in his journal in June, August, and October following, and for some time subsequent. Mr. Kolb, a man of retiring disposition, but of ardent patriotism and fearless spirit, was now coming rapidly into notice. He appears not to have had the advantages of education possessed by some of his contemporaries. This circumstance, together with his natural modesty, probably kept him at first from taking a prominent part in the public affairs of the time. His superior qualities of head and heart, however, could not remain unknown to or unappreciated by the people. With the growing exigencies of the times, the popular instinct turned at once to those who were fitted by nature to be military leaders during so stormy a period. Of these, Abel Kolb was soon to take a conspicuous place.

On the 1st of January of this year, Cheraw District lost a worthy and useful citizen in the death of David Williams. Cut off prematurely in his thirty-sixth year, his country could illy afford to be deprived of his services. He had been added, with others, the year previous, to the Committee of Observation for St. David's. His untimely end was much lamented.

With the approach of summer the conflict off the Bar of Charles-town drew near. Many of the Whigs from Pedee responded to the call from the coast.

Major Samuel Wise was in command of troops on Sullivan's Island, and engaged with all his enthusiastic ardor in the preparations made for the approaching struggle.

On the 7th of June he wrote to his friend, Henry William Harrington, Esq., of Pedee, giving some account of the state of things up to that date.

"I am now," he said, "at the lower end of the island with 210 men, while fifty vessels are so nigh that we can see their men; and since I began to write, they have got

---
*Mr. Kolb resided at a point central and important.

under way, and are apparently intending to come in. It gives me pleasure to inform you our men are in the highest spirits. Let the event be what it will, our regiment wishes to engage. The shipping are within random shot, and certainly coming in. It positively gives me fresh spirits."

On the 22nd of June he wrote again:—

"I don't know if I am right in my conjecture, but I do conceive the longer we are kept in the face of an enemy, the less we dread fighting them; but, as our situation here is looked on by every officer in our case as desperate, and that we must certainly fall a sacrifice, I expect we shall either fight like a tiger pent up, or take the marsh for it. However, our officers chiefly declare the first will be their choice, and that they would not quit the island were they certain of death. But it is my hope that our Great Creator, who has appeared so evidently in the behalf of America, will not desert us, though I assure you, it is clear to me we cannot prevent their landing without a direct interposition of heaven. My opinion has been, and still is, that they will land on the lower point of this island from Long Island.

"They have two pieces of cannon mounted, and are this day mounting three more, which will cover their landing in spite of all we can do.

"I did not get over, however, before yesterday morning. I was appointed officer of our advance-guard, and my lieut. was kind enough to officiate for me until I landed.

"Between Long Island and Sullivan's there is at low water a circular sand bar or island about 200 yards across. On this side the creek is not fordable. On the other side I am told it is. Here I went with a canoe yesterday, with Lieut. Smith, and walked to the farther side of the sandbar, and was there within shot of the enemy. I took one Regiment to be Highlanders and the other to be Cornwallis' (common slaves), with some artillery. After I returned, Smith, with Wm. Jordan, one of my privates, went over again, which brought on a small skirmish, seven or eight of their Highlanders running down as fast as possible towards them, with a view of getting between them and the canoe. Smith fired at them without effect. Jordan likewise fired, and his man fell, but whether to dodge, or because wounded, I know not. The enemy fired fourteen guns without effect, crying to Smith in Scotch, 'Stop, you cowardly rascal;' on which he, suiting his actions to his words, said, I retreat like a Guinea Lion. He deigned not to run, which made me uneasy for him. He likewise had a private of the artillery with him, without arms, who fell down at every shot, and caused much laughter to the enemy, as they thought they had killed him.

"We fired five shots from our two field-pieces, which were very well directed, and nearly reached their main body, but did no damage.

"One of the enemy's bullets came very nigh me. I really wished to engage them, the more so when I found them to be a set of people who have ever been friends to tyrants.

"The enemy have just now sent an armed schooner opposite our two field-pieces at the point of the Island (she came down the creek from Dewees Inlet), and anchored her within point-blank shot of the same. On which, our two field-pieces are just ordered to be removed. Their guns fight under deck, consequently our rifles cannot touch them, and a number of flat-bottomed boats, it is said, are following her, in which we are ordered to the point of the Island. I expect their next movement, after landing their men, will be along the creek to the bridge.

"I have sent Bob with this letter and the gun I promised you. I am rather afraid of losing him. I could wish him to stay with you a day or two. I value not myself, but want not to hurt my child; and from the enemy's preparation I expect our fate on Sullivan's Island will be determined in two days at most. I surely think Mr. Chesnut will come down. I have therefore sent on my papers, for should I be unfortunate, you will want them. If you do but escape, my dear friend, I shall be well satisfied, for I am not doubtful of your care of my child.*

"I am most sincerely,
"Your affectionate friend,
"Saml. Wise."

---

*This was an only child, a daughter, afterwards Mrs. Ball, who was sent to England to be educated. Upon the death of Major Wise, his executors, General

Under date again of June 27th, he addressed his friend as follows:—

"Why, my dear Sheriff,* were I to give you an account of our little skirmishes, I might write daily, for we have had it these two days; but do excuse me if my ability is not equal to my inclination, for I describe it the best I can.

"On Monday morning the enemy brought an armed schooner within seven or eight hundred yards of the point of the island. The ensuing night we carried an 18-pounder and two field-pieces to the point, and attacked her early in the morning, and out of eleven shots fired at her, I believe three struck her. Finding we could not destroy her, the firing was discontinued, and at eleven o'clock, about twenty of the enemy, seemingly American renegade Tories, came down to the Oyster Bank with clubbed muskets, and took shelter behind it, at which time the Indians were on the return in a string from the point of Sullivan, and your humble servant was walking along the open beach to the point of Sullivan. At this instant the enemy began to fire, and aimed their shot directly at the Indians, who caused us to laugh heartily by their running and tumbling, several of them whooping and firing their muskets over their shoulders backward. I confess, though the bullets poured round me, I laughed against my inclination. I walked up to our slight breast-work, where I sheltered myself and happened to be the oldest officer. The enemy really aimed well. Their shots went excessively nigh us, and very often struck the top of our breast-work, and frequently dropped close over it within a few yards of us.

"I cannot help doing justice to the superiority of their musketry, for I could not observe that our shot in the least affected them; and I believe they might have been blazing away at us yet, had it not been for our artillery, which was loaded by Lieut. Spencer (a brave officer) with grape and other shot, and dislodged them, it is supposed, with the loss of two or three men; but this is only supposition. But

---

Harrington, and Messrs. Boulk and Hayne, found the estate nearly insolvent. Mr. Ball was not satisfied, and brought suit against them, but recovered nothing.

*It will be remembered Mr. Harrington was now Sheriff of Cheraw District.

they by no means behaved like cowards, for they turned and fired in their retreat, and gained the end, I suppose, they desired, to haul off the schooner while they amused us. Last night they threw up two entrenchments behind the Oyster Bank, and attacked us with howitzers, field-pieces, and musketry from the same, and one 8-pounder from South Island. Being ordered on business to the fort, I was absent at the time of the fray; but was informed by every officer the firing was not near so sharp as yesterday. That of yesterday continued incessantly from musketry from 25 to 30 minutes. This morning it was much longer, but very few muskets were fired, being at about one hundred yards greater distance. Indeed, on our side, only two rifles were fired, and the 18-pounder about three or four times; after which our artillery was hauled off, and are now placed at about a quarter of a mile from the point of Sullivan's Island, where the hills begin. We, fortunately, had nobody killed or wounded either day; but had blankets, &c., shot through, and the stock of a gun broke in a man's hand. We picked up many of their bullets, for they fell so nigh us we saw their whiz in the sand.

"I must to you do justice to Capt. F. Boyakin—(nay, I am in conscience bound to do it). He came down to us in the very hottest of the fire yesterday. I believe there were about sixteen to twenty guns on our side. The enemy are now busy improving their entrenchments.

"I suppose we shall have another brush to-night or tomorrow. Several of our people have, with them, mutually laid down their arms, and walked to the edge of the creek and conversed—a proceeding highly criminal, and now put a stop to. The Highlanders in these conversations always asked after, and sent their compliments to their countrymen. They likewise frequently give us scurrilous language. Their sentries were so nigh us last night, that we could hear them hail quite distinctly, and their drums &c. are almost as familiar to us as own own.

"I am afraid I shall have some uneasiness about Bob. Our field-officers objected to my having so much pay for him, and I did not propose taking any more for him as that was the case, after the last return, which was the 20th instant. But he certainly was a slave to the regiment, and the best drummer in it. He is consequently now missed and inquired after, and I have told them I never intend to take any more pay for him, as they grumbled at it. But they tell me I have no right to withdraw him, and I really think their reply is reasonable, as I have received pay for him. You know the number belonging to J———. I think there is really great risk in his being here; and you, as his parent by adoption, and guardian by my choice, will do as justice directs you about him, for he is now in your hands.

"I am, my dear Captain,
"Your ever sincere and affectionate friend,
"SAML. WISE.

"P.S. Remember me to every inquiring friend, particularly the two Mrs. Pegues.

"N.B. I might have informed you that a report prevails there is a larger fleet off than that already here, which I believe not;—that our regiment have never pulled off their clothes by night since we left Haddrell's Point;—that we have been constantly up for several nights past from 12 or 1 o'clock to sunrise, and on guard, fatigue, or alarm all day. But we are still Rangers, and must do everything, and yet are not worth our rations, though masons, &c., from town, &c., say, they are sure we may easily kill five hundred of the enemy before they reach the fort. Pretty language this, to troops they despise! Remember, we are here three hundred and ten privates, and are to kill five hundred by task work. Adieu! My patience bears no more; but place me where they will, I'll go. I hate to be tasked. We are now in the hands of Omnipotence, and to this must we look for redress through our own endeavours, and not to our own ability; and may the Sovereign of the universe protect and defend you, my dear friend! I might have told you our brave Rangers hauled off the three pieces of artillery to-day, in spite of their musketry and bombs; but to-day they were Highlanders that engaged us. I may likewise inform you a large vessel is this instant run aground in coming over the bar."

This letter* was addressed to "H. W. Harrington, Esq., Haddrell's Point, or elsewhere." Captain H. had come down since the early part of June, in command of a company of volunteers from St. David's Parish, and was now at Haddrell's Point; Major Wise, as it appears, not having been informed of his arrival, or exact locality. He did not take part, however, in the action of the following day, Friday, 28th June—a day rendered ever memorable for the signal victory obtained over a proud and powerful foe!

This repulse of the enemy led to a state of comparative repose for the inhabitants.

There were many suspicious characters, however, to be looked after, and not a few to be confined.

The following order was issued soon after, viz.:—

"The Sheriff of Cheraw District will receive and detain in the Gaol of said District, Henry Machie, John Champneys, and James Carson, whose going at large is dangerous to the liberties of America and the safety of the colony.

"J. RUTLEDGE.

"Charles-town, August 2nd, 1776."

A few days after, another order was also despatched with reference to the same matter, to this effect:—

"The State Prisoners sent to Cheraw Gaol are to be treated with humanity and kept only under the restraint necessary to prevent their escape—their confinement being intended only to secure them and prevent their going at large.

"J. RUTLEDGE.

"August 6th, 1776."†

On the 5th of August, President Rutledge issued a Proclamation, requiring the Legislative Council and General Assembly to meet at Charles-town, on Tuesday, 17th of September, for the despatch of divers weighty and important affairs. An election having been ordered, to fill two

---

*The letter of Major Wise forms a part of the collection of General Harrington, in possession of his son, Colonel H. W. Harrington, of Richmond County, No. Ca., who kindly gave the author access to the whole.

†Harrington manuscripts.

vacancies for the Parish of St. David's, Henry Wm. Harrington and George Hicks, Esqrs., were duly returned, and with Col. Powell took their seats. Mr. Pegues appeared on the 19th. Col. George Pawley and Col. M'Intosh, the other members for St. David's, were absent, the latter doubtless being engaged in military service.

On the 30th of Sept., "the Speaker laid before the House a letter, which he had received from George Gabriel Powell, Esq., and the same being read, was as follows: —

" 'Sir,—I understand there are charges of an extraordinary nature against me, laid before your honorable House. I humbly request, therefore, that I may be heard in my defence by a committee, before any resolution is taken thereupon, trusting that I shall be able so to acquit myself, as to stand fair in the opinion of my country, which is above all things desirable, to

" 'Honorable Sir,
" 'Your most obt. humble servant,
" 'G. G. POWELL.'

" 'Charles-town, Sept. 30th, 1776.

"Whereupon, it was ordered, that the consideration of the said letter be postponed."

Of the character of the charges referred to, nothing is known. The subsequent records of the House make no mention of the matter; and the probability is, that having been found to be a groundless slander or the work of some malicious enemy, no further notice was taken of the affair. There is at least no evidence that Col. Powell suffered at all in the public estimation.

On the 10th of October, it was resolved by the House, "that the Committee of St. David's Parish do take into their custody the salt now in Mr. John Mitchell's store, at Cheraw Hill, paying for the same at the rate of fifty shillings currency per bushel." "And that they sell and distribute the said salt to and amongst such of the inhabitants of this State, as have not lately received a dividend of the salt in Charles-town, or at Winyaw, who shall apply for the same, in the proportion of one half bushel to six white persons in a family." This action indicates the extreme scarcity of this article, and to what shifts the distressed inhabitants were driven, alike destitute to a great extent of the means of defence and necessaries of life.

At this Session of Assembly, an Act was passed, making a change as to the places of election for St. David's. The preamble was in these words:—"Whereas, the great extent of the Parish of St. David's renders it exceedingly inconvenient for all the inhabitants thereof to attend the elections at the parish church, and it would greatly conduce to their ease if the election was held one day at the court house in the said parish, and the other day at the parish church thereof," &c.: and thus it was arranged.

After the adjournment of the Court for Charles-town District in October, Chief Justice Drayton presiding, the Judges commenced their circuits throughout the state.

The charge of the Chief Justice to the Grand Jury of Charles-town was marked by learning and patriotic ardor, and published in the *Gazettes,* producing, as on former occasions, a decided effect upon the public mind. The Court for Cheraws District was opened on Tuesday, 15th of Nov., and the following presentments were made by the Grand Jury:—

"I. When we reflect on the many grievances that the good people of North America have long labored under from the numerous oppressive and unconstitutional acts of the British Parliament, but more particularly some that have been passed since the conclusion of the late war; and at the same time consider, that their most humble and dutiful petitions and remonstrances against these acts have been always answered by a repetition of similar, nay, sometimes greater injuries and oppressions; we find them justified by the laws of God and Nature, and compelled by the dictates of reason and humanity, to dissolve their union with that Government, and to renounce all allegiance thereto. It is, therefore, with the highest pleasure, that the Grand Jury for the District of Cheraws embraces this first opportunity of congratulating our fellow-citizens and American brethren on the late declaration of the Constitutional Congress, constituting the United Colonies of North America free and independent States, and the inhabitants thereof totally absolved from any allegiance to the British Crown, that being the only means now left of securing to themselves and their posterity the inestimable blessings of liberty and happiness, and which we, as freemen, are resolved to support and defend at the hazard of our lives and fortunes.

"II. We present the want of a a new jury list in this district, and recommend that a law may be passed for that purpose.

"Lastly. We return thanks to his Honor, the Judge, for his most excellent charge delivered the first day of this sessions.

"Claudius Pegues, *Foreman*.	L.S.
Charles M'Call.	L.S.
Thomas Ellerbe.	L.S.
John Wilds.	L.S.
Zachariah Nettles.	L.S.
Thomas Ayer.	L.S.
Martin Kolb.	L.S.
Abel Edwards.	L.S.
Philip Pledger.	L.S.
Robert Lide.	L.S.
John Kimbrough.	L.S.
Thomas Lide.	L.S.
William Pouncey.	L.S.
Moses Speight.	L.S.
John Mikell.	L.S.
Martin Dewitt.	L.S.
Magnus Corgill.	L.S.
Aaron Daniel.	L.S.
Richard Curtis.	L.S.
Abel Wilds.	L.S.
Thomas James.	L.S."*

The occasion, memorable as the first presented to the people of Cheraws, since the 4th of July previous, for the expression of their sentiments, was hailed with delight, and rendered worthy, in the improvement made of it, to be

*Gazette.

placed side by side with others that had gone before. Nothing could be added to give weight to what the Grand Jury here declared to the world, but the redeeming the pledge of "life and fortune." This had already been done in part, and was within a few years following to be completed by the costliest oblations on the altar of freedom.

In consequence of the unsettled state of affairs, the Court for Cheraws District did not sit again until the fall of 1778, and after that no more until the war was over.

For more than two years to come, the British confining their operations chiefly to the northward, South Carolina enjoyed a state of profound repose.

A lucrative trade was carried on by waggons with the States south of New Jersey. Commerce flourished and plenty abounded. With the exception of occasional incursions by the Tories along the border, there was little to mar the pleasures of the calm which thus succeeded the opening storm. And even the spirit of the Tories was crushed by the brilliant victory of Fort Moultrie, and the departure of the enemy.

Liberty had risen to the ascendant. And until Carolina became again the scene of hostile operations, no incident of special interest transpired in connexion with the struggle on the Pedee. So long as the Whigs could remain at home, domestic enemies kept at a distance.

On the 18th of Feb., 1777, the parish of St. David lost a prominent man and useful citizen, Arthur Hart, Esq. He died at his residence on Pedee, having served his country faithfully from the commencement of the struggle for independence, leaving a son, James Hart, to transmit his name and spirit to his descendants.

We hear again from Major Wise, now of the Continental line, in the following letter to Capt. Harrington :—

"Nelson's Ferry, 1st March, 1777.

"My dear Friend,—We are once more ordered to Georgia, that State being actually invaded, and a whole company of our regiment at Fort M'Intosh* taken prisoners. Samuel

---

*Fort M'Intosh is a stockade on the St. Jues. Winn, our captain, behaved well.

Williams was with the party that took our people. Tomorrow we leave, and I shall have the command of the main detachment on the march. Col. Thompson goes ahead with a few horse, and Col. Mayson is absent.

"I have no papers to send you. We are out of the latitude of news here.

"Believe me, my dearest Friend,
"Your ever well wisher,
"H. W. Harrington, Esq.   SAM. WISE.
"Pedee."

On the 9th of April, writs of election were issued for filling up vacancies in the General Assembly.

One member was returned for St. David's, in the room of the Hon. Alexander M'Intosh, who had been elected a member of the Legislative Council.

Thus the year 1777 passed on and drew to a close. Attention began to be turned to other matters, now that comparative quiet was restored, and the public mind to some extent relieved from the long-continued agitation to which it had been subjected.

The education of the young, in consequence of the troubles of the past, had been sadly neglected. The evil was sorely felt, and a general determination manifested to provide against its continuance.

Of the efforts made in this direction, in St. David's, some account will be given in the next chapter.

CHAPTER XIII.

St. David's Society—Its organization—First members—Others added—Original subscription paper—Incorporation of the society—Its subsequent history—Origin of "Society Hill"—Character of the community—Military organization on Pedee—Military Acts—Alexander M'Intosh a brigadier general—Letters of Major Wise—Oath of allegiance—Account of it—Original record—Letter of Major Wise—Presentments of grand jury of Cheraws—Representatives elected for St. David's—Letter of Henry William Harrington—Of Major Wise—Death of Colonel Powell—Account of him—State of public affairs—Colonel M'Intosh in service—Correspondence with General Moultrie—Movements of the army—M'Intosh's reply to the enemy—General alarm through the State—Armies in motion—Siege of Charles-town—Colonel M'Intosh a commissoner to treat with the enemy—Siege raised—Public rejoicings—Extracts from Pugh's journal—Attack on Savannah—Major Wise killed—His character—Loss of others from Pedee—Captain Harrington removes to No. Ca.—His promotions—Judge Pendleton elected representative in place of Major Wise—Extracts from Journal of Assembly on subject—Tories in gaol—Maurice Murphy a colonel—Gloomy prospects for the State.

ABOUT this time appears the first mention of a society which was destined to exert an important influence on the welfare of the communities bordering on the Upper Pedee.

But little attention had hitherto been given to the subject of education. With a country recently settled, and most of the inhabitants poor, it was to be expected that matters of material interest would first engage the thoughts of the people. For some years past, too, the public disturbances, so deeply affecting the peace and prosperity of the infant settlements, had seriously retarded their progress.

Being now, however, in a state of comparative repose, and with brighter prospects for the future, the welfare of the rising generation was no longer overlooked.

On the 13th of December, 1777, this entry appears in the Rev. Mr. Pugh's Journal:—"Assembled at the Meeting House, in Society, to promote learning;" and on the 20th, "went to Dr. Mills', about the Society's rules." On the 31st, also, "went to the Neck,* to the Society, signed the rules, chose officers, &c."

The Hon. Alexander M'Intosh was elected president, and George Hicks and Abel Kolb, wardens.

The society took the name of "St. David's," and by that honored appellation continued afterwards to be distinguished.

The names of those who participated in the organization were as follows, viz.:—

Gen. Alexander M'Intosh	Col. George Hicks
Col. Thomas Lide	Capt. Thomas Ellerbe
Wm. Henry Mills	William Terrel
Abel Wilds	Thomas Evans, sen.
Major Robert Lide	Joshua Edwards
Capt. Daniel Sparks	Col. Abel Kolb
Rev. Elhanan Winchester	Nathanael Saunders
Capt. William Dewitt	Thomas James
Rev. Evan Pugh	William Pegues, Esq.
Benjamin Rogers	

On the 31st of January, 1778, were added to the list of members,—

Capt. Philip Pledger	Richard Hodge
Abel Edwards	Col. George Pawley
Thomas Powe	John O'Neall
William Ellerbe	William Thomas, Esq.
Charles Mason	Edward Irby
Jeremiah Brown	Major John Kimbrough
Joshua Terrel	Peter Allston, Esq.
Benjamin Williamson	Captain Simon Connell
Capt. Edward Jones	Cap. George King
John Wilds	Philip Singleton
James Hicks	Capt. Benjamin Hicks
John Thompson	Charles Irby
William Blassingame	Capt. Claudius Pegues, Jr.
Capt. Charles Gee	Edward Blake.
John Hodge	

The organization of the society excited much interest among the inhabitants of St. David's Parish.

An original subscription paper of the date just mentioned,

*The Welch Neck.

with a preamble, has survived the ravages of time, and is in these words, viz. :—

"As the endowing and establishing public schools and other seminaries of learning has ever been attended with the most salutary effects, as well by cultivating in youth the principles of religion and every social virtue, as by enabling them afterwards to fill with dignity and usefulness the most important departments of the State; who that is a lover of his country, as he looks around him, can fail to deplore the great want of this necessary qualification in our youth, especially in the interior parts of it, at this early period of our flourishing and rising state. In the future, when we shall be at liberty to make our own laws without the control of an arbitrary despot, what heart would not glow with pleasure to see a senate filled with learned, wise, and able men, for the want of whom the most flourishing republics have become the tools of arbitrary despots. And whereas, there is a society established in the Parish of St. David, by the name of the St. David's Society, purposely for founding a public school in the said parish for educating youths in the Latin and Greek languages, mathematics, and other useful branches of learning, by those who are not of ability, without assistance, to carry so useful and necessary an effort into effect:

"Wherefore, in order to contribute to so laudable and benevolent an undertaking, we, whose names are hereunto subscribed, do promise to pay, or cause to be paid into the hands of the Secretary of the said Society, the respective sums subjoined to each of our names, whenever the same is called for by the said Secretary or his order.

"Witness our hands, the 31st day of January, 1778.

	£	s.		£	s.
William Lide	100	0	Charles Irby	50	0
John Wilson	50	0	Joseph Johnson	50	0
Philemon Thomas	25	0	John Manderson	50	0
Duke Glen	25	0	John Ogle	500	0
John Jenkins	25	0	Joseph Pledger	50	0
William Jones	25	0	John Pledger	50	0
John Speed	25	0	Benjamin James	20	0
Nathan Savage	100	0	Isaiah Frisbe	50	0

	£	s.		£	s.
Joseph Dabbs	50	0	Moses Fort	25	0
Jethro Moore	25	0	John Mikell	50	0
Charles Evans	50	0	William Forniss	50	0
Joseph Gourley	25	0	David Roach	25	0
Nathanael Sanders	100	0	William Vann	5	0
Tristram Thomas	55	0	Enoch Evans, Jun.	20	0
Charles Sparks	100	0	Ethelred Clary	25	0
John Thompson	50	0	Aaron Daniel	50	0
Edmund Irby	50	0	Samuel Winds	60	0
John Lucas	25	0	Baily Clark	100	0
Samuel De Saurency	12	10	Thomas Deane	50	0
Andrew Dick	15	0	Thomas Ayer	10	0"*

In the sentiments expressed, and the laudable interest taken in so timely and noble an undertaking, this paper does honor to the early days of the Pedee. The most of the subscribers† lived in other parts of the parish, at some distance from Long Bluff.

On the 7th of May, a few names were added to the list of members, viz., James Blassingame, Adam Cusack, John M'Call, Hugh Jones, and Rev. John Cowen.

At a meeting of the society, July 27th, were added the names of David Roach, Alex. Craig, Jethro Moore, Robert Gibson, and Henry Clark; and on 14th September, Rev. John Brown.

In December of this year (1778), St. David's Society was incorporated. The Preamble to the Act was in these words:—"Whereas, sundry inhabitants of the Cheraw District have formed themselves into a society by the name of the 'Saint David's Society,' for the express purpose of instituting and endowing a seminary of learning in the District of Cheraw, to instruct and educate youth in the necessary and useful branches of knowledge, and have made humble application to the General Assembly of this State to be incorporated, and invested with such powers and privileges as may most effectually advance the views of the said Society:

---

*£100, depreciated in May, 1778, was equivalent to £30 8s. 9¾d. £100, old currency in sterling, to £14 5s. 8½d.

†Some of the names on the subscription list appear here for the first and last in the records of the time, as in the case of Dr. John Ogle, the largest subscriber.

Therefore, be it enacted, That the Honorable Alexander M'Intosh, Esq., President of the said Society, and George Hicks and Abel Kolb, Esqrs., the present Wardens, and the several persons who now are, or who shall hereafter be, members of the said Society, shall be a body incorporate."

Subsequent to this time, no further progress appears to have been made, until the troubles of the Revolution were over, when the society was reorganized, and went into vigorous operation.

The first school-house was erected a few yards from the spot where the building known to the present generation was used as an academy until within a few years since. It was near the brow of the first commanding eminence above the river, about three quarters of a mile distant.

Of the first teachers nothing is known. For more than a half century after, the academy of St. David's was of distinguished note in the eastern section of the State. Many were prepared within its walls for a more thorough course of study abroad; and others, not less eminent in after years, looked back to it as their only Alma Mater.

About this time, settlements began to be made still further out from the river, along the line of the present village, and from the society then established, the infant community took the name of "Society Hill."

Formed of planters in easy circumstances, though for the most part yet of small estates, but who continued to grow in wealth and refinement, this community became noted for the intelligence and virtue of its members, and in all the essential elements of character and progress changed less than almost any other to be found. It presented no attractions to men of enterprise from abroad, and opened but little field for the spirit of adventure or speculation to those in its midst, and continued, as a consequence, to be marked by those quiet and conservative traits which an agricultural people, with a sound religious sentiment pervading them, might be expected to display. Since the early part of 1775, the military organization on the Pedee had undergone important changes. At that time, as will be remembered, Col. G. G. Powell was in command of the Cheraw Regiment, one of the thirteen into which the militia of the State was then divided, with Charles Augustus Steward, Lieut.-Colonel, and Abraham Buckholts, Major. In the latter part of 1777, Geo. Hicks was Colonel, Abel Kolb, Lieut.-Col., and Lemuel Benton, Major. Col. Hicks probably succeeded Col. Powell.

The Militia Act of March, 1778, which repealed all former Acts, as well as the "Resolves of the late Provincial Congress," provided for a division of the militia into three brigades, for each of which a brigadier-general and major of brigade were to be appointed. Prior to that time, as already mentioned, the only organization was that of companies, battalions or troops, and regiments.

Under the Act of 1778, no volunteer company was to be formed, and those previously existing were to be disbanded whenever there should cease to be fifty effective men on their muster rolls. No regiment was to be divided unless containing more than twelve hundred men. Lieut.-Colonel Alexander M'Intosh was appointed to the command of the brigade, embracing the eastern portion of the State.

This position he maintained till his death, as appears from the private records and public journals of the day.

Major Wise continued to write to his friend, Capt. Harrington, giving some account of matters as they transpired in other parts of the State, and in Georgia:—

"My dear Friend,   "Charles-town, January 22, 1778.

"You herewith receive the last paper printed, or likely to be for some time, on account of the fire which happened here on the morning of the 15th inst., which burned down all along the Bay, from Queen's Street to Stol's Alley and back in a parallel line to Church Street, except a few scattering houses. The Tories have been by some few accused of it, but the real cause was, I believe, accidental in Union Street, and an excessively high wind. Indigo is very dull sale, at 60s., and rice at 70s.—the embargo still continuing. We have a report of a French war, but nothing certain.

"The Assembly have granted a million to purchase produce to ship for dry goods, to be sold to the public at 25 per cent. profit; and chose the following delegates, viz.,

Christopher Gadsden, A. Middleton, Wm. H. Drayton, H. Laurens, and J. Matthews. The last wanted a few votes, but I am sure will be chosen to-morrow.

"Three companies of our regiment and myself are ordered to town to do duty, with Col. Pinckney. Therefore I shall be stationed here, probably for some time. I have sent for the *Georgia Constitution* for you, and hope to get it.

"24th. Since writing the above, a report prevails that an engagement happened on Christmas-day between Generals Washington and Howe—the particulars unknown. Some say Washington was defeated.

"I am, dear Sir,
"Your ever afft. friend,
"S. WISE.
"Henry Wm. Harrington, Esq., Pedee."

"My dear Sir, "Charles-town, 12 April, 1778.

"The General having ordered me with 200 men to Georgia (notwithstanding he had given me leave to come up), prevents my attending Court, and I fear will be of bad consequence to you in your trial with James. I will be greatly obliged to you if you will deliver the enclosed to Col. Hicks. The Tories here are of opinion they will govern before the summer is over.

"Indeed, Col. Powell told me yesterday he would not go off, for we should have enough on our hands without troubling them.

"Gen. Howe writes from Georgia, that the enemy are collecting at St. Augustine from West Florida and every other quarter, to attack Georgia; and that this affair of the Tories from the back country marching, is a plan settled some time ago. I know it will by the ignorant be attributed to the oath. I don't expect to see you before July, even should we not be attacked.

"I promised myself much satisfaction from this intended jaunt to Pedee, for my wife and son-in-law were coming with me.

"However, you know a soldier ought to be patient under disappointments.

"I understand Hodge brought in several letters and gave

them to Wiley, but none of them have reached me. Were it not that I knew of this circumstance, I might suspect my friends on Pedee had forgotten the man who is resolved never to forget them, or the place where the partner of his heart is deposited.

"We have great hopes of peace from the accounts received from the Southward. God speed it, I say.

"I am, with the most sincere regard,
"Dear Sir, ever your affect. friend,
"S. WISE.

"Henry Wm. Harrington, Esq., Pedee."

The oath referred to in this letter in connexion with the Tories, was that enacted by the Assembly in March of this year, as an oath or affirmation of allegiance, to be taken by every adult made, in the following words, viz.: "I, A. B., do swear or affirm that I will bear true faith or allegiance to the State of South Carolina, and will faithfully support, maintain, and defend the same, against George the Third, King of Great Britain, his successors, abettors, and all other enemies and opposers whatsoever; and will, without delay, discover to the Executive Authority, or some one Justice of the Peace in this State, all plots and conspiracies that shall come to my knowledge, against the said State, or any other of the United States of America. So help me God."

Those who refused this oath were obliged to depart the country, being permitted to leave their families if they desired it, and also to sell or carry off their estates.

It is not surprising that the disaffected were excited by it to the bitterest resolves.

An original certificate* in the printed form, which appears to have been distributed throughout the State, is in these words, viz.: "I do hereby certify, that Thomas Quick hath taken and subscribed the Oath of Allegiance and Fidelity, as directed by an Act of the General Assembly of the State of South Carolina, entitled, "An Act to oblige every free male inhabitant of this State, above a certain age, to

---

*In the author's possession. It was found among the papers of Thomas Quick.

give assurance of Fidelity and Allegiance to the same, and for other purposes therein mentioned.

"JAMES HICKS, Capt.

"May, the 29th day, 1778."

Again Major Wise writes:—

"Charles-town, 18th April, 1778.

"My dear Friend,

"I wrote you by Mr. Strother of my being ordered to Georgia, for which place I set off to-morrow, with 150 rank and file of ours—58 of the 1st and 50 of the 6th, under command of Col. C. C. Pinckney—a circumstance I like much. The Tories are said to be assembled there to the number of 500—nay, some accounts say, 1700.

"Remember me to all your family, and believe me,

"Your ever sincere Friend,

"S. WISE.

"Henry Wm. Harrington, Esq., Pedee."

The Court for Cheraw District opened on the 16th of November. The Grand Jury made the following presentments:—

"I. We present, as a great grievance, the number of Representatives in the General Assembly, humbly apprehending that thereby the State is put to an unnecessary expense, and that if the representation was smaller it would be thereby more respectable, and the public business be done with facility.

"II. We present, as a grievance, the want of a public post throughout this State.

"III. We present, as a grievance, the want of a bridge over Black Creek, and over Thompson's Creek, near Roger's Ferry, and over Crooked Creek.

"Lastly we recommend that these presentments may be published in the *Gazettes*.

"William Henry Mills, *Foreman*. L.S.
George Hicks. L.S.
John Hodge. L.S.
Peter Roach. L.S.

Thomas Ellerbe.	L.S.
William Dewitt.	L.S.
Claudius Pegues, sen.	L.S.
Benjamin Hicks.	L.S.
Thomas Hicks.	L.S.
Thomas Ayer.	L.S.
John Pigot.	L.S.
Joseph Pledger.	L.S.
William Blassingame.	L.S.
Claudius Pegues, jun.	L.S.
Henry Council.	L.S.
Joshua Edwards.	L.S.

"Ordered that the said presentments be printed and published.

"By the Court,
"Thomas Powe, C.C.T."

By the Constitution, adopted in March previous, the representation had been reapportioned, and provision made for the election of senators. The parishes retained, in most instances, the number of representatives they had before. No change was made in the case of St. David's, which was now entitled to one senator and six representatives. The grand jury called in question the wisdom or expediency of this feature of the new Constitution, and were bold enough to recommend the change. Elections were ordered for the last Monday in November; and for St. David's, Hon. Alexander M'Intosh was returned as senator; for representatives, William Standard, Charles Evans, Wm. Henry Mills, William Pegues, and Abel Kolb, Esquires; leaving a vacancy, which was subsequently filled by the election of Major Wise.

The Legislature was to meet on the first Monday in January ensuing, in Charles-town.

The following letter will convey some idea of the trying wants of this period, as experienced by the people of the interior:—

"Colonel Joseph Kershaw.

"Dear Sir,—Our friend, Claudius Pegues, Esq., is so greatly distressed by an unfortunate accident that happened to his eldest son last Tuesday, that he cannot write on the subject; but well knowing your friendship for him, has desired me to beg the favor of you, Sir, to give Mr. John Wright, the bearer of this, all possible assistance in obtaining amputating instruments at or near Camden. The young man received a load of Bristol shot, from his own gun, in his right arm, just above the wrist, by which both bones are much shattered; and notwithstanding the immediate assistance of two doctors, we, from certain appearances, are apprehensive of mortification; and our doctors having no instruments, in order to be prepared for the worst, we now make this application to our friend to assist us in obtaining an amputating saw for the arm, and a needle. Your brother, Sir, has been so good as to write on our behalf in a pressing manner to Mr. Duncan McRae; but our fears suggest to us, as there is a possibility of that gentleman's being from home, that that may now be the case; and as a disappointment of this nature may greatly endanger the life of my young friend, permit me, Sir, to entreat you to interest yourself in this matter; and then, if instruments are to be had, I doubt not but we shall be so far happy as to obtain them.

"I am, with high regard,
"Your most humble and
"Most obedient Servant,
"HENRY WM. HARRINGTON.
"Decr. 13, 1778."

Soon after this, Major Wise writes from Purysburg. The conflict was waxing warm in that quarter.

"Head-quarters, Purysburg, 18th January, 1779.

"Dear Harrington,—I write you merely because, when an opportunity offers, I wish it not to escape me. We gather here pretty fast; but you know what militia are, no sooner come, than for going again. We may have here now nearly or quite 3000, and expect 1500 more in two or three days from your State.* Our back country militia has not yet joined us. Howe is gone, regretted by none. Our present

*Captain Harrington had removed to North Carolina.

general (Lincoln) seems to command for himself, and I hope will do better.

"The living was never so well found. He lets us want for nothing that is necessary to be had. Nor are we turned out and harrassed for every trifle. The army is as little fatigued as possible. The enemy have their full swing in Georgia, and are in possession of all the ferries, which, I apprehend, will make it very difficult re-entering Georgia. The Georgians have joined them in shoals, and have taken arms against us. Yet I am satisfied it is more through necessity than choice, for we really abandoned them and their property to the enemy. And should we now leave this place (such is our present situation), and march up the country to cross the river high up, the enemy might, in the interim, enter Carolina here, and take the two remaining galleys, which have been warped up here just above the tideway. We lost in Sunbury Fort, which is taken, upwards of 100 more prisoners, with the cannon and everything there. I never before could imagine it possible that such showers of bullets could have been fired without doing more execution. The enemy fired on us thirty-eight minutes in flank, front, and rear; and so nigh as to abuse us with their tongues; and we scarcely ever returned the fire, and had to retreat over a causeway across an impassable swamp a full quarter.

"Of our regiment, we had but one sergeant killed, and four privates wounded, and sixty-four made prisoners.

"I am, my dear friend,
"Yours most sincerely,
"SAMUEL WISE.

"Remember me to your family.

"The enemy and we are frequently corresponding by way of flags, and they seem in this respect more ready than is judged expedient. It is suspected they send, through this means, to gain intelligence.

"However, they are polite, and it is said, use our prisoners well."

The parish of St. David was now to mourn the loss of one who had been long and prominently connected with its history.

No man of the time had occupied a more conspicuous or honorable place in all connected with the public interests of the Pedee than George Gabriel Powell. On the 21st of January his useful life was brought to a close in Christ Church Parish. Having early won the confidence and affection of the people on the Pedee, he retained his place in their esteem with singular uniformity through years of eventful changes, relinquishing at times, in their behalf, positions of more commanding influence, returning to their service as his first love, and devoting to it his maturest labours to the end of his career.

His memory should never cease to be cherished with admiring gratitude by the descendants of those whom he so faithfully served.

The Legislature was now in session in Charles-town, and in February elected William Strother Sheriff of Cheraws district.

Attention, however, was now to be turned from civil affairs to the reapproaching struggle for liberty and life, and the comparative calm which had been enjoyed for two years past was to be no more known until the close of the war.

After the failure of the British Commissioners to effect a reunion of the Colonies with the Mother Country, the struggle was recommenced on a new system. The order of procedure was changed, and the South became henceforth the principal theatre of offensive operations.

The close of 1778 saw more active and vigorous preparations than before for a decisive blow upon the South. In December of that year Savannah was taken, and South Carolina became a frontier state, calling for redoubled efforts on the part of her people. The public spirit was roused to the highest pitch, and everywhere military movements were being made. The churches were deserted, and the inhabitants generally in a state of commotion and alarm. Lieut.-Col. M'Intosh was now actively engaged in the service of the State. After the evacuation of Augusta by the enemy, he was detached, in command of a company of regulars, with a party of militia under Col. Howard, in all about 200, to follow the enemy and harass them in the rear.

Col. M'Intosh appears to have possessed, in an eminent degree, the confidence and affection of Genl. Moultrie. About this time the following correspondence took place between them.

"(Sent by express).

"Black Swamp, Apl. 29, 1779.

"Dear Sir,

"You must endeavor to join us, if you can without any great risk. I wish you could have given me an account of the enemy's number. I could better judge how to act; the light horseman informs me you imagine them upwards of three hundred men. I think you were right to retreat in time, as your force would not be equal to theirs by any means. I expect soon to have accounts from you and more particulars; as you have no baggage, you may cross the country to this.

"I am, &c.,
"WILLIAM MOULTRIE."*

To this letter, Col. M'Intosh replied as follows:—

"Coosahatchie, Apl. 30th, 1779.

"Dear General:

"Last night two deserters from the enemy came to Bee's Creek; they were of the light infantry. They say Col. Maitland commanded yesterday, that he had the light infantry, and the 2nd battalion of the 71st regiment, amounting to eight or nine hundred men; that they were to send for three field-pieces and three six-pounders, with a reinforcement to make them up 1500 men; that they did not know the Colonel's plan, but that they heard it said that he intended to proceed to Charles-town, and that he had thirty or forty Indians with him. I have given Genl. Bull and Col. Skirving information of these particulars; the men are so lame that I cannot be up before tomorrow night. We are all safe.

"I am, &c.,
"ALEXANDER M'INTOSH.†

"Brig.-Genl. Moultrie."

*Moultrie's "Memoirs," p. 389.
†Ibid., p. 401.

On his retreat from Black Swamp immediately after, having learned that the enemy had crossed the river at the Two Sisters in great force, General Moultrie marched with all possible expedition to Coosahatchie, giving notice to Colonel M'Intosh, who was posted at Purysburg, to march immediately, so as to join him, which he did that night.

Colonel M'Intosh gained no little note upon the opening of the campaign in Georgia, by a reply to the enemy, which became a well-known saying in the army. It was in February, 1777, when a body of British troops, arriving at Sunbury, a party of them were detached to demand the surrender of a fort, of which M'Intosh was in command. His answer was, "Come and take it;" which they deemed it expedient not to attempt to do.

The militia were now marching to Charles-town from different parts of the back country.

Captain James Gregg, among others, went down on this occasion, in command of a company from "Old Liberty," just below the line of St. David's, on the west side of the river.

General Prevost was now in pursuit of General Moultrie with an army of 4000 men, General Lincoln marching with hasty strides to come up with the British, Governor Rutledge hurrying down from Orangeburg with about 600 militia, hastening to get to town, lest he should be shut off.

Never was there such consternation and confusion, five armies moving through the lower parts of the State at the same time, and all for different purposes.

A large proportion of the militia of the State had been drafted, put under the command of Colonel Richardson, and marched for the American head-quarters.* A portion of this draft doubtless formed the expedition from Pedee, long after spoken of as the "Black Swamp Voyage."† Its destination was Black Swamp, Beaufort District, or the neighborhood, toward which a general movement had been made. The term "Voyage" was used by writers of a previous age for expeditions either by land or sea, and being

*Ramsay's "Revolution," vol. ii. p. 12.
†Ayer's "Narrative."

gradually adopted into the spoken language of the day, was retained for a long period after, as in this instance, though it had become obsolete with contemporary writers.

The retreating and invading forces concentrated towards Charles-town, and but for a remarkable delay on the part of General Prevost, when not far from the city, it would, as all accounts agree, undoubtedly have been taken. In the disposition of the troops for the defence of the town, Colonel M'Intosh, with the 5th Regiment, was commanded to take post in the redoubt, on the right side of the line.* On the 12th of May, when the question was carried for giving up the town on a neutrality, a respectable merchant and citizen of Charles-town was affected to tears at the humiliating spectacle.

Colonel John Laurens was requested to carry a message from the Governor and Council to General Prevost, but begged to be excused, saying, that though he would do anything in his power to serve his country, he could not think of carrying such a message as *that*. General Moultrie then sent for Colonel M'Intosh, and requested he would go with Colonel Roger Smith, who had been called on by the Governor with the message. They both begged to be excused, but were at length pressed into compliance. Colonel Prevost acted on the part of the British.

The message was to this effect: to propose a neutrality during the war between Great Britain and America; and the question, whether the State should belong to Great Britain or remain one of the United States, was to be determined by the treaty of peace between the two powers. The commissioners held their conference a quarter of a mile from the American gate. The enemy would accede to no other terms but the surrender of the Americans as prisoners of war. The result was speedily known, and at daylight the next morning, the joyful report was spread along the lines that the enemy had gone.†

The news of the seige was carried rapidly through the State, and many were filled with alarm and gloomy forebodings.

*Moultrie's "Memoirs," p. 412.
†Ibid., p. 431.

This entry occurs in the journal of the Rev. Evan Pugh, under date of May 11th: "Have news of Charles-town being besieged by the enemy. I feel melancholy about the fate of Charles-town and my friends."

Sounds of rejoicing, however, were soon to follow. On the 14th of July, Mr. Pugh preached a thanksgiving sermon for the signal deliverance from the foe. But the joyous respite was of short duration.

With the approach of October, preparations were made for an attack on Savannah by the combined forces of the French and Americans. On the 9th of that month the assault was made, and many sealed their devotion to liberty with their blood. Among the number of these was Major Samuel Wise, a gallant soldier of freedom and a cherished son of Pedee. He served the country of his adoption with enthusiastic ardor, and was ever true to those instincts which he brought with him from the land of his birth. Major Wise was possessed of a generous disposition and high sense of honor. Scrupulous himself in his dealings with others, he exacted a like course of conduct in return, which involved him at times in serious difficulties. His last years were saddened by reverse and bereavement. His end was such as he desired it to be, at the post of duty and in the thickest of the strife.

Leaving no son, his name disappeared, except in its records, from the history of Carolina, but will ever be cherished as one on that extended roll of patriot worthies which these stirring times produced. The death of this good soldier was not the only one for which the inhabitants of the Pedee were called to mourn on this occasion.

In his journal, November 9th, with reference to the siege of Savannah, Mr. Pugh wrote: "We lost many youth;" and on the 21st, preached (Job xiv. 1, 2) "A funeral for those youths lost at Savannah, 9th October past, from these parts."

Captain Harrington, having removed some time previous to this from the Welch Neck on Pedee, to Richmond County, North Carolina, was, on the 25th of November, commissioned colonel of the militia of that county; and, in June of the following year, promoted to the brigadier-generalship of the Salisbury District, which embraced an extensive territory. His head-quarters afterward were chiefly at Cross Creek; a part of the time also at Haley's ferry, and for a short period near Cheraw Hill.

The Legislature was now in session in Charles-town, giving all the aid in its power to the defence of the State. The death of Major Wise created a vacancy in the representation from St. David's, which was filled by the election of the Hon. Henry Pendleton. Judge Pendleton had been on the Law Bench since April, 1776; but at this time, and until the adoption of the Constitution of 1790, a judge was eligible to a seat in the Legislature. He was, however, not a resident of St. David's Parish, and the Constitution of 1788 made the ownership of a settled estate and freehold in his own right, of the value of three thousand four hundred pounds currency, clear of debt, in the parish or district for which a non-resident should be elected, necessary to his eligibility. Whether he actually owned such an estate, or was made for the time a nominal possessor, is not known. There *was* a difficulty, however, connected with the election, as appears from the following proceedings in the House of Representatives, Jan. 24th, 1780, viz.:—"Mr. Justice Burke presented to this House a Petition of the Hon. Henry Pendleton, Esq., and the same was received and read, setting forth, that the Petitioner is informed by several inhabitants and freeholders of the Parish of St. David's, that he was unanimously elected by a majority of the electors of the said parish, to be their representative in the General Assembly, and that, by some accident or neglect, the writ of election has never been returned. The Petitioner therefore prays that he may be admitted to his seat, and that the right of representation may be reserved to the said parish, notwithstanding any accident that may have befallen the said writ, &c.

"Read also the following affidavit, which was presented with the said Petition, viz.:—

"South Carolina.

"George Cogdell maketh oath, that he was at the election in St. David's Parish for a member to serve in the

General Assembly in the room of Major Wise, deceased, about the latter end of November, held in consequence of a writ issued for that purpose, when the Hon. H. Pendleton, Esq., was, as he understands, unanimously elected, and supposes the said writ, if not returned, must have been lost or neglected."

The campaign of 1779 ended without any decisive result on either side. The Tories, as usual, had been actively at work, the Whigs having been called away from their homes, and some of the former were now paying the penalty, as the following record shows:—

"Received of Thomas Powe, Commissary of my Regiment, 10 lbs. corn flour, 750 lbs. beef, and 450 lbs. corn flour, for use of my Regiment, guarding the Tories in jail—Oct. 30th, 1779. GEO. HICKS, Colonel."*

This was the jail at Long Bluff, and these Tories had doubtless been engaged in some attack or plundering expedition, and captured.

Maurice Murphy was now in command as acting Colonel in the lower part of St. David's Parish, on the east side of the river, embracing probably a portion of Liberty Precinct. He was a man of reckless daring and ardent patriotism, and performed a most influential part throughout the war. Every available resource of men and means was now called into requisition.

The prospect was most inviting for the enemy.

The French had taken their departure; and no sooner was this known, than a grand expedition was set on foot from New York, under Sir Henry Clinton, for the reduction of Charles-town, and the subjection of the State. The Continental Regiments in South Carolina had been greatly reduced by the casualties of war and the expiration of their terms of service. From twenty-four hundred in 1777, the number was diminished to eight hundred in 1780. The future was full of gloom for the Whigs. Nevertheless, the resolution was adopted, in full House of Assembly, to defend Charles-town to the last extremity.

---

*Comptroller's office, Columbia, S. C.

The militia were ordered to rendezvous, and every man who could to take up arms. There was an ominous calm, now that the conflict of 1779 had passed away; and every one felt that the last and decisive struggle was soon to begin. The Whigs of Pedee were prepared for the strife, and another chapter will show how nobly they responded to the call of their country.

CHAPTER XIV.

Opening of year 1780—Response from Pedee for defence of Charles-town—Movement of forces—No. Ca. militia under Colonel Harrington—The colonel leaves for Newbern—His letter—Effects of fall of Charles-town on the people—Incidents connected with it—Extracts from Pugh's Journal—Feeling of the British—Wemys's Expedition up Pedee—Houses burned—Adam Cusack hung—Reaches Cheraw—Extracts from Pugh's Journal—Oath of allegiance—Incidents connected with it—Wemys returns—Indulgence shown him afterwards by General Sumpter—Extract of letter of Sir H. Clinton—Cornwallis takes command—Disposition of British troops—M'Arthur sent to Cheraw—Cornwallis's despatches—Account of Harrison, a Tory colonel—M'Arthur at Cheraw—Letter of General Caswell—M'Arthur at Long Bluff—Attempt to capture Thomas Ayer—The result—Stirring scene—Capture of Nathan Sweat—His escape—M'Arthur returns to Cheraw—Plundering parties at General Harrington's and Thomas Ellerbe's—Colonel Bryan, a Loyalist, marches to Cheraw—Enemy alarmed —M'Arthur to fall back—Cornwallis and Tarleton on subject—General Gates arrives at Pedee—Proclamation—M'Arthur leaves—Expedition down the river—Its failure—Whig exploit—Major Thomas distinguishes himself —Colonel Mills escapes—Cornwallis's and Tarleton's accounts of it—Sickness of British at Cheraw—Account of 71st Regiment—Safe conduct for Mrs. Harrington—Skirmish in Anson County—Remarkable negro—Letter of J. L. Gervais—Letter of Spence Macay—Accounts preceding battle of Camden—Effects of Gate's defeat—Extracts from Pugh's Journal—George M'Call—Movements about Long Bluff—Colonel Kolb—Samuel Bacot's adventure with Tories—Elias Du Bose's capture—Tories plunder Mrs. Harrington—Subsequent flight—General Harrington marches to Pedee—Letter of Colonel Nicholas—Of General Gates—Notice of Wemys—Letter of J. Penn—Of Colonel Brown from Beauty Spot—Of General Gates—Of Colonel Martin—General Harrington reaches Haley's Ferry—Marches to Cheraw—General Smallwood's letter—Letter of Colonel Brown—Account of Major Barfield—Colonel Davidson's letter to General Harrington—Colonel Brown's letter to same—Extract from *Gazette*—General Smallwood to General Harrington—Colonel Marion's letter—Colonel Kolb's—Return of his regiment—Cornwallis's letter to Sir H. Clinton—List of negroes in British service—General M'Intosh's death—Account of him—Colonel Donaldson to General Harrington—Arrival of General Green at Charlotte—Divides his forces—Marches to Pedee—Position there—Cornwallis to Tarleton—Tarleton's view of American movements—Close of 1780.

THE year 1780 opened upon Carolina under the most threatening aspects. The approach of a greatly increased force of the enemy filled the inhabitants with dire apprehensions, which, notwithstanding the most heroic efforts for their defence, were soon to be realized. Promptly responding to the call from Charles-town, all the available troops from

Pedee were soon in motion, as from other parts of the State. The first division of Col. Hicks's regiment, under the command of Lieut.-Col. Kolb, was on the march.* The second division, under Col. Hicks, moved in February. Tristram Thomas was major in this command, and John Andrews, adjutant. Edmund Irby, Thomas Ellerbe, Stephen Jackson, and Maurice Murphy commanded companies.

Capt. James Gregg's company formed part of a detachment under Major Thornby. They remained at the Ten mile House (near Charles-town), two months, when their term of service expired. Just then Sir H. Clinton approached the city, when Major Thornby and other officers proposed to their men to volunteer for its defence. They did so unanimously, and marched in and remained in the city until the capitulation. The late George M'Call,† of Darlington District, then quite a young man and active in every patriotic service, was a member of Capt. Gregg's company. He was also under his command in Charles-town during the previous year.

On the 6th of April, a body of North Carolina Militia under Col. Henry Wm. Harrington, reached the city, having entered by way of Addison's Ferry. Major Lemuel Benton‡ appears to have remained on the Pedee, with a sufficient force for the protection of the inhabitants against the Tories. Col. Harrington left Charles-town before the fall of the city for urgent public reasons, as appears from the following letter to Mrs. Harrington.

"George-town, 30 April, 1780.

"I am now in George-town, sixty miles nearer . . . than I was last Friday morning, at which time I left Charles-

---

*The following record remains:—"Recd. of Thomas Powe, Commissary of Colonel Hick's Regiment, 1600 pounds of corn flour, three large steers, 200 lbs. of pork, 20 busls. of corn, for the use of 1st division of said Regt., on march to Charles-town.

"ABEL KOLB."

†George M'Call was born on Lynche's Creek, in 1760. Immediately after the Revolution, he removed to Georgia, and remained until 1789, when he returned to South Carolina, and settled in Darlington District, where he resided until his death.

‡In Rev. Mr. Pugh's journal, April 10th, 1780, appears this entry, viz.:— "Preached at the Lake, Zach. ix. 12, to army under Major Benton." This was doubtless Lowder's Lake, in Darlington District.

town, with the advice and unanimous consent of the Lieut.-Governor and Council, and by Genl. Lincoln's order, and am now on my route for Newbern, there to take my seat in Assembly; and to request, in behalf of South Carolina, a large and immediate aid of North Carolina Militia.

"H. W. HARRINGTON."

The news of the fall of Charles-town spread rapidly through the State, causing the wildest alarm among the desponding, and for a time almost despairing inhabitants. Families were thrown into a state of the deepest anxiety for their absent members, not knowing what had befallen them, or how, though their lives had been spared, they would be treated by the foe. The most exaggerated reports were put in circulation, growing as they went, which added much for a short time to the general distress. As an example of this, the case of Major Robert Lide may be mentioned. He had been hurried with a detachment from Pedee at the last moment, for the relief of the beleaguered city; but, before reaching it, the capitulation took place.

His anxious wife was walking out when the news reached her of the sad reverse; and with a feeble constitution already giving way under the burden of previous suspense, she passed into a swoon, was borne insensible to the house, and never recovered from the shock.

In the journal of Mr. Pugh, the following entries appear:—

"May 17. Had the news of Charles-town taken.

"May 18. Preached at Cashway—a fast day.

"May 22. At home—much terrified about the English Light Horse coming.

"May 23. Had certain news of Charles-town being in the hands of the British army. Our men came up. Mr. Hart up."

The report of the Light Horse coming was but too well founded. It proved to be the rapid and devastating march of Major Wemys, to reap the first fruits on the Pedee of the recent success, and to fasten upon the popular mind the idea that the State was lost beyond recovery. The British conceived themselves in possession of the rights of sovereignty over a conquered country, and that therefore the efforts of the citizens to assert their independence any further, was chargeable with the complicated guilt of ingratitude, treason, and rebellion.

Influenced by these opinions, and transported with indignation against the inhabitants, they violated rights which are held sacred between independent hostile nations. In almost every district their progress was marked with blood, and with deeds so atrocious that they reflected disgrace on their arms. This was emphatically true of Major Wemys, of the 63rd regiment. He marched, soon after the fall of Charlestown, from George-town to Cheraw, on the west side of the river, destroying property of every description, and treating the inhabitants with relentless cruelty.

The dwellings of Nathan Savage at the mouth of Lynche's Creek, of Jordan Gibson at Little Bluff, or Wiggin's Landing, and of Moses Murphy in the same neighbourhood, with many others, were burned. Among the first to feel the effects of the fury of this merciless officer, was Adam Cusack, a noted Whig, who had rendered himself particularly obnoxious to the enemies of his country. He had neither taken parole as a prisoner nor protection as a British subject; and was charged with no other crime than refusing to transport some British officers over a ferry, and shooting at them across a river.* Another account states that he had shot at the black servant of a Tory officer, John Brockington, whom he knew, across Black Creek. He was taken prisoner soon after, and for this offence tried by a court martial, and, on the evidence of the negro, condemned.† His wife and children prostrated themselves before Wemys as he was on horseback, for a pardon, who would have ridden over them, had not one of his own officers prevented the foul deed. From this scene he proceeded on to superintend the execution. Cusack was carried to Long Bluff and hung.‡ Dr. James P. Wilson made an earnest effort to save his life, and came very near involving himself in a serious difficulty with the British officer. Wemys lost no time in pursuing

---

*Ramsay's "Revolution," vol. ii. p. 156.
†James's "Life of Marion," p. 58.
‡He was hung about the spot first occupied by the depot of the Cheraw and Darlington Railroad, at the foot of the hill, below the village of Society Hill, then on the public road leading from Cheraw to George-town.

his way, and calling the people to submission. He reached Cheraw early in June.

The following extracts from Mr. Pugh's journal will give, in few words, the sad picture of the conqueror's progress.

"June 11. Went up to the Cheraws to surrender myself to the British; lodged at Col. Lide's.

"Monday, 12th. Signed parole, as a Prisoner of War."

Agitated and distressed, and scarcely knowing what to do, he appears to have repented of his course, as a subsequent entry indicates.

"Thursday, 22. Went to the Court House in order to give up my parole, but could not do it.

"Thursday, 29th. Went to Dr. Mills's, took the Oath of Allegiance to the King; and home.

"Saturday, July 2. Went to preach at Cashway, began my sermon, but the congregation broke up by the re (bels!) taking the horses."

Dr. Mills had either not sympathized heartily with his country at the first, or was possessed of one of those easy consciences which adapts itself with facility to a change of circumstances. He gave in his adhesion at once to the enemy; and from that time became a determined foe to the American cause. He was an evil counsellor for every desponding patriot within his reach, but, in due season, paid the penalty of his guilt. The declaration of allegiance imposed upon many of the people, was in these words:—

"I, A. B., do hereby acknowledge and declare myself to be a true and faithful subject to his Majesty, the King of Great Britain, and that I will at all times hereafter be obedient to his government; and that whenever I shall be thereunto required, I will be ready to maintain and defend the same against all persons whatsoever."

While Wemys was in the neighbourhood of Long Bluff, Dr. Wilson's house was burned, and such of his property as came within the reach of the enemy, was destroyed. His wife was forced to seek shelter at Charlotte, North Carolina.

The dwelling of Capt. Wm. Dewitt,* on Cedar Creek, on

---

*About the spot where the late Judge Evans resided. The late Major John Dewitt, of Society Hill, was a lad of fourteen or fifteen, and went with his father's family to Guilford.

this, or a subsequent occasion, was also destroyed. On the approach of the British, Capt. Dewitt took his family to Guilford, N. C., but immediately returned himself, and took an active part to the close of the war.

When called upon to take the Oath of Allegiance to the King, he is said to have drawn with his sword a circle on the ground, indicating that spot to be his country, and standing thereon, to have uttered words, of proud defiance to those who would thus have prohibited him from his sacred fealty as an inhabitant of Carolina and an American citizen. Similar to this in tone, was the spirited reply of Thomas Ayer, who, when urged by Magnus Corgill and other neighbours to take protection, and told, that if he refused, his property would be confiscated, warmly replied, "the question was not one of *property,* but *liberty!*"

Many of the inhabitants submitted, others yielded nominally, intending to resist upon the first opportunity, while not a few hurriedly removed with their families, servants, and other personal effects, to places of safety, leaving their dwellings to the mercy of the enemy, but returning themselves to repel the foe.

Those of the Whigs who so far submitted as to take the oath, intending not to keep it, felt, that being forced upon them, it was not binding. John Wilson and James Gillespie, then young men, with a neighbour, had been to Cheraw to swear allegiance. After crossing the river on their return, they rode for some time in silence, as if absorbed in thought, and afraid to utter their sentiments; at length one of them said, "Well, I don't think that amounted to much"—and thereupon, all joined in a hearty laugh, finding a perfect agreement of opinion on the subject.

The atrocities perpetrated by the British and Tories, for the latter gladly followed in the train of the conqueror, only served to drive the Whigs to desperation, and led to a terrible revenge when the time arrived for throwing off the yoke. And that time was not long in coming; for no sooner had the British withdrawn, than the spirit of liberty, crushed, but not subdued, began to rise to the ascendant

On the 25th of July, Mr. Pugh wrote these few but pregnant words: "The people in arms against the English."

Major Wemys, after accomplishing the objects of his bloody visit, returned to George-town, to pollute no more the upper parts of the Pedee with his presence. And yet, this man, who had been guilty of so many atrocities, was made the recipient of that generous return which the injured people of Carolina so often extended to their heartless oppressors.* On the 12th of the following November, in attempting to surprise General Sumpter, near Fish Dam Ford, on Broad River, he was taken prisoner, having been severely wounded in the engagement. He had in his pocket a list of the houses he had burned at Williamsburgh and Pedee: with great trepidation he showed it to Sumpter, and begged he would protect him from the militia. Notwithstanding his atrocities, he was treated with indulgence, but became a cripple for life.†

Up to this time, the nearest posts to the Cheraw District held by the British, were George-town and Camden. A position was now to be taken on the Upper Pedee, to add to the lengthening and tightening chain, and to the alarm and suffering of the inhabitants.

The following extract from a letter of Sir Henry Clinton, of June 4th, 1780, to the Hon. George Gervain, one of his Majesty's principal Secretaries of State, will convey some idea of the condition of things in Carolina, as viewed at least by the British Commander, and the feeling of the enemy:—

"With the greatest pleasure," he said, "I farther report to your lordship, that the inhabitants from every quarter repair to the detachments of the army, and to this garrison (Charles-town), to declare their allegiance to the King, and to offer their services in arms for the support of the Government. In many instances they have brought in as prisoners their former oppressors or leaders; and I may venture to assert, that there are few men in South Carolina who are not either our prisoners or in arms with us."‡

*Ramsay's "Revolution," vol. ii. pp. 188, 89.
†James's "Life of Marion," p. 73.
‡Tarleton's "Memoirs," p. 80. This interesting work, and one indispensable

Sir Henry Clinton now left for the North, and his command devolved on Lord Cornwallis. A temporary period seems to have been put to any organized resistance in Carolina. A partisan warfare, however, was here and there kept up, especially with the Tories, who were now bold and constantly marauding, wreaking their vengeance with bitter malignity on the Whigs of Pedee.

Emissaries were despatched by Lord Cornwallis to North Carolina, with instructions to some of the leading Royalists of that State, to "attend to the harvest, to prepare provisions, and to remain quiet till the King's troops were ready to advance, about the latter part of August or early in September; that interval of time being deemed indispensably requisite for the construction of magazines, with properly secured communications, for a clear establishment of the militia, and for a final adjustment of their civil and military regulations which in future were to govern Georgia and South Carolina."*

Early in June, Lord Cornwallis made such a disposition of the British troops as to establish a thoroughly organized line of posts upon the frontiers of the State.

"Major M'Arthur, with the 71st Regiment (Highlanders), was stationed at the Cheraws, in the vicinity of the Pedee River, to cover the country between Camden and Georgetown, and to hold correspondence with a friendly settlement at Cross Creek,† in North Carolina." It was also said, "Besides the defence of the frontiers, another material advantage resulted from this disposition of the king's troops. The officers and men of the different regiments and corps were supplied by the flour and cattle, whilst the horses were foraged by the produce of the country; any expenditure of the provisions brought across the Atlantic was unknown, except in Charles-town and Savannah."‡

In a letter of the 30th of June, to Sir H. Clinton, Lord

---
to a thorough understanding of the Revolution in Carolina, is written in the best style of military history, and throws much light, not otherwise to be had, on all connected with the movements of the British forces, and the general plan of their campaigns.

*Tarleton's "Memoirs," p. 85.
†Now Fayetteville.
‡"Tarleton," pp. 87, 88.

Cornwallis said: "I have agreed to a proposal made by Mr. Harrison, to raise a provincial corps of five hundred men, with the rank of Major, to be composed of the natives of the country between the Pedee and Wateree, and in which it is extremely probable that he will succeed."*

The Tories on Lynche's Creek, in the neighbourhood of M'Callum's Ferry, committed many murders and depredations. They were headed by the two Harrisons, to one of whom Cornwallis refers. It was he, doubtless, who was afterwards a colonel, the other becoming a major, in the British service, and both called by Tarleton, men of fortune. They were, in fact, two of the greatest banditti that ever infested the country. The proposed plan of a provincial corps was never carried out. Before the fall of Charlestown these brothers lived in a wretched log hut, by the road near M'Callum's, in which there was no bed covering but the skins of wild beasts. During the contest the major was killed; after it was over, the colonel retired to Jamaica, with much wealth, acquired by depredation.†

M'Arthur reached Cheraw some time during the month of June. The parish church was called into requisition for a portion of his force, and traces are yet to be seen some distance out on the southern line of the town of the temporary barracks erected. According to tradition, M'Arthur and other officers were not wanting in courtesy to the ladies of the vicinity, and as a consequence were treated with such a degree of civility as the necessities of the case made imperative. The soldiers, however, were not restrained; and many persons in the neighbourhood were plundered and treated with indignity.

Numerous incidents are related of the sufferings and losses of the inhabitants during the brief sojourn of the enemy.

The report reached Western South Carolina, at Camp Catawba,‡ Old Nation, about the 4th of July, that Gen. Caswell,

---

*Tarleton, p. 177.
†James's "Marion," p. 45.
‡Letter from a Mr. Williams to his wife, of 4th July, from Camp Catawba. Gibbes's "Documentary History," 1776-82, p. 135.

of the North Carolina line, had defeated the British at the Cheraws, and cut off the 71st Regiment entirely. But this was a mistake. The enemy was yet to remain there for a brief season triumphant.

On the 5th of July, General Caswell wrote to General Harrington from "Camp ten miles south of Ramsay," as follows:—

"Dear Sir,

"I had your favor from Chatham Court House, and also one from Col. Collier, and am much obliged by your information.

"Nothing new has happened in this part of the country since your departure. Donaldson's party left him at Cole's Bridge last Friday night, on the approach of 400 horse, they say from the Cheraws, 200 of which were British; since which I have heard nothing from that quarter. I shall wait on the Baron de Kalb to-day, and will fix the time and place of our joining. He is to be this day at Willcox's Iron Works. If it will not be attended with danger to the troops to move from Salisbury, I presume Gen. Rutherford will join me, in consequence of my letter by your favor, on the upper part of Deep River. Pray present my compliments to the General, and let him know I expect to hear from him on that subject daily.

"From you, I flatter myself I shall frequently hear.

"I am, with great esteem, dear Sir,

"Your most obedient servant,

"R. CASWELL.

"Brigadier-General Harrington."

Soon after M'Arthur's arrival at Cheraw, he went down the river with a detachment, and made his head-quarters for a short time at Long Bluff. His force was large enough to admit of division, and to keep the country in awe.

While at Long Bluff, he offered a handsome reward for the capture of Thomas Ayer. Ayer had made himself conspicuous a short time before, as the leader of a company which had been sent out to take some bold and mischievous persons, who had rendered themselves obnoxious to the inhabitants by their lawless depredations.

Having succeeded in capturing a portion of the band, he secured the country against any more of their ravages by hanging them all.

The effect of the reward offered for Ayer, was his capture by a party of Tory neighbours. They kept vigilant watch for him, and caught him while on a brief and cautious visit to his family. He came up at night, and keeping close during the day, intended to leave for camp the following night; but, late in the afternoon, sixteen Tories galloped up to the house and secured him. They tied him with buck-skin strings, furnished by old Magnus Corgill for the purpose, and hurried him off toward the river, intending to take him immediately to M'Arthur. But, by the time they reached Hunt's Bluff, a terrific thunderstorm had blown up, and fearing to cross the river and prosecute their journey through the swamp in the darkness of such a night, they concluded to keep their prisoner in an old unoccupied house on the bank until morning. George Manderson, the leader of the party, apprehending no danger from any quarter, left Ayer in charge of the others, and went down with one of his companions, Tom John, to get supper and sleep at old Jonathan John's. Relief was soon to overtake the now despairing Ayer. A few hours after the Tories left his residence, his elder brother, Hartwell, with five Georgians, rode up very unexpectedly to the family. The names of these timely visitors were—William Cooper, James Nephew, Charles Tharp, John Tharp, and Joseph Plummer.

Upon being informed of what had occurred, Hartwell Ayer and his companions set out in immediate pursuit, and took the Tory party completely by surprise. They approached under cover of the darkness and tempest, and were at the door before being discovered. Most of the party within were asleep. Shooting first those who were up, they continued to fire and despatch with the sabre and bayonet until all were killed, except Asal John. Being a son of his old neighbour, who was a peaceable man, Thomas Ayer protected him with his own body, and induced the captors to spare his life. Then mounting the horse of Dick Owen, one of the Tories just killed, he returned with all possible speed to his family, not knowing what might have befallen them. Upon learning the whereabouts of George Manderson and Tom John, Hartwell Ayer and his companions went off in pursuit. Riding up cautiously to old John's residence, they civilly inquired for Captain Manderson,* who, as he appeared at the door, was saluted with a shower of bullets. Though struck by several balls, the wounds inflicted were slight; and springing through the back door of the house, he made his escape to the swamp, which was near at hand. Tom John was not so fortunate. He was knocked down with the butt of an old musket, and then pinned to the floor with the bayonet, remaining in that condition as the gun was jerked off, and supposed to be dead. But, on the bayonet being removed, he arose, and proved to be not seriously injured. He lived several years afterwards. When informed of the rescue of Ayer, and the slaughter of the Tories, M'Arthur was more enraged than ever. He determined to go in person and take vengeance. Crossing the river with a strong party, he came very near surprising the family, then at home, consisting of Mrs. Ayer and her sons, Lewis Malone and Zaccheus, both of whom were lads. They made a timely escape, however, to the swamp, which was near by, and there remained in concealment several weeks, being supplied with food by their good neighbour, James Sweat.† M'Arthur took possession of the deserted premises, killed the stock, destroyed most of the fencing, and burned all the buildings except a large crib, which he spared on account of the corn it contained, meaning to appropriate it to the use of his troops.

---

*Captain Manderson removed after the Revolution to Georgia, and settled on the Savannah River. He died about the year 1794. William Cooper and James Nephew, of the band of Georgians, were half brothers. They lived at Sapello, Georgia, long after the war was over.

†Mr. Sweat was then quite a young man. He afterwards became a Baptist preacher, and removed to the south-western part of the State, where some of his descendants are still living.

Nathan, an elder brother of William Sweat, was a brave and active Whig. Their father, who was then an old man and infirm, lived quietly, and was undisturbed by any one.

It was, however, subsequently taken off and secured by the friends of the family. Every valuable negro was carried away, with others belonging to different persons in the neighbourhood. The now empty crib became the dwelling of the family to the close of the war.

Nathan Sweat was captured by M'Arthur's party, and carried to their quarters on the west side of the river above. He remained long enough with them to discover their fleetest horse; and, watching a favorable opportunity, mounted the animal and bade his captors adieu. He was pursued, but succeeded in reaching the swamp below, and made his escape. On the following morning, while sitting on his horse at his mother's door, and in the act or receiving food from her hands, the old lady discovered the approach of a hostile party, and cried out, "Nathan, the enemy are upon you." Again putting spurs to the noble steed, which had outstripped his pursuers the day before, he made good his escape, congratulating himself, doubtless, as the distance widened between them, on his correct judgment of a horse, to which he owed his life.

After his return to Cheraw, M'Arthur sent a detachment up the river on a plundering expedition. On their approaching the residence of General Harrington, in Richmond county, Mrs. H., who was at home, discovered them in time to have a horse secreted in an out-building, which, fortunately, was not disturbed. Such of the negroes as did not escape were taken, and carried, with the live-stock, to Cheraw. The overseer was tied, and made to accompany them. Mrs. Harrington, who was most distressed at the capture of the servants, fearing they would be carried entirely away, followed on, to recover them, if possible. M'Arthur told her she could have them if they would go with her. But, being probably captivated with the idea of freedom, they preferred remaining where they were, with the exception of a woman and her family, who went back with their mistress.

The most of these and other negroes taken by the enemy were recaptured upon the breaking up of the British post at Cheraw. The difficulty in the way of the enemy was to get any considerable body of slaves to the coast. The only apparently feasible means was by the river in boats, and the attempt thus to transport them proved to be ineffectual. A few negro men were carried off with the troops, and never recovered.* Captain Thomas Ellerbe, who lived a few miles below Cheraw, suffered severely in the loss of property. Many horses were taken from him, of which he had a large number. Having become obnoxious as an active Whig, he was obliged to secrete himself from the enemy. As marauding parties would go to the house to demand a fresh supply of horses, Mrs. Ellerbe, who would not have dared flatly to refuse, was sometimes relieved by the faithfulness and sagacity of one or two servants, who kept the horses in the recesses of the swamp, driving them from place to place, their mistress not being informed of their movements; she could only plead ignorance, and thus her husband's property was saved. Captain Ellerbe lost not a few negroes. Claudius Pegues had also a number taken by the enemy while at Cheraw, the most of whom escaped, and subsequently returned to their master. One of these was treated with great cruelty by the British. His account was, that they ordered him to ride, and because he fell off several times, they hacked him with their swords, leaving him, as they supposed, dead by the road-side. He managed to crawl home, and eventually recovered, though shockingly mangled.

The form of legality was sometimes given to acts of plundering. An original† receipt or certificate is in these words:—

"Got at Philip Pledger's house, eight horses for his Majesty's service.

"By THOMAS HAMILTON,
"July 23, 1780.   "Lieut. 71st Regt."

*Of those taken off on this occasion, was a servant of General Harrington, named Cuffee. He was noted for his remarkably valuable traits of character. He was supposed to have been carried with the British on their return to Camden. He subsequently passed into the hands of Captain Campbell, a British officer, who settled after the Revolution on Pedee.
General Harrington brought a suit in Cheraws District for his recovery. The damages found were large, and only to be discharged by the delivery of the negro. Rather than pay the amount, Captain Campbell sent to Jamaica for Cuffee, where he had been transported, and delivered him to his master.
†The original is in the Author's possession.

But the Whigs in this section were not to contribute much longer to an imperious and unsparing foe. A change was rapidly approaching.

In a letter to Sir Henry Clinton, dated Charles-town, July 14th, 1780, Lord Cornwallis said: "The Government of North Carolina is likewise making great exertions [he had referred to Virginia] to raise troops, and persecuting our friends in the most cruel manner; in consequence of which, Colonel Bryan, although he had promised to wait for my orders, lost all patience, and rose with about 800 men, on the Yadkin; and by a difficult and dangerous march, joined M'Arthur on the borders of Anson County. About two-thirds only of his people were armed, and these, I believe, but indifferently."*

Colonel Bryan was a noted loyalist, and great things were expected of him; but, being of a timorous and undecided spirt, he accomplished little. On the march to Cheraws, he was actively pursued by General Rutherford, but had the address to elude him.†

"The news brought by these loyalists created some astonishment in the military, and diffused universal consternation among the inhabitants of South Carolina. They reported that Major-General De Kalb, a French officer in the American service, was advancing from Salisbury with a large body of Continentals; that Colonel Porterfield was bringing State troops from Virginia; that General Caswell had raised a powerful force in North Carolina; and that Colonel Sumpter had already entered the Catawba, a settlement contiguous to the Wacsaws. These accounts being propagated and artfully exaggerated by the enemies within the Province, caused a wonderful fermentation in the minds of the Americans, which neither the lenity of the British Government, the solemnity of their paroles, by which their persons and property enjoyed protection, nor the memory of the undeserved pardon so lately extended to many of them, had sufficient strength to retain in a state of submission or neutrality. Whilst the Americans were collecting

---

*Tarleton's "Memoirs," p. 119.
†Lee's "Memoirs of Southern Campaign," vol. i. pp. 158, 159.

their forces, Lord Rawdon made occasional alterations upon the frontier, in order to confirm the adherence of the loyal inhabitants, and to obviate the designs of the enemy. . . . Some detachments were sent out; others drawn in. . . . Major M'Arthur's position in the Cheraws was deemed too forward, and he was desired to retire some miles into the Province."*

So Tarleton afterwards wrote. The subject of M'Arthur's position and movements was now exciting no little anxiety at head-quarters. On 15th July, Lord Cornwallis wrote to Sir H. Clinton: "I have just received intelligence from Lord Rawdon that De Kalb has certainly joined Caswell at Coxe's plantation on Deep River; his lordship in consequence has withdrawn Major M'Arthur's detachment over the Black Creek, where he means to join him with two battalions, and post Lieut.-Col. Webster on Hanging Rock Creek. This will make his situation pretty compact, but I fear the enemy will make incursions into the country."† Appearances were daily becoming more threatening for the enemy. A considerable number of the militia of North Carolina had taken the field, and agreed to rendezvous at Anson Court House on the 20th of July, that they might be in readiness to co-operate with the Continental army.‡ Anson Court House was about thirty miles above Cheraw on the river.

"On the 24th of July General Gates arrived in the American camp. His name and former good fortunes re-animated the exertions of the country; provisions were more amply supplied by the inhabitants; and the Continental troops now reached the frontiers of South Carolina."§

It was now manifest that M'Arthur would be forced to make a precipitate retreat from Pedee. The inhabitants were greatly encouraged, and ripe for revolt. The advance of Gates was rousing into activity all the latent energies of the State. The most resolute of the militia, indignant at the treatment they had received, and convinced by Sir

---
*"Tarleton," pp. 91, 92.
†Ibid., p. 120.
‡Ramsay's "Revolution in S. C.," vol. ii. p. 139.
§"Tarleton," p. 97.

Henry Clinton's proclamation, which had been faithfully acted on by Lord Cornwallis, that repose during the war was a chimerical expectation, determined from concealed enemies to become open foes. On the day that the British relinquished their post at Cheraw, the inhabitants, distressed by their previous depredations and disgusted with their conduct, took up arms. Preparatory to his departure, M'Arthur had made an arrangement for transporting a number of his sick, with the captured negroes, by boats to George-town. They were to be under the care of Lord Nairne, and the whole under the new-made British colonel, William Henry Mills,* with a military escort, composed of a portion of the militia of the country who had taken the oath of allegiance.

Hearing of the projected expedition down the river, a party of neighbouring Whigs, under the lead of James Gillespie, collected at Bedingfield's,† a short distance from Cheraw, and determined to gather a larger force and surprise the enemy. As they went on their numbers increased, and the command was assigned to Major Tristram Thomas. In the meantime, with the departure of the boats, M'Arthur commenced his retreat towards Black Creek.

The Whigs fixed upon Hunt's Bluff as the most favorable point for intercepting the expedition. A battery of wooden guns was hastily constructed, and placed immediately on the bank, in a sudden bend of the river. In due season, as the slowly-moving flotilla appeared, the most imposing demonstration that they could present was made by the command of the gallant Thomas, and an unconditional surrender demanded. It is not improbable that there was a secret understanding with some of the leading men of the militia under Colonel Mills. However this may have been, no resistance was attempted, and the surprise was complete. At the same time, a large boat coming up from George-town, well stored with necessaries for Major M'Arthur's force, was seized for the use of the American army. Colonel Mills succeeded in getting away, and made his escape to George-town.‡ The other new-made British officers of the militia

---
*Lee's "Memoirs of the Southern Campaign," vol. i. p. 162.
†Now Irby's Mills, three miles from Cheraw.
‡Ramsay's "Revolution in S. C.," vol. ii. p. 140.

were taken prisoners by the party under Major Thomas, and with some of their men and the sick, more than a hundred in number, carried prisoners into North Carolina. The British Commander, and Tarleton also, as will be seen, spoke of it afterwards as a mutiny, making no allusion to the well-planned surprise by the Whigs, but for which the expedition might have reached George-town in safety. The negroes, of course, were recaptured and returned to their owners. This effective blow struck increased terror into the enemy, already alarmed, and encouraged the inhabitants to more determined and unyielding resistance. It was the first brilliant exploit yet achieved upon the Pedee, and occurred just at a time when the most important moral effects were likely to follow in its train.

Lord Cornwallis, deeply chagrined, very naturally attempted to give the most favorable version of the affair. In a letter to Sir H. Clinton, from Charles-town, August 6th, he thus wrote:—"The general state of things in the two Provinces of North and South Carolina, is not very materially altered since my letters of the 14th and 15th of last month were written." Alluding to matters in other parts of the State, he proceeds: "In the eastern parts of the Province, Major M'Arthur, seeing the great importance of the post at Cheraw Hill, and finding himself perfectly secure from any attack of the enemy, desired to continue there longer than it was intended he should, when I had the honor of writing to you on the 15th. At last, however, the 71st Regt. grew so exceedingly sickly, that he found it absolutely necessary to move, and marched on the 24th to the east branch of Lincoln's (Lynche's) Creek. Gates, who had taken the command of De Kalb's Corps, was still on Deep River; and Rutherford no farther advanced than Rocky River, Pedee. Knowing of no enemy within many miles, he ventured to send about 100 sick in boats down the Pedee to George-town. Col. Mills, who commanded the Militia of the Cheraw District, though a very good man, had not complied with my instructions in forming his corps; but had placed more faith in oaths and professions, and attached less to the former conduct of those he admitted. The instant the militia found that M'Arthur had left his post, and were assured that Gates would come the next day, they seized their own officers and the hundred sick, and carried them all prisoners into North Caralina. Col. Mills with difficulty made his escape to George-town."* In his memoirs of the time, Tarleton says: "The approach of Gen. Gates with an army of six thousand men, induced Lord Rawdon gradually to contract the posts upon the frontier, in order to assemble his forces. Major M'Arthur was directed to draw nearer to Camden; the two batallions of the 71st Regiment, under his orders, were at this period considerable sufferers by the unhealthy climate of Carolina. To disencumber himself for movement, he collected some boats on the river Pedee, and committed upwards of one hundred sick men to the care of Col. Mills, to be escorted to George-town by the militia under his command. After the sick were embarked, Major M'Arthur commenced his march. In less than ten days the militia mutinied, and securing their own officers and the sick, conducted them prisoners to Gen. Gates, in North Carolina. This instance of treachery in the east of the Province followed the perfidious conduct of Lieut.-Col. Lisle, on the western border, and strongly proved the mistake committed by the British, in placing confidence in the inhabitants of the country where acting apart from the army. The only probable way to reap advantage from the levies made in Carolina, would have been to incorporate the young men, as they were raised, in the established provincial corps, where they could be properly trained, and formed under officers of experience. By such a line of conduct, all the British regulars would have been saved, the king's troops in general would have been augmented, and considerable service might have been derived from their additional numbers."† It is not surprising that such free comments on the British movements in Carolina, which Tarleton could very well make by the light of experience after the war was over, drew down the severest strictures upon his work. Such was the result of the freedom, altogether proper on the part of a historian, in which he indulged. It was manifestly a most hazardous

*"Tarleton," pp. 137, 138.
†Ibid., pp. 97, 98.

step to have entrusted the fate of such an expedition to the militia of the country, most of whom were burning with long-smothered feelings of revenge. It taught the enemy a lesson, however, which was not afterwards forgotten. In his letter of August 6th, already quoted, Lord Cornwallis went on further to say: "The wheat harvest in North Carolina is now over, but the weather still is excessively hot; and, notwithstanding our utmost exertions, a great part of the rum, salt, clothing, and necessaries for the soldiers, and ammunition for the troops, are not very far advanced on their way to Camden. However, if no material interruption happens, this business will be nearly accomplished in a fortnight or three weeks.

"Our assurances of attachment from our distressed friends in North Carolina, are as strong as ever. And the patience and fortitude with which these unhappy people bear the most oppressive and cruel tyranny that ever was exercised over any country, deserve our greatest admiration."*
The reader of these latter days, will form his own opinion upon the remarks of his lordship in the closing paragraph above. That the Loyalists and Tories of North Carolina at this time suffered much, there can be no doubt, and that they deserved to suffer, is quite as certain. But, that they groaned under the most oppressive and cruel tyranny ever exercised over any country, few now will be prepared to admit. But, thus the mortified Commander wrote.

The allusion made both by Cornwallis and Tarleton to the sickness from which the British suffered while at Cheraw was sadly true. Tradition tells how the soldiers, unaccustomed to a southern climate, sickened and died. And the spot is now pointed out, quite a perceptible sink in the earth, in front of the parish church of St. David, where many, placed, it is said, in one common grave, lie buried.

The number of sick sent off on the breaking up of the post indicates a season of unusual fatality. The return of the 71st regiment also on the 15th of August, the eve of the battle of Camden, about three weeks after it left Cheraw, told how their ranks had been thinned by death. Of the

*"Tarleton," p. 128.

1st battalion, the return was, 2 captains, 4 lieutenants, 1 ensign, 1 adjutant, 1 quarter-master, 1 mate, 14 sergeants, 6 drummers, 114 rank and file. Of the 2nd battalion, 1 captain, 3 lieutenants, 3 ensigns, 9 sergeants, 94 rank and file.*

Leaving Cheraw, the tide of war turned rapidly towards Camden. The accounts given by the British commander at the time, and subsequently by Tarleton, of that conflict, of such tragic consequence for a season to the American cause, are of exceeding interest, and form a thrilling chapter in the history of the war in Carolina.

After the loss sustained by the ravages of M'Arthur's plundering party in the neighbourhood of her husband's residence, Mrs. Harrington took refuge with her friends in South Carolina. General Harrington was then in camp at Cross Creek, and wishing to have her there, an escort was sent to conduct her thither, as the following record shows:—

"State of North Carolina,
"The Honorable Richard Caswell, Esquire, Major-General and Commander-in-Chief of the militia of the said State, in service,

"To the Commanding Officers of his Britannic Majesty's Forces, in South Carolina, and all others whom it may concern.

"These are to certify, that Col. John Donaldson and Lieut. Reuben Wilkinson are permitted to proceed with a flag of truce to South Carolina, in order to conduct the lady of Henry Wm. Harrington, Esquire, and her family to the interior parts of this State. All officers, civil and military, in this State, and others concerned, are requested to take notice thereof, and govern themselves accordingly.

"Given under my hand and seal, in the camp at the Cross Roads, near Deep River, the 21st day of July, 1780.
"R. CASWELL.

"By his Honor's command,
  "John Sitgreaves, A.D. Camp."

---

*"Tarleton," p. 137, 138.

Upon his arrival Col. Donaldson probably found the enemy breaking up, or already gone. His mission was successfully accomplished.*

During the struggle on the Pedee Gen. Harrington sent a detachment of Whigs to Anson County in charge of a negro. He was the property of Michael Crawford, of Anson, had been in the service of Col. Donaldson, and was exchanged for one of the general's servants. Shortly before they reached the river the Whigs were surprised by a party of Tories, who lay in ambush; and upon the first fire were dispersed. The negro was taken off by the Tories and lost. The Whigs soon rallied, and returned boldly to the conflict.

The Tories, satisfied with their booty, retreated after a brief skirmish. They were pursued, and a riderless horse, with a bloody saddle, was captured. Of the Whigs, one named Curtis was killed, and Daniel Hicks wounded in the thigh, from which, however, he afterwards recovered. After the war Crawford brought a suit against Gen. Harrington for the negro, but recovered nothing.

The scattered Whigs kept up an occasional correspondence. On the 26th of July, John Lewis Gervais, then at Williamsburg, Virginia, wrote to his friend, Gen. Harrington, as follows:—

"Dear Sir,—After a fatiguing journey I have at last joined my family here, who have undergone great hardships and difficulties. John and Sinclair have both been sick, but are better. I have not heard from your quarter since I left it, and am anxious to know the fate of our friends at Pedee. Mrs. Gervais wishes to hear if the articles she sent up in the boat are safe, and begs you to have them secured in some safe place till we return. Gov. Rutledge I found gone to Philadelphia, and I have not heard from

---

*Colonel Donaldson was accompanied on this occasion by Toney, the body servant of General Harrington throughout the war, a negro of remarkable character, honest and faithful in the highest degree. He was the father of Cuffee, of whom mention has been made. General Harrington purchased him from John Mitchell, about 1776. After the Revolution, he was sent by his master on horseback from Pedee to Newbern, N. C., with 1500 Spanish silver dollars, to pay for a tract of land which General H. had bought. The money was delivered in safety. The British had no conception of such devotion in a slave.

him since. I should be glad to hear from you, and the situation of our affairs to the southward, if we have any prospect to return soon to Carolina, &c. Mrs. Gervais joins me in best regards to you and Mrs. Harrington; and we most sincerely wish to assure you by word of mouth of the perfect esteem with which we are

"Your most obliged and most obedient Servants,
"JOHN LEWIS GERVAIS.

"Please to direct any letters to the care of Col. Griffin, at Williamsburg."

On the 27th of July Gen. Gates arrived at the Pedee from the northward, and on the 4th of August issued a proclamation, inviting the patriotic citizens of Carolina to assemble under his auspices and vindicate the rights of America; holding out an amnesty to all who had subscribed paroles imposed upon them by the ruffian hand of conquest; and excepting only those who, in the hour of trial, had exercised acts of barbarity and devastation upon the persons and property of their fellow-citizens. To this appeal there was a general and hearty response. New life was infused into the lately desponding patriots, and many came forward without delay to join the advancing army. On the 28th of July, Major Spence Macay, aide-de-camp of Gen. Rutherford, addressed Gen. Harrington as follows: —

"Camp at Clarke's, July 28, 1780.

"Dear General,—Last night Gen. Rutherford received a letter from Gen. Caswell, informing him that Gen. Gates desired Gen. Caswell, Gen. Rutherford and yourself to meet 27th instant, at Cox's Mills, in order to settle a plan of future operations to the southward. The general says 'that he is happy to acquaint Gen. Caswell that the Virginia Militia, with such continental corps of cavalry and infantry as Congress have allotted to serve with the Southern Army, are in full march, and will speedily join it; and has also the satisfaction to think that the measures taken by the Executive Council of Virginia in conjunction with that of this State, will shortly relieve our distresses, and put it amply in our power to push the enemy from their advanced posts even to Charles-town.'

"Governor Nash has written to Gen. Rutherford, requiring the attendance of all the members of General Assembly at Hillsbrough, on the 20th of August next, and especially those who are in the army. The Governor's letter is big with caution, the enemy numerous, and much danger is to be apprehended from them.

"I am, dear General,
"Your most obedient and humble Servant,
"SPENCE MACAY.

"To Brig.-Gen. Harrington,
"Richmond County."

Gen. Gates, confident of victory, lost no time in advancing toward the enemy near Camden. Lord Cornwallis's account of preliminary movements and the fortunes of that ill-fated day for the American cause, forms an interesting link in the chain of events at this period. On the 21st of August he wrote from Camden to Lord George Germain:—

"It is with great pleasure that I communicate to your Lordship an account of a complete victory, obtained on the 16th instant, by his Majesty's troops under my command, over the rebel Southern Army, commanded by Gen. Gates.

On the 9th instant, two expresses arrived with an account that Gen. Gates was advancing towards Lynche's Creek, with his whole army, supposed to amount to six thousand men, exclusive of a detachment of one thousand men under Gen. Sumpter; who, after having in vain attempted to force the posts at Rocky Mount and Hanging Rock, was believed to be at that time trying to get round the left of our position, to cut off our communication with the Congarees and Charles-town; that the disaffected country between the Pedee and Black Rivers had actually revolted; and that Lord Rawdon was contracting his posts, and preparing to assemble his forces at Camden. In consequence of this information, after finishing some important points of business at Charlestown, I set out on the evening of the 10th, and arrived at Camden on the night between the 13th and 14th, and there found Lord Rawdon with all our force, except Lieut.-Col. Turnbull's small detachment, which fell back from Rocky Mount to Major Ferguson's posts of the militia of Ninety-six, on Little River. . . . After consulting with some intelligent people, well acquainted with the ground, I determined to march at 10 o'clock on the night of the 15th, and to attack at daybreak, pointing my principal force against their Continentals, who, from good intelligence, I knew to be badly posted close to Col. Rugeley's house. Late in the evening, I received information that the Virginians had joined that day; however, that having been expected, I did not alter my plan, but marched at the hour appointed, leaving the defence of Camden to some provincials, militia and convalescents, and a detachment of the 63rd regiment, which, by being mounted on horses they had pressed on the road, it was hoped would arrive in the course of the night. I had proceeded nine miles, when, about half an hour past two in the morning, my advanced guard fell in with the enemy. By the weight of the fire, I was convinced they were in considerable force, and was soon assured by some deserters and prisoners that it was the whole rebel army on its march to attack us at Camden. I immediately halted and formed, and the enemy doing the same, the firing soon ceased."*

Tarleton says, "On the 15th, the principal part of the King's troops had orders to be in readiness to march; in the afternoon Earl Cornwallis desired Lieut.-Col. Tarleton to gain circumstantial intelligence by intercepting a patrol, or carrying off some prisoners from an American picket. About ten miles from Camden, on the road to Rugeley's Mills, the advanced guard of the Legion in the evening secured three American soldiers. The prisoners reported that they came from Lynche's Creek, where they had been left in a convalescent state, and that they were directed to join the American army, on the high road, that night, as Gen. Gates had given orders for his troops to move from Rugeley's Mill to attack the British camp next morning near Camden. The information received from these men

*"Tarleton," pp. 128-131.

induced Tarleton to countermarch before he was discovered by any patrol from the enemy's outpost.

"The three prisoners were mounted behind dragoons, and conveyed with speed to the British army. When examined by Earl Cornwallis, their story appeared credible, and confirmed all the other intelligence of the day. Orders were immediately circulated for the regiments and corps designed for a forward move, to stand to their arms.

"The town, the magazine, the hospital, and the prisoners were committed to the care of Major M'Arthur, with a small body of provincials and militia, and the weakest convalescents of the army. . . At 10 o'clock the King's troops moved from their ground, and formed their order of march on the main road to Rugeley's Mills. Lieut.-Col. Webster commanded the first division of the army. . . At 12 o'clock, the line of march was somewhat broken in passing Saunders's Creek, five miles from Camden. A short halt remedied this inconvenience, and the royal army proceeded in a compact state with most profound silence. A little after two, the advanced guard of the British charged the head of the American column; skirmishing followed; but, except a few occasional shots from the sentries of each army, a silent expectation ushered in the morning. At dawn, the two commanders proceeded to make their respective arrangements for action."*

Before the close of that eventful day, the American army was routed, the unhappy Gates escaped by a hasty flight into North Carolina, and general consternation again seized the minds of the inhabitants.

Many of the most devoted Whigs removed their families with haste to North Carolina and Virginia, returning themselves to the conflict. The Tories were more emboldened than ever, and from this time on was waged a sanguinary and desperate warfare on the Pedee. From Drowning Creek and the Little Pedee, from certain neighbourhoods on Lynche's Creek and the parts lower down, marauding bands were ever and anon pouring in on the river settlements, which were true almost to a man. A spirit of

*"Tarleton," pp. 103-105.

unsparing revenge took possession of the Whigs, and many a plain from the line of North Carolina above to the upper limits of Marion's field of action below, were to be watered with blood.

In the brief entries made in his Journal, the Rev. Mr. Pugh doubtless gave expression to feelings which very generally prevailed:—

"Friday, 18th August. Got the news of Gates's defeat; moved to Lide's quarter.

"Saturday, 19th. About in great trouble.

"Sunday, 20th. Over the river, moved home my goods.

"Tuesday, 22nd. Bad news.

"Sunday, Sept. 3rd. Went to Kolb's; men met there upon a scout after Tories.

"Saturday, 16th. Had news of the British at Black Creek.

"Sunday, 17th. At home; melancholy day. Am plundered severely; but, blessed be God, am spared yet.

"Tuesday, 19th. At home; all day full of trouble.

"Thursday, 21st. At home; went to Lide's in great trouble.

"Monday, 25th. Went to Mr. Kimbrough's; sorrowful.

"Wednesday, 27th. At home; British left the Long Bluff.

"Thursday, 28th. At home, after my cattle.

"Tuesday, 10th Oct. Whigs flying, or retreating from here."

The approach of Gates to Pedee, as already remarked, was hailed with delight by every ardent patriot. George M'Call and four youthful companions, upon hearing that Gates had crossed the Yadkin, started up the river to join the army and take part in the expected conflict at Camden. They had proceeded but a short distance, when intelligence reached them that Col. Giles was raising a volunteer force below to swell the columns of the American commander. Hastening back, they found the colonel with his party at Giles's Bluff, some distance below on the Pedee. They remained in that locality two weeks or more, and were joined during the time by Colonel Marion with an additional force. Having collected a few old field-pieces, Marion crossed the river and commenced a redoubt. While engaged upon this work, where a temporary stand was intended to be made, the news reached them of Gates's defeat. As a consequence, the plan of operations previously agreed upon was broken up; and the brilliant career in which he was to become so distinguished as a partisan leader, already successfully commenced, now opened in larger outline and bloodier prospect upon Marion. With the force hastily collected and now under his command, a few sallies were made against the Tories in Williamsburg and the region east of the Pedee. Col. Giles received orders to march with such a volunteer force as would accompany him, to Long Bluff, there to join Col. Kolb, for a retreat into North Carolina, or any other movement which the course of events might determine. The result was, that Col. Kolb remained in the neighbourhood of Long Bluff, for the protection of the lives and property of the inhabitants there against the Tories. Young M'Call, who met Col. Marion for the first time on the occasion alluded to, was so deeply impressed with his superior military sagacity, that he determined to join his command, and share the fortunes of the future with him to the close of the war. Col. Hicks had gone with his family to Virginia, leaving the active command of the forces on the Pedee to Lieut.-Col. Kolb, a position which the latter appears to have retained until his death, in the early part of the following spring.

The depredations by the Tories were secretly committed, except in those cases where they had the advantage of overpowering numbers, or the Whigs were absent from their homes.

Samuel Bacot was one of many sufferers, though sometimes eluding the enemy, or sharing with others the benefit of their cowardly fears. On one occasion, a party of Tories were seen approaching his house. He seized a well-charged musket, and, giving a few hasty directions, was in the act of escaping, when the distress of a favorite child detained him for a moment, and until the enemy were dismounting; a little more, and it would have been too late. He succeeded however, in reaching a thick covert in the rear of the dwelling in safety. His directions were observed by the family, and as the Tories entered and were about to make search, the loud report of a musket was heard, and the clatter of shot against the walls and door facings as they came through the open passage from the rear, confirmed the impression of a murderous surprise. A panic followed, and the cowardly wretches ran for their lives, leaving even their horses behind them, to the amusement and relief of the family.

On another occasion, Mr. Bacot was taken prisoner and carried to Camden, where he suffered much from a cruel confinement. About thirty others were at the same time imprisoned, and it was determined to send them all to Charles-town, for safe keeping, in charge of a detachment double their own number. His companions were known to Mr. Bacot, and a few of them as determined spirits on whom he could rely in effecting an escape by the way.

To these his plans were communicated soon after the march commenced. They were to take advantage of any favorable circumstance which might occur, for effecting their liberation. A long and wearisome day passed away, the party halting in the evening near a deserted log house by the road side, which was to be occupied during the night. The arms were stacked in front, near the steps. There were two apartments, separated by a thin partition. In the one which opened on the piazza, the guard took lodging, placing the prisoners in the other, with which they communicated by a door. From the latter room, a window opened upon the road.

The weary captives had now a better opportunity for consulting together, and it was soon determined to carry their plans into execution. "Saturday night" was agreed upon as the watchword and signal for action. To take possession of the guns, when the main body were asleep, was a matter of the first importance. About midnight, Mr. Bacot tapped at the door, and upon its being opened, begged the captain for a drink of brandy, a ready excuse being given for the request at so unseasonable an hour. He perceived at a glance that the moment for action had come; and taking the glass which was handed him, said, as he raised it, with emphasis on the last words, "Here is success to *Saturday night,*" and dashed the liquor in the officer's face.

As the words were uttered, his eager and impatient comrades rushed out, and seizing the arms, were opposed by the nearest sentinel, who was speedily overpowered. The rest of the prisoners, not understanding the cause of the confusion, and thinking it a suitable time for escape, began to leap out of the window. The whole guard being roused, their surrender was peremptorily demanded, and so sudden and complete was the surprise, that they yielded at once. They were then paroled and dismissed; and the captives, once more at liberty, lost no time in finding their way homeward.*

Elias DuBose, on Lynche's Creek, had many adventures with the Tories. On one occasion, before the removal of his family to Virginia, he had returned from the camp on furlough. The Tories, being apprised of his movements, approached his house in the dead of night, and demanded admittance. Well knowing their designs, Mr. Du Bose presented himself, gun in hand, with a heroic wife by his side, also armed, and refused them admittance, threatening to shoot the first man who made the attempt to enter, and adding that he would sell his life as dearly as possible. They then threatened to burn them, and made preparations to carry the threat into execution. In this desperate emergency, no alternative was left but a compromise; the dauntless Whig proposing to surrender, on condition that they would not tie or confine him, but that he should be carried to old Mr. Wilson, a neighbouring magistrate and friend of the King, who resided on the opposite side of the creek, and by whose sentence he consented to abide.

Supper was then provided for them. Upon arriving at Mr. Wilson's, and submitting the case to him, he said such a neighbour should not be injured, and told his friend Du Bose to go at large; upon which he returned to his family the same night.

The warfare with the Tories extended up into the neighbouring counties of North Carolina.

Some time after Gates's defeat, Mrs. Harrington had an adventure with a band of marauders, some of the conse-

---

*In an account of this incident given in Johnson's "Traditions of the Revolution," the name of Peter incorrectly appears, instead of Samuel Bacot.

quences of which she had reason to deplore to the end of her life. The general, then absent on duty, had sent an urgent message to her to take the negroes and such other moveable property as could be transported, and start immediately for Maryland. She did so with all possible expedition; and bidding adieu to home, had proceeded as far as Mountain Creek, in Richmond County, when she was met by Captain John Leggett, a noted Tory, of Bladen County, near the line of Robeson, with his party. They at once began their work of plunder, destroying such of the property as they could not take with them. Some of the negroes made their escape, and remained under cover until all danger was past.

The books, and a valuable library which General Harrington was particularly anxious to preserve, were scattered along the road, and not a few, with many valuable papers, were lost or destroyed. The horses were all taken. Fearing a pursuit, the Tories soon took to flight. One of them, named M'Koy, received a young negro man as his share of the spoils, and fled by way of the Grassy Islands. In crossing the river at that point, the horse stumbled, throwing the negro off, who was drowned. After the war, judgment was obtained against this man, but nothing recovered. Mrs. Harrington made her way back as well as she could to her father, Major James Auld, in Anson County. Her brothers, John and Michael Auld, started with a company in pursuit of the Tories, but did not overtake them or succeed in getting any of the property back.* Some time before the march of General Gates to the South, General Harrington had his head-quarters at Cross Creek. The object of his position there was to keep the Tories in awe, and protect the public stores, collected and sent forward from time to time. On the advance of Gates to Camden, he summoned

---

*After the war, General Harrington brought suit against Leggett, and obtained judgment. Leggett, in the meantime, had transferred his lands to another to prevent their being taken. Upon its becoming known, they escheated to the State. An Act was afterwards passed by the Legislature of N. C. giving General H. title to these lands. Upon going to Bladen, he found two daughters of Leggett, and gave them deeds for their homestead. Leggett, with others, had escaped to Nova Scotia, but had now returned. General H. received very little in the end—but a few hundred dollars for one or two tracts of land.

General Harrington from Cross Creek with all despatch to his assistance. The latter immediately took up the line of march; but, upon arriving at Haley's Ferry, on the Pedee, received intelligence of the disastrous defeat and general dispersion of the American forces. His head-quarters for a time were in this neighbourhood.

On the 18th of August, Colonel Nicholas, of the Virginia Militia, wrote to General Harrington as follows:—

"Mark's Ferry,* Aug. 18th, 1780.

"Sir,—As I command at this point, I took the liberty of opening your letter to General Stevens. My orders from Colonel Harrison were to stay and command this pass, in order to enable the stragglers of our army to cross the river; and I doubt not, on your considering the necessity of rallying our men, who generally seem to pass this way, and which would be rendered entirely ineffectual by giving up the ferry to the command of the disaffected people, you will render me all the assistance you can, both by giving me advice and falling on some plan for the safety of the troops here and at Cole's Bridge, the former consisting of about 300 men badly armed. Colonel Harrison directed me to march on for Hillsborough as soon as I supposed the men had all passed that were likely to come this way.

"P.S. I just saw a letter from General Caswell to Colonel Seawell, which I have forwarded to him, and which will put it out of his power to act with me, I expect.

"Sir, I am, with respect,
"Your most obedient servant,
"J. NICHOLAS,
"Lieut.-Col. V. Militia.

"Brig.-General Harrington, on Pedee."

On the 10th of September Gen. Gates, now on his retreat through North Carolina, wrote to Gen. Harrington.

"Hillsborough, 11 in the forenoon, 10th Septr., 1780.

"Dear Sir,—This moment I received your letter, dated the 6th inst., 8 P. M., from Cross Creek. I am much pleased

---

*Mark's Ferry was fifty miles above Cheraw.

with the good news it contains, and hope it will prove true; in the mean time it is our duty, by every means, to know with certainty if the fleet of our allies is, or is not, upon this coast. I desire you will immediately do everything in your power to satisfy me in that particular. Such necessary and unavoidable expense as is incurred in procuring this intelligence, I will cheerfully pay.

"I am, dear sir,
"Your affectionate, humble Servant,
"HORATIO GATES.

"Brigadier-General Harrington.

"P.S.—Continue your spies toward Camden and down Pedee."

The enemy were now much emboldened, and renewed their plundering expeditions, as they had done after the fall of Charles-town, in the spring and early part of the summer. Again Major Wemys made his presence felt in the country above George-town. The *South Carolina and American General Gazette* of September 20th, contained an extract of a letter from that place of the 16th, saying: "Major Wemys has been scouring the country to the northward of this. Several of the inhabitants who, after giving their paroles, joined Marion and Horry in their late incursion, have gone off with them. Some of their houses, &c., have been destroyed in terrorem. The persons of others, equally culpable, are secured, as they have, by their recent base conduct, shown themselves unworthy of being allowed to go at large."

Soon after this, the Board of War of North Carolina addressed to Gen. Harrington the following cummunication:—

"Hillsborough, Octr. 1st, 1780.

"Sir,—Gen. Gates will give you directions how you are to conduct yourself in your military operations. As he understands that business much better than I do, you will obey his orders. There are a number of militia at Col. Scamlock's, in Chatham, left by Gen. Sumner, many of them unable to do duty. I have written to the colonel to send all that appear able to go to you, to Cross Creek, as they may act as a guard—those that are unwell, to be discharged, as they are only an incumbrance.

"You will give such orders relative to any that join you as you think proper.

"I am, your obedient servant,
"J. Penn."

Gen. Gates also wrote on the same day: "As the enemy are advancing by the route of Salisbury, I recommend it to you, to collect your force immediately at Cross Creek, and be prepared to march by Chatham Court House the moment you receive orders."

By order of the Governor of North Carolina, Col. Thomas Brown, of that State, had marched to Pedee, and soon after his arrival wrote to General Harrington, informing him of his movements.

"Camp at the Beauty Spot, 10th Octr., 1780.

"Dear Sir,—I have, agreeably to your order, marched as far as this place, eight miles below Hick's Mills; but meeting with a letter here, informing me of your retreat back to Cross Creek, I conclude to proceed no farther; but shall, as directed by his Excellency, Gov. Nash, drive off all the beef cattle that I can possibly collect. I have received no orders from you since the 3rd inst., which, together with your unexpected retreat,* has left me so much in the dark how to act, as to determine me as above. The inhabitants about this place seem perfectly still, except about ninety, who are said to be collected at Spike's Mill, on Jeffrey's Creek; but we learn there is a party gone out this day in order to dislodge them, under the command of Capt. Delany. Captains Murphy and Council, with their companies, are ranging up and down this river in order to keep the Tories in awe. I hope shortly to hear from you; and am,

"Dear sir, with much respect,
"Your most obedient, humble Servant,
"Thos. Brown.

"P.S.—Since I concluded I have been lucky enough to meet with the person who furnishes the following deposition. He is a son-in-law to Capt. Henry Council, and is said to have been compelled into the British service, and has returned home in consequence of Ford's orders. 'Tis confi-

---

*The unexpected retreat here referred to, was from Haley's Ferry, on Pedee, to Cross Creek.

dently asserted by a person lately from Georgia, that six thousand French are landed there, and have taken Sunsbury. We further learn that the Tories about Little Pedee are summoned to meet on Thursday next, by one Jesse Barfield. I shall endeavor to watch their motions, and if possible, disperse them.

"I am, as before, yours, &c.,
"T. B.

"To Brig.-Gen. Harrington,
  "at or near Cross Creek."

It appears from this letter, that the Whigs on Pedee were now rendering effective service against the Tories. This conflict was fiercely waged, and only to close with the termination of the war.

On the 11th of October, General Gates wrote to General Harrington as to a change of position.

"Hillsborough, Octr., 11, 1780.

"Dear Sir,—Last night I received your letter from Cross Creek, dated the 6th instant. Colonel Kolb was then here. He is of opinion that you might securely take post with your brigade upon the Pedee, opposite the Cheraws; to this, if it meets with your approbation, I have not the smallest objection. On the contrary, I recommend to you to do it immediately. I desire you will acquaint Colonels Marion and Giles with your intentions, and recommend it to them to make diversions against the enemy's posts below. It is not improbable but you may, soon after your arrival upon Pedee, hear something from General Sumpter. You may, thereupon, with proper caution being taken, correspond and co-operate with him. But this information must be kept a profound secret to every one but yourself.

"I am, Sir,
"Your affectionate, humble Servant,
"Horatio Gates.

"Brigadier-General Harrington,
  "near Cross Creek."

On the day this letter was written, Colonel Martin, in behalf of the Board of War of N. C., addressed General Harrington on the same subject.

It was a matter of great importance to the inhabitants on the Pedee.

"War Office, Hillsborough, Octr., 11th, 1780.

"Sir,—General Gates's orders for your retreat from the Pedee were unknown to the Board of War until your arrival at Cross Creek; a post so essential to be kept up for the support of this State, and protection of our neighbouring friends in South Carolina, that the Legislature had this object particularly in view.

"On the remonstrance of the Board, General Gates has countermanded your orders, which you will receive with this. As Mark's Ferry seems rather too high up the river for the purposes intended, you will therefore please to exercise your own discretion as to your main post on the Pedee, so that it be not far above or below the boundary, and your particular detachments. The army stand in great need of provisions, particularly cattle.

"Colonel Brown hath a particular command from the Governor, by direction of the Assembly, to collect all the cattle on or near Pedee, so as not to distress private families or individuals, and have them driven into the interior parts of this State. You, Sir, will have the superintendence of Colonel Brown and all other officers serving in your quarter, to direct their particular movements, and detachments to join you or otherwise.

"Other officers and men from you may be employed in the like service, which is so important and pressing at this juncture.

"Mr. Amis is directed to attend and receive the cattle, and have them driven to this post. You have a hint dropped you from General Gates, which perhaps may shortly be carried into execution.

"General Smallwood has accepted the command of our militia, with whom you will please to correspond. He, with Colonel Morgan, has marched for Salisbury.

"I am, with respect,
"Your most obedient, humble Servant,
"ALEXANDER MARTIN.

"Brigadier-General Harrington,
    "Cross Creek."

The movements of the British were at this juncture a subject of much uncertainty with the American commanders. As a consequence, counter-orders were constantly being given. Soon, however, this state of things was to pass away, and the plans of the enemy to be more clearly developed. About the latter part of October, General Harrington reached the Pedee with his command, and took post at Haley's Ferry, but soon removed to a point on the river, immediately opposite Cheraw. He was kept in constant communication with the Board of War of North Carolina, as well as with the commanders of the South Carolina forces lower down the Pedee. General Smallwood addressed him soon after.

"Camp New Providence, 31st Octr., 1780.

"Sir,—Since my acceptance of the command of the militia, I have not had an opportunity of writing you, and am still at a loss to know your position, or where to direct for you. I am apprehensive the particular quarters to which our military operations have been confined, have jointly obstructed this, as the intermediate country has been in possession of the enemy.

"It is necessary I should know your strength, resources, and views, before I could with propriety point out any particular mode to govern your conduct, or regulate it under the general scale or system to be adopted in our future operations. I have taken this opportunity, therefore, by Colonel Davie (who is ordered for particular purposes to that part of the Tory country lying between us), to write you, to be transmitted, if necessary, by a few horsemen, upon whose return you will be so obliging as to favor me with the necessary information above required.

"The British, two days ago, were encamped at or near Lee's Mill, said to be fifteen or twenty miles below the cross roads from that place. Roads lead to the westward —Congaree, Charles-town, and Camden—so that no just conclusion can be drawn of their next movement or views.

"Our strength is so small here, and without artillery, that nothing can be attempted against them, especially as we should have a river in our rear, and our supplies principally to be drawn from this side; but I shortly expect General Gates on with the concentrated troops, when perhaps something may be effected. We have just received advices from Governor Jefferson, of the arrival of a large fleet of the enemy within the Capes of Virginia, that they were debarking on the 22nd instant; but he does not mention their number, or where they were landing, though, I imagine, at Portsmouth, and the number to be the same lately embarked at New York, and recently destined against West Point; but the capture of André, the British Adjutant-General, who acted as a spy, and the discovery of Arnold's treachery, changes their course for Virginia.

"You have no doubt heard of Arnold's perfidy, and the deep plot laid by him and André of trepanning our excellent Commander-in-Chief, and betraying the forts at West Point, with 4000 men.

"The conquerors of Ferguson and his party I expected to join me here, but they have generally dispersed.

"I am, very respectfully,

"Sir, your obt. humble Servant,

"W. SMALLWOOD, Secretary.

"Gen. Harrington."

Colonel Brown was still on the Pedee, rendering effective service against the Tories. He wrote again to the general, from

"Camp, Bear Swamp, Novr. 4th, 1780.

"Dear Sir,

"I received your favor of the 26th of October, dated near Haley's Ferry. It gives me pleasure to hear you have marched to a part of the country that so much wanted your assistance; and I can assure you, I have been ever since I received your first orders, upon the march after those scoundrels, and can inform you the report concerning Capt. Moore is partly false, as he did not lose one man, and but one slightly wounded. But Barfield did surprise him and took several of his horses; but I have paid them tolerably well for it. I have killed Miles Barfield, wounded two others of the Barfields; and, it is said, Jesse

Barfield is shot through the hand, but the certainty I cannot tell. I have got four more of the Barfields well ironed and under guard, whom I am very choice of. You mentioned you would be glad to know how I came on in collecting cattle. I have got 259 head and sent them to Headquarters, and have just got to collecting again, as Barfield hath prevented me for a fortnight past. I hope you will write to me by every opportunity, and I will not fail.

"And am, Sir, with respect,
"Your humble Servant,
"THOS. BROWN.
"General Harrington, near Haley's Ferry."

The family of Barfield, to several of whom Col. Brown's letter refers, lived on Little Pedee, and had now become notorious.

The history of their leader, Major Barfield, the most prominent among them, was one, unhappily for themselves and the country, not unfrequent in the days that tried men's souls; furnishing a sad illustration of the fact, how trivial causes are permitted to lead to a decisive and fatal change in the conduct of life. Major Barfield is said to have been a captain in the American service at the first siege of Charles-town. Some indignity was offered him by a superior officer, and he appealed for redress to the general in command.

It was not granted; and becoming morbidly affected, he took revenge by deserting the cause of his country, carrying a number with him, and proving himself ever after, a bitter and relentless foe. He was possessed of superior abilities, with a commanding person and respectable fortune, and became the acknowledged leader of the disaffected inhabitants between Great and Little Pedee.

During the course of the war, he took refuge on some occasion in the British camp, was seized with the smallpox and died. The predatory warfare between the Whigs and Tories was actively carried on in the adjoining parts of North Carolina.

The following letter of Colonel Davison to General Harrington refers to the subject.

"On Brown Creek, near Lanier, 6th Novr., 1780.

"Dear General,

"I proceeded according to your orders, and on Brown Creek we took a grand Tory by the name of Thomas Blake. I put him under a guard and sent him off to James Boggin's; but before they got there, the prisoner endeavoured to make his escape. The guard fired at him and killed him.

"Horses are very scarce in this quarter. I have collected a few very good beef cattle, and put them in my own field about three miles from where the river road crosses Brown Creek. I think I can gather a good many beef cattle in this country, by the information I have. John May came in to me, and promised to be of all the service he can to his country; and, indeed, he has been very useful to me since I have been in these parts; but, as I heard you mention something about him in your camp, I have ordered him down to you.

Dennis M'Clendon was taken yesterday morning and brought to me by Major Miller, &c. By the best authority, the old man intended to come in as soon as he could find some of his own county officers. We have several Tories laying out yet, though I think all will come in except those who have gone to the British.

"Our general muster is on Thursday next, at May's Mill. And then the militia of this county is to be stationed at Lanier's plantation on Brown Creek; and then we will proceed immediately to gather all the beef cattle in these parts, except you order otherwise.

"The bearer hereof waits on you for your orders. Please to send me some salt if possible. I have sent Dennis M'Lendon and Stephen Murphy under a guard, in the care of Lieut. Colter. I have no news worth writing to you. I am just setting off to the head of Brown Creek and Lane Creek, and shall not be back until the muster.

"I am, dear General,
"Your most obt. Servant,
"GEO. DAVISON.

"N.B.—I beg to be excused for not writing to you sooner."

On the Pedee occasional reverses were experienced, but not of very serious consequence. Barfield was roaming through the country, plundering and killing as opportunity offered, though forced to be cautious in his movements. Col. Brown continues the narrative:—

"Dear Sir, "Camp near Caird's Mill, the 9th of Novr., 1780.

"I this evening received yours, dated this day, near Charraw Ferry, with the disagreeable news of Capt. Murphy's defeat, and highly approve of your plan, and will do everything in my power to put it in execution, as it is a most dreadful affair that such a set of scoundrels should be allowed to exist upon earth. I have 162 men, of whom I have about 45 horse, fit for duty. I expect to be to-morrow at Caird's Mill; and would recommend it to the officers commanding your posts, to meet me on Sunday at Jonathan Miller's, as Barfield resorts near that place. Your troops can cross Little Pedee at Gibson's, and then there is a direct road to Miller's. Yesterday, Barfield fell in with 5 of your men that left your camp on Monday, by the names of Robert Vernon, Matthew White, Theophilus Eavens,—Hadley (the other name I cannot tell), and kept them till about midnight, and then took all their horses and arms, paroled them and let them go.

"I would recommend it to you to send a formidable troop of horse, as Barfield can raise 70 or 80 horse himself, and is determined to prevent any cattle being collected amongst them; and, I imagine, there might be two or three hundred head of good cattle got, if they could be once broken up.

"Barfield attacked my regiment last Monday week, at night; but they did us no damage, only slightly wounded two men. I wrote to you a few days ago by Cross Creek, and hope to hear from you by every opportunity. And am, Sir, with respect,

"Your humble Servant,
"THOS. BROWN, C.T.T."

Cautious and rapid in their movements, approaching by stealth and generally under cover of darkness, it was difficult for the Whigs to capture the marauding parties of Tories. Under Barfield, the organization was effective and formidable.

The *South Carolina Gazette and American Journal*, Charles-town, of Nov. 15th, contained the following intelligence:—"We are authorized to inform the public that about 200 of the inhabitants near Pedee River, over whom Mr. Marion and his associates for some time past have exercised the most despotic and cruel tyranny, lately collected together in arms, and fell in with a gang of banditti, whom they routed and entirely dispersed. The leader of the rebels, a Col. Murphy, was amongst the killed.

"A few days since, the victorious Loyalists joined the King's forces posted at George-town. The accounts from that part of the country represent the people eagerly disposed to contribute their assistance towards preventing any future inroads of the rebels."

Fortunately for his country, the report of Col. Murphy's death was false. He survived this and many other bloody conflicts, to see both foreign and domestic foes subdued. "Mr. Marion," so contemptuously alluded to, had already become a terror to the enemy, and was yet to see many a proud officer, with once victorious soldiers, suppliants before him.

Gen. Smallwood continued to write, giving an interesting account of the general progress of events.

"Camp, November 15th, 1780.

"Sir,—I received your two favors of the 28th October and 5th inst., some time after I wrote you on the 31st ultimo. They were delivered by some militia from Gen. Butler's camp, and had been delayed on the road. The expresses you sent never came further than Salisbury, which prevented my writing as I could have wished.

"I must request you in future to direct the expresses to deliver their despatches in person, that they may be immediately answered on their return; but I hope our communication shortly may be opened upon a more direct route through Lynche's Creek.

"I daily expect the arrival of General Gates with the

Continental troops, when our strength will enable us to advance lower down, and it then may be necessary for you to advance across the country, to co-operate with us; and, in the interim, as I am unacquainted with the country, I could wish you would point out, or give your opinion upon the propriety of taking a position somewhere upon Black River, or Lynche's Creek. If such a position could be taken with security, it would have a happy tendency in several respects, particularly in facilitating some plans in view—the suppression of the Tories, and securing supplies, which are much exhausted in this quarter. You will also be so obliging as to favor me with returns of your strength, resources, and views, as I requested in my last. We now draw supplies of forage and provision from the upper part of Lynche's Creek, and the Tory part of the Waxsaw settlement; and I am now extending my views lower down in these quarters and across the Catawbas.

"Lord Cornwallis remains at Wynsborough inactive, Tarleton below on the Santee, wasting and destroying all before him, which indicates an evacuation of Camden. This place, I think, might have been reduced ere this, and Tarleton circumscribed in his deprepations, had the Continental troops been forwarded; but in our present weak state, Lord Cornwallis has taken so judicious a position, either to cut off our retreat or aid his parties, that these enterprises could not be risked.

"I think something may shortly be effected, unless the enemy should be reinforced, which I really am apprehensive of, and that the arrival of the French fleet you mention in yours of the 5th inst. is premature. I wish they may not prove to be British, with a reinforcement, and the firing, salutes or signal guns, as we have no intelligence of a French fleet from the latest accounts from the northward; but I am informed of a late embarkation from New York, conjectured to be destined to Charles-town; and also that some part of the fleet and forces from Portsmouth had sailed for that place.

"Sumpter has lately defeated a party of two hundred British cavalry and infantry mounted, and a small number of Tories, who attacked him at Fish Dam Ford, at 3 o'clock on the morning of the 9th instant. The commanding officer, Major Wemys, a surgeon, and sergeant-major, were taken wounded, with upwards of twenty more prisoners, some valuable horses and arms. Seven were killed and more wounded, who were carried off. Sumpter's loss was only four killed and two wounded.

"I am with very great regard and esteem,
"Sir, your obedient, humble Servant,
"W. SMALLWOOD.
"Brigadier-General Harrington,
"Kershaw Ferry."*

For several months past, Marion† had been actively engaged with the enemy in the parts below, and shortly before this, made an unsuccessful attempt upon George-town. He gave the following account of it to Gen. Harrington.

"Blackmingo, 17th Novr., 1780.
"Sir,

"Since my last to you, Colonel Tarleton retreated to Camden, after destroying all the houses and provisions in his way. By information, I was made to believe there was but fifty British in George-town, and no militia, which induced me to attempt taking that place. But, unluckily, the day before I got there they received a reinforcement of two hundred Tories under Captains Barfield and Lewis from Pedee. The next day the Tories came out and we scummaged with them.

"Part I cut off from the town, and drove the rest in, except the two men killed, and twelve taken prisoners. Our loss was Lieutenant Gabriel Marion, and one private killed. These two men were killed after they surrendered. We had three or four wounded, one since dead of his wound.

"Captain Barfield was wounded in his head and body, but got off. Captain James Lewis, commonly called 'Otter Skin Lewis,' was one killed. I stayed two days within three

---

*Kershaw Ferry was that at Cheraw, so called then.
†Marion is supposed to have been at this time a colonel, though previously called general. In August, he was commissioned by Governor Rutledge to take command of the post at Lynche's Creek, but not appointed general until some time after that, as James says in his "Sketch," p. 46 (note).

miles of the town, in which time most of the Tories left their friends and went home.

"Finding the regulars in the town to be eighty men, besides militia, strongly entrenched in a redoubt, with swivels and cohorns on their parapet, I withdrew my men, as I had not six rounds per man, and shall not be able to proceed on any operations without a supply of ammunition, which I will be obliged to you to furnish me with by Captain Potts, who commands a detachment to guard the prisoners taken. I have not heard anything from General Gates since the letter you sent me.

"A man from the high hills of Santee, within eight miles of Camden, says that Washington's Horse is at Rugely's Mill, one mile from there. I beg to know where our army is, and what news from them.

"I am, with esteem, your most obedient Servant,
"FRANCIS MARION.
"Hon. Brig.-General Harrington, Pedee."

Colonel Kolb was now in command in the neighbourhood of Long Bluff, and the acknowledged leader on the Upper Pedee.

In reply to a call from General Harrington, he made the following return of his force:—

"To Brig.-Gen. Harrington.
    "Dear Sir,
            "You last wrote that you wanted to see me, with a return of my regiment this day in camp. I should be happy in waiting on you at any time after to-day. I think to ride up to-morrow, if I should not be sick.

"Sir, you wanted to ascertain the number of men I had in the regiment.

"Agreeably to my returns, I have but 233 men, besides officers. I shall send you the part of my regiment you require to-morrow, or next day. I shall have them marched up under command of some one captain.

"I am, Sir, your most humble Servant,
"ABEL KOLB.

"27th of Novr., 1780."

The number here returned was small indeed, having doubtless been much reduced by disease and the sword. The exposure and privation endured in the kind of warfare now carried on must have been very great, wasting away imperceptibly what was not at once destroyed.

The spirit of revolt on the Pedee gave much concern to the enemy, particularly in connexion with the holding their post at Camden. On the 3rd of December, Lord Cornwallis, from his camp at Wynsborough, wrote to Sir H. Clinton on the subject. He said:—"Colonel Marion had so wrought on the minds of the people, partly by the terror of his threats and cruelty of his punishments, and partly by the promise of plunder, that there was scarcely an inhabitant between the Santee and Pedee that was not in arms against us. Some parties had even crossed the Santee, and carried terror to the gates of Charles-town. My first object was to reinstate matters in that quarter, without which Camden could receive no supplies.

"I therefore sent Tarleton, who pursued Marion for several days, obliged his corps to take to the swamps, and by convincing the inhabitants that there was a power superior to Marion, who could likewise reward and punish, so far checked the insurrection that the greatest part of them have not dared to appear in arms against us since his expedition."*

Notwithstanding the tone of this communication, Cornwallis had sad forebodings of the future that awaited him, as his correspondence shows. He was much deceived in the opinion, if in reality it was entertained, that the patriots were convinced of a power superior to Marion. The British had exercised so much oppression and rapacity over all those who would not join them, and so much insolence over those who did, that the people of Carolina found there was no alternative between a state of downright vassalage on the one hand, and of unyielding warfare on the other. The men of principle already had done so, or were prepared to take up arms; and in general, only the unprincipled remained with the enemy in expectation of plunder, or from motives

---

*"Tarleton," p. 200.

of fear. They had now learned, besides, that the country might be overrun with more facility than kept in subjection by the necessarily divided forces of the enemy, and that a partisian warfare, such as Marion had now begun, was the best that could be carried on against a foe superior in force and discipline to themselves.*

In common with the inhabitants of other parts of the State, the Whigs of Pedee had been made to contribute their faithful slaves to the working force of the enemy. Among the returns of negroes in the different departments, were the following in the published records of the day:—

"Novr. 1780† Negroes in the engineer department, that joined the army since the landing under Sir H. Clinton, in 1780.

"Sam,   taken from Colonel Hart
Dick,   "   "   "   Kolb
James,   "   "   "   "
Simon,   "   "   "   "
Pompey,   "   "   "   "

"In Barrack Master's department:—
"Abraham, taken from Colonel Kolb,
Jupiter,   "   "   General Harrington."

On the 18th of November, the Pedee country and the State at large sustained a heavy loss in the death of Gen. Alexander M'Intosh.‡

In every relation of life, this patriotic and honored citizen had ever maintained the most exemplary character. A member of the Provincial Congress and one of the Committee of Observation for St. David's Parish; a representative successively, and the first senator elected, for St. David's; the President of St. David's Society from its organization; appointed first Major, then Lieut.-Colonel in the Provincial service, afterwards Brigadier-General of Militia, and member of the Legislative Council, as first established—it was his

---

*James's "Sketch of Marion," p. 84.
†*Gazette* of November, 1780.
‡This entry appears in the journal of Mr. Pugh:—
"Sunday, 19th Novr. preached Gen. M'Intosh's funeral, at the Welch Neck, on 2 Timothy, iv. 7, 8."

happiness to fill every position to which he was called with fidelity and honor. Of superior mental endowments, and well-balanced character, commanding in person, and possessed of an ample fortune, he was enabled to exert a degree of influence beyond most of his contemporaries in the service of his country, in which he was active and prominent from the commencement of the struggle for liberty. Nor, in the midst of so troublous a period did he forget the chief duty of man. In war, he meekly served the Prince of Peace, and died the death of the righteous.

General Harrington was still on the Pedee,* and continued to hold that position until some time in December. He then moved up the river, and was shortly after at Grassey Creek, Roanoke, where he received the following letter from Col. John Donaldson:—

"Richmond County, Pedee, 30th Decr., 1780.

"Dear General,

"This will serve to acknowledge the receipt of your favors, dated the 11th and 19th inst., for which I am much obliged to you. Your order on me by W. Hardick shall be answered the first opportunity. As to news, I am at a loss to inform you of any. As to the enemy's movements, was last night informed that Lord Cornwallis had retreated to Camden, but am not certain as to the truth. Before this reaches you, I imagine you will hear of the Hon. Major-General Green's marching here with a number of Continentals, Virginia Militia, and some cavalry; but as to real number, am not acquainted, for I have never been in camp yet, which is on Hick's Creek.

---

*The following is one of many accounts of articles furnished General Harrington's forces on Pedee:—

"State of South Carolina.
"To George Hicks.

				£	s.	d.
Novr. 6, 1780,	1921 lbs. of pork @ 32s. 8d. per 100,			£31	7	6
„ 15, „	100 bundles corn blades, @ 70d. per 100,			0	15	6
„ 29, „	180 busls. corn, @ 3s. 6d.			31	10	8
				£63	13	8

"The above mentioned pork, corn blades, and corn were impressed for use of N. C. militia, in this State, under command of Brig.-Gen. Harrington, who at that time had the command of the S. C. militia on both sides of the Pedee."

"Brigadier-General Morgan is left with some chosen troops on the Catawba River. Where General Sumpter is, I cannot say. General Marion has had two small skirmishes with the Tories and British, at or near Nelson's Ferry. The enemy retreated towards Camden. He took some prisoners and killed some, the number not known. His Excellency, John Rutledge, Esq., of South Carolina, General Huger, and some other officers belonging to that State, are in camp.

"I am told his Excellency is going to camp at the Cheraws. I hope he will transmogriphy the Northern Tories, and make them know that liberty has not declined altogether her friendship for that State. Col. Thomas Wade has got an appointment to act as Commissary for the South State. He speaks of building 300 flat-bottomed boats, as to the use of which many are the conjectures. I hope for the best.

"If our allies are but near Bermuda, I should think Lord Cornwallis will draw near to Charles-town for support of that place. It was almost without necessary guards a few days ago, as report goes.

"I have spoken to Col. Medlock as to your request, but he says he has not received any satisfactory answer from the Board of War; but as he is coming to the Assembly in the course of the week, he may settle that matter.

"He was appointed, at our Court, Commissioner, and gave security for the same. How far we are justifiable in holding Court, I cannot say. Some necessary things were done—for particulars, shall refer you to Col. Medlock.

"Col. Wade was at my house a few days ago, and hinted he would be willing to be done with the Light Horse Regiment for the three counties. He told me he would write to you on the subject. If so, and any party of horse or foot should be thought proper to be raised, and that for a certain time, not less than six or twelve months, if thought best, and that proper arms might be had for them; then, if you should think that my weak abilities could be of any service to my country, I shall be willing to serve, so that strict discipline may be allowed, when on duty. But shall refer the whole to your good judgment. I rest fully assured

of your doing everything in your power for your much-injured country, and remain, dear General,
"Your most obedient, and
"Very humble Servant,
"JOHN DONALDSON.

"To Hon. Brigadier-General Harrington,
"Grassey Creek, Roanoke.

"P.S.—Sir, please to present my compliments to Mrs. Harrington, and all inquiring friends.—I am yours, &c.
"J. D.

"N.B.—I am in great want of a good sword. In case of employment, will pay any expenses.—I am yours,
"J. D."

General Green, who had been sent to take charge of the Southern Department, arrived at Charlotte, North Carolina, December 2. But, in consequence of the scarcity of food, that region having been greatly plundered, he divided his forces. Gen. Morgan was sent with a strong body to the western parts of South Carolina, while General Green, with the main column, marched on 20th December for Pedee. His force now consisted of not more than one thousand Continentals, and about as many militia. He was bare of ammunition and clothing, and had no money to pay for them.*

He pitched his camp on the southern bank of Husband's Creek,† three miles from Cheraw, on the east side of the river, but moved almost immediately after to a position on Hicks's Creek, a mile higher up.

Lord Cornwallis, in a letter to Col. Tarleton, dated Wynsborough, Dec. 26th, 1780, thus wrote:—"A man came this morning from Charlotte-town; his fidelity is, however, very doubtful. He says, that Green marched on Wednesday last towards the Cheraws, to join Gen. Caswell; and that Morgan, with his infantry, and one hundred and twenty-four of Washington's Light Horse, crossed Biggin's Ferry

---
*James's "Sketch of Marion," p. 85.
†Some remains of his first encampment were to be seen a few years since.

on Thursday and Friday last, to join Lacy.* I expect more certain information."

Of the movements made about this time, Tarleton wrote afterwards:—"During the preparation for the second invasion of North Carolina, emissaries had been despatched into that Province to obtain intelligence of the force and designs of the enemy.

"Near the end of December information was received that Gen. Green had made a division of his troops, which did not exceed one thousand four hundred men, exclusive of the militia; and that he had committed the light infantry and Col. Washington's cavalry to Gen. Morgan, with directions to pass the Catawba and Broad Rivers, in order to collect the militia in the districts through which he marched, and afterwards threaten Ninety-six; whilst he conducted the other division of the Continentals to Haley's Ferry, on the River Pedee, to form a junction with Gen. Caswell, and give jealousy to Camden. This appeared to be the outline of the American design previous to the arrival of Gen. Leslie's reinforcements. The intelligence Gen. Green had procured since his appointment to the southward, and the calculations of his own and the British force, might suggest the propriety of attempting to distress the frontier of South Carolina by a desultory war, till he could acquire a command sufficiently numerous and well disciplined to conduct more decisive operations.

"There could not be an arrangement better chosen, provided the Royalists were not joined by any additional regiments; but the increase of the English army would certainly frustrate such a disposition.

"It is not to be supposed that Gen. Green would have adopted the hazardous plan of dividing and advancing his troops, if he had received authentic information of Gen. Leslie's command being withdrawn from Virginia and united to the force in South Carolina; because such an accession of strength would naturally produce a movement from Wynsborough, which, if executed with tolerable rapidity, might separate the two divisons of the American

*"Tarleton," p. 207.

army, and endanger their being totally dispersed or destroyed."*

The disposition of his forces made by Gen. Green may have been hazardous, and was doubtless done in ignorance of the transfer of Leslie; yet the enemy failed to take advantage of it, so as to accomplish the results most confidently anticipated.

The advance of Green to Pedee inspired general confidence in that part of the State, and gave a new impetus to the partisan warfare already successfully waged. Thus the year 1780 drew to a close, victory, in the main, having followed the invader's steps. And yet the spirit of liberty had revived; the division of the British forces to keep the State in subjection, only developed the weakness of the enemy, and pointed out the way, by such a conflict as Marion, Kolb, and others were now carrying on, of ensuring a certain and not very remote victory in the end.

---

*"Tarleton," pp. 207, 208. It would seem, from what Tarleton here says, that General Green's first design might have been to go to Haley's Ferry, or possibly that report was circulated to mislead the enemy. His movement was directly to Cheraw.

CHAPTER XV.

General Green on Pedee—His retreat into North Carolina—Progress of British arms—Extracts from Pugh's journal—Colonel Murphy and the Tories—Gideon Gibson's death—Difficulty and co1·respondence between Captain Snipes and Colonel Kolb—The latter writes to General Marion—Whigs surprise the Tories on the Three Creeks—Harry Sparks killed—Tories routed—Whig expeditions against them to Drowning Creek and Cat Fish—Tories retaliate on Colonel Kolb—His death—Adventures of Lewis Malone Ayer—Other scenes of that day—Outrages by the Tory party—Kolb's character—Account of Captain Jones, the Tory leader, and others—Cartel for exchange of prisoners between General Green and Cornwallis—Cornwallis's movements—His declining fortunes and his correspondence—Colonels Benton and Murphy, and other leaders on Pedee—Extracts from Pugh's journal—Murphy's fight with Tories at Bass's Mill—Derangement of civil affairs—Ordinary appointed for Cheraws—Gainey's difficulty with Murphy—Treaty between Gainey and General Marion—Gainey's character—Incident connected with battle of Eutaw—Legislative elections for Cheraws—Colonel Steward's case—Mrs. Steward's petition—Steward's character and death—Confiscation Bill—Extract from *Royal Gazette*—Citizens of Cheraws included in the Bill—Extracts satirical from *Royal Gazette*—General Pinckney's letter to General Matthews.

The year 1781 opened upon strangely varied scenes throughout the State. The enemy was confident, though suffering from reverses, and preparing for decisive movements. The presence of Gen. Green on the Pedee kept the disaffected in awe during his brief stay, and brought with it a state of comparative repose to the inhabitants in the adjacent region. Col. Kolb was now in the full tide of his successful career as the honored champion of the cause of America in the Cheraw District. Col. Murphy was doing valiant service in the parts lower down on the east, Major Benton had his post on the west of the river, while Marion was actively engaged from Lynche's Creek to George-town.

The wearied army was recruiting in camp on Hicks's Creek. John Wilson, then a young and active Whig, was appointed captain of a small company of trusty men, called the "Munchausen Corps," as a light troop, to scour the country around during Green's sojourn on the Pedee. This, however, was to be of short continuance. The pursuit of Morgan by Cornwallis, after the battle of Cow-pens, of which Gen. Green received early intelligence, induced him to break up his encampment on the Pedee and move with all possible despatch in order to join Morgan.* He went in advance, with a small party, leaving the main body to follow on. The march commenced on the 28th of January, 1781. Of the almost incredible hardships endured during the rigors of this memorable winter, and particularly on the retreat from Guilford Court House, the historians of the time have written. Nothing of special interest occurred during the month's stay of Green on the Pedee. The only remains of his correspondence while here which have appeared, are a few brief letters to Marion, Sumpter and others.

His departure threw the Whigs of Cheraw District once more upon their own strong arms for protection, and the warfare with the Tories was renewed with unsparing ferocity.

Called off, as many of them were to the assistance of Marion, advantage was taken of their absence by marauding parties to ravage the country, and plunder their defenceless homes. Alarming accounts were also spread abroad of the progress of the British arms, keeping the public mind in a state of constant agitation. Mr. Pugh's journal furnishes some extracts descriptive of the time.

"Thursday, 25th January. At home all day. Had certain news of Tarleton's defeat at Broad River. Many people here all day.

"Saturday, 3rd February. Went to the Mill,† and Lide's. Met Lee's horsemen at the Mill.

"Thursday, 22nd. Murphy's company ran from the Tories.

"Wednesday, 28th March. Had the news that Marion's camp was taken.

"Thursday, 29th. Camp not taken. The British at Burch's."

---

*James Gillespie, a staunch and active young Whig, who resided near Green's Camp, acted as guide to the general on his march from Pedee.

†Long after known as Gibson's Mill, on the road from Long Bluff to Georgetown.

Lower down, on the east side of the river, the Tories made frequent incursions from Little Pedee, finding ready co-operation on the part of some in that immediate region.

The Whigs were driven in some cases to acts of cruel retaliation. One instance of this kind is related of Col. Maurice Murphy. He was a man of ungovernable passion, which was often inflamed by strong drink. On the occasion alluded to he went to the house of a noted Tory, named Blackman, then somewhat advanced in years, and inoffensive. He had several sons, however, who were active against the Whigs. Murphy's real object, doubtless, was to discover where these and others of their companions were. Having tied Blackman, he asked him who he was for; and upon his replying, "for King George," gave him fifty lashes. The question was repeated with the same reply, and the like punishment inflicted, until the fourth time, when, upon finding the old man unyielding, Murphy was compelled to desist. Blackman lived on Cat Fish, and the place is yet called "Tory's Camp."

Gideon Gibson, the uncle of Murphy, blamed him for his conduct on this occasion.

Subsequently Murphy stopped with his company at Gibson's for breakfast, and while there the subject was resumed. A quarrel ensued, and as Murphy mounted his horse to start off, Gibson followed him to the door and said something offensive, whereupon Murphy shot him dead. Three of Gibson's sons were present in Murphy's company, and were men of undoubted courage; but knowing his violent temper and desperate resolution, did not interfere. Nothing was done to Murphy afterwards.

In the early part of the year Capt. William Clay Snipes, from the Lower Pedee, applied to Gov. Rutledge for permission to raise an independent company to operate westward of the Santee. The Governor wrote to Gen. Marion, 28th January, from Cheraw, on the subject, giving his sanction to the undertaking, and Gen. Sumpter subsequently issued instructions to the same effect.

In raising his company, Captain Snipes induced some of the men under Col. Kolb's command to join him. This led to a correspondence and protest on the part of the colonel against such a proceeding.

"Sir,—I am informed you are taking all the young men that I have ordered to join Gen. Marion with you to the southward. I must now beg leave to inform you of Gen. Marion's orders against such proceedings, which I have just received, forbidding any person leaving his brigade without his leave. "I am, sir,
"Your most obedient, humble Servant,
"A. KOLB.
"To Capt. Snipes."

To this the following tart reply was made:—

April 16th, 1781.

"Sir,—I received yours, and this will inform you that I have instructions form Gen. Sumpter, who commands Gen. Marion, to raise men where I can; and as to Gen. Marion's orders, in this case it avails nothing.
"I am, sir,
"Your most humble Servant,
"WILLIAM CLAY SNIPES."*

Two days after this Col. Kolb wrote to Gen. Marion on the subject, complaining of Captain Snipes' course.

"April 18th, 1781.

"Dear Sir,—Through much difficulty I have sent you Captain John Wilds with a few men, though not the number you expect.

"I expressed a few days ago the opinion that I should not be able to send you a single man, for as soon as the men were ordered to join you, Snipes and some officers whom he had appointed out of this regiment, endeavored to prevent their joining you, by telling them some fine stories, and speaking rather disrespectfully of you, as I have been informed, to prevent their joining you.

"As soon as I received your last orders I immediately

*Gibbes's "Documentary History," 1781-82, pp. 52, 53.

informed Lieut. Lyons, whom I had ordered to join you with the young men that were to have been continued with you, of your orders, informing him that I thought the young men that were ready in turning out with him to join Gen. Sumpter would receive the same advantage by joining you, but this did not avail anything.

"When I found this to be the case, I wrote him again, also wrote Captain Snipes, a copy of which I have enclosed you; also Snipes' answer. I saw Lyons yesterday myself. I asked him about the men that he had raised; he said he had sent them to General Sumpter, and that he would send every other man of the regiment that he could recruit, to him, notwithstanding they were ordered other ways. He damned himself if he would serve under any officer but whom he pleased; that he disregarded any orders that might be issued to the contrary. As soon as I received your orders, I ordered my men to have half of their men in readiness to join you, by a certain time. Just as they were ready to march, the said Lyons immediately impressed several of their horses, and sent them off, which prevents many of them coming to you, and the scarcity of horses at this time and place, prevents their being replaced.

"I should be glad to know what method you would have me to take with such persons. I shall endeavor to send some few men on to you as soon as horses can be had, as we are obliged to stop ploughs to get horses at this time to do patrol duty. We have no news, only of a party of Tories, who have been in Captain Murphy's company, commanded by a Captain John Brockington.

"I am, dear Sir,
"Your most humble Servant,
"ABEL KOLB."*

General Marion wrote to General Sumpter immediately, and in reply, General Sumpter said:—"You gave your opinion in that [a previous letter], it is true, with respect to raising troops upon the State establishment, which opinion it appears you have resumed, not from the ill policy of the

---

*Gibbes's "Documentary History," 1781-82, pp. 54, 55

measure, but because Major Snipes might have disobliged you. Whether he gave a cause of umbrage I know not; he was acting by no particular direction of me. If he has transgressed, he is amenable, and may, as an officer, be punished with great propriety, notwithstanding there is neither executive nor legislative body in the State; yet I think their powers exist, and whoever denies it is dilating the almost mortal wound our laws have received, and directly admits what Major Snipes may have done to be just, or that what he prevented another from doing, was unjust. I revere the citizen who is tenacious of the laws of his country. I lament their being so much abused. If I have done it, I think myself accountable, and shall no doubt be called upon by the gentleman to whom you say you shall represent the matter; and if he is unacquainted with my motives and the step I have taken, should be happy to have his opinion upon that head. To his judgment and authority, I pay the greatest respect; but I have not a doubt but that he and all impartial men, will applaud an undertaking which promised so much good to the United States, and this in particular; especially as it was the last and only measure that could be adopted for its security, or possession of even the least part of it. As to the powers by which I act, they ought not to be called in question by any man, until gentlemen whom it might concern had used proper means to obtain information."* Here the discussion of the matter appears to have dropped. Even before these lines of General Sumpter were penned, Col. Kolb was no longer among the living. One of those bloody acts of the Tories, so characteristic of this period, led to a series of retaliations on the part of the Whigs, which ended in a mournful catastrophe for the inhabitants of the Pedee.

A party of Whigs, shortly before this, went out in search of a noted band of Tories who were known to occupy a stronghold in the swamp of the Three Creeks, from which frequent incursions had been made into the river settlements. At that time, the swamp was an almost impenetrable morass, rendering it a secure retreat for such outlaws.

*Gibbes's "Documentary History," 1781-82, pp. 64, 65.

Upon approaching its border, the Whigs remained quiet for some time, hoping to discover some sign of the enemy; but in vain. To penetrate it in a body, not knowing the exact location of the Tory camp, would have been a most hazardous undertaking. They were at a loss what to do, and as painfully impressed with the necessity of striking an effective blow. At length, after a tedious delay, one of their number, Harry Sparks, noted for his activity and courage, volunteered to go in alone and bring back a speedy report to his companions. He succeeded in reaching the camp;* and after a careful inspection, was in the act of retreating, when he was discovered and captured. His protracted absence excited alarm, and at length, becoming desperate at the thought of Sparks' fate, the whole party dashed into the swamp together, determined to rescue him, if alive, or perish in the attempt.

Following his trail, they succeeded without difficulty in reaching the spot, and there found the camp deserted, and, to their horror, the lifeless body of their comrade hanging from a tree. A cry went up for vengeance, and, not long after retribution came. Captain Daniel Sparks, a brother of Harry, succeeded in capturing subsequently one of the ringleaders of the Tory gang. Upon being charged with the act, which he promptly acknowledged, Captain Sparks told him he should be hung. "Very well," said the undaunted fellow, "as soon as you please."

Sparks ordered his men to proceed with the execution of the prisoner, who assisted with apparent cheerfulness in adjusting the rope about his neck, sprang on the back of the horse brought to elevate him from the ground, asked if the rope was well secured to the limb, and upon being told it was, kicked the horse, making him move suddenly from under him, and swung off into eternity with an oath upon his lips. After hanging Sparks, the Tories fled, fearing the proximity of a large and hostile party, well knowing that instant pursuit would be made. They were followed without delay by Col. Kolb, in command of a chosen band,

---

*The locality of this once celebrated hiding place is now pointed out near the "Mineral Spring" in Marlborough District, seven miles below Bennettsville, a favourite resort of some of the planters of the neighbourhood.

among whom were James Gillespie and Josiah Cantey, and were overtaken on Drowning Creek, in the neighbourhood of a famous Tory rendezvous. On their way, while passing a house a short distance from the road, Cantey rode up to inspect the premises. As he approached, a large mulatto, a noted outlaw, left the house, and mounting his pony, started off at full speed. Soon overtaking him, Cantey rather jokingly said he would shoot him if he did not stop. Without slackening his pace, the fellow discharged his gun at Cantey, who was partially in the rear, striking him in the breast. Cantey fell from his horse, and as others of the party came up, exclaimed, "I am mortally wounded." It proved, however, to be nothing serious. The mulatto was at once overtaken and shot. Another like him was soon after despatched. The expedition ended in a general rout of the Tories, but nothing more.

Soon after his return from Drowning Creek, Colonel Kolb went down the river on the east side, to the neighbourhood of Cat Fish, with a more formidable party. Major Lemuel Benton, Capt. Joseph Dabbs, and John Coxe were among the number who accompanied him. Some daring outrages had been committed in this quarter, and it was necessary to proceed with a strong and well-organized body.

Nothing of importance occurred until they reached Hulin's Mill.* Here they surprised two notorious Tories, John Deer and Osburn Lean. The latter was shot in attempting to make his escape into Cat Fish Swamp, and got off with a broken arm. Deer was overtaken as he reached the swamp, and killed. It was on this occasion, or shortly before, that Caleb Williams, a desperate marauder, noted especially for house burning, was taken by Kolb's party and hung. After proceeding further, capturing other guilty parties, and punishing or discharging them on promise of good behaviour, Colonel Kolb returned home, and dismissed his party, feeling secure for a time at least in the thought that the Tories

---

*This was the site of the mill owned by the late Joseph Bass, ten or twelve miles above Marion, C. H. Hulin was a neutral character. Many persons, actuated by politic motives, found it to their interest to take such a position. They were generally Loyalists at heart.

had been overawed, and would not soon renew their depredations. In this, however, he was most sadly deceived. It was natural that such acts of retaliation on the part of the Whigs should excite a desperate spirit of revenge in the Tories. In this instance their fury was directed chiefly against Colonel Kolb, who had rendered himself most obnoxious by his repeated successes in capturing and punishing some of their most active and notable men. And they were particularly excited against him, now that his path in the late expedition had been marked by the blood of several of their favourite companions. Nothing, as subsequently appeared, was to satisfy them short of his life. No sooner had he departed from the neighbourhood of Cat Fish, than a plan was set on foot to surprise him in the bosom of his family, and put him to death. Knowing that his men would be disbanded for a short time after his return, they determined to follow on without delay, and make sure of their prey.

Accordingly, a company of about fifty Tories collected at the place now known as Tart's Mill, six miles above Marion Court House.

Their leader was Captain Joseph Jones,* a native of that neighbourhood. No time was to be lost. The more rapid their movements, the more certain would be the surprise. A few hours' hard riding would take them to the object of their revenge, about thirty-four miles distant. It was arranged that they should reach Colonel Kolb's at a late hour of the night.

Riding up rapidly under cover of darkness, the surprise was complete. The high qualities of the gallant Kolb, suddenly roused from sleep, with his loved ones around him, and a brutal foe thirsting for blood at his door, were now to be put upon their last and severest trial. His family consisted of Mrs. Kolb, an only daughter,† then a child,

---

*James, in his "Life of Marion," speaks of Gibson and his party as having gone on this occasion against Colonel Kolb. Gibson may have been a prominent character in connexion with the affair, but Jones was unquestionably the acting captain of the Tory party.

†The late Mrs. Anne J. Pouncey, wife of Major James Pouncey, of Marlborough, then but eight years old.

and two sisters.* Two young men, Evans', were also with the family. They had probably accompanied the colonel on his late expedition, and were members of his staff. The house was well secured, and the inmates doubly armed. Well knowing the bloody purpose and desperate character of the foe, Colonel Kolb's first impulse was to sell his life as dearly as possible. A determined resistance was accordingly made, though in the face of overpowering numbers, and as some accounts represent, but incorrectly perhaps, several of the Tory party were killed. Not knowing the number within, and excited to desperation by the resistance offered, if not the havoc made in their ranks, the Tories threatened to burn the dwelling with its inmates, if Colonel Kolb did not at once surrender. It is said by one authority, the house was actually fired. Reduced to the last extremity, and moved by the entreaties of the ladies, whose consternation must have been great, the colonel agreed to deliver himself up as a prisoner of war. The proposition was accepted; and he went forth, accompanied by his wife and sisters, and when almost in the act of presenting his sword, was treacherously shot on the spot. This deed was perpetrated, without the captain's orders, by Mike Goings, a private in the Tory ranks. On some former occasion, Colonel Kolb had excited this man's special hostility, and hence his perfidious revenge. Thomas Evans, upon this murderous breach of faith, attempted to escape, but was shot, and died soon after from the effect of the wound.† The dwelling was then plundered,‡ and after setting it on fire, the Tories made a hasty retreat.

Between the dwelling of Colonel Kolb and the ferry, a few hundred yards below, stood a block house which had been erected by the Whigs for the safe keeping of their

---

*These sisters were Ann James, who married Joshua Edwards, and Sarah, who married Evander M'Iver, as heretofore stated.

†Thomas Evans succeeded in reaching a house on Spot Mill Creek (on the west side of the river), near a point where it is now crossed by the Cheraw and Darlington R. R., and died a few days after. Some authorities state that another person named Evans, a brother probably, was shot on the spot and killed.

‡John Jones, a brother of the Tory captain, was seen on the return of the party, as they passed old John Bethea's, riding Colonel Kolb's horse and saddle, with a feather bed tied before him.

prisoners. It was called the "Bull Pen." On this occasion a number were confined within its walls, among them two British officers, and several soldiers. Simultaneously with the assault on Colonel Kolb, the small guard which kept watch at the "Bull Pen" were surprised, and the prisoners turned loose. Two of the soldiers, on their release, went down the river to the residence of old Mrs. Wilds, opposite Long Bluff, in search of the treasure, which by some means they had learned she kept on her person. Finding her unprotected, they made a rude search and took her gold away. At this stage in the history of this calamitous day, the thrilling narrative of an eye-witness continues the story. Lewis Malone Ayer,* the second son of Thomas Ayer, of Hunt's Bluff, then a lad of twelve or thirteen years of age, was on a visit with his mother to the family of John Downes, a brother-in-law, who lived about three miles above Colonel Kolb's on the river. Mr. Downes having died in the course of the night, young Ayer was despatched at an early hour in the morning to inform the colonel of the sad event.

He had proceeded about half way, when he was startled by the firing of guns in the direction of Col. Kolb's residence. Upon going a short distance further, and alarmed at the unusual sounds he had heard, he saw an old man, William Forniss, riding out from his house to the road. They were well acquainted; and upon coming up, he accosted the youth in an excited, hurried manner, saying, "Lewis, what firing of guns was that a while ago?" Ayer replied, "I do not know;" and just then, upon looking in that direction, they saw Colonel Kolb's residence in flames. Young Ayer then related the errand on which he was going, and the old man replied, "Come along, let us go and see what is to pay there. I will not lead you into danger."

On approaching the path which led out from Colonel Kolb's to the main Welch Neck road down the river, they saw, from a number of fresh tracks, that a company of horsemen had passed rapidly on but a short time before. "Whoever they are," said Forniss, "they are gone, and we may

---

*The venerable Lewis Malone Ayer, of Barnwell, to whom reference has already been made.

LEWIS MALONE AYER,

A courier of Francis Marion in the Revolution, head of a large family which has furnished several sons and daughters of distinction in the State.

now approach without fear." Upon riding up, a mournful spectacle was presented to their view. The dwelling was enveloped in flames, and about to tumble in; and a short distance off were Mrs. Kolb and her two sisters-in-law weeping over their dead.

They told the sad story of the surprise and resistance, of the final capitulation and the closing scene; and how, not satisfied with blood, the Tories had rifled the house of every valuable, set it on fire, and fled. The bleeding corpse the agonized females had been forced to remove beyond the reach of the burning timbers. The lapse of nearly eighty years had not dimmed the eye of memory as the once youthful Ayer looked back from old age upon the shocking scene. His day's adventures had now just begun. Forniss, well aware of the danger to which all those who might come in the way of the retreating Tory party would be exposed, informed young Ayer that a brother-in-law of his (Ayer's), named M'Gee, was that day to come up to Col. Kolb's on business, that he must hasten on, get around and ahead of the Tories, so as to intercept M'Gee and apprize him of the danger, or he would certainly be killed.

The youthful rider was mounted on a beautiful animal, a piebald mare, with flaxen mane and tail, and noted for her fleetness. He was confident she could bear him away unharmed from any pursuit that might be made, having outstripped the Tories on several previous occasions when they had chased him to effect her capture. Excited by the scene just witnessed, and alarmed at the prospect of the imminent peril to which M'Gee would be exposed, he started at once on the hazardous mission, secure, however, in the watchful eye above that guided him, and the fleetness of his mare, which had often eluded the pursuer before. After proceeding a short distance, he met an old man, Willis by name, small of stature, and a shoemaker by trade. Willis lived out in the marshes, and being old and feeble, was allowed to occupy ostensibly the position of a neutral. His heart, however, was with the Whigs, and, as opportunity offered, he rendered faithful service to the cause of liberty. On this occasion he rode a shaggy pony, corresponding in age with himself, and carried on his shoulder an old-fashioned, long-barrelled fowling-piece, which he affectionately called "Old Sweet-lips." Upon meeting young Ayer, he asked what all that shooting was he had heard above. In a few words the story was related to him, and that of the errand upon which the youth had started. "Very well," said he, "hurry on; you will see two of the red-coats lying in the road ahead of you." His words proved true, for a little further on the youth found two British soldiers dead in the road, who had bled profusely. They had paid the penalty of an untimely plundering sally with their lives.

How the old man, feeble as he was, managed to kill them both, he did not relate. Observing that their shoe-buckles had been taken out, young Ayer concluded that they were also stripped of every valuable about them. Hearing a few days after that old Mrs. Wilds had been robbed by two of the soldiers who escaped from the "Bull-pen," the old man went down to see her, and found that they had taken from her person one hundred and one guineas, which she had kept for a long time concealed, supposing that no one out of her own immediate family knew anything of it. Willis then produced the package of coin, which she recognized as her own. On opening and counting it out, not a piece was found missing. She offered a portion to the honest recoverer, which he magnanimously refused to receive, saying it was hers, and he was sufficiently rewarded in being able to restore it to her. From the spot where the soldiers had fallen, young Ayer pursued his way, the road running along a ridge flanked on either side by swamp or boggy marsh land. He hastened on, for there was no time to be lost. A few miles below, at a point where an abrupt turn was made by the road to avoid the marsh, it reached the house of a man named M'Daniel. Riding at a rapid pace, for he expected not to overtake the Tories so soon, he was almost upon them before he could rein his mare in. Some of the party were on the piazza, but most of them within the house. He was immediately discovered and pursued with a shout, the Tories halloing at the top of their voices to the flying youth to stop. Several shots were fired at him, but without effect, having been aimed high, as he supposed, not to kill his mare.

After wheeling round, young Ayer struck out of the main road into a narrow cow-path, which crossed a large and very boggy marsh.

It was so narrow and obscure that his pursuers did not observe it, though he knew, being familiar with the locality, that it was the only track by which a safe crossing could be effected. Seeing him dash through, they attempted to do the same, and by going directly across, hoped to get ahead of him, as the path led around by an angle. But, in this they were sadly disappointed. For as he reached the opposite ridge, and looked back, lying close on the off-side of his mare, the result was what he anticipated. The whole party were in full view, riders and horses floundering in the mud, in hopeless confusion. The chase was at an end, the despicable pursuers deeply chagrined to have been thus out-witted by a boy, and glad to get back to the quarters they had left. The flying youth pursued his way through the woods for several miles, until he reached the road leading from Pledger's Mill* to the Welch Neck road, with which it formed a junction near a house owned by a Mr. Cogdell, but then occupied by a man named Cotton. The Tories, as young Ayer afterwards learned, supposed his object was to pass them in order to give information of their coming to a party of Col. Murphy's men, then at Brown's Mill, on Muddy Creek, and whom the Tories intended to surprise. They hastened on therefore at greater speed, after the escape of Ayer.

The latter had taken a somewhat circuitous route, to elude them the more surely, and in that way the Tories got ahead of him.

After leaving M'Daniel's, they wantonly killed a mulatto man, the slave of Capt. Daniel Sparks, whom they found on the way; and Cotton, taken by surprise, was despatched at his house. A few moments after they left Cotton's, young Ayer came into the Welch Neck road again, but knowing the party had passed the point where M'Gee would enter it, he turned off into the road by which the latter was to come, and after going a short distance, met him on his way.

---

*Since known as the Old Saw Mills, in Marlborough District.

The greater speed of the Tories after the chase of young Ayer, was the means of M'Gee being saved.

The most of Col. Murphy's men had left the post at Brown's Mill some days before.

A few, however, remained; and of these, who were surprised, Capt. Joseph Dabbs,* a useful citizen and well-tried Whig, was killed. Another, Ned Threwitts, escaped with a bullet in his shoulder.

After returning from this bloody expedition, the Tories dispersed, taking refuge, doubtless, for a time in their hiding places, knowing full well the vengeance with which they would be visited by the Whigs. Thus ended for the region of the Upper Pedee, the 28th of April, 1781, one of the saddest days in its history. The leader, to whom all eyes had proudly looked, was no more. Cut off in the prime of his manhood and in the midst of a career of usefulness for his country, before his noble qualities had yet been fully developed, he would doubtless have reached much higher distinction as a partisan leader, had his life been spared.†

He was a man of retiring disposition, but firm and unyielding where principle was involved, decided in his views, and of the highest order of courage. His education was limited; but a sound and discriminating mind made amends for the want of early cultivation. He had amassed a comfortable fortune, and contributed liberally in means as well as personal effort, to the cause of independence. In person he was of medium size, and comely, though not striking in appearance. His death, at such a juncture, was well calculated to fill the minds of the Whigs of Pedee for a time with despondency. A worthy successor, however, was at hand, to revive the public spirit, and nerve those, who had already suffered much, for other conflicts. His command devolved on Major Lemuel Benton, who as Lieutenant-Colonel, nobly sustained it to the close of the war. In a letter to Marion, of the 6th May following, General Green alluded to the death

---

*Captain Dabbs lived on Crooked Creek, on lands near the site of the mill owned in later times by Judge Evans.

†The widow of Colonel Kolb subsequently married Jesse Wilds, a son of the old Mrs. Wilds of whom mention has been made.

of Col. Kolb, with unaffected sorrow. Ramsay, the first historian of the Revolution in Carolina, recorded it briefly. On the hearts of his sorrowing countrymen, who knew him best, his real worth was impressed in characters which time could never efface. Tradition has assigned him the first place, perhaps, in the confidence and affection of the people, among the military men of that day.

Captain Jones,* the leader of the Tory party which surprised Col. Kolb, was a man of some note. He possessed a good property, and was ingenious to a remarkable degree. He is said to have made the first surveyor's compass ever used in Marion District. Notwithstanding his course during the Revolution, he continued to live on Cat Fish until about 1802, and then removed to Colleton District, where he died not very many years since. Old Willis, the shoemaker, an Irishman by birth, lived to a very advanced age, and died, where he had lived, in the marshes.

Prior to these events on the Pedee the shock of arms had been felt again in North Carolina. Shortly before the battle of Guilford Court House, after the two armies had aproached each other, and had some skirmishing, and one or two engagements, Lord Cornwallis and General Green entered into a correspondence for the exchange of prisoners belonging to the Southern armies. Captain Broderick, who was empowered to treat by the former, on account of some difficulties which arose, could not bring the business to a conclusion; and being afterwards revived, it was finished by Captain Cornwallis on the part of the British, and Colonel Carrington as agent for the Americans, when the customary tariff was signed and executed. It was done at the house

---

*Some years after the Revolution, Captain Jones was on his trial at Georgetown for passing counterfeit money. Samuel Wilds, afterwards so distinguished, but then quite a young man, and not yet at the Bar, was present, and proposed to raise a company, take Jones out and hang him, saying he deserved to die for his connexion with the murder of Colonel Kolb. This incident was related to the author by the late John D. Witherspoon, of Society Hill. It seems hardly in keeping, however, with that kindness of heart and noble generosity for which Judge Wilds was so remarkable. He was young, however, and the feeling yet intense against the Tories. Mr. W. also stated that he once spent the night with Kirby, the murderer of Joseph Dabbs.

of Claudius Pegues, on Pedee, May 3rd, 1781.* The declining fortunes of Cornwallis, after the battle of Guilford, as related by Tarleton, is a sad story. It touches the heart even now to look back upon the scene, and contemplate the agonizing trials as he went down, of one who was actuated by generous impulses and sentiments of patriotic devotion to his king and country. After the close of the winter campaign in North Carolina, Cornwallis withdrew his forces into South Carolina, followed by Green. Soon after he advanced to Cross Creek, and then to Wilmington. "The aspect of affairs at this juncture," said Tarleton, "presented various and opposite designs to the noble earl at Wilmington. Upon the different investigations of the subject it was too successfully described, that the country between Cape Fear River and Camden was barren, and intersected with creeks and rivers; that the road to Georgetown was replete with the same difficulties, that an embarkation for Charles-town was disgraceful, and would occasion delay whilst the transports were coming round; and that Virginia was more accessible, where Gen. Phillips commanded a respectable force."† The noble earl was evidently looking with wistful eye toward South Carolina. There he had fondly hoped to maintain undisputed sway, and it was hard to give up the cherished design.

"Hearing of Green's approach, Lord Rawdon, who commanded the frontiers of South Carolina, was greatly alarmed, fearing a total defection of the inhabitants, an interruption of all communication with Charles-town, and the attack of a continental army, superior to his own in numbers." "Though the expresses from Cross Creek did not reach their destination, he gained by some other means such early intelligence of the approach of Green, that he made judicious arrangements to counteract the designs of the enemy, and to advertize Earl Cornwallis of his embarrassed situation at Camden." His leader, however, could render Rawdon no assistance. The unhappy earl was himself in a position of the most trying embarrassment. He knew not where to

*Moultrie's "Memoirs," vol. i. p. 178.
†Tarleton's "Memoirs," p. 283.

look for reviving prospects. On 23rd of April he wrote from Wilmington to Lord George Germaine, as follows:—"Although the expresses I sent from Cross Creek to inform Lord Rawdon of the necessity I was under of coming to this place, and to warn him of the possibility of such an attempt of the enemy, had all miscarried, yet his lordship was lucky enough to be apprized of Gen. Green's approach, at least six days before he could possibly reach Camden; and I am therefore still induced to hope, from my opinion of his lordship's abilities, and the precautions taken by him and Lieutenant-Colonel Balfour, that we shall not be so unfortunate as to lose any considerable corps. The distance from hence to Camden, the want of forage and subsistence on the greatest part of the road, and the difficulty of passing the Pedee, when opposed by an enemy, render it utterly impossible for me to give immediate assistance, and I apprehend a possibility of the utmost hazard to this little corps, without the chance of a benefit in the attempt; for, if we are so unlucky as to suffer a severe blow in South Carolina, the spirit of revolt in that Province would become very general, and the numerous rebels in this Province be encouraged to be more than ever active and violent. This might enable General Green to hem me in among the great rivers, and, by cutting off our subsistence, render our arms useless; and to remain here for transports to carry us off would be a work of time, would lose our cavalry, and would be otherwise as ruinous and disgraceful to Britain, as most events could be. I have, therefore, under so many embarrassing circumstances (but looking upon Charles-town as safe from any immediate attack from the rebels), resolved to take advantage of General Green's having left the back parts of Virginia open, and march immediately into that Province, to attempt a junction with Gen. Phillips."* Broken in spirit, threatened on all sides, knowing from recent experience the strength of Green, and fearing him as an antagonist, Cornwallis, in his desperate extremity, decided upon a step which soon led to his ruin. He was evidently afraid to risk a passage through the country bordering on the

*Tarleton's "Memoirs," pp. 325, 326.

Pedee. For the same expresses which had brought him the disagreeable news alluded to in the opening of the foregoing extract, also informed him "that the upper parts of South Carolina were in the most emminent danger from an alarming spirit of revolt among many of the people." His star was now on the wane, and soon to go down. His favorite legion leader thus commented on the earl's resolution to go to Virginia. "Happy would it have been, as far as general probability can be determined, had Earl Cornwallis directed his chief attention to the critical state of South Carolina, and commenced his return by any route to secure it."

On the 24th of April, Cornwallis wrote thus to Gen. Phillips:—"My situation here is very distressing. Green took the advantage of my being obliged to come to this place, and has marched to South Carolina. My expresses to Lord Rawdon, on my leaving Cross Creek, warning him of the impossibility of such a movement, have all failed; mountaineers and militia have poured into the back parts of this Province, and I much fear that Lord Rawdon's posts will be so distant from each other, and his troops so scattered, as to put him into the greatest danger of being beat in detail, and that the worst of consequences may happen to most of the troops out of Charles-town.

"By a direct move towards Camden, I cannot get time enough to relieve Lord Rawdon; and, should he have fallen, my army would be exposed to the utmost danger from the great rivers I should have to pass, the exhausted state of the country, the numerous militia, the almost universal spirit of revolt which prevails in South Carolina, and the strength of Green's army, whose continentals alone are at least as numerous as I am; and I could be of no use on my arrival at Charles-town, there being nothing to apprehend at present for that post; I shall, therefore, immediately march up the country by Duplin Court House, pointing towards Hillsborough, in hope to withdraw Green; if that should not succeed, I should be much tempted to form a junction with you."

The stratagem as to Green failed most signally, and Virginia became the theatre of Cornwallis's final overthrow.

The partisan warfare on the Pedee continued now to rage

with unabated fury. Colonel Benton, wise in council and efficient in action, possessed of those peculiar qualities calculated to inspire confidence in all who were associated with him, or under his command, was equal to the trying emergencies of his position. Colonel Murphy, on the eastern side of the river below, was battling valiantly; while Major Thomas, and the Captains Sparks, Pledger, Council, M'Intosh, Ellerbe, Pegues, Jackson, and others, on both sides of the river, were doing gallant service for their country. A strong guard had been placed at Kolb's Ferry, an important point on the river, under command of Captain Edward Jones,* and continued there until the close of the war.

The "Bull Pen," which stood very near the Ferry, answered the purposes of a substantial prison house. It was often in use. A stockade was also erected at the gaol† on Long Bluff, and a guard kept there as occasion demanded.

In a letter to Marion, of May 1st, Gen. Green cautioned him to keep a good look-out for Tarleton, saying:— "I think it probable he is in the George-town route; but it is possible he may be on the upper route, as I hear of a guard being lately surprised near the Cheraws."‡ Gen. Sumpter was then at the Congarees, M'Arthur on his way to Camden, and the gallant Lafayette, with a large detachment from the Northern Army and Pennsylvania line, on the march to join the Southern forces.

Mr. Pugh's Journal contains a few brief entries at this period:—

"Tuesday, 17th of April. Had news of the Tories in Cashway.

---

*The following was one of many accounts rendered in after the war:—

"State of South Carolina.

"March 3rd, 1781. Received of Wm. Dewitt, 480 lbs. of pork for use of guard at Kolb's Ferry.
"EDWARD JONES,
"Captain of Guard."

†"State of South Carolina, Cheraw District.
"This may certify that William Dewitt, Esq., furnished a guard of my regt., at the Cheraw Gaol, with 2 hogs, 126 lbs.
"LEM. BENTON,
"Lieut.-Colonel Commandant of Militia.
"20th Decr., 1782."

‡Gibbes's "Documentary History," 1781-82, p. 66.

"Saturday, 28th. Went to the Mill. Col. Kolb is killed, and 6 or 7 men by the Tories.

"Friday, May 4th. All the men come home from Gen. Marion's camp.

"Tuesday, 15th. We hear Camden is burnt. British gone."

The report of six or seven men killed, besides Col. Kolb, if it was true, must have included others who were murdered by the Tory party on their return down the river.

In August of this year, Colonel Murphy was stationed, with a small force, near the mouth of Black Creek. He sent word to old Moses Bass, who kept a noted public-house at the mill on Naked Creek, across the river and about four miles distant, that he would be there with his men on a certain day, and to have a good dinner, with plenty of cider, in readiness. By some means, the Tories in the neighbourhood were informed of the expected visit, and made preparations for attacking Murphy at Bass's. The house stood on a small island, made by a sudden bend of the creek, forming almost a circle, and a canal cut across the neck of land leading out to the main road near by.

On the appointed day, Murphy and his party went over, suspecting no danger.

While at dinner, they were suddenly surprised by the enemy's approach. Two men came rapidly up on horseback, and were in the act of crossing the creek by a causeway when first discovered. They were followed by the main body, under Major Barfield.

Some of the Whigs, who happened to be on the piazza, were fired upon, and for a moment all was confusion. By this time, the Tories had approached within fighting distance, and the conflict began.

The Whigs having the benefit of a cover, soon gained a decided advantage, killing several of the enemy, with the loss, however, of two of their own number, Harper and Mixon. Giving way under the effective fire from the house, the Tories were in the act of retreating, when one of Murphy's men, named Daniel, who had a stentorian voice, cried out, "Good Heavens! what shall we do? the powder is out." Upon hearing this, the Tories returned to the fight; and the

Whigs, no longer able to keep up an equal fire, were forced to escape in every direction across the creek, to the cover of the thick timber beyond. It ran but a short distance in the rear of the dwelling. Reaching it by a few bounds, they tumbled down the steep bank, and got off without further loss.

One of their number, a man named Thompson, from the Poke Swamp settlement, on the west side of the river, as he jumped the fence near the creek, found a large and powerful mulatto, Shoemake by name, pressing closely upon him, with his rifle aimed and in the act of firing. Happily for Thompson, the rifle missed fire, and before it could be readjusted, he made his escape. Twenty years after, Thompson heard of Shoemake's going to Camden, caught him on his return, and inflicted severe punishment. Peter Bozeman, a valiant soldier of liberty, who afterwards settled and died in Darlington District, was one of Murphy's party.

Malachi Murphy was another, and received a wound in the shoulder as he reached the creek, which disabled him for the time. He fell down the bank, and crawling under a large log, remained there undiscovered, though the Tories several times passed near him. Daniel, whose unfortunate exclamation led to the disaster, was a man of powerful frame, and carried Murphy on his shoulders to Black Creek, making some amends thereby for his untimely blunder.

Thus ended their day's frolic for the Whigs, teaching them the lesson which so many have learned too late, that vigilance is the price of liberty.

The civil affairs of the country were now sadly deranged.

No Circuit Court had been holden on the Pedee since November, 1778, nor had any district officers been appointed. The estates of deceased persons were neglected, and for orphans no legal provision was made. On the 13th of August, Governor Rutledge wrote to General Marion, and in the course of his letter alluded to this subject. He said: "I think of appointing immediately an ordinary in each district, by whom wills may be proved, and letters testamentary and administration granted; and other business with the ordinary jurisdiction transacted. The Constitution directs that this shall be done; and I think it is a measure absolutely necessary for a number of reasons. I wish you would recommend proper persons, who are able to undertake the office of ordinary for George-town, Cheraws, and Charles-town Districts."

By proclamation of 13th September, appointments were made, Claudius Pegues being commissioned ordinary for Cheraws District. The *Royal Gazette,* as it was called, of Charles-town, made merry over this business. On the 3rd November, it said: "The following proclamation, appointing ordinaries in the several districts of the Province, has been lately received from the country." Here followed the proclamation, with these comments: "Most of the persons appointed ordinaries are commanders of parties of rebel mounted militia. They, and their followers, have, by the murders they have committed, afforded sufficient business for a Court of Ordinary. Mr. Rutledge seems to think it but fair they should enjoy the fruits of their own labor." The time was not far distant when words of bitter sarcasm were to be heard in reply!

Colonel Murphy, in his active and vigorous movements, was giving much trouble to Major Gainey and the Tories under his command. The latter addressed General Marion on the subject, as follows:—

"Pedee, September 8th, 1781.

"Sir,—Your answer of the 5th of September came to hand this day, and in perusing the same, I understand that your honor wrote to the North Carolinians concerning our truce, which I never received or heard of before; it has miscarried by some means or other. My full desire, Sir, is to be at peace with all parties, if they will with me. I am very sorry, Sir, to acquaint your honor that I am under the disagreeable necessity of complaining to you of Colonel Murphy. I wrote several orders to him to restore their plunder, which they refused to do, except such as is of no service to themselves; all that is of value they keep, so that I found there a stumbling block. The way, just about the time that Murphy first broke out and ruined me, and broke me up, for which reason, I first revolted my constancy to my country, was—he took some horses from me, one of which he has yet in his possession; then I wrote an order, and sent to him for said horse, which he refused to send, without I would hunt up and get all his horses which he has lost, which was six or seven head, he says; and I don't know his horses; I never saw them; and in like manner, they detain several horses and negroes, and a number of cows.

"I have no reason to complain of any of your men, save that same regiment of Murphy's. The list you wrote to me about, you shall faithfully have given up very shortly to Colonel Irvin's order.

"I am, with respect, Sir,
"Your very humble Servant,
MICAJAH GAINEY."

The truce alluded to in this letter grew out of articles of agreement concluded on the 17th June previous, between Colonel Peter Horry, in behalf of General Marion, and Major Gainey, commanding officer of the Tories, or King's subjects —inhabitants lying between Great Pedee River and North Carolina.* By these articles, Gainey and his officers agreed to lay down their arms and remain neutral, to deliver up all those who refused to comply with the treaty, and all deserters from the Americans, and also to restore all negroes and other plundered property. The terms of the agreement were not strictly complied with by Gainey, and hence the course pursued by Colonel Murphy. The continued non-observance of their solemn stipulations led to a projected expedition in June of the next year, concerted between Governor Matthews, of South Carolina, and Governor Martin, of North Carolina, to subdue Gainey and his party, who were marauding in both States. General Marion was to have the command; and as soon as it became known, it brought Gainey to terms. At Burch's Mill, on Pedee, a treaty was signed (June, 1782), by which the Tories agreed to lay down their arms as enemies of the State, to demean themselves thereafter as peaceable citizens, to deliver up all stolen property, to apprehend all who did not accede to the treaty then made, to take all deserters from the American army and deliver them up, to return to their allegiance, and

---

*Gibbes's "Documentary History," 1781-82, p. 98.

abjure that of his Britannic Majesty. From this treaty, Gibson, who killed Colonel Kolb, and Fanning and his party, were excepted, but they escaped.*

In his letter to Marion, Gainey gives a reason for having taken up arms against his country. If that which he assigned was the leading motive, and was founded in truth, it only proved that, like others, he allowed feelings of resentment against an individual, to extinguish every patriotic impulse. But his heart was not right in the matter, and an excuse was readily framed for his traitorous course. As a reward, and because of his influence, doubtless, he was promoted by the British to the position of major, which he subsequently filled. He lived six miles below the site of the present village of Marion, between Cat Fish and the river. His father, Stephen Gainey, was an Englishman, and emigrated at an early period to this part of Carolina. In person, Major Gainey was large and powerful, and in mind above the ordinary standard. He had a respectable property, and might have made, if so disposed, a most efficient champion of liberty. He was, however, a man of violent passions and overbearing disposition, and before the Revolution, had made himself obnoxious to many of his neighbours. After the war, the feeling against him was so strong, that he was compelled to leave, and removed to Richmond County, North Carolina. It is said, that fifty years after the struggle of the Revolution had ended, there were men in Marion who would have killed him on sight.

An incident may be mentioned in connexion with a member of his family, illustrative of the summary method of ending disputes, and of the bloody spirit that marked these days.

Stephen, a brother of Major Gainey, was killed by William Dewitt of the same neighbourhood. They had agreed upon a race with two noted steeds. The winner was to take the horse of his competitor. Gainey won the race, and carried off the stakes. Dewitt claimed and took back his horse with violent hands, on the ground of some unfairness in the race. Gainey succeeded in recovering

---

*James's "Life of Marion," pp. 123, 166.

him, and at the same time took Dewitt, carrying him bound to his house. He went to sleep, leaving his prisoner tied. Dewitt managed to get loose (by the aid, it was said, of his captor's wife), took down Gainey's own gun, and shot him dead on the spot.

In the battle of Eutaw, fought on the 8th of September of this year, some of the militia from Pedee took part. Among them was Captain Claudius Pegues with his company.

Joshua David, a private, was badly wounded in the hand, and permanently disabled. Thomas Quick, also a private, a brave and active Whig, was a near neighbour of his captain, and warmly attached to him. Before the battle commenced, it was agreed between them, that if either should be wounded or killed, the other would take special care of him. During the engagement, Captain Pegues was wounded in the leg, but continued for some time to maintain his ground, seemingly unconscious of the injury he had sustained. But, bleeding profusely, Quick discovered his condition as he was about to fall, and with the aid of Nero, a faithful body servant of the captain, bore him from the field. Quick then requested permission to return, if to take only one shot more at the enemy, and resumed his place in the ranks. Thomas Quick lived many years after the war, and left a son, bearing his name, who was long a worthy citizen of Marlborough District.

On the 17th of September, Governor Rutledge wrote to General Marion, informing him that Benton's regiment had been allotted to his brigade.* This position the regiment continued to hold to the close of the war. Subsequent records show that most of the militia from Pedee were more or less in constant service under Marion. On the 23rd of November, the Governor inclosed to General Marion writs of election for Members of the Senate and House of Representatives, as embraced within the limits of his brigade. Some difficulty was felt in determining upon the best places for holding the elections, in the then unsettled state of the country. It was left by the Governor to Marion and the

---

*Gibbes's "Documentary History," 1781-82, p. 214.

managers appointed, to decide. Tristram Thomas, Philip Pledger, William Dewitt, and William Pegues, were four of the six representatives elected for St. David's, and took their seats in the House, at Jacksonborough, on the 18th of January following. On the 30th of January, John Wilson was appointed Sheriff for Cheraws District. Owing to some accident or oversight, he did not receive his commission for some time afterwards. In a letter to General Marion, Governor Matthews alluded to the subject, saying, "I sent Mr. Wilson, the Sheriff for Cheraws, his commission three months ago, and am surprised to find he did not receive it. It must be lying somewhere at George-town; but if he cannot get it, I will send him another. However, his not having the commission need not prevent him from acting. The appointment by the Legislature is the substantial part; the commission is now a matter of form."* Among the matters to be disposed of at this session of the Legislature, was that relating to the banishment of certain persons, and the confiscation of their estates.

On this proscribed list, was the name of Charles Augustus Steward. While a bill was pending on the subject, the wife of Colonel Steward presented the following petition, viz.:—

"To the Honorable, the Senate of the State of South Carolina:

"The humble petition of Sarah Steward, humbly sheweth: That your petitioner is the wife of Charles Augustus Steward, of the District of Cheraws, whose name, she is informed, is inserted in a list of persons whose estates are to be confiscated, and themselves to be banished from this State, by a bill now before your Honorable House. Your petitioner begs leave to set forth, that her husband, about a year ago, returned to South Carolina from Great Britain, where he went in the year 1775, with leave of the Honorable House of Assembly; that ever since the Revolution, he has entertained the most warm and friendly attachment to the American cause, and on all occasions done every friendly

---

*Gibbes's "Documentary History," 1776-82, p. 191.

office in his power to relieve American prisoners distressed in England, which he has the evidence here to prove. Your petitioner assures your Honors, that after her husband's arrival in Charles-town, the Commandant offered him a military commission, supposing, from his extensive acquaintance in the district where he lived, and having been formerly a colonel of militia, that he might have had considerable influence over the inhabitants; but, that he peremptorily refused to take up arms against the Americans.

"She also declares, that on his refusal to take a commission, he was summoned to mount guard as a private in the garrison of Charles-town; but he refused this, and said he would rather be sent to the Provost; and that, from time to time, he has been, and is now, not only suspected to be an enemy to the British Government, but is shaken off by all his acquaintance; he not only lives retired from society in town, but he has been so much distressed for want of the necessaries of life, that your petitioner, though brought up in ease and affluence, has been for months past obliged to the necessity of making shirts, and even submitting to drudgery, in order to maintain herself, her child, and husband, whose low state of health could not permit him to come out of town.

"Your petitioner now comes before this Honorable House, to beg that he and his family may be restored to the bosom of this country; and she implores the mercy and protection of her countrymen, in behalf of a husband, who has never done a single act of hostility against a country that is dear to him, and of which his wife and child are natives.

"And your petitioner, as in duty bound, &c.

"SARAH STEWARD.

"Jacksonborough, 18th Feby., 1782."

The touching appeal of Mrs. Steward was successful. Her husband, once prominent and highly esteemed, but now broken in spirit and health, was relieved from banishment, and his estate from confiscation. Colonel Steward appears to have been possessed of an amiable character and excellent traits.

His unfortunate error in setting at defiance the resolves of the Provincial Congress, prohibiting the collection of debts, was the turning point in his political career. The fact of his departing soon after for England, and on his return of remaining in Charles-town until action was about to be taken by the Legislature, doubtless tended to confirm the suspicions of the public as to his fidelity to the American cause. He again took up his residence on his plantation near Cheraw Hill, and died in less than three years after.*

The *Royal Gazette* of March 26th, contained the following notice of the action of the Legislature on the Confiscation Bill, &c. :—

"Charles-town, March 20th, 1782.

"The following has been sent to us from the country, as a correct list of those persons whose estates have been confiscated by an Act of the rebel Assembly at Jacksonborough :—
"They are divided into six classes.
"Class I.—Comprehends all British subjects who have property in this country—that is to say, such persons as never have submitted to the American Government.
"Class II.—Such of the former inhabitants of this country, as presented congratulatory addresses to Sir Henry Clinton and Admiral Arbuthnot.
"Class III.—Those who petitioned to be armed in defence of the British Government, after the conquest of this Province.
"Class IV.—Those who congratulated Earl Cornwallis on the victory gained at Camden.
"Class V.—Those who have borne commissions, civil or military, under the British Government, since the conquest of this Province.
"Class VI.—Obnoxious persons."

Under Class V., the names of Daniel Clary, Robert Gray, and William Henry Mills, citizens of Cheraw District, were

---

*The following notice appeared in the *Columbian Herald; or Patriotic Courier of North America,* of January 13th, 1785 :—

"Lately died, at his seat at Fairy Hill, Cheraws, Charles Augustus Steward, Esq."

included. The latter was banished, and his estate confiscated. He was, years after, known to be in Jamaica, engaged in the manufacture of sugar. It is somewhat remarkable, up to how late a period he appears to have retained the confidence of the people. Before his banishment he became very obnoxious.

The *Royal Gazette* sometimes made a show of merriment at the expense of the Whigs.

On other occasions, it indulged in bitter sarcasm, as in the following announcements of 13th March, 1782, under the the head of "intelligence extraordinary from Philadelphia":—

"The following books are in press there, and will speedily be published:—

"A Treatise on Bills of Exchange, with observations on Protests, according to the newest and most approved methods, by Robert Morris, Esq., Financier to the United States.

"A Dissertation on the difference between Mexican and Spanish Milled Dollars, by the same.

"Killing Tories, no Murder. Embellished with a beautiful Frontispiece, representing the death of Mr. Dawkins, and dedicated, by permission, to his Excellency, General Green, by Colonel Wade Hampton.

"The Sacred Obligation of a Military Parole, stated and illustrated, by Brigadier-General Pickens.

"Ways and Means for the year 1782, by a Member of the Assembly at Jacksonborough, with a Supplement by John Rutledge, Esq., on the Advantages of Converting Indigo into Paper Certificates.

"A Topographical Description of the Northern Parts of South Carolina betwixt Pedee and Santee, illustrated with a Map, wherein are accurately delineated all the Thickets and Swamps in that Country from an actual survey, by Brigadier-General Marion.

"Select Manœuvres for Cavalry, to which are added Practical Observations on the most soldier-like manner of swimming rivers on a route, by the same.

"Description of the Strong Brick Castle at the Eutaws, by General Green."

Had these choice volumes been republished a little while

after, it would have been with very marked notes and emendations, and a terrible significance. The delay in getting them out of press was fortunate indeed!

The Government was forced to keep a watchful eye on the retention, for its own use, of the supplies furnished within the limits of the State. The removal of cattle had excited attention, when Colonel Brown, of the North Carolina Militia, was stationed on Pedee for that purpose. On the 19th of May General Pinckney wrote to General Matthews on the subject.

"Pon Pon, May 19th, 1782.

"Dear Sir,

"By a letter this moment received from General Huger, dated the 10th of this month, he desires me to inform your Excellency that a Colonel Perkins, a trader from Virginia, has contracted for five or six hundred head of cattle on Pedee and Cheraw, and which, in a few days, will be driven off for Virginia if not immediately stopped. The consequences of such a speculation (for our Commissioners have it not in their power to go to market with ready money), are truly alarming.

"I am,
"Your Exellency's most obedient Servant,
"CHARLES COTESWORTH PINCKNEY."

The result of the information that was thus given is not known. The trial of the Whigs of Pedee, and the story of their conflicts with the Tories by day and by night would fill a volume, could it be written out in full. The sufferers and actors, however, in these scenes have long since passed away; and amid the uncertainties of tradition but little which is reliable can be collected. Enough remains to continue the narrative through another chapter, and to the commemoration of the terrible strife that chapter will be devoted.

CHAPTER XVI.

Depredations of Tories on Poke Swamp, Jeffrey's, Black, and Lynche's Creeks—James Gregg and Charles Evans among the sufferers—Duke Glen's engagement—Daniel Hicks's encounter—William Pegues's losses—John Wilson's escape—Skirmishes of Benton's forces—Alexander M'Intosh's adventure—His prowess—Close of 1782—Colonel Benton commands on Pedee—His letters to Governor Matthews and General Marion—Marion's Brigade—State of feeling between Whigs and Tories—Whigs attack Tories between Lumber River and Little Pedee—Colonel M'Ree's adventure—William and John Bethea and the Tories—Hawthorne's revenge—Jef. Butler, the Tory captain—Account of him and his punishment—Andrew Hunter's escape from Fanning—Their meeting in Charles-town—Fanning's attack on Robert Gregg—Fanning's character and end—Adventure of General Harrington—Curious sequel of the same—General Harrington's character and death—Singular end of Claudius Pegues—Maurice Murphy—Incidents connected with him—His character and end—Tristram Thomas—Some account of him—Lemuel Benton—His character delineated—His course after the war—Colonel George Hicks—Joshua Ammons—His remarkable career—His meeting with Lafayette—Jacob Brawler—His unequalled gift to his country—Notice of William Shaw—The close of the Revolution—List of some of those from Pedee engaged in active service.

WHEREVER a few defenceless Whigs could be found, or superior numbers seemed to promise the foe an easy victory, there the Tories hovered around. From the lower settlements on Lynche's Creek up to the North Carolina line above, depredations were committed.

Among others, Captain James Gregg had been forced, for a considerable time, to conceal himself in Poke Swamp, where he slept in a hollow log, fed by his family, occasionally visiting his residence under cover of darkness. His house was eventually burned, his property destroyed, and his wife and children turned out of doors.

Along the borders of Jeffrey's and Black Creeks many similar scenes were witnessed. Those neighbourhoods which were remote from the river settlements, and consequently weak and exposed from their isolated position, suffered most. In these instances a few persons here and there, of property and prominence in the struggle for liberty, were made the special objects of this retaliating warfare. The Blakeneys and Evans' on Lynche's Creek, in what is now Chesterfield District, had made themselves particularly obnoxious. Charles Evans* was possessed of a good property, and noted for his fine stock. On one occasion the British and Tories surprised and captured him. His best horses, with other property, were taken. Evans himself was securely tied, put upon an inferior animal, and carried a prisoner to Charles-town, where he remained in confinement until the war was over. Near the North Carolina line, bordering upon the Cheraw District, many bloody conflicts took place with the Tories. Duke Glen, whose name appears before the Revolution as a resident of St. David's Parish, removed to Anson County, and settled near the mouth of Mill Creek, on Pedee. He was a noted captain of the Whig forces in this partisan strife, and especially inimical to the Tories. The latter had been for some time on the look-out for him, and hearing on one occasion of his return, collected a party to surprise and capture him at his own house.

Fortunately, Glen heard of their plan, and prepared for them by gathering a tried company of Whigs. He divided his force into three parts, taking the main body into the dwelling under his immediate command. One portion was stationed in the loft of a stable near the path by which he knew the approach would be made, and the rest in ambush. They were to let the enemy pass, and upon a signal, to be given by Glen, rush up and surround the Tory party. The plan was well laid. Of those in the stable loft, the late Colonel Benjamin Rogers, of Marlborough, was one. The Whigs became so impatient for the attack, as to fire too soon, which enabled the Tories to escape in time to save themselves from serious loss. Only one of their number was wounded; and he managed to get off a little distance and conceal himself through the night. The next morning he was followed by his bloody track, found alive and begged

---

*Charles Evans was the first husband of the late Mrs. Mary Blakeney, of Chesterfield, who continued to reside in that immediate neighbourhood. She lived to a very advanced age, and was remarkable for her physical and mental vigor and activity to the last. When past eighty, she rode over her plantation daily, and superintended in person her own business. Such were the hardy characters formed in the cradle of the Revolution and the times preceding it.

for his life, but William Pratt, of Anson, seized a gun and shot him dead. On the eastern side of the river, near the dividing line between Richmond County, and what is now Marlborough District, lived two young men, named Skipper, of mixed blood, but peaceable and inoffensive. They had taken parol, however, and for no other offence, were seized by the Whigs on both sides of the line, and hung. Such a course was well calculated to excite a feeling of bloody retaliation, and thus the murderous conflict continued. Daniel Hicks, a staunch Whig, married the widow of Colonel John Donaldson, already mentioned, who died about the year 1781. Hicks had excited the special hostility of the Tories, who laid many plans to capture and kill him. In one instance, they collected a party to surprise him at his own house, at night. Having notice of their approach, he directed his wife to say, that no one was at home but herself. They were satisfied Hicks was there, however, and threatened to break the door open if she did not admit them. It was a desperate emergency, but the fearless Whig, brave and collected, was equal to it. Directing his wife to open the door, and stand behind it, as she did so, there was Hicks with his gun ready, but so as not to be perceived in the darkness. As the party advanced, he shot a Tory, named Brigman, who first presented himself, inflicting a desperate wound. Suspecting thereupon, that they were about to be set upon by a party concealed in the house, the wretches immediately fled. Hicks gathered a company of his neighbours forthwith and pursued, but not in time to overtake them. Brigman was found in the morning, and put to death.

William Pegues, was an ardent Whig, and suffered much from the depredations of the Tories. On one occasion as a party of them approached his house, he succeeded in making a hasty retreat to the river, and was pursued, but by means of a canoe, effected his escape. After plundering the dwelling, they set it on fire, and went off, taking forty negroes with them, of whom, only a few were afterwards recovered. Mrs. Pegues, then in delicate health, had to fly with two little children, an infant but a few weeks old, and a young negro girl. She remained some time on the banks of the river, crying for help, until some one from the family of her husband's father came to her relief, taking her helpless party across to a place of safety.

John Wilson, while on a Whig excursion into North Carolina, was taken by the Tories. They started down with him from Haley's Ferry, having given him the benefit of riding an inferior horse.

After proceeding some distance, he pretended to have been hurt in the leg, and putting it across the saddle, rode on for some time, apparently in great agony. His guard having become careless, allowed him to fall somewhat behind, which he soon managed to increase to a respectable distance, when, putting spurs to his horse, he succeded in making his escape.

The troops under Colonel Benton were engaged at different times in skirmishes with the Tories on Black Creek. On one occasion, a detachment of Benton's forces, and those of a Captain Baker, of Georgia, united against the foe. The former happening to be sick, requested Baker to take command. The Whigs were at breakfast when the enemy came upon them near the ferry on Black Creek, on the George-town and Cheraw Road. Thrown for a moment into confusion, they soon rallied, and forced the Tories to retreat, pursuing them some distance. Several of the latter were killed, and some wounded too severely to escape. Among the killed, was a DuBose, the only one of a very large connexion who took sides against his country. A noted Tory, Hughes, was one of the wounded. When the Whigs returned from the pursuit, and were about to despatch him, he pleaded for mercy, and urged that he had often fed the Whigs. The commanding officer replied, that if he could prove this, he would be spared. Peter DuBose confirmed the statement, but added, that he had fed them with the provisions of the Whigs. The old offender was spared, his age probably touching the hearts of his captors. He had been shot on former occasions, and several times left for dead. He was once hung by a Whig, named Baxter, at Daniel DuBose's, to a gate-post. Thus left suspended, his wife came to the rescue, and finding him still alive, cut the rope and saved his life.

Another skirmish took place about this time, higher up on Black Creek, Colonel Benton commanding. The Tories were routed and fled, but being overtaken and surrounded, were forced to make a hand to hand fight, suffering very severely. Colonel Benton had no fire arms except his pistols. One man, pressed by the colonel, turned about, and was in the act of firing his musket, but, before he could do so, Benton discharged his pistol at him, missing him, however, then threw it at him and knocked him from his horse to the ground.

In another skirmish on Black Creek, at a point nearest Society Hill, Captain Alex. M'Intosh,* then a young man, commanded the Whigs. A brother of M'Intosh was wounded, and the latter, excited to desperation, killed every Tory he caught. On this occasion, Hughes was wounded. M'Intosh coming up, fired his pistol at him, but did not kill him, and desisted from any further attempt upon his life. Captain M'Intosh was a man of large size, and extraordinary strength and activity. He is said, in one instance, when hotly pursued by the Tories, to have leaped his horse across Black Creek. Many incidents have been handed down of his personal prowess, some of them in this age almost passing the bounds of credulity. A noted character, known long after as Old Mrs. Croly, lived about this time two miles below Society Hill, afterwards in the flat woods on Black Creek. She often harbored the Tories. John Lucas and a few other Whigs once found a party of Tories at her house, who managed to escape. Lucas took her out, and was about to hang her, when Captain M'Intosh and Major John Mikell came up, and by their intercession, caused her to be released. Thus the year 1782 opened, and advanced. The region of the Pedee was left open to the incursions of the Tories; but, unsupported as they were by any neighbouring British force, their allies, were for the most part unsuccessful, and gradually the light began to dawn upon Carolina, which was soon to grow into a bright day of emancipation from a foreign yoke,

---

*Captain M'Intosh held many offices of trust in after life, but was not a good manager. He lost his property and died about the year 1828. He was the executor of General M'Intosh. George M'Intosh, formerly of Marlborough District, was his only surviving son.

and of a government of their own. Lieut.-Colonel Benton was now the principal leader on the Pedee. He had many difficulties to contend against, some of which were pressing him sorely. In the following letter to Gov. Matthews, while he pays a justly merited tribute to the inhabitants of St. David's, touching allusion is made to certain evils from which they were now suffering.

"St. David's, Great Pedee, August 20th, 1782.

"Sir,—Though I have not the honor of a personal acquaintance with you, I am now under the necessity of humbly addressing you on this manner, in behalf of the Parish and Regiment I have the honor to represent and command; a people that have ever stood among those who are foremost for their inflexible attachment to their country; suffered many capital distresses, nor have ever despaired of success in our greatest extremity. Although we have so long been at such a distance from the enemy's lines, and suffering every murder, plundering, and cruelty that could be perpetrated by a banditti of the most desperate villains and mulattoes, immediately bordering on our settlements, we have, on all occasions, turned out, and kept in General Marion's camp equal numbers with any in his brigade. Part of those who were under a truce that have not surrendered, and many other villains in this part of the country, that still continue their outrages, render the lives and property of the good citizens very unsafe; and this disorder, in all probability, must continue, and the re-establishment of good order and civil law be hindered, except you, in your goodness, will indulge my regiment with a sufficient guard to the gaol, as it is insufficient for its use; with orders for supplies of provisions for that and the poor inhabitants; and an armed party to detect and bring to punishment the refractory and disobedient, which my warm desire for that purpose will induce me to engage to have punctually performed, with all due moderation, for the good of this country, and agreeably to any instructions you may think proper to give me; which I could do, and keep one-fourth on the field on common occasions, and on extraordinary emergencies with cheerfulness turn out one-half. My feelings will not let me omit mentioning to you some characters, among them, of Mr. Gainey's truce men, who have been received by General Marion as citizens, and are now doing military duty, and enjoying equal privileges with your best soldiers and citizens, who have borne the burden and heat of the day. Such, I mean, as were meant to be exempted by an Act of the late General Assembly at Jacksonborough—men, who have burned, plundered, and in cold blood (after many of our worthiest men had surrendered as prisoners of war), in the most ignominious and cruel manner, taken their lives, particularly Colonel Abel Kolb's, my worthy predecessor, and a gentleman formerly a member of the Assembly, a justice of the peace, a good officer, and a useful citizen, and capital loss to this part of the country: and the very villains that perpetrated this wanton, horrid murder, burning and plundering, are now, in the face of his distressed family and friends, received and restored to equal privileges with the men who have suffered everything by them that it was in their power and savage disposition to inflict.

"I am, Sir,
"Your most obedient and very humble Servant,
"LEMUEL BENTON,
"Lieut.-Col. Commanding Cheraw Militia.

"N.B.—Your answer and instructions I shall hope to receive by the bearer, Mr. Vinow, in regard to the above. I do not doubt but General Marion will acquiesce in it, as I mentioned the matter to him not long since, about provisions, men, and ammunition.

"If you will be so kind as to furnish us with the Militia laws, passed by the last Assembly, it will be of singular service, and the people and myself will be instructed."*

Governor Matthews appears to have been sufficiently impressed by this letter to address the following brief note to General Marion:—

"Uxbridge, August 24th, 1782.

"Sir,—I enclose you a letter I have just received from

*Gibbes's "Documentary History," 1776-82, pp. 207-209.

Lieut.-Col. Benton, and wish you to take such orders therein as you shall think proper.

"I am, Sir,
"Your most obedient, humble Servant,
"JOHN MATTHEWS."*

What specific orders, if any, this communication of Col. Benton induced, is not known. Doubtless Gen. Marion did all in his power for the inhabitants of the Upper Pedee.

A few days after, Col. Benton addressed the general again:—

"St. David's, August 29th, 1782.

"Sir,—Yours from Watbo, of the 18th inst., I received, and in answer, assure you, that I have constantly been, since my arrival at home, and still am, using my utmost endeavors to send you the full one-third of my regiment.

"The twenty men with whom I had your permission to guard the jail, have been constantly on hard duty, catching and bringing in the disobedient; so that, inclusive of what you have lately ordered and the guard will bring you, in addition to Major Thomas's class, there will be at least fifty men; and hope to have it in my power, about the 3rd of next month, to send you some more, as I expect by that time to have another squad gathered.

"But, without this armed party to be constantly on duty, and monthly relieved, I cannot do anything; for the district is so extensive, the duty so hard, and the distance to your camp so great, that it can't be expected that the men who have just been discharged from your camp can perform that duty. This mode would have been better executed if the commanding officer of my regiment at home, when I was in the camp, had not have hindered part of my orders (that was in his power) for that purpose. There are but fourteen of the twenty men mentioned that are at this time fit for duty, six of whom I send with the party, and the others will come with the next I have mentioned; though, I hope, you will send them back, as the law cannot be enforced without them. The people are, at this time, very

*Gibbes's "Documentary History," 1776-82, p. 214.

sickly about home, as has appeared by the trials of a number of men by a regimental court I lately ordered, and held four days, when I used every lawful and reasonable method in my power to turn out the men. There are several men, whom the guard will bring down, sentenced to some extraordinary duty, a list of whose names, and their term of service, I will send to Major Thomas.

"I am, Sir, with all due respect,
"Your obedient, humble Servant,
"LEML. BENTON,
"Colonel.*

"N.B.—If you permit me to continue the guard at the jail, please to give some instructions about salt, &c., for them, as it is scarce here."

To what commanding officer reference is made in this letter, is not known. Petty jealousies doubtless affected some who were otherwise patriotic. It was a happy circumstance for the people of this region, that a man of the firmness and unfaltering devotion of Benton was left to plead and defend their cause.

Again he writes to Marion a letter of the same date with the foregoing:—

"St. David's, August 29th, 1782.

"Sir,—Yours from Watbo I answered, and expect it will be handed you with this, as also yours from Lind's Ferry, of the 26th, which is just come to my hands.

"One-third of my regiment I have under orders to join you, and expect with this will come in about fifty men, in addition to Major Thomas's division; and those that may remain behind I will send with all possible expedition, so that if in my power the public service may not be hindered. As to the men being relieved monthly, it is so late now that it will be impossible for me to get them in camp until near the middle of the ensuing month.

"I am very sensible that it will make a considerable confusion in the regiment, as the men do not look upon themselves liable to go to camp yet, and the law will not

---

*Gibbes's "Documentary History," 1776-82, pp. 214, 215.

oblige them until each division does two months' duty agreeably to law; therefore, I must beg to be excused in that particular, and I will send relief early in October, when their tour will be out, according to law.

"I remain, with all due regard,
"Your most obedient Servant,
"Leml. Benton,
"Lieut.-Col. Commandant.*

"N.B.—Excuse my paper, &c., which hindered me from writing more fully.
"L. B."

Marion's brigade consisted about this time of the following regiments: Lieutenant-Colonel M'Donald's, Cols. Richardson's, Irvin's, Benton's, and the regiment formerly Maybank's.

Of the efficient service it performed in the closing work of the Revolution it is needless to speak. Upon Colonel Benton's command developed the additional duty of protecting an extensive territory from the incursions of the Tories.

The Whigs, however, were not to suffer much longer, for the protracted struggle of the patriots of Carolina was now drawing rapidly to an end. The evacuation of Charles-town, though officially announced by General Leslie as early as the 7th of August, was not to take place until the 13th of December, 1782.

Nothing of special note occurred on the Pedee during the remainder of the year. The conflict with the Tories did not cease at once with the withdrawal of the British forces. The state of feeling was too intense, the animosities which had been engendered were too deadly to be suddenly done away.

Old feuds were to be settled and retaliations inflicted, until, by degrees, a state of internal peace and quiet was restored. In the skirmishes which subsequently took place, the Tories were the sufferers. Of these some traditional accounts remain.

*Gibbes's "Documentary History," 1776-82, p. 216.

In the fork between Lumber River and Little Pedee was a noted band of Tories, who continued to hold out against the Government, even after it became firmly established. A party of Whigs, consisting, with others, of Jordan Gibson, William and Thomas Neville, Enos Tart, John Bethea, sen., John Bethea, jun., and Levi Odom, banded together to bring these outlaws to terms. A man named Courtney, who had acted as commissary for the enemy in these parts, was particularly obnoxious to the Whigs. They had often tried to take him, but in vain. He was in the habit of going to old Shoemake's, a noted Tory, and at length, this Whig party in passing found him there. Shoemake lived in an open field, and in order to make sure of Courtney, his pursuers stationed themselves at some distance around. Courtney, seeing their approach, attempted to escape on his horse, which was a very fleet animal. He came first upon Gibson, who fired, but missed him. He then approached Tart, who took better aim, and broke his leg, bringing him to the ground. As they gathered around him, Odom, who was a relative of the Betheas, and had served as a soldier in Virginia, called on the Nevilles to shoot the wounded man, but they refused. He then said if no other would he would shoot him himself, and did so, putting an end to his life. Long afterwards, when sick and in delirium, Odom was seen to exhibit the utmost terror at the vision of the bloody victim of his revenge.

Proceeding from this place, the Whigs, having reached the neighbourhood of the Tories, succeeded in capturing several, and determined to execute them without delay. But, the alarm being given, a sufficient number gathered from the adjacent country to rescue the prisoners, and bring their captors to treat with them. The result was that the Tories, satisfied by this demonstration of the fate that awaited them should they persist in their course of opposition, agreed to submit to the Government of the State, and henceforth keep the peace. The agreement continued to be observed, and no further difficulties of consequence occurred in this locality.

On the east side of the river, in the neighbourhood of Poke Swamp, Colonel M'Ree resided after the war. In company with two others, he succeeded in capturing one Bradley, a Tory, who had been guilty of notorious depredations. M'Ree tied him, and carried him to his house. Soon after their arrival, a party approached for the purpose of rescuing Bradley, one of them, Lewis Johnson, firing upon M'Ree as he sat in his door, but without effect. M'Ree, immediately closing the door, seized his gun, and from a window shot Johnson and killed him.

Bradley was taken the next day to George-town gaol, but afterwards escaped. He was subsequently arrested and hung. During the war several Tories, hearing that William Bethea, who lived near the present dividing line between Marlborough and Marion Districts, had a large quantity of money concealed in his house, set out for the purpose of securing the treasure. They found Bethea at home; but he had taken the precaution to select some other place of security for the fruits of his labor. They used every means to extort the secret from him, and as a last expedient, poured melted pitch upon his head, but all in vain. They found he would pay the penalty with his life, and left without further molestation. Some time after, and when the revolutionary struggle was over, John, a son of William Bethea, met Snowden, who was one of this marauding party, in the woods, and without difficulty overpowered him. With a loose bridle which he happened to have, he attempted to hang his victim, but was not able to get him suspended high enough. He then broke his legs, and carried the murderous design into execution. Bethea, commonly known as "Sweat Swamp John," because of his residence thereon, was a man of remarkable strength and activity. On a previous occasion, he met at night a Tory, who was also a man of much physical power, but, after a short struggle, succeeded in tying him, putting him on his horse, and carrying him as a prisoner to Colonel Hicks.

Another singular instance of revenge is related as having occurred in this neighbourhood. A Whig, named Hawthorne, was plundered and murdered by a party of seven Tories. His son took a vow that he would not sleep on a bed or eat at a table until he had killed five of the seven. He pursued them for years, and followed one or more of them to Tennessee, and is said actually to have fulfilled his vow to the letter.

In the neighbourhood of the DuBoses, on Lynche's Creek, was a famous Tory captain, Jef. Butler. He had been guilty of many acts of plunder, and at different times treated the family of Elias DuBose with great rudeness and cruelty. William Dick, a brother-in-law of Mr. DuBose, who moved to that neighbourhood after the war, went to Butler's with a small party, and found him on the ridge pole of a corn crib which he was covering. Dick ordered him down, and upon Butler's refusal to obey, knocked him off with an ear of corn. He was then tied and carried to DuBose's residence, and upon being confronted with Mrs. DuBose, denied having ever seen her. She knew him, however, too well. He was then taken out, tied up, severely whipped, and told if he did not leave the country in a given number of days, he would be dealt with more severely. Knowing what the result would be, he went off without delay, and was never heard of afterwards. As a Tory leader, the courage and ferocity of Butler were well known on the Pedee.

"During the Whig ascendancy," says Sabine, "in that part of South Carolina, he went into Marion's camp at Birch's Mills, and submitting himself, claimed the protection which the Whig officer had granted to some other Loyalists who had preceded him.

"Against this some of Marion's officers, whose friends had suffered at Butler's hands, protested. But Marion took the humbled Butler to his own tent, and declared that he would protect him at the hazard of his own life. The officers, still determined to indulge their hatred, sent their commander an offensive message, to the effect that Butler should be dragged from his tent, and that to defend such a wretch was an insult to humanity. Marion was not to be intimidated; and though the mutiny among his followers threatened to be formidable, he succeeded in conveying Butler, under a strong guard, to a place of safety."*

How far the account of this partial writer is to be relied upon is very questionable. One thing, at least, the course

---

*Sabine's "American Loyalists," p. 189.

of events subsequently proved, that Butler was not so fortunate upon falling into the hands of the Whigs of St. David's, who but for timely removal, would have made him pay the forfeit of his life.

Towards the latter part of the war, Andrew Hunter, of St. David's, was the chief actor in connexion with the well-known adventure which gave him celebrity. Hunter was a bold and daring spirit, and had gone on the occasion referred to, with a small force, in search of the notorious Fanning, on Drowning Creek, North Carolina. Fanning met him with a much larger party than he was supposed to have at the time. The Whigs were soon routed, and then commenced the memorable flight. Hunter rode a favorite mare, and relied on her fleetness to save him. But Fanning, mounted on as fast a horse, and with better bottom, as the result proved, singled out Hunter as his special object of pursuit. The chase was long, and exciting in the extreme. At length the mare failed, and Fanning overtook and captured her rider. Several of his men soon came up, and all dismounting, made thesmelves merry at the expense of the discomfited Whig, who had engaged in the luckless adventure. The whole party sat carelessly about for some time, resting themselves and their horses. At length Hunter, who knew it to be a case of life or death with him, having watched his opportunity, managed to get near enough to leap astride the horse of Fanning, and putting spurs, very unceremoniously bade his captors adieu. A few shots were fired at him, but without effect, as they were aimed high in order to save the horse.

Hunter had called his mare the Red Doe, and ever after the horse was known by the name of the Red Buck. After the war, Hunter and Fanning met in Charles-town. Fanning demanded his horse, which Hunter had ridden down, and high words passed between them. Fanning challenged Hunter to fight. The latter, having choice of weapons and the mode of combat, agreed to meet his adversary the next morning, on horseback, with swords, on the green near the city. It was soon noised about, and many persons assembled the following day to witness the novel encounter. Hunter rode out on the Red Buck. But Fanning, afraid at heart to meet one who was as active and powerful as he was fearless, did not make his appearance, and kept out of sight during Hunter's stay in town. Afterwards, Fanning brought an action, in Darlington, for the horse, but failed to get a verdict. Hunter was subsequently elected a member of the Legislature from Darlington. He died in his sixty-second year.

On one of his expeditions for the recapture of his horse, Fanning made not a few of the scattered Whigs along his route feel the effects of his vengeance. Robert Gregg, a brother of Captain James Gregg, was one of the sufferers. Upon Fanning's approach to his house, Gregg attempted to shoot him, but his gun snapped. He then endeavoured to make his escape to the swamp, which was near by, but was fired upon and severely wounded in the hip. He fell, and being covered with blood, played his part so well as the Tories came up, that they supposed him to be dead, and left without further molestation. He continued a cripple for life.

Fanning was a notorious marauder, of considerable talent, but reckless and sanguinary in disposition. When Marion admitted Major Gainey and the band of Loyalists and Tories under him to terms, Fanning was specially excluded. But both he and his wife succeeded in reaching Charles-town, which was then in possession of the Royal troops, in safety. Previous to his flight to the coast, he made a fruitless attempt to reanimate the friends of the Crown, with whom he possessed influence. There was, in the region to which he belonged, no more determined enemy of the Whigs and the cause of liberty. He lived to a great age, and died not very many years since, it is believed, in Canada.*

A singular incident is related of General Harrington. He had been on a visit to his family in Richmond County, and was returning with his aids to his command at Cross Creek. When not very far from the end of his journey, and within a mile or two of M'Kay's, a place of public entertainment, he directed his aids to go on there, turning off himself from the main road, to spend the night with an old

*Sabine's "American Loyalists," p. 282.

friend. Early the next morning, while on the way to M'Kay's, and alone, he was suddenly accosted by a man, very near him, who, protected by a tree, should the general attempt to discharge his pistol, presented his gun, and ordered him to dismount. Thus taken by surprise, and completely in the power of the robber, there was no alternative but to obey the command.

The general accordingly dismounted, and asked what was wanted. He was told to deliver up his money. The general put down five guineas; and being questioned, assured him it was all he had on his person. Upon which, having eyed alternately for a moment or two the general and the money, turning the latter about in his hand, he returned three of the guineas, with the remark, that their owner looked like a man who would need some money to get along with. He then told the general to walk off, and not attempt to mount his horse or touch his holsters until he had gone more than a hundred yards, or he would shoot him on the spot. Subsequently, on the removal of his quarters to a point near Wilmington, this individual, with others, was brought in a prisoner to General Harrington's camp. They immediaetly recognized each other, but without any expression of the fact, until after this man, with several other of the prisoners, had been tried and condemned to death.

General Harrington, thinking from what had transpired on the road, that there were some pecuilar circumstances connected with him, and that he was not the abandoned villain which such an act of highway robbery would seem to indicate, took him aside and questioned him closely. In explanation of his course, he said that he lived in a neighbourhood where all had taken British protection, or were Tories, and that it was impossible for him to remain there and be anything else, pleading extreme necessity for the robbery. Upon being asked if he was willing to swear allegiance to his country and serve under General Harrington throughout the war, on condition of his life being spared, he replied that he was; and thereupon took the oath, and proved himself ever after faithfully devoted to the general, and a true soldier of liberty.

After the war, General Harrington was elected a member

of the Legislature of North Carolina, and in that and other positions of trust, served his adopted State with unswerving fidelity. Strongly inclined, however, to retirement, he rather avoided than sought the excitements and distinctions of public life, and gave his latter years to the peaceful pursuits of agriculture, the cultivation of the social relations, and the sweets of domestic life. Happily constituted for contributing to the endearing pleasures of home, he was peculiarly blessed in having to share with him in those delights, one who was not more admired for her understanding and excellence of character, than beloved universally for those beautiful traits by which the life of woman in every relation is adorned.

In person, General Harrington was small, but well formed and handsome. His education was good, and his mind highly cultivated. After a life of eminent public service and private virtue, he died at his seat in Richmond County, on the 31st of March, 1809, in the sixty-second year of his age; spoken of in the papers of the day, "as an active and useful officer, who had acquired honor in the Revolution, which secured to this country its independence."

One of the friends of his earlier and later years, Claudius Pegues, of Marlborough, preceded General Harrington to the tomb. Mr. Pegues was too advanced at its commencement to take an active part in the war, presenting to his country, however, a son, who bore his name, to render gallant service in that cause to which he was ardently devoted. A singular circumstance is related in connexion with his last moments. Residing at the time alone, he sent for both of his sons, and told them he would die that day, although walking about the house, and apparently in his usual health. After conversing with them some time, and while they were talking together on the subject, he took up an arm-chair, moved it a little, and seating himself, quietly breathed his last.

Colonel Maurice Murphy, of whom such frequent and honorable mention has been made, continued, after the Revolution, to serve his country, as opportunity offered, to the close of his life. He was a bad manager, and never possessed much property. On one occasion, when in Charlestown, he was arrested for debt, and while in jail-bounds, met on the streets one Harrison, who had taken many negroes from the region of the Lower Pedee during the French and Indian war, and was then a resident of St. Augustine. Colonel Murphy rushed on him with his sword, saying that he had taken from him property to a larger amount than the debt for which he was then confined, and that if he did not pledge himself to cancel the debt and costs, he would kill him on the spot. Well knowing Murphy's determination, the alarmed and conscience-stricken Harrison at once acceded to the demand, and forthwith carried his promise into execution. In passing Jeffrey's Creek, on his return from Charles-town, it happening to be a muster-day, Colonel Murphy saw in the ranks one who had been a noted Tory, and by whom he had probably been made to suffer. Excited by the recollections of the past, he leaped from his horse and made rapidly towards him, the man only escaping from severe chastisement or death by instant flight. These instances show that Murphy was of quick and ungovernable passion; and yet, notwithstanding the violence of his temper and occasional dissipation, he maintained a character for generosity and integrity, commanding always the confidence of the people, and ever retaining a high place in the popular regard for his active and devoted services throughout the war. There was no more gallant or devoted Whig on the Pedee. In person he was straight as an arrow, rather bald, and of great physical strength. His end was a sad one. Imprisoned for debt, he died in the jail at Long Bluff; a touching example of the charge often made, of the ingratitude of Republics!

Tristram Thomas was a name respected and honored by all classes on the Pedee. General Thomas was modest and retiring in disposition, but firm and decided whenever principle was involved in the conduct of life. Sturdy by habit, and resolute in character as circumstances might demand, he was happily fitted by nature for the perils and labors of the Revolution. The discouragements to which the actors of that stormy period were often subjected, never unnerved

COL. LEMUEL BENTON.

or intimidated his soul. Possessed of a solid understanding, a practical turn of mind, and virtuous principles, he faithfully discharged the duties incumbent upon him in every station to which he was called in the administration of the affairs of his own district and the councils of the State. He was the first Brigadier-General on the Pedee after the war. He lived to a good old age, universally esteemed and died at his residence* in Marlborough District, in 1817.

Lemuel Benton, the compeer of Thomas, and the successor of Kolb as commander of the forces on the Pedee, was a man of very marked character. His early opportunities of improvement were quite limited, but with talents of a superior order, and an energy that flagged under no difficulties, he rose by the native force of mind and character to a position of commanding influence. Ardent in feeling, and of strong and violent passions, he was a bitter enemy and as fast a friend. He had the peculiar faculty, which few possess, of gaining the confidence of the masses and leading them at will. As a stump-speaker he had no superior in his day. On more than one occasion he conducted his own defence in Court with signal success. This talent as a speaker, with his efficient military services, was the means of securing him a seat in Congress as the first member from the Pedee District. He encountered a strong opponent in a Mr. Wilson of Williamsburg, a gentleman of popular manners and influential connexions, but unequal to Colonel Benton before the people, and hence doomed to defeat. Previously to this election Colonel Benton had been returned as one of the first two members of the Legislature from Darlington. At the next canvass for Congress, two years after, he was opposed by Benjamin Huger, of George-town, and defeated. The fact that he had opposed Mr. Adams's administration probably contributed to this result. His career as a public man was now closed. Colonel Benton was about six feet in height, stout, but well formed, and of handsome and commanding person. He died at his residence in Darlington about the year 1819.

---

*General Thomas lived at the place now known as Ellerbe's Mills, near the public road leading from Society Hill to Bennettsville.

Colonel George Hicks survived the Revolution several years, though advanced in age. From the time of his emigration to the Pedee he took a high position in the confidence and esteem of the people. He was distinguished for purity, benevolence, and general excellence of character. Remarkably considerate and humane, conscientious and faithful in the discharge of every trust, his course through life was such as to inspire universal regard, and to call forth the unaffected regrets of all classes at his departure from earth. His name never ceased to be mentioned with affectionate veneration by those of his contemporaries who survived him—an example of the kind which has seldom been known.

A name which should ever be remembered with respect by the descendants of the Whigs of St. David's, is that of Jushua Ammons. Of humble pretensions through life, this man won for himself a position second to no other for active and unceasing devotion to the cause of liberty. He emigrated from Maryland and settled before the war in what is now Marlborough District, but a few miles from the present county seat. No one on the Pedee, perhaps, took a more varied part, or at more distant points in the revolutionary struggle. He appears to have been almost ubiquitous. Engaged actively in the partisan warfare under Marion; then in the Continental line; in most of the battles of Carolina, and under Lafayette's command when hastening to join Washington before York-town, he was continuously in the field, acting most of the time as orderly-sergeant. It was while on the march of Lafayette, between Charlottesville and Scottsville, Virginia, when he encountered the British army which had been stationed on the route to intercept his progress, that the gallant Frenchman received a severe wound. Mr. Ammons happened to be near the person of the general when he fell, and was the first to reach him. He bore his commander from the field, placing him under the shade of a tree. In 1824, when Lafayette visited America as the nation's guest, and journeyed to the southward, Joshua Ammons, with many others, hastened to the North Carolina line to meet the noble old chief. He was introduced to Lafayette as a soldier of the Revolution, and one who had borne him from the field when he was wounded near Scottsville. The name was still familiar to his ear, but the person of the humble soldier forgotten. But this did not matter. The past rushed upon him in an instant and thrilled his soul. Recognising in the lowly individual before him the bold and faithful supporter on the battle-field, he embraced him as a friend, and invited him to head-quarters. There, doubtless, they communed in spirit, calling up stirring reminiscences of the times that tried men's souls, and passing again, though in the evening of life, through the throes of struggling liberty in which they had participated as youthful combatants. The exploits of Joshua Ammons would make an extended narrative if written out in full. Daring almost to a fault, he shrank from no danger, nor shunned any responsibility. Prison ships presented no terrors to his dauntless soul, nor did a view of the gallows affect his nerves. He lived to a very advanced age, and passed away amid the grateful benedictions of the descendants of those with whom he had fought in unwavering devotion to his country.*

Another name which has no place in history, and is now unknown in the region where he lived, deserves, in one respect at least, the first place in the annals of the Pedee, if not in the story of the Revolution throughout the thirteen colonies. Jacob Brawler gave his own life and the lives of twenty-two sons to the cause of liberty in Carolina. He removed from Tar River, North Carolina, to Liberty Precinct, and settled on Cat Fish, sixteen miles below the present village of Marion. He was married twice, and had large families by both wives, of whom all were sons, except one, a daughter. After the fall of Charles-town, some of his sons were drafted; but the old man said there should

---

*When Lee's "Memoirs of the Southern Campaign" first appeared, Mr. Ammons read the book with absorbing interest. His running comments are said, by an intelligent friend and neighbour, who was often with him at the time, to have been extremely interesting and instructive. Many statements he corrected, the memory of numerous incidents was recalled, and the most varied emotions were excited by the perusal. It seemed to revive, as an expiring flame, the spirit of '76—a flame which continued to burn in him with enthusiastic devotion to liberty, dear in the recollection of its early conflicts, until extinguished in death.

be no division among them, that if one went, all should go, and that he would accompany them. Twenty-four in all, they embarked in the strife, and almost incredible to relate, but one of the sons returned to tell the tale of their slaughter. Overwhelmed by the calamity, the frantic wife and mother went off, not knowing whither, in search of her loved ones, but only to return, after a fruitless search, a broken-hearted mourner. She was eventually put upon the parish, and lived to old age. The surviving son, who was of weak mind and body, died a few years after, and the name became extinct in Marion.*

With the close of 1782, the Revolution may be said to have ended in Carolina. The long and anxious struggle was then over. And, with returning peace, prosperity came. Again attention was to be turned to the material development of the State, to the subject of education, and other departments of progress. The halls of justice, long silent, were to be re-opened; and now that those who had been sorely oppressed, were to be henceforth free and independent, they were to feel, in the work and fruits of peace, the full measure of the responsibility assumed, when they solemnly pledged to each other their lives, their fortunes, and their sacred honor.

The following very imperfect list collected from the Archives of the State, will give, in addition to those already mentioned, embracing also some of them, the names of not a few others on the Pedee, who took part in the war, and may

---

*This account, which may appear almost incredible, was related to the Author by the late Hugh Godbold, of Marion, and confirmed, in every particular, by William Shaw, a humble but worthy and respectable man, who was of age at the time, lived in the same neighborhood, and knew the family of Brawler well. Mr. Shaw was born in March, 1759, and in the spring of 1859, when the Author spent a night with him at the house of Mr. Godbold, was possessed of astonishing vigor of body and mind for one of his years. Neither his sight nor hearing was very seriously impaired. He sat up to a late hour, listening, with unabated interest to a conversation about the early days of the Pedee, taking part himself, and was as cheerful as a man in his prime. He said a red oak was then living which stood in Brawler's yard. Brawler was poor, but ingenious. He adopted the following method of catching bears:—Driving sharp nails, pointing downward, in a bee-gum, he baited it at the bottom, having secured it well. The bear, putting his head down, would be caught beyond the possibility of extrication. William Shaw had passed his hundredth year when the Author saw him for the first and last time; and, considering his activity, was one of the most remarkable cases of longevity on record.

HISTORY OF THE OLD CHERAWS.   405

fitly bring this narrative of the Revolution to a close. Other services were doubtless rendered by most, if not all of those included in this list. Many either neglected or declined, after the Revolution, to present any account against the State; while a large number of those who lost their lives during the struggle, were not afterwards represented. The records of the Continental line, had they been accessible, would have added many more names. Fractional as it is, the list here given is well worthy of preservation.

Allen, Jeremiah, lieutenant of Militia, in . . . 1782
Ammons, John, private in Capt. Thos. Parrot's Company of Horse . . . . „
Ammons, Thomas, private, in . . . . „
Andrews, John, adjutant of Col. Hicks's Regt. from Feb. to Nov. 1780
Arnold, William, private, in 1782
Askew, John, „ under Marion . . . . „
Ayer, Hartwell „ in 1778
Bacot, Samuel, 1st Lieut. in Marion's Brigade, in . . 1782
Benton, Lemuel, private in Benton's Regt. „ . . „
Beasley, Daniel „
Beasley, William „
Berry, Wm., sergeant, in . . . . „
Bird, Wm., private „ . . . . „
Blackwood, Abram, private, in . . . . „
Blakeney, John, sergeant in Marion's Brigade . . „
Blakeney, Robert, private „ . . . . „
Blakeney, Thomas, „   „ . . . . „
Bozeman, John „   „ 1783
Bryant, Gray „   „ Benton's Regiment . . 1781
Bryant Hardy „   „   „   . . „
Burkitt, Ephriam „   „   „   . . „
Burkitt, Samuel „   „   „   . . „
Butler, John, Captain
Campbell, James, sergeant, in 1782
Cassity, Zachariah, private in Benton's Regiment . „
Champ, Richard „   „ . . . . „
Cherry, William „   „ Marion's Brigade . „

Clark, Harman, private in Marion's Brigade . . . 1782
Clayton, Lawrence ,,   ,, ... ,,
Clements, Joseph   ,,   ,, ... ,,
Coker, Benjamin   ,,   ,, ... ,,
Coker, Nathan   ,,   ,, ... ,,
Coker, Thomas   ,,   ,, ... 1781
Cole, James, sergeant and private 1782
Coleman, James, private, in . . . . ,,
Coleman, John   ,,   ,, ... ,,
Collier, John   ,,   ,, ... ,,
Conn, Thomas, adjutant and private in Benton's
    Regiment 1781
Cone, Matthew, private, in 1782
Conner, James   ,,   ,, ... ,,
Cook, William, sergeant and private in Continental
    line . . . . ,,
Council, William, private under Marion . . . . ,,
Courtney, Stephen ,, in . . . . ,,
Coward, William   ,,   ,, ... 1780-81-82
Cox, Emanuel   ,,   ,, ... ,,
Cox, James   ,,   ,, ... ,,
Cox, John   ,,   ,, Capt. Standard's Com-
    pany, Benton's Regiment 1781
Cox, Josiah, private in Capt. Moses Pearson's Comp. 1782
Cox, Samuel   ,,   ,,   ,,   ,,   ,,   ,,
Cox, William   ,,   ,,   ,,   ,,   ,,   ,,
Crocker, James   ,,   ,, ... 1780-82
Daniel, Aaron   ,,   ,, ... ,,
Daniel, John   ,,   ,, ... ,,
Darby, Jacob   ,,   ,, ... ,,
David, Azariah   ,,   ,, ... 1782-83
  ,,   Ezekiel   ,,   ,, Marion's Brigade . . . 1782
  ,,   John, sergeant and lieutenant alternately 1779-82
  ,,   Joshua, private, Capt. Thomas Ellerbe's Com-
        pany, Hicks's Regiment 1780
Davis, John, private, in 1782-83
Davis, Thomas   ,,   ,, ... ,, ,,
Davis, William   ,,   ,, ... 1782
Dewitt, Charles, second-lieut. in Marion's Brigade 1781-82
Dewitt, Martin

Dial, John, private, in 1782
Doney, Peter, private, in . . . . „
Douglass, Jesse „ „ 1781-82
Douglass, Joshua „ „ . . . . „ „
Du Bose, Andrew „ „ Benton's Regiment in 1780,
    and captain, in 1781
Du Bose, Daniel
Du Bose, Elias, lieutenant and private
Du Bose, Isaac, private, in Mahan's Cavalry Regiment 1782
Du Bose, Samuel
Du Bose, William, sergeant, Benton's Regiment,
    Marion's Brigade
Duling, James, private, in 1782
Duling, John „ „ . . . . „
Ellerbe, Thomas, captain, in 1781-82
Ellerbe, William, private „ 1782
Evans, Benjamin „ under Major Amos Windham
Evans, Burwell, private, in . . . . „
Evans, Enoch, first-lieut., Capt. Irby's Company,
    Hicks's Regiment, siege Charles-town 1780
Evans, Ezer, private, in Captain Irby's Company,
    Hicks's Regiment, siege Charles-town . . . . „
Evans, George, lieut., in 1781-82
Evans, John, private, in 1782-83
Evans, Josiah „ „ Benton's Regiment . 1781-82
Evans, Thomas „ „ Hick's Regiment, siege
    Charles-town 1780
Evans, William
Fort, Moses, private, Irby's Company, Hicks's Regiment, siege Charles-town . . . . „
Faulkner, John, private, under Marion
Fountain, William, private, in 1783
Flowers, John „ „ 1782
Fitzpatrick, James „ „ . . . . „
Ford, Albert „ „ 1781-82
Frasher, — „ „ . . . . „
Fuller, John „ „ . . . . „
Farmer, Zachariah „ „ . . . . „
Gardner, Stephen „ „ . . . . „

Gardner, William, private in 1782
Gay, —, lieutenant „ 1781-82
Gibson, Thomas, sen., private, in . . . . „
Gibson, Thomas, jun. „ „ . . . . „
Gillespie, James, sergeant, Martin's Troop, Sumpter's Brigade
Gillespie, Samuel, private, Robuck's Regiment
Goodson, Arthur „ in 1782
Goodson, Thomas „ „ . . . . „
Goodwyn, Britain „ „ . . . . „
Goodwyn, David „ „ . . . . „
Goodwyn, Lewis „ „ . . . . „
Gregg, James, captain, Britton's Neck Regiment, Colonel Ervin
Griffith, Joseph, captain
Grimes, James, private, Irby's Company, Hicks's Regiment, siege Charles-town 1780
Hagin, David, private, in Benton's Regiment . . . 1782
Hales, Silas „ „ . . . . „
Harrall, Levi „ „ . . . . „
Harrington, Wm. Henry, commanding South Carolina Militia, both sides of Pedee, November . . 1782
Harrison, Henry, private, in 1782
Hendley, Jesse „ „ . . . . „
Hendricks, William, captain, Marion's Brigade . . „
Hewstess, James, sergeant . . . . „
Hicks, George, colonel 1779-80-81
Hickson, John, private, in 1782
Hindley, Edward „ „ Benton's Regiment
Hinds, John, lieut. and private, in . . . . „
Hines, Samuel „ „ „ . . . . „
Hinson, Clayburn, commanding detachment prisoners to Long Bluff . . . . .April, 1781
Hinson, William, private, Round O Company Militia 1779
Hird, John, lieut., in 1782
Hodge, Elias, private, in 1779
„ Isham, private under Major Tristram Thomas, Hicks's Regiment 1780
„ James, private under Lieut. John Pledger, Murphy's Regiment 1782

Hodge, John, private in Capt. Standard's Company,
  Hicks's Regiment 1780-81
  „ Joseph, private under Major Thomas, and in
    Hicks's Regiment, in 1782
  „ Robert, sergeant, Captains Standard's and
    Pearson's Companies, Benton's Regt. 1780-82
  „ Thomas, private, in 1782
  „ Welcome, sergeant, Benton's Regiment, siege
    Charles-town 1780
Hollis, Moses, lieut., in 1783
Hubbard, Noah, private, in 1782
Huckaby, Isham, sergeant and private, in . . . . „
  „ Samuel „ „ „ . . . „
  „ Thomas, private, in . . . . „
Huggins, John, captain, Col. Hugh Giles' Regt. . . . 1779
Hunt, Criswell, private, Benton's Regiment
Irby, Edmund, captain, Hicks's Regt., M'Intosh's
  Brigade, siege Charles-town 1780
Irby, Charles, commissary 1782
Jackson, John, lieutenant, in . . . . „
  „ Stephen, captain, Kolb's Regiment . . . 1780
  „ Stephen, junr., private, in 1782
  „ William „ „ . . . . . „
James, Alexander, lieut., in . . . . „
  „ George, private „ . . . . „
  „ James „ „ . . . . „
Jenkins, Charles „ „ . . . . „
  „ James „ „ . . . . „
  „ Reuben, lieutenant and private . . . . „
Jinkins, James, lieutenant in Benton's Regiment . . „
John, Azel, private, Benton's Regiment 1782
  „ Jesse „ „ 1783
  „ Thomas „ „ 1782
Johnson, John „ Capt. Standard's Company, Ben-
  ton's Regiment 1781
Johnston, John, private 1782
Jolley, Joseph „ . . . . „
Jones, Edward, Captain of Guard, Kolb's Ferry . 1780-83
  „ James, private 1782
  „ William „ . . . . „

Keil, William, private 1782
Keith, Cornelius   „   . . . . „
Kennedy, Stephen „   . . . . „
Kilgore, Henry   „   . . . . „
Kirby, James   „   . . . . „
Knight, Niglet   „   . . . . „
Kolb, Benjamin, Benton's Regiment 1781
„ John, sergeant and corporal 1780-81
„ Peter, private, in 1782
Large, David „   „   . . . . „
Lee, William „   „   . . . . „
Lide, Robert, Major, Marion's Brigade
Lowther, Edward, private in 1781-82
Lowry, Robert   „   „ Marion's Brigade . .   „   „
Luke, Owen   „   „ . . . . „
Lundy, Drewry   „   „ 1781
„ John   „   „ 1781-82
Lyons, Guthridge, captain, Benton's Regiment . . 1781
„ William,   private 1781-82
Marlo, James   „   1782
Mannings, James   „   . . . . „
Marsh, John Lewis   „   Benton's Regiment . 1781
Martin, Jeremiah   „   „   „   . „
„ William   „   „   „   . „
Mason, Charles, commissary under Marion, and private 1782
„ Joseph, private, in . . . . „
M'Call, George   „   under Marion . . . . . „
„ Henry, sergeant of horse 1782-83
„ John, lieut. and private, Marion's Brigade 1781-82
„ William, private in 1782
M'Carter, James   „   „ . . . . „
M'Cullough, George, captain, in . . . . „
M'Donald, John, private   „   . . . . „
M'Dowell, Samuel   „   „   . . . . „
M'Gee, James   „   „ . . . . „
M'Intosh, Alexander, captain, Benton's Regiment 1781-82
„ Lacklin, private, in 1782
„ William   „ Captain Nelson's Company, Marion's Brigade 1781-82

HISTORY OF THE OLD CHERAWS. 411

M'Iver, Evander, private and clerk in Captain Irby's
    Company, Hicks's Regiment, M'Intosh's Brigade 1780
M'Muldrough, Andrew, private, in 1782
    ,,   Hugh, sergeant-major, in . . . . . ,,
    ,,   James,   ,,   ,, ... ,,
    ,,   William, lieutenant ,, ... ,,
M'Natt, Joel, private, Murphy's Regiment, Marion's
    Brigade . . . . ,,
  ,, Mackey, private . . . . ,,
Mikell, James   ,, ... ,,
  ,, John, jun., lieut. and private, Marion's Bri-
    gade 1780-82
Miles, William, private, in 1782
Mixon, Maraday ,,   under Lieut. John Rushing,
    Benton's Regiment, at Long Bluff, in . 1783
  ,, Samuel, private in 1782
Moody, Andrew   ,,   Captain Standard's Com-
    pany, Benton's Regiment 1781
  ,, Roderick, private in Captain Standard's Com-
    pany, Benton's Regiment . . . . . ,,
Moore, Gully, private, in 1782
  ,, Jeremiah ,,   ,, ... ,,
Munnerlyn, James, lieutenant
Murphy, Maurice, captain in Hicks's Regiment, in
    1779-80, major, in 1780-81, and lieut.-col. com-
    manding, in 1781-82
Murray, William, private, in 1782
Nettles, George   ,,   ,, Pedee Regiment, Marion's
    Brigade 1780-82
Nettles, Joseph, private, in 1779-82
  ,, Robert   ,,   ,, Marion's Brigade
Noland, William   ,,   ,, ... 1782
Northent, William ,,   ,, ... ,,
Norwood, John, captain in Marion's Brigade, in . . ,,
  ,, Samuel, private, in . . . . ,,
Nugent, Thomas   ,,   ,, ... ,,
O'Neal, John, commissary of detachment under Col.
    Benton, in . . . . ,,
Outlaw, Benjamin, private, in . . . . ,,
Parker, Moses   ,,   ,, ... 1781-82-83

Parrot, Thomas, Captain of Horse, in 1782
Pasley, Robert, captain, in 1781
Pearson, Aaron, private ,, ... 1782
,, Moses, lieutenant in Hicks's Regiment, in 1780, and captain in Benton's Regiment, Marion's Brigade, in 1781-82
Perkins, David, private, in 1782
,, Isaac, sergeant ,, ... ,,
,, Lewis, private ,, ... ,,
,, William ,, ,, ... ,,
Pigot, John, sergeant, in . . . . ,,
,, Nathanael, private, in . . . . ,,
Pledger, John, lieutenant in Marion's Camp, 1781-82, and lieutenant commanding in Murphy's Regiment, in . . . . .July, 1782
Poke, Daniel, private, in . . . . ,,
,, John ,, ,, ... ,,
,, Luke ,, ,, ... ,,
Pouncey, Anthony, quarter-master, in 1780
Powe, Thomas, commissary, Hicks's Regiment . . . ,,
Powers, Nicholas, private, in 1782
Preswood, Jonathan, sergeant, in . . . . ,,
,, Thomas, private ,, ... ,,
Purvis, Alexander ,, ,, ... ,,
,, Gilbert ,, ,, ... ,,
,, John, lieut.-col., in 1780
Raburn, John, private, Captain Daniel Sparks' Company 1779-80
Raspberry, John, private, in 1782
Rasher, Michael ,, ,, ... ,,
Rawlinson, John ,, ,, Benton's Regiment . ,,
Rivers, Frederick ,, ,, ... ,,
Roan, William ,, ,, ... ,,
Roberts, Philip ,, ,, ... ,,
Rogers, Edward ,, ,, ... ,,
Rouse, Neal ,, ,, ... ,,
Rushing, John, lieutenant, Benton's Regiment, at Long Bluff, in 1782-83
Russell, Stephen, sergeant and private, in 1782
Sansbury, Daniel, private, in 1781-82

Saunders, Nathanael, lieutenant and private under
    Benton, in 1780-81
Sellers, William, private, in 1782
Sexton, Edward,   ,,   ,, ... 1782
Shoemake, Samuel ,,   ,, ... ,,
Simons, David, sergeant, in . . . . ,,
  ,,   Samuel, private ,, ... ,,
Smith, Charles ,, ,, Capt. Thomas Ellerbe's Comp. ,,
  ,,   John, private   ,,   ,,   . ,,
  ,,   Richard ,,   ,,   ,, . ,,
  ,,   Jeremiah, private, in Andrew Du Bose's and
    Thos. Ellerbe's Companies, Benton's Regiment ,,
Sparks, Daniel, captain, in 1781-82
Spears, David, private, in . . . . ,,
Standard, William, captain in Benton's Regiment 1781-82
Spencer, Calvin, assistant quartermaster-general,
    June to August 1780
Stanley, Shadrack, private, in 1782
Starks, Henry   ,,   ,, ... ,,
Stephens, John   ,,   ,, ... ,,
Strother, George, lieutenant, in . . . . ,,
Teal, Edward, private, in . . . . ,,
Terrell, Edward ,,   ,, ... ,,
  ,,   James, lieutenant, Benton's Regiment at
    Long Bluff 1783
  ,,   Samuel, lieutenant, in 1781-82-83
Thomas, Tristram, captain in Hicks's, Kolb's and
    Benton's Regiments, 1780-81, and major in Ben-
    ton's Regiment 1781-82
Thorp, Eleazer, private, in 1782
Tootles, Obed   ,,   ,, ... ,,
Townsend, Light ,,   ,, Benton's Regiment . ,,
Veal, John   ,,   ,, ... ,,
Vickers, Jacob   ,,   ,, ... ,,
Vining, Jesse   ,,   ,, ... 1782-83
Waddell, Abel   ,,   ,, ... 1781
Warwick, Abraham, private, in 1782
Watkins, Samuel   ,, under Capt. Amos Windham
Weaver, Hartwell, private, in . . . . ,,
White, James, private, in 1782

Whittington, Barnett, private, in 1782
" Ephriam, lieut., Benton's Regt., in 1781-82-83
" Francis, private in 1782
" Levi " " . . . . . . "
" Nathanael " " . . . . . . "
" Richard " " . . . . . . "
Wilds, Abel, private, in . . . . "
.. Jesse, lieutenant, in . . . . "
" Samuel, private, in 1782
Williams, Daniel, captain in Benton's Regiment, in . 1781
Williamson, Jesse, private, Marion's Brigade . . . 1782
" Shadrach, lieutenant and private, in . "
" Stephen
" Sterling, private, in . . . . "
" William " " . . . . . . "
" Willis " " . . . . . . "
Wingate, Edward " " . . . . . . "
Windham, Amos, Captain under Kolb, and major, in "
" Jesse, private
" William " 1782
Wise, James " . . . . "
" William " . . . . "
Wood, Benjamin " . . . . "
Woodward, Thomas " . . . . "
Wright, Amos, private, Capt. Amos Windham's Company . . . . "
" Gillis, private . . . . "
" Joseph " . . . . "
" Solomon, private, Capt. Windham's Company . . . . "
Yates, William, private . . . . "
Youngblood, David, private . . . . "
" Peter, captain . . . . "

CHAPTER XVII.

Members of Legislature elected for St. David's Parish—Petition of Elizabeth Mitchell, and action of Legislature thereon—Petition of Robert Allison—Relief extended—Elections for Cheraws District—First Circuit Court at Long Bluff after the Revolution—Charge of Judge Grimke—Presentments of grand jury—Tobacco inspectors appointed for Cheraws—Ordinance for opening navigation of the Pedee—Commissioners appointed—Ordinance of following year—Commissioners—Course of Legislation on the subject—Elections to Legislature for St. David's—Captain Dewitt resigns his seat—Re-elected—County Court Act—St. David's Parish divided into three counties—Boundary lines—Provisions of the Act—County Justices for Marlborough, Chesterfield, and Darlington—Locations made for the several county sites—Prevailing crime at that day—Presentment of County Court for Chesterfield—Burning of records in Darlington County—Practising lawyers in St. David's—Names of counties—Greenville, why so called—St. David's Society revived—Its history—Teachers—Thomas Park—Life and character—Members of St. David's Society—Notices of Welch Neck Church—Removal of church building—Account of William Falconer—Other settlers in Cheraw District after the Revolution.

The state of public affairs urgently demanded the attention of the Legislature, which was to meet in January, 1783. At an election holden for members on the 25th and 26th of November, Major Tristram Thomas was returned Senator; and Lemuel Benton, Thomas Powe, William Pegues, William Strother, William Dewitt, and Claudius Pegues, jun., Members of the House for St. David's.

"On the 15th of February, was received the petition of Elizabeth Mitchell, widow of John Mitchell, in behalf of herself and the heirs and devisees of her deceased husband, setting forth, that he had been dead almost two years, and left his estate, real and personal, to herself and children—that she had observed, with concern, that his estate was confiscated by an Act of the General Assembly, and begged leave to state, that for many years preceding his death, her husband was of very distracted mind, and if he had been guilty of any acts to occasion the displeasure of the Legislature, such misconduct must have been the result of his insanity—that he was confined frequently as an absolute madman—that he never held any commission under the British—that herself and the heirs are well affected to this State; and one of the heirs, though a youth of tender years, had lately turned out a volunteer in the State service; and she therefore prayed relief from the said Act of Confiscation, &c." The petition was favorably received, and relief extended, except as to such part of the estate as would descend to a daughter who had married Captain Campbell, a British officer.

On the 24th of February, the petition of Robert Ellison was read, setting forth "that he was an officer in the militia before the fall of Charles-town, and always exerted himself in the service of America—that he was made a prisoner in Camden, and confined on James's island under very unhappy circumstances, and therefore prayed relief from the penalties of an Act for amercing certain persons therein mentioned, &c." The case of Mr. Ellison seems to have been misunderstood. He was consequently relieved, and continued to enjoy the confidence and esteem of his fellow-citizens to the close of his useful life.

At this Session of the Legislature, Claudius Pegues, jun., was elected Ordinary for Cheraws District, and William Dewitt, Sheriff. The latter having accepted the appointment, vacated his seat as a member of the House. A new election was ordered for 24th and 25th of March, and Peter Allston returned.

The first court holden at Long Bluff, after the Revolution, was on the 15th of November, of this year. It was an occasion of unusual interest.

Judge Grimke, who had been appointed on the 20th of March previous, appeared for the first time on the Northern Circuit, and made it the occasion of a timely and eloquent charge to the grand juries which came before him. The feelings of animosity, so recently cherished towards the Tories, were deeply rooted in the hearts of the people; and a disposition was manifested on the part of many to keep up the distinction, chiefly for the sake of appeals to popular feeling in connexion with elections.

Judge Grimke did not shrink from what he conceived to be his duty under the circumstances, and gave expression to such wise counsels, mingled with patriotic sentiments, as tended much to quiet the public mind, and convince the reflecting classes of the error and excess into which many had fallen. The Charge, together with the Presentments of the Grand Jury of Cheraws, was published in the *Gazettes* of the day.

The most interesting chapter in our annals, perhaps, except the account of the struggle itself, is that of the few years preceding the Revolution, and next, the narrative of the times immediately succeeding.

The charge of Judge Grimke was as follows:—

"Gentlemen of the Grand Jury:

"This being the first time that I have had the honor of addressing the grand jury of this district in my judicial capacity, I must confess I feel myself impressed with an anxious awe, the offspring of diffidence; and when I reflect upon the respect due to this place, upon the merits and dignified stations of the gentlemen to whom I am delivering my sentiments, upon the honor conferred on me by the voice of my country, and upon the important trusts committed to my charge, the consciousness of my inexperience to perform the momentous duties of my office rushes in upon my mind, and almost overpowers my senses. But, persuaded of this distinguished mark of my country's favor, of the dignity of the office, and of the importance of its obligations, I perceive myself bound by the indissoluble ties of honor to merit the confidence that has been reposed in me.

"I will endeavor to regain those moments which the service of my country employed during the late war, in the military line, and by the most unwearied assiduity, render myself competent to appear in this capacity. It shall be my pride, always to make the law of the State my rule in the administration of justice, and to aim at the most impartial and punctual, though merciful execution of them. And the contemplation of the present situation of this country, excites an ardor in forming such resolutions, and of carrying them, without delay, into execution. For the war which has for so many years suspended our power of opening the courts, has delayed justice to the good citizens of this State; and has protected many daring offenders in the outrages they have committed on the public tranquillity, in their violation of the security of property, and in the repeated insults which they have offered with impunity to our inhabitants. This intermission in the public proceedings of courts of judicature, has been of so long a continuance, and the offences committed since the capitulation of Charles-town so seldom punished, that the idea of the penalties affixed to the crimes, has been absorbed by the familiarity and frequency of their occurrence. Our bewildered minds seemed no longer alarmed at the commission of crimes of the first magnitude; and carnage, and all the havoc of war let loose upon our unfortunate country, had in some degree hardened the hearts of the most compassionate amongst us. But I hope the barbarous mode in which the enemy carried on their war, and which of necessity produced several instances of retaliation on our part, has not totally annihilated the merciful dispositions of our nature, and irremediably tempered our minds to violence, cruelty, and oppression. True it is, that men have long exercised a habit of consulting their own bosoms, their own resentments, and their own arms, for a redress of injuries; but the impolicy and injustice of such appeals are too evident to need a comment thereon.

"At that period, indeed, when such unnatural and alien principles were forced upon us for our creed, and when we were compelled to adopt as the only means of probable salvation (the means which in some instances were used), perhaps we might stand exculpated before God and the nations of the earth. The convulsions of our country, the desolation of our farms, the conflagrations raging through our settlements, and all the ravages of our moveable property, presented a scene capable of agitating the minds of men who were not even sufferers in so general a calamity. But, when the cruelties of these refined barbarians extended themselves to the families and relatives of our countrymen —when women were upbraided and accused as guilty of a crime for the loyalty of their husbands and sons to our great and just cause—when they were turned out of their hospitable dwellings, deprived of every comfort and conveniency of life, robbed of their personal clothing, and even of the necessary covering to intercept the intemperate ardor of the sun, or the mighty falling dews of an inclement sky, without any refuge or asylum than the wild and desolated plains of their country; when their cattle, the only resource of sustaining themselves and infant families, during the exile or captivity of those to whom they looked for succor, were cruelly driven into their barns, and inhumanly consumed by fire with the buildings; when men, whose age and infirmities alone should have been their protection, and who were rather subjects even of an enemy's sensibility and compassion; I say, when such men, who were but lingering out the glimmering remains of a painful life, without the addition of any sharper misery, became the objects of the indignation of an enemy, powerful and in arms, were dragged from their homes, and thrust into the sepulchres of our forefathers; when our brave citizens, who had become captives by the fortune of war, were not allowed the usual privileges annexed to this unfortunate condition, but were daily perishing for the absolute want even of the common necessaries to sustain their miserable lives; when the most repeated and violent infringements of the capitulation of Charles-town were not only practised, but impudently avowed; when British faith had become as proverbial with us, as that of the 'Carthaginians was amongst her contemporary nations;' when even the puerilities of our children could excite the malice of these heroes; when the disgrace and disappointment of the panic-struck Rawdon, flying before the terror of our arms, had instigated them to give a loose to their fury, and to sacrifice, though not even by their mock forms of justice, by an ignominious execution, a martyr to our glorious cause;* when their impious hands were not restrained from pillaging the temples of the Almighty; from disturbing the ashes of the dead, who ought to be in peace; or from polluting the sacramental pales of the Holy Communion, which it is sacrilege to violate;—then were the banners displayed, which aroused men's souls into action. Then it was, that we girded on our swords, and couched our quivering lances. Then it

---

*The noble and devoted Hayne.

was that we became familiar with the din of arms, embraced the fatigues of marches and of the camp, and courted the dangers of the field. These were the alarms that roused our drooping spirits, and quickened our hearts with an enthusiastic spirit of opposition. At this moment, to have remained indifferent or neutral; to have artfully reasoned from moderate, peaceable times, to times which were not moderate, and could not be peaceable; or to repose our fears on the soft lap of hope, would have been deceiving ourselves. For no other alternative (so dreadful was our situation) remained for us, but to await the assassinating arm of our perfidious foe, or resorting to the conditions of a state of nature, to assert the vindication of our wrongs by our own hands. To have been weak enough, affecting the hypocritical mask of moderation, to have silently and obediently acquiesced under such enormities, would have left it problematical to posterity, whether our early and national character was stamped with cowardice or treachery. But now, the scene is changed; the ravages of our country and the afflictions of our friends no longer excite the tumultuous passions of the mind. Our foe is fallen, and hath retired with envy and disgrace to the dominions of their tyrants. Our mighty adversary has been compelled to acknowledge our freedom, our sovereignty, and independence; and we now behold him an humbled solicitor at the throne of the dignity of our State for a return of our commercial favors. Pause, therefore, at this important and critical juncture, and contrast your present situation with that from which you are just emerged. Behold the olive branch of peace extended wide o'er your towns and fields, and all your country reviving under its genial influence. Our citizens can now in tranquillity enjoy the sweet converse of their families and their connexions, and find a peaceable and safe asylum at their own farms. They are no longer alarmed by terror or suspense, but exercise their different vocations without interruption. No longer are their abodes infested by the bloody-minded ruffian, nor our temples turned into a den of thieves; but benevolence and hospitality mark again our plantations, and respect and piety our places of public worship.

"Were I, gentlemen, to pursue this theme, and enter upon a description of the relative and exalted station you stand on with the other powers of the earth, it is a subject yielding so much rapture to the mind of the Americans, I fear I should be tempted to deviate from my original design. With what transport should I relate the admiration which our success has created in the minds of the distant nations! Behold the honor you are held in by them, and with what ardor they gaze upon the new constellation with which you have enriched the political firmament! See their glorious contention; see how they press to your hospitable shores. Look forward to the immense empire, the work of your hands, that you are creating, and hearken to the loud acclamations of your posterity, re-echoed to you by the azure vault of applauding heaven! These are prospects that attract as they dazzle our fascinated attention. These are scenes that the intenseness of reflexion can never be wearied with! These, these are the rewards of your virtue and bravery!

"But I must leave this subject, though with reluctance, and call your attention to an object of more immediate and of very considerable importance. I have described to you the necessity there was of our citizens assuming the reins of justice, and of inflicting punishment upon the unconvicted offender. I have shown you what your situation is at present compared with a former, and reminded you that peace was once more diffused through our commonwealth. This, then, is a conjuncture in which it is incumbent on us to exert our abilities. Here is room for the heart to conceive, and the understanding to direct. It would be a worse than perfidy united with timidity to desert the state vessel which we have anchored in a safe haven after the perils we have voluntarily endured for her sake, and negligently to suffer her to perish by a fatal indifference to her interests. Should we grow remiss in our duty at this period to the Republic, we sacrifice the dignity of our country, and disgrace will be brought upon us for ever.

"The distressed condition of this country calls loudly for the assistance of its individuals, and we have it now in our power to prevent a longer delay to justice, and the consequent relaxation of our laws. Therefore it becomes the pointed and indispensable duty of each of our citizens to endeavor to re-establish the harmony and order of our community, and to revive the good discipline of its members. We must resolve, then, to renounce the empire of the passions, to correct that licentiousness which has pervaded the State, to resign ourselves to the calm operations of our judgment, and to embrace the temperate admonitions of our reason.

"The distempered emotions which alarmed our breasts, like the threatening meteors of the heavens, shall disappear, and our hearts resume their wonted serenity. But, in a more particular manner does it become you, gentlemen of the grand jury, to second and support the judicial departments in the attainment of this important and desirable end. For you are selected by your country for the rank you hold amongst her citizens, and for the superior understanding attendant on your enlightened stations of life. You officially compose the grand inquest of your district, and are here the representatives and guardians of its inhabitants. It is to you that these, our countrymen, look up for advice to pursue, and for patterns to imitate. Wherefore it lies much in your abilities, as I make no doubt you are excited thereto by your inclinations, to divest them of prejudice, to instil into their minds just and constitutional principles, to hold up examples which may deter them from evil, and to impress them with a proper sense of the duty they owe to their magistrates, and of the implicit obedience they should pay to the laws of their country. Were I to undertake the task of pointing out to you minutely, the respective duties of your office as grand jurors, I should enumerate almost all the civil obligations of society; but, as I am persuaded it will be unnecessary for me to detail these exhortations to you, I will leave you to your own hearts and consciences; the best directors, the most irreproachable monitors of mankind. Nevertheless, there is one division of the duties which fall to your lot, which I must request you to consider with me in the most impartial and dispassionate manner. Let us not deceive ourselves, and vainly imagine, because our enemy is fled, that our dangers are over. I fear we have an enemy of a more pernicious tendency amongst us, whom it will require the most obstinate resolution to overcome. I mean the dominion of the passions, the gratification of our private resentment. It is time, however necessary and politic it was lately to draw a bold and visible line of discrimination between the inhabitants of this country, that such a distinction should now be obliterated, wholly and irrevocably. The terms of Whig and Tory are no longer useful, and the commotions of our country, which gave rise to and supported these denominations, having subsided, these popular characteristics must of course be sunk also into oblivion. I will contend, that there cannot at this moment exist such characters as Tories amongst us; for however willing some men, inveterate in folly, might be, even as yet to be considered in that light, the variation of the condition of our State will not any longer justify the appellation. For that person alone, in my idea, may justly be stigmatized with toryism, who basely taking advantage of the subjugation of the government under which he lived, during the suspension of the laws and the jurisdiction of the criminal and civil courts, who joined the enemies of his country, and revelling in its calamities, being sensible of his security from punishment, exercises a wild and brutal dominion over his fellow-citizens, depriving them illegally of their property, and according to the intemperate dictates of his passions, of their precarious lives. Wherefore, then, since our Government is re-established, our laws in full force, and offenders presented to you for punishment, should we cherish so idle, so unprofitable a discrimination? Is it the quality of a good citizen, or the policy of a wise administration, to render the inhabitants of their country inimical to their Government? Surely not; but if you were industriously to keep up the idea that certain persons amongst you are Tories, what is it but declaring that such men are out of the protection of your laws, and that a citizen would be justified in putting them to death without the ceremonies of a trial? Were this the case, in vain have we contended for the sovereignty of this country, in vain have we attained the independency of our State, for the will of each individual is the sovereignty and independency thereof.

"It may be inquired here, and with propriety, what right have we, as individuals, to inflict punishment upon those who have violated the laws, or have injured us in our persons, or property? None but a bad citizen would revolt at the idea of appealing to the laws of his country; they are our protection and redress. And whoever infringes them, be he distinguished by the title of Whig, or stigmatized with that of Tory, can find no refuge from their justice, no escape from the punishment annexed to their offence. Surely there can be so just distinction drawn between those who violate the laws of a country; but the inhabitants thereof must be subject to their operation equally as to the certain and immutable stroke of death.

"To hear the language which has been held forth upon this subject, one would be naturally led to believe that none but Tories could commit crimes, or, at least, that the same actions, if committed by Whigs, are not only pardonable, but commendable. Away with such trivial distinctions, and let us learn again to consider the transgressor of our laws as the only enemy of our State. Let us reflect calmly and deliberately upon the offences of which these persons stand accused. Black as the catalogue is of rapine and murder, I see no offence which did not exist before the commencement of the present war. And were men, who were familiarly guilty of these crimes, branded at that period with the appellation of Tories? What! were murder and the various offences composing our calendar of felonies, deemed Toryism in that age? And were criminals punishable unheard and uncondemned, by the fiat of an individual, barbed, perhaps, with private revenge? No, gentlemen, however illegal their conduct, however enormous their offences, they still had the benefit of a fair trial. The only reason, the impracticability of making examples of offenders, which could justify the conduct of our citizens during the war, exists no longer. If, therefore, notwithstanding this manifest alteration in our circumstances, there are any who still dare industriously to irritate men's minds by this discrimination, I shall class them with those offenders, artful knaves, who, despairing of mining our commonwealth by the force of arms, sow the secret and insidious seeds of jealousy and suspicion amongst us. These are the detestable weapons of designing men, whose ambition or avarice is not yet stated. They but make a plea of this cant language to embroil again in civil discord our peaceable citizens, that they, forsooth, may once more reap the harvest of our confusion. I cannot take my leave of this subject without reminding you that many of the persons hitherto designated by the title of Tories, and remaining amongst us, have thrown themselves upon the mercy of their country, and are entitled to the benefit of our laws.

"In future, therefore, if any man commits murder, or robs a citizen, or perpetrates any other enormous offence, let him be apprehended, examined before a magistrate, and committed to gaol. Let him take his trial by his compeers, and be condemned by the justice, as well as by the voice of his country. But, if there is any one so lost to his duty as to seek for redress by an extra-judicial vindication of his wrongs, or by any other mode of proceeding more summary than a trial by jury, I will not hesitate to affirm that he is in effect a more dangerous enemy to the constitution of this State than the implacable adversary we have just driven from our shores. But here, then, I must beg leave to assure you that if any citizen has been injured during the late British usurpation over this country, although I will discountenance any man's arrogating satisfaction to himself by force of arms, that I will use every encouragement in my power to bring the offender to trial, and cause him to make exemplary compensation for the injury committed. For the pardon, which such men may have received from the Legislature, extends only to offences against the Government, and by no means to injuries done to individuals. But, above all, let us recollect our national characteristic of humanity, and preserve it untainted in the bosom of peace. The enemy, because we would not rival or countenance them in their barbarities, during the course of a long and bloody war, have uniformly charged us with a want of spirit. And should we not give them just reason to suppose that the charge was well grounded, if, as soon as they who pretend to have been a restraint upon our inclinations, have retreated, we give a loose to the wanton dictates of our passion and revenge? Let us examine what we owe to ourselves as men of sense and humanity, and what is due to the dignity of the State, rather than what such offenders deserve to suffer from our hands for their manifold misdeeds.

"I have already, gentlemen, taken up so much of your time, that I will not delay you longer than to take a cursory view of the duties incumbent on you as a grand jury, and to recapitulate the offences cognizable by you.

"You are entitled, according to the uniform and established custom of this State, to the privilege of first enquiring into the crimes committed within the jurisdiction of this Court. And the oath which has been just administered to you, requires your diligence and activity in investigating the truth of all such matters and things as shall be given you in charge, or shall come to your knowledge, in examining the evidences which are brought against the accused, and in forming a conscientious decision, after mature deliberation, upon the testimony supporting these allegations, or upon the knowledge which you yourselves have respecting the subjects of your inquiry.

"It is then prescribed to you to make a true and just report thereof, for your determination (formed privately amongst yourselves, and in which twelve of your number must indispensably concur to give weight and effect to the indictments) is the great spring that sets in motion all the wheels of prosecution. Your reports furnish the Court with subject-matter to proceed on, are the first means of introducing the citizen into a secure situation, and lay the foundation of bringing offenders to their merited punishment. But it is not to be understood that you are to make so minute an investigation into such matters as are the proper subjects of your inquiry, as to establish the fact itself. You are to find the bill, though founded only on probable grounds of suspicion, that the accused is guilty. For, notwithstanding the Petit Jury cannot exceed the crime laid in your indictment, yet they have the power, nevertheless, of extending it to the least degree of offence that can be in that kind. Your report, therefore, is an information or declaration in favor of the State, founded upon an *ex parte* inquiry against the accused, which precludes the least possible chance of an offender escaping without punishment. And in conformity to that wise maxim which declares, that it is better that ten guilty men should elude the justice of the courts of law, than that one innocent person should suffer unmeritedly, it is likewise preferable that ten guiltless persons should undergo the inconvenience of an examination before you, than that one offender should triumph in his crimes with impunity. Since, therefore, you are authorized to examine only the evidences against the prisoner, and that your verdict can neither acquit nor convict, it is not necessary that you should find the specific crime of which the prisoner stands accused. For instance, if one has by accident killed a person, it does not lie with you to discriminate the degree of offence.

"You are further, gentlemen, obliged by virtue of your oath, to be secret in your councils, and silent upon the reasons of your decisions; unless the Court demand some questions of you. You should not divulge whatever has been debated upon in the course of your business, nor the sentiments which are delivered; nor make public the persons who made use of these arguments, nor the opinions which you yourselves held in discussion of the point in question: for certain it is, that such discovery is accompanied by perjury. The remainder of the oath illustrates with what integrity you ought to conduct yourselves in the execution of your duty.

"You must not suffer your minds to be clouded by the passions, but suppress all emanations of prejudice or malice, and give a full and absolute sway to the dictates of reason and justice. You must not omit presenting for punishment offenders against the law, either through partiality, favor, love, reward, or any expectation thereof.

"This, I confess, is a very difficult task; but, notwithstanding the repugnant impulses of our tender nature, be assured that your oath will cause you to make a free inquiry, and to deliver a just account of the result. For it is also enjoined you to present the truth, the whole truth, and nothing but the truth, according to the best of your skill and knowledge. If, therefore, there is any mental reservation, any concealment of the truth, or any part thereof, any suppression of facts which have come within your own knowledge, you betray the trust which your country has generously committed to your prudence, fidelity, and integrity.

"But, at the same time that you are required to present all that you shall learn relative to the subject of your inquiries, you shall not report anything but what is true; that is, no known falsity, no unjust accusation, which might be the occasion of drawing on an innocent person the suspicion of being criminal, and of subjecting him to the reproaches of his fellow-citizens. For it is as much incumbent on you to protect the virtuous, as to accuse and bring to trial the guilty transgressor.

"If, therefore, it appears to you that the evidences are false, or that the charges appear founded in prejudice and malice, you ought to present such notorious offender. The consideration of this part of your duty, is a sufficient compensation to the generous and humane, for the disagreeable office imposed upon you of pointing out the wicked for the animadversion of the Court, since nothing surely can yield a more substantial gratification to virtuous minds, than the reflection that, besides being naturally possessed of the inclination, the laws of the country have invested them with the power of shielding the weak, unprotected, and honest from the calumnies and unmerited aspersions of the base and flagitious.

"The crimes which are cognizable by you are two-fold: the first are capital, for which the offender loses his life; the second are fineable, to answer which the goods and lands of the guilty are subject, and to the fine is sometimes annexed corporal punishment.

"It will be sufficient, at present, that I only mention to you in general terms, the denominations of the crimes which comprise many more of an inferior degree. The capital offences are felony; the fineable offences are those committed against the public justice, against the public peace, against the public profit, against the public health, and also such as introduce nuisances to the damage and destruction of the property of the good citizens of this State.

"And now, gentlemen, I take my leave of you, congratulating you on the great event, which we have been so instrumental in accomplishing by the succor of divine Providence.

"It is with pleasure we look back upon the difficulties and dangers we have been obliged to undergo in the establishment of our independence, and our perils and labors for the sake of our country, will render it dearer to us. Let us therefore exert ourselves to cherish and preserve that freedom, which has cost us such an expenditure of blood and treasure. Let us emulate those martial efforts of which we now are experiencing the benefits, and endeavor to secure the civil peace, order, and tranquillity of the State. The former have made us a free people; the latter will render us forever happy."

This charge, in the generous feelings and moral courage exhibited, was highly honorable to the character of the judge; and though doubtless, with other efforts of the kind, productive of beneficial results, could not allay the deep feelings of animosity and revenge which had taken possession of many of the people, or save society from the unhappy scenes attending the redress of a varied class of wrongs sustained during the war, which the ordinary administration of justice could not possibly reach. Only the lapse of time could extinguish resentment, and the passing away of the actors in other days, bring repose. For more than a generation the evil was sorely felt.

The grand jury made the following presentments:—

"State of South Carolina.—We, the Grand Jurors for the District of Cheraws, present, as a grievance, the want of a road leading from the Long Bluff Court-house, the most direct way to Camden; also, another road, leading from the Long Bluff Court-house to Murray's Ferry on Santee; likewise, another road leading from Kolb's Ferry to Rain's Bridge on Gum Swamp, to meet a road leading from Cross Creek to that place.

"II. We present, as a grievance, the want of a bridge over Black Creek, on the road leading from the Long Bluff to George-town.

"III. We present, as a grievance, the dangerous navigation of the River Pedee, arising from the great number of logs lodged in the different parts of the same.

"IV. We present, as a very great grievance, the want of the laws now in force in this State to be printed, and the magistrates and other officers to be furnished with the same.

"V. We return our most hearty thanks to his honor, the judge, for his learned charge delivered to the grand jury, and request that it, together with these, our presentments, be printed in the *Gazettes*.

   "George Hicks, *Foreman*.
    Morgan Brown.
    Moses Pearson.
    Richard Brockington.
    Thomas Lide.
    Tristram Thomas.
    Philip Pledger.
    John Pledger.
    Thomas Ellerbe.
    Aaron Daniel.
    Joseph Ellison.
    John Andrews.
    William Ellerbe.
    John Westfield.
    John M'Call."

At the following Session of the Legislature, January, 1784, Thomas Powe was appointed Commissioner of Location for Cheraw District. Under an Act passed to regulate the inspection and exportation of tobacco, the growth and produce of this State, and for other purposes, a warehouse or warehouses were ordered to be established at Cheraw Hill; and Benjamin Hicks, jun., John Westfield, and William Pegues appointed inspectors. The presentments of the Grand Jury of Cheraws, the November previous, called the attention of the Legislature to the important subject of making some provision for improving the navigation of the

Pedee. The matter had been pressed upon it before, but no relief yet afforded. In an ordinance passed on the 26th of March of this session, for appointing commissioners to clear out certain streams, the Great Pedee was included. Benjamin Hicks, sen., George Hicks, Thomas Powe, William Kershaw, and William Pegues, were the commissioners appointed under the same for Cheraws District, and empowered to contract for the removal of all obstructions in the Pedee as high up as the North Carolina line; and for that purpose were authorized to draw on the Treasury for any sum of money not exceeding 300*l.* sterling.

Of the action of the commissioners, nothing is known. The same subject, as will be seen, continued to receive the attention of the Legislature; but, either from the want of adequate appropriations, or the inefficient execution of the work, or other causes perhaps beyond the control of those entrusted with it, the navigation of the river continued to be seriously obstructed until a period long subsequent. By an ordinance passed the following year, for clearing out certain rivers, Benjamin Hicks, sen., George Hicks, Thomas Powe, William Pegues, Captain William M'Cotry, James Grier, Francis Greaves, Colonel John Ervin, Colonel Hugh Giles, Henry Davis, sen., and Archibald Odom, were appointed commissioners for making navigable the Great Pedee from Euhany to the North Carolina line. To defray the expense thereof, they were authorized to assess what further sum might be requisite on all lands, in proportion to their value, as assessed for the payment of the general tax, situated within six miles of the said river, from Euhany to the Warhee Bluff, and within ten miles of said river, from the said Bluff upwards; and on all male inhabitants, from sixteen to fifty years of age, living within six miles of the river, from Euhany to the Warhees, and within ten miles from the Warhees upwards. They were also authorized to make the like assessment afterwards, from time to time, to keep the river navigable. The history of the legislation of the State on this subject, like that of some of its judicial decisions, will be found to have gone through a certain course of changes, returning at last to the plan first adopted, as the courts have done to principles, once established, then modified, and finally made the settled rule of law. Commissioners were first appointed to improve the navigation of the river, then a board of public works, then a general superintendent, and at length, after the failure of these plans to a great extent, commissioners, as at the beginning, the system of all others that has proved most effective.

At an election for the Legislature, held on the 29th and 30th of November, 1784, William Dewitt was returned Senator, and Morgan Brown, Elias Du Bose, Colonel Lemuel Benton, William Pegues, Thomas Powe, and Calvin Spencer, Representatives for St. David's Parish. One of the seats having been subsequently vacated, Tristram Thomas was elected a member for the session of the following year. The Legislature met on the 20th of January. On the 29th of that month, Captain Dewitt, who was sheriff of Cheraws at the time of his election, appeared, and having taken the oath, informed the House of the fact; upon which, it was resolved, that, agreeably to the constitution, he was not qualified to take his seat. Having returned home, and resigned the office of sheriff, he was re-elected, and took his seat in March. Allen Chapman was elected Sheriff, and George Hicks, Robert Lide, and William Thomas, Commissioners of Caveats for Cheraws District.

The Session of 1785 was rendered memorable by the passage of the celebrated County Court Act. As the population of the country extended, the Circuit Court system, established in 1769, was found inadequate to the due and equal administration of justice. To remedy this evil, it was proposed to establish Courts of Inferior Jurisdiction, ofter the model of the County Court system of Virginia and North Carolina. Mr. Justice Pendleton, one of the Associate Judges, and an active member of the House of Representatives (for these offices were not then incompatible) was the able advocate of this scheme. By his influence and strenuous exertions, it was adopted.*

By this Act, it was provided "that the District of Cheraws should be divided into three counties, that is to say,—one county lying and being on the south-east side of

---

*Introduction to Brevard's "Digest," p. xvi.

EXTRACT FROM AN ACCOUNT BOOK

In the store of Bright Williamson, at Mechanicsville, 1804.

Pedee River, bounding on the said river on the one side, the district line of George-town on the other side, and on the other side, the North Carolina boundary, and shall be called and known by the name of Marlborough County; one other county, beginning at the mouth of Cedar Creek, on Pedee River, thence up to the head of the southernmost branch of the said creek, and thence by direct line to the fork of Lynche's Creek, being the upper county of the said northern division of the District, and shall be called by the name of Chesterfield; one other county, beginning at the mouth of Cedar Creek, thence down Pedee to the District line, thence along the said line to Lynche's Creek, thence up the same to the fork, being the lower county of the said division, and shall be called Darlington County." By the 11 sec. of the Act, the Justices of the said counties were empowered to build Court Houses, &c., to cause taxes to be laid for the erection of public buildings, and to select for the same the most convenient part of each county. The County Courts, thus established, were to be held once in every three months, by the justices of the peace of the several counties respectively; and their jurisdiction extended to the hearing and determination of all causes at common law, to any amount where the debt was liquidated by bond or note of hand, or where the damages in certain actions did not exceed fifty pounds, and in other personal actions where the damages did not exceed twenty pounds, or where the titles of land did not come in question. In criminal cases their jurisdiction was extremely limited. The modes of proceeding were prescribed, the forms of process, and the manner of trial. The right of appeal to the superior, or Circuit Courts was provided.*

On the 21st of March, the joint committee of the Senate and House, appointed for that purpose, reported a list of justices for the several counties. For Marlborough, Claudius Pegues, sen., Geo. Hicks, Morgan Brown, Tristram Thomas, Claudius Pegues, jun., Moses Pearson, and Thomas Evans.

For Chesterfield County, Thomas Powe, William Pegues, Benjamin Jackson, William Strother, Calvin Spencer, Joseph Pledger, and Charles Evans.

---

*Introduction to Brevard's "Digest," p. xvi.

For Darlington County, William Dewitt, Lemuel Benton, Zachariah Nettles, James P. Wilson, Elias Du Bose, Robert Lide, and Charles Dewitt.

The office of justice, under this Act, was one of high trust, and much importance. Men of experience and position were selected. The school of the Revolution had brought out conspicuously not a few citizens of solid judgment and unblemished integrity on the Pedee. At no period since, perhaps, in proportion to the population, have as many such characters been known.

For the Court House of Marlborough, a location was first made near Gardner's Bluff, the most of the settlements being then on the river, or in the region adjacent. Afterwards, it was removed lower down, to the site of the old Court House, as it has since been known, on the main river road, above Crooked Creek; and there continued until the extreme unhealthiness of that locality rendered a change necessary, the population also having extended out from the river into the pine lands; and the present county seat, Bennettsville, was selected. For Chesterfield, the site of the present Court House was chosen. For Darlington, there was some difficulty in effecting an agreement among the justices. Col. Benton made strenuous efforts to have the location fixed at Mechanicsville. Elias Du Bose, an influential justice, was as anxious to have Coffee Town, a point on Swift Creek, six miles above the present Court House, selected. As a compromise, the present site, nearly midway between the other two, was chosen. So sparse were the settlements in that neighbourhood, that only a few years before, nothing but an old Indian trail led from that point to Camden. The Courts for Marlborough were to be holden on the 1st Mondays in March, June, September, and December. For Chesterfield, on the 2nd Mondays of the same months; and for Darlington, on the 3rd Tuesdays in January, April, July, and October.

Such records of the County Courts as have been preserved, exhibit but little matter of interest. The country was sorely embarrassed with debt, and suits were numerous. There were many prosecutions in the County Courts, particularly for cow stealing, which appears at that period to

EXTRACT

have been the most frequent crime. The only presentment which has been found, was one made in Chesterfield, March 13, 1787; and the only subject matter of it, certain persons therein named, as having been guilty of offences against the public morals. The grand jury on this occasion, so far as the names appear on the records, consisted of the following persons:—

      Thomas Ellerbe, *Foreman.*
      Wm. Lyons.
      Ephraim Horne.
      Abraham Cook.
      John Evans.
      Thomas Leonard.
      Benjamin Outlaw.
      Jason Meadow.
      Joel Yarborough.
      Joseph Booth.
      Joseph Powell.
      John Blakeney.
      Moses Hollis.
      John Carter.

Many of the records of Chesterfield County remain in a good state of preservation. But few are to be found in the public offices of Marlborough, and unfortunately for the history of justice as administered in Cheraws District, all the Circuit Court records, with those of Darlington County, were destroyed by the burning of the Court House about 1804.* The fire occurred during Court week, and an old woman, who was party to a cause then pending, and whose interest it was to get rid of the records of the Court, was suspected of having been privy to the burning. Beyond this suspicion, however, no clue was ever discovered as to the origin of the conflagration.

---

*A strong wind blew in the direction of the gaol, carrying a burning shingle to the roof and setting it in a blaze. The late John D. Witherspoon, of Society Hill (who related the circumstances to the Author), was present, and being then a young man, and of great activity and decision, rendered very efficient service on the occasion. There being no ladder at hand, he ascended by a smooth pole to the roof of the gaol, and saved it, with the prisoners in it, from destruction. The loss of documentary matter, connected with the history of the Pedee, was irreparable.

The Circuit Court for Cheraws District continued to sit at Long Bluff. The lawyers whose names appear in the records of this period at the Cheraws Bar, were Elihu Hall Bay, Joseph Brevard, Thomas Waties, and Thomas Parker; a few years later those of William Falconer and John Dibble are frequently mentioned, and John Caulkins. By the close of the century a number of others were added to the list.

In 1785 there was no resident lawyer within the bounds of Cheraw District.

The three counties are supposed to have been named, respectively, in honor of the Duke of Marlborough, the Earl of Chesterfield, and Col. Darlington, who distinguished himself in the war of the Revolution.* By the County Court Act, that portion of the Judicial District of Georgetown, now constituting Marion District, was formed into a county under the name of Liberty Precinct, and the site of the present Court House selected. The name was most appropriately given, as in that region, under Marion, the struggle for liberty on the Pedee was chiefly waged.

About this time the name of Greenville appears for the first in the records of the day instead of Long Bluff as before. It was so called in honor of Gen. Green, to whom South Carolina was largely indebted for the successful issue of the struggle which secured her independence.

The St. David's Society, which had been suspended during the latter years of the war, was now revived, and immediately took rank among the most distinguished schools of learning in the State.

From its walls, in subsequent years, went forth those who were to fill the highest positions of usefulness and distinction in Carolina.

The following notice appeared in the *South Carolina Gazette and Public Advertiser* of Aug. 13, 1785:—

"The St. David's Society met on the 23rd ultimo, at Greenville, in the District of Cheraw, and chose the following gentlemen as officers for the year then commencing:— James P. Wilson, Esq., President; William Dewitt, Esq., Vice-President; Thomas Powe, Esq., Treasurer; and Evan-

---
*Mill's "Statistics of So. Ca.," p. 512.

der M'Iver, Secretary. They also appointed the following gentlemen a committee to superintend the erection of suitable buildings, engage tutors, &c. Thomas Powe and William Dewitt, Esqrs., Rev. Edmund Botsford, Mr. Abel Edwards, and Mr. Evander M'Iver. This laudable society, formed for the benevolent purpose of erecting an academy, was instituted in the year 1778; but, owing to the calamities of the late war, had been entirely neglected. However, we hope, from its happy revival, and the very liberal subscriptions already made, that it will soon flourish, and that their intended plans may be prosecuted and carried into effect." In the following year William Pegues, Esq., was elected President, Samuel Wilds, Treasurer, and Enoch Evans, senr., Secretary; which offices the two latter continued to hold for years afterwards.

Andrew M'Culley took charge of the academy in the early part of 1786, and taught until October of the following year. Of Mr. M'Culley nothing more is known than that he appears to have discharged his duties to the satisfaction of the society. He was succeeded for a short time by Ezekiel Hitchcock, who had probably been his assistant.

Eli King was Principal for three years, beginning with 1788. He was from New England, and a friend of Thomas Park, who succeeded him in 1791. Samuel Wilds assisted Mr. King in 1788, and was afterwards, for a time, the Principal. Mr. King, after giving up the school, embarked in mercantile pursuits. Thomas Park had charge of St. David's from 1791 to 1800. About that time he engaged with Mr. King in business. Better fitted, however, for teaching than merchandizing, their enterprise proved a failure. Mr. Park then took charge of the academy at Ebenezer, in the lower part of Darlington, and was transferred from that position, upon the organization of the South Carolina College, to the Professorship of Languages, having been elected in November, 1806. There he continued in the uninterrupted discharge of duty until 1834-5. He was then elected Treasurer and Librarian of the College, and faithfully discharged the duties of these offices until his death in 1844, in the 79th year of his age. Mr. Park was a native of Uxbridge, Massachusetts, and graduated at Brown University, Providence, R. I., in 1791. In the latter part of that year he came to the Pedee. Without experience as a teacher, but with a well-trained mind, correct scholarship, particularly in the ancient classics, and conscientious devotion to duty never surpassed, he entered at once upon that highly useful and most successful career as a teacher of youth, which was only to terminate with his declining strength more than forty years afterwards. With neither genius nor learning, few men did more than Thomas Park for the education of the youth of Carolina, and no one ever retired from a position so difficult to fill, whether in the academy or the college, with a larger share of the confidence and affection of those with whom he had been connected. A just and beautiful tribute has been paid to his character and services by Professor Laborde in his History of the South Carolina College. It was a tribute richly deserved, and touchingly rendered by the writer of that work. Mr. Park was succeeded in St. David's by the Rev. Frame Wood, who continued in charge until 1804. He was followed by Enoch Hanford in 1804-5, and the latter by Elias Jones in 1806-7.

After the revival of St. David's, in 1785, it continued to flourish. Public examinations were held annually, and committees appointed to act on such occasions. The exhibitions of the pupils excited much interest in the country around for a considerable distance, and were numerously attended. The records of its early history would serve as a model for many of the academies of more recent times, which, though more pretentious, are not so thoroughly conducted as was this noted school of old.

In 1795, an Act was passed by the Legislature, providing that all the confiscated property to which the State was then entitled in the Circuit Court District of Cheraws, as also all the property already escheated, or which might thereafter escheat, should be invested in the incorporated society of St. David's.

Death had already hade sad havoc among the members of the society. Between the years 1780 and 1788, the following, as entered on the records, had died, viz.:—General Alexander M'Intosh, Colonel Thomas Lide, Abel Wilds,

William Terrell, Thomas Evans, sen., Joshua Edwards, Colonel Abel Kolb, Thomas James, Captain Philip Pledger, Richard Hodge, Charles Mason, Joshua Terrell, Captain Edward Jones, Philip Singleton, William Blassingame, Rev. John Conner, Adam Cusack, Hugh Jones, Benjamin Williamson, Captain Edmund Irby, Charles Irby, Captain George King, Captain Simon Connell, and John Thompson.

The following members were dismissed from the society at their own request, for the most part, doubtless, because of the distance at which they lived, rendering it inconvenient to attend the meetings:—May 3rd, 1787—Benjamin Rogers, Colonel George Hicks, Colonel Lemuel Benton, Captain William Pegues; May 1st, 1788—Major Robert Lide, Captain Thomas Ellerbe, William Ellerbe, Captain Benjamin Hicks, Josiah Evans; May 6th, 1790—Alexander Craig, David Roach, Jesse Wilds; June 18th, 1791—William Thomas; August 6th, 1792—Rev. Evan Pugh, and Major John Kimbrough.

The following were members after 1788:—Daniel Sparks, Rev. Elhanan Winchester, William Dewitt, Rev. Evan Pugh, Nathanael Saunders, John Hodge, Abel Edwards, Thomas Powe, John O'Neal, William Thomas, Jeremiah Brown, John Kimbrough, Peter Allston, Charles Gee, Claudius Pegues, James Blassingame, John M'Call, David Roach, Jethro Moore, Alexander Craig, Robert Gibson, Moses Pearson, Rev. Edmund Botsford, Morgan Brown, Evander M'Iver, James P. Wilson, Maurice Murphy, Peter Kolb, Benjamin James, Tristram Thomas, Jesse Wilds, Benjamin Kolb, Thomas Evans, Enoch Evans, sen., Enoch Evans, jun., Samuel Wilds, Edward Duke, Henry Clark, and William Falconer.

The cause of religion partook largely of the general depression caused by the troubled state of things during the Revolution. After the resignation of Mr. Winchester, in September, 1779, the Rev. Edmund Botsford took charge of the Welch Neck Church. Mr. Botsford was very highly esteemed. He remained until the 1st June, 1780, when, upon the threatened approach of the British troops, he went to Virginia; returning to Pedee, however, in 1782. During his absence, the church was supplied a part of the time by the Rev. Joshua Lewis, an excellent man, who long continued his faithful labors in this region. It is mentioned in the records of the church, that of the 220 white members left by Mr. Winchester in September, 1779, only 48 remained in March, 1793, showing the sad havoc of death, and the unhappy results of a protracted war.

In 1798, the inhabitants on the river very generally gave up their plantations as residences, and retired to the hills in the neighbourhood of the present village. About the same time, a movement was made to abandon the spot which had been consecrated as a place of religious worship for nearly three quarters of a century, and erect a suitable building on Society Hill.

Before the close of the century it was probably done. The records of the church, for a few years following 1798, were lost or destroyed, and no account remains of the completion of this design.

The first building erected after the removal was near the St. David's Academy, and remained for almost half a century. The more imposing structure of the present day is upon a spot very near the original site. Sad are the changes which time brings with it. The signs of progress are linked with the memorials of decay. The associations of the past it is well to cherish—and let the earlier days of the old Welch Neck never be forgotten.

Shortly before, and soon after the Revolution, some valuable accessions were made to the population of Cheraw District.

The Rev. Timothy Dargan settled on Jeffrey's Creek, in charge of a church there, prior to the year 1780.* He was a native of Virginia, but came to South Carolina in his youth, and in the early part of his life bore a commission in the Provincial troops, which were raised for the defence of the Province during the French and Indian wars. He remained on Jeffrey's Creek until his death, in 1783. He was the grandfather of the late Chancellor Dargan, of Darlington.

Colonel John Smith settled in Darlington District after

---

*Wood Furman's "History of the Charleston Association," p. 78.

VIEWS AT SOCIETY HILL.

1. *Welch Neck Baptist Church.*
2. *Gateway to Governor D. R. Williams's Home.*
3. *Library Building.*
4. *Judge Wilds's Tomb, Baptist Church Cemetery.*
5. *Judge Wilds's First Law Office.*

the war. He was a native of Maryland, and served during the Revolution in the Maryland line. He distinguished himself in the battles of Monmouth and Hobkirk's Hill, and in the disastrous conflict at Camden, where he was taken prisoner with De Kalb. When General Washington accepted the command of the army, in 1798, during the impending difficulties with France, Mr. Smith received the appointment of colonel, which he accepted at the earnest solicitation of the commander in chief.* Colonel Smith filled several offices of honor and trust in Darlington, and was highly respected to the close of his life. He left no descendants bearing his name. Andrew and Ralph, two brothers, followed him to Pedee. Colonel Andrew Smith also served in the Maryland line. He was a prominent merchant in the early history of the town of Cheraw, and died there. Ralph Smith settled and died in Marion.

Captain Campbell, who had been an officer in the British service, settled in Marlborough, and continued to reside there until his death. The family became prominently connected with this region. His sons, Robert and John, who were gentlemen of amiable traits and large popularity, became distinguished, having both been members of Congress from the Pedee District.

Gavin Witherspoon removed, after the war, to Darlington. He was a true soldier of the Revolution, having served under Marion. Many incidents are related of his prowess. The late John D. Witherspoon, so well known in Darlington, was his son.

The name of William Falconer, afterwards so distinguished on the Pedee, appears about this period. He was a native of Scotland, and educated in or near Glasgow. Mr. Falconer came first to Charles-town, as amanuensis for a Scotchman, Dr. Black, a man of some literary attainment, but blind. In 1785, William Falconer advertised in the Charles-town papers as writing master, not, as it would be now-a-days, a professor of penmanship. His aspiring genius, not content with such a position, soon looked in another direction, and in 1787 his name appears as an attorney in

---

*Mill's "Statistics of So. Ca.," p. 517.

the records of Cheraw District. He settled first at Long Bluff, and soon afterwards married a daughter of Thomas Powe, selecting a home four miles above Society Hill, in Chesterfield, where he continued to reside. Mr. Falconer became a prominent member of St. David's Society, and the leader of the Bar on Pedee. His career as a lawyer and public man was one of marked success, as will appear hereafter.

Major Drury Robertson came to Marlborough after the war, and was prominent there for many years, taking a leading part in the affairs of that district. He was a maternal grandfather of the late Colonel William T. Ellerbe, of Marlborough.

The name of Alexr. Craig appears in the records of Chesterfield during the Revolution. His brother, John Craig, then quite young, was long after known as a worthy man and useful citizen, having been connected for many years with the Court of Common Pleas, and Ordinary for that district. He married a Miss Chapman, and reared a large family, the most of whom, or their descendants, yet reside in Chesterfield.

Allen and John Chapman emigrated shortly after the Revolution, from Westmoreland, Virginia, to Chesterfield. The former was a trooper in the Virginia line during the war. He settled first in the lower part of the district, and afterwards moved a few miles above Cheraw, where he lived and died. His first wife was a daughter of Thomas Powe. He afterwards married Eleanor, a daughter of Captain William Dewitt, and reared a large family, as did his brother John. They were useful and respected citizens.

Baron de Poelnitz, moved by the spirit of his distinguished countrymen, Kosciusco, Pulaski, and others, came from Poland, to join the American standard in the cause of freedom. He made a large purchase of land on the Pedee,* and soon after the war, settled on the east side of the

---

*The nut-grass, now so formidable an enemy of many of the planters in this region, is said to have been first brought by William Allston, to the place which Baron de Poelnittz afterwards purchased.

The first English settlers brought the hawthorn with them for hedges. Some remains of it are yet to be seen in certain localities on the river.

river, in the lower part of Marlborough. He came up the river, with his effects, in a boat from George-town. The baron had three sons—Charles, Alexander, and John. The first died early. His only daughter, Elizabeth, is said to have been a very beautiful and accomplished lady. She married, first Charles Stuart, then Colonel Thomas Evans, and finally became the wife of Robeson Carlos. Mr. Carlos emigrated from Virginia to Pedee about 1790, and was a prominent and useful man. Baron de Poelnitz died about the close of the century. None of his descendants, who bear the name, remain on the Pedee.

William Harllee, the first of the name who came to Carolina, was, in early life, a captain in the British navy. He took an active part in the rebellion of the Stuarts in 1745, and was forced to emigrate to America. He settled in Richmond County, North Carolina, near the State line. His son Thomas came to Marion about the close of the century, and was the father of the late Colonel David S. Harllee, of Cheraw, and other members of the family, who have been prominent citizens of Marion.

Soon after 1790, Adam Marshall settled at Long Bluff. He had previously taught school on Poke Swamp, in Marion. He married, in May, 1791, Mary, a daughter of Captain James Gregg. Mr. Marshall entered upon a successful career as a merchant, and amassed a large fortune. He died in Charles-town, where he had gone on a visit of business.

John Punch, in 1793, and Drs. Oliver Hawes and Miles King, were soon after added to this community. Dr. Hawes came from Wrentham, Massachusetts, and married Mary Lee, of George-town. He secured an extensive practice, and was esteemed for all those virtues which adorn the life of the man and citizen. A Federalist by early sympathy, he took an active part in the political excitements which followed this period. Dr. Hawes was for years President of the St. David's Society. His useful life was brought to a close in 1821.

After the war, George and William Strother settled near Cheraw Hill. They were sons of Charles Strother, who emigrated, at an early period, from Virginia to Charleston, where he continued to reside, though interested in, and giving some assistance to, St. David's Parish. During the Revolution, George Strother was an officer in Capt. Thomas Ellerbe's company. Soon after, he married a daughter of Captain Ellerbe. Mrs. Strother survived her husband many years. William, the other brother, after residing some time in Charles-town, moved to Cheraw, and married a third wife, Lucy Hicks, who survived him. She afterwards went, with her children, to Alabama.

CHAPTER XVIII.

Senators and representatives elected for St. David's—Justices appointed for the three counties—Other elections—Ordinance for opening navigation of Lynche's and Black Creeks—Commissioners for same—Results of these efforts—Number in Pedee and Cheraw Regiments—Delegates from St. David's to Convention in Charles-town to ratify Federal Constitution—Vote of St. David's—Petition to Legislature from Cheraws for a circulating medium—Senator and representatives elected for St. David's, October, 1788—Petition from Cheraws for light troop of horse—Proceedings thereon—Officers of same—Delegates from St. David's to Convention for framing new State Constitution—Elections, and justices appointed, for Cheraws District—Senators and representatives elected—County Court system re-modelled—County Court Judges appointed, and Justices of Peace—Act for opening navigation of the Pedee, and Lynche's and Black Creeks—Commissioners for same—Exhibition of St. David's Academy—Death of Dr. James P. Wilson—Equity circuits established—That for Cheraws—Population of Cheraws District—Representatives elected for the three counties—Petition as to the paper medium, and action thereon—County Judges elected, and other officers—Colonel Benton in Congress—Tristram Thomas elected brigadier-general—Colonel Benton resigns in consequence—Inhabitants of Cheraws meet about Jay's Treaty—Great freshets in Pedee—Embankments on the river—Representatives elected—Petition for navigation of Lowder's Lake—Commissioners—Results—Regiments of Cheraw Brigade—Petition as to inspectors of beef, &c., at George-town, and result—County Judges elected—Petition for canal from Roger's Lake to Pedee, and result—Petition of Robert Ellison—Elections for Cheraws District—Legislative canvass in Darlington—Elections for Legislature—William Falconer—County Courts abolished—Circuit Courts established—Officers elected for the three districts—Dividing line between Chesterfield and Darlington—Canvass for Legislature in Darlington—Samuel Wilds—Elections for Legislature—Chesterfield regimental return—Cheraw Brigade—Colonel Spencer—Account of, and anecdote—Town of Cheraw—History of—Name of Chatham dropped—Its later history—Population of Cheraws District—Citizens commemorate death of Washington—Account of Mr. Pugh—Cheraws District passes away—William Falconer, notice of, letter to Alexander Craig, and death.

AMID the blessings of peace and returning prosperity, the country was henceforth to progress, and a settled course of legislative administration to be adopted. The preceding forms of government having been of a temporary character, important constitutional changes were to be made. In November, 1786, William Thomas was elected Senator; and Calvin Spencer, Robert Baxter, Morgan Brown, Andrew Hunter, Lemuel Benton, and William Strother, Representatives for St. David's. Mr. Thomas was opposed for the

Senate by Dr. James P. Wilson. With the exception of Morgan Brown, the members elect took their seats in January following. In March, the following justices were appointed, viz.:—for Marlborough, Hon. William Thomas, Colonel Thomas Lide, William Easterling, and Samuel Brown; for Chesterfield, Thomas Ellerbe, Samuel Taylor, Robert Lowry, and David Perkins; for Darlington, John M'Call, Robert Brounfield, Albert Fort, Robert Allison, and Enoch Evans. Some of the justices, formerly appointed, retained their positions. At this session, Benjamin Rogers was elected Sheriff for Cheraws District, and Lemuel Benton, Escheator. A petition was presented to the House from sundry inhabitants in the Counties of Marlborough and Chesterfield, for the establishment of a ferry between Long Bluff and Cheraw Hill. An ordinance was passed, March 27, for opening the navigation of Lynche's and Black Creeks. For the former, James Marshall, John Dick, Elias Du Bose, Roger Wilson, Daniel Du Bose, John Smith, Zachariah Nettles, Robert Ellison, John Day, Josiah Cookfield, Lewis Harrall, James Brown, Austin Stone, John James, John Piggott, Robert Carter, James Snow, and William Goddard, were appointed Commissioners. For Black Creek, Henry Cannon, John Peoples, James Williamson, Michael Russell, William M'Muldrough, Andrew Hunter, Albert Fort, John Powell, William Williams, John King, and Edward Cooper. In the absence of better facilities for transportation, especially in the case of the inhabitants residing on Lynche's Creek, the navigation of these streams, it was supposed, would be a great public benefit. No important advantages, however, were obtained. This and other efforts in the same direction, show, at least, that the work of internal improvements was not neglected.

According to the general return of the militia of the State, as reviewed in 1787 and 1788, of the brigade, embracing Berkeley and Craven Counties, the Pedee Regiment, Colonel John Baxter, numbered 1000, and the Cheraw Regiment, Colonel Lemuel Benton, the same.

At the session of the Legislature, January, 1788, the same members appeared as the year previous for St. David's. The most important subject brought up for consideration at

WILLIAMSON'S BRIDGE ON BLACK CREEK.

Site of Ferry where Skirmish Between Benton's Forces and the Tories Occurred.

this session was the ratification of the Federal Constitution, adopted in September of the previous year by a convention of delegates assembled in Philadelphia for that purpose.

It was resolved, that elections should be held in April, for delegates (to consist of a number equal to that of the senators and representatives from the several districts and parishes respectively), to meet in Charles-town the following May. For St. David's Parish, the following gentlemen were elected delegates to this convention, viz.:—Colonel Lemuel Benton, Major Tristram Thomas, Captain William Dewitt, Captain Calvin Spencer, Captain S. Taylor, Doctor R. Brownfield, and Benjamin Hicks, jun.* The Legislature adjourned on the 29th of February, to meet in Charles-town 7th of October.

The delegates met in convention the 12th of May. On a motion for the ratification of the Federal Constitution, it was carried by a vote of 149 to 73—the delegates from St. David's voting in the affirmative. Major Thomas was absent. On a motion made by Mr. Justice Burke, and seconded by Major Snipes, to restrict the re-eligibility of the president of the United States after the first term, the vote of St. David's was in the negative.

At the meeting of the Legislature in October, Major Thomas presented a petition, signed by John Pledger, William Standard, and many others, in these words, viz.:—"The petition of the inhabitants of Cheraws District, humbly sheweth, that your petitioners labour under many and great grievances, for the want of a circulating medium to enable us to discharge our debts; for the want of which, many of our fellow-citizens have had their property seized and sold at sheriff's sale, not to the amount of one-tenth of its value, and many others are expecting the same fate. We, your petitioners, therefore humbly pray, that your honorable body will take our distresses into your serious consideration, and pass a law, that the creditor shall take the

---

*The election was held for St. David's on the 10th April, at Kimbrough's Mill, afterwards known as Gibson's Mill, on the road from Society Hill to Georgetown; on 11th April at Chesterfield, C. H.; on the 12th at Marlborough, C. H. William Pegues, Lemuel Benton, and Tristram Thomas were the managers appointed to conduct the election at the several places named.

property of his debtor at its value; or strike a circulating medium, and exchange it for indents, and that the medium shall be received by sheriffs at their sales; or that you will grant us such other relief, as to you, in your wisdom, shall seem meet, &c."

The Act which had been passed in 1785, to establish a medium of circulation by way of loans, afforded only temporary advantages. It caused the ruin of many, and the public suffered seriously in the end.* Hence the petition of the inhabitants of Cheraws.

At the November election, 1788, for St. David's, Morgan Brown was returned Senator; and Robert Ellison, Charles Evans, Thomas Evans, Robert Brownfield, Drury Robertson, and Henry Cannon, Representatives. The Legislature met in January, and continued to sit about three months. During the session, a petition was presented to the Governor from several of the inhabitants of Cheraws District, setting forth, "that the good citizens in these extreme parts of the State are much exposed to the depredations of horse-thieves, and other violators of the laws, which are thereby rendered less vigorous, and are more contemned than is consistent with the welfare and safety of those who live under their protection. That infantry, of whom the militia is composed, have, from the tardiness of their motions, been found by the experience of many years, insufficient to apprehend and bring to justice many depredators, who therefore act almost at discretion, with impunity; that there are several instances of notorious offenders, after search warrants and other precepts have been issued against them, exulting, nevertheless, in their crimes, and openly threatening the murder and destruction of peaceable citizens; who yet, for want of a force sufficient to apprehend them, elude the punishment which, in such cases, the law provides. That your petitioners humbly conceive, that an independent, volunteer troop of horse, composed of the inhabitants, properly accoutred, subject to the command of their own officers, and commissioned by the Commander-in-Chief, would contribute much to remove, if not entirely to pre-

---

*Introduction to Brevard's "Digest," p. xvii.

vent, the aforesaid grievances, and others of the like nature. That several of the principal inhabitants have agreed to form themselves into such a troop, to consist of a captain, two lieutenants, a cornet, and forty privates; and have elected Samuel Taylor, captain, to command them; and have also agreed, that from and immediately after their officers shall have been commissioned, as aforesaid, they will, with all possible despatch, co-operate with and assist within their own district, each and every officer of this State in the legal discharge of his or their duty, when thereunto required. Wherefore, your petitioners humbly pray your Excellency to establish the said troop of horse, by the name of the Chatham Light Horse; to commission the aforesaid Samuel Taylor, captain; Holden Wade, 1st lieutenant; Benjamin Hicks, sen., 2nd lieutenant; and Thomas Godfrey, cornet, to command the same, &c."

          Signed by

Thomas Powe	Leml. Cox Jepson
Samuel Taylor	Nathan Leavensworth
Holden Wade	Benjamin Rogers, jun.
Benjamin Hicks	Alexander Powe
Thomas Godfrey	William Powe
William Pegues	George Hicks
Allen Chapman	Claudius Pegues, sen.
William Falconer	Claudius Pegues, jun.
Frederick Fort	Duncan M'Rae
Erasmus Powe	Thomas Ellerbe
Benjamin Hicks, jun.	William Ellerbe.
Alexander Craig	

Whereupon, the Governor, Thomas Pinckney, made the following communication to the Upper House:—

"Mr. President, and Honorable Gentlemen of the
                      "Senate.

"Honorable Gentlemen:

"As it does not appear to me that the Executive is vested by the existing militia law, with power to grant the prayer of the petition, which accompanies this communication, and as I think the establishment desired would be beneficial, I have referred the matter to the determination of the Legislature.

"THOMAS PINCKNEY.

"Charles-town, 17th Jany., 1789."

The foregoing was referred to a committee, consisting of Mr. Brown, Mr. Walker, and Colonel Hampton; and in the House, to a committee, consisting of Mr. Justice Grimke, Mr. Waties, Dr. Irvine, with the members for St. David's.

Favorable action was taken, and the troop organized, much, doubtless, to the relief of the good citizens of Pedee, and the increase of the military ardor of the people.

Another matter, affecting the interests of some of the inhabitants of Cheraws, as well as the public at large, came before the Legislature, under a petition, setting forth, "that a tobacco inspection, on the north-east side of the Pedee River, about ten miles above Cheraw Hill, at the head of navigation, would be a considerable advantage to the State, there being a large quantity of tobacco made on that side of the river; and the inconveniency of crossing to the Cheraw Hill, occasions it to be carried to Cross Creek. We, therefore, recommend Parker's Ferry as a convenient place, and William Pegues, Thomas Powe, and Claudius Pegues, jun., Esqrs., for commissioners; and as the proprietor will build warehouses, and furnish scales and weights at his own expense, we hope that your honorable body will establish it there, &c."

Signed by

Thomas Powe
William Pegues
Allen Chapman
Claudius Pegues, sen.
Claudius Pegues, jun.

George Hicks
Tristram Thomas
Samuel Taylor
Lemuel Benton
William Thomas.

The committee reported favorably, and an Act was passed accordingly. At this session, the important subject of a new State Constitution was agitated, resulting in the determination of the Legislature that an election should be holden on the 26th and 27th of October ensuing, for delegates to a convention, to meet in Columbia, on the 2nd Monday in May, 1790, to consider the matter of the said Constitution. For St. David's Parish, Calvin Spencer, Benjamin Hicks, Lemuel Benton, Robert Ellison, Charles Evans, Morgan Brown, and Rev. Evan Pugh were duly elected delegates.

At the session of 1789, Lemuel Benton was elected Sheriff for Cheraws District, and Benjamin Hicks, Clerk of the Court of Common Pleas. And the following Justices, viz.:—for Marlborough, Drury Robertson; for Chesterfield, Duncan M'Rae and John Brown; for Darlington, Alexander M'Intosh and Absolom Sauls. Robert Baxter, one of the Representatives from St. David's, died during the session.

At a meeting of the Legislature, Jan. 1790, Henry Cannon and Charles Evans appear to have been the only members present from St. David's. On the 20th of Jan. the following County Court Justices were appointed:—for Darlington, Samuel Mathis, Henry Cannon, and Dr. Robert Norris.

The Convention met in Columbia in May. The Constitution was adopted on the 3rd of June. It gave the Counties of Marlborough, Chesterfield, and Darlington two representatives each, and for the three, two senators. At the ensuing election, Morgan Brown and Robert Ellison were returned Senators. Thomas Evans and John Jones James, Representatives for Marlborough. Thomas Powe and Charles Evans for Chesterfield. John Huggins and Moses Fort for Darlington. John M'Ree was elected Representative for Liberty. The Legislature met on the 4th Monday in Nov. Under the classification of the Senators elect, which had been adopted, Morgan Brown took his seat for four, and Mr. Ellison for two years. During this session, an Act was passed, remodelling the County Court system. "Three Judges or Justices of the County Courts were chosen for each county, by joint ballot of the two Houses of the Legislature, to preside in the respective Courts, which were held semi annually for the trial of causes; but they were allowed no compensation for their services. Two intermediate courts were holden annually, for the transaction of business relating to roads, taverns, and the poor.

"Although the administration of justice in these Courts was irregular, and in many instances unequal, owing chiefly to the want of legal information in those who were appointed to preside therein, yet they were a great convenience to the community, considering the defects of the Circuit Court system of that day; and much good, as well as some evil, resulted from their establishment. It was an important step towards the attainment of that improved system which afterwards existed."*

The number of justices for each county, being now limited to three, the position became correspondingly responsible and important.

In Jan. 1791, the Legislature elected, as County Court Judges, for

Marlborough, Morgan Brown, Tristram Thomas, and William Thomas.

For Chesterfield, Wm. Pegues, Thos. Powe, and Calvin Spencer.

For Darlington, Robert Ellison, Lemuel Benton, and John Smith.

And as Justices of Quorum and the Peace,

For Marlborough.

Geo. Hicks
Thos. Evans
Drury Robertson
Moses Pearson
John Wilson
Samuel Brown
Wm. Easterling
Richard Brockington
William Legg

For Chesterfield.

Samuel Taylor
Charles Evans
Wm. Strother
Robert Lowry
David Perkins
Christopher Vernon
Thos. Blakeney
Wm. Powe
Benjamin Rogers

For Darlington.

John B. Turner
Absolom Sauls
John M'Call
Albert Fort
Henry Cannon
Alexander M'Intosh
Wm. M'Muldrough
L. Stanley, jun.
Wm. Dewitt

*Brevard's "Introduction," p. xvi.

On the 15th of January, the House was informed by Thos. Powe, one of the members elect for St. David's, that he declined taking his seat; and a new election was thereupon ordered. Lemuel Benton was elected Sheriff for Cheraws District. At this session, an Act was passed for improving the navigation of certain streams. Among others, Great Pedee River, and Lynche's, Black, Jeffrey's and Cat Fish Creeks. Tristram Thomas, Morgan Brown, Wm. Pegues, Baron de Poelnitz, Alexander M'Intosh, Moses Pearson, Wm. Strother, Nathanael Saunders, Samuel Benton, Thomas Evans, and Richard Brockington, were appointed Commissioners for the work on the Great Pedee, from the North Carolina line down to the mouth of Black Creek, under the name of the Upper Board of Commissioners on Pedee. The Lower Board, from the mouth of Black Creek to Euhaney Ferry, consisted of William Wilson, John M'Kee, Moses Murphy, Gavin Witherspoon, John Witherspoon, John Dozier, John Porter, Shadrach Simons, John Gregg, Thos. Benton, Abel Goodman, and Jas. Green.

For Black Creek, from its mouth up to the Fork, the Commissioners appointed, were Lawtermore Edwards, Wm. M'Muldrough, Andrew Hunter, Henry Cannon, John King, John Saunders, and Albert Fort. For Lynche's Creek, from the plantation of Capt. Charles Evans, down to the Effingham Mills, to be known as the Upper Board; Needham Lee, Daniel Du Bose, John Castle, John Huggins, James Marshall, Charles Evans, George Evans, John Pigot, Elias Du Bose, and Absolom Sauls. And from the Effingham Mills to the mouth of the Creek, as the Lower Board, were William Goddard, Austin Stone, John Saunders, Lewis Harrall, John Smith, Robert Ellison, John James, James Brown, Isaiah Cookfield, Zachariah Cato, and Zachariah Nettles.

Saturday, 18th of June, of this year, was a day famous in the history of the St. David's Society. The exhibition of the students attracted a very large audience, gathered for a distance from the country around, and was said to have surpassed any ever witnessed before. On the 27th of July, this society lost one of its active and prominent members, and Cheraw District a useful citizen, in the person of Dr.

James P. Wilson. He died at his residence, Long Bluff.*

In 1791, the Circuit Court for the District of Cheraws, was, by Act† of Assembly, ordered to be holden at "The Cheraws." This, however, was not done. The Court continued to sit at Greenville, as before. In the same year, it was enacted,‡ that the Court of Equity, hitherto sitting in Charles-town, should be held at Columbia, for the Districts of Camden, Orangeburg, and Cheraw. In 1799, the State was divided into four Equity Circuits. Of these, the Northern was composed in part of Marlborough, Chesterfield, and Darlington, the Court for which was to be held at Greenville. At the meeting of the Legislature in November, the following Justices of the Peace, &c., were appointed, viz.:—for Marlborough, Geo. Cherry; and for Darlington, Robert Lide, John Huggins, Evander M'Iver, and Elias DuBose. The census of the State was taken in 1792; and the return of population for Cheraw District, was as follows:—

Free white males of 16 years and upwards	1779
" " " under 16 years	1993
" " females, including heads of families	3646
All other free persons	59
Slaves	3229
Total	10,706

In October of this year, Robert Ellison, whose term as senator had expired, was re-elected. And, as Representatives, for

Marlborough,
John Jones James,   Benjamin Hicks.
Chesterfield,
Wm. Falconer,   Wm. Pegues.
Darlington,
Alexander M'Intosh,   John Smith.

---

*The funeral of Dr. Wilson took place on Sunday. The Rev. Edmund Botsford preached, on the occasion, an appropriate discourse, from 1 Cor. vii. 29.
†"Statutes at Large," p. 261.
‡Ibid., p. 288.

The Legislature met on the 4th Monday in November, and on the 3rd of December, Mr. Ellison presented a Petition from sundry inhabitants of Cheraw District, praying the passage of a law, for extending the time limited for the payment of the paper medium loaned to the petitioners, who had suffered so much in their crops by the extraordinary drought and freshets which had prevailed during the previous summer, as to deprive them of the means of discharging the same. It was referred to a Committee, consisting of Mr. Ellison, General Barnwell, and General Pinckney, who reported favorably; and a bill was introduced and passed accordingly. At the session of the following year, 1793, the same members appeared for St. David's, and took their seats. For Liberty, John Baxter, and Gavin Witherspoon for west part of Liberty. Alexander Craig was elected County Judge for Chesterfield in place of Samuel Taylor, who had left the country; and Wm. Falconer, in place of Christopher Vernon, who declined serving. For Marlborough, Benjamin Hicks, in the room of Morgan Brown. Robert Ellison was elected Sheriff, and Alexander M'Intosh, Commissioner of Locations for Cheraws.

Col. Benton was now in Congress, the first representative in that body from the Pedee District. His political sentiments were very decided, and honestly and fearlessly maintained on all occasions. In certain traits of character he was not unlike his near relative, the late Senator Benton, of Missouri. Col. Benton was one of the party violently opposed to the administration of John Adams. He returned from Philadelphia in the latter part of April, 1794, to become involved for a time in a warm personal controversy. An extra session of the Legislature had been called to meet in Charleston, in May. A few days after it opened Major Tristram Thomas was elected General of the Cheraw Brigade. Col. Benton felt this very keenly, his friends attributing it to the fact of his absence, and to the use of unfair means on the part of his opponent. General Thomas, however, was worthy of the position and of all honor, receiving a reward justly due for his past services. It was a matter deeply to be regretted, that these gentlmen, who had so lately fought side by side for their country, should thus have been brought into antagonism, and especially as to a point so deeply touching the sensibilities of an old soldier as that of military precedence. Col. Benton resigned his command of the Cheraw Regiment, and was succeeded by Calvin Spencer. An election having been ordered, April 30th, to fill the place of senator, made vacant by the resignation of Mr. Ellison, who had been elected sheriff, Thomas Powe was returned, and took his seat at the meeting of the Legislature in Charleston.

On the 8th of August a large number of the citizens of Cheraws District met at the Court House, to consider the matter of Mr. Jay's celebrated treaty. Of the result of their action no record remains.

On the 18th of August there was a destructive freshet in the Pedee. The river was higher than had been known since 1776. In the latter part of May of that year many of the inhabitants were forced to abandon their residences in the swamp, and fly for safety to the highlands. That rise was the greatest known since the settlement of the country, of which traditional accounts were handed down to a recent period. There has been some like it since. In January, 1796, another memorable rise occurred. It was not until a period long subsequent that attention began to be turned to the important subject of embankments. The means of the earlier settlers, however, were not equal to works of that kind on a large scale. The late Gen. D. R. Williams, of Darlington, is believed to have led the way in this kind of enterprise. He constructed very extensive embankments, which have proved of incalculable value since.

In October of this year (1794) some very serious trouble (probably insurrectionary) was anticipated, and a strong guard stationed at Long Bluff. Of the history of it, however, nothing more is known.

At the Fall elections the following representatives were returned, viz.: for

Marlborough,	Chesterfield,	Darlington,
John Jones James.	Wm. Falconer.	Richard Brockington.
Drury Robertson.	James Blakeney.	Ezekiel DuBose.

At the ensuing session of the Legislature Gen. Thomas

presented a petition from sundry inhabitants of Darlington, for opening and making navigable Lowder's Lake, from Herring Creek to the mouth thereof. A favorable report was made on the subject, and an Act passed appointing Richard Brockington, Wm. Brockington, George M'Call, and Charles Dewitt, commissioners for carrying the same into effect. This legislation resulted in no material benefit. The work, if begun, is supposed to have been abandoned soon after. At this session £1000 were appropriated for repairing the Court House, and the erection of a new gaol at Long Bluff.

Thomas Evans was elected County Judge for Marlborough in place of Wm. Thomas, resigned.

Of the militia of the State, now divided into nine brigades, that of Cheraw, being No. 9, consisted of three regiments, viz. :—

> The 37th, Col. Thomas Evans.
> „ 38th, Col. Robert Ellison.
> „ 39th, Col. Calvin Spencer.

At the session of the Legislature of the following year the same senators and representatives appeared for Cheraw District and the three counties.

At this session Gen. Thomas presented a petition from sundry inhabitants of Cheraw District, praying that the House would not grant the petition of the inhabitants of George-town, respecting the appointment of commissioners to elect a Measurer of lumber and an Inspector of beef, pork, and flour for said town. The petition from Cheraws was successful, as no act appears to have been passed on the subject. County Judges were elected as follows:—for Marlborough, John Jones James, in place of Benj. Hicks, who had left the country; and for Darlington, Alex. M'Intosh, in place of Robert Ellison, who had been elected Sheriff for Cheraws.

At the election holden in October, 1796, the same representatives were returned, with the exception of Richard Brockington, who was succeeded by Andrew Hunter, for Darlington. For Liberty were returned John M'Ree and Thomas Wickham. Wm. Thomas appeared as senator in place of Thomas Powe, and with Gen. Thomas, took his seat. At this session a committee was appointed, consisting of Drury Robertson, Joshua Saxon, and Mr. Nott, to report how the amount appropriated for repairing the Court House and building a new gaol at Long Bluff had been expended. William Thomas was chosen one of eight electors to cast a vote for President of the United States. Sundry inhabitants of Marlborough had petitioned the Legislature for a canal to lead from Roger's Lake into Pedee River, and an Act was passed for that purpose, appointing Robert Allison, Edward Croslin, and Tristram Thomas commissioners, who were authorized to "open and keep in repair a canal of not more than fifty feet in width, to lead from any part of the said lake to such point on the river as they might deem fit," and also, "to stop up Naked Creek at any point deemed most convenient, diverting the waters of the same through the said lake and canal, provided the expense should be defrayed by voluntary subscriptions, and the canal, when so opened, be free to all citizens and the country at large." The proviso of the act probably led to the failure of the scheme.

At the meeting of the Legislature in November, 1797, the same members appeared from Pedee. A petition was presented from Robert Ellison, to be allowed to erect mills on Black Creek. A counter petition was also offered, objecting to the same, on the ground that it would obstruct the navigation of said creek. The matter was referred to a committee, who recommended that the petition of Mr. Ellison should be granted, but with such restrictions and limitations as would obviate the objections raised.

Alexander M'Intosh was elected Sheriff for Cheraws in the place of Robert Ellison, resigned, and Drury Robertson a County Judge for Marlborough.

In the memorable canvass of 1798, in Darlington, for the Legislature, a name appeared which was destined to become distinguished in South Carolina. Samuel Wilds was one of four candidates. His competitors were Andrew Hunter, of revolutionary note, Ezekiel Du Bose, just of age, and Wm. Zimmerman. Mr. Wilds was then in his twenty-third year. His early struggles against what seemed to be the most adverse fortune (for he was very poor, and left in charge of a large family of younger children, for whom their mother could not otherwise provide), had of necessity kept the sphere of his labors and acquaintances alike limited. He was scarcely known beyond his immediate neighbourhood, and to the few who had learned to appreciate him, only known as a young man of promising parts, of noble character and high aspirations. Mr. Zimmerman was already a public man of prominent position, and young Du Bose, in addition to attractive personal traits, had the advantage of a very extensive family connexion in his favor. He led the ticket, followed by Mr. Zimmerman. Young Wilds defeated, but not disheartened, for he was moved by an emulation worthy of his future success, was soon to take the lead in turn, and reach the high position he attained, with a rapidity unprecedented, perhaps, in the history of the State.

The former members, William Falconer and James Blakeney, were returned for Chesterfield, and Drury Robertson for Marlborough. William Whitfield appeared as a new member for the same county, in the place of John Jones James. For Liberty, John Ford and Lewis Harralson were elected. Captain John M'Iver was returned a senator in place of General Thomas.

Mr. Falconer, who for several sessions had been a member of the House from Chesterfield, now occupied a leading position in that body. Well educated and thoroughly trained, cool and fearless, shrewd as he was sarcastic, and ready and powerful withal in debate, he had few equals, and no superior in these respects, perhaps, in the halls of legislation or the forum. He was acknowledged head of the Cheraw Bar, and was henceforth to have his name indissolubly connected with the most important change in the system of judicature of the State which had yet taken place. "At this time," says Judge Brevard, "the administration of justice was extremely tedious and defective. The jurisdiction of the County Courts was very limited, and in many of them justice was dispensed in a very loose and imperfect manner. The accumulation of business in the Circuit Courts had greatly increased, and the manner of despatching it was not always the best that might be practiced to answer the purposes of public justice, and give satisfaction to the people.

"In order to establish a uniform and more convenient

system of judicature, a bill was brought forward in the Legislature for instituting District Courts, in the several counties of the State, and in small sections of that part wherein County Courts were not established, and to arrange those Courts into several circuits or ridings.

"The most zealous and able advocates of this project, were William Falconer, Esq., a member of the House of Representatives, from Chesterfield, and William Marshall, Esq., late one of the Judges of the Courts of Equity, a member of the Senate. It was carried, and passed into a law."*

At the following session, the same members appeared from Pedee. The Circuit Court Act of the previous year was revised and amended, and the County Courts, which had been retained in it—with very limited powers, however—were now for ever abolished. The system for the administration of justice, thus essentially charged, was to be carried into effect as speedily as possible.

Sheriffs were to be elected for them, and Courts of Ordinary also established in the several districts, and other important regulations adopted.

The term county now was laid aside, and that of district took its place, which has since been retained. The following gentlemen were elected sheriffs, viz. :—For Marlborough District, Robert Allison; for Chesterfield, Joel Bullard; for Darlington, Alexander M'Intosh. The Commissioners appointed for building and repairing the several Court Houses and gaols, were :—

For Marlborough,

William Thomas,	Thomas Evans,
Tristram Thomas,	Benjamin Rogers.
Drury Robertson,	

For Chesterfield,

William Falconer,	Thomas Powe,
Calvin Spencer,	Robert Lowry.
William Pegues,	

For Darlington,

| Robert Ellison, | Andrew Hunter. |
| William Zimmerman, | |

*Brevard's "Digest," Introduction, p. xix.

The dividing line between Chesterfield and Darlington had not, up to this time, been run out.

An Act was accordingly passed at this session, appointing Alexander Craig, William Falconer, and Erasmus Powe, Commissioners on the part of Chesterfield; and Robert Ellison, William Zimmerman, and D. R. Williams for Darlington, to establish said line. For some reason the work was not done; and a second Act was afterwards passed, appointing for Chesterfield, William Falconer and Major John Dewitt, and for Darlington, John Norwood and Alexander M'Intosh, to run out and mark the line, as fixed by law.

On the 11th of April, 1800, a very considerable shock of an earthquake was felt by many of the inhabitants on Pedee, the weather at the time being cloudy and warm for the season.

In the canvass of 1800 for the Legislature, another exciting contest took place in Darlington. The same candidates appeared as in the fall of 1798; also Richard Brockington. Samuel Wilds, having been since at the Bar, was becoming more widely known, and being superior as a speaker to all his competitors, was elected without difficulty. William Zimmerman retained his seat. In the canvass of 1802, which was also warmly contested, such was the popularity of Mr. Wilds, that he received the unanimous vote of the district, with but one exception, and that the vote of a man whom he had severely, and, doubtless, very justly scourged in Court. The same members were returned for the other districts, except Drury Robertson, of Marlborough, who was succeeded by David Stewart. For Liberty, Philip Bethea, sen., and James Ervin were elected. Alexander M'Intosh was returned for the Senate, in the place of William Thomas, of Marlborough. William Zimmerman was elected sheriff, in place of Alexander M'Intosh, now in the Senate.

About the year 1800, the total militia of the State, according to the most reliable returns, was supposed to be 35,785. The Cheraw brigade, No. 9, numbered 2224. On the 29th of November, of this year, the following return was made of the Chesterfield regiment, Colonel Spencer commanding, viz.:—

A General Return of 39th Regiment of the South Carolina Militia, Commanded by Colonel Calvin Spencer.

		Field and Commissioned Officers.						Regimental Staff.			N.C. Officers.	Rank and File.						Arms, &c.						Remarks.
		Lieutenant-Colonel.	Majors.	Captains.	Lieutenants.	Ensigns.	Total.	Paymaster.	Surgeon.	Total.	Sergeants.	Drummers.	Fifers.	Rank and File.	Rank and File above the age of 45 or Alarm Men.	Pioneers.	Total.	Total, General.	Colors.	Swords.	Espontoons.	Firelocks.	Drums.	Fifes.	
1st Bat.	Capt. John Dewitt	1	2	1	1	1	3	1	1	2	4	..	..	26	12	3	41	53	1	3	..	15	1	..	There is deficient in this return two entire companies (to wit)—the 2nd Company in the 1st Battalion, commanded by Capt. William Ellerbe, deranged for the want of officers; supposed to contain about 40, total; and the 2nd Company in the 2nd Battalion, commanded by Capt. Owens, deranged on account of the officers not being commissioned; supposed to contain about 66 total.
	Capt. Joel Bullard	..	..	1	1	1	3	..	..	..	4	1	1	83	20	..	105	112	..	2	1	45	1	1	
	Capt. John Jones	..	..	1	1	1	3	..	..	..	3	1	1	46	12	..	60	66	..	1	..	20	1	1	
2nd Bat.	Capt. Cadr. Lucy	..	..	1	1	1	3	..	..	..	3	..	..	70	15	..	85	91	..	1	..	18	1	1	
	Capt. Runnalds	..	..	1	1	1	3	..	..	..	4	1	..	35	15	..	51	58	..	2	..	16	1	..	
	Capt. Daniel Cook	..	..	1	1	1	3	..	..	..	4	1	..	50	20	..	70	77	..	3	..	20	1	..	
Total		1	2	6	6	6	18	1	1	2	22	4	2	310	94	3	412	457	1	12	1	134	5	3	

29th November, 1800.

I, John P. Rushing, 2nd Major in the 39th Regiment of the South Carolina Militia, being Commandant of the day at a Regimental parade of said Regiment, had this day by order of the Brigadier-General, do certify the above to be a true state of said Regiment, or six companies thereof, agreeable to the returns by the respective officers to me made.

JOHN P. RUSHING, *Major*.

Colonel Spencer became actively connected with St. David's Parish before the war. During the Revolution, he served in several military capacities. About the commencement of the struggle, he contracted an engagement with Rebecca Ford, of the neighbourhood of George-town, and saw her but once while the conflict continued. It was on this occasion that the British, then in possession of that region, hearing he was to be at the family residence, laid a plan for his capture. Coming suddenly up, they surrounded the dwelling; the active lover, however, managing to escape in time to reach a mill-pond near by, into which he plunged so as to swim across and elude his pursuers. He was as swiftly followed and fired upon, and so pressed, that, finding escape hopeless, he surrendered himself, and was kept in confinement until a final exchange of prisoners at the cessation of hostilities. Soon after this, he married Miss Ford, and settled in Chesterfield District. After a long life of private virtue and public service, having filled various positions of honour and trust, his career was finished in January, 1801.* Mrs. Spencer subsequently married Thomas Powe, the friend and companion, in peace and war, of her late husband. She survived Mr. Powe many years, and died about 1844, at an advanced age.

The town of Cheraw was laid out, as heretofore mentioned, about the year 1766. Called Chatham soon after, it seems, even in the popular language of the day, not long to have retained it. The name does not often appear among the records of the country immediately succeeding that period. An attempt was made many years after to revive

---

*Among the effects of Colonel Spencer were several trunks of papers, among which were many letters and other manuscript matter of an early date, and beyond doubt of much historical value. Mrs. Spencer, during her widowhood and afterwards, to the close of her life, preserved these papers with scrupulous care.

Soon after her death, the trunks, the contents of which seem never to have been carefully examined, were opened by her representatives. Such land papers as were supposed to be of value were taken out, and the rest destroyed.

To much disappointment of this kind was the Author doomed, in his search among family records for documentary matter connected with the history of the Pedee, but in scarce another instance, to one like this, with the exception of Colonel Benton's, the most valuable collection, perhaps, in this region.

and continue it, but failed. It was generally called Cheraw Hill, and the Cheraws.

It was supposed at first, by the inhabitants of the neighbouring country, that on account of its position, being at the head of navigation on the river, and its proximity to a large and fertile region in North Carolina, it would become a place of permanent and increasing commercial importance. It was, from an early period of its history, the seat of several extensive trading establishments; but the expectation of the public was in the end, or for a long time at least, disappointed. Having failed to become the seat of justice for Cheraws District, though strenuous efforts were made to have it so, and proving at times very unhealthy; neither its population nor commerce increased as rapidly as was anticipated. It was described by one* who remembered it, as it was about 1792, to have contained then not more than a dozen houses. In 1802, a writer of that day, alluding to Chatham, said: "It is a small village, situated on Cheraw Hill, at the head of navigation of Pedee River. It contains a few stores, and gives encouragement to the trade of that part of this State, which is partly drawn from North Carolina, by the Yadkin river. When the navigation of this river becomes open, it is probable this settlement will secure advantages from the additional trade which will then be carried on."† The navigation of the river, for the improvement of which several acts had at different times been passed by the Legislature, was not effectually opened, until the work was subsequently undertaken by General D. R. Williams, and the late David Gregg, of Society Hill, who carried it successfully into execution. There were not only formidable obstructions in the shape of logs, often of very large size, the accumulation of ages; but in many places the channel had to be turned or cut deeper, with a bottom sometimes almost as hard as rock. With the improved navigation of the river, the town revived, and continued to advance until it reached a considerable degree of commercial importance for the interior. The efforts which had been

---

*The late Lewis Malone Ayer, already mentioned.
†Drayton's "View of Carolina," p. 212.

made, by means of a canal a part of the way, to open the navigation of the river above the town, and through the Yadkin, into North Carolina, had failed of success, and the waggons from that region continued to be the only means of transportation.

In 1820-21, the town was incorporated, and chiefly through the exertions of the late Governor John Lide Wilson, then a member of the Legislature, and deeply interested in this as the region of his nativity, retained its early name of Cheraw instead of Chatham, as some desired, and to a certain extent it had been called. The first line of hills* rising above the river bottom were unfortunately cleared and built upon in the early settlement of the place, increasing its unhealthfulness ever after.

In 1800, the population of Cheraw District, according to the returns of a Federal census then taken, showed an increase of nearly one hundred per cent. over that of 1792. It was as follows:—

Free White Males.

	Under 10.	Of 10, and under 16.	Of 16, and under 26.	26 to 45.	Over 45
Marlborough,	839	334	299	341	184
Chesterfield,	889	367	261	371	178
Darlington,	1086	440	423	493	264

Free White Females.

Marlborough,	700	270	427	328	158
Chesterfield,	716	335	365	369	144
Darlington,	1001	435	454	499	168

Entire White Population.

Marlborough, 3880; Chesterfield, 3995; Darlington, 5263 13,138

Colored.

Marlborough, 1393; Chesterfield, 1148; Darlington, 2336 4877

Total . . . 18,015

*One of these, many years since abandoned, has been long known as "Yankee Hill." Among the early settlers, many came from the north for purposes of trade. Few of these, however, were very successful in business.

The year 1799 was rendered memorable in the history of the country as the last in the life of Washington. The event which plunged a nation into mourning was commemorated by the citizens of Pedee, the Rev. Evan Pugh having preached to a large concourse of people at Darlington Court House, a discourse appropriate to the occasion.*

Mr. Pugh himself, after a long life of useful and honorable service for his fellow-men and his country, was two years after to follow the way of him to whom he had paid so just a tribute. Not more quiet in manner and unobtrusive in character, than assiduous in the discharge of duty and efficient in action, he was highly appreciated and revered, wherever known.†

With its division into the three judicial districts of Marlborough, Chesterfield, and Darlington, the name of the Old Cheraw District was to pass away, and the stirring incidents and exciting scenes connected with its earlier history to be forgotten.‡ Long Bluff continued to be the seat of the

---

*The text of this discourse was from 2 Timothy, ix. 7, 8, showing that this venerable divine entertained no doubt as to the fact, which some of late years have made a question, whether Washington was a Christian.

†The following obituary, which appeared at the time, paying a just and truthful tribute to the memory of Mr. Pugh, will fitly give the closing chapter of his history:—

"George-town, Wednesday, Jany. 19, 1803.

"Died, on the 26th December last, at his plantation on Pedee River, Darlington District, in the 71st year of his age, the Rev. Evan Pugh, A. M., pastor of the Baptist Church at Mount Pleasant. This venerable divine was a native of Pennsylvania, and educated in the principles of the Quakers; but when he arrived at the years of manhood, and experienced what he believed to be a renovation of heart, by divine grace, he became a member of the Baptist Church. Soon after this, on his coming to this State, he engaged in a course of private studies for several years; and having acquired a good acquaintance with the dead languages, and the most useful arts and sciences, but especially with theology, he entered on his ministerial labors in the year 1763, so that he had been nearly forty years in the public character of a gospel minister, and the whole of the time resident in this State. He was a man of sound judgment, of plain, unaffected manner, and of a cheerful, entertaining conversation. His character was unimpeached and amiable, his benevolence extensive, and his piety fervent.

"He was an affectionate relative, a good citizen, and an evangelic, excellent divine. 'Mark the perfect man, and behold the upright; for the end of that man is peace.'"

‡It is almost incredible how entirely the knowledge of the leading events in the earlier history of the Pedee country, especially those immediately preceding the Revolution, and of the judicial history of Cheraw District, had passed away. They are believed to have been entirely unknown to the older and more intelligent citizens.

Court of Equity "for the Cheraw Equity Circuit," until the year 1824, when the Court was ordered to be holden at Darlington Court House.

A few years after the breaking up of the Cheraw District, its most distinguished advocate, William Falconer, was to pass away also. Mr. Falconer had acquired a large and lucrative practice. He was the terror, however, of the younger members of the Bar, as well as a formidable adversary of the more able and experienced. Astute and learned, unsparing and sarcastic, he was well qualified to take advantage, as a special pleader, of every defect or informality, and to make the most of the weak points in his opponent's case.*

The advantages taken in this way, especially of the younger lawyers, led to a general combination against their common enemy, to which he was at length forced to succumb, so far, at least, as to change his practice essentially in the particulars mentioned. The justice of the charge, so often made of latter days, against the system of special pleading, as contracted and dishonorable, may well be questioned.

A strict adherence generally to this system, would doubtless have led to a more thorough training for the Bar, a clearer conception of cases, and with the narrowing of the issue by such a process, to a sharpening of the intellect, and a corresponding development of the logical powers, as well as a great saving of time and expense, by the exclusion of irrelevant evidence in the administration of justice. The social life of the Bar seems to have had no charms for Mr. Falconer. His friends and intimate companions were confined chiefly to the clients whom he faithfully served.

---

*Mr. Falconer is said, by those of late years who remembered him, to have been overbearing, as well as morose. He could not brook opposition. Sometimes he had to give way, when prudence dictated it. An anecdote is related illustrative of this. On one occasion, on his way to Camden, he met on the highway an up-country waggoner, of unpretending appearance, and a poor turnout withal. The road was narrow, and the dignified attorney pursuing his course in his sulky, was not disposed to give way. They met, and not a word passed. Mr. Falconer then ordered his servant to hand him his holsters, whereupon the waggoner, quietly reaching back, brought forth his rifle; and Mr. F., not willing to give battle, turned out of the road, and allowed the stranger to pass on.

To an incident which occurred in his private history, soon after his settlement at Long Bluff, the moroseness of his disposition afterwards has been in part attributed. The respect and confidence of the public, however, he never lost, and his talents and acquirements were brought into constant requisition in the service of society and the State, until the close of his career. The chairman for years of the Examining Committee of St. David's Society, he was the terror of the young, and not less held in awe by the teachers of his day. Such was the appreciation of his attainments, that he was elected a member of the first Board of Trustees of the South Carolina College in 1801. Of his leading position in the Legislature, and the part he took in effecting a change in the system of judicature of the State, mention has been made. The following letter, written on his return from the Legislature in 1800, will give some idea of his style and business habits, as well as furnish an interesting relic of that period.

"Montrose, 25th December, 1800.

"Dear Sir,—Upon my arrival at home, I hasten to give you such information, concerning our public affairs, as I think may contribute either to your information or amusement. For this purpose, I submit the inclosed papers and remarks. The democratic ferment, concerning which I shall have the pleasure of remarking personally to you, having, in some degree, after the elections, subsided, a strict and laborious investigation of the state of our finances occupied the attention of the Committee of Ways and Means. We scrutinized the report of the Comptroller General (marked No. 1), and the reports contained therein of both the Treasurers of the State. We personally examined those officers, fully and minutely; and observed on the subject matter, and on their conduct, respectively, in our report of Ways and Means (marked No. 2).

"Appropriate clauses for carrying into effect the spirit and intention of the said report of ways and means, have been inserted in the Act for raising supplies for the year 1800. The reason of my mentioning the contingent fund is to meet a variety of unforeseen, small demands, continually incident to the executive department, which might be more easily and advantageously discharged with ready cash than by contracting, as heretofore, on credit; and, that the application of that fund might, in future, undergo legislative examination. The inclosed papers exhibit a more correct statement, and a more comprehensive view of our fiscal arrangements than any heretofore which I have seen. And I notice, not without pleasure and becoming pride, how far the upper exceeds the lower division of the State in punctuality in the collection and due arrangements of the taxes. (See Nos. 3 and 4.)

"In the Lieutenant-Governor's message (No. 2) herewith sent, you may perceive the correspondence which passed between him and the Governor of North Carolina on the subject of boundary. In consequence of the said message our Legislature resolved, That our State now, as heretofore, and particularly as expressed in a resolution on that subject, in the year 1792, professing the utmost readiness to appoint commissioners with full powers, to terminate, in a speedy and friendly manner, all differences with her sister State so soon as North Carolina shall appoint commissioners, with similar powers, to meet the commissioners of our State for that purpose; will, and hereby does, the more to manifest her said intention, authorize and direct the Governor of this State to invite the Government of North Carolina, in the event of that Government still adhering to her Bill of Rights, to meet our State in the Court of the United States, where the claim of territory may be constitutionally examined and adjusted: and to inform the Government of North Carolina that this State has appointed commissioners to take care of her interest, and to defend her claims in the said court. But, as it appeared from the documents which accompanied the said message, to be the intention of North Carolina, to open only that part of the line which is to the westward of the Catawba River; the commissioners of our State are authorized to commence and prosecute, in the said court, such process as may effect an adjustment of the whole line. The above is, as nearly as I can recollect, the substance of the adopted resolution. It is generally believed that this State will, along that part of the line which lies to the eastward of the said river, gain territory: for it is said that the commissioners who originally made the last-mentioned part of the line, among other mistakes, were either ignorant of, or inattentive to, the difference between a statute and a geographical mile.

"The taxes this year are fifty cents per centum *ad valorem* on land, and fifty cents per head on slaves. The debt, for which one quarter dollar was separately imposed on slaves, is fully provided for, and the act imposing it is, therefore, repealed. The next payment of the paper medium is, again, as usual, transferred. That money is now in such good credit that a great part of the interest of last year was paid in specie. This money ought never to be destroyed, for it may produce a fund which may, after some time, be sufficient to pay, without the aid of taxes, the whole expenses of Government!

"I applied so intensely to the business before the Legislature, that, during its session, I could not find time to detail the proceedings thereof.

"I am, with great regards,
"My dear Sir,
"WM. FALCONER.

"Alexander Craig, Esquire."

The "democratic ferment," to which allusion is made in this letter as "having subsided, in some degree, after the elections," was a subject touching Mr. Falconer sorely. Decided in their maintenance, and active in the propagation of his political sentiments, it was his lot, with many others, to fall with the Federal party in South Carolina in the final contest of that period.

An eminent measure of success continued to reward his efforts at the Bar. But, after his political disappointment, his habits became dissipated. In May, 1805, he drove from his residence in Chesterfield to Camden, a distance of more than fifty miles, as counsel in the case of Henry Rochelle, indicted for murder, and returned home the same night. This extraordinary effort brought on a fever, from which he died.*

---

*This day's work not only ended in Mr. Falconer's death, but killed the mare he drove, which was a remarkable animal.

"Thus perished," as Judge O'Neall justly remarks in his interesting sketch,* "one of the early luminaries of the law"; and, as may with equal truth be added, the most distinguished advocate and public man, Samuel Wilds,† perhaps, excepted, who had yet appeared upon the Pedee!

---

*O'Neall's "Bench and Bar of South Carolina," vol. ii. p. 344.
†Samuel Wilds was now much younger, and could hardly, therefore, be compared as a public man with Mr. Falconer.

CHAPTER XIX.

Closing chapters—Pupils of St. David's afterwards distinguished—Ezra Pugh—His brilliant prospects and premature end—Charles Motte Lide—His early life—Preparation for the Bar—Application for admission—Obstacle in the way—Speech on the occasion—Subsequent success—Removal to Georgia as a planter—His account of the undertaking, and locality there—Farewell—Return to Carolina—Memorable suit growing out of his father's will—Extracts from speeches during progress of the case—Memorial to the Legislature for relief—Appearance before a joint committee—Effects of his speech—Disappointment and Death—His habits and tastes, and opinions respecting him.

WITH the close of the century the concluding chapters of this history must begin. Already much protracted beyond the design with which the work was originally undertaken, it cannot be pursued further (even did the continuous course of events on the Pedee abound in matter of sufficient interest to the present generation to invite to the task), than the presenting sketches of a few of those who, having been pupils in the Academy of St. David's prior to the year 1800, gave promise of a brilliant future, but passed away before most of those now living appeared upon the stage.

Of others who subsequently emerged from the walls of that early school of learning, and rose to high distinction, filling a large place during the greater part of the first half of the present century in the history of the State, it will be unnecessary to speak. Their names, for there were not a few of these identified with the Pedee, can never be forgotten. With their marked traits of character, the results of their labors, and the leading incidents of their lives at the Bar, on the Bench, in Legislative Councils, in professional pursuits, and in other branches of the public service, we are yet familiar. While of others, who preceded them in the paths of usefulness or the race for fame, but little is now generally known. The first of these, in the order of time, was Ezra Pugh. He was the second son of the Rev. Evan Pugh, and born on Pedee in the year 1771.

As a youth, he was not more remarkable for amiability and excellence of character, than for those intellectual endowments which inspired the hope of a high degree of usefulness and success in life. One of his early companions in the school of St. David's, who was afterwards distinguished for solidity of understanding, was often heard to say, that when students together, while he was applying himself closely, young Pugh, either unengaged or reading some other work, would, at the last moment, take up the text-book, glance over the subject matter of the lesson, and grasp it as if by intuition; and that with slight effort, he would readily solve the most difficult mathematical problems.

Dr. Park, who was his early instructor, and afterwards associated during their college career with many of the most distinguished men of the State, frequently remarked of Mr. Pugh, that he was, intellectually, the most remarkable young man he had ever known. After his graduation, he appears to have devoted himself for some time to literary pursuits, preparatory to a profession, then studied law, was admitted to the Bar, and settled at George-town. The fond hopes of his friends, however, and the well-founded anticipations of the public, were blasted by his premature death, on the 29th of January, 1802, in the 31st year of his age.

In a notice published at the time of this sad event, it was said: "a love of literature induced him, while young, to turn his attention to the study of a profession. This he accomplished with but very little pecuniary aid; and by unwearied diligence, he acquired a fund of useful information, which would have done honor to better circumstances.

"A benevolent disposition, added to a strong memory and sound judgment, qualities rarely united in the same person, caused him to be esteemed by all who knew him, and beloved by his more particular acquaintances."

Another, to whom tradition has assigned the highest place as a genius, though in its erratic form, was Charles Motte Lide, the third son of Col. Thomas Lide.

He was born in what is now Marlborough District, during the times which preceded the Revolution, and seems to have exhibited in his character and subsequent career the impress of that unsettled period. After an academical course in St. David's, he determined to apply himself to the study of the law, and remained in the office of Judge Brevard of Camden eighteen months. Intense application, with sedentary habits, led to a serious decline of health, which made it necessary for him to suspend his studies for three years. With returning strength, he went to Litchfield, Connecticut, and attended a full course of law lectures under the celebrated Judge Reeve. Returning to South Carolina, he entered and remained nine months in the office of Thomas Parker, Esq., one of the leading lawyers of Charleston, with the intention of applying, at the end of that time, for admission to the Bar. But, an unexpected obstacle to the immediate accomplishment of his long cherished wishes, was here interposed. For, after the commencement of his legal studies (in the year 1796), an Act was passed by the Legislature, requiring of every citizen of the State, who had not graduated in some college or university of the State or of the United States, or in some foreign university, to have served a regular clerkship, and read law in the office of a regular practicing attorney of this State four years, as an indispensable preliminary to admission to the Bar. With this exacting requisition, young Lide could not comply, without a more protracted preliminary confinement in some law office than he was now willing to undergo. For, deducting the time of his sickness, he had studied but three years and a half, of which one was spent out of the State. In this dilemma, he claimed admission as a matter of right, under the Act of 1785, during the operation of which he had entered the office of Judge Brevard, and which prescribed no time. In deference to this claim, it was proposed by John B. Holmes, Esq., one of the gentlemen appointed on the examining committee, that Mr. Lide should argue the point before the Court. The suggestion of a proceeding so novel, doubtless originated, in part, in the desire to hear this gifted aspirant for legal honors, whose peculiar powers were already known. He cheerfully acceded; and in the course of a week prepared an elaborate speech,* which was delivered before the Court, composed of Judges Waties, Bay, Johnson, and Trezevant.

The exordium and other portions of this speech, delivered under such extraordinary circumstances, as to clothe it with peculiar interest, were as follows:—

"May it please the Court:—Plutarch informs us, that the first appearance of Demosthenes at the bar, was in his own cause. In this respect, may not I, without vanity, note the similarity of fortune. 'Kindred objects kindred thoughts inspire.' The same may be said of kindred situations. Oh, that I could feel the sympathy of situation so strongly, as to catch but a faint spark of that sublime fire which inflamed the breast of this illustrious prince of eloquence, and gave to his tongue that vehemence of speech, which seldom fails to impart the persuasion of the soul.

"After serving a faithful apprenticeship to the common law, after preserving in my legal pursuits through difficulties and trials the most severe and afflictive—through poverty, through sickness, and almost through death—and having at length arrived at the gates of the court—at length presented myself at the portals of the law—does the iron finger of technical construction point my inadmissibility? Am I told of an intervening statute, which operates as a complete foreclosure on all the equities of my situation —confines me to a state of sub-infeudation, without hope of ever aspiring to the dignity of a tenant *in capite*—that this imaginary stumbling block which lies *in limine,* at the threshold of the Court, must be removed, before I am permitted to take a seat with the venerable fathers and worthy sons of the Common Law—that this supposed Chinese wall must be scaled on the ladders of reason, argument, and law, before I can be entitled to a passport to the temple of legal science? This is literally and emphatically my situation; and it is for this purpose, to remove this stumbling block,

---

*For the manuscript papers of Mr. Lide, embracing his speeches, with much other matter of interest, all prepared with much care, and as would appear, originally designed for publication in book form, the author is indebted to the kindness of a relative, a Mr. Lide, of Alabama.

to scale this ideal wall, that I now appear, for the *first* time, before the awful brow of a Court of Justice. I crave an indulgent hearing. I crave a respect for my feelings on this delicate and interesting occasion; those feelings of *my* nature which constitute the acme of my happiness or misery.

"Previous to the Act of 1785, the admission of attorneys to the Bar depended on a rule of court. By that Act, *examination* is the only preliminary to the admission of *natives*. Under that statute I claim admission, and contend, that as I commenced my legal studies while it was in full operation and vigor, a right, a perfect right of admission attached instanter, indefeasible by any subsequent Act of the Legislature. This point, I hope to render luminous to the court, by the clearest rays of legal demonstration. And though it is a question of immediate personal concern, I trust I shall be able to forget my own interest in it, and moving out of myself, found my arguments on the true explanation and sound exposition of the doctrine of *ex post facto,* and the principles of analogy, adopted by the English courts of justice, and recognised by our own in a great variety of cases. The definition which Judge Blackstone gives of an *ex post facto* law, relates only to crimes, notwithstanding the term itself is general and comprehensive, and *ex vi termini* embraces all acts as well civil as criminal. Making of law *ex post facto,* he tells us is—'when after an action (indifferent in itself) is committed, the Legislature then for the first time declares it to have been a crime, and inflicts a punishment upon the person who has committed it.' But, immediately after remarking on the cruelty and injustice of such laws, more cruel and unjust than even the laws of Caligula, he forgets the particularity of his definition and draws his inference generally in the following words: 'all laws,' mark the change of his language, 'all laws should be therefore made to commence *in future* and be notified before their commencement; which is implied in the term *prescribed.*' It would be no difficult task, were it necessary, to point out other instances in which even Judge Blackstone himself, this most learned and eloquent expounder of the law, has fallen into contradictions. Let me, therefore, a stripling, a little David, when compared to this Goliath of the law, be on my guard. This will also serve to show, that I am not deterred by high-sounding names, from a thorough investigation of legal principles. But to return, I lay it down in as general terms as any rule can be laid down, that all laws, whatever may be the subject matter of them, should have a prospective, and not a retrospective operation. It is easy to show, that in those few instances in which there have been deviations from this sacred principle of all legitimate legislation, they have been bottomed, either upon principles of policy, or upon the broader and more benevolent principles of humanity. They have been temporary and partial sacrifices of principle to principle. Shall I say that I have in my eye, the two principal cases of limitations and bankruptcy? Abstractly and independently considered, these laws and others of a similar nature are a direct violation of the principles of natural justice; but in their general tendency, are salutary, equitable, and beneficial. The first is founded on the maxim, *interest respublica ut finis sit litium.* The last is a noble sacrifice of justice at the shrine of humanity; or to speak with more propriety, justice is of a composite nature, and includes necessarily in itself the principles of humanity. They are a *sine qua non* to each other, constituent parts of the same unity. In Great Britain, if no period is fixed for the commencement of a statute's operation, it is of course considered binding from the first day of that session in which it was enacted."

After arguing the point, he proceeds:—"I repeat it again and again: there is but one tense in legal philology, and that is the future; there is but one vision, and that is prospective. The eye of the law, like that of the eagle, should be fixed on the sun, not on the earth—should look straight forward, taking no note of anything behind. If laws are allowed to have a *Janus* form—to have a double aspect, looking before and after, we may bid a final and mournful adieu to life, liberty, property, justice, and all those rights which mankind have hitherto held in the highest veneration, and purchased at an incalculable expense of blood and treasure. . . . Was it possible for my dim eyes to penetrate the shades of time and discover that Act, rising on the surface of futurity? Is not prescience an acknowledged and essential attribute of the Deity—of that awful Being, with whom time and eternity are the same, and all knowledge merely intuitive? Present circumstances are the only *data* of civil, as well as moral action. We must, from the very constitution of our frame, predicate all our hopes and all our plans, of whatever nature, upon what *is,* and not upon what *is to be.* This is the only firm basis of action, and those who do not build upon this rock will find themselves and all their works, sooner or later, involved in one large, promiscuous ruin.

> " 'Oh blindness to the future! kindly given,
> That each may fill the circle marked by heaven.'

. . . "If they can divest the student of a right of admission at one time, they can surely do it at another; if at one stage of his legal progress, at any and always. Where, then, is his security,—where his guarantee,—where the rock of his legal salvation?

"At the very instant he fancies himself standing on *terra firma,*—behold! the ground, by the magic touch of a legislative wand, in the twinkling of an eye, converted into a Serbonian bog, in which he is awfully sunk, swallowed up and lost for ever,—

> " 'And in the lowest depth,
> A lower deep still opens to devour him.' "

Having argued the legal point at length, he concludes:—

"Standing, as I conceive I do, upon an unshaken basis, and girt with the double belt of principle and precedent, I might now enjoy the calm serenity of a mind confident of success, were I not too sensible that all human confidence is vain. Let me therefore earnestly and pathetically entreat the Court, to give this question the most mature consideration before they make a decision, which, if in the negative, involves consequences to me of the most serious import, and will give an entirely new modification to my situation, hopes, and future prospects."

This effort of Mr. Lide was unavailing. For, on the day after the delivery of the speech, Judge Waties, calling him up to the bench, politely complimented him, and privately delivering the opinion of the court, expressed regret that they could not comply with the prayer of his petition. He observed, that some of the judges refused to pay any attention to the Act of 1796,—Judge Burke, in particular, having publicly declared, that he would not be bound by that Act. Accordingly, after the passing of that statute, admissions had been made to the Bar of students who could not comply with its requisitions; several having been admitted but a short time previous to the application of Mr. Lide. Judge Waties declared, that, as to himself, he revolted at the idea of disregarding a solemn act of the Legislature. Mr. Lide then entreated the judge to bend the law so as to accomodate it to the peculiar circumstances of his case, urging that the long suspension of his legal studies by sickness, was the only thing which brought him under its operation; that this was the visitation of Providence, and the maxim would apply, *Actus Dei nemini facit injuriam.*

"Sir," said Judge Waties, in reply, with some degree of resentment, "we do not grant favors." "Sir," replied Mr. Lide, "I am better acquainted with the office and duty of a judge, than to ask them. All I request is, that the Court will bend, not break the law: the expression is legal and proper, and frequently used by the judges of England."

"At this stage of the conversation," continues Mr. Lide in his narrative, "Judge Bay, with that natural goodness and politeness which sometimes outstrip his understanding, expressed to me his regret that I had not made my application for admission sooner. Upon which, I observed that the law and the circumstances were the same; that I knew there was a tide in human affairs, but had no conception that it extended to and influenced courts of justice. This was decisive, and admitted of no reply." Perceiving the inflexible determination of the Court, Mr. Lide retired, both mortified and disappointed; but feeling, as he said, that it was one of the proudest days of his life. He was not only complimented by the Judge, but immediately after the delivery of the speech, John Julius Pringle, one of the most distinguished advocates of Charleston, who was present and attentive throughout, approached the youthful pleader, and entering into conversation, very familiarly and obligingly asked him several questions respecting his future intentions and prospects, adding, that in consequence of some expressions used in the exordium of the speech, the gentlemen of the Bar stood ready to furnish him with any pecuniary means which might be needed to prosecute his legal studies, and requested him (Mr. Pringle) to communicate their disposition in this respect, but that he had informed them there was no occasion for it, as Mr. Lide's means were fully sufficient. After quitting the office of Mr. Parker in the spring of 1800, Mr. Lide went to Columbia as a student, and soon after, on his own affidavit, covering the deficiency as to time, was admitted to the Bar during the same year. He had intended settling in Columbia as a lawyer, but during the delay caused by the unexpected obstacle thrown in his way, another gentleman came in and establishing himself there in full practice, marring the prospect, as Mr. Lide feared, for his own early success. He, therefore, unfortunately determined, after remaining at th Bar twelve months, to relinquish the pursuit, and established himself as a planter on Crooked River, Camden County, Georgia. This, as he says, "was an enterprise of the most arduous, romantic, and alpine nature. But industry and perseverance conquered every difficulty. I called the tract of land which I purchased of Mr. James Seagrove, 'the Asylum.' Shortly after my arrival there, in a letter to a friend, I thus correctly depicted the existing scenery: 'On my first debarkation at this place I found it completely under the dominion of nature. The hand of culture had not presumed to intrench on her rights, nor the axe to violate the long and sacred silence of the forest. Here the owl has long maintained his ancient and solitary reign, and from his nightly court still issues dreadful proclamations to warn me against encroachments on his territory. I pitched my tent of moss under a large white oak, which afforded me a kind and protective shelter till a few days ago, when I decamped under my present habitation. In gratitude I have suffered him to retain his ancient and venerable seat, though his neighbours have long since fallen around him. When he does fall, he shall fall with all the leafy honors of the forest at his side."

"After transforming a wild wood into a cultivated field, in the fall of 1803," he afterwards wrote, having remained there only eighteen months, "I disposed of land, negroes, and crops to Messrs. Wood and Drysdale, two gentlemen from the Bahama Islands. When the sale was completed my spirits underwent a remarkable and visible depression; and in this melancholy mood I composed the following valedictory, which breathes something of the tenderness of Ossian.

"Farewell, sweet Asylum, which received me into your friendly bosom at a time when anxiety and despondency corroded my health, and poverty grinned upon my heels. Farewell, ye lovely flowers, ye golden blossoms,* which daily expand your little bosoms to kiss the mid-day sunbeam. Farewell, thou surrounding forest, that hast so long darkened my solitude, and cast a browner horror on my cares. How often have you listened with anxious dread to the cry of my axes and the crash of your contemporary trees! You, too, must soon yield to the persevering vigor of the axe. You, too, must soon lay your tall heads low and moulder into dust! And thou, majestic and venerable White Oak, under whose protective wing, on the broad platform of nature, I have so often reposed, adieu!

"It is true that I have stript you partially of your leafy honors;† but it was done from a benevolent motive, to extend your branches, and to clad you with more luxuriant foliage. Farewell, thou meandering stream, on whose silent, sacred banks I have so long lived. How often have I floated on the full swell of your rapid, boiling tide! Once did I sleep upon your bosom. No longer will you contribute to my health, convenience, or repose. No longer will you pass in sympathetic silence the door of my moss-stuffed hut. And thou, good genius of the hommock who, after witnessing all my cares, and all my toils, hast at length smiled upon my labors and crowned them with success, farewell, a long farewell!

---

*"Cotton blossoms."
†"I had it topped."

"Think not that I am ungrateful for your favors. No, far be it from me. Necessity alone has compelled me to renounce my allegiance to you, to withdraw from your solitary domain, and to relinquish the cultivation of your favorite plant. Be still propitious. Let your smiles accompany me while I go to revisit friends who have long known and loved me, and scenes which have been familiar to my earliest youth!"

The profession of the law not appearing to Mr. Lide, as he says, "to promise a remuneration by any means adequate to the great sacrifices of time, of property, and above all, of health, that he had made in order to qualify himself for it," he resolved to abandon it. "At that time," he remarks, "the long staple or black-seed cotton was held in high estimation, and generally regarded as the shortest and surest road to wealth. The South of Georgia was considered by Col. Hampton and myself the finest theatre of success." Col. Hampton furnished him with letters, advice, &c. Accordingly, in the early part of the following year, 1802, he went to Virginia to purchase negroes, and soon after removed to Georgia. But having invested a part of his funds in another undertaking, it led to financial embarrassment, and the breaking up of the cotton enterprise just as it had progressed to a point to become remunerative.

In the fall of 1803 he returned to Carolina, and resumed the practice of the law, but irregularly and without that spirit and determination which alone could ensure success. The memorable and protracted suit, growing out of the will of his father, Col. Thomas Lide, from its beginning in 1806, appears to have absorbed all his energies and called forth all his powers.

Col. Lide had contracted a third marriage with Mrs. Mehitabel Irby. By a will, executed during his last illness, provision was made for an annuity to his widow. It was alleged that this was done on the ground there would be a posthumous heir, which proved not to be the case; and that false representations had been made, and undue influence brought to bear upon the testator when in a very weak state of mind, to that end. The representatives of Mrs. Lide afterward claimed the annuity, with interest, for a term of years. The claim was resisted by the heirs of Col. Lide, chiefly on the grounds mentioned, and hence the suit. Charles Motte Lide was, therefore, personally and deeply interested in the result. During the progress of the case he delivered the most elaborate speeches, full of legal learning and abounding in classical lore, rising at times to a degree of pathos, which, with his peculiar manner and brilliant powers, made a deep and lasting impression on those who heard him. The extracts already given from his pen, with those of the speeches which are to follow, will convey some idea, though of course imperfectly, of what he was at the Bar. Contemporaneous testimony, as well as tradition, assign him a very high place in point of oratorical power, not only before the juries of the country, but the more enlightened audiences of the day. As often the case with those who have been highly gifted, the most brilliant flashes of his wit and eloquence were doubtless called forth under the stimulus of the occasion, and hence not preserved.

In June term, 1814, he pronounced before Judge Thompson, and a deeply interested and profoundly attentive audience, a speech, of which the following was the exordium :—

"May it please your Honor: after revolving like a planet, and like this case, through all the signs of the zodiac, after experiencing all the changes of changeful fortune, after passing through a vast variety of untried being and of woe, I am at length, through the capricious revolution of time and of accident, reluctantly driven back to the 'dull debate, the noisy bar,' and placed in this forum in order to raise my hand and voice in a cause, in which I would cheerfully expend the last cent of my property, and heartily shed the last drop of my blood.

"Fortunate, indeed, is the coincidence, and singularly happy is the man, though the necessity in this particular case is ever and deeply to be regretted, in whose favor duty and inclination are thus made, providentially, to unite and co-operate. In this arrangement and concurrence I see distinctly the hand of Providence. *Cui Bono,* for what good end, or for what wise purpose, have I been protected and preserved through unparalleled difficulties, through unprecedented afflictions, misfortunes and trials but for this high argument, this unattempted theme. Rely upon it,

> "There is a Providence that shapes our ends,
> Rough hew them as we will.'

"To correct injustice is at all times and on all occasions to discharge a pleasing, a beneficient, and even a god-like office. In this instance it is also to perform a moral and a political duty. It is a duty I owe to myself, it is a duty I owe to the other devisees and co-defendants, it is a duty I owe to my country. But a stronger, a higher, a more sacred motive animates me. Filial piety demands it of me. Methinks I see the shade of my father looking down with indignation on the ungrateful ruin and unmerited devastation of his family, frowning upon me for unavoidable inattention and delay, impatiently beckoning, and imperatively demanding of me to make this exertion, in order, to use the forcible language of Judge Buller, to 'blot out the blot' which has been so unworthily affixed by the decree now to be reviewed, to his memory and understanding; and as far as possible to mitigate and to correct the calamitous effects which it has so unjustly wrought and accomplished."

"On this solemn occasion," he subsequently exclaimed, "I act a far more interesting and important, though less conspicuous part, than the eloquent Symmachus when he pled before the throne of the Emperor Valentinian for the Gods of Rome. *He* advocated the cause and reign of polytheism; *I* advocate the cause and dominion of justice and of law. *He* prayed and entreated for the restoration of the altar of victory; *I* supplicate for the restoration, or rather, recognition of the remedies by rehearing or bill of review. He plead for the continuance and preservation of an idle superstition, already undermined by the then new light of Christianity; I plead for the conservation and perpetuation of our whole system of equity. It is not, then, my cause alone which I this day plead; it is the cause of my family, it is the cause of justice, it is the cause of the constitution and laws, it is the cause of the entire mass of the community. 'Whatever, therefore,' in the words of a memorable and distinguished orator, 'can best encourage and animate to diligence and to energy; whatever is most powerful and influencing upon a mind not callous to every sentiment of gratitude and honor, demand at this moment the exercise of every function and faculty that I am master of.'"

The counsel for the defendants having given up all hope of success in consequence of an adverse decision previously made, and virtually abandoned the cause, he proceeds to comment upon their course: "under this chilling impression, after the second verdict in the Court of Common Pleas, and the consequent decree in Equity, both of which were adverse, their counsel imprudently and suicidally abandoned the cause in despair. Never, surely, was there less room for the indulgence of this last freezing sentiment of the human heart. On the contrary, their motto or principle of inspiration should have been that which encircles the arms of the State, *Dum spiro spero*. Most unfortunately, however, the breasts of the defendants' counsel did not glow with this noble, manly, soul-inspiring, magnanimous, and Spartan-like sentiment. Just in this awkward, timorous, and short-hand way, was the best and most hopeful cause in the world cruelly, unnaturally, completely, and prematurely butchered and sacrificed by those who were entrusted with its defence, and who should have cherished and sustained its precious being to the last period of its legal existence. To the bright morning of its commencement, there unexpectedly succeeded a long and dreary night of terrible gloom, of clouds and thick darkness.

"Had the counsel for the defendants, instead of being struck with dismay, have again carried the case up, in their turn, to the Constitutional Court, as in this mode of procedure they ought to have done, the good nature, if not the good sense of the Court, there being verdict against verdict, and the scales of justice, abstractly considered, hanging in equipoise, would, upon mere motion and as a matter entirely of course, have granted a second new trial. In fact, it is reasonable to suppose, that they would have exulted in the opportunity of reviewing their former decision.

"But, instead of this having been done, the cause was, as just stated, horribly smothered and strangled to death in its cradle. During the whole of these latter proceedings I was at a distance from the scene of decision, and in absolute ignorance of them. For, after the first verdict, I had supposed on good authority that the cause was at an end. Nor was I awakened from this state of tranquil ignorance and agreeable delusion until the execution against myself arrived at Laurensville, near to which place I at that time resided, and announced to me the mournful result of the contest. I immediately determined on resistance; but owing to pecuniary embarrassments, was compelled to postpone it to a more convenient time. In confirmation of this assertion I shall make an extract from a letter, a copy of which I preserved, addressed, very shortly after the arrival of the execution, to Duncan M'Rae, Esq., the administrator, *cum testamento annexo,* of the estate of the devisor, in which I distinctly and strongly announced this resolution and intention. It is in these words: 'This business,' alluding to this suit, 'shall not stop here; these waters must be troubled; and, if necessary, it shall be the occupation of the remaining part of my life, to keep them in constant and boiling agitation.' . . . Having finished the woeful, Romeo and Juliet tale of this short-lived and luckless case, thus prematurely terminated, I will now attempt to give, what should have been, according to my ideas, its actual history. This will be best accomplished by the criticism on the proceedings both at law and in equity, which have just been briefly narrated.

"Disdaining then all idle ceremony and the vain impertinence of forms, let us utter our sentiments with freedom but not without respect."

He then proceeds to a most detailed, elaborate, and able examination of the facts of the case from the beginning, with the principles of law and equity involved, citing with learned comments, a vast array of authorities, occasionally digressing, as in the following instance. Referring to Blackstone, he adds:—"Having frequently had occasion to cite this great authority, I can no longer refrain from giving expression to those strong and ardent feelings of gratitude, which are so justly and eminently due, not only from myself, but from the whole legal corps, to this illustrious author, for the immense advantages derived, and to be derived, 'to the last syllable of recorded time,' from his toilsome labors and erudite lucubrations. As Mr. Cumberland observes of Dr. Johnson, *Etiam mutuas loquitur,* I take no notice of the labors or attempts of Sir Matthew Hale, though they are not without their value or utility. The incomparable Blackstone first educed order out of chaos, and elevated the study of law to the rank and dignity of a science. His successors, and they are many, and great, and learned, are only treading in his footsteps.

"He first, a poor orphan boy—let not the great and wealthy plume themselves too much; this orphan boy, I say, first erected this vast, magnificent pile, and they, his successors, are merely adding the superficial ornaments.

> " 'With nice distinctions glossing o'er the text,
> Obscure in meaning, and with words perplext;
> With subtleties on subtleties refin'd,
> Meant to divide and subdivide the mind;
> Keeping the forwardness of youth in awe,
> The scowling Blackstone bears the train of law.' "

He finally concludes in these words:—

" 'There is,' says a feeling orator, 'a principle of resistance in mankind, which will not brook such injuries, and a good cause and a good heart, will animate men to struggle in proportion to the size of their wrongs, and the grossness of their oppressors. On this principle, like Hamlet, I have pried with an eager, inquisitive, insatiable, and unsatisfied curiosity, into the most obscure, hidden, and minute circumstances of this cause. . . .

"On this principle, I have attempted faintly to imitate the sublime conduct, the exalted and devotional patriotism of Curtius, and have leaped into, in order to close for ever, this dreadful, yawning gulf to the best hopes, interests, and prospects of myself and family. On this principle, I have struggled, and on this principle, will I continue to struggle, till the last expiring, convulsive gasp of this singularly unfortunate cause. I will exhaust, before I have done, all the resources of which I am possessed, of information and learning, of genius and judgment, of invention and argument. If possible, I will, as far as relates to this cause, exhaust even the legal and equitable codes. I will exert every nerve, strain every muscle, rouse and display every power and every principle of energy which exist in me, whether corporeal or mental.

"In this case, I am a torrent shooting down the sublime slope of the Andes, a mighty river overwhelming its grand and elevated banks, and pouring its accumulated flood into the capacious and expansive bosom of the ocean. To arrest such a torrent, to oppose such a river, would be almost as idle and vain, as to stop the sun in mid-career, or nature in her rapid and majestic course. To fall by such proceedings and decisions as I have exhibited to your honor, would indeed be to be 'brained by a lady's fan,' and to perish in the style of the mock-heroic. Such a contemptible dénouement of this drama, would completely take away all dignity from distress, would be not less ridiculous than calamitous. To avoid this fate, to prevent such a 'heel and catastrophe' to this wretched cause, are the true objects of that unwearied industry, of that patient toil, of that midnight research, to which I have so long and cheerfully submitted, in its investigation and development. But, if after all shall have been said and done, I cannot ultimately command, it must, at least, be universally admitted, that I shall have deserved the most rare, the most signal, and the most glorious success."

This speech, of which only a few extracts have been given, must have occupied the greater part of the day in its delivery. Major Blanding, afterwards so distinguished at the Bar, was the opposing counsel. The decision of the Judge was adverse, ordering and decreeing that the application for a rehearing be rejected. In the delivery of the opinion, however, the Judge admitted "that a bill of review would lie, provided a case was made out, competent to warrant and sustain it." This Mr. Lide considered a "great point gained," in the final prosecution of the cause. "It gave me," as he said, "what Archimedes wanted for his instruments, in order to move the earth—a place on which to plant my legal and argumentative machines before the Court of Appeals in Equity."

To this last appeal to the courts of the country, he now applied himself with unwearied and extraordinary assiduity, knowing that if against him, the decision would be final. The result of his preparatory labors in the effort made, was an enduring monument to his patient research, his sleepless application, his inventive power, and legal erudition.

The cause was argued before the Appeal Court in Equity, at Columbia, on the 25th and 26th of November, 1814. "It is with a mixed feeling of pride and gratitude," Mr. Lide remarks, "that the Equity Chamber was crowded and adorned with the wisdom and gravity of age, as well as with the sprightly intelligence and laudable curiosity of youth."

The argument was introduced by a few observations, which he deemed appropriate, as follows:—". . . 'We hold it,' says Junius, addressing himself to Dr. Blackstone, 'that the cause of an injured individual,' and I may presume to add, much more that of an almost ruined family, 'is interesting to the public.' I recall to the recollection of your Honors this just, wise, politic, and truly patriotic sentiment, because I am extremely anxious to secure to myself the attention and respect of the Court. For on this occasion I am sadly serious. Pardon then, in the course of this great struggle, something to my feelings. My old literary friend, Burke, has taught me, that such is the complexity of human affairs, that men semetimes unavoidably find themselves in strange situations; 'but the Judges,' says he, 'should always be the same.' And Curran has also informed me, 'that had it not been for the boldness of Nathan's parable, his candor might have cost him his head.' But truth speaks with such a lofty warning voice, in accents so strong and so awe-inspiring, that she astounds the callous front of guilt, disarms the hand of power, and places conscience at pleasure, and in submissive acquiescence, under the mighty sway of her awful sceptre.

"Besides, may it please your Honors, I am about to contend for all which can interest me, whether considered as an isolated being, or as a member of a private family, or, of that greater family of my fellow-citizens, the community.

"And therefore, I shall follow an example, which on no other occasion would I even think of following—the example of Richard the Third, and mount 'black Surrey for the field to-day.'

"I took the liberty to allude to my family. One member of that small family has fallen, partly, I think, under the corroding effects of this decree, and is now sleeping with his fathers. Peace be to his ashes, and eternal rest to his soul. Another member of that unfortunate family still survives, on whom Providence, in his mysterious and inscrutable dispensations, for wise purposes, no doubt, hath grievously inflicted his chastening rod. It is on his account that I am chiefly solicitous. For myself, I am under no apprehensions. That Being who feeds the raven, yea, even the young raven, will take care of me. For we are assured that a sparrow falls not to the ground, unnoticed by his vigilant and parental eye.

> "'Oh, for a muse of fire,
> To ascend the brightest heaven of invention,
> An empire for a stage, heroes to act,
> And princes to behold, the swelling scene.'

"May it please your Honors:

"From the great importance and extreme length of this case, it was absolutely necessary to follow the rules of the dramatic art, and to distribute into three acts this vast and tragic drama. Already, twice in valiant conflict have I encountered the foe. Once, at Chambers, did I startle and touch him with the point of Ithuriel's spear. The argument in the Circuit Court of Equity, at Cheraw, appalled the adverse counsel and his——client. This worthy duumvirate looked like wretches, smitten and blasted by the lightning of heaven. They trembled! good God, how they trembled! It was the couching of the Norman lance, before the degenerate Greeks, of the Roman-Eastern empire. Again I enter the lists, with my loins girt about, and my lamp trimmed and burning—emaciated, it is true, but not exhausted. No, may it please your Honors, my genius for legal warfare is not yet exhausted, nor will it be, nor can it be, so long as a single patch, or thread, or particle is left of this Sybilline record—so long as a single question out of it starts up, dares to raise its hydra head, to be cut off by the giant arm of law and logic. This well-fought field is not yet abandoned with dismay and despair, the hostile armor of attack and defence is not yet broken to pieces and cast away by either conflicting party, nor will it be until this honorable Court shall interpose, and by its decision put a final period to the contest. Twice, I repeat, have I already, at great length, argued this cause, and this is my third, formal, and I trust last effort. Under this cheering hope, I do therefore enter this Court, with the heart-felt joy of a sailor, 'long tossed at sea and all his viands spent,' on the discovery of land, of *terra firma,* and with the buoyant prospect of a speedy termination to his rough and toilsome voyage. Incessantly agitated, and wearied in mind and in body, it may readily be supposed and believed that I enter this august hall of justice with the ecstacy and fluttering wings of the stray dove, in its return to Noah's Ark, to find a resting place, a home and a nest, in the fond wish and expectation of final dismission hence, with lightsome heart, with my 'crest elevated by hope and heightened by joy,' and my temples bound around and decorated with the laurel wreath of victory, won in all 'the pride, pomp, and circumstance of glorious war'—to pursue, in peaceful silence and improving solitude, that plan of legal studies which I have crayoned out for myself. Should this, however, not be the case, and this ray of hope be dashed to the ground—but I will not anticipate the judgment of the Court.

> " 'The dawn is over-cast, the morning lowers,
> And heavily in clouds
> Brings on the day, the great, the important day—
> Big with the fate of Cato, and of Rome.'

"I cannot help reflecting on the peculiarity of fortune, which perpetually imposes on me the necessity of appearing and re-appearing, in my own case. With Burke, I may truly say, *Nitor in adversum* is the motto for a man like me. I am not, however, without consolation and encouragement from high examples. Demosthenes and Cicero were both subjected to the same fortune, though, I believe, not in so great degree. Cicero pleaded *pro domo,* for his own house, burned down by a faction; and Demosthenes made a noble stand *in persona,* against his guardian, who had defrauded him of part of his estate. I, too, may presume to venture on the same ground, and draw my weapon, in self-defence, surely,—

> "'Unless self-charity be some time a vice,
> And to defend ourselves it be a sin,
> When violence assails us.'

"This circumstance reminds me of my professional *debut* in Charleston, some ten, or twelve, or more years ago, when one of your Honors, whom I have in my eye,* was then and there, one of my judges. And although I was defeated, and hardly defeated, still, I retain a vivid recollection of the dignified sympathy and sensibility of his Honor, Judge Waties, on that trying occasion. His Honor, Judge de Saussure also, then at the bar, at the instance of my friend Lightwood, alas! since dead and gone to his account, had the goodness, with the kindest promptitude and alacrity, to make some introductory and very favorable observations on my subject. And I hope, their Honors will not be displeased at the liberty I take in presenting to their minds, this, to me, at least, pleasing image of agreeable reminiscence. I know where I am. I understand perfectly well the genius of this Court. Nothing burns here, but the lamp of legal science. Lighting, then, my slender taper at this glorious fountain of illumination, and holding it in my hand, I propound for the consideration of the Court the following questions, namely:—

"First, whether a will or devise may be revoked or invalidated *pro tanto,* or in part only?

"Secondly, whether the one or the other may be revoked or invalidated, in whole, or in part, by importunity or undue influence alone?

"Thirdly, if neither can be so revoked or invalidated by importunity, singly, whether, if with this strong circumstance of improper influence, there be connected facts or transactions indicative of fraud, a will or devise may not be in whole, or in part, revoked or invalidated?

"Fourthly, whether, for this purpose, parol evidence may be admitted to prove fraud, or undue influence?

"The fifth and last question which I shall propose, arises out of the construction of the Act of eighteen hundred and eight,—the institutional and organic Act of this Court. It is this: whether upon a fair, rational, and correct con-

---

*Bowing to Judge Waties.

struction of that Statute, the old, firmly established, long practised remedies by re-hearing or bill of review, should be considered and adjudged to be abolished, and the right or privilege of appeal to this Court substituted *in loco,* or in place of those remedies?

"Numerous other questions, out of this case, might no doubt be raised and suggested by subtle and learned ingenuity,—for what subject may not be infinitely ramified?—but these, and particularly the last, as being a preclusive question, if decided against the remedies by re-hearing or bill of review, appear to me to be the principal or most important."

After treating these questions at great length, in which not only many legal authorities, but other authors, as Shakespeare, are learnedly discussed—he goes on to notice in much detail, and expose the many errors connected with the previous proceedings both at law and in equity, and concludes in the following strain:—

"May it please your Honors,—Shall I be permitted to subjoin a few words more, on my own little subject? Yes. *Ipse de me scribam.* Inheriting a very delicate constitution, suffering almost perpetual ill-health, possessing a disposition, not of the most Socratic kind, and a temper not formed of the sternest stuff,—subjected before twelve years of age to that orphanage which springs from the grave,—cast out, at this late day, from the moorings of the hearth, and dismissed from the 'mild majesty of private life,' is it a matter of the smallest wonder that I should have run into some eccentricities; that I should have indulged in some little aberrations from the strict line of perfect rectitude; that I should have yielded for a moment to those amiable frailties, those 'sweet follies, which should be known to friends alone, and men of generous minds'? Have not some of the finest and fairest characters in history, been guilty of still stranger deviations from the rigid rules of morality?"

(*Collateral Remarks.*)—"May it please your Honors, in making this observation I did not intend, merely to appeal to the general reading and opulent memory of the Court. But, passing by the case of Cæsar, who wept before the statue of Alexander, because, at his age, he had performed no action worthy the pen of the historian; and descending a long tract of time, I cannot refrain from citing, as a most signal instance, the character and conduct of Charles James Fox. With him, as with most other elevated souls, prudence was not the favorite virtue. Nor is this to be wondered at; for genius, generally built on strong passions, is the most sublime and effervescent principle in nature.

"That great and amiable man, after having lost and won, and lost again, his immense patrimonial estate,—after having been abandoned by all his friends as a victim to his vices,—possessed so much sensibility, so much fortitude, so much intelligence, such a just and manly confidence in his many virtues, in his fascinating manners and his gigantic talent,—that, recalling his recollection, and shaking himself into returning energy,—like another phœnix, he arose out of his own ashes, and presided over the destinies of a great empire. Achilles was vulnerable in the heel. Nations are subject to strange and frightful ebullitions. Nature herself is irregular. A superior influence, irresistibly, and at will, guides and controls the destinies of the physical and moral world. The lofty stem of the pine yields like a sapling to the force of the tempest. The robust poplar, with his vigorous roots, also bows before the overruling energies of nature. So, even so, it is with man. The great Napoleon himself,—that unrivalled master of the sublime science of war, that moral volcano, which has thrown out such bitter substance,—submits, with profound and dignified humility to a ruthless climate,—fairly and greatly acknowledges, in the face of Europe, and of the world, the imperious power of inveterate circumstances. At a still later period, on the final catastrophe of the grand tragi-comic drama of France, and of Europe, this distinguished personage, this modern Cæsar, exhibited no less strikingly and gloriously for himself, the fortitude, combined with the sensibility of a man, and of a hero. But to return—As for myself, may it please your Honors, in the peaceful, noiseless tenor of my way, I have been for years rolling the stone of Sisyphus. Once did I flatter myself, that I had securely planted it on the summit of the mountain, and assumed a commanding attitude. But, fortune frowned, the political horizon thickened and blackened, this disastrous case, like the ghost of Brutus, stalked before me,—these successive causes, eventually combining and co-operating, with united and irresistible energy seized me by the top, and again hurled me to the bottom. In this humble and prostrate posture, whilst I feelingly own with Cardinal Wolsey,—making all due allowance for comparative elevation and depression,—'the blessedness of being little,'—let me, at the same time, surpass in religious resignation that ambitious prelate, and submit to the revengeful reverses of fortune, with manly dignity and philosophic fortitude. The master orator of the French Revolution, no less forcibly than beautifully observes that, 'reputation is the flame upon the altar; cease to feed it, and it expires.' Sincerely penetrated and deeply impressed with this great truth,—it is my firm and fixed resolution to weave up all my follies, and in future, to hold, if possible, my 'course unfaltering, up the steep ascent of virtue,' and manfully and steadily to direct all the energies of my mind and body, to the enviable acquisition of a 'local habitation and a name.'

"With this view, and for the accomplishment of this high purpose, I should have selected, had health permitted, this city, on account of its many great and singular advantages, as the place of my permanent residence, and the theatre of my future exertions. The College Library, of itslf, would have been a great consideration and inducement. That superb and spacious accomodation of science, which reflects so much honor on the wisdom and liberality of the State, is destined, in a few years, to produce a wonderful revolution in the state of society and of literature in our infant Republic. No longer will the eye of liberal curiosity and anxious inquiry be directed to a particular city, or a particular section of the State, in search of men of genius and of learning. They will be found here; they will be found everywhere; they will be found seated at the foot, and under the black and frowning brow of bald and sterile mountains,—contemplating the sublime beauties of nature, and causing her to startle at the vast penetration of man, which can lay open and reveal her own mighty and occult secrets, and even probe her to the quick.

"May it please your Honors: after this exertion, may I, dare I, lay hold of a small corner of the skirt or robe of fame, and holding that in my hand, and following the high example, and supporting myself by the great name and authority of Montesquieu, assume and repeat, with him, and after him, the lofty sentiment of Correggio,—'And I also am a painter!'

"May it please your Honors: I close in the style—excuse the association—of Sheridan, and of our Saviour: 'I have done'—'It is finished.'"*

To this speech Major Blanding replied, and Mr. Hooker concluded the pleadings for the appellants.

On the last day of the term, the opinion of the Court, adverse to Mr. Lide, was pronounced by Chancellor de Saussure—precluding all further appeal to that tribunal. This was in December, 1814. As a last alternative, Mr. Lide presented a memorial to the Legislature during the session of 1816—setting forth briefly the history of the cause from its beginning—urging the errors into which the Courts had fallen, and the example of a celebrated case in England, in which, the parties having failed in the Courts, Parliament granted relief. Referring to this precedent, he says in conclusion: "That was nobly done. Now, I ask, will a republic be less generous than a monarchy? Surely not. Your memorialist, therefore, in honest confidence, respectfully prays this honorable body, to refund to him out of the treasury of the State, in imitation of the British example, the amount of which your memorialist has been thus wrongfully deprived by a Court of ulterior decision,— or to grant him such other relief as to your wisdom shall seem meet.

"And your memorialist further suggests, that before such a state of things should any longer be suffered to exist,

---

*"The concluding sentences," Mr. Lide adds in a note, "from their brevity, and from a natural wish to close with dignity, were pronounced recitatively; but I was not a little mortified on being informed that that tone of voice, between common speech and song, should have been mistaken by the audience, respectable and enlightened as it was, for actual singing. Considering the greatness and solemnity of the occasions on which these expressions were used, and also their conciseness, I am, myself, convinced that I acted with taste and judgment."

your memorialist, for one, would rejoice to see the proud temples of legal science topple on their warders' heads, thorns and thistles grow and flourish on their consecrated foundations, and the mournful turtle-dove utter her melancholy note, where the goddess of justice should have sat enthroned."

The memorial was referred to a special joint committee of both Houses, of which the late Governor John Lide Wilson was one. Mr. Lide was requested to appear and plead his cause before the committee. He did so; and came in a costume as singular,* as his appearance was wild and haggard. Every exertion of his genius and eloquence had hitherto failed. Breaking forth, as a final effort, with expiring splendor, his varied powers were all brought into commanding requisition. It was to be the triumph, or the failure of his life. The committee gave him a long and patient hearing, for the case had now become one of peculiar and mournful interest,—added to which, his character, his genius, his declining fortunes, and previous efforts in the cause, had given him a sad celebrity. With the progress of his speech, the excitement, even with that select body of legislators, became painfully intense, and when he closed, in the words and recitative style of his last effort before the Court—"I have done—It is finished,"—every member of the committee was bathed in tears.†

Though the personal interest he excited was deep and universal, relief was not granted; and shortly after, the flickering taper, which had thus been kindled by the stimulus of the occasion into a flame of unearthly brightness, was extinguished in death!

It was equally a misfortune for himself and the State, that adverse circumstances at an early period should have given a morbid direction to Mr. Lide's character and subsequent course. Continued disappointment only served to increase this disposition and, as a fatal canker, it ate out his

---

*He appeared in a blanket, as his outer garb, with hair dishevelled, sunken, piercing eyes, and huge folios of the law in strong array.

†Governor Wilson described it to the Author, with evident emotion even then, though nearly forty years had passed away, as a scene surpassing the power of language to pourtray.

life. It led to an irregularity of habit and unsteadiness of purpose, which precluded the possibility of success.

He was not more fond of the law as a study, than devoted to literary pursuits. His speeches throughout abound with allusions indicative of a richly stored mind. Shakespeare, of all others, was his text-book, and in the depths of that universal genius, few, perhaps, have ever been more profoundly versed. His familiarity with, and command on all occasions of this great author, are said by those who remember him, to have been extraordinary.

The late Hugh S. Legare, of Charleston, the Cicero of Carolina, who heard him on one of the memorable occasions connected with the case to which attention has been given, is reported to have said, that Mr. Lide was the greatest genius he had ever seen! A similar remark was also made by the celebrated Dr. Maxcy. In his death Pedee mourned her most erratic, but one of her most gifted sons. His mantle, rare and peculiar as it was, has fallen upon no other since.

CHAPTER XX.

Samuel Wilds—His early life—Filial devotion—Admission to the Bar—Unbounded popularity—His election to the Legislature—Made Solicitor—Promotion to the Bench—Impression made upon the people—Charge to the Grand Jury of Abbeville District—Feeling expressed by the Grand Jury—Sentence on Slater—Sentence on John Tollison—His last Court in Charleston—His death—Its effect on the public mind—Proceedings of Bar of Charleston—Proceedings at Sumpter—Obituary notices—Lines suggested by his death.

MENTION has been made of a few of the more distinguished of those who had been among the early pupils of the academy of St. David's. There was another, the brightest of the rising stars in her firmament when the sun of the last century went down on the Pedee.

Samuel Wilds is a name, in the language of the late venerable Chief Justice of South Carolina, "which challenges respect even after he has rested in the silnce of the grave for nearly fifty years." He was the second son of John Wilds, and born March 4th, 1775, in that part of Cheraw District which subsequently became Marlborough County.* His father died early, leaving a large family, whose support devolved chiefly on Samuel, who was then a youth.

In mind and character his mother was no common woman and from her, doubtless, the superior traits of the son were inherited. Her virtues inspired respect in all who knew her, and commanded, on the part of her noble son, the most affectionate and touching veneration. She is said by one who knew her, to have been "a distinguished lady for her day." His brother, John, was a young man of remarkable promise, but died just as he had prepared himself, as a physician, for entering on the work of life.

---

*Judge O'Neall is mistaken in supposing Darlington the place of his nativity.

To his education and advancement, the subject of this notice had devoted himself with unsparing solicitude.

The early life of Samuel Wilds was a period of sore and continuous struggle against seemingly adverse fortune. The fruits of his youthful labors were mainly devoted to the support and comfort of his mother and her helpless family. But a portion of his time and slender means, as a consequence, could be devoted to his own improvement. He acted, when quite young for such a position, as local deputy sheriff of the district, was also assistant for a time under Thomas Park, in the academy of St. David's, and afterwards became the Principal. This school was his only alma mater. The filial devotion which he exhibited with unwavering constancy, through years of trying privation, was the most beautiful trait in the character of young Wilds, and continued to be its brightest ornament, after he had reached his maturity and was crowned with the lustre of august position and distinguished fame. It was a solid basis for greatness, other elements of strength being added, and a model for the young of every generation. It was not until his twenty-third year, every difficulty having been surmounted, that the first summit in his nobly aspiring career was reached, in his admission to the Bar, of which he was soon to become the ornament and pride. During the same year, he became a candidate for popular favor, but being yet comparatively unknown, and with strong influences opposing him, lost his election to the House of Representatives by a small minority. About this time he married Elizabeth, daughter of Captain Wm. Dewitt, who contributed largely to his happiness, and survived him many years.* One of his first speeches was made at the Bar of Sumpter, in a case for which he had been retained by Daniel Du Bose. His success was complete. It was in the early stage of the court; and such was the effect of his eloquence, that many clients came to him at once and secured his services, giving him a good practice at the start, and an

---

*This excellent lady subsequently married Dr. Thomas Smith, of Society Hill; a pattern of the wife, mother, friend, and Christian. Dr. Smith yet remains, after a long life of usefulness and honor, one of the very few left of that generation.

established reputation as a lawyer throughout the circuit. It was an almost unexampled instance of the kind. His popularity, the spontaneous tribute paid to his exalted worth, was now so great, that in the election of 1802, as already stated, he was triumphantly elected to the Legislature.

In December of that year, he was made solicitor of the Northern and Eastern Circuit. This position gave him a wider field for the display of his peculiar powers, and brought him more generally into notice. The result was, that two years after, he was elected judge, and took his seat on the bench before the completion of his thirtieth year. He had then been but six years at the Bar, to which he was admitted with slender opportunities for preparation. Yet, so rapidly had he mastered that system and those principles which he was now to administer and elucidate, that the ermine sat as easily and gracefully upon him as if he had passed through the most thorough course of study and a practice of many years. A deep impression was made upon the people of the State wherever he travelled his circuits for the first. To a commanding and handsome person were added a dignity and simplicity, with a winning ease and grace of manner,* which inspired profound respect and captivated every heart.

His charges were learned and instructive, and his sentences pathetic and eloquent. Of the former, one specimen is fortunately yet extant. It appeared in the *Charleston Courier*, of May 5, 1807, with some prefatory remarks by the Editors, showing the impression made upon the public mind at the time.

---

*It is related of him, that while holding his first Court in Charleston, a large ball was given, to which, with other dignitaries, Judge Wilds was invited.

He was not provided with the usual dress for such an occasion, and pleaded that as an excuse for not attending. His friends, however, furnished from their own wardrobe what was wanting, and no alternative was left but to make his *debut*. Chancellor De Saussure, himself a model of elegance, felt some apprehension how his brother, for whom he had a high regard, and raw, as he thought, from the country, would sustain himself, and with another friend, kept near him for a while as a support. He was introduced to a lady, who complained that the lights were not burning brightly. He instantly replied, in his happiest manner, "that with such brightness as he saw beaming from the beautiful eyes around him, the light could not grow dim ;" upon which, the Chancellor remarked to his companion, "That is enough ; Wilds can take care of himself, and we may go about our business."

The estimate placed upon it by the grand jury, to whom it was addressed, is sufficiently indicated by the language of the presentment and the request appended to the charge.

"We call the attention of our readers to the very excellent charge of Judge Wilds, which occupies so large a part of this day's paper. The good sense, sound policy, and genuine patriotism which it contains, render it deserving of the most attentive and serious perusal.

"We sincerely hope that his liberal sentiments may be productive of all the good they are so well calculated to produce.

"Charge delivered by Judge Wilds to the Grand Jury of Abbeville District, on Monday, 16th of March last, and published at their request.

" 'Gentlemen of the Grand Jury:

" 'You have so often, I apprehend, had your duties as grand jurors explained to you, and the regular organization of our courts has given such frequent occasions to the exercise of these duties, that perhaps it may be unnecessary for me, at this time, to address you on that subject; however, as I consider them of great importance, both to the community and to yourselves, and believe it impossible that their nature and extent can be made too familiar to your minds, I claim the indulgence of a few observations.

" 'The great outlines of your duty are strongly marked in the solemn and impressive oath which has been just administered to you. "You shall diligently inquire and true presentment make of all such matters and things as shall be given you in charge. You shall present no one from envy, hatred, malice, or ill-will; neither shall you leave any one, unpresented, from fear, favor, affection, or hope of reward."

" 'As the Grand Inquest of your District you are charged with the inquiry, whether the laws have been faithfully observed and executed; and this delicate trust you are sworn impartially to discharge. Upon your accusation alone will the Court entertain even the suspicion of guilt against the most obscure individual: and, on the other hand, when once you have preferred such accusation, neither the most dignified station, nor the most exalted endowments, can screen the person accused from the necessity of publicly vindicating his innocence, or of submitting to the penalties prepared for guilt. Under this stern despotism of the law are completely levelled all those artificial distinctions which the refinements of civil society are continually imposing on mankind.

" 'It is, after all, gentlemen, in the temple of justice alone that the high and the low, the rich and the poor, are brought to feel their original equality. Well has the patriot and philanthropist regarded the trial by jury as one of the strongest evidences of national freedom; for so long as the benefits of this mode of decision are within reach, neither the bold attacks nor the secret approaches of lawless power can long oppress with impunity. In proportion, then, to the importance of your present functions, should be your exertions for their faithful discharge. Whilst, on the one hand, no artifice should secure the guilty from your animadversion, your cautious scrutiny, on the other, should form a rampart of security around the innocent.

" 'It is no apology for an over-hasty and groundless accusation preferred by a grand jury, that the person accused, before he can be made liable to the penalty of the law, must be again found guilty by another jury after a more strict and solemn inquiry; for besides the expense and vexation which it may occasion to procure a discharge, an acquittal by the petit jury will not entirely wipe away the reproach of having been esteemed guilty by a grand jury, equal at least in number and equally bound to do impartial justice. You all know and feel the value of character, and I can recommend no better rule by which you should discharge your present duties than that which should influence the discharge of every other duty, namely, "do unto others as you would have them do unto you."

" 'Besides the examination of such bills as shall be laid before you by the attorney on behalf of the State, there are a variety of other matters subject to your cognizance and animadversion; and though this power, in its first exercise, be merely censorial, not of itself subjecting those against whom it is directed to legal punishment, I will venture to promise, should your investigations present to view offences requiring corrections more forcible than censure, such corrections will not be withheld.

"'Everything relating to the internal policy of your district is properly a subject of your inquiry; such, for instance, are your public roads, highways, and bridges. The great importance of good roads to every country none will deny. But, to a country situated like yours, remote from every advantage of water carriage, good roads are all-important. The widely-spreading progress of population and agricultural improvement in your district, well adapted by nature to the cultivation of our staple commodity, renders inexcusable the present state of your public roads. Perhaps there is no circumstance which so strongly marks the progress of a country in civilization as attention to their public highways. We find amongst the first objects which have attracted the attention of nations but just emerging from barbarism, some rude attempt to facilitate their intercourse by roads; and it is one, among the first instances, in which the solitary, selfish independence of the individual is brought to yield something for the public good. But, were this the only test by which to ascertain the advancement of a country in civilization, I should greatly flatter you, gentlemen, did I not tell you your progress was small indeed.

"'If you should think as I do, that those to whom the laws have confided this branch of police, have shamefully neglected their duty, it becomes yours to say so; and upon your presentment, the Court will direct such measures as will, in all probability, occasion more attention to this subject in future. Such, also, are the laws relative to the performance of patrol duty, and the government of slaves. These laws are strict, and policy requires they should be strictly observed; and it will be a departure from duty in you to suffer any known violation of them to pass unnoticed; and such are all offences against the laws, either of omission or commission, either in any of your public functionaries, or in private individuals, which may come to your knowledge, and which have not otherwise been brought to the view of the Court. Another branch of jurisdiction which I hold to be legitimately yours, is the office of Censors, exercised by grand juries, over the private vices and immoralities of individuals. It is my duty, however, to inform you, that this power, as incidental to your body, is questtioned by many, and denied to you by some. Under institutions like ours, resting entirely upon public opinion, where so much depends upon public virtue, I consider its existence somewhere of first necessity. The spiritual censures to which, in other countries, many of these offences are consigned, in a country like ours, where every person worships his Maker as he pleases, or impiously refuses to worship him at all, would indeed be feeble; and I am aware of no rule, legal, political, or moral, which denies to you the right to express, either as a body or individuals, either privately or publicly, to individuals, to the Court, to the Legislature, or to the world, your abhorrence of vice and its perpetrators. There are a great variety of duties which society imposes on us, upon the performance of which its welfare very much depends; and as many vices, destructive of its interests, which should be prevented, that acknowledge not the coercion of municipal law. The impossibility of reaching the evil by legal remedy has left the performance of these duties, and the prevention of these vices, entirely dependent upon moral rule. That drunkenness, lying, duplicity, ingratitude, lewdness, and debauchery, amongst a variety of other offences of the same description, are evils seriously injurious to society, none will deny; and that any adequate punishment is provided for them by the laws, none will pretend. They can only be prevented, then, by their strong repugnance to the moral sense of the community, and by the reprobation of the influential and virtuous. The dread of being dragged into public view by the penetrating scrutiny of an impartial grand jury, and of having their vices exposed to the animadversion of the world, will prevent many from offending. Should you feel it your duty to exercise this power, you will at once see the importance of proceeding with great delicacy and caution. Grand Juries frequently exercise the privilege of expressing, as a body, their opinions on matters of public concern; and Legislatures, as far as I have observed, uniformly treat such opinions with respect. As from the manner of their organization, grand juries have every opportunity of expressing the public sense of their respective districts, it would, indeed, be a very great want of wisdom in Legislatures to preclude themselves from such correct sources of information.

" 'Should you be of opinion that any particular vices stalk with impunity through the land for want of legal power to punish them—should you be of opinion that any of your rights, either public or private, are not sufficiently acknowledged and protected by the laws of your country, you have the privilege to tell the Legislature so.

" 'In making you acquainted with your privilege in this respect, I have done my duty; to attempt to direct the exercise of this privilege, would be a departure from it. Should you conclude to address the Legislature, there is one subject, however, to which I will venture to invite your attention, particularly as it is not likely to awaken any of those discordant passions which so often convulse the social fabric, and render man the enemy of man, but will more likely soothe existing asperities, by producing one honorable instance at least, in which the enlightened and virtuous of every party do cordially unite.

" 'The subject to which I allude is education; and I suggest to you the propriety of recommending to the Legislature the adoption of some general system by which the blessings of information may be widely disseminated through our country. This interesting subject has, for a considerable time past, deeply occupied the public mind; and though, from the novelty of the thing, and the particular local circumstances of our country, difficulties have arisen which have not been obviated, yet I am confident they must shortly yield to reflection, experience, and perseverence. The prosperous situation of our finances invites to the present as an auspicious time for effecting some arrangement of this sort; and the warm recommendation of grand juries will keep alive the generous propensity for some time entertained on the subject by the Legislature; and receive the support of every enlightened patriot and good man. The importance of knowledge, particularly in a government like ours, is felt by all; for besides ameliorating the affections of the human heart, and amplifying the range of social enjoyment, knowledge is the only sure correction of the diseases to which our body politic is ever liable. The abuse of public confidence will be best prevented by enlightening the public mind. The great bulk of the people, in matters of public concern, always act from honest motives, and never do wrong but in the endeavour to do right. General information, by enabling them to discriminate the modest pretensions of merit from the hollow professions of the designing demagogue, by discovering to them that, in political philosophy, there is a point in improvement at which abstract speculation should yield to practical experiment, would certainly prevent many improprieties into which they are unintentionally, but sometimes unavoidably led.

" 'The important stations which the individuals of our community occupy, render it not only a matter of humanity, but of sound policy, to extend to those who lack the means of acquiring information, the public assistance. Born every man in a measure his own legislator, the public bounty surely could not be better employed than in qualifying each, as far as practicable, for the exercise of such dignified privileges.

" 'However the sports of fortune, or the tendency of civil institutions, have rendered unequal the conditions of men; as to political rights *all* are equal. The arrogant pretensions of rank and the haughty domination of hereditary folly are not acknowledged in our system of government. The highest offices are open to the claims of the most obscure individuals; and you need not be told, gentlemen, that upon such individuals a generous public have sometimes bestowed their confidence, even in advance. There is, therefore, every inducement to direct the public patronage towards the education of our youth. Much, very much, it must be conceded, has already been done by the Legislature establishing, under their own immediate auspices, at the seat of Government, a seminary of the first respectability. From its central situation, its benefits are equally accessible to every part of the State; and from its liberal support, an education may be finished here with equal advantage, in my opinion, and perhaps with less expense, all things considered, than at any institution of equal rank on the Continent. Placed under the immediate direction of the principal officers of Government, with other trustees of equal responsibility, its success and their reputation are closely united. The sons of this institution enjoy the singular advantage of exhibiting to their countrymen, annually assembled, from every part of the State, the earliest testimonies of their talents, and of having ascertained, before they step forward in the theatre of life, their probable success on it.

" 'The child of but yesterday, nursed but a short time by the public affection, the South Carolina College, rises rapidly into eminence, exhibiting a success which its enemies never feared, and its most sanguine friends scarce ever hoped.

" 'The probable consequences resulting from this institution, render its establishment, in my estimation, amongst the most important acts of our State Legislature. Here, a liberal education may be acquired, without contracting habits and sentiments not native to our clime, nor congenial to its interests. Here, the young men of our State are formed, as it were, into one large family, and the early friendships contracted will unite them through life as brothers, without regarding the places of each others' residence; and the present jarring suspicions and supposed contrariety of interests between different parts of the State will be found to yield to offices of mutual kindness and more enlightened policy. Intellectual worth will no longer be ascertained by geographical boundaries, weakly conceived, and wickedly marked out; nor political rights depend upon propinquity to the sea, the sand-hills, or the mountains. Few, I apprehend, who possess the means, will neglect the present favorable opportunity of educating their sons, and fitting them for future usefulness.

" 'But, unfortunately, gentlemen, even in our own favored country, a very large portion of its citizens are not possessed of these means; poor and friendless, they aspire not to the procuring for their sons blessings never enjoyed by themselves. And shall these numerous children of misfortune be entirely excluded from those dazzling meeds with which science rewards her votaries? Shall our country be deprived of the intellectual services of that class of our fellowmen on whom genius is most apt to lavish her favors?

" 'Policy and humanity forbid it. Those astonishing endowments of mind which exalt the human character are, perhaps, oftener found beneath the humble cottage than in the stately mansions of the great. A very large proportion of those sages and heroes who have adorned the ages in which they lived, were educated in the schools of adversity. A benevolent Providence is, by this means, continually levelling down those haughty arrangements which the pride of families, and vanity natural to man, are ever willing to raise up.

" 'You are called together, gentlemen, for the purpose of punishing vice and protecting virtue. You are intended to be a terror to those who do evil—a praise to those who do well. It cannot, I hope, be necessary to remind you to act worthily of the character you have assumed; and that it would be unpardonable in you to neglect those virtues which you have promised to promote, or to practise those vices which you have sworn to punish.' "

The Grand Jury, having made presentments on education, roads, &c., as suggested by his Honor, concluded with these words:—"We beg leave to return our thanks to his Honor, Judge Wilds, for his deliberate and punctual attention to the business of this Court, so far as it has progressed.

"We sincerely reciprocate his sentiments, delivered at its commencement, so strongly expressive of his wish for the promotion of the harmony and happiness of our common country. We hope we may be permitted to request a copy of his charge to our body; and recommend that it, together with the foregoing presentments, may be published in some public newspaper in this State.

"JOHN ARNOLD, Foreman.

"Abbeville, March Term, 1807."

The utterance of such sentiments, so well expressed, as were those of this charge, was well calculated to touch the popular heart, and lead the public mind aright. When it is remembered how limited his own opportunities of education had been, the few years of study which had followed his admission to the Bar, and the yet comparatively early age of Judge Wilds, this production, both as to excellence of matter, and correctness and dignity of style, is worthy of all praise.

The famous sentence* passed upon Slater for the murder of his own slave, gave to the name of Judge Wilds a worldwide celebrity. It made a deep impression, not only in this country, but in England. It appeared soon after its delivery, or portions of it, in the books of oratory of the day; and as Judge O'Neall justly remarks, "is a beautiful and eloquent specimen of his powers." It was in these words:—

"John Slater!

"You have been convicted by a jury of your country for the wilful murder of your own slave; and I am sorry to say, the short, impressive, uncontradicted testimony, on which that conviction was formed, leaves but too little room to doubt its propriety.

"The annals of human depravity might be safely challenged for a parallel to this unfeeling, bloody, and diabolical transaction.

"You caused your unoffending, unresisting slave, to be bound hand and foot, and by a refinement in cruelty, compelled his companion, perhaps the friend of his heart, to chop his head with an axe, and to cast his body, yet convulsing with the agonies of death, into the water! And this deed you dared to perpetrate in the very harbor of Charleston, within a few yards of the shore, unblushingly, in the face of open day. Had your murderous arm been raised against your equal, whom the laws of self-defence and the most efficacious laws of the land unite to protect, your crime would not have been without precedent and would have seemed less horrid. Your personal risk would at least have proved, that though a murderer you were not a coward. But you too well knew that this unfortunate man, whom

---

*It is not a little singular that this production is not to be found in the newspapers of Charleston of the time. The Author, at least, after a diligent search, failed to find it, or any allusion to it, in the files of newspapers in the Charleston Library. It was found by Judge O'Neall in the "Key to Uncle Tom's Cabin," after a vain search elsewhere.

chance had subjected to your caprices, had not, like yourself, chartered to him by the laws of the land the same rights of nature; and that a stern but necessary policy had disarmed him of the rights of self-defence. Too well you knew that to you alone he could look for protection, and that your arm alone could shield him from oppression or avenge his wrongs; yet that arm you cruelly stretched out for his destruction.

"The counsel who generously volunteered his services in your behalf, shocked at the enormity of your offence, endeavored to find a refuge, as well for his own feelings as for those of all who heard your trial, in a derangement of your intellect. Several witnesses were examined to establish this fact; but the result of their testimony, it is apprehended, was as little satisfactory to his mind as to those of the jury to whom it was addressed. I sincerely wish this defence had proved successful; not from any desire to save you from the punishment which awaits you, and which you so richly merit, but from the desire of saving my country from the foul reproach of having, in its bosom, so great a monster.

"From the peculiar situation of this country, our fathers felt themselves justified in subjecting to a very slight punishment him who murders a slave. Whether the present state of society requires a continuation of this policy, so opposite to the apparent rights of humanity, it remains for a subsequent Legislature to decide. Their attention ere this would have been directed to this subject, but, for the honor of human nature, such hardened sinners as yourself are rarely found to disturb the repose of society. The grand jury of this county, deeply impressed with your daring outrages against the laws of both God and man, have made a very strong expression of their feelings on the subject to the Legislature, and from the wisdom and justice of that body, the friends of humanity may confidently hope to see this *blackest* in the catalogue of human crimes pursued by appropriate punishment."*

---

*Judge O'Neall adds the following note (see his "Bench and Bar of S. C.," vol. i. p. 104):—"The punishment under the Act of 1740, § 38, under which Slater was convicted and sentenced, was a fine of £700, currency—equal to £100 sterling—which, at 4s. 8d. to the dollar, is $428, 57-100—and incapacity to

"In proceeding to pass the sentence which the law provides for your offence, I confess I never felt more forcibly the want of power to make respected the laws of my country, whose minister I am.

"You have already violated the majesty of those laws. You have probably pleaded the local law, under which you stand convicted, as a justification of your crime. You have held that law in one hand and brandished your axe in the other, impiously contending that the one gave a license to the unrestrained use of the other.

"But though you will go off unhurt in person, by the present sentence, expect not to escape with impunity. Your bloody deed has set a mark upon you which I fear the good actions of your future life will not efface. You will be held in abhorrence by an impartial world, and shunned as a monster by every honest man. Your unoffending posterity will be visited for your iniquity, by the stigma of deriving their origin from an unfeeling murderer. Your days, which will be but few, will be spent in wretchedness, and if your conscience be not steeled against every virtuous emotion—if you be not entirely abandoned to hardness of heart—the mangled, mutilated corpse of your murdered slave will ever be present in your imagination, obtrude itself into all your amusements, and haunt you in the hours of silence and repose.

"But, should you disregard the reproaches of an offended world—should you hear with callous insensibility the gnawings of a guilty conscience—yet remember that an awful period is fast approaching, and with you it is close at hand, when you must appear before a tribunal whose want of

---

enjoy or receive the profits of any office, place, or employment, civil or military, and if unable to pay this fine, then imprisonment for seven years. The Act of 1821 changed this trifling punishment for what Judge Wilds justly called 'the *blackest* in the catalogue of human crimes,' to death." His eloquent tongue had been silent in death nearly eleven years, when the "wisdom and justice" of the Legislature yielded to the "hopes" of the "friends of humanity." "At my instance," continues the judge, "my friend Daniel Horlbeck, Esq., caused the records to be examined, to ascertain when the above sentence was pronounced, and strange to say, nothing can be found. There is no Sessions docket or journal, until 1833, now extant. No indictment against Slater can be found. I presume the sentence was pronounced in 1807." This is confirmatory of the fact stated in the preceding note, that the sentence was not published in the city papers of the time.

JUDGE SAMUEL WILDS.

power can afford you no prospect of impunity—when you must raise your bloody hands at the bar of an impartial, omniscient Judge.

"Remember, I pray you remember, whilst you yet have time, that God is just, and that His vengeance will not sleep for ever."

An occasion like this called forth the peculiar powers of Judge Wilds, touching, as it did, the tenderest sensibilities and stirring up the emotional depths of his nature. The sympathies of the man were not swallowed up in the stern sense of duty in the upright judge. It was here that he appeared good as he was great.

Another production, and the last of those emanating from him which has been preserved, though it seems not to have attained such celebrity, deservedly takes rank with the sentence passed on Slater. It was published in the *South Carolina Gazette,* of Wednesday, May 3rd, 1809, with the following remarks prefixed, viz. :—

"Eloquent and Impressive.

"At the Court of General Sessions of the Peace, holden at Union Court House, in March Term last, before the Honorable Judge Wilds, John Tollison was tried and found guilty of the wilful murder of John Mathis; and when the unhappy criminal was brought to the bar, to receive the sentence of the law, the following eloquent and impressive address was delivered by the judge. The serious impression it made on all who were present,—the faithful, correct, and forcible view it exhibits of the awful and terrific situation of the wretch, who, abandoned to the feelings of humanity, imbues his hand in the blood of his fellow-creature—induced the members of the Bar attending that Court, earnestly to request the honorable judge to commit it to writing, and favor them with a copy; which request he politely complied with, and by those members of the Bar it is now offered to the public :—

"John Tollison:

"The duty which yet remains to be performed towards you, of all others to me the most awful and distressing, it is my misfortune to be obliged to perform alone. The laws of our common country have commissioned me to announce to you your doom: I hold your death-warrant in my hand. Death, the great destroyer of man, is terrible even in its mildest forms; though we behold its destructive ravages spread wide around us—though we behold the rich, the poor, the old, the young, the virtuous, the vicious, fall indiscriminately before its deadly scythe, and feel our own fate inevitable,—still we cannot contemplate its frightful approaches, but with the most fearful apprehensions. The awful uncertainties of a future state, the untried vicissitudes of an unknown world, whence none who have gone, have ever returned, appall the strongest hearts; and like cowards, we groan under the pressure of life's many ills, fearful to draw aside the veil which hides the future from us. But, though death be always dreadful, it is not always equally so. To yield our lives to Him who gave them; to wait the dread moment on our beds of sickness, surrounded by those we love, whose affectionate concern, whose sympathizing tears, soften the anguish of expiring nature—to die for our native land, to guard its honor on the field of danger, and meet the grim tyrant at the cannon's mouth, though not enough to make him welcome, robs him of half his terrors. But, unfortunately for you, these are consolations which will not support you in your approaching doom. The life which God hath given you, you have yourself most wickedly destroyed—the tender love, the sympathetic tear which would have cleaved to your departing spirit, and winged it for its flight, you have banished by your public disgrace, to pine in hopeless solitude over your untimely fate; and to the offended justice of that country, for whose honor to have died would have been heroic, you fall a victim. Hung up between the heavens and the earth,—heaven's oldest, greatest curse stamped on the deed you have done; no friendly voice to bid a long farewell; no friendly hand to close your eyes in death; you will exhibit an awful, but instructive spectacle to the world, and prove that the arm of avenging justice is swift to overtake him who sheds a brother's blood.

"I need not remind you, for you cannot have forgotten the circumstances which led to this fatal catastrophe. Your hands yet smoke with the blood of murder, and Mathis's new-made grave makes an impressive appeal to your memory. Think not to find a palliation for your offence in the intoxication under which it is said you labored; nor hope to extenuate its horrors, in the irritation of passion which you endeavored to establish. Your drunkenness but aggravates your crime; the diabolical fury which drove you on to perpetrate this fatal deed, seems not to have had any exciting cause; and the insidious, cowardly manner in which you made the attack, the deadly weapon which you wielded, and your unmanly perseverance in inflicting the deepest injuries on an adversary, who had not made the slightest resistance, nay, who was even unable to raise his hand against you, argue a most savage temperament of soul—a heart black with malevolence, and more than ordinarily depraved. You have had a fair and impartial trial by juries of your own choice, in the selection of whom even your caprice has been tenderly indulged: you have had the benefit of able counsel, whose manly address to the understanding, whose eloquent appeals to the heart, must have saved you, if even a doubt of your guilt could have been excited; but alas! it has all been in vain; you have been pronounced guilty of the horrid crime of murder, for which you die unpitied.

"It will be hardly generous to remind you, for it can now only aggravate your distress, of the many strong inducements which you had to a different conduct. Living in a land of light and liberty, where every right is securely protected, every virtuous exertion liberally rewarded,—in the vigor of health and prime of manhood, and surrounded by all the means of honest enjoyment, life was surely worth preserving. You have, but my heart sickens at the thought, a wife, who tenderly loves you—you are a father of children, who look to you for bread; for them at least you ought to have lived. Cruel, thoughtless man, what have you done? Besides robbing these objects, justly dear to your heart, of their only protection and support; besides turning them on a wide and friendless world, exposed to all the buffetings of scoff and adversity, you have unkindly loaded them with disgrace, which, though they do not merit, they must for ever feel.

"But, if the laws of your country, and your country's

God; if the love of life, and its varied enjoyments; if the distress and disgrace of a family you love, were unable to withhold your murderous arm; yet, believe me, when I assure you, a reason yet more powerful than all, ought to have made you pause! You have an immortal soul at stake, and have, by this fatal deed, to the manifold transgressions of an ill-spent life, added a mountain of guilt.

"Your days on earth are now numbered. The sword of death, which hangs uplifted over the frail thread of your existence, ready to drop, will quickly cut it in twain, and those who have known you, will know you no more! But, though you feel the fatal stroke, hope not in it to find a termination of your woes. It will be the mere prelude to another trial, awfully terrific. Again you will be arraigned at the bar of justice, and the black record of a thousand crimes spread in your view. Again you must raise your trembling hand, but before a Judge, whose penetrating eye will spy the secret corners of your soul, whose power is fearful indeed! Again you will be confronted with witnesses—and, horrible thought, the bleeding, murdered Mathis, probably dragged from the howling regions of despair, will appear in the number; should you again be found guilty, your doom will be interminable woe! Let me conjure you by every tie which yet has a hold upon your heart, to devote the scanty remnant of your days to serious preparation for your approaching doom! Strive importunately, I beseech you, to secure that Advocate, whose merits are all powerful, whose services alone can save you; for in the exhaustless fountain of redeeming grace, even the foul stain of murder may be washed clean!

"The sentence of the Court is, that you be now carried from hence to the place from whence you came, and that on the last Friday in May next, between the hours of eleven in the forenoon and two in the afternoon, you be carried to the place of public execution, in the district of Union, there to be hanged by the neck until your body be dead, and may the Almighty God have mercy on your soul!"

The end of a brilliant career was now rapidly approaching. It is needless to remark, how much was crowded into a life not more brief than successful, not more singularly marked by its rapid rise to eminence, than the manner in which the highest honors thus early won were borne! It will suffice to say, that no man was ever more deservedly popular, more universally beloved, or more profoundly regretted in his departure from earth than Samuel Wilds.

There was, as we must conclude from tradition and contemporary testimony, a charm in his manner and conversation—in his countenance, his words, his actions, his life—about the whole man, in short, which has seldom, if ever, had a counterpart in any public character.

Taken altogether, judged by what he was and what he did, for his life was short—he had scarcely completed his 35th year when death overtook him—it may well be questioned whether his native State has ever produced a better or a greater man.

His last Court was held in Charleston. It was a most laborious session, tasking his vigorous powers to the uttermost. The work, however, was faithfully done, seventeen hundred suits having been disposed of, to the satisfaction of every party interested. To the last a brighter lustre was being added to his name. But, his race was finished! The first intelligence received in the city from the home to which he had returned with fond anticipations, was the announcement of his death. The blow was deeply felt. In all parts of the State his name had become a household word, and was gratefully and admiringly cherished. Adapting himself, without effort, to all classes, he commanded the love and the homage of all. In Charleston, the seat of intelligence and refinement, where he won every heart from the first, the feeling produced by the tidings of his sudden and untimely end, was intense, and the public manifestations of regard, affecting and impressive. In the country, meetings were also held, and every demonstration of respect and sorrow was made for one who was, in truth, a universal favorite.

Of the action of the Charleston Bar on this melancholy occasion, the *Courier* of March 21st, 1810, contained the following notice:—

"At a meeting of the gentlemen of the Bar in Charleston, convened on Monday forenoon, for the purpose of expressing their respect for the memory of the Honorable Judge Wilds, recently deceased, Timothy Ford, Esq., was called to the chair, and a committee appointed to frame resolutions, expressive of the object of the meeting, consisting of the following gentlemen, viz.:—The Hon. Langdon Cheves, William Loughton Smith, Esq., Keating L. Simons, Esq., and Charles Fraser, Esq., who reported the following resolutions, which were unanimously adopted, viz.:—'The members of the Bar of Charleston, being convened on the melancholy occasion of the death of the Honorable Samuel Wilds, one of the Judges of the Court of Common Pleas and Sessions of this State, have entered unanimously into the following resolutions:—Whereas, the Bar of Charleston have received with emotions of heart-felt sorrow the mournful intelligence of the death of Judge Wilds, and deplore this sad event, not only as a calamity to the public, who are thereby bereaved of an able, upright, and assiduous minister of justice, but as being particularly afflicting to themselves, who were personally and cordially attached to him, as well from a high sense of his professional merit, as on account of his numerous private virtues, and of an uncommon amiableness of disposition and suavity of manners, happily blended with the dignity of deportment suitable to his high station:— Therefore, resolved, that they do, in testimony of their sentiments, most sincerely entertained by them, and as a tribute of affection and respect for his memory, wear crape on the left arm one month from the date of this resolution.

" 'Resolved, that the Rev. Mr. Flinn be requested to deliver a sermon[*] on the melancholy occasion, and that the members of the Bar do attend the same.' "

The *Carolina Gazette* of April 6th, 1810, published the following proceedings in Sumpter:—

"Sumpter Court House, March 16th, 1810.

"The gentlemen of the Bar at Sumpter Court, having heard of the death of the Honorable Judge Wilds, called a meeting of the members present, to take into consideration in what manner they should express their regret for his loss,

---

[*] Mr. Flinn preached an admirable discourse, as requested, which was afterwards published.

and their respect for his memory. The Honorable Judge Brevard was pleased, at their request, to attend the meeting, and preside, when they came to the following resolution:— 'We, the members of the Bar of South Carolina, convened at Sumpter Court House, deeply impressed with the loss we have sustained in the death of the Honorable Judge Wilds, deem it equally a privilege and a duty to give expression to our feelings by some public mark of the respect we entertain for his memory; to mingle our tears with those of his family and relatives, to sympathize with his friends, and to deplore, with our fellow-citizens at large, the calamity which has befallen the State, in the loss of one of its greatest ornaments. As a faint emblem, therefore, of the tribute due to departed merit, we do hereby resolve, that we will testify the grief which we feel at the loss of a man so virtuous and beloved, of a judge so able and so distinguished in the discharge of the duties of his office, by wearing crape on the left arm until after the next sitting of the Constitutional Court.

" 'Abraham Nott	J. G. Mathis
John S. Richardson	Abraham Blanding
John D. Witherspoon	James Ervin
James S. Dees	John B. Miller
R. L. Witherspoon	Thomas R. Mitchell
James Caldwell	James G. Spann.' "
William Grant

The *Raleigh Star,* of March 22nd, 1810, contained the following truthful and touching obituary notice:—

"Died, at his seat near Cheraw Court House, on Friday, the 9th of March, the Honorable Samuel Wilds, one of the Associate Judges of the State of South Carolina. In this gentleman, his family, his friends, and his State have sustained a loss which will be as deeply regretted as it is irreparable.

"He seemed formed by nature to conciliate affection and excite admiration; for such was the benevolent sunshine of his countenance and the fascination of his manners, that to know him was to love him; and such was the strength and disinterested liberality of his mind, that to converse with him was to receive edification and feel the admiration due to superior intellect. He possessed a *vis vivida animi,* a richness of imagination, which, while it decked with eloquence whatever it touched, displayed with better energy and grace the offspring of his judgment. His progress in life was proportioned to the superiority of his endowments. Holding the first place in the friendship of all who knew him, and the idol of his fellow-citizens, he rose with rapid strides, though still in his youth, to the first honors of his profession. But, inscrutable are the ways of Providence. He was permitted to rise like the sun, enough above his horizon to give anticipations of the splendor of his meridian elevation, when the dark cloud of death passed over his face, and wrapt him for ever from our view. But he lives, and long will live in the fond and disconsolate affection of his amiable consort and connexions, in the admiration of his friends, and his State will long deplore the loss of the most promising of her sons."

The fullest tribute to the memory of the departed jurist, who was, indeed, one of the noblest of men, appeared in the *Carolina Gazette,* of Charleston, March 30, 1810. It will aptly close the brief sketch of his life which has been given.

"Sic transit gloria mundi.

"Died, on Friday, the 9th inst., after a short and violent illness,* the Honorable Samuel Wilds, one of the Judges of the Court of Common Pleas, and Sessions of this State; within a few hours of the day which would have completed his thirty-fifth year. The death of this amiable gentleman and excellent citizen, was as unexpected and afflicting, as his elevation to public esteem and distinction, had been rapid, brilliant and well merited. Some account of the rise and progress of a man, so deservedly esteemed and generally lamented, cannot but be acceptable to the community he hath so well served, and particularly to the inhabitants of this city, who have been so recently benefited by the able and assiduous discharge of his public functions, as a minister of justice.

---

*The disease was pneumonia.

"He was born in Marlborough District, in this State, of parents, who were of Welch extraction; and was the eldest of a numerous family of young children, whom his father left, at a tempestuous season, to the care of a fond and exemplary mother, with little other inheritance than his own honest fame; with scarce other bequest than a parent's blessing! But these were enough for the lamented subject of our remarks. A shrewd, sagacious boy,—a docile, obedient child—ere long he began to divide with his mother, the cares of her family, and by a degree of diligence and good management, seldom found in one of his age, he continued to regulate the affairs of their narrow fortune, so as to lessen the toils of his surviving parent, and to augment the sum of her comforts. Yet, he was not contented. 'The young idea beginning now to shoot,' his ardent mind parched with the thirst of knowledge. Alas, his parent had not withal to sustain its appetite. Too kind, however, not to sympathize, too generous not to fan its noble flame, her maternal love, by dint of frugality and privation, found the means of gratifying the longings of her darling boy. He was placed by her at the St. David's School, in Cheraws, under the tuition of Mr. Park, a learned and respectable gentleman, now one of the Professors at the College at Columbia. His aspiring and teeming genius at once carried him ahead of all his young companions, in so great and rapid a proficiency, in all the branches of his studies, that he was soon, under the liberal patronage of his preceptor, promoted, with the allowance of a small salary, to the place of an assistant teacher. An incident here occurred, of which he ever spoke to his friends with delight. It was his lot to educate the lady who afterwards became his wife, and to whom, during a happy union of near twelve years, it may be truly said, he never gave 'a pang, but when he died.' Thus advanced, his pittant salary glowed like a mine in his eyes. It now afforded him the means for which he had often sighed, of opening the spring from whence he had tasted, with so much pleasure, to an only and beloved brother, a boy of promising parts. John Wilds was accordingly put to school by his brother. Some time afterwards, the latter succeeded to Mr. Park, as principal teacher. His mind, now expanding as he advanced in years, began to explore the path he was to tread in his walk through life. Endowed with an uncommon share of sagacity, with a sound judgment, a quick discrimination, and a large fund of native elocution, he selected the profession of the law, as the best theatre for his talents, and as presenting the readiest course, under the genius of our government, for his rise to distinction.

"He accordingly entered on the study of the law, with the late Wm. Falconer, Esq. Still more the favorite of genius than of fortune, he was not enabled to devote his time and thoughts entirely to the study of his profession, but was obliged to divide them between that and the economy of the little patrimony which sustained his mother and sisters, and the duties of a place in the sheriff's office of the district of his residence, from whence he derived a maintenance for himself and his brother. The time at length arrived for his entering upon the career which he hath run with so much honor to himself and usefulness to his country.

"He was called to the Bar in the spring of '98. It is needless to state that he was, immediately after his admission to the Bar, engaged in every cause of importance in the districts adjacent to the place of his nativity. He had been so long and so much a favorite in these, that this circumstance affords no test of his professional merit. In the remote districts of his practice, he quickly ranked among the most eminent in his profession; and by the unaffected simplicity of his manners, and the native amiableness of his disposition, became in them as much beloved as among his own neighbours.

"His first and most earnest wish now, was to establish and bring forward his brother. The latter being inclined to the study of physic, was, after having received the rudiments of his profession from Dr. Hawes, a gentleman of science resident in his neighbourhood, and a friend to the family, sent by his brother to Newport, in Rhode Island, to complete his professional education, under the late Dr. Seuter, and was also supplied by him with the means of occasionally attending the lectures of Dr. Rush, at Philadelphia. Having finished his studies, he returned home, and commenced the practice of physic. The fondest wishes of his brother's heart were now about to be consummated. This promising plant, cultivated with so much labor and anxiety, put forth its tender buds,—fair to the eye; but there came 'a frost, a killing frost,' that nipt it in the flower. The amiable subject of our notice derived consolation from preserving his memory in honorable recollection.

"Having unavoidably incurred some debts in beginning the practice of his profession, which he had done on the faith of the brightest prospects, now closed in the grave too soon for the performance of his engagements, it was felt by his brother as a sacred duty, to see them discharged; and this he did in the spirit with which he accomplished all his duties. This rude shock, which closed for ever the channel wherein the benevolence of him who is our theme had delighted to flow, did not, however, dry up or impoverish its abundant source. It became, as soon as his pecuniary resources would admit, a maxim with him, to which he strictly conformed in practice, always to have flourishing under the genial warmth of his bounty and patronage, some tender shoot of genius that had been exposed to the frost of poverty.

"Honored by the virtuous, and blessed by the poor, he still pursued the track of his bright destinies. In the autumn of 1800, he was unanimously elected a member of the House of Representatives of the Legislature of this State, from the district of Darlington.

"Unbending, yet liberal in his public principles, it was his uncommon felicity to be cherished with pride and delight by his own party, at the same time that he enjoyed the general esteem and confidence, and in numerous instances, the cordial affections of his political opponents.

"Under such circumstances, it could not be long ere his influence would become important and distinguished in the body of which he was a member. He accordingly enjoyed this distinction, not only with the consciousness of deserving it, but the heartfelt satisfaction of knowing, that the sense of this merit was a universal sentiment. This honorable height he reached, as well by an instinctive repugnance to all the bubbling devices of popular intrigue, as by the noble independence of his character, the abundant resources of his mind, and an upright, direct, manly pursuit of the measures he believed to be connected with the public advantage; which held out to all that marked his course, 'the assurance of a man,' bent only on the welfare of the State.

"In aid of those excellent qualities, and so estimable a character, were a frankness of mind, without the least mixture of guile—an openness of heart, without the slightest tincture of bitterness or acrimony—a fascinating playfulness of temper, that banished all semblance of harshness or austerity, and a presence beaming with the most happy mixture of benignity and sense—while withal, he carried himself with so modest a port, and with so much native, unassumed dignity, that he was wont, at the first introduction, to seize upon the esteem and regards of his acquaintance, and bind them to him with a gordian knot.

"Indeed, such was the unaffected simplicity of his manner and lively 'sunshine' of his countenance, that he could, at the same moment, win the esteem of hoary age and draw lisping infancy to his bosom.

"Nor shall it be forgotten, that his eloquence, like the herald of the morn, precursed his race to the bright meridian of his public honors. His eloquence owed much to nature; as much to the care with which he cultivated it. Ready, perspicuous, manly, and flowing, its general type partook of the amiableness of his disposition, being inclined, 'by winning words to conquer willing hearts'—although it was susceptible, when he pleased, of a degree of elevation and energy, that stamped on it the features of a commanding character.

"It shone most in a chaste and nervous expression of sentiment, imbibing nourishment rather from the passions than the fancy, and delighting more in the glowing regions of the heart, than the serene fields of the imagination; though even hence it were wont to inhale many a fragrant breath, and to weave many a graceful wreath. It was, however, only the dress and ornament to his masculine reason. Endowed with a vigorous and ample understanding, which had surmounted every difficulty in its way, and profited by every occasion of enriching itself with precious lore—and being no less delighted with the fruit of logic, than charmed with the flowers of rhetoric—he exhibited in discursive power, a degree of strength and solidity, that was unrivalled by the flight of his elocution.

"His mind always embraced a clear and comprehensive view of his subject, and his ratiocination was generally conducted from cause to consequence, by a beautiful and regular concatenation, though sometimes, it must be owned, its method was disturbed by an overruling bias to declamation—the eloquence of which, however, never failed to atone for his transgression of order. His moral excellences are sufficiently portrayed in the traits that have been given already of his character. The sentiments of filial piety and affection (it shall still be remarked), could but have deep root in a heart of so soft and generous a mould. One habit, which was fixed with him, will suffice to show this. It was his custom, ever, on returning home from a journey, especially after he had risen to distinction, at whatever hour of day or night it happened, immediately to visit his mother, who resided at a short distance from his own dwelling, that he might taste the joy his dutiful and affectionate demeanor was wont to kindle in her aged bosom, and feast his soul with a parent's blessing.

"Possessed of the qualities of mind above noticed, it would seem that a popular assembly had been a better theatre for his talents than the solemn bench of justice, and that they would have been attracted to the national councils as their most suitable sphere of action; but his destiny ruled otherwise.

"After having served for two years as Solicitor of the Northern Circuit, to which post he was almost unanimously elected, in December, 1802, and faithfully discharged the duties thereof—in fulfilling which he combined the softest feelings of humanity with an inflexible adherence to the claims of public duty—he was, in the year 1804, elected a judge of the Court of Common Pleas and Sessions of this State.

"Seated now on a noble eminence, his mind seemed to grow to the prospects around him, and although the cast of it may have appeared better adapted to another, but no less distinguished part, it was, nevertheless, here that it displayed its highest energies. How well he discharged the duties of this important station, may be seen in the records of our Courts, and will be read hereafter, in the juridical history of our State. How happily he performed them, may be read now in the sorrowful countenances of his brethren of the profession, in the effusions of their grief, and in the public honor they have conferred on his memory.

"It seemed, indeed, the pleasure of Providence, that this favored genius should mount to the skies, clothed in the radiance of a star.

" 'Within a month, a little month,' after having accomplished important services for the State, as a minister of justice; after having displayed the powers of his mind, and the resources and readiness of his learning, during a long and laborious term, in examining and determinining, with the soundest judgment and most accurate discrimination, the multifarious topics springing out of seventeen hundred suits, in which, though many were not litigated, many were, and some involving questions of a complicated and difficult nature; after having sealed his labors with the affectionate adieus of his fellow-laborers, while yet on every tongue the living theme of praise, his soul rushed from its abode of clay, and sought its native heaven.

"Oh, where is now the light of those eyes that beamed with so lovely a lustre? Where that benignant smile? Where the 'sunshine' of soul that for ever played on that manly face? Cease weeping, folly!—they have fled with his spirit from the circles of men to the spheres of angels.

"Yet it were allowable to shed on their departure some natural drops. Their image yet lives with us; it is engraven on the hearts of his numerous acquaintance; it is embalmed in the tears of his mourning friends and relatives."*

To this touching record of departed worth, watered with the tears of him from whom it emanated, may be added the

---

*This tribute of affection was doubtless from the pen of that noble man and distinguished lawyer, Keating L. Simons, Esq., of Charleston, between whom and Judge Wilds the truest sympathy and most cordial and endearing friendship existed.

effusion of another,* who born and reared in the same region with Judge Wilds, and probably his pupil in St. David's, knew and loved him in his earlier years, and now joined, with all the generous ardor of his nature, in the general grief over his untimely end!

"FOR THE *COURIER.*

"Lines occasioned by the lamented death of the Hon. Judge Wilds.
"Come, grief, with thy funeral train,
  Thy heart-afflicting sigh,
And pity's elegiac strain,
  And sorrow's swollen eye.
Cease pleasure's gay, deceitful sound,
Our brows with cypress leaves be bound,
As bending sad o'er virtue's bier,
We wake the plaintive song, and shed the sorrowing tear.

"With ceaseless hate, terrific foe,
  Death wields his vengeful arm;
He lays the pride of valor low,
  And rifles beauty's charm.
Yet why, insatiate tyrant, why
A mark so noble and so high,
To strike with vent'rous arrow dare,
And folly's giddy tribe with cruel fondness spare?

"Virtue in vain her boast would save,
  And shield her favorite son;
Alas, he sinks into the grave,
  Heaven's holy will be done!
The wreath that learning had prepared,
The patriot's brightest, best reward,
Torn from his living brow, shall bloom
A laurel ever green around his grassy tomb.

"Though here his silent relics sleep,
  Cold in the chill embrace of earth,
His early fate shall genius weep,
  And justice tell his worth.
Where shall his mourning country find
So good a heart, so strong a mind?
A life so pure, such honorable fame,
As that which shed its beams 'round Wilds's modest name?

"Ah! why in quest of classic lore,
  Does wisdom idly toil;
The flow'ret scarcely blooms, before
  It withers in the soil.
Yet still its fragrance shall survive,
And still the fame of genius live,
While fond remembrance on her grateful breast,
Its various worth records with deathless force imprest.

---

*Supposed to be John Lide Wilson, then in his twenty-sixth year.

"There still his voice shall charm the ear,
 And still in memory's tearful eye
His form shall to his friends appear,
 And wake the mournful sigh.
From earth removed, his manly soul,
Far, far above the earth's control,
On seraph's wings to heaven has flown,
And joys in virtue's meed, religion's sacred crown!

"W.

"March 17th, 1810."

INDEX

ADAMS, among settlers on Pedee, 99
Allison, Rev. Mr., notice of, 69
    ,,   Dr. Robert, elected Sheriff for Marlborough, 460
Alston, Peter, settles on Pedee, 105; his removal, 106
    ,,   Peter, Representative for St. David's, 416
Ammons, Joshua, notice of, and meeting with Lafayette, 402-403, and *note*
Andrews, John, Adjutant under Kolb, 301
Assembly, Commons House of, elects deputies to Congress, 206
    ,,   General, under new form of government, convened, 258
    ,,   Address of Speaker of House and Council to President, 258
    ,,   Summoned to meet in Charles-town, 274
    ,,   Vacancies in, for St. David's filled, 275
    ,,   prescribes Oath, its effects, original certificate of, 287-288
Auld, John and Michael, pursuit of Tories, 330
Ayer, Thomas, settles on Pedee, his family, 93 and *note*
    ,,   ,,   reply when asked to take oath of allegiance, 305
    ,,   ,,   reward offered for by M'Arthur, 309
    ,,   ,,   capture of, and escape, 309-311
    ,,   Lewis Malone's narrative of Kolb's death, and of pursuit by Tories, 362-368
    ,,   ,,   removal to Barnwell, and death, 93 *note*

BACOT, SAMUEL, settles on Pedee, origin, and family, 105-106
    ,,   ,,   adventure with Tories, 327-328
    ,,   ,,   imprisonment and escape, 328-329, and *note*
Baker, notice of family, 75
    ,,   Captain, of Georgia, skirmish with Tories, 386
Bar of Cheraws, 204; Lawyers at, 436
Barfield, noted Tories of the name, 337
    ,,   Major, account of, and his perfidy, 338
    ,,   fight with Murphy at Bass's, 372-373
    ,,   notices of, 334, 337-338
Baxter, James, settles on Poke Swamp, 79
    ,,   Colonel John, distinguished, 79; Representative for Liberty, 455
    ,,   one of the name hangs a Tory, 386
    ,,   Robert, Representative for St. David's, 445; his death, 451
Bedgegood, Rev. Nicholas, notice of, and family, 96 and *note*, 97
    ,,   ,,   preaches Sessions sermons at Long Bluff, 196
    ,,   ,,   extract from his journal, 96, *note*
Benton, Lemuel, settles on Pedee, marriage, his family, 104
    ,,   ,,   a Major in command on Pedee, 352
    ,,   ,,   with Kolb after Tories on Cat Fish, 359
    ,,   ,,   Lieutenant-Colonel, 371
    ,,   ,,   his regiment allotted to Marion's Brigade, 377
    ,,   ,,   on Black Creek, skirmish of his force with Tories, 386
    ,,   ,,   another skirmish on Black Creek, 387
    ,,   ,,   writes to Governor Matthews, 388-389

Benton, Lemuel, writes to General Marion, 390-391, 391-392
" " opposed successively by Mr. Wilson and General Huger for Congress, 401
" " Representative for St. David's, 415, 432, 445
" " County Court Justice for Darlington County, 433, 452
" " Escheator for Cheraws, 446
" " delegate to Convention in Charleston, 447
" " delegate to Convention in Columbia, 451
" " Sheriff for Cheraws, 451, 453
" " in Congress, and difficulty with Major Thomas, 455-456
" " resigns commission as colonel, 456
" " traits of character, 371; sketch of, and death, 401
Bethea, William, settles on Little Pedee, his family, 86
" " attacked by Tories for his money, 394
" John, sen., and jun., after Tories, 393
" " punishes Snowden, a Tory, 394
" Philip, Representative for Liberty, 461
Blackman, a Tory, punished by Colonel Murphy, 354
Black Creek, Acts to improve navigation of, and commissioners, 446, 453
Blakeney, John, settles on Lynche's Creek, his family, 100
" " family of, suffer from Tories, 383-384
" Mrs. Mary, notice of, 384, note
" James, Representative for Chesterfield County, 456, 459
Boundary line between North and South Carolina, 37-41, 469
Botsford, Rev. Edmond, notice of, his marriage, 88, note
" " removes his family to Virginia, 439-440
Braddock's defeat, followed by removals to Pedee, 92
Bradley, a Tory, taken and killed by Colonel M'Ree, 394
Brawler, Jacob, unequalled gift to his country, 403-404, and note
Brevard, Joseph, at Cheraw Bar, 436
Brigman, a Tory, killed by Daniel Hicks, 385
Brockington, Richard, his settlement and family, 90
" Mrs. Mary, 90, note
" Richard, Representative for Darlington, 456
Brown, Rev. John, comes to Pedee, notice of, 64
" Colonel Thomas, ordered to Pedee, 333
" " writes to General Harrington, 333, 334, 337-338
" John, County Court Justice for Chesterfield, 451
" Morgan, Representative for St. David's, 432-445
" " Senator for St. David's, 448
" " County Court Justice for Marlborough, 433, 452
" " delegate to Convention in Columbia, 451
Brownfield, Doctor Robert, delegate to Convention in Charleston, 447
" " Representative for St. David's, 447, 448
Bryan, Colonel, a Loyalist, notice of, 314
Buckholdts, Jacob, Mention of, family, 54, and note
" Creek, 76
" Abraham, Major of Cheraws Regiment, 226
Bull Pen, notice of, 361-362, 364, 371
Bullard, Joel, Sheriff for Chesterfield, 460
Butler, Jef., Tory Captain, notice of, adventure with Whigs, 395-396
" " protected by Marion, 395

CAMPBELL, Captain, settles on Pedee, 441
" " his sons, Robert and John, notice of, 441
Cannon, Henry, Representative for St. David's, 448
" " County Court Justice for Darlington, 451
Cantey, Josiah, adventure with Tories, wounded, 359
Carlos, Robeson, settles on Pedee, 443

Cashway, origin of name, 78, *note*
Caswell, General, writes to General Harrington, 309
Cat Fish creek, Act to improve navigation of, and commissioners, 453
Caucasian race, progressive, 108
Caulkins, at Cheraws Bar, 436
Chapman, Allen, settles in Chesterfield, 442
    ,,   ,,   Sheriff of Cheraws, 432
    ,,   John, settles in Chesterfield, 442
Charge of Judge Drayton, 211-215
    ,, of Judge Grimke, 416-429
    ,, of Judge Wilds, 502-509
Charleston exposed to attack by sea, 251
    ,, siege of, incidents of, effects on State, 295
    ,, fall of, effects, and incidents, 302
Charles-town, evacuation of, 392
Chatham, when and why so called, 119, 179; origin and history of, as name of town, 463-465
Cheraw settled, town laid out by Kershaw, 118, 119
    ,, when and why called Chatham, 119, 179
    ,, commissions for erecting Court House, &c., 185
    ,, petition and counter-petition, as to location, and action of assembly, 185-192
    ,, progress of buildings at Long Bluff, 194
    ,, regiment, officers of, 135
    ,, officers elected by Provincial Congress, 236
    ,, Stockade Fort at, history of, 240-244
    ,, prisoners sent to gaol of, 174
    ,, sickness of British soldiers there, 319, 320
    ,, Circuit Court for, continues to sit at Long Bluff, 436
    ,, district, population of, 454, 465
    ,, town of, its history, 463-465
Cheraws, judicial district, bounds of, 185
Cherry, George, settles on Cat Fish, 101
Chesterfield County, boundaries of, 433
    ,,   ,,   after whom named, 436
    ,,   ,,   site of Court House, 434
    ,,   ,,   Courts, when to be holden, 434
    ,,   ,,   County Court, justices for, 433, 446, 451, 452, 455
    ,,   ,,   presentment of grand jury for, 435
    ,,   ,,   representatives elected for, 454, 456, 457, 458, 459, 460
    ,,   ,,   dividing line with Darlington run, 461
Circuit Court continues to sit at Long Bluff, 436
Circulating medium, petition for, 447, 448; time extended, 455
Civil affairs, derangement of, 373
    ,,   ,, Marion writes to Governor Matthews about, 373, 374
Clary, Daniel, estate confiscated, 380
Clinton, Sir Henry, writes to Honorable Geo. Gervain, 306
    ,,   ,, goes to the North, 307
Colt, William, a settler, 79
Colson, Abraham, early settler, 79
Commerce, state of, in province, 121; revived in 1776, 278
Commissary receipts for provisions furnished during war, 298, 301 *note*, 347 *note*, 371 *notes*
Confiscation of estates to be made, 378
    ,, Mrs. Steward petitions in behalf of her husband, and result, 378, 379; notice of by *Royal Gazette*, 380
    ,, Mrs. Mitchell petitions for husband, 415, 416
Convention in Charleston to ratify Federal Constitution, 447
    ,,   ,, election for, where held, 447 *note*

Convention in Charleston, delegates from St. David's, their votes, 447
,, in Columbia for State Constitution, delegates from St. David's, and their votes, 450, 451
Cornwallis, Lord, succeeds Sir H. Clinton, 307
,, ,, disposition of troops, 307
,, ,, writes Sir H. Clinton, 308, 314, 315
,, ,, account of failure of expedition on river, 317, 318
,, ,, his prospects in Carolinas, 319
,, ,, writes Honorable Geo. Gervain of Gates's advance, 323, 324
,, ,, account of opening of battle of Camden, 324
,, ,, writes Sir H. Clinton of spirit of revolt in State, 345
,, ,, feelings and prospects, 345-346
,, ,, writes Tarleton about Green, 349, 350
,, ,, cartel with Green for exchange of prisoners, 367
,, ,, declining fortunes, retreat to Wilmington, 368
,, ,, account of his embarrassed situation, 369
,, ,, writes General Phillips, 370
Cotton, its cultivation, 116; specimens of cloth, 116
Council, Captain, commands on Pedee, 333, 371
Counties, first in Carolina, 31, 32
,, Marlborough, Chesterfield, and Darlington, boundaries of, 433
,, origin of three names, 436
,, sites selected for Court Houses, 434
County Court Act, provisions of, 432, 433
,, ,, system remodelled, 450-452; abolished, 460, 461
Court District, system established, account of, 459-460
Court of Equity, how arranged, where to sit, 453
Courtney, a Tory, killed by Whigs, 393
Courts, want of, sorely felt, 121
,, held only in Charles-town, evils of, 126, 127 and *note*, 128
,, first petition for from Pedee, 131-132, and *note*
,, ,, ,, action of council thereon, 132-133
,, second petition for, from Pedee, and account of, 135
,, next petition for, how disposed of, 137
,, Circuit Court Act passed, account of, 137, 138
,, ,, ,, ,, progress of bill in Parliament, 155
,, ,, ,, ,, gaining ground, Governor's address, 182-183
,, ,, ,, ,, provisions of and benefits, 184, 185
,, ,, ,, ,, officers created, and appointments, 195, 196
,, opened at Long Bluff, the occasion, 196
,, last circuit of his Majesty's Justices, 230
,, opened under New Constitution, 263
,, suspended by war, 278; re-opened, 288
,, closed again, 373; opened after war, 416
,, ordered to be holden at Cheraws, not done, 454
Coxe, Emanuel, notice of family, 99
,, John, with Kolb after Tories, 359
Craig, Alexander, notice of, 442
,, ,, County Court Justice for Chesterfield, 455
,, John, in Chesterfield, marriage, &c., 442
Craven County, its limits and settlement, 32
,, ,, first parochial organization in, 32, 33
,, ,, Prince George Winyaw, 33
,, ,, Prince Frederick's, 33
,, ,, line between two parishes, Act of, 33-35
,, ,, St. Mark's, its limits, 36
,, ,, line between St. Mark's and Prince Frederick's, 36
,, ,, Regiment of, 120
,, ,, extent of Prince Frederick's and St. Mark's, 166, 167

Crawford, John, notice of, and the family, 71 and *note*
    ,,   James, captain in Revolution, 71
Croly, old Mrs. spared by Whigs, 387
Crosland, Edward, notice of, family tradition, 99
Culloden, battle of, followed by emigration to Pedee, 87, 88
Cusack, Adam, his execution by Wemys, 303 and *note*

DABBS, Joseph, on Pedee, marriage and descendants, 101
    ,,   ,,   with Kolb after Tories, 359
Dabbs, Joseph, killed by Tories, 366
Daniel, a Whig, blunder at Bass's, 372; atones for it, 373
Dargan, Mr. Timothy, settles in Darlington, 440
Darlington County, its boundaries, 433; the name, 436
    ,,   ,,   site of Court House, 434
    ,,   ,,   Courts when to be holden, 434
    ,,   ,,   fire at C. H., account of, 453 and *note*
    ,,   ,,   County Court Justices for, 434, 446, 451, 452, 457
    ,,   ,,   Justices of Peace for, 433, 452, 454
    ,,   ,,   Representatives for, 454, 456, 457, 458, 459, 460, 461
    ,,   ,,   dividing line with Chesterfield, 461
David, first of this name, account of family, 51 and *note*
    ,,   Joshua, wounded at Eutaw, 377
David St., account of name, 162 and *note*
Davd's, St., Parish established, 163-165
    ,,   ,,   nature and objects of organization, 166
    ,,   ,,   some of Commissioners decline acting, 167
    ,,   ,,   Journal of Vestry, organization, 166-167
    ,,   ,,   action as to church building, 174-175
    ,,   ,,   officers elected, 175; subsequent elections, 177-181
    ,,   ,,   efforts to procure a clergyman, 175
    ,,   ,,   church occupied by British, 176
    ,,   ,,   taxes laid on Parish, 177-178
    ,,   ,,   parish expenditure, 178, 180
    ,,   ,,   organization ceases, 181
    ,,   ,,   ,,   fails to meet wants of people, 182
    ,,   ,,   notice of Bill altering bounds of, 181
    ,,   ,,   church building, 181; grand jury presents it, 203
    ,,   ,,   subscription in, for poor of Boston, 220-222 and *note*
    ,,   ,,   Committee of Observation for, their duties, 227-228, 229
    ,,   ,,   Members added to Committee, and duties, 237
    ,,   ,,   action of Committee as to Col. Steward and John Mitchell, 237-239
    ,,   ,,   Commissions issued for Volunteer Companies in, 244-246
    ,,   ,,   ammunition provided for, and want of, 244, 249, 253, 254
    ,,   ,,   entitled to six representatives under new Constitution, 257
    ,,   ,,   salt provided for inhabitants, 275
    ,,   ,,   retains former number of representatives, 289
    ,,   ,,   change in places of election, 276
Davison, Colonel George, writes to General Harrington, 339
Delaney, Captain, commands company on Pedee, 333
Dewitt Martin, settles on Pedee, his family, 97
    ,,   Thomas, settles lower down, his family, 98
    ,,   William, notice of, and family, 97 and *note*
    ,,   ,,   his house burned by British, 304 and *note*
    ,,   ,,   removes his family, 305
    ,,   ,,   conduct as to oath of allegiance, 305
    ,,   ,,   representative for St. David's, 378, 415
    ,,   ,,   Senator, 432; Sheriff for Cheraws, 416
    ,,   ,,   County Justice for Darlington, 434

Dewitt, William, delegate to Convention in Charleston, 434
,, Charles, County Justice for Darlington, 434
,, William, kills Stephen Gainey, 376-377
Dibble, John, at Cheraw Bar, 436
Dick, William, notice of, 92; punishes Jeff. Butler, 395
Diseases, which first known on Pedee, effects of climate, &c., 117, 118
Donaldson, John, 1st Lieutenant of Rangers, 236
,, ,, escorts Mrs. Harrington to Cross Creek, 320
,, ,, writes to General Harrington, 321
Dopson, Joseph, first settler on Upper Pedee, 50
Drayton, William Henry, account of appointment as Judge, 200
,, ,, presides at Long Bluff, 209, 210
,, ,, charge to grand jury, 211-215
,, ,, ,, its effect on petit jury and their charge, 215-217
,, ,, ,, in Charles-town noticed in Parliament, 219
,, ,, ,, to grand jury in Charles-town, 263, 276
,, ,, ,, character public service and death, 220
Droughts, remarkable instances of, 117
Du Bose, John, first of name on Pedee, family, &c., 91 and *note*, 92
,, Elias, notice of his family, 92
,, ,, adventure with Tories, 329
,, ,, ,, with Jeff. Butler, 395
,, ,, Representative for St. David's, 432
,, ,, County Justice for Darlington, 434
,, Isaac, 2nd Lieutenant in Regiment of Foot, 236
,, ,, Ezekiel, Representative for Darlington, 456, 459

EARTHQUAKE, felt on Pedee, 461
Education, sons of planters sent abroad, 122
,, want of, sorely felt, 299
Edwards, Rev. Joshua, emigrates to Pedee, notice of and family, 82, 83 and *notes*
Elections, for Assembly, trouble at, apprehended, 154-156
,, ,, action of Vestry of St. David's, 167
,, ,, elections held, and names of voters, 169, 170, 171, 172, 173
,, ,, within limits of Marion's Brigade ordered by Governor, 377
Ellerbe, Thomas, petitions for land, difficulty with Welch, 62, 63
,, ,, account of name and family, 63 and *note*, 64 and *note*
,, Thomas, a captain under Kolb, 301; under Benton, 371
,, ,, suffers from British, 313
Ellison, Robert, petitions for relief under Amercing Act, 416
,, ,, Representative for St. David's, 448; senator, 454
,, ,, delegate to Convention in Columbia, 451
,, ,, County Court Justice for Darlington, 452
,, ,, elected sheriff, 456; resigns seat in Legislature, 456
,, ,, petitions for mills on Black Creek, and results, 458
Embankments on river, 456
Ervin, James, Representative for Liberty, 461
Evans, notice of family, 52 and *note*, 64
,, Nathan, his family, 75, and *note*
,, Charles and George, settle on Lynche's Creek, 100
,, Thomas, wounded at Kolb's, dies, 361 and *note*
,, Charles, carried prisoner to Charles-town, 384
,, ,, County Court Justice for Chesterfield, 433
,, ,, Representative for St. David's, 447
,, ,, delegates to Convention in Columbia, 451
,, Thomas, County Court Justice for Marlborough, 433, 457
,, ,, Representative for St. David's, 447

HISTORY OF THE OLD CHERAWS. 535

Exports, first articles of, 110

FALCONER, Wm., at Cheraws Bar, 436, 441; sketch of, 441, 442
,, ,, Representative for Chesterfield, 454, 456, 459
,, ,, C. C. Justice for Chesterfield, 455
,, ,, connexion with District Court system, 459, 460
,, ,, letter to Alex. Craig, 468-470
,, ,, character, anecdote, and death, 467 and *note*, 468, 470 and *note*, 471
Fanning, the Tory, excepted from truce, 376, 397
,, adventure with Hunter, 396, 397
,, character and subsequent history, 397
,, attack on Robert Gregg, 397
Ferries, petitions for, 446
Flax, why abandoned, 111
Fletchers, the family, 99
Forniss, William, notice of, 101
Ford, John, Representative for Liberty, 459
Fowler, Rev. Andrew, visits Cheraw, notice of, 166 *note*
Foulis, Rev. Mr., notice of, 175 and *note*
Freshets, in Pedee, 456

GAINEY, Major, difficulty with Murphy, 374
,, ,, writes to Marion on subject, 374, 375
,, ,, truce with Marion, 375, 376
,, ,, defection, character, and history, 376
,, Stephen, killed by Wm. Dewitt, 376, 377
Galespy, James, petitions for land, his family, 61, 62
,, ,, jun., anecdote of, 305
,, ,, ,, raises a force against expediton on river, 316
,, ,, ,, guide for Green, 353, *note*
Gates, General, arrives at Pedee, proclamation, 322
,, ,, advances towards Camden, 323
,, ,, Cornwallis's account of the movement, 323, 324
,, ,, defeat and flight, 325
,, ,, writes to Gen. Harrington, 331-334
Gazette, Royal, merry over Governor's proclamation, 374
,, ,, notice of Confiscation Act, 380
,, ,, merriment at expense of Whigs, 381
,, ,, sarcastic notice of books to be published, 381
Gervais, John Lewis, writes Gen. Harrington, 321, 322
Gibson, Jordan, his removal, 73
,, Gideon, notice of, and family, 73, 74, and *notes*
,, ,, connexion with trouble at Mars Bluff, 139, 140, 145, 146
,, ,, killed by Murphy, 354
,, Jordan, after Tories, 393
,, alleged murder of Kolb, excepted from truce, 376
Giles, Col. Hugh, notice of, 70
,, ,, raises volunteer force, 326
Glen, Duke, adventure with Tories, 384, 385
Godfrey, Richard, notice of, and family, 103
Godbold, John, early settler, notice of, and family, 68, 69 and *note*
,, Hugh, notice of, 69 and *note*
Goings, Mike, murderer of Kolb, 361
Government retains supplies, 382; Gen. Pinckney's letter on subject, 382
Governor, Royal, flight from Charles-town, 374
Grand Jury, first presentment at Cheraws, 196-198
,, ,, subsequent presentments, 198, 199, 201-203, 217, 218, 230-233
,, ,, of Cheraws, only one making presentment, 233 and *note*

Grand Jury presentments, under new Constitution, 264-266, 276, 277, 288, 289, 429, 430
,, ,, effects of presentments on people, 200, 277, 278
Grants, earliest to lands on Pedee, 50; others made, 54, 56, 57, 73, 81
,, curious reservations in, 115
Gray, Robert, estate confiscated, 380
Gregg, John, petitions for land, notice of, and family, 86, 87, and *note*
,, Joseph, his family, 87, and *note*
,, Captain James, marches to Charles-town, 294, 301
,, ,, ,, suffers by Tories, 383
,, Robert, attacked by Fanning, 397
Green, General, movements of, marches to Pedee, 349
,, ,, effects of presence there, 351, 352
,, ,, leaves Pedee, his march, 353; effects on people, 353
,, ,, cartel with Cornwallis, 367
,, ,, cautions Marion against Tories, 371
Greenville, time and origin of name, 436
Grimke, Judge, charge at first court after war, 416-429

HANFORD, Enoch, teacher in St. David's, 438
Harrallson, Lewis, Representative for Liberty, 459
Harllee, William, emigrates to America, 443
,, Thomas, settles in Marion, 443
Hart, Arthur, account of and family, 105, and *note*
,, ,, his death, 278
Harrington, Henry William, emigrates to Pedee, his family, 104, 105, and *note*
,, ,, ,, commissioned captain, 239, and *note*
,, ,, ,, at Haddrell's Point, 274
,, ,, ,, elected Member of Assembly, 275
,, ,, ,, writes to Colonel Kershaw, 289, 290
,, ,, ,, military promotions, 296, 297
,, ,, ,, head-quarters, where, 297
,, ,, ,, marches N. C. Militia to Charles-town, 301
,, ,, ,, writes to Mrs. Harrington, 302
,, ,, ,, loss of and notice of valuable negro, 313, *note*
,, ,, ,, suit after war for negro, 313, *note*
,, ,, ,, sends detachment with negro to Anson, 321
,, ,, ,, account of his servant, Toney, 321, *note*
,, ,, ,, movements after Gates's defeat, 330, 331
,, ,, ,, arrives at Haley's Ferry, and Cheraw, 336
,, ,, ,, moves up river, and to Grassey Creek, Roanoke, 347
,, ,, ,, adventure with robber, 397-399
,, ,, ,, character and death, 399
,, Mrs., adventure with British, 312
,, ,, ,, with Tories, and suit, 329, 330, and *note*
,, ,, ,, safe conduct to Cross Creek, 320
,, ,, notice of, 399
Harrison, two brothers, Tories on Lynche's Creek, 308
,, Major, adventure with Murphy in Charles-town, 400
Hawes, Dr. Oliver, settles at Society Hill, notice of, 443
Hawthorn, brought to Pedee, 442, *note*
Hawthorne, murdered by Tories, his son's revenge, 394, 395
Hemp, cultivation of abandoned, 111
Hewstiss, name known early, true Whigs, 98
Hicks, George, petitions for land, notice of and family, 79, 81, and *note*
,, ,, captain in King's service, 119
,, ,, as major starts with detachment to Congarees, 249
,, ,, marches to Charles-town, 256
,, ,, Chairman of Committee of Observation for St. David's, 238

HISTORY OF THE OLD CHERAWS.

Hicks, George, Warden of St. David's Society, 281
,, ,, removes with family to Virginia, 327
,, ,, Commissioner of Caveats for Cheraws, 432
,, ,, C. C. Justice for Marlborough, 433
,, ,, sketch of, 402
,, Daniel, adventure with Tories, 385
,, Benjamin, jun., Inspector of Tobacco at Cheraws, 430
,, ,, ,, delegate to Convention in Charles-town, 447
,, ,, ,, delegate to Convention in Columbia, 451
,, ,, ,, Representative for Marlborough, 454
,, ,, ,, C. C. Justice for Marlborough, 455
Hodge, notice of family, 101
Horse-pen, origin of name, 110
Hughes, a Tory, spared by Whigs, 386
Hunter, Dr. Robert, notice of, 69
,, Andrew, adventure with Fanning, 396, 397
,, ,, Representative for St. David's, 445; for Darlington, 457

INDIAN tribes in Carolina, 1
,, territory, of tribes on Pedee, 2; language, 19
,, remains in Pedee, 21, 22, 23
,, mode of clearing lands, 24; grave opened, 25
,, habits and customs, 23, 26-29
Indians, Catawbas, tradition, 2; origin, 3, 19
,, ,, removal, settlement, territory, and language, 3-5
,, ,, visit to Charles-town, with Cheraws, 9
,, ,, murder of some by Notchees, 10, 11
,, ,, Governor's visit to them and others, 11, 12
,, ,, their effort for union with other tribes, 13, 14
,, ,, visit by John Evans, 15, 16
,, ,, smallpox among them, its effects, 16, 17
,, ,, union with Cheraws, 18; their town, 18
,, ,, decline and number, 18
,, ,, removal to North Carolina, 19
,, Cheraws, how name called at different times, 1
,, ,, their territory, 2; first mention of, 5
,, ,, advised to unite with Catawbas, 17
,, ,, meaning of Cheraw, 19, 20
,, Kadapaws, where found, 2
,, Pedees, locality, 2; first mention of in public records, 8
,, ,, murder of one by Wm. Kemp, 8, 9
,, ,, visit to Charles-town, and presents to them, 10
,, ,, address by Governor at Congarees, 12
,, ,, owners of slaves, 13
,, ,, urged to settle among Catawbas, 13, 14
,, ,, murder of some by Notchees, 15, 16
,, ,, meaning of Pedee, 20, 21
,, travellers among them, Lederer, 5-8
,, ,, ,, ,, Bartram, 2, 5; Lawson, 26-28; his end, 29
,, ,, ,, ,, Adair, 5
,, Sara, its locality, 6-8
,, Winyaws, their locality, 2
Indigo, account of, 111, 112, and *note*
Insurrection of slaves, 234, 456
Internal improvements, necessity for, 109
,, ,, roads, bridges, and ferries, 112, 113, 114
,, ,, ,, ,, grand jury notice them, 197, 198, 201
Irby, Charles, notice of, family, 92, and *note*
,, Edmund, commander under Kolb, 301

36—H. O. C.

Irish Protestants, their petition and locality, 74, 75; Irish town, 75
Izard, Walter and Ralph, early settlers, removal, 75

JACKSON, Stephen, captain under Kolb, 301; under Benton, 371
   ,,   Benjamin, C. C. Justice for Chesterfield, 433
James, James, leader of Welch colony, 52
   ,, Rev. Philip, account of, 52
   ,, John Jones, Representative for Marlborough, 454, 456
   ,,   ,,   ,, C. C. Justice for Marlborough, 457
Jamieson, Colonel, early settler, 75
Jay's treaty, meeting at Darlington to consider, 455
Jeffrey's Creek, act passed for navigation of, and commissioners, 453
Jolly, Joseph, early grantee of land, 54
Jones, Captain Joseph, leads Tory party against Colonel Kolb, 360
   ,,   ,,   ,, subsequent history, 367, and *note*
   ,, John, one of party at Colonel Kolb's, 361, and *note*
   ,, Captain Joseph, commands guard at Kolb's Ferry, 371
   ,, Elias, teacher in St. David's, 438
Justices of Peace, first appointments of, 133
        ,, for Cheraws, under new Constitution, 257-258
        ,, for three counties, 433, 452, 454
        ,, importance of office under C. C. Act, 434

KERSHAW, Eli and Joseph, settle at Cheraw, 104
   ,,   ,, elected captain of rangers, 236
   ,,   ,, advertises property, removal, 119, *note*
Kimbrough, John, notice of, and family, 90-91
King, Eli, teacher in St. David's, 437
   ,, Dr. Miles, settles at Society Hill, 443
Kolb, Jacob, petitions for land, 50
   ,, Henry, petitions for land, his family, 83, 84, and *note*
   ,, Jehu, his character, 84
   ,, Abel, family and residence, 84 *note*, 268
   ,,   ,, Warden of St. David's Society, 281
   ,,   ,, marches troops to Charles-town, 301
   ,,   ,, commands at Long Bluff, after Gates's defeat, 327, 344
   ,,   ,, return of his force to General Harrington, 344
   ,,   ,, in full tide of success on Pedee, 352
   ,,   ,, difficulty and correspondence with Captain Snipes, 354-355
   ,,   ,, writes to General Marion, 355-356
   ,,   ,, pursues Tories to Drowning Creek, 358-359
   ,,   ,, goes to Cat Fish after Tories, 359-360
   ,,   ,, surprised by Tories, his death, 360-361, 363
   ,,   ,, character, effects of his death, 366, 367

LAFAYETTE, General, marches to join Southern forces, 371
        ,, interview with Joshua Ammons, 402-403
Lands, first advertisements for sale of, 54, 74, 75
Legislature, canvass for, in Darlington, 458-459, 461
Lewis, Rev. Joshua, pastor at Welch Neck, 440
Lide, notice of, family, 77
   ,, John, his family, 77
   ,, Thomas, his character and family, 78 and *note*
   ,, Robert, settles on Pedee, his descendants, 78, 79, and *note*
   ,,   ,, marches detachment to Charles-town, 302
   ,,   ,, incident of Mrs. Lide, and death, 302
   ,,   ,, Commissioner of Caveats for Cheraws, 432
   ,,   ,, C. C. Justice for Darlington, 434
   ,, Charles Motte, notice of, 473

HISTORY OF THE OLD CHERAWS. 539

Lide, Charles Motte, seeks admission to Bar, speech on occasion, 474, 480, 482
,, ,, goes to Columbia, admitted to Bar, 480
,, ,, removes to Georgia, account of enterprise, 480-482
,, ,, farewell, on departure from, 481-482
,, ,, suit growing out of his father's will, history of, 482-483
,, ,, speech in 1814, 483-488
,, ,, ,, before Appeal Court in Equity, 480-496
,, ,, ,, remarkable peroration, 496 and *note*
,, ,, memorial to Legislature, 496-497
,, ,, appearance, and speech before joint committee, 497 and *note*
,, ,, character, genius, and end, 497-498
Light Horse Troop, petition for, action thereon, and officers, 448-449
Long Bluff, origin of settlement there, why called so, 118 and *note*
,, Court House there, 193
,, stockade, with guard there, 371
,, appropriation for public buildings at, 457 ; repaired, 458
Lowder's Lake, petition for opening, and commissioners, 457
Lowry, notice of family, 179, *note*
Loyalists, character of, 267
Lucas, John, adventure with old Mrs. Croly, 387
Luke, John, grantee of land in Welch Neck, 79
Lynche's Creek, Acts to improve navigation of, and commissioners, 446, 453

MACAY, Major Spence, writes General Harrington, 322, 323
Magistrates for Cheraws District, 225 ; why names published, 225, 226
,, vindication of by grand jury, 232, 233
Manderson, Capt. George, escape at Hunt's Bluff, 311 and *note*
,, John, notice of, 104
Manufactures, first specimen of, and prospects for, 116
Manufactures, domestic, efforts to promote, 157, 158
,, notice of Christopher Gadsden, 158
,, subscription for papers in St. David's, 159 and *note*, 160 and *note*
Marion, Col. Francis, operations before and after Gates's defeat, 326-327
,, ,, notice of his defeat in *Royal Gazette*, 341
,, ,, attempt on George-town, 343
,, ,, his military status at this time, 343, *note*
,, ,, writes to General Harrington, 343, 344
,, ,, writes General Sumpter about Capt. Snipes, 356, 357
,, ,, correspondence with Major Gainey, 375, 376
,, ,, troubled about writs of election in brigade, 377
,, ,, regiments composing his brigade, 392
Markets, for first settlers, 110
Mars Bluff, origin of name, 69, *note*
Marshall, Adam, settles at Long Bluff, 443
Marlborough County, its boundaries, 433 ; after whom named, 436
,, ,, site for Court House, 434
,, ,, Courts, when to be holden, 434
,, ,, C. C. Justices for, 433, 446, 451, 452, 455, 457, 458
,, ,, justices of peace for, 433, 452, 454
,, ,, representatives for, 454, 456-461
Martin, Col. Alex., writes Gen. Harrington, 334, 335
Matthews, Governor, writes Marion in reply to Benton's letter, 389, 390
Mathis, Samuel, C. C. Justice for Darlington, 451
M'Intosh, John, settles on Pedee, his family, 88, 89 and *note*
,, Alexander, notice of him, his family, 89 and *note*
,, ,, union of family with Welch, 90
,, ,, captain in King's service, 119
,, ,, elected major by Provincial Congress, 236

M'Intosh, Alexander, receives letter from Council of Safety, 251, 262
,,   ,,   elected lieutenant-colonel, 256
,,   ,,   Member of Legislative Council, 279
,,   ,,   President of St. David's Society, 281
,,   ,,   made brigadier-general, 285
,,   ,,   commands in Georgia, 292
,,   ,,   reply to Gen. Moultrie, 293
,,   ,,   celebrated reply to enemy, 294
,,   ,,   commissioner at Charles-town, 295
,,   ,,   his character and death, 346, 347
,,   Capt. Alexander, commands under Benton, 371
,,   ,,   in skirmish on Black Creek, 387
,,   ,,   notice of him, 387, note
,,   ,,   C. C. Justice for Darlington, 451, 457
,,   ,,   Representative for Darlington, 454
,,   ,,   Commissioner of Locations for Cheraws, 455
,,   ,,   Sheriff for Cheraws, 458; for Darlington, 460
M'Iver, Roderick, notice of, his family, 88 and note
   ,,   Sarah, early settlers, 88
   ,,   union of family with Welch, 90
   ,,   John, elected senator, 459
M'Arthur, Major, reaches Cheraw, 308
   ,,   ,,   goes to Long Bluff, 309
   ,,   ,,   offers reward for Thomas Ayer, result, 309-311
   ,,   ,,   at Cheraw, sends party to General Harrington's, 312
   ,,   ,,   retreat from Pedee, 315-318, 371
   ,,   ,,   sends expedition down the river, 316, 317
M'Dowell, William, notice of, 100, and note
M'Call, George, notice of, 301, and note
   ,,   ,,   joins Marion, impression of Marion, 326, 327
M'Rae, Duncan, C. C. Justice for Chesterfield, 451
M'Ree, Colonel, adventure with Bradley, 393, 394
   ,,   ,,   Representative for Liberty, 457
M'Culley, Andrew, teacher in St. David's, 437
Medal of Pitt, account of, 122, 123 and note, 124
   ,,   statues and rings, and statue in Charles-town, 124, 125, and note
Mills, earliest in Pedee country, 63, note; 110, 111, note; 118, 119, note
Militia, first review on Pedee, officers, 120; from Pedee in constant service, 377
   ,,   returns of, 446, 457, 461
   ,,   return of Colonel Spencer's regiment, 462
Military condition of Province, 119, 120; organization, 120
   ,,   further Acts on organization of, 285
   ,,   ardor in Province, 236, 292
   ,,   strength in Carolina at close of 1779, 298
Mills, William Henry, elected to Provincial Congress, 254
  ,,   ,,   ,,   takes sides with British, 304
  ,,   ,,   ,,   made colonel by Royal Government, 316, 318
  ,,   ,,   ,,   escape to George-town, 316
  ,,   ,,   ,,   estate confiscated, banishment, and history, 380, 381
Mikell, John, notice of and family, 89 and note, 90
Mitchell, John, a trader, 106
   ,,   Mrs. Elizabeth, petitions for her husband, result, 415, 416
Moultrie, General William, writes to Colonel M'Intosh, 293
Murphy, first of the name, and its change, 71, and note
   ,,   Malachi, notice of, and family, 71, 72, and note
   ,,   Maurice, and his sons, 72
   ,,   Michael, petitions for land, 72, 73
   ,,   Colonel Maurice, commands on Pedee, notice of, 298, 333, 352, 371
   ,,   ,,   ,,   punishes Blackman, a Tory, 354

Murphy, Colonel Maurice, kills Gideon Gibson, 354
",, ",, ",, adventure with Tories at Bass's, 372, 373
",, ",, ",, difficulty with Gainey, 374
",, ",, ",, attacks Harrison in Charles-town, 400
",, ",, ",, attacks Tory at Jeffrey's Creek, 400; his end, 400
",, Malachi, wounded and escapes at Bass's, 373

NAVIGATION of Pedee, earliest account of, 62
",, ",, Acts passed on subject, and commissioners, 430, 431, 446, 453
",, ",, history of legislation on subject, 431, 432
",, ",, effectually opened, 464
Negroes, remarkable, instances of, 313 *note*, 321 *note*, 377
",, returns of, in British service, 346
Nettles, Zachariah, C. C. Justice for Darlington, 434
Neville, William and Thomas, after Tories, 393
Newberry, District, why so called, 53, *note*
Nicholas, Colonel, writes to General Harrington, 331
Norris, Dr. Robert, C. C. Justice for Darlington, 451
Nut Grass, notice of, 442, *note*

OATH of allegiance after fall of Charles-town, 304
",, ",, course of people in connexion with, 305
",, ",, incidents connected with, 304, 305
Odom, Levi, a Whig, kills Courtney, 393

PARISH organization, want of, felt, 125
Park, Thomas, teacher in St. David's, 437; subsequent history, 437, 438
Parker, Elisha, notice of, family and descendants, 98
",, Thomas, at Cheraws Bar, 436
Pawley, Colonel George, notice of the family, 100
Pearson, family settlement, 179, *note*
",, Moses, a noted captain, 79, *note*
",, ",, C. C. Justice for Marlborough, 433
Pegues, Claudius, his arrival, settlement, and account of family, 94, 95 and *note*
",, ",, active in affair at Mars Bluff, 147
",, ",, elected to Assembly from St. David's, 171
",, ",, declines seat in Provincial Congress, 254
",, ",, suffers from British at Cheraw, 313
",, ",, C. C. Justice for Marlborough County, 433
",, ",, his singular end, 399
",, William, Representative for St. David's, 378, 415, 432
",, ",, suffers from British, Mrs. Pegues's escape, 385, 386
",, ",, inspector of tobacco at Cheraw, 430
",, ",, C. C. Justice for Chesterfield, 433, 452
",, ",, Representative for Chesterfield, 454
",, Claudius, jun., capt. under Benton, 371
",, ",, ordinary for Cheraws, 374, 416
",, ",, incident at Eutaw, 377
",, ",, Representative for St. David's, 415, 432
",, ",, C. C. Justice for Marlborough, 433
Pendleton, Honorable Henry, elected Representative for St. David's, account of, 297, 298
",, ",, ",, active in passage of County Court Act, 432
Penn, J., wrtes to General Harrington, 332, 333
Petitions for Ferries, 446; for tobacco inspection at Cheraw, 450
",, for circulating medium, 447, 448; for its extension, 455
",, for troop of light horse, action thereon, 448, 449

Petitions for opening Lowder's Lake, 456, 457
,, against measurer of lumber, &c., at George-town, 457
,, for canal from Roger's lake to Pedee, 458
,, from Robert Ellison, for mills on Black Creek, 458
Piney Grove, where, 93
Planter's club, notice of, 119
Pledger, Philip, arrival, notice of family, 85 and *note*, 86
,, ,, captain in king's service, 119
,, ,, adventure with Driggers and his gang, 194, 195, and *note*
,, ,, horses taken by British Lieutenant, 313 and *note*
,, ,, Representative for St. David's, 378
,, John, captain under Benton, 371
,, Joseph, C. C. Justice for Chesterfield, 433
Poelnittz, Baron de, settles on Pedee, his family, 442, 443
Population of Cheraw District, 454, 465
Posts, British, nearest to Charles-town, 306
Pouncey, William, his family, 84, and *note*
Powe, Thomas, account of, and family, 102, 103
,, ,, Representative for St. David's, 415, 432
,, ,, Commissioner of Location, 430
,, ,, C. C. Justice for Chesterfield, 433, 452
,, ,, declines seat for St. David's, 453
Powell, Colonel G. G., visit to Mars Bluff, and letter, 146-149
,, ,, visit to Broad River, 150
,, ,, member of Assembly for St. David's, 173, 177
,, ,, appointed Judge, 173, 184
,, ,, deputy from St. David's in Provincial Congress, 208
,, ,, Colonel of Cheraws Regiment, 226
,, ,, in Provincial Congress, 240
,, ,, declines seat for St. Philip's in favor of St. David's, 247
,, ,, ordered with regiment to Congarees, 248
,, ,, elected judge under new Constitution, 259
,, ,, retains seat for St. David's, 259
,, ,, letter to Assembly as to charges against him, 275
,, ,, character and death, 292
Pratt, Wm., with Duke Glen, against Tories, 385
Presentments of Grand Jury, 196-198, 198-199, 201-202, 203, 217-218, 230-233, 264-266, 276-277, 288-289, 429-430, 435
,, of Petit Jury, 216
Prices, early notice of, 60, 61, and *note*
Prices of slaves, 117
Province, general prosperity of, 115, 116
Provincial Congress, first meeting, account of, 207-208
,, second meeting, and objects, 208-209
,, deputies from St. David's, 209
,, meeting 1st January, 1775, action of deputies of St. David's, 226-227
,, circular letter to St. David's, 234
,, Association formed, other action, 235-236
,, military organization by, 236
,, meeting, Nov. 1775, and action, 247-249
,, orders payment to Major Hicks, and others, 255, 256
,, action for defence of colony, &c., 255, 256
,, oath prescribed, effects on people, 263
Public Buildings, appropriation for, 457; repaired, 458
,, Commissioners for buildings, &c., in three districts, 460
Pugh, Rev. Evan, notice of, and family, 102
,, ,, officiates in St. David's Church, 175

Pugh, Rev. Evan, extracts from Journal of, 267, 268, 296, 301 *note*, 302, 304, 306, 326, 346 *note*, 353, 371, 372
,, ,, preaches thanksgiving sermon, 296
,, ,, elected delegate to Convention in Columbia, 451
,, ,, preaches sermon commemorative of Washington, 446 *note*
,, ,, character and death, 466 and *note*
,, Ezra, notice of, talents and death, 472-473
Punch, John, settles at Society Hill, 443
Purvis, John, petitions for land, and settles, 81-82

QUICK, notice of the family, 101 and *note*
,, Thomas, a gallant Whig, 101
,, ,, incident of at Eutaw, 377

REGULATORS, origin and history of their movements, 128, 129, 137, 155, 160, 161
,, troubles in North Carolina, 129, 153, 154
,, in other parts of South Carolina, 130, 135
,, about Camden, 134
,, notice of outlaws, &c., 134, 135
,, Governor's address about, and Assembly's reply, 136, 137
,, Lieut.-Governor's remarks about, 136, 137
,, accounts of from back country, 138, 139, 144, 149, 151, 152, 153, 154, 155, 182, 194 and *note*
,, character of leaders, 138, 146
,, accounts of affair at Mars Bluff, 139, 140, 144, 145, 155, 156
,, traditional account, 150 and *note*
,, Governor's proclamations and efforts, 141, 142, 143, 144, 145
,, Col. Powell's mission and letter, 146-149
,, demands of the people, 154, 155
,, Governor's address and Assembly's reply, 156, 157
Revolution, incipient causes of, 122, 126, 127, 128
,, progress of feeling, 205, 206
,, effects of repeal of Stamp Act, 206
,, Scheme of East India Company, and course of Parliament, 206, 207
,, Town Meeting called, 207
,, list of some from Pedee in service, 404-414
Roach, Henry, petitions for land, 62
Robertson, Major Drury, settles in Marlborough, 442
,, ,, Representative for St. David's, 448
,, ,, County Court Justice for Marlborough, 451, 458
,, ,, Representative for Marlborough, 456, 459
Rogers, Nicholas, grantee of land, family, 65, 66 and *note*.
,, Benjamin, one of Glen's party, 384
,, ,, Sheriff for Cheraws, 446
Royalty, last days of, in Carolina, 224
,, Royal Governor's flight, 240
Rushing, John, notice of, 240
Rutledge, Governor, writes to Marion about Benton's Regiment, 377
,, ,, sends Marion writs of election, 377

SANDY BLUFF Settlement, account of, 70
,, subsequent history of, and visit there, 74 and *note*
Sauls, Absolom, County Court Justice for Darlington, 451
Saunders, one of the families at Sandy Bluff, 71
,, John, notice of, and family, 73
,, George, his untimely end, 73 *note*
Settlements, made first on coast, and extension, 31
,, where first made in interior, 51, 66, 70, 117

Settlements, inducements held out to emigration, 42
,, in lower part of Welch Tract, 69
,, settlers and church building, 69, and *note*
,, on Little Pedee, 86
,, on Lynche's Creek, 100
,, whence their elements derived, 108
,, on Black Creek, 100
Shaw, William, notice of, 404 *note*
Shoemake, a Tory, notice of, 373, 393
Slaves, increase of among first settlers, 73
Smallwood, Gen., writes to Gen. Harrington, 336, 337, 341-343
Smith, Col. John, settles in Darlington, 440
,, Andrew and Ralph, notice of, 441
,, John, C. C. Justice for Darlington, 452; Representative, 454
,, Dr. Thomas, notice of, 500, *note*
Snipes, Capt. Wm. Clay, difficulty and correspondence with Kolb, 354, 355
Snowden, a Tory, punished by John Bethea, 394
Society of St. David's, organization and history of, 280-284
,, ,, subscription paper in aid of, 282, 283
,, ,, first school-house, 284
,, ,, revived after war, 436; officers, &c., 436, 437
,, ,, escheated property given to, 438
,, ,, deceased members of, 438, 439
,, ,, members dismissed, 439; added, 439
,, ,, academy building, 440
,, ,, famous exhibition, 453
,, ,, later pupils of, alluded to, 472
Society Hill, origin of, 440
Soldiers, list of, in war, 404-414
Sorrency, Samuel, petitions for land, 58
Sparks, four brothers, account of, 98, 99
,, Daniel, his character and family, 98 and *note*, 99
,, Harry, hung by Tories, and fate of one of Tories, 358
,, Daniel, captain under Benton, 371
Spencer, William and Calvin, notice of, 106
,, Calvin, Representative for St. David's, 432, 445
,, ,, C. C. Justice for Chesterfield, 433, 452
,, ,, delegate to Convention in Charles-town, 447
,, ,, delegate to Convention in Columbia, 451
,, ,, colonel of Chesterfield Regiment, 461
,, ,, notice of engagement, marriage, and death, 463 and *note*
Stewart, David, Representative for Marlborough, 461
Steward, Charles Augustus, settles near Cheraw, 106 and *note*
,, ,, elected to Assembly, 177
,, ,, lieut. col. of Cheraw Regiment, 226
,, ,, before committee of St. David's, 237, 238
,, ,, his character, 379; error, and subsequent career, 380 and *note*
,, Mrs. Sarah, petitions for her husband, &c., 378, 379
Stock raising, most profitable business, 76
,, wild, found by settlers, how taken, 109, 110
,, remarkable incident related of Malachi Murphy, 110, *note*
Strother, notice of, family, 179 *note*
,, George and William settle near Cheraw, 443, 444
,, William writes to Council of Safety, 253
,, ,, Sheriff of Cheraws, 292
,, ,, Representative for St. David's, 415, 445
,, ,, C. C. Justice for Chesterfield, 433
Stubbs, John, settles on Cat Fish, 87

Sumpter, General, writes to Marion, 356-357
Sweat, Wm., notice of, 101
 ,, James, account of, 311 and *note*
 ,, Nathan, capture and escape, 312
Sweeney, notice of the, family, 91
 ,, Barney, his descendants, 91

TARLETON, Colonel, account of affairs in Carolina, 314, 315
 ,, ,, ,, failure of expedition on river, 318, 319
 ,, ,, ,, British movements before Camden, 324, 325
 ,, ,, ,, American movements and Green's advance, 350, 351 and *note*
 ,, ,, ,, Cornwallis's situation, &c., 368
 ,, ,, ,, ,, error, 370
Tart, Enos, after Tories, 393
Taxes, notice of, 115 and *note*
Taylor, Captain S., delegate to Convention in Charleston, 447
 ,, ,, leaves the country, 455
Terrell, account of the family, 53 and *note*
Thomas, Tristram, emigrates to America, 93
 ,, ,, removal of his family to Pedee, 93 and *note*, and 94
 ,, Rev. Robert, notice of, 94
 ,, Tristram, notice of, 94; Major under Kolb, 301
 ,, ,, commands party on river against boats, 316, 317
 ,, ,, his active service on Pedee, 371
 ,, ,, Representative for St. David's, 388, 442
 ,, ,, Senator for St. David's, 415, 459
 ,, ,, C. C. Judge for Marlborough, 433, 452
 ,, ,, delegate to Convention in Charleston, 447
 ,, ,, difficulty with Colonel Benton, 455-456
 ,, ,, sketch of, and death, 400, 401 and *note*
 ,, William, settles on Pedee, marriage and family, 94 and *note*
 ,, ,, Commissioner of Caveats for Cheraws, 432
 ,, ,, senator, 445
 ,, ,, C. C. Justice for Marlborough, 452
Thornby, Major, commands detachment to Charles-town, 301
Tobacco, its cultivation, 112 and *note*
 ,, inspection at Cheraws, 430
Tories on Pedee, and punishment, 298
 ,, pursued by Kolb, 358-359, 359-360
 ,, revenge on Kolb, 360-362
 ,, on Jeffrey's and Black Creeks, 383
 ,, between Lumber River and Little Pedee, pursued by Whigs, 393
Townsend, notice of, 101
Township, plan of, 42, 43
 ,, on Pedee, name and locality, 43, 44
 ,, proceedings of Council, 43, 44, 45
 ,, first settlement in Queensborough, 44, 45
 ,, locality of the town, 45
 ,, form of grant for plots in, 45 *note*
Trade, points of note for, 112
Troops, British, sickness at Cheraw, 176, 319, 320
Turbeville, Rev. William, notice of, 70, 71, and *note*
Turnage, William, 98

VOYAGE, use of term, 299

WATIES, Thomas, at Cheraws Bar, 436
Webster's notice of, 99

Welch emigration to America, 46
,, remove from Pennsylvania to Delaware, 46
,, first visit to Pedee, when and why made, 45, 47
,, tract assigned them, 47, 48 ; its extension, 48-51
,, settlement on Cat Fish, 51
,, Neck, its locality, why selected, 51
,, account of colony in Welch Neck, 52, 53
,, organization of first church, 53
,, records of church, 53 *note;* many lost, 440
,, appeal to Council for protection against Indians, 53
,, inducements held out by Government to others to come, 54, 55
,, increase of settlers, list of grants, action of Council thereon, 55-58
,, difficulties in their way, 58
,, petition to have lands surveyed and granted free of expense, 59
,, action of Council on petition, 60
,, upper limits of their settlement, 62
,, exclusive in their feeling and policy, 61, 66
,, relics, 67, and *note;* a few names only left, 162
,, their first articles of cultivation, 111
,, encouraged by Government to produce certain exports, 60
,, removal of their church building to Society Hill, 440
Wemys, Major, his march up Pedee, incidents of, 302, 303, 304
,, returns to George-town, 306
,, indulgence shown him by General Sumpter, 306
,, again on Lower Pedee, 332
Westfield, John, notice of, 62 *note*
,, Tobacco Inspector at Cheraw, 430
Whigs and Tories, when the distinction between them took its rise, 266, 267
,, ,, conflicts between, 257, 298, 305, 325, 326
,, ,, ,, 357, 358, 370, 371, 382, 383, 387, 392
Whitfield, William, Representative for Marlborough, 459
Wickham, Thomas, Representative for Liberty, 457
Wilds, notice of family, 52 *note*
,, Samuel, petitions for land, 118
,, Mrs., robbed by British soldiers, 362
,, Samuel, birth and early years, 499-500
,, ,, teacher in St. David's Academy, 437, 521
,, ,, candidate for Legislature in Darlington, 458, 459
,, ,, Representative for Darlington, 461, 501
,, ,, marriage, success at Bar, 500, 501
,, ,, anecdote of, 501, *note*
,, ,, elected solicitor, then judge, 501
,, ,, charge to Grand Jury of Abbeville, 502-509
,, ,, sentence on Slater, 510, and *note*, 513
,, ,, ,, John Tollison, 513-516
,, ,, holds last court in Charleston, 517
,, ,, his death, and feeling produced by it, 517
,, ,, proceedings of Bar in Charleston, 517, 518
,, ,, ,, ,, at Sumpter, 518, 519
,, ,, obituary notices of, 519-526, and *note*
,, ,, lines commemorative of, 527, 528
Wilks, John, grantee of land, 79
Williams, Rev. Robert, notice of, and account of family, 64, 65, and *note*
,, David, his death, 268
,, General D. R., notice of, 65, *note*
Willis, Old, kills British soldiers, and returns money to Mrs. Wilds, 363, 364
Wilson, Dr. James P., notice of, and family, 102
,, ,, house burned by British, removes his family, 304
,, ,, effort to save Cusack, 303
,, ,, C. C. Justice for Darlington, 434

Wilson, Dr. James P., opposes Wm. Thomas for senate, 446
,, ,, ,, his death, 453, 454, and *note*
,, John, settles on Pedee, his family, 103, and *note*
,, ,, feeling after taking oath of allegiance, 305
,, ,, commands Munchausen corps, 352
,, ,, Sheriff for Cheraws, 378
,, ,, taken prisoner and escapes, 386
Wise, Samuel, settles on Pedee, 104
,, ,, elected captain by Provincial Congress, 236
,, ,, elected major, 236
,, ,, resigns commission, 246, 247
,, ,, marches to Charles-town, 252
,, ,, writes to Gen. Harrington, 268-273, 278, 279, 285-287, 289-291
,, ,, his character and death, 296
Winchester, Rev. Elhanan, pastor of Welch Neck church, 180 *note*
,, ,, preaches anniversary sermon in St. David's church, 180
,, ,, addresses, with Rev. Mr. Hart, President Laurens, and President's reply, 261-263
,, ,, resigns his charge, 439; state of church, 439, 440
Witherspoon, John D., active at fire in Darlington, 435, *note*
,, Gavin, settles in Darlington, notice of, 441
,, ,, Representative for West Liberty, 455
Wood, Rev. Frame, teacher in St. David's, 438
YANKEE Hill, 465 *note*
Young, Francis, account of, petitions for land, 61
ZIMMERMAN, Wm., Representative for Darlington, 459, 461
,, ,, Sheriff for Darlington, 461.

1. Tomb of Col. Abel Kolb, in Marlboro County, just across the Pedee River from Society Hill.
2. Tomb of Bishop Gregg, in St. David's Churchyard, Cheraw.

HISTORY

OF

THE OLD CHERAWS

ADDENDA

Comprising Additional Facts Concerning the Eight Pedee Counties, and Sketches of the Persons for Whom They Are Named

BY
JOHN J. DARGAN

Assisted by Representatives of the Local Branches of
THE PEE DEE HISTORICAL SOCIETY

Columbia, S. C.
THE STATE COMPANY, PUBLISHERS
1905

COPYRIGHT 1905
BY
THE STATE COMPANY

THE EIGHT PEDEE COUNTIES

WITH

SKETCHES OF THE PERSONS FOR WHOM THEY ARE NAMED

NOTE.

Extract from the Preface to Dr. David Livingstone's Travels in South Africa:

"The preparation of this narrative has taken much longer time than, from my inexperience in authorship, I had anticipated. . . .

"Those who have never carried a book through the press can form no idea of the amount of toil it involves. The process has increased my respect for authors and authoresses a thousand-fold."

The Secretary of the Pee Dee Historical Society adopts the above as his word of apology and explanation to the many-times disappointed people who have been long looking for the appearance of this volume.

"Misery loves company," and especially highly respected company, like that of Dr. Livingstone.

Too much praise cannot be bestowed upon the publishers for the kind and generous assistance extended the Society in all its undertakings.

PREFACE.

The foregoing pages are a literal reprint of the "History of the Old Cheraws, containing an account of the aborigines of the Pedee, the first white settlements, their subsequent progress, civil changes, the struggle of the Revolution, and growth of the country afterward; extended from about A. D. 1730 to 1810: with notices of families and sketches of individuals, by the Right Rev. Alexander Gregg, D. D., Bishop of the P. E. Church in Texas, formerly rector of St. David's Church, Cheraw," which appeared in 1867. Even the numbers of the pages of the present volume correspond exactly with those of the old volume.

This work was done by The State Company, at the suggestion and with the assistance of the Pee Dee Historical Society. This literal reproduction was made in compliance with the request of a few persons and a very generally understood desire throughout the Pedee section for a verbatim reprint of Bishop Gregg's work, but as there were some errors in the book, which it was important to correct, and a good many facts of interest which had not been embodied in that work, and two counties of the Pedee not included in it, the Society has undertaken to bring out with the book the following Addenda, which it is hoped will afford additional interest and information. Wherever correction is made of an error, the number of the page in the original will be given, as a guide to its discovery.

The counties have furnished, through their local committees, the accounts which appear under their respective names. The sketches of the counties, with a portrait of the person for whom the county is named, is work done by the Pee Dee Historical Society. The illustrations of the original text, which appear in the present volume, were placed there, with their descriptive words, by this Society.

It has been the aim of the Society and The State Company not to displace or supersede in any way the old issue of Bishop Gregg's book, but to give a new issue that is not a revision or alteration in any particular whatever, but with only such matter as is properly named Addenda—things added to what has gone before.

The word "Pedee" is spelt two ways, as the reader observes. In the name of the Society it is "Pee Dee," as under that name the Society was formed; but upon reflection it is thought to be better to spell it as it is in the original text and in most of the early writings, this being the recognized spelling for the Indian name, and excluding the initial theory. See page 20 of "The Old Cheraws."

It is the purpose of the Society to bring out another volume as a continuation of Bishop Gregg's good work, starting where he left off at the year 1810, and coming down to 1880. It is the confident expectation of the Society that the people of the Pedee section, through the helpful agency of the county branches which have been formed, will make this second volume one of great thoroughness, valuable information and much interest.

ADDENDA.

BISHOP ALEXANDER GREGG.

There is nothing in the Addenda to Bishop Gregg's book which will afford the same degree of interest to the readers as a sketch of the author's life. The feeling of gratitude toward him for the work which he did in preserving the history of this section of South Carolina is intense, profound, and enduring. Had he not done this work, as far as we can now see, complete oblivion would have covered many of the most interesting occurrences in the history of our State and nation. No one can read the pages of "The Old Cheraws" and not discover that the people who have lived in the Cheraw District were a substantial, patriotic, enlightened, enterprising, self-respecting, and highly respectable body of citizens. In all the great crises of the country's history they have performed a creditable part—a part that displayed an intelligent understanding of their obligations and opportunities for service, and that service has been discharged with a fidelity that affords a high and just pride to their descendants. A distinguished member of the Cheraw Lyceum (Judge Henry McIver) said to the Secretary of the Pee Dee Historical Society, at the time of its organization, that but for the existence of the Cheraw Lyceum, Bishop Gregg could not have carried through the work which he had so nobly undertaken; that it was at the suggestion of the Lyceum he undertook it, and no one would ever know the degree of toil, the self-denial, the discomforts, the perseverance, the delays, the vexations, that had characterized the performance of this work by that devoted author. It is not claiming too much to say that the work which he has done for his people of the Pedee section (from whom he was called away to service in a distant State for his church), is unequaled in value by that of any other person who ever lived within its borders.

At the time of his death a lengthy tribute appeared in the papers from the town of Cheraw, from which the following is a short extract:

"Bishop Gregg was the son of Mr. David Gregg, a well-known and highly respected citizen of Society Hill, in Darlington County, and was born there in 1819. He graduated with the first distinction in the South Carolina College when that noble institution was in the very zenith of its fame and its glory. He was married to Miss Charlotte W. Kollock, a daughter of Mr. Oliver H. Kollock, of Marlboro County, and a sister of our distinguished fellow citizen, Dr. Cornelius Kollock. He was admitted to the bar and practiced in co-partnership with Gen. J. W. Blakeney, in Cheraw, until he decided to enter the ministry of the Episcopal Church. He was for thirteen years the popular and faithful pastor of St. David's Church. During his pastorate here he received several urgent invitations to more lucrative and important charges, but could not be induced to sever his connection with the people of his first love, until the call of his church to the arduous and responsible office of the bishopric presented to him its superior claims to his services. In 1859, just before the storm cloud of war had burst upon his native State, he entered with all the energy of his soul upon his great life-work in Texas, far away from the scenes and associations of his youth and the friends of his early days.

"As Bishop of Texas he went, as it were, a pioneer through an unexplored desert, and gallantly planted the standard of his church all over that great State.

"As rector of St. David's Church he brought the neglected poor to feel that there were places for them in the sanctuary of God, and won the hearts of every class. As a citizen of Cheraw he was the persistent advocate of the best interests of the whole people, and a leader in the promotion of the moral, social and literary institutions, nor is there anyone to whom we are more indebted for the impetus which was given to efforts in this direction. His contribution to our historic literature in 'Gregg's History of the Old Cheraws,' is recognized as an invaluable record of an honorable past, and will stand as a monument to his indefatigable industry and his devotion to the home of his youth.

"Throughout his honored life he was always actuated by the highest and purest motives and governed by the noblest principles—ever ready to sacrifice everything but principle that he might aid his fellow men in their struggles and trials. The fearless champion of truth and right, he was also a firm and trusty friend and faithful counselor."

From the church paper in Texas is taken the following extract from the notice of his death there:

"The first Bishop of Texas was born in Society Hill, Darlington District, South Carolina, on the 8th day of October, A. D. 1819.

"He graduated at South Carolina College, A. D. 1838, and entered at once upon the study of law. He was admitted to the bar, and practiced at Cheraw, in the Northeastern Circuit, embracing the Districts of Chesterfield, Marlborough, Darlington, and Marion, in South Carolina.

"He was baptized and confirmed in St. David's Church, Cheraw, South Carolina, A. D. 1843, and immediately thereafter became a candidate for holy orders.

"Ordained deacon in St. David's Church, Cheraw, on the 10th day of June, A. D. 1846, by the Right Rev. C. E. Gadsden, D. D.

"Ordained priest in St. Philip's Church, Charleston, South Carolina, on the 19th day of December, A. D. 1847, by the same prelate. Immediately upon his ordination to the diaconate he took charge of St. David's Church, Cheraw, of which he became the rector, and he remained in that position until his elevation to the episcopate.

"He received the degree of Doctor in Divinity from South Carolina College, in A. D. 1859.

"Alexander Gregg was consecrated first Bishop of Texas in the Monumental Church, Richmond, Va., October 13, 1859, during the session of the General Convention. In 1874 his vast See, territorially sufficient for a College of Apostles, was divided by the setting off of two missionary jurisdictions, which were committed to two Bishops of their own.

"He continued in the full exercise of his apostolic work until July 11, 1893, when, after a long and trying illness, he fell asleep.

"His administration had been judicious, devoted, and abounding in self-denying labors. He was a man of strong intellectual powers, a graceful writer, a careful and accurate historian, and of unusual energy and force. He has left his impress on the great State which received him as her first Bishop, and she remembers in love and gratitude his devout and devoted life."

The following is taken from the proceedings of the Board of Trustees of the University of the South, at its meeting in 1893:

"The Bishop of Texas presented the following minute, which was heard standing, and the resolutions appended were unanimously adopted:

" 'In the providence of Almighty God, this Board is called upon to mourn the death of the Rt. Rev. Alexander Gregg, D. D., Bishop of Texas, and Chancellor of this University. . . . In the death of Bishop Gregg the church and the University lose a man of rare mold. . . . Bishop Gregg became identified with this University before its bright prospects were blighted by the War Between the States, and upon the return of peace he joined in with enthusiasm to help build it up. Sewanee was always in his heart, and no visitation from him was complete without a word in its favor. His devotion to this University was a most conspicuous factor in his life, because of his deep conviction that its work and the work of the church were one. For nine years he enjoyed the distinction of being the Chancellor of the University, and as such was the presiding officer of this Board. We shall ever remember him with reverence and affection, and we shall ever hold dear, as becomes us, our kindly and profitable association with this truth-loving, duty-doing, and god-fearing man.'

"Bishop Gregg fixed his summer home in Sewanee in 1868. He became Chancellor upon the death of Bishop Greene, in February, 1887, but for the last few years of his life his mind was clouded by illness, and the duties of the Chancellor were performed by others. He died July 11, 1893."

These exhibits from the records of his life, far away from his home in South Carolina, conclusively demonstrate that the same zeal, devotion, and ability characterized him in those distant fields as marked his career here. His precious remains were brought back to his native State and committed to the earth in the cemetery of St. David's Church at Cheraw. The spot is marked by a handsome memorial stone. It should be one of the shrines of the Pedee section. When the Chiquola Club, traveling in the cause of South Carolina history, and visiting all points of interest in its reach, stood at the tomb of Bishop Gregg, with heads uncovered, the manager said: "Here is the most sacred spot in the Pedee territory. It marks the burial place of a historian who has done more for his people than has ever been done by any other individual who has ever labored for them. For it is the written words that endure, and inspire in the long ages the millions who could not witness the deeds they record. The service of the faithful historian is, therefore, unequaled in extent of benefit, in the long life of the world. The tomb of this man should be the mecca of the patriotic people of the Pedee, for by his work they are enabled to see and to transmit to all succeeding generations the glorious lives of the fathers who laid the foundations of the homes and the public institutions of the grand country we now enjoy."

GEORGETOWN.

Georgetown County is named for George II., the King of England from 1727 to 1760. George himself is rather an interesting character, and his reign full of persons and events never to be forgotten.

George was taking his accustomed afternoon's nap, when Sir Robert Walpole arrived to announce his succession to the throne. Aroused from his sleep, he roared out his answer to the announcement: "Dat is one big lie!" This was the best he could do in speaking English, just one better than his father, who could not speak it at all. But this German Prince, King of England, had at least one admired point in his character. In personal bravery he was equal to Caesar; he was ever eager for war, and would have brought England into many a conflict but for peace-loving Robert Walpole, his prime minister, and the gentle control of his wife, Caroline. He was the last English sovereign to engage personally in battle. During his reign the battle of Culloden was fought, the event of which brought many Scotch people to South Carolina, and the heroine, Flora MacDonald, to North Carolina.

His reign saw the rise of William Pitt, and the death of Alexander Pope, the defeat of the French by Wolfe at Quebec, and the establishment of British power in India by Clive's victory at Plassey, the career of the great Frederick of Prussia, the change in the calendar making January instead of March the first month of the year, the rise of the Methodists under the leadership of the Wesleys, and that "social condition characterized by want of faith, by coarseness, and brutality," so vividly portrayed by Hogarth's pencil and Fielding's pen, when placards over the doors of the gin-shops read in this fashion: "Drunk for a penny; dead drunk for two pence; clean straw for nothing." And men and women lay on the straw in beastly helplessness night after night, while in the most fashionable homes the hospitality of the host would find description in Goldsmith's couplet:

GEORGE II.

"Here, waiter, more wine, let me sit while I'm able,
Till all of my guests sink under the table."

So the life and times of George II., in connection with the County of Georgetown, will afford very interesting and instructive reading.

MARLBORO.

Named for the famous first Duke of Marlborough (John Churchhill), who descended from an aristocratic but impoverished ancestry. He made his fortune by his talents and good looks. His conscience seems to have been devoid of scruples, and he is, perhaps, as the historian Green says, the only instance of a man of real greatness who loved money for money's sake, and his lack of learning ever made it harder for him to pen a dispatch than plan a battle. Though his early success as a soldier was remarkable, he won no great victories until he had passed his fifty-second year. After this, Voltaire tells us truly, "he never besieged a fortress which he did not take, or fought a battle which he did not win," or as some one has expressed it in rhyme, with the inaccuracy of poetic license,

> "In battles a hundred and one,
> He never lost an English gun."

Nothing could exceed his natural poise, grace and dignity. In the rage of battle the soldiers saw their leader, with no sense of danger or appearance of hurry, giving his orders with perfect calmness. In the council chamber, he was as cool as on the battlefield.

"He met with the same equable serenity the pettiness of the German princes, the phlegm of the Dutch, the ignorant opposition of his officers, the libels of his political opponents."

There was but one thing on this earth that he seemed to fear, and that was the frown of his spouse, Sarah. One reproving look from her eye would blanch his cheeks. Yet it is said of him that he loved but three things—glory, wealth, and Sarah—and Sarah reciprocated the love given so unstintedly, and aided his every effort at the accumulation of money, and reach for station and fame, and when left a widow seemed to have but one great object, and that was to

THE DUKE OF MARLBOROUGH.

increase the renown attaching to his name. His most brilliant victory was won at Blenheim, when he humbled the pride of Louis XIV., of France, dreaming of universal empire, and became the idol of the hour, receiving from a grateful parliament the manor of Wood-Stock and a palace erected in the park at a cost of two hundred and forty thousand pounds—something over a million dollars. In this gift he verily got a reward after his own heart, and today, though he left no male issue, his descendants hold that property, as proud a possession, of the fashionable sort, as is on the globe.

The Scotch pedagogue, Mathison, did well to name the village where he taught in Marlboro County. Blenheim, and the people of Marlboro should be stimulated to follow this suggestion and study the history of the great duke and his beautiful, talented, and imperious wife.

Queen Anne's famous reign has nothing in it quite so conspicuous as the Marlboroughs, for while the ambitious duke was winning victories, at which "all the world wondered," on fields of battle, the intelligent and forceful Sarah was carrying to triumph her schemes in social and political life, to such an extent that is was said that "Anne reigns, but Sarah rules," and her influence extended so far as to bring the expression from the critical Hallam, author of the "Constitutional History of England," "that the fortunes of Europe were changed by the insolence of one waiting-woman and the cunning of another," and that other was the duchess's cousin, Mrs. Masham. Perhaps no European victories in arms and at court ever did as much for America, in relieving it of the dread of French and Spanish domination, as those of Marlborough and his wife.

CHESTERFIELD.

Lord Chesterfield (Philip Dormer Stanhope), was a close friend of George II. when the latter was Prince of Wales, and his career is intimately connected with the reign of this monarch. He was prominent in his day as a politician, and his speeches in the House of Lords were characterized by wit, eloquence, and elegance; but his life was devoted, in the main, to the pleasures of literature and society, in both of which he became a lustrous figure. It was his special ambition to be the British Maecenas, and the rebuff which he received in this effort, when exerted on Dr. Samuel Johnson in behalf of the Dictionary, brought forth one of the spiciest pieces of writing from the doughty doctor that we have in our tongue.

Though Chesterfield did service of note as an administrative officer in Ireland and Holland, and as an orator in the House of Lords, he is yet best recollected by his six hundred letters to his son. The manners and morality of the times are brought very vividly to light by the birth and careers of Chesterfield himself, and this son of his. The letters are truly abounding in worldly wisdom, shrewd observation, fruitful suggestion, and though occasionally enjoining morality, in precept, yet they display a familiarity with vice and an encouragement to licentious indulgence that render them unfit for detailed discussion.

Let the reader inquire into Chesterfield's own genealogy and the lineage of his son, to whom these letters are written, if he would note the vast progress that has been made in family relations from that day to this. Neither of them was of legitimate birth. But the six hundred letters, fortified as they are with sagacious hints on outward bearing, worked no beneficial effects whatever on the son's life. The familiar lines seem not to have done any great injustice to father or son when they declared:

LORD CHESTERFIELD.

"Vile Stanhope, demons blush to tell,
   How in twice three hundred places,
You showed your son the road to hell,
   Conducted by the Graces:
But little did the ungenerous youth
   Concern himself about them,
For, mean, degenerate, basely bad,
   He sneaked to hell without them."

Celebrated as a writer of these letters, and as the impersonation of politeness, beyond these he is scarcely known to the world of today.

The letters were published by the widow of the son in order to make amends for the Lord's failure to provide, as she thought properly, for her in his last will and testament. Thus we see them, taken all in all, a very ill-flavored set. Fortunately the character of many of the prominent people from Chesterfield County has been such as to relieve the name of its unsavoriness in South Carolina.

FLORENCE.

It would be impossible to think of Florence County, historically, without the name of Gen. W. W. Harllee being in greatest prominence before the mental eye, for as President of the Wilmington and Manchester Railroad, afterwards known as Wilmington, Columbia and Augusta, he became the founder of the town, being allowed the privilege of locating and naming it. He named it for his daughter, Florence, whose modesty denies us the privilege of putting her portrait on the opposite page. So, to her great gratification, instead thereof appears that of her revered father. Refusing likewise any mention of her own life, we take pleasure in recording, in substitution, some of the many distinctions which mark the name of Gen. W. W. Harllee.

If he had done nothing else but construct the long railroad from Wilmington to Columbia, he would have deserved grateful remembrance. But besides this service he was distinguished as an advocate at the bar; as Lieutenant-Governor of the State, before the Confederate War; as a signer of the Ordinance of Secession; as an officer of devotion and ability during the war; as a citizen of commanding influence and leadership before and after the war, in the section where he resided. Called frequently to preside over conventions of the people (notably over that which nominated Wade Hampton for Governor in 1876), when fierce opposition assailed the movements which he led, bold in thought, fearless in action, absolutely beyond the influence of popular clamor, he followed the light of his convictions in a manner to excite universal admiration.

It is a privilege to place this tribute here to the fearless patriot, and enterprising business man, the father of Florence.

General Harllee died in the town of Florence in his eighty-fourth year, in 1897. His daughter, Miss Florence, is now a resident of the town named in her honor.

GEN. W. W. HARLLEE.

DARLINGTON.

Every effort has been made to find the origin of the name of Darlington, as applied to a county of the Pedee section. Bishop Gregg (on the authority of Mills in his "Statistics") says: "The county is supposed to have been named in honor of Colonel Darlington, who distinguished himself in the War of the Revolution," and Mills says this was a mere surmise of his.

The historian McCrady, in an article to *The News and Courier,* thus speaks of the name of Darlington: "Strange to say, the name of Darlington cannot be found elsewhere in Gregg's book, which deals so largely with the names of persons and families of that region. Nor can we recall ever having met with the name, as that of either officer or soldier in the Revolution. It is safe to say that if such a person ever existed, he certainly did not distinguish himself in the Revolution, or in the history of his country. There was no Colonel Darlington, of South Carolina, in the Revolution. We are rather inclined to think that the name was taken from Darlington County, in England, for some reason of which we have lost the history."

An examination of the map of England will show that there is no county of Darlington; but there is an interesting town in the County of Durham by that name, 335 miles north of London. We find this town first in history, full 1,000 years ago, when it is asserted that the monks who fled with the body of St. Cuthbert from the invading Danes rested for a short time on the site of the present town. It was celebrated for its rigid ecclesiastical conservatism for several hundred years, and then as being the home of Edward Pease, the head of a noted Quaker colony, and to him it owes its still greater distinction of having been the birthplace of the modern railway. A short line of twenty-seven miles from Darlington to Stockton was unquestionably the first railroad in the world. This railway, of which George Stephenson (the inventor of the locomotive engine) was the engineer, was projected in 1818. So besides the "Collegiate Church," which dates from the beginning of the thirteenth century, another relic of the past of very great interest is the "Locomotive No. 1," the first that ever ran on a public railway, which stands now on a pedestal of stone at the North Railroad Station, and there is also a monument to Joseph Pease, "the first Quaker member of Parliament."

The town of this date (1905), with its 40,000 inhabitants, is celebrated for its textile and iron manufactures of many kinds. An interesting town it certainly is, with its historic relics and its up-to-date industrial enterprises. Why should not the effort to have an undiscoverable military hero, for whom the "Pearl of the Pedee" might be named, be abandoned, and the interesting old town of England, celebrated as the residence of the lovers of peace and prosperity, rather than of "war with its train of evils," furnish a guiding inspiration to its namesake on this side of the Atlantic, which may likewise become a leader in the anti-war spirit of the present day, and in splendid industrial progress?

INDEPENDENCE OAK,

Near Mechanicsville, from a limb of which it is said was had the first reading to a public assembly in Darlington County of the Declaration of Independence.

WILLIAM III.

WILLIAMSBURG.

William of Orange, a prince of Holland, came to the throne of England in his thirty-ninth year, and reigned thirteen years, holding the crown jointly with his wife, Mary, both being grandchildren of Charles I., who lost his head in the days of Cromwell. No more striking contrast exists in history than that in the tastes and conduct of these two grandchildren of Charles I. and his son Charles II. The latter was devoted to the pursuit of pleasure, indulged until it caused his premature demise, while William and Mary carried abstemiousness and aversion to the pursuit of pleasure to the opposite extreme. King William, like President Roosevelt, loved hunting of the dangerous sort—wolves, wild boars, and ferocious bears, were his favorite game—and cared for no other recreation whatever, while Mary showed attachment to embroidery, playing on the spinet, reading the Bible and the "Whole Duty of Man," rather than to feminine trifles and levities of fashion. Their matrimonial alliance, when formed, was purely for political advantage, and yet it grew into a bond of genuine affection, and there are few things more beautiful than Mary's surrender of the power of her crown to her husband, that he might feel that he was not only the stay of the loving wife, but also of the confiding queen. In closing her words of surrender, she said:

"But now I promise you that you shall always bear rule, and in return I ask only this: that as I shall observe the precept which enjoins wives to obey their husbands, you will observe that which enjoins husbands to love their wives." From that day to the day death separated them, their love for each other was almost idolatrous.

As Marlborough won glory by his victories, William won a rarer glory out of defeats, and in the midst of these disasters, formed coalitions which brought on three long and bloody wars, in which all Europe, more or less, was engaged, and which profoundly influenced the course of European history. It was he who projected the schemes for humbling the arrogant Louis XIV. of France, which Marlborough completed at Blenheim. It was his skillfully formed combinations, though death defeated his intention of personally participating in them, that prostrated Louis's purpose to be the Emperor of all Europe.

His opposition to France was as Hannibal's to Rome, and Bruce's to England; for Louis's devastations in Holland generated in the patriotic heart of William a hate that beggars language to describe, and hence it was that in the fiercest conflicts of battle gayety took the place of sullenness, and grace his usual bluntness of expression, as he literally joyed to see the Frenchmen fall.

His services to England, while only indirect in his purpose (his one thought being the humiliation of France), were yet very marked. It was he who brought England into play as a European power, and it was he that established the most powerful and influential banking institution in the world, known today by the name he gave it, "The Bank of England."

His most uncompromising critics can find only two acts of his reign, the "Glencoe Massacre," and the defeat of the "Darien Scheme," that have left indelible stains, and his apologists have plausible excuses for even these, while foe and friend agree that there never was in so weak a body so indomitable a will, so fearless a spirit.

South Carolina, in the naming of two counties (Williamsburg and Orangeburg), has bestowed great honor on his memory.

COL. PETER HORRY.

HORRY.

Among the counties of South Carolina, Horry is generally known as the "Independent Republic." Its county seat (Conway) may have been named for Henry Seymour Conway, who kept company with Burke, Fox, and others in resisting the oppressions of America in the British Parliament.* The county is probably named for Col. Peter Horry, of Marion's band, "true and tried"; but General McCrady may be right in saying it bears the name of that family of marked distinction in the State's history; for besides the partisan leaders, Hugh and Peter, we find mention of another, Colonel Daniel, on the list of those who had accepted British protection. There were no men more gallant and devoted in patriotic service than the Horrys. The two colonels, Peter and Hugh, both won high distinction in Marion's command, and Colonel Peter has left a glowing tribute to Marion and description of the scenes of the Revolution in South Carolina, that show he could wield a pen (while protesting rather violently that he could not) as mightily as he did his sword. We make this extract: "The Washington of the South, he steadily pursued the warfare most safe for us, and most fatal to our enemies. He taught us to sleep in the swamps, to feed on roots, to drink the turbid waters of the ditch, to prowl nightly round the encampments of the foe like lions round the habitations of the shepherds

---

*This is an inference, as two other towns of South Carolina were named for the friends of America in the British Parliament. Cheraw was for a time called Chatham, until by the efforts of Governor Wilson it was "changed back" to Cheraw in 1820-21 (see "Old Cheraws," page 465), while the name Camden still remains as a grateful tribute to Lord Camden, who, in the House of Lords, with Chatham, nobly advocated American rights, as did Burke, Fox, Wilkes, and others in the House of Commons.

I do very much wish that our town of Conway did perpetuate the name of the noble mover of the repeal of the Stamp Act, of whom in the hour of triumph Burke wrote:

"I stood near him, and his face, to use the expression of the Scriptures of the first martyr, his face was as it were the face of an angel."

And again in 1780, when he so severely denounced the bishops for favoring the continuance of war and bloodshed, Conway was brave and independent and stood stoutly forward for justice and American rights.

who had slaughtered their cubs. Sometimes he taught us to fall upon the enemy by surprise, distracting the midnight hour with the horrors of our battle: at other times, when our forces were increased, he led us on boldly to the charge, hewing the enemy to pieces, under the approaching light of day. . . .

"But lovelier still wert thou in mercy, thou bravest among the sons of men! For soon as the enemy, sinking under our swords, cried for quarter, thy heart swelled with commisseration, and thy countenance was changed even as the countenance of a man who beheld the slaughter of his brothers. The basest Tory who could but touch the hem of thy garment was safe. The avengers of blood stopped short in thy presence, and turned away abashed from the lightning of thine eyes."

We know of nothing that would be more grateful to the generous spirit of Peter Horry than to record here this tribute to his beloved chief, Marion.

Frequent mention has to be made on the pages of history, where details of battles are given, of the two Horrys. In their brilliant dash and devotion, they remind us of the Percys of England. "What could Marion have done without these two lieutenants?" is a question that will frequently come to the mind in the study of Marion's career.

We select Col. Peter Horry's portrait for the opposite page, as the most appropriate to be there. His tomb is in Trinity Church Cemetery in the city of Columbia.

Every effort has been made to find the origin of the name as applied to the county seat of Horry, and some inferences are the only practical results.

Upon request of the Secretary of the Pee Dee Historical Society, Mr. A. S. Salley, Secretary of the Historical Commission of South Carolina, furnishes the following with reference to the name of Conway:

"Conwayboro, the district seat, now known as Conway, undoubtedly obtained its name from Robert Conway, a colonel in the Sixth Brigade, who succeeded Horry as brigadier-general of the Sixth Brigade in 1802, and who, between the years 1787 and 1803, obtained grants for 2,989 acres of land in what is now Horry County, in eleven grants ranging from 100 to 1,000 acres each."

This opinion is also held by Hon. R. B. Scarborough, of Conway, for the same reason given by Mr. Salley.

MARION.

Marion County is named for one of the three most noted partisan leaders of South Carolina. The trio was, Francis Marion, Thomas Sumter, and Andrew Pickens. Marion and Sumter have an advantage over Pickens, as they did not take British protection after the fall of Charleston, but no one could have fought harder than Pickens when he returned to the patriot cause. Marion operated mostly in what is now the Pedee District. His favorite rendezvous was Snow Island, at the confluence of Lynches and Great Pedee Rivers, in Williamsburg County.

There are few finer characters than Francis Marion anywhere in history. While he possessed perfect courage, he was never reckless. His perseverance had its equal in his patience. He truly learned to labor and to wait: and to fight and run away, that he might fight another day. Never was man better fitted for the task allotted him than Marion for the military operations in South Carolina, after the fall of Charleston and the defeat at Camden. There was no seat of government, no commissariat, no ordnance department, no military supplies of any kind. Rutledge was made Dictator because the government had to have its seat in a rapidly moving machine, with no time for consultations or debatable questions. So, well has it been said of Marion:

"His fortress was the good greenwood,
His tent the cypress tree."

Old saws furnish his swords, pewter dishes his bullets, and from fallen foes he got his guns.

"A moment in the British camp,
A moment and away,
Back to the pathless forest,
Before the peep of day."

His soubriquet of "Swamp Fox," given by Tarleton, was well earned.

GEN. FRANCIS MARION.

But marvelous as was the celerity with which he could move from place to place, matchless as were his courage and caution, effective as were the blows which he dealt, skilful as he was in those he avoided, and splendid as were his achievements in war, accomplished after having been saved, as if by a special Providence, from death on the seas and from capture at Charleston, and again at Camden, for the great work awaiting him, yet interesting as his life is, in all that relates to these scenes of adventure and stirring strife, we must insist that his chief glory rests at last in his conduct in the Legislature after the war, when the question arose as to what treatment the Tories should receive at the hands of the triumphant patriots. For if there be any truth in the teachings of the Christ, it is grander to forgive than to fight, to lift up the fallen than to strike down the mighty, to relieve the distressed than to conquer the defiant. It was Marion who led the few noble spirits in the effort to protect from confiscation the property and from death the lives of the mistaken but sincere believers in the divine right of kings, who then resided in South Carolina. Never was the maxim exemplified more fully, "the bravest are the tenderest," the fearless are the forgiving, than when Marion entered so zealously into the protection from cruel penalties of those with whom he had contended most fiercely in battle. Many a fine family in South Carolina owes its presence here today to Marion's generosity and magnanimity. He saw then, fresh from the field of strife, as distinctly as we see now, that the residents of the State who took the side of the king were in many instances as conscientious as those who resisted his authority: and besides with his truly brave heart, he could not consent to striking a fallen and helpless foe.

Write, therefore, the name of Francis Marion high on the roll of the State's worthies. Magnificent in war, he was peerless in his patriotic work after the war. Great as is the State's debt to him as a soldier, it is greater still as a civilian. His service in the field, unsurpassed in brilliancy there, is surpassed only by the wisdom and magnanimity displayed in the legislative halls in the treatment of his prostrate foes.

THE CONTRIBUTIONS OF THE PEDEE COUNTIES

TO THE ADDENDA OF

GREGG'S HISTORY OF THE OLD CHERAWS

THROUGH THE LOCAL BRANCHES OF

THE PEE DEE HISTORICAL SOCIETY

HISTORY OF WILLIAMSBURG COUNTY.

First traces of what is now known as Williamsburg County appeared about 1731, when a settlement was attempted by two men, Finley and Rutledge, from Charleston. A few miles north of the present site of what is now known as Kingstree are two bays which still bear their names.

The first permanent settlement, as far as can be traced, was between 1731 and 1734. John Witherspoon brought from Scotland a colony which had received grants of land from the King of England. They laid out the town of Williamsburg on the present site of Kingstree, which they named in honor of William III., Prince of Orange. The name Kingstree came from a large white pine on the bank of Black River, which forms the western boundary of the town. This species of pine, along "with all gold and silver mines," was reserved for the king—hence the name King's tree, first given to the tree, then the town.

The colony, led by John Witherspoon, was mainly Scotch Presbyterian, and one of their first duties was to build a house of worship, and the edifice erected was called Williamsburg Church. It was situated just across the road from the church bearing the same name that replaced that of the original structure. About 1890, the Presbyterian Church was removed from its historic site on the eastern boundary of Kingstree, and a new building constructed on Academy street, more accessible to the congregation. The ancient structure was torn down and the lot is now used as a place of interment for the dead. The names of the followers of John Witherspoon to this country are some of them still familiar patronymics, such as James, Wilson, Bradley, Frierson, Gordon, Porter, Pressley, McRae, Plowden, McDonald, Ervin, and Stuart.

The first offshoot of the Williamsburg Presbyterian Church was the Presbyterian Church at Indiantown, which was built about 1750, and is still in a fair state of preservation, and is used as a house of worship.

The first civil division of South Carolina was into four counties, viz.: Berkeley, Colleton, Craven, and Carteret. In 1769 the province was divided into seven precincts, of which Georgetown included five parishes and also the township of Williamsburg. The latter, as a whole, was settled mainly by emigrants from Scotland, Ireland, and England.

When the colonies resolved to throw off the British yoke of oppression, Williamsburg, being near the seacoast, was directly in the path of the foraying parties both from Charleston and Georgetown, when those fell into the clutches of the British, and bore the brunt of much hard fighting. Marion's men included a large number of citizens of Williamsburg, and Snow's Island, on the northeastern border of the county, was the private camping ground and recruiting place of the forces of the redoubtable "Swamp Fox." Three of his most distinguished partisan lieutenants, Maj. John James, Capt. Henry Mouzon, and Capt. William McCottry, were of Williamsburg County.

Of this famous camp William Gilmore Simms says: "Marion's career as a partisan in the thickets and swamps of Carolina is abundantly distinguished by the picturesque, but it was while he held his camp at Snow's Island that it received its highest colors of romance. In this snug and impenetrable fortress, he reminds us very much of the ancient feudal barons of France and Germany, who, perched on castle eminence, looked down with the complacency of an eagle and marked all below him for his own." We also have the assertion of this same author that, before the defeat of General Gates, Marion received a message from the Whigs of Williamsburg, asking him to be their leader, and he left Gates's camp in response to the invitation before the Battle of Camden, which resulted so disastrously to the Whigs, to penetrate into the interior of the State in advance of the army.

Simms thus describes the men of Williamsburg at the time of Marion's appearance: "They were sprung generally from Irish parentage, and inherited, in common with all the descendants of the Irish in America, a hearty detestation of the English name and authority. This feeling rendered them excellent patriots and daring soldiers whenever the British lion was the object of hostility. Those of whom we are now to speak, the people of Williamsburg, were men generally of courage, powerful frame, well-strung nerves, and audacious gallantry that led them to delight in dangers, even when the immediate object by no means justified the risk. They felt the rapture of the strife in which the god delighted. In addition to these natural endowments for a brave soldiery they were good riders and famous marksmen, hunters that knew the woods as well by night as by day. They possessed resources of knowledge and ingenuity while in swamp and thicket, not merely to avoid the danger, but in frequent instances to convert to their own advantage." It was in keeping with the esprit de corps thus indicated that the oft-told encounter between Maj. John James and the British officer, Ardesoif, occurred, the main facts of which are as follows: In the midst of the demoralization attendant upon the fall of Charleston, when everything appeared to be lost and a proclamation was issued by Sir Henry Clinton, the British commander, offering pardon to the inhabitants and a reinstatement by "his gracious majesty, King George," in their rights and immunities heretofore enjoyed, when many accepted the offer with alacrity and soon found to their sorrow that they were to bear arms in the service of the king against their countrymen, that the people of Williamsburg, before closing with this magnanimous proposition of Clinton, decided to investigate it, and sent Maj. John James to Georgetown, then held by the British under Captain Ardesoif, to find out just what the offer meant.

Under this appointment James, attired as a plain backwoodsman, called upon Ardesoif and in plain terms set forth his errand. To his inquiry whether the inhabitants were to be allowed to remain on their plantations, the British officer responded negatively, adding: "His Majesty offers a free pardon, of which the rebels were undeserving, for they all deserved to be hanged; but this pardon was granted only on condition that they take up arms in the British cause." James very cooly replied that the people whom he came to represent would hardly accept such terms. This reply provoked Ardesoif, who in a fury exclaimed: "Represent! you d—d rebel; if you dare to use such language to me I'll have you hung to the yard-arm." Major James was entirely weaponless, while Ardesoif was armed with a sword, but the plucky patriot quickly rose and, seizing the chair on which he had been sitting, knocked down the British officer who had insulted him, and escaped into the woods before the British officer recovered from the shock. When Major James returned and reported the result of his interview with Captain Ardesoif, the people of Williamsburg, to whom the thought of imbuing their hands in the blood of their countrymen was abhorrent and a breach of one of the commands of God, resolved to submit to no such tyrannical measure as was being attempted, and prepared to resist to death the ruthless invaders of their homes.

They had at this time placed over them two Tory officers, Amos Gaskins and John Hamilton, whom they hated and despised.

About this time news reached them of the coming of Gates's army into the State, and at the meeting which was held they resolved unanimously to take up arms in the defense of their country. Major James was chosen as commander, and William McCottry, John James, Henry Mouzon, and John McGauley were chosen as captains of four companies which were formed, comprising about two hundred men.

This was the situation when Marion was invited to take command. It will be noted that Marion accepted the invitation even after the disastrous fiasco of Gates. The men of Williamsburg, under his leadership, were by no means disheartened, but more than ever determined to continue their resistance against the British oppression.

Thus, it will be seen, at that time of gloom and despondency, the single ray of light that shone in the darkness of despair was the little band of Williamsburg patriots, undaunted by disaster to their cause, who formed the nucleus of that historic army which, under their bold and dashing leader, became a veritable scourge to the enemies of their country. Prior to Marion's arrival they made prisoners of

House in which Major James knocked down the British Officer.

the British officers appointed over them, practically declaring their independence and demonstrating the quality of their courage.

At this time the Tories on Lynches Creek were committing all manner of depredations and murdering inoffensive citizens. Captain McCottry was posted in advance at Witherspoon's Ferry, and Colonel Tarleton, having crossed Lenud's Ferry on the Santee, heard of the meeting in Williamsburg, and advanced at the head of seventy men to surprise McCottry, who, nothing loath, advanced to give him battle with only fifty men. Tarleton had been posted at the King's Tree (Kingstree). When he heard of McCottry coming with 500 men he marched away a few hours ahead of the advancing army of McCottry, burning the house of Captain Mouzon on his way, and never stopped until he reached Salem, thirty miles away.

Shortly after this Marion came and took command, his first move being against Britton's Neck, where he surprised and defeated Major Gainey, a Tory leader. In this attack Major James commanded what cavalry could be mustered, and in the melee which followed he singled out Gainey to engage in personal encounter.

At his approach Gainey fled, and James pursued him into a thicket, where some of the Tories had rallied. Although alone, James with great coolness called out, as if addressing his followers: "Come on, boys; here they are!" The whole body of Tories broke and fled into Pedee Swamp before James's imaginary army.

As is generally the case, the heroism of the men of Williamsburg was equaled by that of the women, as the following incident forcibly illustrates. A party of Wemys's men, in one of the barbarous invasions of that cruel Tory leader, came to the house of Mr. John Frierson, near Kingstree, where Mr. H. H. Kinder now lives. Mr. Frierson had barely time to escape and hide himself in a tree in full view of his dwelling. The officer in command threatened Mrs. Frierson in the most profane and insulting language, telling her that unless she disclosed her husband's hiding-place he would burn her up in the house. She refused to do so and was forced to enter the house with her four-year-old son, when the building was set on fire and sentinels posted at the doors to prevent her escape. The roof was soon in flames, and although flakes of fire fell thick and fast about her, the heroic wife remained firm in her refusal, until the intense heat of the fire drove the sentinels away and she was suffered to escape with her child.*

The engagement at Black Mingo took place in September, 1780. The Tories were commanded by Capt. John Coming Ball. The action was so closely and sharply contested that the loss on both sides was nearly one-third killed and wounded. Capt. Henry Mouzon and Lieut. Joseph Scott were, by their wounds, rendered unfit for future service.

During the Revolution there were three invasions of Williamsburg, in each of which her sons proved their mettle by the stout resistance they offered, and many heroic deeds were enacted in the way of individual prowess.

The last invasion was in the spring of 1781, when Rawdon, getting between Sumter and Marion, undertook to crush the latter in his rendezvous on Snow's Island. Two forces were sent after him under Colonels Watson and Doyle—one down the Santee and the other along Lynches Creek. By means of superior numbers Watson forced his way down the Santee, his route to Snow's Island lying through the heart of Williamsburg, and the struggle on the part of the wily "Swamp Fox" was to arrest his career. One of the two bridges across Black River was to be the Thermopylae, and there a Spartan band was placed to dispute the passage. Watson chose the lower bridge, fearing an ambuscade on the west side of the river, opposite Kingstree. Making a feint of continuing down the Santee, he fell below the Broomstraw road to deceive his opponent, and soon after wheeling his column, he made a rapid push for the lower bridge; but Marion anticipated this strategic maneuver and dispatched the gallant James with seventy men, thirty of whom were McCottry's riflemen, by a near route, directing them to de-

---

*The Secretary of the Pee Dee Historical Society has seen Mr. Frierson's commission as Lieutenant in the Second South Carolina Regiment, given by Congress in 1782. It is still in the hands of his descendants, now living in Stateburg, Sumter County, S. C., and is in a good state of preservation. Few indeed of this kind of things are kept and valued as they should be in South Carolina!

stroy the bridge and post the riflemen so as to frustrate the attempted crossing. Meantime Marion arrived with his army to support James's little force. When Watson arrived and tried to cross he was met by a deadly fusillade from Marion's riflemen, and, after trying to carry the ford by storm, his ranks were thrown into utter confusion by the fatal volleys.

When the British were about to evacuate Charleston, having tired of the war, they were laying in stores of provisions. A numerous fleet of small vessels under convoy sailed, supposedly against Georgetown. Marion hastened in that direction for the purpose of removing the public stores to a place of safety. Black Mingo was preferred as the depot for the honorable reason, as given in Marion's own words, that it was "a settlement of good citizens and of my earliest and most faithful followers."

GREGG-GORDON.

(Williamsburg.)

Margaret Gregg, daughter of John and Eleanor Gregg, first married Samuel Scott. Their only child, Elizabeth, first married John Cunningham, and after his death married McElveen.

Margaret Gregg married the second time, William Gordon; their children were:

Eunice, who married William Wilson, of Marion County.

Margaret, who married Alex. Gregg, of Marion County.

Samuel Scott, who married Katherine McConnell.

Rebecca Ervin, who married first Arthur Cunningham. Their children were: David, William, and Tahpenas. Rebecca Ervin married the second time, John Scott. Their only child was John Ervin Scott.

Margaret Gregg married the third time, William Flagler. Their children were William, Gordon, and John.

William Gordon was a captain in the army. While a party of Tories were plundering his house once, the alarm was given that the ships were coming. The whole party fled, but one of them became fastened in some way on the fence, and was unable to get over. Mrs. Gordon ran and caught the fellow and, pulling him down on her side of the fence, detained him until help came and he was secured.

At another time they came and carried off all of Captain Gordon's horses, while he was absent fighting the battles of his country. Mrs. Gordon followed the party at a distance and observed where the horses were inclosed. That night she went alone, caught the best horse in the lot and rode away in safety.

MARION COUNTY.

The first legislative notice taken of Marion District by that name is to be found in the Act of 1798, Section 1, Vol. VII, Statutes at Large, page 283, by which the name was changed from Liberty County to Marion District, on page 284 of the said Vol. VII of the Statutes at Large. In the said Section 1 of the said Act are the following words: "One other district to be named Marion District, to comprehend the county now called Liberty County, according to its present limits." This Act changes the name in some instances, as well as also the counties, to be called districts for the whole State. By Section 2 of the said Act courts were established in the following words: "That in each of the said districts by this Act established, there shall be held, from and after the first day of January, in the year of our Lord one thousand eight hundred, by one or more of the Associate Judges of this State for the time being, and at such places as shall be appointed by or under this Act, a Court of Sessions and a Court of Common Pleas, to possess and exercise, respectively, each court in its respective district, the same power and jurisdiction now held and exercised by the several Circuit or District Courts of this State in their respective districts, and shall sit at the time following, that is to say: for Marion District, at Marion Courthouse, on the first Mondays in March and October in every year." Section 4 of the Act distributed the courts into circuits: "And that the several courts of Marion District, Darlington District, Marlborough District, Chesterfield District, Fairfield District, Kershaw District, Sumter District, shall form one other circuit, to be named the Northern Circuit, and that the Solicitor of the said Northern Circuit shall attend each of the courts of the said Northern Circuit, and prosecute therein, respectively, all suits and prosecutions on behalf of the State, according to the usage and custom of the existing Circuit Courts of the State." These courts were made courts of record, jurors provided for, clerks and sheriffs to be appointed, and their duties prescribed. The County Courts, after January 1, 1800, were to have no jurisdiction, original or appellate, of any causes, civil or criminal, and after 1800 all causes, civil or criminal, pending in the County Courts were transferred to the Court of Sessions or Common Pleas, as the case might be, to the courts hereby established. It was further enacted: "That from and after the first day of January, one thousand eight hundred, the several Courts of General Sessions of the Peace, Oyer and Terminer, Assize and General Gaol Delivery, and of Common Pleas, now established and held in this State, shall be, and the same are hereby, forever abolished; and that all suits, appeals and indictments then depending in any of said courts (except the Court of Charleston District, in which the business already commenced shall be continued in the District of Charleston, established by this Act), shall be transferred in the manner following, that is to say: when any District shall contain two or more of the Districts established by this Act, the suits, appeals and indictments depending in the Superior Courts of law of such Districts shall be transferred to that new District established by this Act, within such District wherein the defendant or appellee resides; and where there are two or more defendants or appellees residing in different new Districts, as the plaintiff or appellor shall direct, and where more of the defendants or appellees reside in such District, then to such of the new Districts therein as the plaintiff or appellant shall direct; and all indictments to the new District where the offense was committed, and all the said suits and indictments, shall be continued, proceeded on and determined in the respective courts to which they shall be transferred as aforesaid; and all records of the said Superior Courts hereby abolished shall be transferred to the nearest district established by this Act, there to be kept and continued." (Section 11 of Act of 1798, Vol. VII, Statutes at Large, an Act to establish a uniform and more convenient system of judicature.)

Section 22 of said Act appoints commissioners to locate courthouses and gaols, and to superintend building the same, and for Marion District the following named gentlemen were appointed: "Col. John McRae, Dr. Thomas Wickham, John Ford, John Orr, Benjamin Harrelson, James Crawford, Thomas Harley, and James Rie; that they be, and are hereby, appointed commissioners for the purpose of fixing on a convenient and central location whereon to establish and build a courthouse and gaol in the District of Marion, and to superintend the building of the same." A very good commission, as is supposed. The men appointed set about the work they were appointed to perform. They only had the year 1799 to perform the work assigned them. The time was too short, with the facilities then to be had for such undertakings. By the terms of the Act, the first court was to be held first Monday in March, 1800. Tradition informs us that the first court held in the county, and under the terms of this Act, was held about two miles below the present courthouse, just across Smith Swamp, on the plantation owned and occupied by Col. Hugh Giles, afterwards owned and occupied by Samuel Stevenson, and now by W. W. Baker. The very spot where the house stood was shown the writer by Mr. Stevenson while he owned it. The new courthouse, then in course of construction, was not in condition to be used; therefore, this log house, probably sixteen feet square, was improvised for holding the first court ever held in the county. Philip Bethea, the father-in-law of the writer, told him often that he attended the first court held. It was supposed that the courthouse was completed during the year. That courthouse is still in existence and in a good state of preservation. It was located somewhere on the public square not far from where the present courthouse stands—a wooden building. It was occupied as a courthouse until 1823, when it was replaced by a brick building, which was built that year and was located about the place where the new fireproof building, lately constructed for the clerk's office and for the Probate Judge, now stands.

As already stated, the first courthouse was a wooden structure, which, doubtless, did very well as an initiatory courthouse, but was soon found to be insufficient for the purposes of its erection, and the powers that then were had the brick one of 1823 built. Who the contractor was for the one built in 1800 we have not been able to find out. The contractor for the one built in 1823 was Enos Tart, a prominent man in his day. The courthouse of 1800 was sold or given to the late Thomas Evans, Sr., who moved it out of the public square and reconstructed it on his own lot, and converted it into a commodious dwelling. The house still stands on said lot, and, though one hundred years old, seems to be perfectly sound and still in a good state of preservation. The writer supposes it was built of the very best material; if it had not been it would have gone to decay before this time. It was built before the day of turpentine vandalism. It is an evident fact that the timber from which the turpentine has been extracted soon rots—its very life is taken from it. It is like taking the blood from the animal, man included; life is destroyed, and it soon goes into a state of decay. One hundred years ago the uses of turpentine had not been discovered, nor had the cupidity of man been excited to the destruction of our pine forests.

The courthouse and jail located according to the Act of 1798 formed or made a nucleus for the building up of a county town, at and around the courthouse. We do not know who resided near the county seat before the courthouse was erected; as we are informed by tradition, Col. Hugh Giles, a distinguished character during the Revolutionary War, lived just over Smith Swamp, south of the site of the Marion courthouse. It was for him that Marion was first called Gilesboro, and was so called till away up into the thirties, and even after that by some of the older people. The town of Marion was not incorporated until long after. At the time of which we are now writing, we suppose others were in the vicinity. These were descendants of John Godbold, who settled just below where Marion courthouse now stands, of whom more will be said hereinafter; also the descendants of Nathan Evans, who was one of the early settlers of that region, of whom more will yet be said. In connection with the name of Gilesboro, the writer will relate what his father-in-law, Philip Bethea, told him. Before Marion courthouse was located and established as the county seat, there were no public roads leading to it from the upper end of the county. The courthouse being located there, it became necessary to lay out and build roads to the seat of justice. The road now leading from Marion up by Moody's Mill, and on up by what is now Ebenezer Church, and on up by John Bethea's (now John C. Bethea's plantation), and up by Harlleesville (now Little Rock), then on by Gibson's (Stephen, the writer believes), was ordered by the road authorities to be laid out, opened and put in condition for travel. In cutting out and opening the road, the overseer in charge of the work had much trouble in getting those liable to perform road duty to work; the hands, the poorer white people, alleging that they did not want to work and build the road for old Colonel Giles and John Smith, who lived where Moody's Mill now is, to go up to old John Bethea's to drink cider (old John Bethea made quantities of cider, peach and apple brandy); that no one else wanted the road or would use it, the white hands alleging that they did not want the road. He said that such was the opposition that it almost amounted to a rebellion, and that the law had to be invoked in order to get the work done. The road is one of the most useful roads we have in the county, and none so poor that he would not be affected by closing it up, and would not have it abandoned. The writer's informer, Philip Bethea, was a man grown at the time, and a son of old John, the cider maker, and one of the road hands. We have a few such people among us yet, and perhaps you will often meet them— men having no public spirit, and caring for no one but themselves.

Before 1721 all courts were held only in Charleston. This was an ample arrangement at the time and answered all the purposes of said courts. Charleston was then the State, and at that time was convenient to the settled parts of the province. Some modification or amendments to the Act of 1721 were made in 1746, which it is not necessary to notice. To the Courts of Equity, no special changes were made until 1784, after the Revolution. In that year the Legislature passed an Act abolishing the former Courts of Equity, and conferring all its powers and duties on three judges or chancellors, to be elected by the General Assembly, and to be commissioned by the Governor. (It will be remembered that in 1784 there was no such thing as "His Majesty's Counsel.") The powers and duties of the courts were the same as under the Act of 1721. The change was made to suit the condition then existing. The court established by this Act, 1784, was to be held only in Charleston. The three chancellors provided for in this Act, and elected by the Legislature, were John Rutledge, Richard Hudson, and John Matthews.

The next Act of the Legislature to establish a Court of Equity within this State is the Act of 1791 (Vol. VII, Statutes at Large, page 258), Section 1 of which provides: "That all laws now of force for establishing the Court of Chancery within this State, be, and they are hereby, declared to be and continued of force in this State, until altered or repealed by the Legislature thereof," etc.

Section 2 of this Act, 1791, after reciting the great inconveniences to the remote inhabitants of this State resulting from the fact that the Court of Equity is held only in one place within the State, to wit, Charleston, enacts: "That all future sittings of the Court of Equity for the full and solemn hearing of cases shall be held at the time and places hereinafter directed, that is to say: at Columbia, for all causes wherein the defendant shall reside in Camden, Orangeburg, or Cheraw Districts, on the 15th days of May and December; at Camden, for all causes wherein the defendant shall reside within the District of Ninety-Six, on the 5th days of May and December; and at Charleston, for all causes wherein the defendant shall reside in either of the districts of Charleston, Beaufort, or Georgetown [our district], on the second Monday in March, and the same in June, and the third Monday in September, and the same days in every succeeding year," etc. It further provided that each and every judge should ride the circuit, unless prevented by sickness or other unavoidable disability.

The next Act in regard to the Equity Courts is the Act of 1799 (Vol. VII, Statutes at Large, at page 297), which divides the district as then established into four equity circuits, to be called the Eastern, Northern, Western, and Southern. Marion County was placed in the Eastern Circuit; the

Courts of Equity for this circuit were to be held for Marion and Georgetown, at Georgetown, on the first Monday in February in each and every year.

The next Act in reference to the Court of Equity is that of 1808 (Vol. VII, Statutes at Large, page 304). Section 1 of said Act divides the State into three equity circuits, viz., the Southern, Northern, and Western. Our county, Marion, is placed in the Northern Circuit, composed of Georgetown, Horry, Marion, and Williamsburg, which shall form one other Equity District, to be called the Georgetown District, the Courts of Equity for which shall be held at Georgetown, on the first Monday of February and June in every year. This Act of 1808 also provides for the election of two additional chancellors to be commissioned and perform the same duties as the present chancellors. The two elected were Henry William DeSaussure and Theodore Gaillard.

The Act of 1824 established an Appeal Court for both law and equity, to consist of three judges. It also divided the State into four Equity Circuits. Marion District was assigned to the Fourth Circuit, and the courts to be held for "Georgetown, at Georgetown, for the Districts of Williamsburg, Horry, Marion, and Georgetown, on the first Monday after the fourth Monday in January, to sit for two weeks, should so much be necessary." (Vol. VII, Statutes at Large, Section 9, page 327.) From which it appears, as well by this Act of 1824 as by the Act of 1808, supra, that from and after the year 1799 the business of Equity Courts for this section of the State was on the decrease, for by an Act of 1799, only Georgetown and Marion were united for equity purposes; while by the Acts of 1808 and 1824, Georgetown, Marion, Williamsburg, and Horry were united for the same purpose.

It can be truthfully said that the judiciary of South Carolina, from the earliest times as a State, have been filled, both Circuit and Appeal Courts, by men of high character, distinguished alike for integrity, dignity, learning, and ability. Many of them would have done credit to any country, in any age of the world. Their names stand prominent on the rolls of fame. Such a galaxy of eminent names is scarcely to be seen anywhere. Where all are so eminent, it would seem invidious to mention any. Without disparaging others, the writer cannot forbear to mention some. Going back to the days of the Revolution, we have John Rutledge, Henry William DeSaussure, Hugh Rutledge, Thomas Waties, Joseph Brevard, Samuel Wilds, Jr., Abraham Nott, Charles Jones Colcock, Langdon Cheves, William Harper, David Johnson, John S. Richardson, John Belton O'Neall, Josiah J. Evans, Job Johnston, B. F. Dunkin, D. L. Wardlaw, Frank Wardlaw, John A. Inglis, and George W. Dargan. To this list of eminent jurists others might be added. Of such an array of talent as this, any people might justly be proud. Most of these judges performed circuit as well as appeal duty. Their names are imperishable.

Marion County has been an essential factor in all that affected the State; for whatever affected the State, for good or evil, affected her. She has borne her troubles and misfortunes with marked equanimity. She has subordinated herself to the powers that be, and has ever been in favor of law and order. Her people are a law-abiding people—lynch law finds no place among us. Her citizenship, as a whole, is composed of honest, industrious men, who live by honest means, who are enterprising, each in his vocation trying to live and let others live. She is fast coming to the front among her sister counties in the race for distinction and preferment—a model county. If she progresses through the twentieth century as she has during the nineteenth century now closed, she will have attained a prominence in everything that makes a people great, prosperous, and happy. Her resources are unbounded, and not yet half developed. These, used, as they may and will be, by her people for another century, will make her a star of first magnitude among the many stars of the commonwealth, and her citizens, when they travel, will be proud to say, "I am from Marion County, South Carolina."

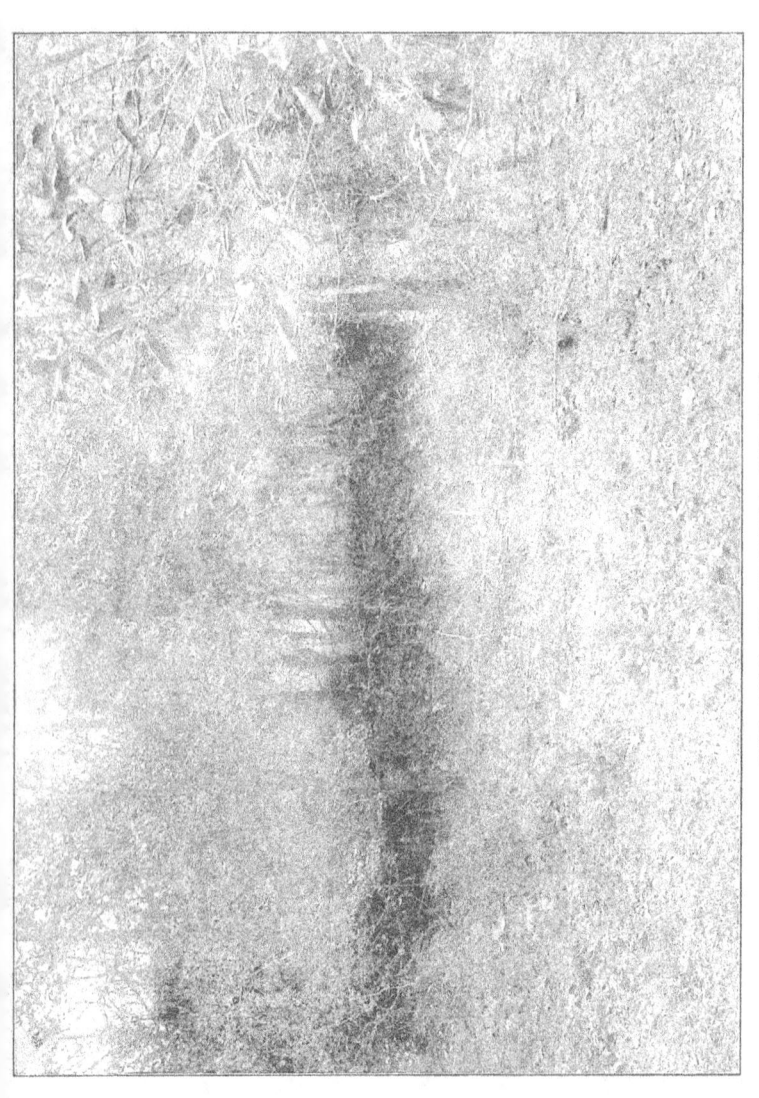

THE SITE OF MARION'S REDOUBT,

Near Port's Ferry, at Dunham's Bluff. The shaded part among the trees is part of the old breastwork.

ADDENDA. 595

BATTLE OF PORT'S FERRY.*

(Marion.)

On August 10, 1780, Marion arrived at the post of Lynches Creek and took command of the party there.

He was soon on the move. On the second day after his arrival—that is the 12th of August, 1780—placing white cockades upon his men to distinguish them from the Tories, he crossed the Pedee at Port's Ferry† to disperse a large body under Major Gainey, stationed on Britton's Neck, between the Great and Little Pedee Rivers. He surprised them at dawn in the morning, killed one of their captains and several privates, and had two men wounded. Major James was detached at the head of a volunteer troop to attack the Tory horse. He came up with them, charged, and drove them before him. On this affair he singled out Major Gainey as the object of his attack. At his approach Gainey fled and James pursued him closely, nearly within the reach of his sword, for half a mile, when behind a thicket he came upon a party of Tories who had rallied. Not at all intimidated, but with great presence of mind, Major James called out: "Come on, boys; here they are! Here they are!" and the whole body of Tories broke again and rushed into the swamp.

BATTLE OF BLUE SAVANNAH.‡

(Marion.)

After the fight at Port's Ferry, Marion did not suffer the courage of his men to cool. In twenty-four hours he was again in motion. Hearing of the proximity of another body of Tories under Captain Barfield, he advanced against him with as much celerity and caution as before. But he found Barfield strongly posted in greater force than he expected,

---

*McCrady's History, Vol. III, p. 651.
†Port's Ferry is a ferry (now not used) on Pedee River, about twenty-five miles south of Marion, S. C.
‡Simms's "Life of Marion."

THE ESCAPE OF ANDREW HUNTER.*

(Marion.)

The story comes down from the days of old
Of Marion's scout, so fearless and bold.
He laughed to scorn the price on his head,
And called it a "Crown of Gold" instead.

He went his way, whether right or wrong;
His heart was warm and his will was strong.
When the longing came o'er him for bairns and wife,
He sought their kiss at the risk of his life.

But alas for the scout so brave and true!—
The history of Judas is ever new—
There were dastards then as there are now,
And the love of gold is the cause, I trow.

They had dogged his steps, in fear and dread,
From the camp in the swamp to his home and his bed;
So he waked one day from his fatal rest
With his enemies' bayonets close to his breast.

He scanned the faces, so fierce in their hate,
And his heart beat wildly at the thought of his fate.
They jeered and derided him, called him a fool,
Said they would eat before hanging him, as breakfast might cool.

The guard led him out and sat down to wait,
While Hunter paced restlessly, pondering his fate.
Each tread brought him nearer the steps, broad and low,
Where, champing her bit, stood the famous "Red Doe."

Not far from the door stood her mate, the "Red Buck,"
And the scout, as he saw them, thanked God for his luck.
"I take chances of bullets instead of the rope."
And his glance sought his guard as he inwardly spoke.

To think was to act, as he dashed for the "Doe,"
Who leaped wildly ahead through the midst of the foe.
"Hunter's escaped!" rang the clamorous cry,
While their captain, with curses, bid them shoot high.

"Don't hit the mare!" "He can't cross the Bluff!"
The bullets sang round him and the riding was rough,
But Hunter sped on in mad haste for the bluff—
To reach it in safety would be more than enough.

The "Doe," like her rider, was gallant and bold.
Hunter gave her the rein, wound her mane in his hold,
And as he neared the high bluff, with the waters below,
Wth a wild, mocking shout he looked back at the foe.

For over the bluff leaped the high-blooded mare,
While his foes stopped shooting to wonder and stare;
And as the "Doe" and her rider swam across the Pedee
There rang o'er the waters the cry, "I am free!"

*The author of the above is Mrs. Dr. Samuel J. Blackwell.

The "Red Buck," whom Hunter had freed as he passed,
Neighed shrilly in recall of his mate going fast.
She answered his call while clambering ashore,
And they parted just there to meet nevermore.

For Hunter exultingly whirled his cap in the air
And called o'er the waters to his foes gazing there:
"Go tell Captain Fanning—that Tory accursed—
That before the said hanging, to catch Hunter first.

"Better hold the 'Red Buck,' or I'll have both today,
For the 'Red Doe' is mine to be kept for alway,"
And scornfully laughing he rode off on the mare
Which afterwards, ever, was his pride and his care.

And 'twas said that in time she shared his alarm,
For when he would sleep, with her rein on his arm,
That at any strange sound she'd jerk sharply about,
As if alert to the danger which threatened the scout;
And he, starting from sleep, would ride off in haste,
For he knew by the "Doe" there was no time to waste.

When the fierce war was ended and America free,
The "Doe" and her master still roamed the Pedee.
Fanning, the Tory, offered slaves and red gold—
"In return for the 'Doe' he would pay sevenfold."

"Dog! Hound!" said Hunter, "Dare he parley with me—
He who imprisoned my wife because I got free?
Tell him 'if ever again on him I lay eyes,'
The score is bitter and one of us dies.

"No, never again shall he have the 'Red Doe',
My freedom and life to her do I owe.
She shall live out her life in close touch with me,
And in dying shall sleep beside the Pedee."

Fanning blustered and swore, and to fight was quite keen.
"Swords in Charleston!" On the Citadel green,
Like the true knight of old, Hunter rode to the fray,
But Fanning took care to shun the array.

They have long passed away, the scout and his foe,
And on the banks of the Pedee sleeps the "Red Doe."
But the story still lives, and is told as of old,
Of Hunter, the scout, so fearless and bold.

HUNTER'S ADVENTURE WITH FANNING.*

(Marion.)

I have been requested to furnish a correct account of it as handed down not only by tradition in the Hunter and Blackwell families, but as preserved in manuscript from among the family records, copies of which I have before me at this entry.

Andrew Hunter was one of Marion's boldest and most daring scouts. His home was in Marion County (now Florence County), on the west side of Great Pedee River, not far from the present station of Mars Bluff, on the Atlantic Coast Line Railroad, and from four to five miles from Mars Bluff Ferry, on Great Pedee River.

On one occasion, not dreaming of danger, or reckless of it, he left camp and visited his family. The Tory Fanning, by some means hearing of his movements, and eager for his capture, followed him and surrounded his house. At daybreak the next morning Hunter found himself in the hands of his most hostile enemies, whom he well knew would not hesitate to hang or shoot him without even the form of a trial, and such was Fanning's determination. He ordered him hung at once, but after a moment decided to have breakfast before carrying out the order. He required the family to prepare his breakfast and left Hunter under guard on the front piazza.

Now Fanning, and not Hunter, was the owner of the blooded mare "Red Doe," as well as her mate, the "Red Buck," and he was riding the mare on that occasion, while one of his lieutenants rode the "Red Buck." Traditions says that this mare was presented to Fanning by a rich Tory in Chatham County, North Carolina, while another tradition says he paid 500 guineas for her. At any rate, she was regarded as the finest and fleetest animal in the Pedee country. She was on this fateful morning loosely hitched to a small oak within a few feet of the piazza where Hunter

---

*Contributed by R. J. Blackwell, Marion, S. C., in order to correct an erroneous account of Andrew Hunter's adventure with the notorious Fanning, described in Gregg's History, on page 396.

paced restlessly up and down, surrounded by the Tory guards, who only awaited the return of Fanning from the dining-room to carry out his cruel order and string the scout to the most convenient tree. Realizing that his situation was desperate, and seizing a favorable opportunity, he sprang from the piazza, mounted the mare, and before the astonished guards were aware of his object was tearing down the road with the speed of the wind. The cry went up: "Hunter's escaped! Hunter's escaped!" and Fanning rushed out with curses on his lips, but seeing him (Hunter) on his favorite mare he cried to the men who were in hot pursuit: "Shoot high." Hunter, hearing this, bent himself forward and made direct for Mars Bluff Ferry, crossing on his way an old mill, the site of which is in existence still, where he found to his horror that the dam was broken, when too late to go around. Tradition says the gap was thirty feet, but that seems incredible. He slackened the mare's gait for her to gather strength for the effort, and then, when within a few yards of the bridge, rushed her forward with all possible speed. She cleared the chasm with a bound and left his astonished pursuers to find their way by another route, thus gaining considerable advantage. He sped on towards the ferry, plunged headlong into the river and swam across to the eastern shore. As the mare with her reckless rider scrambled up the bank, the trooper on the "Red Buck" appeared on the opposite shore. Raising himself in his stirrups, Hunter yelled defiance at him and said: "Tell Captain Fanning the mare is mine, and he must catch Hunter before he can hang him," and was lost to sight in Pedee Swamp. The Tories, unable to cross the river, and realizing the utter uselessness of further pursuit, gave up the chase.

The excitement of the affair wearing off, and as Hunter continued his course eastward, he felt a stinging pain in his back, when it was found that one of the enemy's bullets had struck him there and had come out just above his shoulder blade. This wound was dressed by a woman whose name is now unknown, but who lived in what is now Wahee Township.

Fanning regretted the loss of his mare more than he did

the escape of Hunter, and did everything in his power, first by threats and then by the offers of rewards, to get his mare back. Now he offered $1,000 in gold for her, and afterwards offered seven negroes for her, but Hunter refused all his offers, and kept the mare during the remainder of the war, during which she took him safely out of many a close place and saved his life by her sagacity and fleetness on several other occasions.

After the close of hostilities, hatred for each other still rankled in the breasts of these two men, and Fanning challenged Hunter to a sword duel on the Citadel Green in Charleston, S. C. Hunter, with his friends, repaired to the spot at the appointed time, but Fanning, well knowing that his chances would be slim in a contest with so formidable an antagonist, failed to put in an appearance.

The "Red Doe" was tenderly cared for until she died of old age, and was buried on the banks of the Pedee, where a sandstone slab marks her grave.

Andrew Hunter was descended from the Lairds of Scotland, and his family now have three records, taken from Burke's Heraldry, of the family coat-of-arms, consisting of a silver dog, horses, etc. He was the son of David and Martha Hunter, who came from Virginia in 1749. His wife was Matilda Hickman, and his children by her were John Hunter, Mrs. George W. Dargan's grandfather; Hamilton Hunter, drowned; James Hunter, who was the father of Mrs. Mary McClennaghan; Irene Hunter; Amelia Hunter, who married Ellerbe and died without heirs; Andrew Hunter, who died; Isaac Hunter, who was the grandfather of Dr. Samuel J. Blackwell, Martha Blackwell (Mrs. W. K. Ryan), and Capt. John C. Blackwell, now sheriff of Darlington County. He had other children later in life by a subsequent marriage, whose descendants are still among us.

After peace was made, Andrew Hunter was sent to the Legislature to make laws adapted to the government of a people who had thoroughly demonstrated the fact that "they were and of a right ought to be free and independent."

BLACKWELL.

(Darlington.)

The first we know of the Blackwells in America is their settlement on the island which bears their name to this day, Blackwell's Island, near New York City.

Families, dividing, came southward into Virginia and South Carolina. In the old records of the early settlers the name Blackwell is followed by the word "gentleman," in contradistinction to that of cavalier, bond slave, etc. The Blackwells are of English extraction; in the old part of London there is a quaint old hall called, even to this day, Blackwell's Hall. This old part of London was once the scene of gayety and fashion. It is in the direction of Hampton Court on the Thames River. This hall was built before the days of Queen Elizabeth.

The Blackwells who came to South Carolina settled at Haddrels Point, now called Mount Pleasant, near Charleston. They married into the family of White (of Whites Bridge fame).

Previous to the Revolutionary War, the White who married a Blackwell was a member of the Indigo Society, one of the first societies of educated men formed in this State. The Blackwells also settled near Georgetown and took up lands on Black Mingo Creek. They became rice planters, and were there when the war broke out. Samuel Blackwell and his oldest son, Thomas, were in the war under General Marion. Thomas Blackwell was a commissary officer in Marion's Brigade. The house of Samuel Blackwell was burned by the Tories and his slaves stolen. While his house was on fire, one of the Tories, angered at being unable to find him, snatched his little son, Samuel, from the nurse, a young girl named Ginny. Taking him by the feet, he thumped his head violently on the ground and made as if he would throw him into the flames. His nurse, who lived to be nearly one hundred years old, and was known to the succeeding generations as old Mauma Ginny, took great delight in rehearsing this story.

This Mr. Samuel Blackwell, whose house was burned, had five sons: Thomas (Marion's commissary); Michael, who went to Edgefield County, and whose descendants are now there; Boutwell, who died young; Samuel (whose head was thumped by the Tories); Josiah; and several daughters. Rachel married Mr. Lane; her son was Dr. James Lane, of Marlboro; her daughter married Timothy Pettigrew. Hannah Blackwell, who never married; and another, who married first a Mr. Duke, then an Adair, and afterwards a McLeary, all of Williamsburg. Many of her descendants are still in that county.

Samuel married a Miss Commander, of Georgetown, who was quite an heiress for her day. By her he had two daughters. One married Dr. McBride, of Darlington County, and the other, Elizabeth, married James A. Pettigrew, also of Darlington County. After the death of his first wife he married Mary Ann Hamlin, whose mother was Joanna White, of Whites Bridge. He then came to Darlington County, bought a plantation on Jeffries Creek, just across what was then the Marion County line. Here he spent the remainder of his life and accumulated considerable property. After his death his widow moved to Darlington village, and spent the remainder of her life there, dying at the age of eighty-four years. His children by this last marriage were: Joanna, who married Edward Burch; Martha, who married Eli Hugh Lide, and went west; Hannah, who married Mr. Gee, and afterwards married Gen. Joseph Nettles, of Darlington; Samuel, who married Caroline Hunter, granddaughter of Andrew Hunter; Isabella, who married William Wingate, one of whose sons was Prof. Manly Wingate, for a number of years President of Wake Forest College, and who was so much beloved in North Carolina that a number of papers came out in black border when his death was announced.

Dr. John Hamlin Blackwell, the youngest child, married first in Alabama, Miss Aletha Windom, by whom he had two children, Edward Burch Blackwell and Carrie Aletha Blackwell. After the death of his first wife he married Sarah

Pettigrew, daughter of Robert Pettigrew, whose mother (Robert Pettigrew's mother) was the daughter of the Rev. Timothy Dargan. By this, his second wife, he had three children: Robert J. Blackwell, of Marion; Elizabeth, who married, as his second wife, George W. Lee, of Sumter; and Anna, who married Louis M. Pettigrew, son of W. Brantley Pettigrew, who was a son of Timothy Pettigrew.

Robert Pettigrew and Timothy Pettigrew were brothers, and were grandsons of the Rev. Timothy Dargan.

Dr. John H. Blackwell studied medicine under Dr. Timothy J. K. Dargan, of Darlington; graduated at the Charleston Medical College, and practiced medicine for about forty years in Darlington and Florence Counties. He was also prominent in public life prior to the Civil War, having been a member of the Legislature in 1850 and 1851, and also in 1860 and 1861. He died at his home in Florence County at the age of seventy-six, in the year 1891.

GEORGETOWN COUNTY.

It is a matter of great regret to the Executive Committee of the Pee Dee Historical Society that no "County Branch" was ever organized in Georgetown. As Georgetown and Williamsburg were not included in "Gregg's History of the Old Cheraws," not being counties of that district, but are Pedee Counties, the Committee felt a special desire to have Williamsburg and Georgetown fully written up for the Addenda, and were fortunate in securing a lady member for Williamsburg (Mrs. D. C. Scott), who accomplished, under many difficulties, all that the Committee could desire for her county, but after repeated efforts Georgetown is still without a branch organization, and will have, in consequence, a very defective account of its rich historical possessions. Leaving out Charleston, there is no county in the State that has a greater abundance of historical material than Georgetown, and it is the earnest hope of many people in the State that a volume will be given to the history of the old town, some thing similar to that recently appearing as "Historic Camden." Georgetown, Cheraw and Camden are old towns that should be fully written up as towns, and each could furnish a volume in itself. Herein will be given only a few hints of the material in Georgetown.

The place upon which the town now stands was originally settled, in the year 1710, by the Rev. William Screven, one of the most interesting characters in American history. Similar in type and experiences, he is the full equal in intellectual and moral endowments of the far-famed Roger Williams. But how different their treatment in history! The one who settled the State of Rhode Island, though driven from place to place by New England persecution, as Screven was, remained a New Englander, and his name and fame are known to "earth's remotest bounds"; the other, settling in South Carolina, is scarcely known to one-tenth of the most intelligent people who live on the ground he settled; his face gone forever from the sight of man, while that of Roger

Williams is familiar to the intelligence of the world in all quarters. What a commentary this is on South Carolina's neglect of the worthies in her history! It would seem that the Baptists of South Carolina would rescue this name from the oblivion which covers it, as one of the proudest connected with this church's noble history. The names of Roger Williams, of Rhode Island, and "William Screven, of Kittery," should stand side by side, blazoned on the pages of history, as devoted, self-sacrificing advocates of religious liberty in America.

Georgetown was the scene of many of Marion's most brilliant exploits during the Revolutionary War. It is the interesting point where Lafayette first touched American soil, and the house is still standing where Major James knocked down the British officer, Ardesoif, for his insolence in an interview about the protection of the Americans after the fall of Charleston. (See Williamsburg's contribution to this Addenda for details of this.) In it stands the Winyah Indigo Society building, erected by the Society of this name, which was chartered in 1753 under King George II., and having as one of its presidents Thomas Lynch, subsequently one of the members of the Continental Congress and father of Thomas Lynch, Jr., one of the signers of the Declaration of Independence. It is one of the most interesting buildings on the American continent, and in it has been entertained world-renowned guests through the long years of its existence to the year 1905, when President Cleveland, for the third or fourth time, graced its halls by his presence and oratory.

Its old "Church of Prince George Winyah" is one of the most venerable buildings to be found in this country.

Being a seacoast town, there were occurrences within its town limits and adjacent territory of memorable character during the Confederate War.

While the list of Georgetown's interesting names would take more space than can be afforded here, we may be permitted to mention that it was the home of two Governors of the State, of the same family (Joseph Alston and R. F. W. Allston); that one of these, Joseph, married the only daughter of Aaron Burr, the beautiful, accomplished, charming

WASHINGTON ALLSTON,
Painter and poet.

Theodosia, who set sail from Georgetown, never to be heard of again after years of the most diligent, wide, and thorough search possible to be made. Her father, known the world round, because of his high official station, brilliant talents, and ambitious political exploits, though wrecked and ruined in his fall, had the abiding affection of his daughter while her life lasted.*

On that narrow strip of land, the Waccamaw Neck, was born the most celebrated painter that America ever produced, Washington Allston, known throughout the world of art as the American Titian; pronounced by Samuel Taylor Coleridge, than whom there is no superior critic of painting and poetry, as "unsurpassed in poetic and artistic genius by any man of his age." Eulogies have been pronounced upon him in language as glowing as sincere admiration and high genius could make them, by Wordsworth, Southey, Wilkie Collins, Washington Irving, Prescott, Longfellow, Holmes, Lowell, Dana, Channing, Greenough, Mrs. Jameson, Dickens, Lord Napier, and others of as high order of fame. He was their associate, their equal in the noblest endowments of humanity. Yet as poet and painter he is but little known to South Carolinians of today. If Georgetown had no other than his name to take care of, it would seem that no effort would be spared to do that work thoroughly, and we make no doubt that this is to be done in the near future.

But it is needful that Georgetown should be written up in its social aspects, for it was with no exaggeration that Hugh S. Legare said, while in the midst of European aristocratic circles, that he had not yet seen any society altogether equal to that of the country around Georgetown. They preserved there, for a longer time than elsewhere, the fashions and customs of old England's social life, and even to the present day the habits of the private home and public hall are strongly marked with the old features of English conviviality; and though its enjoyments conflict somewhat violently with the doctrines of teetotalism, there is such a grace and charm of

---

*In this connection it would be interesting to read, on page 103, and the note, in "The Old Cheraws," of Governor John Lide Wilson. Governor Wilson signalized his life by his book on "The Code Duello."

manner still lingering there that it brings regret to every observer to witness the passing forever of such fascinating style from our people.

In the course of a few years, let us repeat, there will come from Georgetown itself those who will make its proud past known to readers of history the world over.

LAFAYETTE'S FIRST VISIT.

(Georgetown.)

The following is contributed by a descendant of Col. Francis Huger, touching the interesting fact of Lafayette's first landing in America:

In 1794 Mr. Huger, having obtained the consent of his friends to travel on the Continent, crossed over to Amsterdam; he was led by his interest in military affairs to go to Antwerp, then the great seat of war, the army under the Duke of York being actively engaged in Flanders. He would have been pleased to have obtained some military employment, greatly preferring the profession of arms to that of medicine; but finding that impossible, and that surgeons were much needed, he offered his services, and was engaged on the medical staff for some months, attending the crowded hospitals, and doing all in his power to succor the wounded soldiers intrusted to his care. Having at length seen them embark for their homes in England, he gladly resigned his situation and pursued his journey to Vienna, where he found that he could procure ample means for recreation and improvement. At the coffee house that he frequented, persons of various acquirements, character and nationalities were to be met with. Among them a gentleman he made acquaintance with soon proved of peculiar interest to him—Dr. Justis Eric Bollman, a native of Hanover, who spoke English well, and German and French fluently, and who appeared to be highly esteemed by the Society of the coffee house for his intelligence, acquirements and gentlemanly deportment. He occasionally made inquiries about America, its institutions and distinguished men, and spoke of General Lafayette and his attachment and service to the Republic. In Mr. Huger's own words, he said: "We conversed freely, and I was led to inform him that General Lafayette had first landed at my father's house on North Island, in the harbor of Georgetown, in South Carolina. The small vessel in which they had sailed from France made the land off that part of the coast lying, as they knew, to the north of Charleston, to which port they were bound; but they feared to proceed without information to that city, which might have fallen into the hands of the British during their voyage. They sent a boat to obtain information, and, observing a canoe fishing outside the breakers, desired it might be brought to their vessel. The negroes in the canoe were people of my father's, who, alarmed at observing the boat make for them, endeavored to escape to the shore, but were intercepted and carried on board the vessel; they then piloted the boat with three gentlemen in it, who were General Lafayette, Baron DeKalb, and (I think) Steuben, to my father's house on the island, which they reached about nightfall. The first impression of the servants, that it was a privateer's boat, had been communicated to the family, who were soon agreeably relieved from their anxiety. These circumstances were told me by my mother. Their guests remained with them another day and night, until a carriage and horses could be brought from the plantation, and my father accompanied them by land to Charleston."

THE TOWN OF CARLISLE.

(Marlboro.)

The little town which grew up around the first courthouse in Marlboro was called Carlisle. Just when it was given that name is not known. In most of the records of the time it is called simply "the courthouse," as Bennettsville is even yet sometimes called by residents of the county. There are on record, however, in the clerk's office, conveyances for two lots from Tristram Thomas to Robert Lide, "in the village of Carlisle." One of the lots was bounded by "John Murdock's lot," "the street" and "James Field's storehouse." The other adjoined "the public lot." This was in 1817, three years before the courthouse was moved to its present site in Bennettsville. The name of the Long Bluff courthouse was then Greenville, and Cheraw was Chatham. The town of Carlisle, when John Murdock paid $600 for a half-acre lot, and when Robert Lide paid "fifty pounds sterling" for the lots above described, is now a cultivated field, owned by A. J. Matheson.

Carlisle was named for Richard Carlisle, who came from Virginia about the close of the eighteenth century, and settled in the neighborhood of Dyer's Hill, on the opposite side of Crooked Creek from the courthouse. He was an exemplary and useful citizen, and raised several sons and daughters, all of whom went to Alabama about 1825. They left in Marlboro Richard's aged mother, Phoebe, and a nephew, James, who had then grown to manhood.

James Carlisle spent most of his life near Salem Church, where he was a deacon and leading member for many years. He was noted for his decisive views, candor of expression, energy and hospitality. He was four times married: first to Isabella Johnson, daughter of Peter Johnson, who died leaving one daughter, Mary Ann. His second wife was Willie Johnson, daughter of William Johnson. She died, leaving an only daughter, Celia Ann. He married a third time, Charlotte McDaniel, daughter of George McDaniel. To this union were born Elizabeth, Ellen, Susan, Thomas Franklin, Joseph A., Benjamin and Jane. His fourth wife was Mary, daughter of John G. Graham. She died childless.

James Carlisle died in 1883, at the age of eighty-two. His daughter Susan was burned to death when a child. His other sons and daughters married and have many descendants. His oldest son, Franklin, volunteered at the age of sixteen, and was in the thickest of the fighting throughout the Civil War. He is now a highly respected citizen of the Tatum section. Joseph and Benjamin moved to North Carolina several years ago.

The parents of Phoebe Carlisle were among the Puritan settlers of New England. One day they were walking in the primeval forest and lost their way. They wandered around for nine days without food. They finally found their way home. The husband ate so much that he died that night. The wife was more temperate in her dinner, and lived. The people of the community declared that they had been bewitched, for it was found that they had been all the time within a short distance of home, and had been walking round and round in a circle.

Phoebe Carlisle's husband was among the first to volunteer to resist British oppression, and was mortally wounded at Bunker Hill. After the battle she went on the scene of the conflict in search of her companion, and found him near a creek, which was running red with human blood. This must have been the little creek between Breed's Hill and Morton's Point, where most of the fighting occurred.

A LETTER FROM DR. S. D. SANDERS TO A RELATIVE IN MARLBORO COUNTY.

Georgetown, Texas, September, 1898.

My Dear Sam: Your highly esteemed letter and present of Capt. J. A. W. Thomas's History of Marlboro came in due time, and both were such a delightful treat to me. For several reasons, the reading of the history has given the highest pleasure. I have a passion for the old-time things and places and people. Captain Thomas and I were about the same age. I have known him from early manhood, and often heard him preach in Cheraw and elsewhere, and then during the war we entered the Confederate service at the same time and in the same regiment. He was captain of Company F, and I a lieutenant of Company D, in the Twenty-first South Carolina Regiment. During these four years of hard service in field and camp we became intimate friends, and I loved him as a brother. Though never our appointed chaplain, he was ever our pastor and often our preacher. I never knew a better, truer, braver man.

The original settlers of Marlboro were, with few exceptions, an exceedingly worthy and respectable people, and their descendants have perpetuated the family traits. I regard the settlement of the "Welch Neck Baptists" fully as important to American goodness and greatness as I do the settlement of the Pilgrim Fathers at Plymouth Rock.

I had lost sight of the fact that our family had descended, on the maternal side, from the founder of the Welch Neck colony. My mother and your grandmother, Gillespie, were daughters of Nancy Hicks, wife of Thomas Godfrey. Nancy Hicks was the daughter of Col. George Hicks, who married the daughter of Rev. Philip James, the first pastor of the Welch Neck Baptist Church, who was a son of James James, the founder and leader of the Welch Neck colony. Mr. James James was a man of large estate and high character and great influence; he owned large landed estates on both sides the Pedee at Society Hill Ferry, and lived, first, above the ferry, on the Marlboro side. Col. Abel Kolb, the hero of Hon. A. D. Sims's novel called "Bevil Falcon," who was killed by Tories during the Revolution at his own house, was a descendant of Mr. James and consequently a relative of ours. He inherited from Mr. James the plantation in Marlboro opposite Society Hill, his elegant brick house being on the bank of the Pedee, just above the ferry.

Captain Thomas was not able to get much information concerning the Pegues family. The original Pegues (so far as we know) was a Huguenot French gentleman, of large wealth, superior education, and fine personal appearance. He married a Swiss lady of accomplishments similar to his own. Despairing of any relief from the Roman Catholics' persecutions in France, he moved over to London and died there

His only son and namesake, Claudius Pegues, in the early part of the last century, while a young man, moved over to America, bringing a good estate with him. In the same vessel with him were a young English gentleman named Butler and his sister, Miss Butler. Mr. Pegues and Miss Butler fell in love with each other and were married in Charleston, S. C. Young Mr. Butler moved up to Edgefield, S. C., and became the ancestor of the Butler family, which has given so many distinguished men to South Carolina in political and military life; among them the two Senators (United States) Butler, and Col. P. M. Butler, who was killed in the Mexican War, and also Hon. Preston Brooks, and also, I think, some of the later Hagoods.

Claudius Pegues moved to Georgetown, S. C., and soon after to Marlboro, and, being the only man of his name who came to America, is the ancestor of all the Pegues's in our country. He lived and died and is buried on the plantation now owned by Frank P. B. Pegues. He was an old man in the Revolutionary War, but did what service he could for his country. His two sons, William and Claudius, were active soldiers in the war. William was the father of the Sneedsborough branch of the family, and Claudius of the Marlboro branch. Your ancestor had four sons: your grandfather, James Pegues, and Malachi, William, and Christopher, all men of high social position and useful lives. The family extended from the Virginia line almost to the Rio Grande River, in Texas. There are many of them living in Texas. I have met with a few of them, and, so far as I know, they are elegant, pretty women. The blessings of a good and pious ancestry have to a large extent descended to their posterity.

. . . I am holding up well for an old man of seventy-six years, feeling only a little the infirmities of old age. I would like so much to go out to South Carolina again, but not much hope of accomplishing it. There are not often found in one family so many elderly persons as in ours. . .

In conclusion, Sam, I thank you so much for your kind letter and the history of Marlboro. We all join in much love to you and all the dear relatives at home.

        Yours most affectionately,
                (Signed) S. D. SANDERS.

MATERIAL TOWARDS A HISTORY OF THE BAPTISTS IN DELAWARE STATE*

Introduction.

Delaware became a State independent of Pennsylvania at the Revolution in 1776; it contains three little counties, viz.: Newcastle, Kent, and Sussex. In the first was a Baptist church as early as the spring of 1703. They settled near the Iron Hill; from thence their religion took a spread, northward as far as London Tract in Pennsylvania; northeast to Wilmington; east to Bethel; west to Elk, in Maryland, and southward to Duck Creek and Pedee, in South Carolina.

The *Delaware Baptists* are *Calvinistic* in doctrines, and differ little or nothing in discipline from their brethren in the neighboring States. Five of their churches have been received into the Association of Philadelphia; the other three belong to the Salisbury Association. These eight churches have been constituted at different times, which order of time we shall observe in treating of them; and, therefore, begin with

Welch Tract.

This church is distinguished as above from a large tract of land of the same name, on the western border of which, at the foot of the Iron Hill, the meeting-house stands, in the hundred of Pencader and county of Newcastle, about forty-two miles southwest by west-quarter-west from Philadelphia. The house is of brick, built in 1746, on a lot of six acres, four of which were given by James James, Esq. His conveyance is dated January 20, 1709. The rest was purchased from Abraham Emmet; the conveyance of this is dated April 20, 1768, and signed Andrew Fisher. The dimensions of the house are forty feet by thirty; it is finished as usual,

---

*Extracts from the records of the Old Welch Church of the State of Delaware, by Morgan Edwards, A. M., made by James D. Evans, Esq., at Philadelphia, at the request of the Pee Dee Historical Society, because it throws light on the history of the Welch who settled on Welch Neck, on the Pedee River.

ADDENDA. 615

excepting galleries, and accomodated with a stove. The families belonging to the place are about ninety, whereof 108 persons are baptized and in the communion, here celebrated the first Sunday in every month. The minister is Rev. John Boggs; the salary unknown, because Mr. Boggs would have it that he receives no pay for preaching, from a consciousness of his vehement exclamations against paying preachers before he himself turned preacher. However, it was proposed to Rev. John Sutton when he came among the people (in 1770) that his salary should be £100. This church was raised to a body politic February 9, 1788. The above is the present state of Welch Tract Church, October 5, 1790.

History.

To come at the history of this church we must cross the Atlantic and land in Wales, where it originated in the following manner: "In the spring of the year 1701 several Baptists in the counties of Pembroke and Caermarthen resolved to go to America; and as one was a minister (Thomas Griffith) they were advised to be constituted a church. They took the advice. The instrument of their confederation was in being in the year 1770, but is now lost except one copy in possession of Mr. Isaac Hughes, and that without a date. The names of the confederates follows: Thomas Griffith, Griffith Nicholas, Evan Edmond, John Edward, Elisha Thomas, Enoch Morgan, Richard David, James David, Elizabeth Griffith, Lewis Edmond, Mary John, Mary Thomas, Elizabeth Griffith, Jr., Jennet David, Margaret Mathias, and Jennet Morris. These sixteen persons (which may be styled a church emigrant and saliant) met at Milford in the month of June, 1701, and embarked on board the good ship James and Mary, and on the 8th of September following landed at Philadelphia. The brethren there treated them courteously, and advised them to settle about Pennepek; thither they went and there continued about a year and a half. During their stay at Pennepek the following persons joined them, viz.: Rees Rhydarch, Catherine Rhydarch, Esther Thomas, Thomas Morris, Hugh Morris, Peter Chamberlain, Mary

Chamberlain, Mary Chamberlain, Jr., Mary Sorensee, Magdalen Morgan, Henry David, Elizabeth David, Samuel Griffith, Richard Seree, Rebecca Marpole, John Greenwater, Edward Edward, John James, Mary Thomas, Thomas John, Judith Griffith, and Mary John.

"But finding it inconvenient to tarry about Pennepek, they, in 1703, took up land in Newcastle County from Messrs. Evans, Davis, and Willis (who had purchased said Welch Tract from William Penn, containing about 30,000 acres), and thither removed the same year and built a little meeting-house on the spot where the present stands. The same year were added to them from Wales, Thomas John and Rebecca John; and by baptism John Wild, Thomas Wild, James James, Sarah James, Jane Morgan, Samuel Wild, Mary Nicholas, Richard Bowen, David Thomas, Mary Bentley, and Jane Edwards.

"In 1709 were added from Kilcam, in Pembrokeshire (Samuel John, pastor), John Devonallt, Mary Devonallt, Lewis Phillips, Catherine Edward; and from East Jersey, Philip Trueax and Elizabeth Tilton; and from Pennepek, David Miles and Alce Miles.

"In 1710 the following Baptists were added from several parts of Wales, viz.: from Rhydwilim (Jenkins Jones, pastor), Lewis Philips, Rees David (a deacon), Thomas Evans, Thomas Edmund, Arthur Edward, Eleanor Philips, Susanna David, and Mary Wallis; from said Kilcam, John Philips (an elder), Thomas Morris, Jenkin Jones (afterwards minister of Philadelphia), John Harry, John Boulton, Richard Edward, Eleanor Philips, Mary William, Elizabeth Harry, Susanne Owen, Mary Owen, Elizabeth John; from Lantivy (James James, pastor), John Griffith (an elder), Rees Jones, Hugh Evan, David Lewis, Samuel Evan, Rachel Griffith, Esther John, Mary Evan; from Langenych (Morgan John, pastor), Hugh David (afterwards minister of the Great Valley), Anthony Mathew, Simon Mathew, Simon Butler, Arthur Melchoir, Hannah Melchoir, Margaret David; from Lanwenarth (Timothy Lewis, pastor), Jane James, Mary David; from Blaeneu-givent (Abel Morgan, pastor), Joseph James.

ADDENDA. 617

"In 1711 were added, from said Rhydwilim, Elizabeth John; from Lanvabon (Morgan Griffith, pastor), William Miricks; from said Lanwenarth, James Jones, Ann Jones. The same year were added by baptism, Thomas Rees, Thomas David, Margaret Evan, Sarah Emson, Rachel Thomas, Daniel Rees, William Thomas, John Thomas, Martha Thomas, John Evans, Lydia Evans.

"In 1712 were added from Pennepek, Nicholas Stephens, Mary Stephens, John Pain, Elizabeth Pain.

"In 1713 were added from said Pennepek, John Eaton, Jane Eaton, Joseph Eaton, Gwenllian Eaton, George Eaton, Mary Eaton; and the same year from said Lantivy, Elias Thomas, Thomas Evan, Ann Evans, and from said Kilcam, Philip Rees.

"In 1714 were added by baptism, John Bentley, James James, Jr., Eleanor David, Mary Thomas, Ann Thomas, David John, Richard Lewis, Sarah Nicholas, Mary Lewis; from Philadelphia, Benjamin Griffith (afterwards minister of Montgomery), Emlin David, Catherine Hollinsworth; from Cohansey (Timothy Brooks, pastor), John Miller, Joanna Miller.

"In 1715 were added by baptism, James James, Esq. (aged 16), John Jones, Richard Witten; and the same year from said Rhydwilim, Griffith Thomas; and from Radnor (Pennsylvania), Mary Robinet.

"In 1716 were added by baptism, Elizabeth John, David Davis, Thomas Richard and wife, Mary Price.

"In 1717 were added from said Pennepek, Cornelius Vansant, Richard Herbert, and by baptism his wife Sarah."

NOTE (1)—The paragraphs in quotations are translations from the records of Welch Tract, which have been kept in the Welch tongue (with some intermixture of English) down to the year 1732.

NOTE (2)—I have transcribed more out of said records than my design required in order to gratify my old friend Joshua Thomas (of Leominster, in Herefordshire), who thinks he may avail himself of them relative to his history of the Welch Baptists.

Remarkables.

Having followed Welch Tract Church from Wales to Pennepek, and from Pennepek to its present station, let us now attend to what has been most remarkable in its progress down to the present time. (1) It has existed for about ninety years, and increased from sixteen to one hundred and eight, besides deaths and large detachments to form other churches. (2) It is a mother church; for that of *Pedee, London Tract, Duck Creek, Wilmington, Cowmarsh,* and *Mispilion* may be considered as daughters. Pedee is a large river in South Carolina, remarkable for its meanderings, so as to form many peninsulas; on one of which settled the Welch Baptists in 1736, and, therefore, called the *Welch Neck.* To form a church on said neck the following persons were dismissed in the month of November, 1736, viz.: "Abel Morgan (late minister of Middletown), James James (a ruling elder), Thomas Evans (a deacon), Daniel James, Samuel Wilds, John Harry, John Harry, Jr., Thomas Harry, Jeremiah Rowell, Richard Barrow, James Money, Nathaniel Evans, Mary James, Sarah James, Ann Evan, Mary Wilds, Elizabeth Harry, Eleanor Jenkin, Sarah Harry, Margaret William, Mary Rowell, Sarah Barrow. The next year (April 30, 1737), Samuel Evan, Mary Evan, (and November 4th following) Daniel Devonallt, Thomas James, Philip James (late minister), David James, Abel James, David Harry, Simon Peerson, Mary Boulton, Catherine Harry, Elizabeth James, Elizabeth Jones, Eleanor James, Mary Hugh. The next year (November 3, 1738), Jane David, Mary Devonallt. And in 1741 (November 1st), John Jones, Philip Douglas, Oliver Alison, Walter Down, Elizabeth Jones, Lettice Douglas, Rachel Allison, Rachel Down; in all forty-eight souls. Pedee Church had shot into seven branches in 1772. In 1780 (November 22d), about eighteen members of Welch Tract were constituted a church at London Tract. Several were dismissed to form a church at Duck Creek in 1781, and another at Cowmarsh in 1781; another at Mispilion in 1783; and another at Wilmington in 1785. (3) Welch Tract Church was the principal if not sole means of introducing *singing, imposition of hands, ruling elders,* and *church cove-*

nants into the Middle States. The *Century confession* was in America long before the year 1716, but without the articles which relate to those subjects; that year they were added by Rev. Abel Morgan, who translated the confession into Welch. It was signed by 122 of Welch Tract members. The said articles were retained in the next English edition, and the whole adopted by the Association of 1742. *Singing psalms* met with some opposition, especially at Cohansey; but *laying on of hands* on baptized believers, as such, gained acceptance with more difficulty, as appears by the following narrative translated from the church book: "But we could not be in fellowship (*at the Lord's table*) with our brethren of Pennepek and Philadelphia, because they did not hold to the *laying on of hands*: true, some of them believed in the ordinance, but neither preached it up nor practiced it; and when we moved to Welch Tract and left twenty-two of our members at Pennepek, and took some of theirs with us, the difficulty increased. We had many meetings in order to compromise matters, but to no purpose till June 22, 1706; then twenty-five deputies met at the house of Brother Richard Miles in Radnor and agreed (1) That a member of either church may transiently communicate with the other church; (2) That every member who desireth to come under imposition of hands may have his liberty without offense; (3) That the votaries of the rite may preach or debate upon the subject with all freedom consistent with brotherly love. But three years after this meeting we had cause to review the transaction, because of some brethren that came from Wales, and one among ourselves (John Devonallt), who questioned whether the first article was warrantable; but we are satisfied that all was right by the good effects which followed: for from that time forth the brethren held sweet communion together, and our minister was invited to preach at Pennepek and to assist at an ordination after the death of our Brother Watts. He proceeded from thence to the Jersey, where he enlightened many in the good ways of the Lord, insomuch that in three years after, all the ministers and fifty-five private members had submitted to the ordinance."

Rev. Elisha Thomas.

His name is written *Elizeus* in the first records of this church; but on his tomb *Elisha*. He was born in 1674 in Caermarthen County; arrived in this country with the church whereof he was one of the first members; he died November 7, 1730, and was buried in this graveyard, where a handsome tomb is erected to his memory. The top stone is divided into several compartments, whereon open books are raised, with inscriptions and poetry in Welch and English. He had two daughters, Rachel and Sarah. Rachel's first husband was Rees Jones, by whom she had children Rees, Mary, Deborah. Rees and Deborah died childless. Mary married the Hon. John Evans, Esq., and is dead with all her children. Her aunt, Sarah (the other daughter of Rev. Elisha Thomas), married Daniel James, and went with him to Pedee in 1736; she had a son Elisha James, who also went to Carolina.

Note—Rev. Morgan Edwards was born May 9, 1722, in the Parish of Trevethin, Monmouthshire, Wales, and was reared in the doctrines of the Church of England. He became a Baptist in 1738. He received his early education at Bristol and was ordained in Ireland June 1, 1757. He arrived in Philadelphia on May 9, 1761, and had charge of the church until 1771; then he resigned and went to reside in Pencader Hundred, near Newark, Delaware, where he lived until his death, January 28, 1795. He was the founder of Brown University, at Providence, R. I.

The original of the above manuscript is now deposited in the archives of the American Baptist Historical Society, No. 1420 Chestnut street, Philadelphia, and the above was published by the Historical Society of Pennsylvania, in the Pennsylvania Magazine of History and Biography, Vol. IX, pp. 45-61, etc. (1885). J. D. E.

FAMILY RECORDS.

LIDE.

Hartsville, S. C., December 6, 1904.

Corrections, pages 78 and 79, Gregg's "Old Cheraws," made by James Lide Coker:

Maj. Robert Lide married first Prisalie Fort, by whom he had no children. His second wife was Sarah Kolb, aunt of Col. Abel Kolb, who was murdered by the Tories (see pages 360 and 361), Gregg's "Old Cheraws." By this marriage he had five sons: John, Robert, James, Hugh, and Peter; and two daughters, Mary, who married Robert Hodge, and Ann, who married Samuel Wilds. Maj. Robert Lide's third wife was the widow Holloway (nee Mary Westfield), who was the mother by her first husband of Jesse Holloway, who married Rachel McIver, and of Mrs. James Pugh, and Mrs. Cyrus Bacot, and Jane, who became the wife of James Lide, the son of Robert Lide. The children of Maj. Robert Lide and Jane Westfield Lide were: Sarah Ann Lide, John Lide, who never married, and Hannah, who married Thomas Hart. Thomas Hart settled on Black Creek, and for him the town of Hartsville is named.

The above is taken from the family records of Mrs. Hannah Lide Coker, formerly of Society Hill, S. C., who was the granddaughter of Maj. Robert Lide.

McCOWN.

Columbia, S. C., November 16, 1904.

In Gregg's "History of the Old Cheraws," on pages 90 and 91, the name McCown is spelled "McKown." Will you please be so kind, in the edition which you are now preparing for publication, to see that notice is called to this correction and give the name the correct spelling, "McCown"?

Yours very truly,

R. M. McCOWN.

SPARKS.

From a letter from Rev. Dr. J. L. Stokes, dated July 4, 1905, the following extract is taken with reference to Captain Sparks and others:

Capt. Daniel Sparks came from Virginia to South Carolina some time before the Revolution. He was one of four brothers, Daniel, Charles, Samuel, and Harry. The last named was a noted Whig and daring scout. He was captured and hung by the Tories near "Mineral Springs," Blenheim, Marlboro County, S. C. (See Thomas's "History of Marlboro County," pp. 34-35 and 105-106.) Gregg says (Chapter V, pp. 98-99), "Capt. Daniel Sparks was a noted captain of militia in the Revolution." Now I wish to call your attention to that word "militia" in the text. It strikes me as misleading in this connection, and tending to degrade the character of service this "noted captain" rendered. The truth is he was one of Marion's famous partisan band. This I have from the unimpeachable authority of Mrs. L. M. Keitt, daughter of the venerable Samuel Sparks (who died within recent years), who was a son of the "noted captain." As you well know, South Carolina was redeemed, not by the "Continental Line," but by the "partisan bands," misnamed "militia" by Gregg.

Captain Sparks first married Miss Stephens in Virginia. There was one child, Elizabeth, by this marriage. She married Silas Pearce. Of this pair my wife is great-granddaughter, through their daughter, Loretta Pearce Cook, and her daughter, Susan Cook Barentine. Captain Sparks subsequently married Martha Pearce, sister of his son-in-law. This elect body survived until October 25, 1852. Of this couple Mrs. Keitt is a granddaughter.

HARLLEE.

Peter Harllee was the first of the name to come to America. His father, bearing the same Christian name, was a younger brother of Robert Harley, the Earl of Oxford. Peter took an active part in the rebellion of the Stuarts in 1745. This being very obnoxious to his powerful kinsman, the latter obtained a pardon from the government, upon certain conditions—requiring, if Peter would change his name, he would obtain a commission for him in the Royal Navy. He consented to change the name to Harllee. Being promoted to a captaincy of a British man-of-war, he served until 1758, when he resigned his commission, and came to Virginia, where he settled. He there married Anne Leake and died when quite old, soon after the close of the American Revolution. His family then moved South, and settled in Marion County.

His only son, Thomas, married Elizabeth Stuart, the daughter of a Scotch emigrant, David Stuart, who, with his sons, David and Hardy, fought through the War for Independence under Marion. David, Jr., having been taken prisoner, was among the few survivors of the terrible incarceration in the prison ships in Charleston harbor.

There were born to Thomas and Elizabeth Harllee nine children who lived to maturity.

John, the eldest, lived to extreme old age, and was a well-known man in the Pedee country.

When quite young he was appointed a lieutenant in the United States Army, and served some years under General Jackson in the War of 1812 in Louisiana, and later in Florida. He never married. The other sons were David S., Peter, Thomas, Dr. Robert, and Gen. William W. Harllee. These were prominent citizens, and all, except Thomas, left large families. The daughters were: Anne, who married John McNeill, and moved to Alabama; Elizabeth, who married Parker Bethea, of Marion; Harriet, who married George I. W. McCall, of Darlington.

BACOT.

Correction of date in Gregg's "History of the Old Cheraws," page 105: Pierre Bacot came to Carolina 1685, not 1694.*

*Correction made by Mrs. H. L. Charles, of Darlington.

On page 106, "History of the Old Cheraws," after the words in the second paragraph, "The late Samuel Bacot, and Cyrus Bacot, of Darlington, were his sons," insert the words: "And Maria Allston Bacot, a daughter, who in 1801 intermarried with Matthew Brunson."

Matthew Brunson was noted among his fellow citizens for his manliness and honesty. Peter A. Brunson, the only surviving son of the latter, is now living at Florence, at the age of eighty-eight years. When a youth he traveled through the Creek Nation, in Alabama, before their removal west, and has listened to the stories of "'76" Goodson, of the Continental Line, and John Boseman, of Marion's Brigade.*

PERKINS-ZIMMERMAN-KEITH.

Extracts from a letter of Miss Elizabeth Zimmerman to the Secretary of the Pee Dee Historical Society:

John Perkins, a native of Kershaw.

Margaret Perkins, daughter of John Perkins, married, first, James Dozier, of Georgetown. There were two children of this marriage: Mary Dozier, who married William F. Zimmerman, and James Dozier (who died in infancy).

Mary Dozier Zimmerman had a large family: James Dozier, William F., John Perkins, Daniel, Eliza (Mrs. T. J. Flinn), Sarah (Mrs. W. R. Davis), and Malvina (who died in infancy).

Margaret Dozier married, the second time, Colonel Keith, of Georgetown, and had two daughters, Lydia Keith, and Harriet Keith.

Lydia Keith married Timothy Dargan and had quite a large family: G. Washington, Jeremiah, Timothy, John, Julius, Edwin, Sidney, Theodore, Charles, and Mrs. Furman (Henrietta), and Mrs. Sims (Margaret).

Harriet Keith married Mr. Samuel Ervin, of Darlington, and moved to Georgia. They had one child, Harriet, who married a Mr. Burch. Mr. and Mrs. Burch had one child,

---

*Correction made by Hon. W. A. Brunson, of Florence, S. C.

Rosalie. Mrs. Burch died in Darlington at her aunt's, Mrs. Lydia Dargan's.

The tragic fate of Colonel Keith should be remembered. He was murdered by his body-servant on his way from Georgetown to his home in Darlington. This occurred not far from the place where Mr. Mat. Muldrow afterward lived. The murderer was burned near the spot where the deed was committed.

ANNOUNCEMENT.

The following are the members of the Executive Committee of the Pee Dee Historical Society—the officers being officers of the Society and ex-officio members and officers of the Executive Committee:

J. L. Coker, LL. D., President, Hartsville, S. C.
H. M. Ayer, Vice-President, Florence, S. C.
Bright Williamson, Treasurer, Darlington, S. C.
John J. Dargan, Secretary, Hartsville, S. C.
Hon. R. B. Scarborough, Conway, S. C.
Hon. J. H. Hudson, Bennettsville, S. C.
Rev. A. H. McArn, Cheraw, S. C.
P. Y. Bethea, Marion, S. C.
A. G. Kollock, Darlington, S. C.
W. A. Brunson, Florence, S. C.
Mrs. D. C. Scott, Kingstree, S. C.
Hon. Walter Hazard, Georgetown, S. C.

A commission signed by all the members of the committee was given to the Secretary to bring out a reprint of "The Old Cheraws," with Addenda, and a second volume extending the work to the year 1880. The Society was organized at Florence, on July 2, 1903.

The second volume will follow this one as soon as the immense task can be accomplished with very limited means.

ADDENDA.   627

INDEX TO ADDENDA.

Allston, Washington, painter, native of Georgetown County, 607.
Ardesoif, Captain, British officer, interviewed by Major John James, 581.

Bacot, family history, 623.
Ball, Capt. John Coming, Tory leader, 584.
Baptists in Delaware State, extracts from history, 614.
Blackwell, family history, 602.
Blakeney, Gen. J. W., law partner of Bishop Gregg, 556.
Blenheim, village in Marlboro County, origin of name, 563.
Blue Savannah, battle of, 595.
Bowling Green, battle of, 596.

Camden, origin of name, 571, *note*.
Carlisle, first name of the town of Marlboro, 610.
Carlisle, Richard, family history, 610.
Charleston, the seat of all courts prior to 1721, 591.
Cheraw, change of name, 571, *note*.
Chesterfield County, named for Philip Dormer Stanhope, Lord Chesterfield, 564.
Chiquola Club, tribute to Bishop Gregg, 559.
Churchill, John, Duke of Marlboro, short account of life and career, 562.
Conway, county seat of Horry County, origin of name, 571, 572.
Conway, Henry Seymour, friend of America in parliament, 571 and *note*.
Conway, Robert, colonel in Revolution, 572.
Courts, equity, 591; divided into circuits, 592; appeal court, 593; eminent jurists in the State, 594.

Dargan, genealogy, 624.
Darlington County, origin of name uncertain, 567.
Darlington, town in England, 567.
Dozier, genealogy, 624.

Edwards, Rev. Morgan, Welch Baptist settler in Delaware, 620.

Florence County, named for the daughter of Gen. W. W. Harllee, 566.
Frierson, Mrs. John, escapes burning by Wemys's men, 583.

Gaskins, Amos, Tory officer, 582.
George II., King of England, account of life and reign, 560.
Georgetown County, named for George II. of England, 560.
Georgetown County, history, 605.
Giles, Col. Hugh, for whom the town of Marion was first called Gilesboro, 590.
Gordon, Capt. William, in Revolutionary army, 585; his wife's brave actions, 585, 586.
Gregg, Bishop Alexander, birth, 556, 557; marriage, 556; admitted to the bar, 557; rector of St. David's Church, 556; first Bishop of Texas, 557; tribute in Cheraw papers, 556; tribute in Texas church paper, 557; tribute by Board of Trustees of the University of the South, 558.
Gregg, Margaret, descendants, 585.

Hamilton, John, Tory officer, 582.
Harllee, Gen. W. W., account of life and career, 566.
Harllee, Florence, for whom Florence County is named, 566.
Harllee, family history, 622.
Horry County, origin of name, 571.
Horry, Hugh, Peter, and Daniel, colonels in the Revolution, 571.
Huger, Col. Francis, description of Lafayette's first landing in America, 608.

Hunter, Andrew, one of Marion's scouts, adventure with the Tory Fanning, 597, 599; genealogy, 601; elected to the State Legislature, 601.

James, Maj. John, with Marion's men, 580, 582; defeats a band of Tories under Major Gainey, 583, 595; defeats Rawdon's men under Colonel Watson, 584.

Keith, family history, 624.
Kingstree, origin of name, 579.
Kollock, Charlotte W., married Bishop Gregg, 556.

Lafayette's first visit, 608.
Liberty County, name changed to Marion District, 587.
Lide, family history, 621.
Lyceum, Cheraw, aid to Bishop Gregg, 555.

McCottry, Capt. William, with Marion's men, 580, 582.
McCown, correction in name, 621.
McGauley, Capt. John, with Marion's men, 582.
McIver, Judge Henry, tribute to Bishop Gregg, 555.
MacDonald, Flora, Scotch heroine, emigrates to North Carolina, 560.
Marion, Col. Francis, account of life and career, 574; accepts command of Williamsburg troops, 582; defeats a body of Tories under Captain Barfield, 595; defeats the Loyalists under Major Gainey, 596.
Marion County, named for Francis Marion, 574.
Marion County, history, 587; commissioners to locate and build courthouses and gaols, 588; first court held in county, 589; difficulty experienced in opening roads, 591.
Marlboro County, named for John Churchill, Duke of Marlborough, 562.
Marlboro County, history, 610; letter from S. D. Sanders, 611.
Mouzon, Capt. Henry, with Marion's men, 580, 582; house burned by Tarleton, 583; wounded by Wemys's men, 584.

Orangeburg County, named for William III., Prince of Orange, King of England, 570.

Pease, Joseph, first Quaker member of Parliament, 568.
Pee Dee Historical Society, officers and announcement, 626.
Pegues, Claudius, family history, 613.
Perkins, family history, 624.
Port's Ferry, battle of, 595.

Scott, Lieut. Joseph, with Williamsburg troop in Revolution, wounded by Wemys's men, 584.
Screven, Rev. William, first settler of Georgetown, 605.
Sewanee, Tenn., Bishop Gregg's summer home, 558.
Simms, William Gilmore, description of Marion's camp and men, 580.
Sparks, family history, 622.
Stanhope, Philip Dormer, Lord Chesterfield, account of life and career, 564.

Thomas, Rev. Elisha, Welch Baptist, settler in Delaware, 620.

Welch Neck Baptist Church, history, 618.
William III., Prince of Orange, King of England, account of life and reign, 569.
Williamsburg County, named for William III., Prince of Orange, King of England, 570.
Williamsburg County, history, 579.
Witherspoon, John, leads a colony from Scotland, settling in Williamsburg County, 579.

Zimmerman, family history, 624.

ADDENDA.

INDEX TO ILLUSTRATIONS.

	Opposite page
Bishop Alexander Gregg..,	Frontispiece
Judge Josiah J. Evans	52
Gen. David R. Williams	65
Hugh Lide	78
James Lide	79
Lewis Malone Ayer	362
Williamson's Bridge, on Black Creek	386
Col. Lemuel Benton	401
Extract from Bright Williamson's Account Book	433
Extract from the Cashway Church Book	434
Views at Society Hill	440
Judge Samuel Wilds	513
Tombs of Col. Abel Kolb and Bishop Alexander Gregg	549
George II	560
The Duke of Marlborough	562
Lord Chesterfield	564
Gen. W. W. Harllee	566
Independence Oak, near Mechanicsville	568
William III	569
Col. Peter Horry	571
Gen. Francis Marion	574
House in which Major James knocked down the British Officer, Georgetown	582
First Courthouse of Marion County	589
Site of Marion's Redoubt, near Port's Ferry	595
Bowling Green, near Marion	596
Washington Allston	607

www.ingramcontent.com/pod-product-compliance
Lightning Source LLC
Chambersburg PA
CBHW071214290426
44108CB00013B/1178